Ella Mae Meech
W R H. Nort
E. g. Sheppard

Y0-ARR-461

PRINCIPLES
OF
ECONOMICS

Fourth Edition
A RESTATEMENT

Raymond T. Bye
PROFESSOR OF ECONOMICS
UNIVERSITY OF PENNSYLVANIA

F. S. CROFTS & CO.
NEW YORK · · · · 1944

COPYRIGHT 1924, 1926, 1932, 1934, 1941 BY
F. S. CROFTS & CO., INC.

FOURTH EDITION

Twenty-seventh Printing, August, 1944

*No part of the material covered by this copy-
right may be reproduced in any form without
permission in writing from the publisher*

MANUFACTURED IN THE

UNITED STATES OF AMERICA

PREFACE

PREFACE

Since my *Principles of Economics* was first published, in 1924, there have been a number of striking and important new developments in economic theory. In the field of monetary economics, the almost universal adoption of managed currency systems throughout the world has necessitated the giving up of some of the older reasoning, based on the assumption of an automatic gold standard, and has led to increased emphasis on the nominal character of money. Also, it has gradually come to be recognized that money is not the passive, neutral factor in the economic process it was once thought to be, but an active agent, playing a decisive rôle in the level and balance of the economy. So, modern writers stress the flow, rather than the mere quantity, of money, and they emphasize the influence of the monetary circulation upon the level of production and the phenomena of business cycles. In that branch of economics which deals with individual prices, or values, there has developed a new technique of analysis, based on the adjustment of the individual firm to the price situation, and using curves of marginal receipts and marginal costs. Along with this, the broad zone of monopolistic competition, which was neglected by the older writers, has been explored. Finally, the theory of international trade has been considerably changed. The classical explanation of the basis for trade, resting on a discarded labor theory of value, has given way, in part, to a new approach, resting on the differences in price structures in different countries, and on the principle of opportunity costs. In this field, too, the changes in monetary systems, and the growth of trade restrictions, have necessitated some revision of the older teachings concerning the mechanism of foreign exchange and the balance of international payments.

It became apparent to me several years ago that my older work would have to be revised in the light of these developments. Not until I had gotten well into the task, however, did I realize how sweeping the revision was to become. As the work progressed, I found that I was rewriting the greater part of the earlier book. Hence, it seemed wise to modify the title, so that it now reads, *Principles of Economics: A Restatement*. The change in title is not meant to imply that I, out of my own thinking, have recast the framework of economics; it is merely a recognition of the significant contributions which a number of brilliant writers have recently made.

In the present work, I have rewritten the chapters dealing with the topics mentioned above, as well as those dealing with certain other subjects in which my thinking has undergone some development. So, the chapters devoted to the time element in production, the combination of productive agents, the monetary system and its relation to the problem of economic instability, individual prices (or values), and international trade, are almost entirely new (in the sense that they differ from earlier editions of my *Principles*). I have also rewritten considerable portions of the chapters dealing with the scope and definition of economics, and the sharing (distribution) of income, with particular reference to interest. To make room for the expanded discussion of these subjects, I have found it necessary to omit some of the less important parts of the previous editions, and to condense and rearrange certain other portions. A few of the chapters, however, remain substantially as they were before. Taking the book as a whole, about two-thirds of it consists of new material and about one-third stands with only minor changes.

My chief task in this, as in the original book, has been to explain current economic principles in such a way as to make them teachable. If I have made any other contribution, it can probably be summed up in two words—refinement and synthesis. When new ideas are first announced, they seem to represent radical departures which threaten to uproot the views which have previously been held; but it is my belief that constructive change in economic principles (as in most things) comes about by evolution, rather than by revolution. Therefore, it is to be expected that the current doctrines, some of which seem so novel, must be integrated with the existing body of principles. It will then be seen that the new developments do not constitute an uprooting of established teachings, but a series of corrections and additions which improve and perfect the older theory. Since this work of integration has not hitherto been fully accomplished, I have endeavored to further it, by weaving the modern views into the traditional fabric of economics. This has called for some reformulation of the old ideas, as well as of the new; but I hope that I have not dealt unjustly, or too violently, with either. Examples of what I have called refinement may perhaps be found in my chapter dealing with *The Time-consuming Production Process*, and in my treatment of *Say's Law*. There may be some work of synthesis in my chapters on *Individual Prices* (where I have tried to unify the recent teachings concerning the individual firm and monopolistic competition with the Marshallian type of value theory), and in my discussion of *The Basis of International Trade* (where I have tried to restate the law of comparative costs in terms which will reconcile it with the scarcity and price structure approach of Ohlin).

I have also ventured to introduce a few changes in terminology which I hope will make for greater accuracy of statement and clarity of thought. Throughout, it has been my endeavor to reveal the unity that characterizes the body of economic principles.

It is somewhat unfortunate for both teacher and student that, as economic principles evolve, they become more complex. Value theory is not quite as simple, when the individual firm and monopolistic competition are introduced, as it was without those elements. The mechanism of international trade becomes more involved, when nominal currencies and exchange controls have to be considered, in addition to gold standard monetary systems. However, it has always been my view that difficulties in economics should be met, not by omission, but by clarity of presentation. Therefore, I have not tried to simplify at the expense of accuracy or realism. I have endeavored, rather, to help toward the understanding of complexities by orderly arrangement, careful, step-by-step development of ideas, numerous diagrams, and copious illustrations.

Some of the material here incorporated was intended to make its first appearance in another work, upon which I have been engaged for some years with the collaboration of my friend and colleague, Professor William W. Hewett. Because the completion of that work has been somewhat delayed, Professor Hewett has kindly consented to my use of it here. I am further indebted to him in other ways. He and his staff have used certain chapters of this book in their classes at the University of Cincinnati, and have given me the benefit of their criticism and advice. As a result of this, the chapters dealing with individual prices have been considerably improved. More than that, Professor Hewett and I have exchanged ideas on so many phases of economic theory over a period of years that each has greatly influenced the thinking of the other. Therefore, he is entitled to credit for a share in whatever there may be of constructive contribution in this volume. I have also benefited by Professor Raymond T. Bowman's helpful criticism of my chapters on prices.

It goes without saying that the source of most of my thinking is to be found in the writings of the many economists, past and present, who have built up, through the years, the structure of economic principles. Moreover, I owe specific debts to particular writers, here and there, which I have tried to acknowledge in the *References and Suggestions for Further Reading* appended to each of the chapters within. I am also grateful to Messrs. James M. Dawson and Irving B. Kravis for assistance with the proofreading.

RAYMOND T. BYE

University of Pennsylvania, May 1941

NOTE

Sales of this work have been so gratifying that several new printings of the Fourth Edition have become necessary. I have taken advantage of these to make some minor improvements. A few passages have been reworded so as to secure greater accuracy and clarity, some refinements have been made in the drawings, and a number of typographical errors that escaped the original proofreading have been corrected.

R. T. B.

June 1944

CONTENTS

CONTENTS

Chapter I

INDUSTRY AND ECONOMICS

A. An Illustration of Modern Industry

The Stages of Production. — The nature and scope of economics can be explained by an illustration. Consider some familiar article of common use, such as a textbook. It seems a simple object, yet a moment's reflection on its origin, and the means by which it comes into its owner's possession, will serve as an admirable example of the complex workings of modern economic activity.

One obtains the book, probably, from a dealer, who keeps a retail shop for the sale of such articles. His store in itself is a complex affair. On his shelves are thousands of books of various sorts, representing many departments and derived from numerous sources. Behind the counters are a number of clerks to wait upon the customers' needs, and the shop is equipped with fixtures, show windows, and numerous facilities created to aid in bringing the book readily into the possession of purchasers.

The dealer secured the book from a publisher, who attended to the business of having it printed, bound, advertised, sold, and shipped to its destination. The materials for the book were obtained from various sources further back in the stages of industry. The paper on which it was printed was obtained from a paper mill, which rolled it from pulp, crushed from spruce timber, cut, possibly, in the vast forests of western Canada. He secured the cloth for the cover of the book from a dealer in such goods, who acted as a middleman between him and the manufacturer who wove the cloth. If we trace this to its beginnings it will take us, through the various stages of weaving, spinning, baling, and ginning, back to the cotton plantations of the sunny South. But the color of the cloth leads in other directions, through the processes of dye making in this country, or, possibly, to the chemical industry of Germany. The title on the cover is stamped in gold leaf, derived, it may be, through many intermediate stages, from the gold mines of South Africa. The ink used in the printing will lead us to the making of lampblack and linseed oil; the glue used in the binding can be traced to the great meat-packing houses of Chicago, and from there to the cattle ranches of Texas or Argentina. Thus the book is a combination of many materials, each produced through a long train of processes from some elementary product of mine, forest, or farm.

The Auxiliary Industries. — Nor is that all. Indirectly, many other industries have contributed to the process. The store where the book was purchased, the establishment in which it was printed and bound, and the many other factories along the intricate path of its production, were built of stones, brick, glass, lumber, and similar materials which lead through the building trades to the clay pits, stone quarries, sand beds, and timber forests of various parts of the nation. The marvelous presses used in the printing, and all the other machinery that entered into the paper making, cloth weaving, ink manufacture, and so on, lead back to the iron and steel industry, and the iron and coal mines of Pennsylvania or other states.

Entering still more indirectly into the manufacture of the book, but no less important, are certain other agencies which are vital to the activities of modern industry. The materials which come from so many different parts, not only of the United States, but of the world, were brought together by ocean steamships, railroads, motor trucks, delivery wagons, and similar conveyances. Each of these involves a vast industry which has thus contributed to the manufacture of the product. Modern industry is not limited to a single region, but extends its enterprise over the entire globe. In such industry, efficient means of transportation are of primary importance, and without it the civilization of today could not exist. The railroads have justly been called the arteries of commerce.

It is likely that the merchant from whom we bought the book borrowed money from a bank in order to lay in his stock, in anticipation of its future sale. The publishers of the book had similar dealings with banking institutions, and throughout the whole chain of industrial processes the closest relations between bankers and manufacturers would be found. The whole banking system, then, was involved in our purchase of the book, and indirectly was a very important aid in its production.

Even the government was involved. The dealer, who sold us the book, was able to depend upon the security of his business contracts by the power of the state; his stock of books was protected from robbery by policemen employed by the city. He probably paid a license fee to the government for the privilege of maintaining his store, and this fee was one of the items that went into the price which he charged. If the dyes were imported from abroad, a tariff was paid to our government and this was a factor in the price of the cloth that went into the binding. So we would find that in many other ways the activities of the government were concerned in the processes by which our book came into existence.

Labor. — A great deal of labor, both physical and mental, went into the making of the book. The author put into it not only his own thought and effort, but drew upon a great fund of knowledge accumulated by many writers both past and present. The dealer, and all the managers of the various factories and establishments in the chain of auxiliary processes, used their training, experience, and managerial skill, each in his own field. The actual handling of the materials, from their origin in mine, forest, and field to the finished book, was done by countless laborers, skilled and unskilled, who contributed to the final product.

Sharing the Product. — Each individual who had any share in the process received a reward for that share. The dealer from whom the book was purchased made a profit on the transaction; so did the publisher, the paper manufacturer, and all the other business men whose part in the production of the book we have analyzed. The clerks in the bookshop, the compositors and pressmen in the printing room, the railroad men who handled the goods in transit, and all the other laborers were paid for their services. The bankers who helped to finance the various undertakings, the landowners of the various properties, and everyone else who in any way played a part in the production of the book, received a compensation, taken out of the price that was paid for it.

The Flow of Money and Goods. — This was made possible by the use of money. When one purchases the book, he pays for it, let us say, two dollars. These dollars, and those of many other purchasers who buy his wares, the dealer passes on to his publishers, his clerks, his landlord and other creditors; and a portion he retains for himself. The publisher, with the dollars he receives from the dealer and many other dealers, pays his employees, and buys his paper, ink, cloth, glue, gold leaf, etc. The producers of these latter commodities, in turn, pass on a share to persons in the preceding stages of production. Little by little, portions of the money are diverted from the stream in the form of wages to employees, profits to employers, and so on, to be spent by them for more books—or food, or clothing, or any other needs, instead of being passed on to producers further down the scale of production. Eventually all of it is thus restored to the hands of men and women who would spend it, not in the production of books or other goods, but in purchasing things for their own use. Thus, in the pur-

chase of the book, a flow of money is started from the users of the
book, down through all the stages of industry until finally it gets back
into the hands of users again. There is a corresponding flow of cloth,
glue, paper, ink, gold leaf, dye, and finished books in the opposite
direction. At every stage in the process of producing the book there
was an exchange of money for commodities or services. Throughout
all of modern industry there is thus a continual flow of money in one
direction and of goods in another. We are so accustomed to the use of
money that we seldom stop to think of the nature of the functions it
performs. It is an all-pervasive feature of the modern industrial world.
Its importance can hardly be overestimated.

Industry a System. — Our consideration of so common an object
as a book and the way in which it comes into one's possession has led
into a maze of complexity. We have seen that the purchase of the book
is only the culmination of a long and intricate series of operations
which extends into the printing, cotton, paper, meat-packing, iron and
steel, building, dye, banking, transportation, and many other industries, and which reaches into various parts of the United States and
even into far distant portions of the globe. It is probable that, if we
were to push our analysis far enough, it would be found to reach
throughout the whole of the modern industrial system and into the
four corners of the civilized world. The same is true of any other
object. Had we chosen a pencil, a necktie, or a lamb chop, our study
would have pushed us through the same long chain of production
and into equally distant regions. In short, every one of the commodities in use in our daily life is here as a result of the vast, intricate, and
far-reaching modern industrial system.

The most remarkable fact about this complex industry is that *it is a
system*. Vast labyrinth of intricate, winding paths, it yet moves with
precision towards a set purpose, and from its workings there emerges
a continuous flow of finished commodities to meet the needs of human existence. In some mysterious way its various parts are so co-
ordinated as to coöperate towards definite ends, and while at times its
actions may be clumsy and inefficient, on the whole it accomplishes its
purpose. Moreover, its activity is entirely spontaneous. No conscious
hand directs its processes. No autocrat or far-seeing mind dictates how
each of its parts shall move to produce the desired result; yet by the
separate actions of each individual part, working in its own way, the
result is attained. The system just grew naturally; yet it possesses
order, and therefore it must be working in accordance with principles
that observation and study will reveal.

B. The Development of Modern Industry

Conditions Preceding the Industrial Revolution. — We can understand better the workings of this order if we first learn something of the historical development which brought it about. A detailed knowledge of this history is not necessary to an understanding of economic principles, so only the barest sketch of it will be attempted here.

The beginnings of the present industrial system are to be found in England. That country, prior to the middle of the eighteenth century, was mostly rural. The masses of the people were little better than serfs, living on the great landed estates of those days under the domination of a proprietor or lord. These estates were called manors. The simple people devoted themselves mainly to agriculture, cultivating the scattered plots of land assigned to their families by long established custom. As the methods of agriculture were crude, they made but a bare living for themselves. The important thing to bear in mind about these early English manors is that they were rather isolated communities, having but little contact with other parts of the country. Each was an economically self-sufficient unit; that is, it provided most of its own needs by the produce of its own labor. The peasants—or villeins, as they were called—raised enough food for their simple diet, made their own clothes and built their own small cottages or huts. Only a very few commodities, such as salt and iron, had to be obtained from outside the boundaries of the manor. Consequently there was very little trade. Being little trade, there was not much use for money, and not much of it circulated in those days. The people had few luxuries, except the lords, who were comparatively well-off because of the contributions in labor and goods which the villeins had to make to them. In all respects the industry and life of the people were simple and primitive.

Some towns existed, but they were nothing like the great cities of modern times. They were primarily for purposes of defense and trade. There were shops and traveling merchants, but no great manufacturing enterprises such as we are accustomed to. What industry there was was carried on by skilled artisans, who were carpenters, smiths, wheelwrights, tailors, and so on, fashioning their products by hand without complicated machinery. A number of these artisans would be employed in a single shop. At the head of the shop was a master workman; his assistants were apprentices who must serve under his direction for a term of years before they could become masters in their turn. We can see that in this association of master and apprentice there was a relationship very different from that which exists today between the wealthy capitalist employer and his wage-earners. This early type of artisan industry was known as the handicraft system.

We see, then, that England prior to the Industrial Revolution possessed a number of distinct economic characteristics: it was mainly rural and therefore agricultural; its manorial communities were economically independent; hence, there was little trade or use of money; its towns were small and few, characterized by some commerce and handicraft industry.

The United States at this time, while it did not have the feudalistic system of manors, with their lords and villeins, was in some respects very much like England. Frontier conditions prevailed. At first each individual was his own master, wresting from nature, very largely by hunting, trapping, and chopping, his own means of livelihood. There developed then a crude kind of agriculture, in which the land was roughly cleared and, because of its virgin richness, it grew abundant crops with very little effort on the part of its cultivators. In time a more careful system of agriculture developed. As in England, there were few towns, little commerce or manufactures, economic self-sufficiency, and not much use of money.

For some time prior to the middle of the eighteenth century several developments in European affairs were taking place which were destined to have effects on both sides of the Atlantic. The discovery of America opened up rich mines of gold and silver. The Spaniards, who obtained most of these precious metals, traded them with other European countries for merchandise of which they were in need, and so they came into general circulation as money. Money made trade much easier to carry on, and so stimulated its growth. Other things were happening to increase this trade development. The Crusades had given Europeans a taste for oriental wares, and some commerce with the East developed as a result. Englishmen also began to discover that they could carry on a profitable trade selling wool on the continent of Europe. This was stimulated by a great plague, known as the Black Death, which in 1348 killed from a third to a half of the population of England, causing a scarcity of labor on the manors. Sheep-raising requires large land areas but not much labor. The lords therefore turned their manors into the paying sheep ranches, expelling the remaining peasants from their small land holdings and forcing them into the towns.

This made possible a new development in industry known as the domestic system. The presence of a labor supply in the towns caused an employer class to spring up who assumed the direction of simple industrial processes, such as weaving, and hired other workers to carry on the labor. Since the process required no elaborate machinery or factory building, the employer usually merely furnished materials to the workers, who took them home to work upon and brought back the finished product, for which they were paid wages. The artisans who did this work often were small agricultural peasants whose main industry was farming, but who had a loom upon which they did weaving on the side. It is easy to see that in this domestic system the beginnings of a factory system are to be found. All that was needed was a larger extension of commercial markets, making it possible to carry on production on a large scale, and the development of machinery and steam power. The former expansion was already in process because of the growing trade between England and the rest of the countries of Europe which has been described. The latter development was about to take place.

The Industrial Revolution. — Beginning with 1767 there began a series of remarkable inventions in spinning and weaving machinery in England which completely revolutionized the woolen industry of that country. The most important of these were the spinning jenny, the mule, the water frame, and the power loom. The perfection of the steam engine at about this same time made possible the application of steam power to this mechanical spinning and weaving machinery, and ushered in the modern factory system. Soon the new power was applied to other industries, until gradually it came into general use. The development of machinery must of necessity be based upon the use of iron and steel. Of no little importance in hastening the change that took place, therefore, were various improved processes for the production of iron and steel which were introduced during this period. The invention of the locomotive and steamboat were equally significant. Stephenson constructed a practical locomotive in 1814. Within the next twenty-five years there was a tremendous development of steam railroads throughout the country. In 1819 the first steamboat crossed the Atlantic and ushered in the era of fast ocean transportation.

The transformation which these various inventions and improvements, following each other in rapid succession, made in the industry of England was rapid and violent. The old handicraft and domestic industries were completely displaced by the machine process. The growth of large factories took place by leaps and bounds, and the cities of England increased in population at a rate which was truly remarkable. Within less than a century the manorial, handicraft, and domestic systems of industry were swept away; great manufacturing cities sprang up in their place, and England became an urban rather than a rural nation.

These changes were soon echoed in the rest of Europe and in the

United States. As has been pointed out, in the early days of the American colonies manufactures were almost unknown, and such manufactured goods as were needed had to be imported from the mother country. Manufactures began to develop in New England, however, prior to the Revolutionary War, and after the United States became independent they rapidly expanded. This took place at about the time when the Industrial Revolution was beginning to make itself felt in England, and the new mechanical devices, the steam engine, and the locomotive, were not slow to find a fertile field in America. Great cities grew up like mushrooms along the harbors, such as New York and Philadelphia. The period from 1830 up until almost the end of the century was one of great railway building and general industrial expansion, which rapidly transformed the United States into a great manufacturing and commercial nation. Meanwhile agriculture became much more productive, due to improved methods that were introduced. Thus was the modern system of industry born.

C. THE NATURE OF ECONOMICS

The Subject-Matter of Economics. — The preceding paragraphs have sketched very briefly some of the characteristics of our industrial system, and something of the historical development by which it came into being. Two aspects of this system will henceforth engage our attention, viz.: its structure, or organization, and its functioning, or process. We shall want to learn of what the wealth and income of a nation consist, how business enterprises are organized, what is the nature of banks, what different kinds of money are in use, and so on. These things constitute the anatomy of the industrial body—its flesh and bones, as it were. But if we are to get a real understanding of economic life, we must look into its physiology—that is, the functioning of its various parts. We must inquire how business organizations operate, what influences guide production into its various channels, how money circulates from hand to hand in the processes of exchange, and what are its effects, how prices come to be established for different products, how the various participants in industry get paid for their services, and all the many activities of the business world. These are the types of questions which economics considers. The industrial organization and its processes constitute its subject-matter.

Desires and Scarcity. — The term "economics" naturally calls to our minds the familiar words "economy" and "economize." There is a kinship between all three of these words because the economic processes that go on in society are, in fact, performing an economizing function for human society. It is necessary to economize because the desires of man outrun the means of satisfying them which are at his disposal. Most of us are so constituted that we want a great many things, and our wants are capable of almost indefinite expansion. We are not satisfied with the mere necessities of food, clothing, and shelter, but we want a richer and more varied diet, more beautiful and elaborate wardrobes, more substantial and luxurious houses, more comfortable and more elegant furnishings; we want automobiles, radios, sporting goods, theaters, motion pictures, cameras, and many other things too numerous to mention. If we are fortunate enough to improve our mode of living, our ambition leaps ahead to still more delectable possessions, so that our desires appear to be quite insatiable. On the other hand, the means of satisfying those desires are limited in quantity. Most of the things we want have to be produced by human labor, and there are only a certain number of human beings to do the work, and they have a rather limited amount of energy to devote to productive activity. The natural resources upon which they must depend for the materials out of which to make the many products which we desire are likewise limited. There is only a certain amount of land available for use, and the minerals or timber that can be obtained from it, or the crops that can be grown upon it, are likewise limited. Therefore, the quantity of things which industry can produce is somewhat scarce, in relation to the desires of the people.

It is this scarcity which confronts us with the problem of economizing. Since we cannot gratify all of our desires, we have to decide which ones are to have priority. Somehow, decisions must be made as to the directions which productive activity shall take, what things shall be produced and in what quantities, and what things shall be sacrificed. Moreover, in carrying on production, we must strive, as far as possible, to avoid waste, in order that the scarce means at our disposal may go as far as possible toward meeting our multifarious wants. The industrial system has been evolved to perform this function. Its processes constitute the means adopted by human society to reconcile the antithesis between unlimited desires and scarcity. For this reason, economics is sometimes called *political economy* or *social economy*—that is, the economizing process of a political state or of society.

Economics a Social Study. — It is important to emphasize the social aspect of this subject. The term social refers to people in groups, in societies, in their relations with one another, rather than as separate individuals. Some branches of learning are confined primarily to the study of individuals. For instance, physiology and psychology (except social psychology) analyze the behavior of the individual body and the individual mind as separate units. But economics, like history and sociology, deals with human beings in their relations to each other, and it describes group phenomena. Because most of us have viewed economic life from our own individual standpoint and studied the effects of the business world upon our own interests, the social point of view of the economist may seem a little strange, at first. The head of a business concern sees himself as the center of a little world, and he thinks of business operations in terms of how they affect him; he is not likely to see himself as part of a great system, as a cog in a machine of vast proportions. The economist takes the latter point of view; he is not much concerned with the individual business man; he sees only a whole class of business men performing a certain social function and behaving in certain ways that affect the community. He analyzes the relation of such business men to other parts of the industrial system, and looks at it all from a community standpoint. Consequently, the economist's description of a business is very different from the picture which any individual business man, relying upon his own experience, would draw—just as a human being, viewing a forest from a trip through it and around it and above it, would get a very different picture of the woods from that seen by a tiny insect living upon a single leaf within it. To this broad point of view the student must adjust himself. This will become natural and clear as we proceed with our study.

A Definition of Economics. — If we gather together the ideas concerning the nature and subject-matter of economics developed in the immediately preceding paragraphs, we will see that it can be defined in the following terms: *Economics is that branch of learning which deals with the social organization and process by which the scarce means of production are directed toward the satisfaction of human wants.* This is not the only possible definition of the subject; other writers may prefer a somewhat different statement. It does, however, express clearly enough the nature and scope of economics. There is no reason, therefore, to confuse the student by discussing the various other definitions which have been proposed.

The Scientific Attitude in Economics. — Economics is sometimes represented as a branch of science, but not all economists would so designate it. The essence of science is the method which it uses, and the method is one that is not entirely applicable to all aspects of economic investigation. Let us look into this.

The scientific method consists essentially of four steps, namely—observation, classification, generalization, and verification. Scientific observation must not be of a casual or vague sort; it must be painstaking and accurate. The scientist accepts no conclusions about phenomena that he cannot establish as a fact by the evidence of his senses, and which cannot be verified by the similar observations of others. In order to get his facts, he examines the things he is studying with the utmost care, under conditions most likely to prevent error arising from possible bias, carelessness, or self-deception. For example, the physicist studies the operation of mechanical forces in a laboratory where ideal conditions can be set up, and he measures the behavior of the forces he is studying with the most precise instruments his ingenuity can devise. The biologist dissects each plant and animal and examines its parts under the microscope, taking careful notes, or possibly photographing what he sees. When the basic facts are once clearly established, the scientist arranges and classifies them, guided by the natural relationships revealed by the likenesses and differences which he finds. This classification, in turn, suggests to him principles, or generalizations, which appear to characterize the behavior of the phenomena he is investigating. The generalizations at first are merely tentative—theories which seem to describe the phenomena—but if, after further testing, no exceptions to the principles so developed are found, they then become scientific laws whose truth has been established by verification. Charles Darwin established the law of evolution in this way. In studying the different species of plants and animals, he observed that they merged into one another in such a way that it was impossible to draw sharp lines between them. This suggested to him that they may have had a common origin, from which they had gradually diverged. So, he was able to set forth the theory of evolution as a tentative generalization. Biologists have since been attempting to verify this theory by seeking evidence of intermediate forms between species apparently separated, and by hunting for evolutionary changes now going on in animal life. Enough evidence has now been gathered, probably, to justify the scientist in setting forth the doctrine of evolution as a law.

The economist, in studying the industrial activities of man, must follow this same careful method, as far as possible. However, he is somewhat hampered in doing so by the nature of the phenomena with which he deals. He cannot establish laboratories where human beings, corporations, money, and the various other phenomena of economic life, can be examined in test tubes or under the microscope. Therefore, he must limit himself to such general facts as can be established by careful observation of what he sees going on around him, and by statistical records. In the present stage of its development, economics does not possess a sufficiently large body of painstakingly and accurately measured facts to permit of the strictly scientific procedures which are common to chemistry, physics, and biology. The economist must, for the present, rely more upon general observation and rigorous logic. He can, however, maintain a scientific attitude toward his subject, and work in a scientific way as far as possible.

It is important to emphasize this attitude in approaching the study of economics, because most persons already have in their minds many unscientific ideas and beliefs about the industrial world. They start out with certain assumptions and prejudices, gathered here and there from faulty observation or hasty guesswork, which are likely to lead them to erroneous conclusions. For instance, a banker has had intimate personal contact with his little narrow sphere in the business world, and may know how to run his institution well; but, because he has never made any careful and systematic study of industry as a whole, his ideas about the industrial system and its operations may be very erroneous and incomplete. The average business man knows fairly well how to manage the details of his own business, but he knows little of the underlying forces of economic life. He has been so absorbed with the tiny niche which it has been his function to care for, that he has never had the time or the facilities to study more broadly the great mechanism of which he is a part. Just as an electrician can wire a house satisfactorily without any knowledge of the science of physics, so one can be a successful manufacturer or merchant without a reliable conception of economic principles. The student of economics must not be biased by a narrow point of view. He must have the open mind of the scientist, ready to see the facts as they are, and prepared to modify many ideas which he now possesses. This is not easy to do, but it is necessary if one is to arrive at any real understanding of the subject.

Pure Economics, Economic Ethics, and Applied Economics. — The final end and justification of all learning is to be found in its contribution to human welfare. Knowledge of economics should, therefore, enable us to improve the economic process, so that it may satisfy more fully the wants of man. However, investigation must precede reform. Just as the physician must have a thorough understanding of anatomy and physiology, before he can diagnose diseases and prescribe remedies for human ailments, so the student of economics must first become thoroughly familiar with how the industrial system now functions, before he is able to appraise its merits and defects or suggest measures of reform. There are, indeed, three phases of economics, which represent successive steps that must be taken in dealing with the practical problems of the economic world. These may be called pure economics, economic ethics, and applied economics, respectively.

It is the first task of the economist to explain *how* the industrial system works, and *why*. At this stage, he seeks merely *to describe* the business world and its workings. That is *pure economics*. To explain how the system works is neither to justify it nor to condemn it; it is a simple statement of facts, a mere description of phenomena. This is comparable to the work of the pure chemist, who studies how the elements of matter behave, their combinations and relationships, regardless of what use is to be made of this knowledge. In his laboratory he discovers that a certain combination of substances will produce a high explosive and announces this fact to the world. The coal operator can use this knowledge to blast coal from its bed, but so can the militarist use it to blow up a ship. The chemist has no concern, as a chemist, with the ethics of either application. So, in economics, we can discover principles which explain what fixes the amount of a man's wages, regardless of whether the wages of a given workman are high enough to keep him in comfort, or so low as to keep him in poverty. We must not allow our sympathy for the poor to bias our analysis of how wages are fixed and what functions they perform in the economic process.

After we have acquired a knowledge of economic institutions and processes, however, it is important to ask whether they serve their purpose well or ill. We must appraise them in the light of our standards of right and wrong, and try to reach some conclusion concerning their effects upon human welfare. This is *economic ethics*. It is comparable to the work of the physician in studying the effects of different foods upon the human body. It is not solely a question of economics, but also of ethics, and it requires intuitive insight and personal opinion, as well as mere knowledge of facts and economic principles. It is thus somewhat less scientific in character than pure economics.

After we have acquired an understanding of the economic process, and have analyzed it from the ethical point of view, certain desirable changes will be indicated. It is then our task to formulate programs of betterment based on our knowledge of how the economic system functions. This is *applied economics*. Applied economics seeks to utilize the knowledge obtained from pure economics and economic ethics so as most effectively to promote welfare, just as applied chemistry takes the results of laboratory investigations and puts them to work for men's purposes in industry, and just as the physician prescribes treatment for a sick patient. But it is important to recognize that, before we can undertake to pass judgment on present economic arrangements, we must understand thoroughly just what those arrangements are and how they work. If we seek to remedy industrial defects without such knowledge, we are likely to come to grief. A study of pure economics, therefore, should precede the study of economic ethics and applied economics.

This book is primarily a text in pure economics. Its purpose is to give its readers a knowledge of the fundamental principles at work in the industrial system. For the most part, it will avoid questions of welfare, it will refrain from passing judgments of praise or condemnation upon our institutions, and it will not suggest remedies for defects. This is not because these things are not important—they are of vast importance; but it is because they cannot be considered intelligently until after the student has grasped thoroughly the first principles of pure economics. If human interest compels us at times to depart from this rule to indulge in a little criticism or praise, or to make a suggestion for reform, it must be regarded as a digression which lies outside the main task to which this work is devoted. In another volume, the author (in collaboration with one of his colleagues) has considered some of the fascinating problems of economic welfare with which applied economics deals.[1]

In the present work, then, we shall discuss such questions as how production is carried on, what are the nature and functions of banks and of money, what fixes the prices of commodities, what determines the size of the incomes of different individuals, and many similar matters. In the other volume referred to are considered some of the problems that arise out of these phenomena, such as, how our productive system can be rescued from the periodical cycles of prosperity and depression to which it is subject, what system of banking and currency is best, how prices can be regulated and monopolies controlled in the interests of social justice, whether or not the present inequality of incomes is fair and how a just system of income distribution should be regulated, whether socialism or some other form of economic organization promises hope of greater welfare than our present system, and a host of equally important and interesting questions.

SUMMARY

A simple example of an ordinary commodity, such as a textbook, showed us that the processes of modern industry are exceedingly intricate, reaching back from consumers, through a long line of producers, auxiliary industries, and institutions, to points distant in both time and space. This intricate complex of processes is nevertheless a somewhat orderly, systematic whole, working in accordance with discoverable principles, to provide us with the necessities and conveniences of life.

Our industrial system originated in England, where a series of remarkable inventions, extending from the middle of the eighteenth to the middle of the nineteenth centuries, overthrew the old manorial

[1] Raymond T. Bye and William W. Hewett, *Applied Economics*, 3rd edition, 1938.

system of agriculture and the handicraft and domestic systems of industry, and set up the factory system in its place. These inventions, carried over to America, transformed the United States from a frontier agricultural nation into a great industrial country. These changes are known as the Industrial Revolution.

The industrial organization so developed, and its processes, constitute the subject-matter of economics. Economics is sometimes called social economy, because the function of economic activity is one of economizing scarce resources, in order to make them go as far as possible toward satisfying our boundless wants. Economics is a social study—that is, it deals with men in their relations with each other; it looks at things, not from the individual, but from the community, viewpoint. Economics may be defined as that branch of learning which deals with the social organization and process by which the scarce means of production are directed toward the satisfaction of human wants. As far as possible, economics follows the scientific method of careful, unbiased observation, classification, generalization, and verification. Pure economics describes the industrial system as it is; economic ethics appraises its effects for good or ill; and applied economics develops a program for improving it. This book deals primarily with pure economics.

REFERENCES AND SUGGESTIONS FOR FURTHER READING

In Henry Clay's *Economics, an Introduction for the General Reader* (American edition, 1920), Chapter I, there is an interesting survey of the nature and purpose of economics, from which I have gained some helpful ideas for the first part of this chapter. A more exhaustive analysis is that of J. N. Keynes, *The Scope and Method of Political Economy* (London, 4th edition, 1917). Some very illuminating discussion is also contained in Lionel Robbins' *An Essay on the Nature and Significance of Economic Science* (London, 1932). I have set forth more fully my own ideas on the nature of economics in an article entitled *The Scope and Definition of Economics,* published in the Journal of Political Economy, Vol. XLVII, pp. 623–647 (October, 1939).

H. L. Beales presents an excellent, concise summary of the development of modern industry in *The Industrial Revolution, 1750–1850* (1928). Arnold Toynbee, *Lectures on the Industrial Revolution* (new edition, London, 1908) is still a valuable reference on this subject. See also the article *Industrial Revolution,* in *The Encyclopedia of the Social Sciences.* A useful short summary of the evolution of modern industry is in the opening chapters of J. R. Turner's *Introduction to Economics* (1919).

NOTE: The references and suggested readings appended to each chapter of this work are not at all intended as a complete bibliography. Rather, as their title implies, they are meant only to guide teachers and students in selecting collateral reading or in finding further information, where there is a wish to probe a little deeper into the subjects discussed. At the same time I have taken advantage of this opportunity to make acknowledgments, where due, to particular sources from which I have obtained material or suggestive ideas.

Chapter II

PRODUCTION AND RELATED CONCEPTS

A. PRODUCTION AND INCOME

Goods and Utility. — It is the task of industry to supply society with the products which its people desire. Some of these products are tangible, material things—such as foodstuffs, articles of clothing, houses, furniture, radio receiving sets, medicines. Others are non-material—such as medical advice, theatrical performances, radio broadcasts. We shall call the material products *commodities,* and the non-material ones *services.* Both commodities and services are known in economics as *goods.* If we use the term *utility* to denote *that quality of anything which makes it desired by human beings,* we may define a *good* as *anything that has utility.* A dwelling house, a plate of ice cream, and the air we breathe are all goods, because people desire them.

Some goods, such as air, or ocean water at the seashore, are so plentiful that everybody can have all that he wants of them. No one has to exert any effort to produce them, and they are not the object of economic endeavor. Therefore, the economist is not concerned with them. They are called *free goods.* Other goods are not so plentiful. Either there is a natural scarcity, as in the case of diamonds and deposits of rare metals, or they can be produced only by the exertion of human effort, as in the case of shoes, steel rails, or bread. These are the object of economic endeavor; hence they are called *economic goods.* Economic goods may be formally defined as *those goods which are scarce, relatively to the desire for them, or whose production requires effort.*

It should be pointed out that the term utility, as used in economics, has no ethical significance. When we say that a good has qualities which make it desired, we do not mean to imply that its effects upon us are necessarily beneficial. Men desire things, sometimes, which they would be better off without. They may crave stimulation or deadening of the senses, as well as nourishing food. Whiskey and opiates gratify the desire for the former just as bread gratifies the desire for the latter. Regardless of the injurious effects of the former and the beneficial effects of the latter, they are all goods, and possess utility.

Production. — It is the function of industry to produce economic goods. Such goods, therefore, constitute *the product* of industry. This statement needs some further explanation, for it involves a conception of industry, and of production, somewhat at variance with popular usage. Many people confine the term industry to manufacturing operations; they do not include such activities as agriculture, wholesale and retail trading, lecturing and teaching, within the ordinary meaning of that word. But we shall use the word industry in the broadest possible sense, to denote all kinds of economic activity.

There is a similar difference in usage of the term production. It was formerly thought that production consisted in the creation of material objects, and the labor of a person that did not result in some tangible commodity was regarded as unproductive. For instance, a tailor who made a suit was considered a producer, but the boy who delivered it to the customer was not. Some uninformed persons still hold this view. Yet a moment's reflection will show convincingly that the mere making of material things is not the essence of production. A child may make mud pies, or a lunatic may carve curious figures from a stick of wood; yet we would not think of these acts as productive. Moreover, it cannot really be said that man *creates* anything material. Matter is here, and is both indestructible and unincreasable. We can alter it in kind, but not in quantity. All that the tailor does when he makes a suit of clothes is to take matter which already existed in one form— that of cloth, thread, buttons, and hair—and change it to another form. The product has been made, therefore, only in the sense that a change in the form of matter has taken place. But even this is not in itself production, for the child has also changed the form of matter without producing anything in an economic sense. The difference between their two actions is that the tailor has made the matter more useful to man, while the child has not. The real essence of production, therefore, is in the doing of something useful. What, then, of the delivery boy? Has he not met this test? Surely the suit is more useful in the customer's hands than in the tailor's shop; therefore in delivering it he has done something productive, just as much so as the tailor in making it.

We have learned that when a thing possesses the quality of being useful to (desired by) man, it has utility. We can say, then, that both the tailor and the delivery boy have imparted utility to the suit of clothes. This makes their activity productive. *We may define production, therefore, as the creation of utilities.*

The full significance of this idea of production may be made clearer by an illustration. Consider again the production of a textbook. What is its purpose? It is to impart knowledge. The ultimate product, then, is not the book, but the dissemination of that knowledge, to which the book is only a preliminary means. The teacher who uses the book in the classroom is also working toward the same result. He and the author, and all those who had any part in the printing, binding, and marketing of the book are engaged in the one process of producing a particular kind of knowledge. The teacher does not produce a material object, although the printer does; but both are part of the same process of production. The theater is another illustration. One may think that the carpenter who constructs the stage is a producer, while the actor who performs upon it is not. Yet what is the real product of the carpenter's labor? He and the actor are combining their energies toward a single goal—entertainment of the public. It is in the enjoyment of the theater-goers that the product of the carpenter's skill and the actor's art are alike found. Since both contribute to this, both are producers.

A utility is not complete when a commodity is in its final physical form. The book is not completely produced when it is printed and bound, although no further changes in its physical structure will take place. For production is not alone the making of the book, but the creation of the gratifications which the book helps to yield. It yields none while on the publisher's shelves; not until it is packed and shipped to various parts of the country and gotten into the hands of its ultimate users can we say that the process of production is complete. Each individual who has had any share in the packing, shipping, transportation, or sale of it, by bringing it a degree nearer to the point where it is capable of gratifying the desire of the user, has shared in its production, and that production is not complete until it is in the hands of the consumer. The economist does not regard it as a finished good until that point has been reached.

Kinds of Production. — The contributions of these various individuals in the production of the book are not all of the same sort. The printers and binders, the packers and carriers, the wholesalers and retailers, and the various persons who handle it in the many stages between the raw material and the finished utility, all are helping to gratify the desires of consumers by quite different sorts of labor. Some are making the material thing itself, others are transporting, handling, or selling it, while the teacher who later makes use of it in the classroom is engaged in still another sort of activity. There are thus a number of different ways in which the wants of consumers may be supplied, and hence, in which production may be carried on.

It has already been shown that, in the printing and binding of a book and in the processes which preceded these operations, the laborers were simply transforming the shape or composition of matter. This is known as the production of *form utilities*. This kind of production consists in changing matter from a raw state into a more usable form. More persons probably are engaged in this production than in any other. It includes agriculture, manufactures, mining and quarrying.

It has also been shown that, before the production of an article can be said to be complete, it must be gotten into the hands of the consumers who are to use it. This usually involves shipping or transporting the article from one place to another. It may be manufactured in New England, for use in the South. This textbook, printed in the East, may be employed by students in a western university. The process of adding to its usefulness by transporting it from the place where it is made to the place where it is to be used is the creation of *place utility*. All industries engaged in the transportation of merchandise or of people are creating utilities of this kind.

In modern industry, the processes of production are split into many stages, each under the direction of different persons. This entails the repeated exchange of economic goods from the possession of one producer to another, and finally to that of the consumer himself. It used to be thought that an exchange of goods must entail a loss to one of the parties concerned. If one individual could make a profit by a trade, it was held, the other person in the transaction must suffer a loss corresponding to the former's gain. The truth is, however, that a fair exchange is advantageous to both parties. If I buy a book from a dealer, its utility to me is greater than that of some other thing that my money would have bought, or I would not make the purchase. I have added to my satisfactions by the exchange of my dollars for the book. Similarly, if the dealer did not expect to receive more utilities from the use of my dollars than he does from the book, he would not sell it to me. Both of us, therefore, have increased our enjoyments as a result of our bargain. The process of exchange, therefore, adds to the utilities of the community, and is a productive operation. Such production may be said to create *possession utilities*. Wholesale and retail merchants, and dealers and brokers of every description, are producers of this kind of utility.

There are some commodities whose utility to men increases with time. Old wine is preferred to new because of its superior flavor. A musician prizes very highly the violin whose great age gives it unusual tone and resonance. Ice, which in the winter is a free good because of its great abundance and slight usefulness, has great utility if kept until summer, when it is more scarce as well as more useful. It is possible, therefore, to add to the gratifications of a community by simply storing goods for a time. Such an operation is properly spoken of as production, for it adds to society's income. This kind of production is known as the creation of *time utilities*. The storage industries are representative of this type of activity.

The kinds of production and the corresponding industries so far discussed have all dealt with the handling of material goods—the extraction and making up into consumable commodities of raw produce, their storage, transportation, and sale. If the student has carefully followed the conception of production outlined, however, he will realize that many persons in the community are yielding utilities not directly associated with the handling of commodities at all. For lack of a better term, we may group the activities of all these persons under the general head of *service utilities*. Embraced under this head are all forms of professional and personal service. The learned professions include some of our most important producers. Physicians, lawyers, teachers, authors, musicians, actors, philosophers, preachers, scientists, artists—these and many others give us some of the priceless things of our civilization. The personal service group is also productive. It includes cooks, waitresses, chambermaids, chauffeurs, valets, bootblacks, butlers, manicurists, hairdressers, and the thousand and one occupations of similar type. Here, also, are some of the less desirable characters, such as the gambling-house proprietor or the prostitute, who, injurious and immoral as their activities may be, are nevertheless gratifying human desires and are, therefore, producers. The officers of government, from president or emperor down to the bureau clerk or the policeman on his beat, are performing another kind of want-gratifying service for the community. Insurance may also be included under the head of service production.

Unproductive Activity. — Not all the activities of men in industry are productive. Some activities do not result in utilities; some, indeed, actually destroy them.

The most obvious cases of this type are predatory activities, such as robbery, piracy, embezzlement, swindling, and the like. Here the aggressor acquires utilities for himself, but he does so at the expense of his victims; there is no net addition to the utilities of society as a whole. Often predatory activities are so combined with productive enterprise that it is difficult to separate the two. This is the case with shady and "sharp" business practices, where the business man endeavors to get something for nothing. Whenever a monopolist exacts an exorbitant price for his wares, or when goods are adulterated or represented to be what they are not, there is predatory business, and such activity is not productive.

Certain types of speculation fall in the same category. The legitimate speculator is productive, because he assists in the creation of time utilities. By buying goods when they are plentiful and holding them for sale later, at a time when they are relatively scarce, he makes them available to consumers when they are most needed, and thereby performs a useful function. This will be explained more fully in Chapter VII. However, there are always some persons in the speculative markets who cannot be classed as legitimate dealers. Some are amateurs taking a plunge on the market; others are bucket-shop gamblers, who bet on a rise or fall in the price of a commodity or of a share of stock, without actually making a purchase or sale. These activities, together with gambling, are to be classed as unproductive. This holds also for speculators in real estate. They may gain by a rise in the value of land, but there is no addition to the utilities of the community.

Advertising presents a mixed case. In some cases advertising definitely adds to the utilities of consumers. By helping them to find the goods they need, by calling new products to their attention which they might not otherwise know about, and by educating them in the use of available goods, it undoubtedly yields utility. A vast amount of advertisement, however, is purely competitive. Its purpose is not to inform consumers where goods can be purchased, nor to educate them to new ways of gratifying their desires, but merely to persuade them to purchase the wares of one producer instead of the similar goods of a rival. The tremendous amount of display advertising maintained by tobacco producers is an example. It is a matter of comparative indifference to society which of several brands of tobacco one buys. The essential thing is that his wants should be supplied. They would be supplied without such strenuous advertising. This competitive display, therefore, is wasteful, and not productive.[1]

Military activity may or may not be productive. In so far as troops are used in preserving order, they are performing police functions, which, as has been shown, are productive effort. Warfare, however, is essentially destructive. From a world viewpoint it is doubtful if it can ever be productive. It may conceivably be productive from a national viewpoint. Defensive warfare, if successful, would be productive to a nation, in the sense that it would prevent the destruction of wealth. Aggressive warfare could be productive to a nation only if it brought

---

[1] Competitive advertising might be considered productive indirectly, in that competition stimulates efficiency and weeds out the inefficient producers, but, even if this be granted, it must be conceded that there is some unnecessary waste.

an increase of utilities greater than its cost. The costs of modern warfare are so terrific that it is doubtful whether the gains can ever compensate for the costs. Certain it is that, even if successful, nations very seldom increase their economic goods by war. Whether or not there are other sorts of gain, political, ethical, social, or racial, which compensate for the material costs, it is not within the province of the economist to decide.

Money Income and Real Income. — The stream of goods which flows from the productive operations of industry constitutes the income of the people. This is not at first apparent, for we ordinarily think of income as receipts of money during a certain period of time. Ask any man what is his income, and he is likely to reply (if he does not tell you it is none of your business!) that it is so many dollars per week per year. However, in economics, it is important to realize that money is primarily a kind of accounting device, like the chips in that game or a ticket to the opera. It gives the holder a claim to a good and it is the goods which are the really important thing. Therefore in the case of most money transactions, we must look behind the money for the goods to which it gives claim. Much confusion is likely to result if we do not do this. For instance, a man's money income may increase, and we are likely to think that he is more prosperous; but if the prices of the goods he buys have risen correspondingly, he is no better off than before. We have to look at the goods he gets in order to tell how he is faring. Again, a church may supply a house rent free to its minister, in addition to the salary it pays him. If we looked only at the salary, we would have a false idea of his true income. We must, then, look beyond the money for the goods which make up *real income*.

Let us be inquisitive, and probe further into the income of the individual who tells us that his income is, say, three thousand dollars yearly. Let us ask him to tell us, not what are his money receipts, but his receipts of goods. We can get the best picture of his real income by an analysis of the things he buys with his money.

With a part of his three thousand dollars he may obtain seats at the theater, hire a cook to prepare his dinners, employ a lawyer to look after his legal affairs, have his shoes polished by a bootblack, and set other individuals to work performing services for him. Evidently, then, the services are a part of his real income. All of us are expending a part of our income in similar ways. The services of human beings, therefore, are one of the constituents of real income.

With another part of his purchasing power he may rent a house, take a vacation trip by railroad and steamboat, pay dues to the golf club of which he is a member, and so on. In this case he could not consider the house, the railroad, the steamboat, and the golf links as part of his income, for he does not own or have exclusive possession of them. He merely enjoys the use of them along with many other persons. Here again we may say that he is receiving services; but in this case, they are the services of wealth, instead of human beings. From the house he gets shelter and all the comforts of home, from the railroad and the steamboat he obtains transportation and from the golf links he derives the pleasure of exercise and play which their use affords. We may say, therefore, that the services of which are part of his real income.

With a third part of his money income he may pu[rchase] various forms of wealth outright. He may buy clothes, food, new automobile, a radio set, a piano, furniture, and many others, an[d] articles. These new commodities, which he acquires during the peri[od of t]ime we are considering, are also included in his real income.

Finally, it is possible that he may save part of his earnings and [invest] them—perhaps in the capital of some business enterprise, perha[ps in] a new house for himself. This case does not differ essentially from [the] ordinary purchase of commodities. For instance, if he invests his sa[v]ings in the stocks or bonds of a corporation, the latter will spend th[e] money so obtained in enlarging its plant or in purchasing equipment; then the investor may be said to have acquired part ownership of, or an interest in the new wealth so accumulated. If he puts his money in a bank, the bank will lend it to business men, and again new wealth will be purchased with it. If he invests it in a house for himself, it is plain that he has bought a new commodity, just as he buys a piano or a suit of clothes. Saving, therefore, is simply one way of acquiring wealth.

We now see what is involved in the concept of *real income*. It refers to the services performed for us by human beings, the services we derive from the use of wealth, and the new wealth we obtain during a certain period. We may define it as *a stream of services and commodities acquired during a period of time.*

Gross and Net Income. — It is sometimes desirable to distinguish between gross and net income. Gross income refers to total real income. Net income is the gross income less the costs which may be incurred in obtaining it. The acquisition of an income usually involves some outgo in the form of costs. These costs consist of payments for wealth used up, for labor expended, or similar charges incident to the getting of the income in question. Thus a physician has to buy various drugs and instruments which he uses in treating his patients. The cost of such supplies and equipment would have to be deducted from his fees in the computation of his net income.

The concept of net income is particularly useful to business men in judging of the profitableness of a business enterprise. The gross money income of a business consists of the proceeds from the sale of the products. Subtract from this the costs of carrying on the enterprise, and the remainder is the net income which accrues to the proprietors as profit. By the net income of a nation is meant its total production or acquisition of goods and services, less the cost of capital used up (depreciation) in obtaining them.

Individual and Social Income. — The real income of a social group or nation consists of the sum of the real incomes of the individuals who compose it. Taking human society as a whole, this is the same as its total production, for all individual incomes are ultimately derived from the goods produced in industry, and all the goods produced must go to someone and must constitute, therefore, individual real income. Hence, income and production are merely two different ways of looking at the same thing. When we speak of production, we are thinking of the source from which goods are derived. When we think of income, we have in mind their destination. Production constitutes the creation of goods, and income is their receipt. It follows that the money value of all the individual incomes must equal the money value of the social product. This gives us two ways of measuring social income. One is to add together the money incomes of all the individuals, making due allowances for real incomes that do not involve money payments, such as the services of housewives, the services of houses occupied by their owners, food provided by farmers from their own gardens, and wages paid to employees in products or services instead of in cash. The other is to ascertain the total money value of the annual production. If the calculations are carefully made, the totals should agree.

At first sight, it is not obvious that the totals reached by these two different methods would be equal, for many individuals receive money income without making any contribution to the social product. A college student may have all his expenses paid by his father, the student himself adding nothing to the community's stream of goods. One may inherit a large sum from a deceased relative, or receive a gift. A thief obtains income without giving anything in return. How, then, is it possible for the sum of individual incomes received to equal the sum of commodities and services produced? The answer is that no item of income must be credited to more than one person. If the allowance received by the college student is regarded as income to him, it cannot be considered income to the father. All cases of income which is transferred by its original recipient to someone else must be deducted from the receipts of the former. Individual incomes must be computed as net. Deducting amounts transferred to others, the total money measure of individual incomes received should equal the total money value of goods produced.

In computing the products of the various business establishments care must be exercised. For instance, what is the product of such an industry as baking? Is it the total value of the bread and pastries which flow from it? No, for some of the production was carried on by other industries in earlier stages of production. Part of the value of the final product is to be attributed to the farmers who grew the wheat, the millers who ground the wheat into flour, the railroads that transported the flour, and so on. There is danger of double counting here; for if we put into the computation the value of the flour produced by the miller, and the value of the bread produced by the baker, we have counted the flour twice, since its cost is included by the baker in the price of the bread. To avoid such duplication we must find the part of the total value of the bread added by each producer who has a part in its production. The value added by the baker, for instance, can be ascertained by subtracting from the value of the bread the value of the flour and other ingredients when the baker received them. The value added by the miller can be found by subtracting from the value of the flour the value of the wheat. A similar method must be followed for each industry. We then get a total of the *value-products* of the various industries, which is the income figure we are seeking. The data for such a method of estimating income are to be found in statistics of agricultural and mineral production, imports of merchandise, censuses of manufactures, statements of railway traffic, etc., all of which are issued from time to time by various government bureaus in most of the civilized nations.

Statistics of total national income are often useful. They enable us to determine a nation's prosperity, whether this is increasing or decreasing, and how it compares with that of other nations. Estimates of national income can also be used to determine the ability of a people to pay taxes, debts, or indemnities. The whole question of the wages of labor and the possibility of their increase, which so agitates the economic and political life of our times, is closely dependent on the size of the national income from which wages must be paid.

In computing national income an allowance must be made for imports and exports. If we add to the total product of the United States the value of all goods imported into it from abroad, and deduct the value of all goods exported to other countries, the resulting figure would give us a measure of the national income. Estimates of this are annually published by the United States Bureau of Foreign and Domestic Commerce. These estimates tell the story of the rise and fall of our national prosperity from year to year.

B. WEALTH AND CAPITAL

The Concept of Wealth. — Closely related to the concept of income is that of wealth. This relationship will become clearer as we proceed. We must first inquire into the meaning of the term. Its definition presents certain difficulties because the word is used in common speech quite loosely.

The United States is said to be a nation of great wealth. Of what does its wealth consist? Certainly its fertile soil, its rich mineral deposits, its factories and farms, its homes, and the various commodities owned and used by its inhabitants are a part of it. Are we also to include its temperate climate, its abundant rainfall, its natural waterways? And what of the intelligence, strength, accumulated knowledge, and training of its citizens? Clearly all these *contribute* to its wealth, but are they a part of it? These are nice questions to which common usage gives no definite answer, because it employs the word wealth in more than one meaning. In one sense the character of the people, the salubrious climate and abundant rainfall of our country might well be considered a part of our national wealth; but we would not consider that person "wealthy" who possessed a fine character, plenty of fresh air and sunlight, but little else. We would consider him "wealthy," however, no matter how puny in health and physique and ability—in fact, even if he were shut up in a dingy prison cell—if he possessed a large quantity of the world's material goods. It is obvious, therefore, that wealth, as it is generally used, is an elastic term and that its meaning varies according to circumstances.

Great precision of language is not often necessary in ordinary conversation, but in systematic analysis exactness of thought is required, and this is possible only when words are clearly and carefully defined. Let us, therefore, proceed to develop a careful definition.

In its broadest sense, we might include under the term wealth everything which possesses utility. Such a definition would embrace everything that contributes either directly or indirectly to the gratification of desires. The sunshine about us, a beautiful landscape, a gold mine, a suit of clothes, and a palace, would all be wealth. For the purpose of economics, however, this concept is too broad. As has previously been explained, in economics we deal only with things that have to be economized, that is, with things which are relatively scarce, or which require effort to produce. Hence, the term wealth should be confined to economic goods. This is the first requirement of a satisfactory definition.

A second is that the term be confined to goods whose ownership is transferable. Only transferable things enter directly into the processes of economic life; only they are bought and sold. The intelligence or character of a human being is a very desirable and useful possession, but it is not a salable commodity; its owner cannot offer it in the markets of commerce. It rests forever in his person. But it may be used to help produce wealth, or to yield services which are bought and sold. Thus an artist's talent is not wealth, in the economic sense of that term; but it is a *source* of wealth, and, as such, is of economic importance.

Finally, wealth is material. It consists entirely of concrete, tangible commodities, such as a house, a cake of soap, or a plot of land. We included non-material goods in our concept of income, for they clearly constitute part of the things for which money income is spent; but such things are not usually included in the category of wealth. Wealth is usually conceived as something having material existence.

Economic wealth, then, consists of scarce, transferable, material goods. This is the formal definition to which we shall adhere. It implies four tests by which we can determine whether or not any given thing is to be regarded as wealth. We have but to ask: Is it a good? Is it scarce? Is it transferable? and, Is it material? If the answer in each case is yes, the thing in question is wealth. If the answer to any of the questions is no, it is not wealth.

Public Goods and Private Goods. — In which category are we to place such things as public parks, highways, harbors, etc.? They are free in the sense that everyone is at liberty to enjoy them equally and without limit, yet they were not obtained without effort, and in fact they were paid for and are maintained out of taxes levied on the people. They are economic wealth in the sense in which it has been defined, yet they differ from those forms of wealth which are in the private possession of individuals. We may distinguish here between *private wealth* and *public wealth;* between *private goods* and *public goods.* Both are economic wealth or economic goods.

Wealth and Title to Wealth. — If the average individual were asked to list those of his possessions which he regarded as wealth, he would probably name, first, all of his material goods, such as his house and furniture, his automobile, his clothing, jewelry, and similar commodities. He would also be likely to include any intangible property he might own, such as stocks and bonds, the mortgage he holds on some piece of real estate, and items of like nature. In addition to these, he would further include the money in his pockets and the deposits to his credit in the bank. Are all these wealth, in the economic sense of that word? The first group mentioned, the material commodities in his possession, clearly fall within the meaning of the term as we have just defined it—but how about the intangibles, and the money? We may consider the former of these first.

What is a share of stock? Suppose I buy five thousand dollars' worth of stock in the Mineral Oil Corporation. With my money, and that of many other stockholders (if it has fallen into honest hands), the corporation will drill oil wells, install pumps, lay pipe-lines, and build refineries. In return for it, I will receive certain pieces of paper which certify to my investment in the company. These are shares of stock. In effect they are simply evidences that I am a part owner in the oil wells, pipe-lines, refineries, and other physical properties of the concern. These physical properties are wealth; the shares of stock are not wealth, but are simply instruments of title. The shares are certificates of my title to five thousand dollars' worth of the wealth of the corporation, and that is all. The case of a mortgage is similar; it certifies to someone's title or partial title to a piece of real estate. The real estate is wealth, the mortgage is an evidence of claim upon that wealth. The same is true of all securities, negotiable papers, etc. The individual looks upon them as wealth because he knows they can be bought and sold—he can obtain wealth with them; but they are only salable because of the title they convey to some form of goods, not for any virtues inherent in themselves. The goods are the wealth, therefore, and not the papers.

The error of including such securities under the term wealth is easily seen if an attempt is made to count the wealth of a community. If we were to calculate the value of the wealth of a city like Pittsburgh, we should have to list all the factories, iron and steel mills, and other industrial establishments; we should also have to include the private personal property of the various citizens, such as their houses, automobiles, and so on. But if we included the stocks and bonds they owned in, let us say, some of the Pittsburgh industries, we should be counting the value of those industries twice—once when we listed the physical properties and again when we set down the stocks and bonds covering those properties. Jones may have $25,000 worth of stock in the Pittsburgh Plate Glass Company. His $25,000 went into the plant of that corporation. We counted it once when we figured the glass works in our record; to count Jones' stock when we come to his personal belongings would be to count his $25,000 a second time. It would make it appear as if there was $50,000 worth of wealth where in fact there would be but $25,000. Stocks, bonds, other negotiable papers and similar evidences of title, therefore, are not economic wealth.

There are certain other intangible assets which the individual or corporation would regard as part of its wealth, but which are not in themselves wealth, although they represent some sort of claim upon wealth. A street railway company might consider its franchise as a part of its wealth. A franchise is simply a privilege, conferred on the company by the city, granting it the right to lay its tracks on the city streets. It is of value to the company because the latter cannot do business without it, but it is not wealth to the community. The tracks and the cars are wealth to the community, but not the franchise. Similarly, a long established business firm may have obtained the "good will" of a clientele; the "good will" brings in business to the company and it can be sold. It is thus one of the assets of the business, and the owners thereof would probably regard it as part of their wealth. But this "good will" is of no importance to the community. It simply means that a portion of the public will deal with this particular firm instead of some other, but this is a matter of indifference to the community, though it is very valuable to the business. All such assets—franchises, patent rights, monopoly power, good will, etc.—are in the nature of titles to wealth. They give their owners power to control wealth or gain possession of wealth; they cause wealth to be transferred from one person to another, but they are not in themselves wealth.

Wealth and Money. — In the case of income, we found it necessary to distinguish between money receipts and the goods of which real income is composed. We must do likewise in the case of wealth. Wealth is commonly measured in dollars, and because of that, we are apt to think of it as consisting of a sum of money; yet a moment's reflection will show that the two things are not identical. The wealth of the United States, for instance, is said to be somewhere in the neighborhood of three hundred billion dollars, but the total quantity of money in this country is but a small fraction of such a sum. The figure three hundred billions merely expresses the money value of the land, buildings, railways, and stocks of commodities that do constitute the wealth of the nation. Wealth, then, is not synonymous with money, and the expression of wealth in terms of money is only a way of measuring its value.

Does the money which is in circulation in the country, however, not constitute a part of its wealth? So far as metallic money—the gold, silver, nickel and copper coins—are concerned, the answer must be in the affirmative. Such money is made of useful, and, for the most part, of precious metals. These materials are clearly wealth, for they are possessed of great utility, they are scarce, and they are readily transferable. Undeniably they conform to our definition of wealth. It is not because they are money, however, that such coins are wealth;

they are so simply because they contain valuable metals. It is not their money-nature, but the substance of which they are made, that makes them so.

How are we to classify paper money and bank deposits, which in modern communities constitutes the greater part of the currency actually in circulation? So far as the substance of which it is composed is concerned, it is practically worthless. The fraction of a cent's worth of paper in a ten dollar bill is such an infinitesimal portion of wealth that we can safely ignore it. But are we to class these pieces of paper as wealth simply because they are money? Let us consider what is a piece of paper money. A gold certificate, for instance, is a piece of paper certifying that gold has been deposited in the treasury of the United States, payable to the bearer on demand. It represents wealth, therefore, but is not wealth itself. A bank note, as we shall learn later in our study, is simply the promise of a bank to pay a stated sum of money on demand. We shall find that the same is true of a bank deposit. Thus, these forms of money are similar to stocks, bonds, and other negotiable instruments. Back of them as security there lies somewhere some real wealth, but they are merely representatives of wealth; they are not wealth themselves.

Capital. — A stock of wealth is frequently referred to as *capital*. Thus we speak of the capital of the United States, by which we mean all the wealth in existence in our country. An individual may refer to his house, furnishings, and personal possessions as his capital. The term is most frequently employed in business, where it refers to the stock of wealth with which the business enterprise is carried on. A railroad has its roadbed and track, its terminals, depots, sidings, locomotives, cars, equipment, coal, tools, and so on. All this wealth is the capital employed in the business. Similarly, the capital of a department store will consist of the land upon which its buildings are situated, the building itself, its fixtures, and the merchandise on its shelves. By capital, we mean, therefore, a stock of wealth.[2]

Individual and Social Capital Accounts. — Individuals, particularly business men, find it expedient to ascertain the amount of their capital from time to time. This is particularly useful in managing a business enterprise, for it enables those in charge to follow the progress and prosperity of their business. Business men, in keeping such accounts, however, are more interested in the wealth to which they have title, or upon which they have a claim, than in the wealth actually in their physical possession. They accordingly draw up a *capital*

[2] Economists, like doctors, sometimes disagree, and one of their points of disagreement concerns the appropriate use of the term capital. See the section entitled *Some Categories of Wealth*, in Chapter IV, and the footnote appended thereto.

balance sheet or *capital account,* upon which are shown not only the physical property of the business, but also the titles to wealth, or property rights. Over against these must be set any debts which are owed to others, for these represent claims by outsiders upon wealth in the possession of the business, and are not, therefore, part of the wealth really owned by the business at all. Such a capital account is drawn up in two columns, one showing the assets (wealth and claims upon wealth) of the business, the other the liabilities (debts to outsiders, for claims they hold upon the wealth of the enterprise). The difference between these two amounts is the "net worth" or capital-value of the enterprise. The following is a simple example of the capital account of a small corporation operating a department store:

Assets		*Liabilities*	
Real estate (plant) . . .	$100,000	Mortgage against company's plant	$ 50,000
Stock of merchandise .	100,000		
Cash on hand or in bank	50,000	Note to bank	50,000
Notes of customers for goods purchased . . .	25,000	Capital (owed by the business to its owners, the stockholders)	
Good will	25,000		200,000
Total assets	$300,000	Total liabilities	$300,000

The "net worth" or capital balance of this enterprise is $200,000. If the company be regarded as an artificial person which "owes" to its owners all of its net assets, this sum can be carried on the books as a liability and both sides of the account will then balance. This is the customary method. Had the company started business with capital to the amount of $100,000 subscribed by the stockholders, the remainder of the $200,000 would represent additional capital accumulated by the business out of its earnings. It would then usually be carried on the books as "surplus" or "undivided profits," or both. Thus, instead of the item "Capital—$200,000," there might appear on the account the following:

Capital	$100,000
Surplus	50,000
Undivided profits	50,000

All this, however, would be included in the "net worth" or capital balance of the business.

It is now apparent why a business man or an individual includes intangible property rights or titles to wealth as a part of his wealth or capital. It is because he may not own outright all of the wealth he possesses, claims against it being held by other persons; and, because of someone's debt to him, he may hold claims against wealth which is not in his possession. He, therefore, regards his net property rights, or titles to wealth, as his capital. This is perfectly correct for him to do; but as economists we must not lose sight of the fact that all of these rights have their basis in real wealth—are in themselves merely claims upon wealth, and that the real capital concerned in all this accounting consists of material goods.

Let us suppose now a community whose people own all the wealth contained within its borders (none of it being held by outsiders), and who own no wealth outside of its limits. If we were to add together the "net worths" of all these people, and in a separate calculation were to add up the values of every concrete article of wealth in that community, the two totals would be exactly equal. This is because every liability on any individual's account would be offset by a corresponding asset on the account of someone else, and every *intangible* asset or property right would be offset by a liability on another account. It must be so, since every debt implies a credit and every claim to wealth in the possession of someone else must be carried by that person as a debt. Therefore, in combining the accounts of the different members of the community, the intangible or non-material items will cancel each other and disappear. Only the material items of real wealth will remain as the capital of the community.

In an actual society such as the United States, however, the combined "net worths" of our residents would not exactly equal the total capital located here. It would show the total capital *owned* by our people, but since they own some property abroad, while some of the wealth situated within our territory is owned by foreigners, the two results would not agree. For this reason such a term as the "wealth of the United States" is somewhat ambiguous. It may refer to the wealth owned by the people of the nation, or the wealth existing within our boundaries, which may be called our *internal wealth*.

The Capital of the United States. — It is frequently desirable to ascertain the amount of a nation's wealth, or capital. Ordinarily in making estimates of this it is the internal wealth that is sought. The necessary information can be obtained from numerous statistical sources, such as census reports, tax assessments, and so on. Such an estimate of national wealth or capital would include:

All the valuable land and natural resources.

All permanent improvements upon land, including buildings, canals, tunnels, roads, railways, etc.

Railway rolling stock, automobiles, and vehicles of all kinds.

Machinery, tools, and other equipment.

Horses, cattle, sheep, poultry, and livestock of all kinds.

Seed, raw materials, and partly finished goods.

All material consumers' goods, such as food, clothing, furniture, etc.

All metallic money.

Estimates of the wealth of the American people in recent years placed it in the neighborhood of 250 or 300 billions of dollars.

Capital and Income. — We have seen that new wealth, created or acquired, constitutes a part of the stream of goods which go to make up real income. If, out of this year's money receipts, we buy meats and vegetables, hats and coats, a comfortable chair, or an automobile, those things constitute part of our real income for that year. To that extent, the concepts of wealth and income overlap. Indeed, so far as perishable commodities are concerned, the distinction between the two is of little significance, for perishable commodities, like services, are used up and disappear within a single income period. But the case of durable wealth is different. If an article of wealth lasts beyond the year in which it was acquired, it yields services which constitute income in succeeding years. For instance, if one buys a house in 1940, it is likely to yield shelter for some decades thereafter, during all of which time its services constitute real income to the occupant. Hence durable wealth is a source of income. It is when we are thinking of wealth as a source of income that we are most likely to employ the term capital. The business man thinks of the wealth invested in his business—his factory, machines, and stocks of material or partly finished goods—as capital because he derives income from them. The house one owns is capital to him because he derives income from it; if he rents it to another, he gets money income; if he occupies it himself, he gets real income.

On the other hand, income is likewise a source of new wealth, for capital may be accumulated out of income, by saving. When we "spend" our income we consume commodities and services. We buy food and eat it, we purchase clothes and wear them out, we go to a concert and listen to music which disappears as fast as it is produced. In "spending," therefore, wealth and effort are used up and dissipated. When we "save" our income, on the other hand, we refrain from consuming goods, and accumulate wealth instead. As a result we have more wealth than before. This may take the form of a store of consumable commodities for future use, as a barrel of apples or a few reserve suits of clothes; or it may take the form of some permanent, durable capital which can be used continuously over a period of many years, such as a house; or it may take the form of productive capital, such as a factory building and equipment, which will continue to produce more goods until it wears out. This capital, which is so saved, is again a source of future income. Income saved, therefore, is abstaining from consumption now, in order that we may enjoy additional consumable income in the future. We shall have more to say about this in a later chapter.[3]

Capitalization. — There is a close relation between the value of capital and the income which it yields. In the case of perishable commodities, like apples or soap, the two values are identical, because the capital and the income are the same thing; but in the case of more durable commodities, they are different. A piece of land, for instance, will ordinarily last forever, continuing to yield income throughout its perpetual life. A factory building yields products through a period of several decades. In such cases, the relationship between the value of the capital and the income derived from it is expressed through the rate of interest; that is, the money value of the income can be represented as a certain percentage of the value of the capital. If a factory building, costing $100,000 to construct, yields a net income of $5,000 yearly to its owner, the income is 5 per cent of the capital.

In the market where goods are bought, sold, borrowed, and loaned, a certain rate of interest comes to be established as the prevailing one. With such a rate as a basis of reckoning, it is possible to construe any source of income as representing a certain capital value. Suppose, for instance, that the money rent derived from a piece of real estate is $200 yearly. If the rate of interest is 5 per cent, this income would be $\frac{5}{100}$ of the corresponding capital value; the latter would be, therefore, $\frac{100}{5} \times \$200$, or $4,000. Putting it a little differently, the income of $200 is equivalent to an investment of $4,000 yielding 5 per

---

[3] This twofold relationship between capital and income presents an ambiguity which has led some writers to say that savings should not be included in real income. These economists argue that only the services of wealth and of human beings should be counted as income; for if we count material commodities as income at the time they are acquired, and also count the services of wealth as income, we may count the same thing twice. For instance, if we say a man's house is a part of his income in the year in which he buys it, we must also count the services which he derives from the use of that house in future years as income; therefore, we have been guilty of double counting. They would only consider the benefits derived from the use of the house from year to year as income. It would seem, however, that this definition confuses income with consumption. It is true that income can only be consumed once; but when the term income is ordinarily used, it is not only consumable income that is meant. If, for instance, savings are not to be included in income, then the phrase "saving a part of one's income" is ridiculous. Hence a majority of economists incline toward the definition of income adopted in this text. Moreover, this concept of income is more useful for most purposes; for it is easier to measure statistically, and it shows better the real earning or productive power of an individual or a nation in a given year than does the other concept.

cent (for $200 is 5 per cent of $4,000). Hence, the real estate would be worth that sum. This process of computing capital values from incomes is known as *capitalization*.[4]

Acquisitive Capital Values. — Through the process of capitalization, a capital value can be derived from any source of income whatever. It is even possible to compute the value of a man, by capitalizing the earnings which he can make during his lifetime. (For this reason, some economists favor including human beings in the definition of capital, although most of them do not.) However, not every receipt of individual income can be attributed to some individual person or particular item of wealth, because sometimes income is obtained in a way which does not permit it to be traced to a tangible source. For instance, a street railway may have secured from its city government a franchise which gives it the exclusive right, in perpetuity, to use the city streets for the operation of street-cars. This gives the company a monopoly of transportation facilities. Unless the city has taken precautions to protect its citizens from the abuse of this privilege, by suitable regulations concerning charges to be made for service, the company can use its monopoly to exact a high rate of fare which will yield it a handsome profit. This profit would constitute a source of income which could be capitalized at a high figure, and the company might sell its exclusive privilege to some other company at this capitalized price. Here the income is not derived from any particular piece of wealth. It rests in the franchise, which gives the monopolist power to extort money from the car riders; yet, to the company, it represents a capital value.

Somewhat similar is the item of "good will," which sometimes appears in the capital balance sheet of a business. Often this is a purely fictitious item, inserted into the account in order to make the assets of the business appear larger than they really are. Sometimes, however, it is a genuinely valuable asset, representing established reputation and business connections which bring patronage to the enterprise, and which, therefore, represent earning power. Other intangible claims of similar nature, such as patents, copyrights, and trademarks, are likewise to be found. We may call all such assets *acquisitive capital values,* because they represent mere power of acquisition on the part of the owner, not resting in any actual wealth or productive capacity.

The existence of these intangible assets makes it necessary to qualify our previous conclusion that, in combining capital accounts, intangible items will cancel each other and disappear, leaving only the material items of real wealth as the social capital. Acquisitive values on the asset side of the accounts will not be canceled by corresponding lia-

---

[4] Capitalization is more fully explained in Chapter XXI.

bilities on the accounts of debtors, for the assets in question are not claims upon any particular individuals. The result is that the total of individual net worths so calculated would exceed the total social wealth. Hence, all such acquisitive values would have to be stricken from the accounts in computing the social capital. This case presents the only real discrepancy between the business concept of capital as net worth, and the economist's concept of it as a stock of wealth.

SUMMARY

A good is defined as anything that has utility. Goods may be either material or non-material, which we call commodities and services, respectively. Economics deals only with economic goods, *i.e.,* those which are scarce relatively to the desire for them, or whose production requires effort. Production is not the making of material things, but the creation of utilities, either of form, place, possession, time, or service. Predatory activities, speculation of the gambling type, competitive advertising, and aggressive warfare are unproductive.

Money income must be distinguished from real income; the latter consists of a stream of commodities and services acquired during a period of time. Gross income is the total of real income, while net income is gross income less the costs of obtaining it. Social income is identical with total production; individual income is the share of total income acquired by an individual. The sum of individual incomes equals the social income. A nation's real income consists of its annual production, plus its imports, and minus its exports.

Wealth consists of scarce, transferable, material goods. Private wealth is that which is owned by individuals; public wealth is owned by the community in common and open to the use of all. Mere titles to wealth, or property rights, such as stocks, bonds, mortgages, and good will, are not wealth. Metallic money is wealth, but paper money and bank deposits are not.

Capital is a stock of wealth. Business men keep records of the capital they own, by means of capital balance sheets, or capital accounts. These show assets (wealth possessed, plus claims on the wealth of others) and liabilities (debts owed to others) in parallel columns. The difference between these two is the net worth, or capital-balance of the individual or the business. In combining capital accounts to get the aggregate capital owned by the community, the total intangible assets are offset by corresponding liabilities, causing the intangible items to cancel out. Thus the real capital of the community, lying back of these accounts, consists of real wealth. However, it does not exactly coincide with the internal wealth of a nation, because some of its people own wealth in other countries, while people in other countries may own wealth in it.

Durable capital yields future income, and income saved and invested becomes durable capital, which again yields income in the future. Any flow of income can be capitalized at the prevailing rate of interest, thus giving rise to a capital value. Some capital values so derived represent acquisitive gains made at the expense of the community; they are not embodied in real wealth or in human productive capacity. Such acquisitive values must be excluded from capital accounts in computing social income.

REFERENCES AND SUGGESTIONS FOR FURTHER READING

There is a brief survey of productive and unproductive labor (to which I am indebted) in Chapter II of F. W. Taussig's *Principles of Economics* (4th edition, 1939). A stimulating and original discussion of this topic is also to be found in Thorstein Veblen's essay on *Industrial and Pecuniary Employments,* reprinted in his *The Place of Science in Modern Civilization and Other Essays* (1919).

The best analysis of income with which I am familiar is to be found in William W. Hewett's *The Definition of Income and Its Application in Federal Taxation* (1925), which has contributed to my thinking on this subject. In the analysis of wealth I have followed, for the most part, Irving Fisher's able work, *The Nature of Capital and Income* (1906), but I have been unable to accept his analysis of income.

Chapter III

SPECIALIZATION, COMPETITION, AND COÖPERATION

A. SPECIALIZATION

Specialization a Result of the Industrial Revolution. — In the opening chapter it was pointed out that the families of earlier days produced by their own labor most of the commodities which were required for their daily existence. Our forefathers in colonial America lived on their own farms, built their own houses, raised their own food, and made their own clothes. In fact, each family was a little economic world to itself, capable, without assistance from others, of meeting most of the needs of its existence. Today, as a result of the Industrial Revolution, each person produces very few of the commodities he consumes. He is rather a specialist, concentrating his labors upon some particular branch of production, and relying upon others to provide him with the other needs of his life. This characteristic of modern industry is called *specialization*. It is also frequently styled the *division of labor*. This division or specialization of labor takes on a number of different forms.

Specialization by Trades. — In the first place industry is divided into a number of different branches or trades, in which the worker carries out the whole of one stage or process of production, but confines his activities to that alone. This kind of specialization is developed in an early stage of civilization, and was characteristic of the handicraft industry in England. In those days the whole of a shoe was made by the shoemaker, a complete suit of clothing by the tailor; and those who followed the various trades of that time, such as the millers, weavers, carpenters, masons, tanners, etc., were skilled workers, each devoting his labors to a single product, which he carried out to completion himself. In our economic system it is still to be found, and is represented by such occupations as that of the farmer, the village blacksmith, the corner grocer, the doctor, the teacher, and similar trades or professions. This type of specialization may be called *specialization by trades,* or *simple division of labor.*

Specialization by Tasks. — But in the typical manufacturing enterprises of the modern world, specialization has become much more complex, so that each branch of production itself is subdivided into minute tasks. One of the best examples of this is to be found in the marvelous processes which have been developed by the huge beef-packing concerns of Chicago. Here the slaughtering of meat has been so carefully systematized that the work formerly done by a single butcher is at present performed by scores of workers, each of whom has a distinct part to play in the process of getting the meat ready for the market. In the preparing of beef, the steer is driven from the stock-yards into a pen, where it is one man's task to kill the animal with a blow from a hammer, and he performs no other operation but this, dispatching each steer as it comes before him. The carcass is then passed on by means of a gravity trolley through a long series of workers, and as it is carried along each one performs some allotted task of cutting and removing the hide, and dressing, washing, and storing the meat in the refrigerator. Each worker has one task and one only to perform, and he does this all day long on thousands of animals day in and day out.

A visit to almost any other producing establishment, such as an automobile plant, a bakery, a department store, or a shoe factory, will show a similar minute division of labor. The process is split into simple operations, each one of which is performed by a special worker whose task it is to do that one thing and that alone. Each task tends to become a specialized operation. This type of specialization may be called *specialization by tasks,* or *complex division of labor.*

Specialization by Stages. — There is a third form, in which the labor of industry is divided into the various stages of production. It was pointed out in the opening chapter that in the manufacture of a book the timber must first be cut, the wood ground into pulp, the pulp pressed into paper, the paper printed and bound, and the book finally delivered to customers. Each of these stages is carried out by a separate group of workers, and the various operations may take place at widely distant points. This is so in nearly every industry. The various processes from the extraction of raw material to the sale of the completed product are handled by separate groups of workers, each constituting an industry in itself. This may be called *specialization by stages,* or *successive division of labor.*

It is characteristic of this kind of specialization that each person looks upon the commodity which he produces as a finished product. The product of the forest is timber, and so far as the lumberman is concerned, the process of production ends when the lumber is obtained. To the paper manufacturer the process is complete when the wood is crushed into pulp and pressed into paper; he thinks of that as the final product of his activities. Similarly, the publisher looks upon the book as the end of the process of production. These, however, are but preliminary stages in a continuous chain of production, and no commodity is finished in the economic sense of the term until it yields enjoyments to the consumer. This does not take place until the final article is placed in the consumer's hands.

Specialization by Geographic Districts. — So far we have spoken only of the specialization between individuals. But there is also specialization between geographic districts. In the United States, the workers in each part of the country tend to specialize on a few products. New England we think of as a manufacturing center; Pennsylvania as an iron and coal producing state. Various parts of the South are devoted to the production of tobacco, cotton, and sugar cane, respectively. We have our corn belt and our wheat belt in the Central West, the beef-raising district of Texas, the tropical fruits of southern California, and the timber products of the Northwest. Moreover, within each of these regions various towns will frequently be found which are devoted almost exclusively to a single industry. Meriden, Connecticut, is known as the Silver City, because its chief product is silverware. Gloversville, New York, contains scores of glove factories, and is the center of the glove-making trade in this country. Philadelphia is famous as a textile city; Minneapolis, Minnesota, as a milling town; Gary, Indiana, as a steel community; and so on.

Not only do the laborers and the workers of each nation and local region become specialists in certain industries, but the labor of the world likewise shows considerable division into different branches. The people of England are engaged primarily in manufacturing enterprises, while those in the British Colonies of Canada, Australia, India, and Africa are producers of raw products, such as wheat, timber, wool, rubber, and the various products of the Orient. One naturally associates certain products with certain nations. We think of Brazil as a producer of coffee. China is noted for its rice and silks; the Philippine islands for their hemp; Argentina for its beef; South Africa for its diamonds and gold. Thus the earth is divided into a great number of specialized areas. This is known as *geographic specialization,* or *geographic division of labor* (also called sometimes territorial division of labor).

Specialization Limited by the Extent of the Market. — The degree to which specialization can be carried depends largely upon the size of the market for the products. A person cannot be kept occupied doing so simple an operation as making a certain cut on the carcass of a steer unless thousands of pounds of beef can be sold by one producer. Otherwise the workman would be idle most of his time and he would have to turn to other work. Such large quantities of merchandise cannot be sold within a narrow territory, for there are not enough people in a small area to use so much meat. Modern methods of communication and transportation have brought far distant places into such close contact with each other that the market for a progressive manufacturer's goods today is almost unlimited. It is only because people over all the United States buy meats produced in Chicago that the plants of that city have been able to specialize to so great a degree. The market for many goods is now world-wide in extent, making very huge output and minute specialization of labor possible.

Greater Abundance of Goods. — Specialization has been universally adopted by business organizations because it lessens the cost of production. It lessens the cost of production because it enables a given amount of work to be done with less labor than otherwise. In short, it increases the efficiency of labor in production. The result is that the labor of society produces a far greater abundance of economic goods than would be possible without it. Two great circumstances are responsible for the great productivity of modern industry—the use of power-driven machinery, and the specialization of functions. These two are to a great degree associated with and dependent on each other. They go hand in hand. The result is a far greater abundance of goods in the modern world than was formerly available.

The common workman of today enjoys many forms of goods which were utterly unknown to even the richest persons of medieval society. For three cents he may have spread out before him each morning the news of all the world. For a quarter he is furnished with moving pictures which bring within his reach forms of wholesome amusement unlike that of anything enjoyed by his forebears of a few generations ago. He is better clothed, better housed, and better fed than the peasant of the old English manor. The latter, forced to live from the meager produce of a backward agriculture, unassisted by the tools we now possess, was dressed in the coarsest of homemade garments, housed in a rude hut, and lived on the plainest of food. The workingman of today has plenty of fairly attractive clothes, colored to suit his fancy and woven in a variety of textures which adds to their attractiveness. Though his house is simple, it usually contains running water, bathing facilities, and a quality and variety of furniture that is far superior to that of ancient times. He has meats and vegetables in greater variety and more convenient facilities for their tasteful and wholesome preparation. Even though he may be in relative poverty as compared with some of the wealthier members of society, his condition has greatly improved. Add to this the many luxuries, the automobiles, fine homes, and other comforts enjoyed by some of the more fortunate members of the population, and it can readily be seen that the income of modern civilization is immeasurably greater than that of the older world.

This, of course, is to be attributed to the Industrial Revolution, with its marvelous inventions, but in part also to the development of specialized production. Machinery is an adjunct of specialization; it makes specialization possible, and is made possible by it. Specialization, therefore, was and is an important factor in the abundance of goods which we enjoy. A few moments' reflection will show why this is so.

How Specialization Contributes to Greater Productivity. — (1) It is an old proverb that practice makes perfect. The specialization of labor makes possible the application of this principle on a wide scale in industry. He who specializes upon a given task becomes highly skilled at that work and can perform it much more efficiently than one who does not devote his whole energies to it. The more minutely the division of labor is extended, the greater the possibility of the application of this principle. The young woman in a glove factory who sews the seams of the fingers of a glove soon becomes so skilled at that delicate work that she can perform the operation with remarkable speed and accuracy, which never could be attained by a person who divided his attention among many operations. In short, *specialization develops an acquired skill* in each productive operation that greatly increases the output.

(2) *By specialization it is also possible to suit the occupation to the ability of the individual.* All persons are not born with equal talents or propensities, nor have they by training and environment developed equal abilities. Suppose that one person is endowed with marked musical talent, while another is naturally gifted with a mechanical turn of mind. If there were no specialization the musical individual would be obliged to spend the greater part of his life upon meeting his more material wants and would have very little time left for his music. Moreover, because of his artistic temperament, he would probably be but a very indifferent workman, and the quantity and quality of the material products which he produced for himself would be quite mediocre. Similarly, the mechanic would have to devote his time not solely to those skilled tasks for which his natural bent equips him best, but would have to divide his labors among many different operations, some of which he could perform but poorly. Where there is specialization, however, each of these individuals can devote his efforts exclusively to that one occupation for which he is best equipped, and then by trading his products for the products of others he will get more

goods, and of better quality, than he would ever have obtained otherwise. Thus the musician will be provided with better commodities and the mechanic will have better music.

It does not follow, however, that under the present organization of industry each person always is placed in that position for which he is best fitted. Often we are not good judges of our own abilities, and many a young person makes a choice in early life which he later realizes was a mistake. But on the whole it is probably true that by means of specialization the majority of individuals are placed in tasks which are more nearly suited to their qualifications than could be the case under a primitive system of industry, where each individual or family group provides all of its own needs. If this is so, specialization must serve greatly to increase the income of the world.

(3) It has already been stated that *specialization makes possible the use of machinery* to a greater degree than could be accomplished without it. When a productive process becomes split into many simple operations, oftentimes of a routine character, it is comparatively easy to devise a machine which will perform one of these operations mechanically. Indeed, the complex division of labor which is characteristic of the twentieth century has developed side by side with the application of steam and electric power and the marvelous mechanical contrivances which have been ushered in since the advent of the Industrial Revolution.

(4) *Geographic specialization enables the industry of a given region to be adapted to the natural resources of that region* in much the same way as individual specialization makes possible the adaptation of the occupation to the natural abilities of a person. Pennsylvania is rich in coal beds. The South is naturally suited by soil and climate to the raising of cotton; the Central West to the production of wheat and corn. If the people of each of these regions concentrate on the production of its specialty, trading it for the products of the other regions, all parties will gain and the general wealth be greater. It is upon this principle that geographic specialization is based.

(5) It is not so easy to explain how it comes about that some communities develop particular industries, which do not appear to rest upon any natural advantage. The cases of Meriden, Connecticut, and Gloversville, New York, have been referred to above. One of these is a silver-manufacturing town, the other a glove-producing community. In neither case, apparently, is there any particular resource or natural circumstance which makes these towns better suited to the development of their respective industries than any other locality. Why, then, have these industries become centered there? Is there some advantage which these communities enjoy that causes them to be specialists in

these occupations? It seems here that there must be some gain to the community analogous to the acquired skill of individuals which enables them to maintain their position of prominence as specialists in certain lines of production. Whole families of workers for generations have been trained in these occupations, so that there is available in these localities a supply of labor of the right type for the carrying on of those industries. A manufacturer of gloves opening up a new plant would naturally settle in Gloversville, because of such an available supply of labor; because, also, of the fact that buyers naturally come to this town to make their purchases; so that the producer located elsewhere would be out of the market, so to speak. It thus appears that geographic specialization is based in part upon certain *advantages acquired by the whole community* which make it better able to carry on that industry than other places.

Uniformity. — Where a manufacturing process is split up into minute tasks, the product must be standardized in order to render the task as simple as possible. The advantage of large output is in part based upon the continuous repetition of identical movements by the worker. The same process is repeated over and over again, exactly the same in the case of each unit of the article being produced. In consequence of this we find hundreds of thousands, even millions, of units turned out all exactly alike. But human nature is so constituted that it loves variety, and this uniformity which the division of labor brings about runs counter to the esthetic sense of man. In the days of handicraft industry each article was produced independently of other articles of the same sort. The result was that there was plenty of room for individualization and variety. Such is no longer the case. While it is difficult to measure such a loss as this in economic terms, there can be no doubt that some loss is there. Consider the sameness and mediocre fit of ready-made clothing, which is manufactured on a large scale, with minute division of labor; then contrast it with the variety and better fit of made-to-order clothes, where more individualization is practiced. It is this individualization that makes the latter dearer than the former. In the one case, the advantages of specialization have brought economies in production, while in the other it has not been possible to utilize these advantages so fully. The same uniformity is to be found in almost every article of common use—in the rows of city houses, in our furniture, books, etc. That this characteristic of our civilization results in a loss of individuality, prevents the fullest development of personality, and tends to keep in check the expression of beauty, can hardly be denied. But on the whole it seems probable that we have gained more from the increased output which specialization has brought than we have lost by the greater standardization and uniformity which has been its accompaniment.

Moreover, there is another sense in which the specialized production process has increased, rather than diminished, variety. In giving us greater income it has widened the total range of commodities at our disposal, affording us a great variety of products of which we would be deprived if we had to depend on less efficient methods. Take again the matter of clothing. While the modern process makes many suits or dresses that are exactly alike, they are so much cheaper that each person can have more garments than would have been possible if each were made individually. Today we have street clothes, working clothes, sportswear, evening dress—often several kinds of each, to satisfy our craving for variety. So specialization, while it makes for uniformity and lack of individuality in goods of a particular kind, has the merit of providing many more kinds.

Increased Dependence. — Another effect of specialization is to be found in the loss of versatility which it has brought to the individual worker. Each laborer under our industrial system is a specialist. Often he is trained to do a particular task and no other. He comes to look upon the task as his occupation. The result is he is almost entirely dependent for employment upon the demand for labor of his particular type. If anything happens to interrupt that demand he is deprived of employment. Being untrained for any other occupation, he must either remain unemployed until such time as there is again found a place for him in industry, or he is obliged to fall into some type of work which calls for no particular grade of skill or previous training, and in which the rate of remuneration is probably lower. This sometimes presents a very serious problem to whole groups of workers. For instance, up until a few years ago glass blowing was a highly skilled trade and yielded good pay to those who were trained in this occupation. Then a machine was invented which would blow glass mechanically. The skilled glass-blowers found themselves out of work. Many of them were middle-aged men with families dependent upon them for support. Trained for their special occupation and unfitted for any other equally skilled trade in other lines, their position was a very difficult one and many of them were forced to accept common laborers' work at low wages. Students of the employment problem know that there is always a considerable amount of unemployment caused by the fact that our workers are so highly specialized that they are peculiarly dependent upon the fluctuations in the limited demand for their type of work.

Under specialized industry, consumers are also dependent to a considerable extent upon other human beings for the goods which they need for their very existence. Hence, if anything happens to interrupt the smooth workings of the productive process in any important industry, the consumer is severely affected thereby. Consider the inconvenience that could be caused in other parts of the United States, if some unusual catastrophe were to destroy the wheat crop in our Central West. Think how profoundly our daily lives would be upset by the interruption of our railway traffic for twenty-four hours or more, through a general strike, for instance. Indeed, even whole nations are dependent upon industrial conditions in other nations for their welfare. England would be helpless without the food supplies and raw materials which she obtains in trade from her colonies. Germany was brought to the verge of starvation by the interruption of her commercial contact with the rest of the world in the first World War. Even the United States with its vast and versatile resources was seriously incommoded by her inability to obtain German dyes and other materials. These difficulties did not arise in the simpler system of industry which prevailed prior to the Industrial Revolution. Then each family was dependent only on its own labors. What it consumed it produced for itself, and it did not need to worry about the conditions of production away from its own land. So long as the processes of industry function smoothly we do not feel this characteristic of our present industrial system as an inconvenience, but the moment that anything happens to interfere with the process, it causes at once a grave situation.

The Worker Divorced from His Product. — Under the simpler system of production which formerly existed, the reward that a person got for his labor was his own product. His income consisted of what he produced with his own hands. Today this is no longer true. Each individual produces only one thing (or only a small part of one thing) and depends on others to produce what he needs in his daily life. What he gets depends on what he buys, and how much he can buy depends on how well he is paid for what he produces. In this complicated way of dividing up the social income there is opportunity for many inequalities to arise. In the division some individuals get much more than others. This has led to the claim that under our industrial system the laboring classes do not get all that their product is worth, and are therefore robbed. Whether or not this is true we cannot here discuss. The problem of what determines the share of the various classes in the income of society is so complex that it will require several chapters to describe it later in this volume. It is sufficient here to point out that specialization has divorced the worker from his product in such a way that his income is no longer dependent directly on what he produces, but on what purchasing power his contribution to production can command. This gives rise to the problems of prices and income sharing that will be discussed in future chapters.

Monotony of Specialized Labor. — It is often claimed that specialization, by splitting the processes of industry into simple routine tasks, has increased greatly the irksomeness of labor. Most men like to feel that they are creating things, and, under proper conditions, will take pride in performance. But, as Adam Smith long ago remarked, one cannot be expected to be immensely interested in making the hundredth part of a pin, or to be particularly proud of such an accomplishment. Specialization often requires that a man's work shall be no more inspiring than that; it reduces the human being to a mere automaton or machine. It is claimed that men rebel inwardly at this; and also that it is a severe strain on their nervous systems, producing fatigue and undermining health.

On the other hand, some critics of these views point out that in many ways specialization has lightened human labor by giving the worker only easy tasks to perform, turning the work requiring sheer brute force over to a machine. Carpenters no longer have to shorten their lives handling the back-breaking jack plane, as they used to do. In every factory one can find workers at easy tasks greatly contrasting with the burdensome occupations of rigorous farm or frontier life. It is argued, also, that monotony is not distasteful to persons of phlegmatic, simple minds. The muscles are soon trained to do the routine operations, so that they are performed by habit and without mental effort, leaving the thoughts free to roam at will. Persons of limited intelligence may not be interested in creative activity, and are perhaps better satisfied with the mechanical occupation that specialized industry provides. Finally, it is pointed out that there are many kinds of specialized work calling for high intelligence and of interesting character—such as the operation of complicated machinery, coördinating and overseeing the work of others, and so on.

Which of these judgments is correct we cannot answer here. It is a problem for the psychologist, the physiologist, and the student of labor problems. Probably there is some truth in both points of view. Undoubtedly we have much yet to learn about these matters.

B. Exchange, Competition, and Coöperation

The Nature of Exchange. — Specialization is made possible by the process of exchange. The farmer specializes on the raising of certain food products and raw materials. He produces in the course of a year's time many more bushels of corn than he and his family can possibly consume. On the other hand, being a specialist, he has no time to make for himself the wide variety of other products such as food, clothing, shelter, newspapers, machinery, and many other goods which he needs. What he does is to exchange his corn for those products. It is so with all other producers. The doctor exchanges his professional services, the hod-carrier his muscular labor, the miller his flour, each for the divers products which he needs for the daily activities of his life.

In primitive communities much exchange took the form of barter. That is, one kind of goods was traded directly for another. In colonial America the trapper used to bring his furs to the trading post, where he received in exchange for them flour, clothing, and various provisions. Traders with savage peoples, such as the natives of Africa, lay in a store of hatchets, knives, mirrors, and miscellaneous trinkets, which they barter with the natives for ivory and other of their products.

Barter, however, is a cumbersome method of effecting exchanges. In highly developed communities the process is made very much easier to carry on by the use of money. Exchange thereby becomes indirect. Instead of exchanging one kind of product directly for another, it is now the practice to sell the product for money, then with the money to buy the other goods which are desired. This serves to conceal the true nature of the exchange process, but does not change it in its essentials. True, the farmer sells his corn for money, and then with the money purchases the shoes, clothes, fertilizers, seed, etc., but in effect he has traded his crops for those articles. Money has simply entered in as a convenient medium of exchange, which facilitates the process.

Confusion of Money Phenomena with Goods Phenomena. — This universal use of money in exchange has so effectively obscured the process that it leads to many confusions and errors in our everyday thinking. We sell our services and our material products for money, we buy everything we use with money, we count our wealth and income in money terms, and we think of our savings as a sum of money —until it seems as if money were the very substance of the economic structure. If not on our guard we are likely to forget that the real wealth, about which the economic activities of men revolve, consists of goods. We forget that what the business world is doing is producing goods, exchanging the goods for each other, paying the product in goods over to the various individuals who helped to produce them, and finally using up or consuming the goods so produced. The student has already been warned against confusing money with income and wealth. As we go on with our study we shall frequently have occasion again to emphasize the fact that back of every money transaction there is a goods transaction, and it will be necessary to be ever watchful not to be misled by failing to look behind the money facts to the more fundamental things.

Exchange is Mutually Beneficial. — It is sometimes thought that in an exchange transaction between two parties, one of them must be the gainer and the other a loser. Such is not the case. In a fair exchange both parties are benefited. A farmer who raises corn has more of that commodity than he can possibly use; the surplus above his own needs is of no benefit to him unless he can find someone who will give him, perhaps shoes, in exchange for it. The shoemaker has more shoes than he wants but he lacks corn. In trading, the farmer gives up something of little value to him and receives in exchange shoes of greater usefulness, thereby making a gain. The shoemaker is equally the gainer, however, and for the same reason. It is no different when money is paid by one person for the goods of another. Suppose he pays one dollar for a necktie. He evidently values the necktie more than the dollar, and more than anything else he could have bought with the dollar, or he would not have made the purchase. He has therefore gained something. The seller must also have valued the dollar he received more than the necktie he parted with, because of something he can buy with the dollar which he desires more than the tie. Therefore he, too, has gained.

Competition among Sellers. — Where there is specialization and exchange, each producer is desirous of obtaining a buyer for his wares. The buyer, however, is unable to purchase everything that is offered to him, and is obliged to choose between them. Thus different sellers come into competition with each other for his patronage.

Suppose one desires to purchase a fountain pen. He will find a number of stationers willing to supply him. Here is competition among retailers for his trade. The retailers, in turn, are besought by competing wholesalers seeking to supply them with their stocks of merchandise. The wholesalers may buy from any one of a number of competing manufacturers of fountain pens, and the manufacturers, in turn, find competing producers of raw materials ready to furnish them with the rubber, gold, etc., which they require. Thus, throughout the various stages of production, there is competition for patronage *among producers of the same thing*.

There is also competition *among the producers of substitute things.* In order to write one does not have to have a fountain pen; he can use an ordinary pen and holder, or perhaps a pencil. Hence, there is competition among the producers of fountain pens and other writing implements for the writer's trade. Competition of this sort is widespread. There is, for instance, the possibility of substituting oleomargarine for butter, beef for lamb, cotton for linen or linen for silk, fiber for leather, oil or gas for coal, one kind of metal for another, one kind of wood for another, automobiles for horses and wagons, etc.; and in every one of these cases there is competition among the producers of the substitute commodities.

These cases are fairly obvious, but there is a more fundamental competition just as universal in economic life, although not so noticeable. Every seller is a competitor of every other, even though they be *sellers of totally unlike things*. Since the consumer's income is limited, if he spends it in one way he foregoes another possible expenditure he might have made. What he spends on clothing he cannot use for food, and if he purchases an automobile he may be obliged to go without a piano. The producer of clothing is then competing with the producer of food for the buyer's purchase, and the manufacturer of automobiles with the manufacturer of pianos. Thus, because buyers must choose what things they will buy and what they will not, all sellers compete with each other for business.

Finally, there is competition *among the sellers of the various means of production*. The worker sells his labor. In doing so, skilled workers compete with unskilled, and men compete with women for employment. All of them may compete with machines which are possible substitutes for their labor. The owners of different kinds of machines or tools compete with each other for the patronage of manufacturers, landowners compete for tenants, and so on.

These various kinds of competition may manifest themselves in various ways. Sometimes the competitors are very active. Rival salesmen besiege the potential buyer and endeavor to demonstrate the superiority of their wares. Extensive advertising campaigns endeavor to persuade the consumer to eat more dairy products in the face of equally enticing appeals to eat more fruit, while railroads and steamship lines issue alluring booklets designed to attract vacation travelers to use their respective facilities. Sometimes the struggle becomes more sinister, as business men resort to cut-throat competition, brute force, and underhand methods to drive their rivals from the field. Or the competition may be quite passive, the parties to it even unaware that they are rivals. But it is there none the less, for it exists by virtue of the fact that buyers must choose between them.

Competition among Buyers. — Competition is not a one-sided affair, to which sellers alone are subject; it exists among buyers as well. Goods being scarce, every consumer desires as many of them as possible. In the effort to secure them he comes into conflict with other consumers. There is, for instance, competition *among buyers of the same thing*. Let us go back to the case of the person who purchased a fountain pen. He is not the only individual who has use for such an article. There are many other buyers, and as many more potential ones who would buy if the price were just a little lower. These buyers are competitors with one another, competing for the supply of fountain pens in the hands of retailers. So also the retailers compete with one another for the stocks of wholesalers, and the wholesalers compete for the products of manufacturers. At every stage in the various successive processes of production are many buyers, just as there are many sellers, competing with each other for goods.

There is also competition among buyers for the various resources, materials, and other *means of production*. Coal operators compete with iron and steel manufacturers for the supply of labor, wheat farmers compete with corn farmers for the supply of land, manufacturers compete with domestic consumers for the supply of coal, and so on.

Competition among buyers is sometimes active, sometimes passive. We see it in most active operation at an auction sale where various bidders outdo one another to obtain possession of some desired object. It manifests itself again in the "want-ads" offering to employ labor published in the daily newspapers. It is most acute in times when there is an unusual shortage of something. During the first World War, when housing facilities were scarce, there was a great scramble among tenants to be first to secure a vacant dwelling; and there are times when employers of labor will send out agents to entice workers away from other occupations by offers of better wages. Usually, however, competition among buyers is more passive than that between sellers. But it is there none the less, and every seller knows he can rely upon it to secure him the best price for his product that the market will afford, for if he offers his wares at a certain figure, a certain number of buyers will purchase it, while if he raises the price, some will drop out of the market, while others will continue to buy, showing that there are always some ready to outbid rival consumers if necessary to obtain possession of the available supply of merchandise.

Restrictions on Competition. — Although competition is very widespread, there are often obstacles to its perfect operation. One such obstacle may be the presence of an agreement between sellers not to cut prices, or the control of the supply of a commodity by a monopoly. Such cases as these are very numerous. They restrict the scope of competition but do not eliminate it. A single group of producers may have a monopoly of anthracite coal production, but they must still compete with the producers of bituminous coal, and of other fuels, such as wood and oil. There may be only one hardware merchant in a small town, so that he is freed from competition there, but there is still the possibility that hardware users may buy from merchants in other towns if he tries to take undue advantage of his position. Similarly, a national monopoly may have to compete with producers in another country. Even the most perfect monopoly of a product is limited in its powers by the fact that consumers may stop buying and spend their incomes on other things if it boosts its prices too high.

The sharpness of competition is also dulled by the ignorance or lethargy of people. We are likely to patronize a store near at hand, although we might do better elsewhere, simply because we are too hurried or too lazy to look further. A laborer may accept employment on poorer terms than he might have obtained in some other occupation or at some other place because he is not informed of the other opportunity. The first of these cases frees the seller, the second frees the employer, of a certain amount of competition. There are many similar examples. Particularly in retail trade the customers are influenced by lack of knowledge of market conditions, by inability to judge the quality of similar goods, by habits or personal whims or clever advertising, to give their custom to one dealer in spite of better offers from another. This lessens the rigor of competition for the favored seller. Here again, however, the limitation on the force of competition is not very great. If there are extreme differences in the advantages offered by competitors they will make themselves felt, and the obstacles to the operation of competition will be overcome.

Coöperation among Sellers. — Universal as is competition in economic life, coöperation is equally prevalent and just as fundamental. This may seem paradoxical but it is none the less true. In fact, coöperation arises out of competition. Although the sellers of dairy products compete among themselves for the patronage of purchasers of butter, milk, cheese, ice cream, etc., they have a common interest against the producers of other products which bid for the favor of consumers. It is to their interest to reduce competition within their trade as far as possible and combine their energies in promoting the sale of dairy foods. So we have associations of dairy products manufacturers to advertise their goods and to promote the interests of the trade generally. Throughout the various stages of industry we have similar associations—of retail merchants, of wholesalers, of manufacturers, farmers, bankers, etc. Such coöperation runs not only along the lines of the various trades, but also all the business men in a certain community, although each is engaged in a different branch of industry, may find that they have certain interests in common—such as the desire to "boom" business in their town in competition with other towns, or to secure from the government legislation beneficial to them all. So we have chambers of commerce in our cities, and nationwide organizations such as the National Association of Manufacturers.

Labor unions are a form of coöperation among sellers. The workers in a given trade have their labor to sell to employers. They can bargain with them more effectively if they suppress competition among themselves and present a solid front. By this unity of action employers can be made to grant concessions which could not be obtained from them by individual employees acting alone.

A frequent form of association among sellers is monopolistic combination, of which so many conspicuous examples have been exposed to the public in recent years. All the business men who constitute the monopoly gain by the elimination of competition among themselves, for they can usually produce more economically and sell at higher prices as a result of their union.

Coöperation among Buyers. — Consumers also find it to their advantage to coöperate in buying commodities or services jointly desired by them. Farmers, for instance, find that they can obtain their fertilizers, seeds, tools, and other articles on better terms if they club together for that purpose than if they act independently. So we have farmers' granges and coöperative stores. There are many other coöperative stores, among workingmen, among college students, and among the public at large. In these associations a number of consumers contribute enough capital to lay in a stock of merchandise, appoint people to manage the enterprise, and share in the profits. Usually each person's share in the earnings is based on the volume of his purchases during the year. In this way the members of the coöperative association obtain their goods at less cost than they would have to pay elsewhere. In England the Rochedale coöperative stores organized on this principle are very numerous and successful, carrying on annually a surprisingly large amount of business. Attempts at coöperative buying in the United States have been less successful.

Employers' associations are frequently formed for the purpose of dealing collectively with their employees. By this coöperation they obtain an advantage in bargaining to offset that gained by the organization of laborers into unions. These associations are practically buying associations to obtain the services of labor on the best possible terms. The trade agreements made at stated periods in this country between the coal operators and the miners are a good example of this kind of coöperation. Here is a coöperative organization of buyers dealing collectively with a similarly coöperative organization of sellers. Many other cases of the kind can be found in industry today.

The Coöperation of Specialization. — All the types of coöperation so far mentioned have been consciously adopted by men for the furtherance of certain very definite aims; but there is an unconscious coöperation running through the industrial system which is far more universal and fundamental. It arises out of the fact that industry is specialized and characterized by the processes of exchange. Specialization is often called the division of labor; it is equally correct—and far more significant—to describe it as the coöperation of labor. It is wise to emphasize this very strongly, for in these days of strenuous competition it is apt to be overlooked. The fact that the labor of the community is divided among many individuals for its performance is equivalent to the coöperation of those individuals in the production of economic goods. The kinds of coöperation involved in specialization and exchange may be classified in a manner very similar to that which we found applicable to the different kinds of competition.

There is, for instance, coöperation *among producers of the same thing*. It is easy to see that the workers at given tasks in an industry are coöperating with each other for the making of their common product. The many employees of a shoe factory, some of whom fashion the soles, others of whom sew the various pieces together, while still others put in the eyelets, nail on the heels, and so on, are combining their efforts toward a single goal—the making of the finished shoe. The product is the result of their joint effort.

It is plain that the workers in different stages of a chain of productive processes are likewise coöperators in achieving a final result. The shepherd who tends his flock and disposes of the wool from his sheep, the woolen manufacturer who converts it into cloth, the clothing establishment that fashions the cloth into garments, and the wholesale and retail merchants who bring it into the possession of consumers—all the workers who have a hand in any of these productive operations—are coöperating in the production of the completed article.

But the economic coöperation between the members of society under the present industrial system is much broader and more fundamental than that which is seen in the above two cases, for there is also coöperation *among the producers of entirely different things*. The present organization of society is one in which each individual is a specialist to a very great degree. He produces one product exclusively, or more likely only a small part of one product. As we learned in a preceding paragraph, he secures what other products he needs in his daily life not from the work of his own hands, but by exchanging his product for that of other individuals. The result of this process of exchanges is that each individual is contributing something to the needs of others and receiving a contribution from them in return. All the men in the productive process are really coöperating with each other to gratify their respective desires. The wealthy manufacturer of woolen clothing in a New England town is a sort of partner to the laborer in the Chicago stockyards who spends his days in sticking pigs, for the former is making clothes for the laborer to wear, while the latter is preparing pork for the manufacturer's dinner. They are exchanging products with each other. This is coöperation of a very fundamental sort, and it is inherent and universal in our industrial system. It means, in effect, that persons of all classes in the United States are co-operating with each other, and with those in other parts of the world —even with the meanest coolie in China who is producing rice for their tables. The remarkable fact about this is that it is entirely spontaneous and unconscious. We do not consciously effect an exchange of our products for those of others, because in nearly every case money enters into the transaction. Yet the coöperation is there.

Solidarity. — In spite of the prevalence of competition on all sides in society today, therefore, we live in a world of mutual interdependence. This interdependence was mentioned before as one of the consequences of specialization. We are now better able to appreciate its importance. The economic well-being of every member of society is closely bound up with that of his fellows, and he cannot escape from this association. Economic life is a great process of mutual aid. This inter-relationship is well expressed by the term *solidarity,* which means the oneness or interdependence of human beings in society. The fact of solidarity brings it about that the prosperity of each of us is closely affected by the behavior of others, and our actions affect them in turn. Thus if one works industriously he increases the wealth of his fellows; if he shirks or is idle he is diminishing the prosperity of all. A railroad strike or a business failure affects not only the parties immediately concerned, but reacts upon persons in other occupations and far-distant places; the discovery of an oil well or the invention of a new machine benefits not only their owners but the community as a whole. If everybody realized the significance of solidarity and acted accordingly, many economic fallacies would be avoided and probably everybody would be more industrious. For all the members of society will gain most if everyone is producing to his fullest and best, and everyone loses when anyone does less well than he might. This lesson is not only a moral preachment; it is a plain scientific truth.

SUMMARY

In the modern industrial system the labor of the community is specialized, or divided. It is specialized into trades, tasks, and stages. There is also geographic specialization, by which whole towns, regions and nations concentrate their production upon certain products. Specialization depends upon the size of the market for products, since a high degree of specialization cannot be carried out unless vast quantities of each product can be made in one establishment and widely sold.

Specialization has led to important consequences. It has helped to increase the abundance of goods by increasing the productiveness of labor. It does this because (1) it develops an acquired skill in the worker by concentrating him upon a given task at which he becomes expert; (2) it enables him to concentrate upon that occupation best suited to his ability; (3) it makes possible the use of machinery; (4) in the case of geographic specialization the industry of a region can be adapted to its natural resources; and (5) whole communities can develop technique and skill for certain kinds of production. Specialization has caused uniformity of goods of a particular kind, but has added variety to our lives by giving us more kinds; it has increased the dependence of individuals and communities and nations on each other; it has separated the worker from his product, thereby making his income dependent on prices and giving rise to difficult problems of value and distribution. It is also alleged that it has increased the monotony and irksomeness of labor, although this is disputed.

Specialization is accompanied by exchange, each person trading his product for the product of others, through the medium of money. The use of money conceals the true nature of the process, but at bottom it is essentially an exchange of goods for goods. In a fair exchange both parties are benefited.

In a system of exchange there is competition among sellers of the same thing, among sellers of substitute things, among sellers of quite unlike things, and among sellers of the various means of production. There is competition also among buyers of the same thing, and among buyers of the means of production. Perfect freedom of competition is restricted by the organization of monopolies and by the ignorance or lethargy of people.

Men are often led to coöperate where they have common interests as a group against the competition of other groups. Thus there arises coöperation among sellers of the same product, among laborers, and so on. Sometimes the coöperation takes the form of monopoly. Similarly, there is coöperation among buyers, such as coöperative stores, and employers' associations. More fundamental than these, however, is the coöperation that exists by virtue of specialization and exchange, which means that many specialists coöperate to produce the same things, and that producers of different things are coöperating to provide each other with their several products. Thus the modern world exhibits solidarity, the mutual interdependence of all the members of society.

REFERENCES AND SUGGESTIONS FOR FURTHER READING

The classical basis for all subsequent discussion of the division of labor was laid in Book I, Chapters 1 to 3, of Adam Smith's famous essay on *The Wealth of Nations*. A later analysis, particularly of geographical specialization, is given in Alfred Marshall's *Principles of Economics* (5th and later editions), Book IV, Chapters 8 to 10. Fuller and more up-to-date treatments of this topic will be found in E. L. Bogart and C. E. Landon, *Modern Industry* (1927), Chapters 3 to 6, inclusive. Consult also the article on *Specialization* in the *Encyclopedia of the Social Sciences*.

Chapter 6 of Henry Clay's *Economics, an Introduction for the General Reader* (American edition, 1920) presents a most interesting discussion of competition and coöperation, which has helped me considerably in preparing the present chapter. T. N. Carver's *Essays in Social Justice* (1915) have also been of value. Chapters 1 to 5 of that most stimulating volume set forth very forcefully and convincingly the dominance of competition in modern economic life. On the other side, P. Kropotkin's *Mutual Aid* (English edition, 1902) contains a great deal of valuable information showing the influence of coöperation in social activity.

Chapter IV

THE TIME-CONSUMING PRODUCTION PROCESS

A. THE TIME ELEMENT IN PRODUCTION

The Roundabout Process. — The wants of primitive man were few and simple, and his methods of meeting them correspondingly direct. If he wanted water, he fashioned a crude jug of clay, baked it in the sun, and carried it on his shoulder to the nearest stream. If he needed a habitation, he fashioned a bow and arrow, shot some animal, skinned it with a crude stone knife, and made himself a tent. These processes did not consume very much time, nor did they require much equipment. Hence, the possessions of such people were few and of a rather elementary character.

The wants of civilized man are more varied, and his methods of providing for their fulfillment very much more complex. In order to provide water for a modern city, men must first extract iron ore from the ground, purify the iron, convert it into machinery, with the machinery and more iron make pipes and plumbing fixtures. Prior to most of these operations, rock must be quarried, bricks baked, and cement manufactured, in order that the necessary buildings may be erected. Finally, reservoirs and pumping stations must be constructed, and pipe lines, sewers, and plumbing systems must be installed. When all this has been done, but not until then, water flows freely in every home, and can be obtained by the mere turning of a faucet. The building of a modern dwelling is equally complex; and it is the same with every product that we have. All are obtained in a long, complicated, *roundabout* process.

Or, consider the matter of food. Primitive man needed but a few tools to secure it. A bow and arrow sufficed to obtain his meat; fruit and vegetables he could pluck with his bare hands from the trees and plants. Modern man goes at it very differently. As in the case of the water system, he begins with the mining of iron and its conversion into steel. Then he makes axes, spades, plows, harrows, tractors, reaping, threshing, and binding machinery. He clears the land of trees, plows and harrows it, surrounds it with fences. On the land he erects barns and other buildings, which require the prior making of other tools and securing of various materials. Then he selects the best breeds of animals, and sets them to graze, or the most promising kinds of seeds and plants them in the soil. When the animals are reared and the grain is harvested, they must be transported by trucks and railroads (whose production necessitated another long line of preliminary processes) to meat-packing plants in the one case and to milling establishments in the other. Back of these establishments lie other chains of prior activity, reaching eventually to some sources in forest, field, and mine. Here they go through various processes of manufacture, until they emerge as beef and breakfast food. Finally, through a series of facilities and dealers they get to the consumers' tables. A long and complicated sequence, indeed! Yet such is the process by which modern man procures his food; and it is pretty much the same with every good he uses.

The essential difference between this process and the more direct methods of primitive industry is that modern industry is *spread over a longer period of time* and requires the expenditure of more preliminary labor. The preliminary labor, instead of being directed toward the immediate satisfaction of some want, is devoted to making some kind of implements or equipment from which want-satisfying goods will eventually emerge. This result, however, may be a long way off. Months or years must elapse between the first step in the opening of an iron mine and the eventual flow of water in consumers' homes; and it will be many more years before the total amount of water so obtained is sufficient to compensate for all the preliminary effort that went into the construction of the water system. Similarly, a long time must elapse between the original activity of tool making, forest clearing, and so on, and the appearance of food on our tables.

The Roundabout Process Increases Production. — We go through this devious path because, in the long run, it yields more goods. The roundabout process is vastly more productive than more direct methods. This will be apparent if we make a simple comparison. Suppose we had at our disposal the labor of one hundred men over a period of ten years, which we may assume to be sufficient for all the successive operations necessary to complete a small water system, from the initial mining of iron and quarrying of rock to the final installation of pipes and fixtures. If we keep these men working throughout the decade at carrying water in jugs and distributing it in person to the people of a small community, they may supply enough water for, say ten thousand inhabitants. At the end of the ten years, there would be nothing to show for their labor except that the people would have been prevented from perishing of thirst during this period. But if we take those same men and set them to work constructing pumping stations, reservoirs, pipe lines, and plumbing systems, it is quite certain that the total amount of water made available to consumers *throughout the life of the completed system* would suffice to provide the needs of a population many times as great for many years to come. The same quantity of labor has worked for the same period of time in both cases. In the first case, all the labor was applied directly to the carrying of water. In the second case, it was applied indirectly, and a far greater product resulted. Thus the roundabout process is far superior, and there can be no question that the per capita output of modern industry is tremendously greater than that of primitive industry because the modern method is roundabout.

The Vertical Structure of Industry. — As a result of the roundabout process, industry is divided into successive stages, some of which are near to, others remote from, the ultimate consumer. This succession of stages is sometimes called *the vertical structure of industry.* It can be illustrated by our previous example. The mining of iron and the making of bricks constitute remote, or early, stages in the production of drinking water. The laying of the pipes and installation of the fixtures constitutes a stage somewhat nearer, or later. Finally, the pumping of water into reservoirs, whence it flows to the user, constitutes the nearest, or final stage, in the production of water. The great Boulder Dam irrigation project offers another example. The making of concrete for this dam, the construction of the dam itself, with its aqueducts and irrigation ditches, leading water into the fields of farmers, the growing of vegetables on the fields so irrigated, the marketing of those vegetables through wholesale and retail traders, and, finally, the cooking of those vegetables in consumers' kitchens—these represent different stages of remoteness and nearness in the production of food. We can think of the whole process as one in which the goods at remote stages gradually *ripen* into consumable goods over a considerable period of time.

The division of production into successive stages is closely associated with the specialization by stages that was described in the preceding chapter. Because of this fact, students often confuse the roundabout process with specialization. However, the two are not identical. It is possible to have specialization without time-consuming methods of production. Such would be the case if an Indian tribe were to divide the labor of fruit-gathering, hunting and clothes-making, etc., among its members, each working at one of these tasks, with little or no use of machinery or tools. On the other hand, it is conceivable that there might be roundabout production without specialization. Such was the case, to some extent, with the early American pioneers, each of whom built his own barns, made many of his own tools, and devoted a great deal of preliminary labor to moderately remote stages of production, working pretty much alone. In modern society, however, the two phenomena go hand in hand; we have both specialization and roundaboutness, each facilitating the other.

Durable Goods and the Gradual Release of Services. — The spreading of production over a period of time is not altogether a matter of successive stages. Equally important (if not more so) is the fact that much of the equipment with which industry is carried on is of a durable character. A machine may last for several years, a factory building or a house for several decades, and a railway tunnel or a dam for a century or longer. Parts of the roads built by the Romans are still in existence. During the entire useful life of these durable forms of wealth they continue to yield services to their owners. The machine and the factory building each go on, playing their part in the industry where they are employed, until the one is worn out and the other falls into decay, or until they become so out of date that they are scrapped; the house keeps on providing shelter for its occupants; the tunnel and the dam continue, each in its respective rôle, until they collapse, or are no longer needed.

The creation of durable wealth is usually an expensive undertaking, because it requires a great amount of productive activity. It takes a considerable force of men, working with appropriate tools and materials, three or four months to build a house, three or four years to build a great dam. All this productive effort is merely preliminary to the end-product which will finally emerge from the equipment so created; and it may be a long time before the full fruit of this effort is realized. Not until the last bit of service has been gotten from the durable wealth—months, years, or decades later—do the effects of the original contribution of those who produced it cease. We can therefore think of such wealth as a sort of store of services, embodied in it by production in the past, which services are gradually released during the course of its useful life.

The creation of durable goods must be regarded as production remote in time from ultimate consumption, even though the goods are to be used directly by the consumer. A dwelling house, for instance, yields services directly to its occupant. However, these services are released so gradually that most of them are not enjoyed until long after the house is built. The major part of the productive activity that goes into its construction, therefore, is directed towards a quite distant future; it is remote from final consumption. On the other hand, a more perishable good, even though it be produced at a stage of production several steps removed from the consumer, may not be very remote from him in time. Cotton growing in the fields today may be a shirt on someone's back a few weeks hence, in spite of the fact that it must pass through several stages of production in the meanwhile. It is the passage of time, rather than the succession of processes, that is the significant phenomenon with which we are here concerned, and it is in that sense that the word *remote* will henceforth be used.

The amount of durable goods now at the disposal of society as a result of past production is very great. It has been estimated that the total value of man-made equipment in the United States is equal to three or four times our annual income.[1] This means that if the entire nation were to devote all of its productive efforts exclusively to the task, it would take some three or four years to reproduce this equipment. The latter is an important source of our present income. Its contribution to our material well-being is well-nigh incalculable.

The Time Element in Production Requires Waiting. — The ultimate aim of all production is consumption—that is, the use of goods in the direct gratification of desires. The preceding analysis reveals, however, that production is carried on, for the most part, in preliminary operations more or less remote from consumption. The fact that a considerable period of time must elapse before remote production finally yields its fruit in consumable products presents a financial problem. Production must be paid for while it is taking place. Someone must hire laborers and pay them wages. Materials must be bought. Land must be leased or purchased. Yet these expenditures will not be returned until the consumable products resulting from them can be disposed of. This means that someone must advance the costs of carrying on the preliminary processes and wait for repayment.

In some cases, the waiting period is short. The flour that is used in a bakery can soon be baked into bread which consumers will pay for. But the money invested in the bakery itself is not so quickly recovered. The initial expense of constructing and equipping it is considerable, and many loaves of bread must be sold over a long period of ensuing years before enough is returned to recompense the owner for this expenditure. Almost every business enterprise presents a similar problem.

Surplus Essential to Time-consuming Production. — This waiting would not be possible if there were not a surplus of consumable goods available to support those who are working in the more or less remote operations of industry. For, since their labors do not yield con-

[1] Wesley C. Mitchell, *Business Cycles: The Problem and its Setting* (1927), p. 98.

sumers' goods until some time in the future, they must perforce be sustained now, either from a stock of such goods accumulated in advance, or from the surplus of such goods being currently produced by other workers. It is from the latter source, for the most part, that they are supported.

A community so poor that it was compelled to devote all of its labors to providing the barest necessities for its people could not have a modern water system, for if any of its workers were withdrawn from producing food and clothing to work on reservoirs, pumping stations, and pipe lines, some of its members would have to go unfed and unclothed, which would probably put an end to the adventure. Suppose, however, that a part of the population could produce enough means of subsistence for everyone; it would then be possible to employ the rest of the workers at making equipment for a more efficient water supply. Thus the community could embark on more roundabout production.

The roundabout process, once begun, provides the means for extending it further, for when tools and implements begin to be used, the increased output of consumers' goods releases workers to produce more equipment. Thus the process, at first difficult to embark upon, becomes ever easier. So, highly industrialized nations enjoy increasing prosperity as time goes on, and their standards of living rise progressively.

B. Saving

Saving and Investment Essential to Time-consuming Production. — Although surplus income is essential to time-consuming production, the mere existence of such surplus does not make it certain that lengthy productive methods will be employed. The people who have more productive power than they need for a bare existence may prefer to reduce their hours of work, and so enjoy increased leisure, instead of engaging in remote productive operations; or, they may consume their surplus in extravagant living. If surplus productive power is to be employed in the carrying on of productive operations at remote stages, or in the making of durable goods, there must be willingness so to employ it. The people, or at least some of them, must deliberately choose to work now at producing goods remote from final consumption, for the sake of the increased flow of consumable products that will result in the future. Such an act of choice takes the form of *saving* and *investing*. This statement needs some explanation, for we ordinarily think of saving as the setting aside of money, and it is not at first apparent that remote production is involved.

The money income which a person receives represents a claim on the current product of industry. If it is "spent," this claim is used to buy goods for immediate consumption, such as food and clothing, or admission to a motion-picture show. Producers, responsive to the demand for goods, will meet this expenditure by manufacturing the articles mentioned. "Spending" thus has the effect of directing production toward goods which are near to the consumer. When we "save," we decide to forego the privilege of immediate consumption. Instead of purchasing goods for our present enjoyment, we invest the amount saved in stocks or bonds; or, perhaps, we deposit it in a savings bank. If we buy newly issued securities, the money goes to the corporation which issued them. If we put it into the bank, the latter ordinarily invests it in securities, mortgages, or the like. In either case, the result is that our claim on current product is turned over to business men; or perhaps to prospective home-owners desiring to finance a home-building project. The business men and home-owners now have money, saved by others, which they use to purchase equipment of which they are in need. This causes production to be diverted from immediately consumable goods to more remote products, especially to such durable wealth as factories, power plants, railways, machinery, and houses. The ultimate claim on these remote goods rests with the savers who made this production possible, for they own the stocks or bonds through which the production of the remote goods was financed; or, they have a claim on the banks, which, in turn, hold claims on the bonds or mortgages of the business men and home-owners to whom loans have been made.

This analysis shows that the real difference between "spending" and "saving" (if the savings are invested) is that, in the case of the former, final goods, yielding immediate enjoyment to the consumer, are purchased, while in the case of the latter, remote goods are purchased, yielding utilities sometime in the future. The money is spent, in the sense of being paid out for goods of one kind or another, in both cases.

Hoarding and Spendthrift Loans. — The qualification contained in the above parenthesis, that savings represent money spent for remote goods, "if they are invested," is an important one; for, if the savings are hoarded in the form of money, they obviously are not spent for durable goods. In certain countries of the Orient, a great deal of saving takes the form of stores of gold and silver. Some saving of this sort goes on in Occidental countries, also, but the amount of it is usually negligible. In times of business depression, however, when very little investment is taking place, a great deal of idle money may accumulate in our banks, taking the form of unexpended bank balances. In both these cases, the money is withdrawn from circulation, for the time being, and is not used in the time-consuming process of production. No addition to the community's stock of durable wealth results from it. Hoards of gold and silver do constitute durable wealth, of course, but wealth which is not being productively used.

Sometimes what appears to be an investment, from the point of view of the individual, turns out to be consumption, from the point of view of society. One may lend one's money savings to an improvident man, who borrows to give an elaborate wedding for his daughter. Here goods are consumed, no durable wealth is created. A more important case is that of investment in government war loans. Some of this investment may take the form of arsenals, forts, ships, and other durable equipment; but much of it goes into munitions which are soon used up and destroyed. Loans of this type, which dissipate savings in consumption, are called "spendthrift loans."

Nominal and Real Savings. — In recognition of these unproductive investments, it is well to distinguish between *nominal savings* and *real savings*. Nominal savings consist of money income withdrawn from immediate consumption by its recipients. Real savings consist of accumulated stocks of wealth, resulting from investment.[2] These will take the form of durable goods, such as buildings, railways, bridges, highways, ships, vehicles and machinery, and of stocks of raw materials and partly finished merchandise somewhere on their way through the production process.

The Purchase of Wealth Already in Existence. — Sometimes, when money is saved, it is used to purchase some form of wealth already in existence—a piece of real estate, or stocks or bonds issued some time ago to previous investors, so that they now represent claims to equipment already constructed. In such cases, there is a mere transfer of ownership. Whether or not such savings are real, or only nominal, depends on what is done with the money by the person who receives it in exchange for his property. If he uses it to take a trip around the world, the savings are dissipated in consumption—they are only nominal. If he buys a house already built, there is a second transfer, and we must trace the funds further. But if he, or the next recipient, uses the money to bring new wealth into existence, the savings are real. Sooner or later, the great bulk of saving takes this last form.

Sources of Savings. — In modern communities, most savings arise in the following ways: (1) Voluntary individual saving, by persons who set aside from their current money incomes sums which they put into savings banks or other financial institutions, or with which they

---

[2] This will include hoards of metal, jewelry, etc., but will exclude idle bank balances (in so far as they are not fully covered by specie reserves—see Chapter VIII) and spendthrift loans.

purchase securities. Such savings are the result of personal thrift. (2) Voluntary corporate saving, which comes about through the reinvestment of corporate earnings. When a business firm is making profits, its directors may decide that it is wise not to distribute all the gain to the stockholders, but to use part of it for making additions to the company's plant, or for other purposes conducive to the welfare of the enterprise. Here the stockholders are saving by proxy, as it were, the directors acting for them. Reinvested earnings of this sort are an important source of new equipment in this country. (3) Involuntary, or forced, saving. We shall learn later that the nature of our banking system permits the banks to create funds which they place at the disposal of business men, funds which do not come from the voluntary savings of anyone, but which are brought into existence by the banks themselves. Fuller explanation of this will be reserved for the chapters on money and banking.

The processes of saving and investment are so complicated that special financial institutions have been developed to provide for them. These also will be considered in due course.

Depreciation of Durable Wealth. — After durable wealth has once come into existence, it begins to wear out. Machinery at best has a life of only a few years, and buildings, even of the most substantial construction, eventually crumble and decay. This gradual deterioration is known as *depreciation*. In addition to being caused by wear and tear, depreciation may occur because a particular kind of equipment has become obsolete. The invention of talking pictures made almost useless the expensive pipe organs with which so many theaters were equipped in the days of the silent cinema, and the development of the auto-bus caused many street-car lines to be abandoned and their track torn up. The scrapping of much industrial machinery and plant that is not worn out, but has merely been superseded by something better, is a common phenomenon in a progressive economy.

Since depreciation does occur, our industrial equipment can only be maintained by continual repairs and replacements. Like the original creation of the equipment, such repairs and replacements require saving. So, the owner, if he is to preserve his investment, must continually provide new funds for this purpose. Good business men recognize this, and it is their custom annually to lay aside a portion of their earnings in a "depreciation fund" to replace their equipment when it is no longer fit for use. Failure to provide such a fund will mean larger profits for consumption now, but will bring the business to grief sooner or later, as many a careless investor has found out, to his sorrow. Hence, it is considered good financial practice to regard the maintenance of plant and its replacement as one of the normal costs of conducting the business, which is provided for as regularly as the payment of interest, taxes, wages, or any other business cost.

The Making of Advances. — Not all of those who are engaged in the more or less remote operations of production wait for the fruits thereof. The waiting is done by those who save and invest. The other participants are paid at once for their contributions, even though they are at very remote stages. The laborers employed in the construction of a waterworks do not have to wait until enough water has been sold to consumers to cover the cost of their labor. They receive their wages immediately, or at regular short intervals, long before dams, pumping stations. pipe lines, and sewers have been completed, and, therefore, long before a single drop of water has reached the users. Who pays these wages? They are *advanced* out of the savings of those who invest their money in the enterprise. When a man invests his savings directly or indirectly in a business project, he puts the managers of that business into the possession of funds with which they can set labor to work producing equipment. That is the real object of the investment. Money savings represent a claim on the current income of the community. Part of that income is in the form of consumable commodities and services. Through the business managers, the claim is transferred to the workers who are employed in producing the kinds of wealth which the business needs. They receive immediately consumable goods and the investor obtains equipment in exchange for them. This has been described as an exchange of present for future goods. When an employer pays wages to laborers, he is usually giving them present goods in exchange for equipment which will ripen into consumable goods in the future. This process is continually going on; the spreading of production over time, therefore, involves a series of advances to labor.

Advances are made not only to laborers, but also to many other participants in the productive process. They are made by investors to business men, and by one investor to another. To return to our previous illustration, the payments made in the construction of a waterworks consist not only of wages to laborers, but also of payments for materials used, such as concrete, iron and steel. In paying for these, the builders of the waterworks are making an advance to the people from whom the materials were purchased, for these materials will yield no consumable income until the water system is put in operation at some time in the future. Part of this advance for materials goes to recompense the investors for wages previously advanced to laborers who made the materials, part to business men as profit for their part in making them, and part as interest to compensate investors for their investments in the equipment used to produce the materials. So, the investors in the system are not only making fresh advances for construction work carried on at their stage of the production process, but are repaying others for previous advances made by them in preliminary stages. There is a succession of advances made by the investors at one stage of production to participants in preceding stages throughout the industrial process.

Advances made in the construction of durable wealth are not repaid until the lapse of a considerable period of time. For, as we have seen, the investor must wait a long while for the full services of this wealth to be released, and he is recompensed for his advance only in the installments of income produced by the wealth through its life. On the other hand, advances made in the purchase of raw materials and more perishable goods will be repaid to the investors at that stage soon; for, when such goods have passed through a given stage of production, they emerge as salable products which are paid for by the buyer, even though they be employed at stages somewhat remote from the final consumer. The buyer in this case has taken over the advance made by the seller at the previous stage, and the former must then wait until he, in turn, is repaid by the next buyer. In the making of cotton shirts there is a heavy investment in durable equipment at each stage of the process. There is the cost of the farm on which the cotton is grown, and of the factory and machinery in which the cloth is made into shirts. Only a small part of this cost can be collected in the selling price of each shirt, so it will be a long time before it is all paid for. Not so with the materials used in the several stages of shirt-making. The farmer gets back his investment in seed and fertilizer when he sells the cotton to the weaver; the weaver is paid for his cotton when he sells the cloth to the shirtmaker; and the latter is paid for the cloth which he purchased when he sells his shirts to the dealer.

Abstinence. — The fact that the time-consuming process of production requires people to save their surplus of current income and invest it in industrial equipment, waiting for the reward of this investment in future consumable goods, has led some writers to stress *abstinence* as an attribute of the savers. If one saves a part of his income and advances it to others for the construction of equipment, he is abstaining from consumption of the goods which he might have bought with his surplus had he cared to do so. There is no denying the truth of this analysis, but it does not follow that abstaining and waiting are always accompanied by acute personal sacrifice. While in the case of persons of moderate means the accumulation of savings can be accomplished only by dint of hard working and frugal living, and while much capital is created by this means, many of the savings from which modern industry is financed come from the investments of persons with very large incomes. It probably entails little or no sacrifice upon the part of the multimillionaire to devote a few hundred thousand or even a million dollars of his wealth to roundabout production, for he may still spend enough annually to live in luxurious extravagance, so that he need feel no pinch of economy as a result of his investments. Moreover, much equipment in modern times is provided by the reinvestment of earnings in the way described above. The saving performed by the stockholders in this case is largely unconscious; it cannot be regarded as involving much sacrifice or deprivation. For these reasons the use of the word abstinence to describe the refraining from consumption which is essential to the accumulation of savings is somewhat inapt; at least it is capable of being misconstrued.

Saving and the Agents of Production. — It was shown above that the time-consuming processes of modern production yield more goods than the shorter methods of primitive industry. Who is responsible for this extra product? Some persons answer this question by saying that it is to be attributed to the equipment employed; and they think of such equipment as constituting in itself a separate agent of production, distinct from land or labor. This, however, is superficial thinking, for the equipment is produced by labor, working, of course, with land. Other persons, seeing this truth, say that labor is responsible for the extra product, land being merely an inanimate gift of nature. This explanation, too, is somewhat superficial, for it ignores the part played in the process by those who save and invest. It is really the roundabout process of employing labor which makes the extra product possible, and labor could not be so employed if there were not saving and investment. The savers and investors, therefore, contribute to the extra product, along with the laborers who actually make the equipment. Because of their contribution, the savers are able to claim a share of the product. That share is called *interest*.

It is clear from what has just been said that, in the time-consuming process there is involved an agent of production which is neither labor nor land, but which inheres in the business of saving and investment. What name shall we give to this agent? Some economists call it *waiting*, fixing upon the making of advances and waiting for future return as the distinguishing contribution of the investor. We prefer to use the term *saving*. There are, then, at least three agents of production, which we may designate as land, labor, and saving. We shall presently encounter a fourth agent, which is called *business enterprise*.

Some Categories of Wealth. — In analyzing the phenomena associated with the time element in production, we have had occasion to differentiate between several kinds of wealth, with reference to its availability for consumption, and its durability. Other writers have commonly sought to emphasize the first of these differentiations by distinguishing between *producers' wealth* and *consumers' wealth*. By producers' wealth, they mean all wealth, of whatever description, in producers' hands, including industrial plant of all kinds, as well as stocks of materials, partly finished goods and unsold merchandise. By consumers' wealth, they mean all wealth, of whatever description, in consumers' hands, including dwelling houses, furniture, clothing, coal in the cellar, food in the pantry, and personal possessions.[3]

This distinction is convenient for some purposes, and we may have occasion to employ it, but it does not go to the heart of the time element in production; for it is evident that the purchase of a residence, which is consumers' wealth, involves saving, investment, waiting, and the making of advances, just as truly as does the financing of a factory building, which is producers' wealth. Moreover, there is not much saving and waiting involved in connection with those producers' goods that consist of raw materials soon to emerge in consumable products. Therefore, recent writers have emphasized the distinction between *durable* and *perishable wealth,* whether in producers' or consumers' hands, as being more fundamental. The latter terms do point more nearly to the essence of the matters here being considered, but they,

---

[3] The same writers further divide producers' wealth into two classes, which they call *land* and *capital,* respectively. By *land,* they mean all natural resources and productive power over which possession of the earth's surface gives control. This includes, in addition to the bare land itself, mineral deposits, wild vegetation and animal life, lakes and streams, and climatic advantages to which the land gives access. It excludes all improvements made by man. By *capital,* they mean all man-made producers' wealth. This includes everything made by man which is in the possession of producers—railroads, highways, factory buildings, stocks of raw materials, livestock, partly finished goods, unsold merchandise. It excludes all wealth in the possession of consumers. These writers stress particularly the several stages of roundabout production, and they associate the term "capital" with those stages which precede the final transfer of goods to consumers.

The distinction between natural wealth and man-made wealth is a useful one for some purposes, but the use of the term "capital" to denote the latter is confusing, for this word is also used in the broader sense in which it was defined in Chapter II. Moreover, it is a mistake to associate the phenomena of saving, investment, waiting, and the making of advances exclusively with producers' goods, for the reasons to be set forth above. It is also a mistake to associate land exclusively with producers' goods, for much land is obviously used by consumers. Witness the land on which residences are situated, and golf courses. In view of these considerations, we have rejected the narrower use of the term capital, and have adopted the terminology following above. In reading the works of other economists, however, students will need to remember that they will sometimes find the word "capital" employed in the restricted way just explained.

It is unfortunate for the beginner in economics that economists do not all agree in their use of words; but the disagreement is an unavoidable accompaniment of progress in thinking. As men learn more about the nature of the economic process, their ideas about them change, and new words must be used to express new thoughts, or the meanings of old words must be changed. This need not be confusing, provided each writer defines with care the terms which he employs, and then always uses them consistently in accordance with his definitions.

too, offer a difficulty; for those perishable goods which are used up in the construction of durable goods are as far away, in time, from the rendering of services to consumers as if they were themselves durable. For instance, the coal burned up in a plant which manufactures steel rails, though it perishes, becomes embodied, so to speak, in the rails, which are a long way off from consumption.

Therefore, it is more satisfactory to distinguish between goods which are near and remote from final consumption. We shall call them *near-goods* and *remote-goods,* respectively. By *near-goods,* we mean *those goods which will be wholly consumed in the immediate future in the direct satisfaction of wants.* Food in one's pantry (or in the stocks of retailers), clothing on one's back, an automobile that is not far from the junk heap, are near-goods, as thus defined. By *remote-goods,* we mean *those goods whose final and complete consumption in the direct satisfaction of wants lies some distance in the future.* All very durable wealth is to be classed as remote, even though it is being partly consumed in the present, as in the case of an occupied house, for most of its services will not be released until the future. And all perishable goods that are used in the production of other goods which will not be consumed until the future, as in the case of the coal burned in making steel rails, just referred to, are likewise to be classed as remote. The distinction between near- and remote-goods is a relative one; no hard and fast line can be drawn between them.

One other term has been used repeatedly in the present chapter, and will appear often in subsequent pages. It is the term *equipment.* By this is meant *all man-made remote wealth.* It excludes natural resources, such as building sites and mineral deposits, and it also excludes goods perishing in the act of final, direct consumption, such as food on the dining table. It includes all other wealth, of whatever description. Most of the wealth in existence at a given time, other than land, is equipment.

Human Equipment. — Human beings can acquire certain qualities whose creation and ultimate results involve phenomena very similar to those of the time-consuming production process. A young man may spend some years in college acquiring an education designed to equip him for a particular career. Someone must pay for his board, lodging, tuition, books, and incidental expenses. Someone must have surplus income above his immediately pressing needs to do this. He must be willing to invest the surplus in the young man's training. Such investment requires saving, and it involves advances, for the payments are made now, in the expectation that the training will justify itself in future results. The investor must wait for these results to materialize. He may gain nothing for himself from his investment, but, presumably, the education will some day yield income to the young man—that is, it will increase his earning power. Much the same is true of all training leading to an acquired skill. A piano-tuner's knowledge of his trade, a violinist's proficiency—all kinds of manual dexterity and the intellectual equipment possessed by skilled workers and professional people—these require a certain period of preliminary training which has to be financed in advance and which, therefore, is properly to be regarded as the result of saving and investment.

So far, the case is a close parallel to material equipment. However, there is an important difference. Except where slavery prevails, human equipment cannot be owned by anyone other than the person in whom it resides. Hence, investment in human training is not usually a business venture for anyone but the student himself. Sometimes, to be sure, employers invest money in training their employees for the particular work of their establishments, and occasionally a college student can borrow money for his education on his personal credit, but ordinarily, such expenses are paid by parents, by friends, or by the state, as an act of altruism or as a contribution to the general welfare. By whatever method they are financed, such payments constitute saving, and the knowledge and skill which result are just as truly a part of society's productive equipment as any investment in material plant.

SUMMARY

The roundabout methods of modern industry have caused production to be spread over a relatively long period of time, although it is more productive than direct methods. Time is required for goods at remote stages to "ripen" into consumable products, and the services locked up in durable wealth are only gradually released. This time-consuming process therefore requires waiting for production to yield immediately consumable goods. The succession of stages is known as the vertical structure of industry. There must be a surplus of currently produced consumable goods to sustain those who are working at remote stages.

This surplus is made available to those workers through saving and investment. When savings are invested, production is thereby directed toward the production of material equipment, instead of toward immediately consumable goods; but no addition to equipment results from hoarding or spendthrift loans. Hence, a distinction must be drawn between nominal and real savings. Where money saved is invested in wealth already existing, the money will nevertheless usually be spent to construct new equipment sooner or later. Savings arise from: (1) voluntary savings of individuals, (2) voluntary reinvestment of corporate earnings, (3) credit created by banks for investment purposes (involuntary saving). Equipment depreciates; hence its maintenance or replacement requires fresh acts of saving and investment. Investment involves advances of present goods (in exchange for future goods) by savers to workers and to all those who participate in the preliminary processes of industry. The refraining from consumption, which is involved in saving and investment, is sometimes described as abstinence, but this abstinence does not always require acute personal sacrifice. Since the extra product obtained by time-consuming methods of production is made possible by saving, saving (or waiting) may be regarded as a factor of production, in addition to land, labor, and business enterprise.

A distinction can be drawn between producers' and consumers' wealth, between durable and perishable wealth, and between near- and remote-goods. The last is most fundamental in connection with the time element in production. The term equipment is also useful; it denotes all man-made, remote, wealth. There is human equipment as well as material equipment.

REFERENCES AND SUGGESTIONS FOR FURTHER READING

Our knowledge of the roundabout process owes most to the Austrian economist, Eugen von Böhm-Bawerk; see Books I and II of his *Positive Theory of Capital* (English translation, 1923). The best analysis of this process in brief compass is perhaps that of F. W. Taussig, in Chapter 5 of his *Principles of Economics* (4th edition, 1939), to which I acknowledge my indebtedness. A very illuminating treatment is also contained in Part II, Chapter 3, of H. G. Brown's *Economic Science and the Common Welfare* (1922). F. M. Taylor has treated this problem in a somewhat original way in Chapter 5 of his *Principles of Economics* (1921).

Chapter V

COMBINING THE AGENTS OF PRODUCTION

A. Varying Proportions and Diminishing Productivity

The Agents of Production. — Production is commonly carried on by human beings, working with natural resources, tools, and various other equipment, in some kind of business organization. It was suggested in the last chapter that the various elements involved in this process could be classified into four general groups, namely: labor, land, saving, and business enterprise. In economics these are usually called the *agents* or *factors of production*.

Economists use the term *labor* very broadly. It refers not only to physical toil, but to all effort, either manual or mental, devoted to production. The activities of business executives, shop foremen, accountants, clerks, and stenographers, as well as those of skilled artisans and common pick-and-shovel workers, are all to be described as labor of one kind or another. The professions—medicine, law, teaching, the ministry—are likewise included. Not all human activity is labor, however; some of it is play. The difference between work and play appears to lie chiefly in the object to which effort is devoted. Play is undertaken for its own sake, as a form of enjoyment; labor is a means to an end—the end of earning a livelihood, of acquiring income. Hence, we may define labor as *human effort exerted for the purpose of securing income*.

Economic usage of the term *land* is equally as broad. The word refers, not only to the physical surface of the earth, but to natural resources in general. It includes mineral deposits beneath the surface, bodies of water, natural forests and vegetation, wild game and fish. All these are to be found on the land and can be acquired only by having access to the land; therefore, from the economist's point of view, they are attributes of land, and are so classified. We may think of land, then, as denoting *all natural resources*.

The sense in which the term *saving* is used to denote an agent of

75

production has been sufficiently described in the preceding chapter. It refers to the use of surplus income to promote roundabout methods of production. It is concretely embodied in industrial equipment.

Labor, land, and saving must be combined and coördinated in a functioning business organization in order that production may take place. The combining and coördinating is done by the fourth agent of production, known as *business enterprise*. We can think of business enterprise as personified in business men, whom we may call business enterprisers. Other names sometimes applied to them are entrepreneurs, undertakers, or business organizers. It is the function of the business enterpriser to determine broad questions of business policy and to exercise general supervision over the work of a business organization. We shall learn more about these functions in the next chapter.

The Classification of Productive Agents Is Inexact. — For some purposes it is convenient to separate the agents of production into the four groups just described, but the separation is rather arbitrary. It would be just as logical to divide them into a hundred. Labor is not a homogeneous category. There are mental workers and manual workers, skilled and unskilled; there are often a score or more different kinds of employees in a single factory. So, also, there are good lands and poor lands, mineral lands, agricultural lands, and building sites. Savings are invested in many different kinds of equipment. Even the work of management is divided and subdivided among a number of different persons in a single enterprise. In reality, therefore, the agents of production are legion, and our classification of them into four general types is only valid in the broadest kind of way. It is a device for our convenience, to promote clearness in thinking; but it must not be carried too far.

The various agents of production need not always be represented by different individuals. A farmer, for instance, may own his own land, buildings, and tools, and may perform the functions of laborer as well as manager. Such an overlapping of functions in one individual is of very frequent occurrence. But whether the agents of production are represented by one or several individuals, the functions which each performs are different. It is these functions which immediately concern us, and we shall study the part that each of these general types of agent plays in industry, regardless of the individuals associated therewith.

Variable Proportions of Productive Agents. — To some extent, the way in which the productive agents must be combined in a given industry is determined by technical considerations, involving matters of applied chemistry, physics, or biology. However, considerable variation is possible within the broad limits set by available techniques. In agriculture, for instance, one may farm intensively or extensively— that is, by the very careful cultivation of small plots of land, or by the more superficial cultivation of large tracts. In the first case, the proportion of labor and saving used is large in relation to the land employed; in the second case, it is small. In manufacturing, if there are materials to be moved, such as coal or sand, one may employ men with wheelbarrows or use a chain-bucket conveyor, operated by steam or electric power. Weaving may be done with a hand loom, in which the human operator throws the shuttle back and forth in such a way as to work out the desired pattern, or with an automatic loom, in which the pattern is controlled mechanically. Paint may be applied to a surface with a brush, which is primarily a work of labor, or with a spray, where the paint is pumped through a hose and atomized mechanically. Each of these last three examples involves differences in the proportions in which labor and saving are combined. Hand work requires relatively much labor and little equipment, hence little saving; mechanical work requires more saving and less labor. In practically every industry similar variations are possible.

This leaves a considerable choice of methods open to the enterpriser; the exact technique to be employed is a matter for his discretion. He will be governed in his choice by certain economic considerations. It is our task in the present chapter to investigate the economic effects of varying the proportions in which the productive agents are combined. This will give us some insight into the factors which will influence the enterpriser's decisions in such cases.

Land and Saving Fixed, Labor Varying. — Let us suppose that we have a farm, equipped with the necessary buildings and tools for operating it effectively, and that we are going to experiment by employing different quantities of labor, in order to ascertain the effects of this variation on the output. Let us lay out ten plots of land on the farm, each an acre in size and of equal fertility. We will plant grain of the same seed on each of these plots. On the first plot, however, we will put only one week of labor during the season, and on each of the others two, three, four, five, six, seven, eight, nine, and ten weeks of labor, respectively. We may refer to these as different *inputs* of labor. On the first two or three plots of land we are carrying on rather extensive cultivation; that is, we cultivate the land rather superficially. As a result, we will get a relatively small crop per acre. On the plots where the inputs of labor are larger, we have more intensive cultivation, and, consequently, a somewhat larger output of grain per acre. This larger crop is due to the extra labor, which makes it possible to plow and cultivate the soil more carefully, to keep down weeds more effectively, and to attend to each operation in a more thorough manner. We will find, however, that this increase will not go on indefinitely as more and more labor is applied, for there is a limit to what the land can be made to yield, and as we approach this limit more closely, it becomes progressively more difficult to obtain a larger crop. Finally, a point will be reached where the yield is at its maximum, and no more can be obtained, no matter how much additional labor may be applied. We may assume this to be reached on the ninth plot of land, where nine weeks of labor are applied.

To get a clearer idea of this, let us suppose that the following table represents the results obtained in our experiment:

TABLE I

Inputs of Labor (in weeks)	Total Outputs (in bushels)	Marginal (Extra) Outputs (in bushels)
1	4	4
2	11	7
3	19	8
4	27	8
5	34	7
6	39	5
7	42	3
8	44	2
9	45	1
10	45	0

The first two columns of the table are self-explanatory. They represent the inputs of labor on each of the ten plots of land and the total number of bushels of grain obtained in each case. The third column needs some explanation. It represents the *extra* crop obtained in each case, as compared with the case immediately preceding. For instance, on the first plot of land the total output is four bushels, which is four bushels more than we would get if we employed no labor at all. The extra yield obtained by employing one week of labor as compared with no labor is, therefore, four bushels. On the second plot we obtained a total yield of eleven bushels by the employment of two weeks of labor, which is seven bushels more than we obtained on the plot where only one week of labor was applied. Accordingly, the figure 7 appears in the third column as the extra product when two weeks of labor are employed. The extra yield in each of the other cases is computed in the same way, and the results are given in the third column.

It will be noticed that these are designated at the top of the column as *marginal outputs*. This term is commonly used in economics to denote *one unit more or one unit less* of something. In the present case we are measuring the marginal output or marginal product of labor, which is simply the extra product obtained by an extra input of labor. Another way to find the marginal product would be to ascertain the loss in product that would occur if one input of labor were withdrawn. For instance, when five weeks of labor are employed, the total product is thirty-four bushels. If we take away one input of labor, the product would be reduced by seven bushels. Seven bushels, then, is the marginal product when there are five weeks of labor. The marginal output is significant because by it the business man must judge how far it is wise for him to go in employing labor upon the land. This point will be more fully explained in a later paragraph.

It is to be noticed that the marginal output at first increases, reaching a maximum of eight bushels when three weeks of labor are applied to the land. It is again eight bushels when four weeks of labor are used; but after this the marginal output declines, until finally it becomes zero after the ninth input of labor. It is at this point that total output reaches its maximum. Presumably, if additional inputs of labor were applied much beyond this point, the total yield would actually decline, for the soil might be overworked, or laborers might get in each other's way. The marginal product would then be a minus quantity.

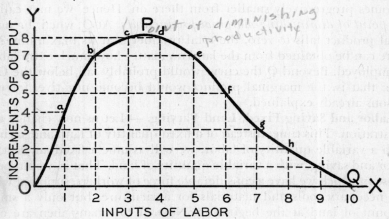

Figure 1. A Curve of Diminishing Marginal Productivity.

The Curve of Diminishing Marginal Productivity. — The above results will be brought out more clearly if we represent them in the form of a graph, such as that of Figure 1. This graph is constructed as follows: Along the horizontal axis (OX) we lay off ten equal spaces, numbered from one to ten, beginning at the point O. These represent the inputs of labor, each space on the line representing one week of labor applied. On the vertical axis (OY) we lay off equal spaces numbered from one to eight (again beginning at the point O) to denote the various increments of output (that is, the successive increases, or marginal products). We know from the table above that the increment of product obtained when one week of labor is applied is four bushels, hence we mark the point *a* on the graph by drawing lines perpendicular to the OX axis at *one,* and to the OY axis at *four.* In like manner we obtain the point *b,* indicating that an extra product of seven bushels is obtained when a second input of labor is used. In the same way we get the points *c* to *i,* inclusive, by plotting on the graph the figures shown in the third column of the table. Now, by connecting these various points by a continuous line, we obtain the curve OPQ, which gives us a general picture of how production in this case is affected by successive inputs of labor. Such curves are frequently used to express relationships between two variables, because the visual picture they give us brings out the behavior of the phenomena under investigation more clearly than numerical tables. We shall have occasion to use many curves of this general type as we go on with our study.

Notice that this curve rises to its highest point at P and thereafter slopes downward until it meets the OX axis at Q. This shows that the marginal product first increases, reaching a maximum at P, and then becomes progressively smaller from there on. Hence, we may call P *the point of diminishing marginal productivity.* At Q, when the marginal product falls to zero, the total product is at its maximum. No more can be obtained from the land no matter how much extra labor is employed. Beyond Q the curve would probably fall below the OX line; that is, the marginal product would become negative, for the reasons already explained.

Labor and Saving Fixed, Land Varying. — Let us now change the illustration. This time, instead of a fixed quantity of land and saving, with a variable quantity of labor, we will assume a fixed amount of labor and saving, with a variable quantity of land. That is, we suppose a case in which we have a considerable force of workers, supplied with the necessary tools and materials for agriculture, but only a small amount of land at the beginning. Now, if too many men are employed on one small plot of land, no matter how well supplied with equipment, not all of the labor can be utilized effectively, for we know from the previous example that the extra workers will add very little to the product if too many of them are used in the combination. Give them more land to work upon, and the marginal laborers whose product is low, can be released to work on the additional land, where their labor will be more effective. As a result, the output will be greatly increased—perhaps more than doubled. Here we have a stage of increasing marginal productivity. However, if we go further with this process, each additional acre of land will lead to farming of a more extensive sort, until presently too little labor is applied on each acre to cultivate it effectively. The increase in product to be obtained by additional acres will then begin to decline. Here we have reached a stage of diminishing productivity, just as in the previous illustration. If the process is continued far enough, a point will be reached eventually where no more product can be obtained at all. Output per unit of labor and saving is now at its maximum, just as we formerly obtained the maximum per unit of land and saving.

If we draw a graph to represent this case, we will obtain a curve similar to the curve of Figure 1. Measuring increments of output on the OY axis as before, and inputs of land on the OX axis, the curve will at first rise to a peak and then decline, until eventually it touches the bottom line. This curve will not coincide with the previous one, but it will behave in the same general way.

An Example from Non-agricultural Industry. — So far, we have dealt only with agriculture. Let us now turn to a case of manufactures. We may assume that we are concerned with a factory designed for the production of rayon fabrics. This will consist of a building, erected on a suitable site, and provided with dyeing vats, a power plant, winding and weaving machinery, storage rooms, and other appropriate equipment. We may suppose, furthermore, that there is on hand a sufficient store of raw materials and fuel to operate the plant for some time. Here, then, is a fixed quantity of land and of saving embodied in equipment. We propose to experiment with varying quantities of labor. A certain minimum number of men will be necessary to operate the plant at all; below this the output would be zero. Three or four men may suffice to keep up steam in the boilers and operate one of the winding machines and one of the looms. It is obvious, however, that these men cannot carry on production very efficiently. Part of the power generated in the boilers will go to waste because there are not enough men to utilize the machines which the plant is capable of operating. Some of the machines will be idle. Each man will have to be a jack-of-all-trades, able to perform the various processes of dyeing, winding the yarn upon cones or bobbins, setting up the work in the looms, operating the looms, inspecting, packing, and shipping the final product. The process will be deprived of the advantages of specialization. If more men are employed, specialization can be developed and each one will become more expert at his particular task. The power generated in the engine room can be used more fully, and so on. Hence, up to a certain point, each extra man employed will make a larger addition to the output of the establishment; but this cannot go on indefinitely. As more and more workers are added, it will be increasingly difficult to find ways to use them effectively. There is a limit to the extent to which division of labor can be carried, and only one operator can be employed effectively upon a given loom or other piece of machinery. Helpers here and there may add something to the efficiency of the other workers, but this too has its limits. Hence, sooner or later, extra product per worker must decline. Eventually, if enough workers are employed, the maximum capacity of the plant will be reached, and no further product whatever can be obtained no matter how many more men are added.

Thus we see that in this case we have the same tendency at work as in the two previous examples. The successive increments of product obtained from successive inputs of labor rise to a point of diminishing productivity, and then decline. A graph of this situation would yield a curve of the type with which we are now familiar.

Labor and Land Fixed, Saving Varying. — Let us now consider a problem in which we have a fixed quantity of labor and land, and in which we propose to experiment with various quantities of saving. This case is much more subtle than any of the foregoing, because of the way in which saving enters into production. It will be recalled that the effect of saving is to cause production to be carried on in roundabout, time-consuming ways. An increase in saving, therefore, tends to lengthen the process. If we want to use more labor in production, we employ more and more men, or we employ the same number of men a greater number of days or weeks, so that the case is simply one of the addition of like units—we have seven units instead of six, or eight units instead of seven. Likewise, in the case of land, we simply add acre upon acre of land of similar qualities. Saving, however, is not a simple instrument of production like a man or a piece of ground; it is a process, and the process takes different forms depending upon whether little or much saving is used. If we wanted to use more saving on a farm, we *could* increase the number of barns, corn cribs, plows, tractors, etc., and in the case of a textile mill, we *could* add to the number of looms; but this would be a very clumsy method of investing additional savings. The process of increased saving would be more likely to take the form of more complicated and durable equipment, requiring the carrying on of more preliminary activity. On the farm, tractors would take the place of horse power, threshing machines would take the place of flails, milking machinery would take the place of human hands. In the textile mill, power looms would take the place of those operated by foot treadles and automatic looms would take the place of those in which the shuttle was thrown by a human operator.

Because of this change in the form of industry, there is no very satisfactory way of measuring the number of units of saving employed. Furthermore, we cannot confine our observation to a single business enterprise, because, in a system characterized by specialization by stages, no one enterprise makes the whole of anything from its beginning to its end, and many of the preliminary operations in which additional savings are employed take place at earlier stages of production. For instance, the tractor is not made on the farm, yet it is the tractor which embodies the increased saving. In the same way, the automatic loom, which represents the application of more saving to weaving, is not made in the textile mill. Therefore, a study of the effects of increased saving upon production must cover all stages of industry from the most remote to those which are nearest the consumer. Needless to say, the fact that saving can be embodied in so many different forms of equipment makes it impossible to define a unit of saving with precision, and hence to measure the successive units of it employed in a productive process. Nevertheless, we can conceive in our minds of increasing degrees of roundaboutness in the production of any commodity resulting from the investment of additional savings.

We learned in the preceding chapter that passage from direct, hand methods of production to more roundabout, time-consuming methods increases the productivity of industry. The use of a tractor represents a more roundabout method than the use of a horse, but it will accomplish more work; the power loom will weave more cloth than one operated with a treadle. It seems reasonable to suppose, however, that not all of the roundabout devices at the disposal of the business man are equally productive. Some are more effective than others. Presumably, if only a small fund of savings were available, it would be devoted to those forms of equipment which would add most to the product. After the more effective devices had been exploited, additional savings would have to be put into forms of equipment which would be less useful. When the farmer is already supplied with a tractor, a reaper-thresher combination, and the other usual farm machinery, additional equipment will not be so obviously advantageous. He could no doubt use additional savings to improve his equipment at many points. If his house and barn are frame structures, they could be built of stone; more durable types of fencing could be employed; roads could be improved, and so on. But it is not to be expected that investment in these things would yield as much return in product as investment in the most necessary equipment. In a textile mill, steam power will be vastly more productive than hand-driven machinery, but the automatic loom, which represents a much more complicated and expensive piece of machinery, will not yield as much surplus over the simpler type as will the power-driven over the foot-operated instrument. Additional savings could be employed in conveying machinery and automatic devices of various sorts, but after the more clearly useful of such investments had been adopted, additional equipment of this sort would be less productive. Likewise, in every other branch of industry, there are some ways in which savings can be used to marked advantage, others in which the superiority over more direct methods is less.

Therefore, we come to the same conclusion that we reached in the other cases. Up to a certain point, the employment of additional savings adds increasing returns to the output of production, but beyond that point the marginal product begins to decline. Presumably, there is a limit in each industry beyond which increasing investment in equipment would add nothing at all to production. Hence, the curve of diminishing productivity presented in Figure 1 is applicable in a general way to increasing quantities of savings also.

The Effects of Science and Invention. — All that has so far been said, about the effects of increasing one agent of production in relation to the others, must be interpreted with a qualification. It is assumed that the cases with which we are dealing do not involve the use of any new discoveries or inventions. We suppose that at the start of each experiment the experimenter has at his command a certain amount of knowledge and certain available techniques, and that he works within the limits set thereby. If, during the course of the experiment, a new discovery is made which greatly improves the efficiency of the industry concerned, the tendency to diminishing marginal productivity may be obscured by the introduction of this new element. For example, a new discovery in agricultural methods, such as an improvement in kinds of fertilizer, might go parallel with more intensive methods, so that increasing increments of product would be obtained, instead of the decreasing increments which would have resulted, had it not

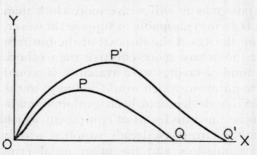

Figure 2. The Effect of Improvement in the Arts upon Diminishing Productivity.

been for this technical change. A new mechanical invention may suddenly provide new opportunities for the investment of savings and lead, for a time, to greatly increased increments of output from extra investment. What happens in these cases is that the new discoveries push the whole productivity curve upward, so that it occupies a higher position than before, and its shape may be altered in such a way that the point of diminishing productivity is pushed further to the right, as in Figure 2. Within the limits set by the new technique, however, the tendency to diminishing productivity will again be operative. The principle has not been destroyed; it merely operates on a new plane. This is comparable to the effect of a current of air upon a moving object. A baseball, thrown from the hand of a pitcher in a dead calm, will follow a certain course, which might be described by a curve plotted on a piece of paper. However, if a sudden gust of strong wind blows across its path after it leaves the pitcher's hand, its course will be distorted, and it will follow a somewhat different curve. The same law of gravity is working upon it in both cases, however, and will eventually bring it to earth.

We must be especially careful about making allowance for changes in techniques when we are dealing with production over considerable periods of time. As the years go by, changes in population and the amount of saving occur simultaneously with changes in the technique employed in industry. We have here a mixture of interacting influences, the progress in the arts of production tending to offset the tendencies to diminishing productivity in such a way that we may get increasing increments of product from year to year. This point will be more fully developed in a later paragraph.

We must also be careful in our interpretation of what is meant by increased roundaboutness of production resulting from increased saving. In any given state of the arts of production, certain choices are open to the producer, some of which involve relatively direct, others relatively roundabout processes. We have already seen, for instance, that he may have a choice between an automatic or a hand loom. At any one time, he can utilize an increased amount of savings only by choosing among the alternatives *then afforded by existing industrial knowledge*. It is within the limits of this knowledge that the tendency to diminishing productivity operates. Let there be some striking change in methods, however, such as the substitution of electric for steam power, and there may be an outlet for a large volume of new savings at an increasing rate of productivity, where previously no such outlet existed.

General Statement of the Law of Diminishing Productivity. — With the qualification just stated, it appears that we have here a general principle that applies to any possible combination of productive agents—to increasing numbers of workers employed in a factory, to increasing amounts of fuel fed into a furnace, to additional equipment of locomotives and cars employed in railroading. It would be easy to multiply instances without number. Always we would find that the effect of increasing any one agent leads first to increasing, then to decreasing additions to output. For most economic problems, it is the phase of diminishing outputs that is most significant, for, so long as the returns to be gotten by adding extra units of a productive agent keep increasing, it usually pays to add more and more of that agent; but when the increments of product begin to decline, a question is raised as to how far it pays to go. Hence, it is the tendency to diminishing productivity which sets limits to the employment of the several agents in any given operation. Because of this, the principle which has here been described is usually known as the law of diminishing marginal productivity, or, more often, simply as *the law of diminishing productivity*. This law may be formally stated as follows: *In a given state of the arts, additional inputs of any productive agent used with a fixed quantity of other agents, will, after a certain point has been reached, yield progressively smaller increments of product.*

Fixed and Variable Costs. — This principle has an important bearing upon the conduct of every business enterprise. A business establishment is usually provided with a certain plant, consisting of a building (or buildings) and machinery or other durable equipment. This plant is of a more or less permanent character, so that it cannot readily be changed until the time comes when it is worn out or in need of drastic alterations. It is, therefore, a fixed agent of production for the time being. The plant has a given maximum capacity, but the owner does not have to operate it to its fullest. Within the limits set by that capacity he can vary his output, according to the volume of orders he has to fill, by employing more or less labor and materials. The labor and materials thus constitute variable agents of production. Here we have, therefore, variable agents used in combination with a fixed agent, so that the principle of diminishing productivity is brought into play.

To the business man, this principle is revealed most tellingly through its effects upon his costs of production. There are certain costs associated with the plant which, because the latter is fixed in character, will run on pretty much the same from year to year, regardless of the volume of business done. Interest must be paid annually on borrowed savings invested in the equipment, and funds must be laid aside regularly to repay the principal of the loans as they fall due. An allowance should also be made for the gradual depreciation of the plant, so that sums may be available to replace it when it is worn out or obsolete. Taxes on the property must be met. Fire insurance must be kept in force. There will also be a certain administrative staff of office executives, foremen, watchmen, and the like, who must be kept employed, and whose salaries must be paid, whether the plant is operating at capacity or only on part time. Some of these expenses may vary slightly as the business expands or contracts. The plant will usually depreciate more rapidly when in active use than when idle, and the administrative staff will be somewhat larger when the volume of business is great. But they fluctuate much less than the output; they are relatively constant. Therefore, they are known as *fixed costs*. They are also called, sometimes, overhead costs, and supplementary costs.

If we divide these costs by the number of units of product turned out by the plant, the cost per unit will decline as the output increases; for, since these costs remain fixed *in the aggregate*, they must be less *per unit*, the greater the number of units produced. If the fixed costs in a given enterprise are $5,000 per year, and the output is 5,000 units, the average of the fixed costs per unit is one dollar, but if the output were 10,000 units, the average would be only fifty cents.

The costs which are associated with the variable agents of production will behave quite differently. In order to produce more of a given product, more fuel must be fed into the power plant of the factory, more materials must be purchased to work up into finished goods, and more labor must be hired to do the work of manufacturing. Hence the bills for fuel, raw materials, and wages will increase. If the quantity of products produced is smaller, all of these costs will be less; if the plant is not operated at all, they will be zero. Costs of this kind, which vary in rough correspondence with output, are known as *variable costs*. Other terms which are sometimes applied to them are operating costs, and prime costs.

If we compute the variable costs *per unit of output*, we will find that their behavior runs opposite to marginal productivity. That is, if a plant is not operated up to the point of diminishing productivity, marginal output keeps increasing as additional expenditures for variable agents are made; therefore, the variable costs per unit of product fall. But after the point of diminishing productivity has been passed, additional expenditures for variable agents bring smaller returns in product; therefore, the variable costs must presently rise. It appears, then, that these unit costs move downward, then upward, as output expands. As the maximum capacity of the plant is approached, variable costs per unit will become very high indeed, until the point is reached where they approach infinity, because the addition to output resulting from any further expenditure would be zero.

Average Costs. — The *total costs* of producing a given volume of output in an enterprise consist of the sum of the fixed and variable costs. If we add these together and divide by the number of units of goods produced, we have the *average costs* of production. The behavior of average costs is a resultant of the behavior of fixed and variable costs. Let us see how this works out in a given case. We shall choose, as an illustration, the agricultural experiment of a previous paragraph. In that experiment we started with a fixed quantity of land and equipment and added varying quantities of labor. Hence, we can construe the costs associated with the land and equipment as fixed, and those incurred for the labor as variable. The fixed costs will then include rent for use of the land, and interest and depreciation on the equipment. Let these costs amount to $5 per acre per year. The variable costs will consist mainly of wages for labor. Let us suppose this to be $5 for each unit of labor employed. If we now apply these figures to the inputs and outputs of our original experiment, as recorded in Table I above, we will get the results shown in Table II.

TABLE II

Inputs of Labor	Fixed Costs	Variable Costs	Total Costs	Total Output	Average Cost per Unit (Bushel) of Output
1	$5	$5	$10	4	$2.50
2	5	10	15	11	1.36
3	5	15	20	19	1.05
4	5	20	25	27	.93
5	5	25	30	34	.88
6	5	30	35	39	.90
7	5	35	40	42	.95
8	5	40	45	44	1.02
9	5	45	50	45	1.11
10	5	50	55	45	1.22

Observe that, in this table, the fixed costs remain the same (at $5), no matter how many inputs of labor are applied, but that the variable costs increase in direct proportion to the number of units of labor employed. By dividing the figure for total costs in each case by the corresponding figure for total output, we get the average costs per bushel of product, shown in the last column. Observe that this average in the beginning is fairly high ($2.50), but drops steadily downward (to a minimum of 88 cents) until five inputs of labor have been used. This is due partly to the fact, above explained, that the fixed costs become less per unit as they are spread over a larger number of units of output, and partly also to the fact that the variable costs per unit at first fall, because of the tendency to increasing productivity. After the fifth input of labor, however, the average costs start upward, and become progressively higher as further inputs of labor are applied. This rise is due to the fact that, after the point of diminishing productivity has been passed, increasing inputs of labor yield progressively smaller increases in product, so that the variable costs per unit rise. At some point, the upward pull of these costs becomes great enough to offset the downward pull of the fixed costs, so that the average costs must rise. In our illustration, this occurs at the sixth input of labor.

The behavior of the average costs is most conveniently represented by means of a graph, such as that of Figure 3. For the moment we are

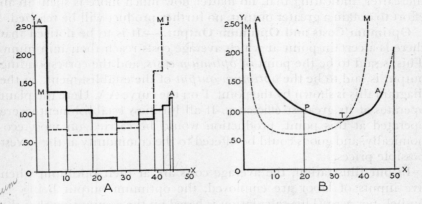

Figure 3. Average and Marginal Costs.

concerned only with the solid lines in this figure; the dotted lines will be explained in a later paragraph. Consider first Part A of this drawing. Here the costs per unit of product are measured on the vertical line OY, beginning at the point O, and units of output on the horizontal line OX, again beginning at O. The heavy stepped line (AA) is drawn with reference to these two axes, the height of the steps in each case indicating the average cost per bushel for the corresponding output. These are plotted from the figures shown in the last two columns of Table II, which we have just been considering. It will be noticed that the line shows average costs falling from $2.50 per bushel, for an output of four bushels, to $.88 for an output of 34 bushels, after which it rises again. Part B of the drawing shows the same phenomenon in the form of a curve. This curve is more satisfactory to work with than the stepped line, because it enables us to see at a glance what the average cost would be for any possible output. For instance, if we take any point on this curve, such as P, and project lines perpendicularly to the two axes, we know at once that the average cost per bushel will be $1 when 20 bushels are produced. Although the exact picture of average costs will vary from enterprise to enterprise and from industry to industry, it will always have a shape somewhat similar to that of the curve here shown; for average costs typically decline to a certain minimum, after which they rise again.

There is, of course, an absolute limit to the amount of product that can be obtained in any given establishment. This marks its maximum capacity. In our illustration this is supposed to be reached at 50 bushels. The average cost curve rises with increasing steepness as this point is approached (see the dotted part of the curve) and becomes vertical thereafter, indicating that, no matter how much more is spent in an effort to obtain a greater output, no further product will be realized.

Optimum Costs and Optimum Output. — It is to be noticed that there is a certain point at which average costs reach their minimum. This is said to be the point of *optimum costs,* and the corresponding output is said to be the *optimum output* of the establishment. In the diagram this is shown by the point T on the curve AA. Here the plant operates at its greatest efficiency. If all business establishments were operated at this point, production would be carried on most economically, and goods could be offered to the community at the lowest possible prices.

In our illustration, the average costs are at their optimum when five inputs of labor are employed, the optimum output being 34 bushels per acre. This calculation is based on the assumption that the costs associated with the land and equipment are fixed at $5, while the variable costs of labor are $5 per input. If these costs were different, however, the optimum might come at some other point. Suppose, for instance, that the fixed costs are $10 a unit, instead of $5, and the variable costs $3 a unit, instead of $5. The calculation would then be as shown in Table III. This time the optimum cost is 72 cents per bushel, and it comes at the sixth input of labor, where output is 39 bushels. Were we to plot this on our diagram, it would give us a curve somewhat lower, and slightly different in slope, from the curve AA of the drawing. This is because land and equipment are dearer and labor is cheaper than in the previous example. Therefore, it is more economical to use less land and equipment and more labor.

In general, we may say that economic efficiency requires that we economize as much as possible on those agents which are dearest. Hence we may expect to find that relatively small proportions of dear agents of production will usually be used in combination with relatively large proportions of those agents which are cheaper, within the limits of variation which existing technology permits. For instance, in the early development of our country, when land was plentiful and cheap and labor scarce and relatively dear, farming was carried on extensively—huge tracts of land were rather thinly cultivated with the use of very small amounts of labor. Now that land is scarcer and more dear and labor more abundant and cheap, farming has become much more intensive—farms are smaller in size and more labor is employed in relation to the land that is used. In manufactures the same thing is true. In a country like China, where saving is scarce and dear and labor abundant and cheap, highly mechanized processes

TABLE III

Inputs of Labor	Fixed Costs	Variable Costs	Total Costs	Total Output	Average Cost per Bushel
1	$10	3	$13	4	$3.25
2	10	6	16	11	1.45
3	10	9	19	19	1.00
4	10	12	22	27	.81
5	10	15	25	34	.74
6	10	18	28	39	.72
7	10	21	31	42	.74
8	10	24	34	44	.77
9	10	27	37	45	.82
10	10	30	40	45	.89

are not much used; goods are made by hand with relatively simple tools. But in the United States, where savings are more abundant and cheaper, and labor less plentiful and, therefore, dearer, complicated mechanical processes are in wide use and relatively few goods are made by hand.

It should now be clear that the point of optimum costs will vary with the prices of the agents of production. That combination of agents which, in a given system of prices, yields the lowest optimum cost is *the optimum combination*. The optimum combination of agents in Table II is five units of labor for each unit of land and equipment, and in Table III it is six units of labor to one of land and equipment. In general, the optimum combination is one in which relatively few units of dear agents of production are combined with relatively many units of those agents which are cheaper in price.

Marginal Costs. — Although, when the output of a business establishment is at its optimum, the product of the enterprise can be furnished to the public at lower cost than at any other point, it does not follow that a plant will always be so operated. Business men are interested in making as large a profit as possible, or, if they must forego profits for the time being, in reducing their losses to a minimum. Considerations of profit and loss may make it advantageous to produce more or less than the optimum output. So long as the sale of extra goods will bring in receipts that exceed the extra cost of obtaining them, it will pay the business man to produce them, no matter how high the costs may be. Therefore, it is important to know what are the extra costs of additional increments of output.

Let·us return now to the case of the farmer whose costs we have been considering. In our original computation, we found his optimum output to be attained when there were five inputs of labor and output was 34 bushels. If he adds a sixth unit of labor, he will get a marginal product of five extra bushels, making a total output of 39. Now we must ask, what do these five extra bushels cost the farmer? Obviously, his only expense in obtaining them was $5 for the sixth unit of labor. Looking at it from another standpoint, he increases his output from 34 to 39 bushels by increasing his total costs from $30 to $35. The cost of the five extra units, therefore, was $1 per bushel. This we call the *marginal cost*. It is the expenditure incurred in bringing forth the extra, or marginal, yield. Likewise, to increase production to 42 bushels, by adding a seventh unit of labor, would mean three more bushels of product, at an extra cost of $5. The marginal cost for those three units would be $5 ÷ 3, or $1.66 per bushel. By similar computations, we may derive the marginal costs for every possible output of our previous illustration. Such a computation is presented in Table IV.

TABLE IV

Inputs of Labor	Total Output	Total Costs	Marginal Costs for the Total Increment	Marginal Product	Marginal Costs per Unit of Output
1	4	$10	$10	4	$2.50
2	11	15	5	7	.71
3	19	20	5	8	.62
4	27	25	5	8	.62
5	34	30	5	7	.71
6	39	35	5	5	1.00
7	42	40	5	3	1.66
8	44	45	5	2	2.50
9	45	50	5	1	5.00
10	45	55	5	0	—

If we plot these marginal costs on our diagram, we can readily compare them with the average costs and observe the differences in their behavior. The resulting curves are shown by the dotted lines

MM in Figure 3. Observe that the marginal cost curve resembles the average cost curve, in that it begins at a high figure, drops to a minimum, then rises thereafter; but the two curves do not coincide. The marginal cost curve at first lies below the average, then crosses the latter and lies above it. Furthermore, the minimum point on the marginal curve occurs at an earlier stage of production than the minimum point on the average curve. This is because the marginal cost curve reflects directly the declining increments of product that result from each successive input of the variable agents. It is, in fact, the curve of diminishing marginal productivity reversed. The other curve, however, represents the average cost of all the increments; therefore, the influence of each successive increment is modified, by being averaged in with the other increments of cost.

The marginal curve crosses the average curve at the lowest point of the latter (T in the drawing). The reason for this is that, so long as the increments of marginal cost are below the average, they continue to pull the average downward; but when they once rise above the average, they thenceforth pull it upward. It is the same as if we had four stones weighing 35, 15, 20, and 30 pounds, respectively. Their average weight would be 100 ÷ 4, or 25 pounds. Now if we added a fifth stone, weighing less than the average—say only 10 pounds, then the new average weight would be 110 ÷ 5 or 22 pounds. The extra stone, because it weighed less than the initial average, pulled the average weight down. However, if the fifth stone had weighed more than the average—say 50 pounds, it would pull the average up, to 150 ÷ 5, or 30 pounds. In other words, when the additional unit is less than the previous average, the new average is lower than before. This means that, so long as marginal costs are less than average costs, they continue to pull the average curve downward, even though the marginal costs themselves are rising. But, just as soon as the marginal costs exceed the average, the average curve must rise. Therefore, the average curve continues to fall until the marginal curve rises above it, whereupon the former turns upward. Consequently, the average reaches its minimum when the marginal curve crosses it. The behavior of these two curves in our illustration is typical. In every business enterprise the relationship between them will be the same, although their exact slopes may differ.

Marginal costs are significant because they enable the enterpriser to estimate his probable profits or losses, and, accordingly, to decide how much he wishes to produce. Assume for the moment that the selling price on the market for the type of wheat being produced by our farmer is $1.05 per bushel, which is considerably above his optimum costs of 88 cents. At this price it would pay him to produce somewhat beyond his optimum output of 34 bushels, for, if he raises 39 bushels, the extra five will cost him only $1 per bushel, adding five cents to his profits for each of the extra bushels. If the price were $1.75, it would pay him to go to 42 bushels, for, by so doing he would add three more bushels at an extra cost of only $1.66, leaving him a further profit of 9 cents on each of the extra bushels. On the other hand, suppose that the price is only $.75, which is less than the optimum cost, and hence below any possible average costs of production. One might think that, under these circumstances, it would be better to stop producing entirely. But this is not so, for he has fixed expenses which he must meet, whether he operates his farm or lets it lie idle, unless he chooses to give up his business altogether, and lose his entire investment. Rather than do this, he is likely to hang on for a while in the hope of an improved situation. He can reduce his losses to a minimum by producing up to, but not beyond, the point where his marginal cost is equal to the selling price, for, so long as the extra increment of output yields a return exceeding the extra cost of producing it, his losses will be reduced by the difference. For instance, an output of 34 bushels would be more advantageous than one of 27, because the extra seven bushels would cost only 71 cents per bushel more than the smaller output, and would thereby reduce his losses by four cents on each bushel. But it would not pay him to produce 39 bushels, because the extra bushels would cost a dollar each, which is more than he can get for them, so that the additional output would only increase his losses.

Our conclusion is that the output of a business enterprise is not necessarily at its optimum, but varies with the price prevailing for the product. The general rule which governs policy here is, that it will pay the enterpriser to expand his production up to, but not beyond, the point where the marginal cost equals the extra receipts obtainable from the sale of the product.[1]

Cost Patterns in Different Types of Enterprise. — It has already been stated that, while costs in different types of business enterprise behave in a generally similar way, there are some differences of detail. In some types of industry, production requires the construction of an elaborate and extensive plant but needs a relatively small proportion of labor and raw materials. A typical example of this is the electric power industry. To furnish electricity to a community there must be an extensive layout, consisting of a building, steam boilers or a large dam for water power, dynamos, transmission wires, poles, transformers, meters, and the like. When the plant is once built, the only raw

---

[1] This principle is more fully elaborated in the paragraph entitled "The General Rule of Policy," in Part B of Chapter XIV.

materials required are fuel for the boilers (if steam is used for power) and a few office supplies and repair parts. Very little labor is required —a small staff of men to operate the plant, to read customers' meters, to make necessary repairs, and to handle the accounts and correspondence of the central office. In an establishment of this kind the fixed costs will be very heavy and the variable costs very light. Hence, the larger the volume of current generated, the lower will be the fixed costs per kilowatt of electricity, and the variable costs will not be great enough to offset this, even though they may increase considerably; the net result will be that the average cost curve will slope downward until the maximum capacity of the establishment has been very nearly reached. The curve of average costs in this case will resemble that

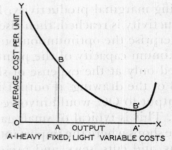

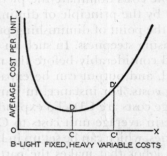

Figure 4. Different Types of Average Cost Curves.

shown in Part A of Figure 4. If the output of such a plant is a small percentage of its total capacity, such as OA in the drawing, the cost of supplying current will be relatively high (AB), and the company will have to charge a rather high rate for its current. However, if it can induce its customers to use more electricity by offering cheaper rates, it may be possible to expand its output to OA' and take advantage of the low unit costs A'B'. In companies of this kind, cheap rates may prove a very profitable policy for the company. Since the life of plants of this kind is fairly long, in a growing community a far-sighted enterpriser will build a plant of sufficient capacity to meet future needs. This means that, in the early stages, the demand for its facilities will not be sufficient to operate the plant at its optimum; therefore, the rates must be high. As the community grows, more and more of the plant capacity can be utilized, and rates can be progressively reduced.

Railroads present a somewhat similar case. The investment in road-beds, trackage, stations, terminals, rolling-stock, signal systems, and repair shops is very large. They have a long life, so that they are likely to be built for a capacity in excess of immediate needs. Variable costs for wages, materials, repairs, etc., are likely to be relatively higher than in the case of the power industry, but are nevertheless overshadowed by the fixed expense of the railway equipment. Hence, the average unit costs will fall as the business of the railroad expands. Waterworks and gas companies are in practically the same position as electric power plants. Manufacturing establishments with heavy, durable plant, such as shipyards, steel mills, and locomotive works, have somewhat the same characteristics, although to a less marked degree.

On the other hand, businesses which operate with relatively simple equipment, and in which labor and materials form the major elements of cost, will have cost patterns more like those of the second curve in the drawing. Here the downward pull of fixed costs is less apparent, variable costs dominate the picture; hence, the curve is governed directly by the principle of diminishing marginal productivity. It falls until the point of diminishing productivity is reached, then rises with increasing steepness. In such an enterprise the optimum output is attained considerably before the maximum capacity of the plant is attained, and output can be expanded only at the expense of sharply rising costs. For instance, in Part B of the drawing, if output is OC, average costs are CD. To expand output to OC' would involve an increase in average unit costs to C'D'. This is typical of small garment factories, which can be set up in little shops where the important agent is the labor that makes the patterns, and cuts, sews, and presses the cloth. The only equipment needed is floor space, a few electric cutters and sewing machines, and perhaps some pressing machines, all of which are relatively inexpensive. If such a shop wishes to enlarge its output, it must employ more labor and use more cloth, trimmings, thread, etc.; as the work is speeded up and more crowded, these costs will rise.

B. Land and Population

The Social Significance of Diminishing Productivity. — We have seen that a business enterpriser may vary in considerable degree the amounts of the different agents of production which he employs. But when we examine the economic position of society as a whole, we find a less flexible situation. After the territory of a nation has once been fully occupied, it finds itself in possession of a fixed supply of land, of which it cannot readily obtain more. To be sure, swamps can be drained and deserts can be irrigated, but these possibilities are rather limited, and the total quantity of land that can be reclaimed by such measures is usually quite small. It is not far from the truth to say that, in most cases, the supply of land is fixed. This is not the case with savings. As a community grows in efficiency, its people usually become more prosperous, and they save an increasingly large proportion of their income. So, industry is carried on with an ever-growing supply of equipment. This is even more true of labor. In most parts of the world, the growth of population is continually adding to the supply of workers. It is a natural tendency of the human race—as of all life—to increase and multiply. The instinct of sex is one of the strongest with which men and women are endowed. Its natural and unrestricted expression leads to a large number of births, which tends to cause a rapid increase in the population. Under favorable circumstances, where a high birth rate and a low death rate prevail, it is possible for the population to double itself by the natural increase of births over deaths every twenty-five years. In the early development of the United States we actually increased at this rate for several decades. Under ideal conditions it should be possible for a population to grow even more rapidly.

We have, then, a situation in which increasing quantities of labor and savings are being applied to a relatively fixed area of land. As a result of this, the principle of diminishing productivity will come into play, unless it is counteracted by sufficient progress in the technology of production. In the absence of such improvement, increasing population will sooner or later crowd the available natural resources, and a decreasing per capita product is likely to result. This may go so far that the social income is insufficient to meet the needs of all the population.

The Law of Population. — The tendency for a growing population to press upon natural resources in this way was given prominence by a clergyman and economist of the nineteenth century, named Thomas Malthus, who was one of the first to describe it. His "Essay on Population" is one of the classic works of economics, and has had an important influence on human thought since his time. In recognition of this, the principle which he described has come to be known as the *Malthusian law of population;* sometimes it is called simply the *law of population.* This law may be stated as follows: *In a given state of the arts of production, population tends to outrun subsistence.* By subsistence is meant the means of maintaining or supplying the needs of the people.

In some circumstances this principle presents a difficult dilemma to a people. Inasmuch as population tends to outrun subsistence, either some way must be found of continually increasing production faster than the natural increase of people, or the growth of population must be checked. Malthus took an over-pessimistic view of the outlook. It did not appear possible to him that production could be enlarged fast enough to provide for a rapidly growing people, and the only result he could see was a difficult struggle for existence, in which poverty and starvation would wipe out the surplus population, and vicious and immoral practices would keep down the number of births. It is said that the picture of this struggle which Malthus suggested was the inspiration for Darwin's later presentation of struggle for existence and survival of the fittest in the world of plants and animals.

Positive and Preventive Checks. — Malthus believed that the growth of population must necessarily be checked in either one of two ways. He called these *positive checks* and *preventive checks.*

Positive checks are those which operate by increasing the death rate. When the pressure of population upon the means of subsistence becomes severe, per capita production is so low that poverty results. Undernourished, insufficiently clothed, and lodged in unsanitary dwellings, the people succumb easily to disease. Infant mortality is great, epidemics decimate the population from time to time, and misery prevails. War is another means of reducing a superfluous population. Some savages deliberately practice infanticide and kill off their aged and infirm. Positive checks usually operate among backward peoples, where hide-bound traditions and a lack of technological progress prevent the rapid growth of production. Such a state of affairs prevails in China and India even today. In these countries dense populations struggle to keep alive in conditions of poverty, eking out a miserable existence. The death rate in these countries is very high.

Preventive checks to population operate by keeping the birth rate low. Vicious means of gratifying the sexual passions, such as prostitution and other forms of immorality, checkmate the natural reproductive processes and keep down the number of births. The postponement of marriage to an age of relative maturity, a condition very prevalent among the more highly civilized peoples, is another cause which tends to reduce the birth rate. More important than these is the growth of contraception, or birth control, a development which Malthus did not foresee. Among more intelligent peoples, parenthood is becoming less and less a matter of blind chance and more and more a matter of deliberate choice and control. This is especially true among the more well-to-do classes, where small families are the rule, but it is becoming more widespread among the working classes as well. Modern parents realize that a small number of children can be better trained and better educated than a large number. Consequently, they restrict their families to a size which permits them to enjoy a high standard of living. In some parts of the world this development has gone so far that the threat of overpopulation seems to be effectively dispelled, and the evil consequences foreseen by Malthus no longer threaten.

Progress in the Technique of Production. — Malthus underestimated, also, the possibilities of improvement in productive methods.

Events since his day have shown that this is a factor of very great importance. With the development of science and invention, the arts of production lead to ever greater productivity. Before the coming of the white man, it is estimated that the entire continent of North America was able to support a bare half million savages; their methods of industry probably could not provide subsistence for a greater number. Today the United States supports more than 130,000,000 people. The machine process, with specialization, has made this continent yield enough for a far larger number of persons than now inhabits it. So long as such progress can continue, there is always the means to support an increasing population. This factor, coupled with the tendency to birth control already mentioned, has made the population problem look very different from what it did in Malthus' time.

Critics of the Malthusian principle have construed the development of progress in the arts of production as proof of the falsity of his law, and of the law of diminishing productivity, from which it is derived. This, however, is an unwarranted conclusion. If the law is carefully formulated, it is still valid. In the above presentation of it, it was stated as a *tendency,* implying that it might be offset by counteracting influences; and it was qualified by the condition "in a given state of the arts," which suggested that changes in the state of the arts might be such an offsetting circumstance. A tendency does not necessarily become an accomplished fact. A weight suspended from the ceiling by a cord tends to fall to the floor, because of the force of gravity; but it does not drop, because the tension of the cords offers an opposing force sufficient to overcome the attraction of gravity. It is similar with the tendency of population to outrun subsistence—it may be overcome by the opposing force of a progressing technology.

The operation of the two sets of forces is illustrated by the drawing of Figure 5. Here the size of the population is measured along the horizontal axis OX, and the per capita product of industry along the vertical axis OY. The tendency to diminishing per capita product, resulting from the pressure of population on the means of subsistence, is represented by the dotted curves P, P', and P". The lowest one of these curves (P) is supposed to represent the state of production as it may have been a century ago. We suppose OA to measure the size of the population at the census of 1840. AB then represents the per capita product at that period. It is supposed that production had already proceeded past the point of diminishing productivity, so that the point B is represented as lying on the declining portion of the productivity curve. Had the state of the arts remained unchanged, an increase in population would have pushed the point B further down the curve to the right, so that per capita production (AB) would have become smaller and smaller as time went on. But technological progress more than kept pace with the growth of population, so that the productivity curve was pushed gradually upward towards P', and eventually to the position P", which is taken to picture the situation as it exists today. The population in 1940 is represented by the distance OC, and per capita product by CD. This is much greater than production in 1840, in spite of the much larger population which we now have, because of the higher productivity made possible by improvement in the arts. If we project the straight line RT through the points B and D, we obtain a picture of the increase in per capita production that has taken

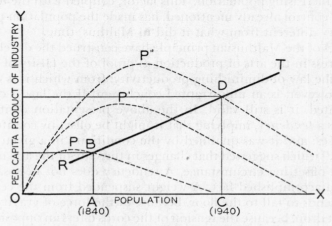

Figure 5. Progress and Population Growth.

place over a century or more, and which may conceivably take place in the future, if it continues at the same rate. This line is a resultant of the two sets of forces, namely: the tendency to diminishing productivity, caused by the pressure of population on a limited amount of land, and the tendency to increasing production caused by technological progress. Were the population to increase from its present figure, without any further progress in the arts, per capita production would fall downward to the right along the line P"D, but if progress in the arts continues, it may be expected to move along the line RT. So, the tendencies to diminishing productivity and the pressure of population are still operative, although they may be offset by counteracting influences.

Partial Escapes from Population Pressure. — The discussion to this point indicates that there are two ways in which the tendency for population to outrun subsistence may be counteracted,—through a decline in the birth rate, resulting from birth control, and through progress in the arts of production.

There are other escapes which may be open to particular countries that feel the pressure of population growth, although they would not constitute a solution to the problem from a world point of view. For instance, a nation may increase its land area by acquiring territory from other peoples. To some extent, Germany, and to a much greater extent, Italy and Japan, are prolific peoples whose dense populations feel acutely the pinch of very limited land resources. They seek to relieve this pressure by acquiring more land at the expense of other nations. Population pressure has always been one of the causes making for imperialistic expansion. The acquisition of colonies provides an outlet for surplus populations without loss of citizenship in the mother countries. Emigration to less densely populated parts of the world, politically independent of the country of origin, affords a similar outlet. The United States, in the nineteenth century, accommodated millions of people, overflowing from their confined quarters in other parts of the world, in this way. South America has played a similar rôle. There still remain some parts of the world which are sparsely enough populated to receive further immigrants. However, emigration is not a very satisfactory solution to the problem of population pressure. New births at home rapidly fill the ranks depleted by the emigrants, while the presence of the latter in the countries to which they go sooner or later complicates the population problem there. Eventually the latter countries become unwilling to receive more immigrants and pass legislation to restrict their admittance.

Some nations have solved the problem of accommodating a large population upon a small area by devoting themselves to manufactures or commerce almost exclusively, selling the products to foreigners and importing in exchange the food and raw materials which they need. England has pursued this policy very successfully, as have also Holland and Belgium. Of course, this is an indirect means of drawing upon a larger land area.

None of these outlets can solve the population problem permanently, because eventually this process would lead to a filling up of all the sparsely populated parts of the world. Eventually the people of the world must face the fact that there is only a limited amount of land on this planet. Even progress in the arts cannot take care of a growing world population indefinitely. An Australian statistician has figured that, if the present rate of population growth throughout the world continued indefinitely, the progeny of a single pair of human beings in 10,000 years would require 1,340,000,000,000,000,000,000,000 earths simply to furnish material for their bodies! It is inevitable, therefore, that some time in the future the increase in numbers must cease. In some countries this seems to be taking care of itself by the simple process of a lowered birth rate. For several decades prior to the World War, the population of France was stationary, and it is estimated that, if present tendencies continue, the population of the United States will cease growing in another generation. In other parts of the world, this tendency has not yet become so manifest, and in these regions the problem of population pressure is even now acute. Eventually it seems probable that tendencies to declining growth will manifest themselves everywhere, and that the human race will settle down to relatively fixed numbers of people. If this is accomplished through the falling birth rate, it need not lead to the distressing consequences which were anticipated by Malthus; and there is no reason to suppose that it cannot be accompanied by ever-rising standards of living, brought about by continual improvement in the arts of production.

The Optimum Population. — It is desirable that the population of a nation be of such numbers that they can utilize most effectively the natural resources at their disposal. If the number of people is too small, they will be unable to exploit their resources adequately, and per capita production will be less than it might be. On the other hand, if there are too many, diminishing productivity is brought into effect, and per capita production is, in this case also, lower than is possible. The first may be called a state of under-, the second a state of over-population. It follows that there is a certain number in which the ratio of population to natural resources is such as to give the maximum possible per capita product. This is known as the *optimum population*. If the optimum number of persons is maintained, the prosperity of the people will be highest. It is, therefore, a very desirable condition. What sized population is best for the exploitation of a given territory depends upon the state of industrial technique prevailing there. If primitive methods of production are in use, only a relatively small population can be maintained without bringing a reduction in per capita income. With modern efficient industry prevailing, a much larger number of persons can be employed economically. The optimum number of people in the United States today is much greater than in colonial days, and in colonial days it was much greater than under the crude industrial régime of the Indians.

A recent writer has attempted to prove that, throughout human history, the various peoples of the world have so controlled their numbers as actually to attain, or closely approximate, the optimum population.[2] Where overpopulation has occurred, he believes, it was the exception rather than the rule. In the judgment of the present writer, the argument is not conclusive. It is probable that many peoples have

[2] A. M. Carr-Saunders, *The Population Problem*, 1922.

maintained themselves at a standard of living, above the merest necessities for subsistence, by conscious control of their numbers, and that is undoubtedly true in some parts of the world today; but this is very different from saying that they have kept their numbers at just the right amount to attain the maximum possible per capita production. It is unlikely that such a desirable state of affairs prevails.

SUMMARY

Production is generally carried on by a combination of four agents of production—land, labor, saving, and business enterprise. This classification can be further subdivided; and, also, one person may sometimes combine the functions of several agents. Within the limits fixed by technology, the proportions in which the agents are combined can be varied. If the inputs of one agent are increased while the others remain fixed, the increases in output (marginal products) will increase, up to a certain point, and diminish thereafter. This principle is known as the law of diminishing marginal productivity. It is applicable to both agricultural and non-agricultural industry, and to any possible combination of the productive agents. However, the tendency to diminishing productivity can be offset by improvements in the arts of production.

The conduct of a business usually involves both fixed and variable costs. The fixed costs remain substantially unchanged, regardless of the volume of output; the variable costs increase in rough proportion to output. The sum of fixed and variable costs, divided by output, gives the average costs. As output expands, average costs at first decline to a minimum, then rise thereafter. The minimum, or optimum, costs denote the optimum output for the business. This optimum depends on the prices of the agents employed; the tendency being to combine relatively small amounts of dear agents with relatively large amounts of cheap agents. Marginal costs refer to the successive additions to total costs occasioned by successive increases in output. Average and marginal costs can be pictured by means of roughly U-shaped curves, the marginal curve at first falling faster than the average, crossing the latter at its minimum point, and rising more rapidly from there on. The exact shapes of these curves vary from enterprise to enterprise.

In society as a whole, population and saving tend to increase, while land remains fixed in quantity. As a result of this, population tends to outrun subsistence (the Malthusian law), unless offset by progress in the arts. Population must then be checked, either by positive means (an increase in the death rate), or by preventive means (a decrease in the birth rate). However, in progressive countries, progress in the arts may enable production to keep pace with population growth in given periods. Particular countries can relieve the pressure of surplus population by territorial expansion, by emigration, or by importing foodstuffs and raw materials in exchange for manufactured goods. For any time and place there is an optimum size of population, which is that size which maximizes per capita production.

REFERENCES AND SUGGESTIONS FOR FURTHER READING

For the first part of this chapter I am indebted in considerable measure to the elaborate discussion of the tendency to diminishing productivity developed by J. D. and A. G. Black in Chapters V and VI of their *Production Organization* (1929). A somewhat different approach is to be found in Chapter 2 of T. N. Carver's *The Distribution of Wealth* (1904). Reference should also be made to J. M. Clark's *The Economics of Overhead Costs* (1923), especially Chapters IV and V.

We owe the law of population to T. R. Malthus' classic *Essay on Population* (6th edition or later), which is still worth reading. Edward M. East's *Mankind at the Crossroads* (1923) is a careful and comprehensive modern presentation of the population problem. Harold Wright gives a briefer survey in his *Population* (1923). Two recent books which express a growing concern over the possibility of a declining population are R. R. Kuczynski, *Population Movements* (1936), and A. M. Carr-Saunders, *World Population* (1936).

Chapter VI

THE ORGANIZATION OF BUSINESS ENTERPRISE

A. Characteristics of Business Enterprise

The Business Enterpriser. — In the last chapter we learned that production is carried on by a number of different agents of production, combined into a working organization. We called those agents land, labor, saving, and business enterprise, and we discovered that it is the function of the last of these to combine and direct the other three. In the present chapter it is our task to look at this fourth agent of production more closely, and to see how business enterprises are organized.

The agent of production with which we are here concerned is personified by that class of business men who are variously known as enterprisers, entrepreneurs, undertakers, or simply business organizers. We shall employ the term *enterprisers.*

It is the function of the enterpriser to obtain such capital as is necessary for the business which he conducts, to employ the appropriate kinds and amounts of labor, and to unite them into a smooth-running productive organization. He may select land of the quality suited to his purpose and in an advantageous location, determine the amount and character of the plant and equipment which he needs, hire and place in their respective positions laboring men, secure foremen and other executives to supervise and direct their labors, and organize the whole into a going concern. He must also find a means of financing the business in order to obtain sufficient capital, much of which may be borrowed.

In doing this work, the enterpriser is performing labor, so that he is, in a sense, a laborer. He may also invest his own savings in his business, so that he is, in part, a capitalist. But he is a laborer and a capitalist of a very special kind, and his relationship to ordinary labor and capital is unique, because of the controlling position which he occupies. It is for this reason that we designate him as a separate agent of production, and set him apart for special consideration.

The labor of superintendence, or direction, as it may be called, is not necessarily carried out in its details or even in its broad outlines by the owners of a business or those who have the responsibility for its existence. The latter may employ superintendents or managers to attend to these matters and leave the actual executive work of running the plant entirely to them; but the responsibility for the selection of these managers rests upon the enterprisers themselves, and in the last analysis, therefore, it is they who in a broad way direct the business. While the enterprisers may pay but little attention personally to the selection of personnel, or to the executive direction of the processes of manufacture and the sale of the product, it is they who determine that a business shall exist in the first place, who choose the field of industry in which its operations shall be carried on, and who determine its general policy. Thus the business enterprisers are primarily responsible for the direction of a business.

The business enterpriser may be defined, therefore, as *the person, or group of persons, who assumes responsibility for the conduct of a business enterprise.*

This responsibility is a very serious one. We shall learn in the next chapter that all businesses entail a considerable element of risk. The capitalists who finance the enterprise risk their savings, which it is always possible they may lose. The employees depend on the industry for a livelihood, and if the business does not succeed will suffer unemployment and deprivation. These two groups entrust their wealth and their earning power to the care of the enterpriser; upon his efficiency or inefficiency depends their prospects of gain or loss. Moreover, the enterpriser himself usually has a considerable investment of his own in the business, so that he not only controls the risks of others, but runs a risk of his own. Even more serious to him, perhaps, is his personal reputation and self-respect. Business success will make him a leader in his community, and place him and his family in comfort and plenty; failure means for him ruin, ignominy, and defeat.

While the enterpriser is usually an employer of labor, there are some forms of business in which he is primarily a speculator or financier, where little labor other than a small clerical and stenographic force is required. In manufactures, transportation, merchandising, and similar industries, the enterpriser controls a large aggregation of capital and of labor, and his function is in great measure one of organization. In banking, brokerage, insurance, and similar financial industries the organization is small, and the principal functions of the enterpriser are centered in the exercise of judgment concerning price changes and the making of investments, and are of a more generally speculative character.

Essential Characteristics of a Business Enterpriser. — The proper performance of these functions calls for qualities of a peculiar and unusual sort. The successful business enterpriser must have executive ability; he must be a keen judge of men and be possessed of capacity for organization, for it is his task to select the personnel of industry and to obtain and direct a staff of men in such a way that they will work together smoothly and efficiently. He must have a broad knowledge of industrial conditions, in order that he may be kept informed as to the possibilities of securing supplies for his business in the most economical way and of forecasting the future market for his product. He must be fearless and bold to take advantage of opportunities when they present themselves, for upon his courage and quickness in making a decision at the right moment much of his success will depend. He must be shrewd in bargaining, for upon it will depend in part the cheapness with which he purchases his raw materials, his labor and other needs, and the possibility of gains in disposing of his wares.

In making their decisions, business enterprisers are dominated by purely economic motives—by considerations of monetary gain or loss, to a greater extent than other men. This is a requirement for success in the world of business. While they are in business partly, no doubt, from the urge of the creative impulse within them, and while they find a source of enjoyment in the enterprise whose growth and development they watch over with almost parental solicitude, and in whose success and expansion they feel a sense of just pride; yet, in the conduct of that business they are very watchful for the chance of profit, and it is pecuniary gain which is the goal, though perhaps not the motive, for their endeavors. While they may be in business for the game itself, it is the game of "making money." So, likewise, the business man may find in his enterprise an outlet for many desires, ambitions, and motives. It may bring him recreation, prestige, social acquaintance, the satisfaction of work well done,—but he attains all of these by working toward the one end of profits. He is very watchful, therefore, of where he can increase his gain, buying where prices are lowest and selling where they are dearest, wherever he finds an opportunity. In his shrewdness at this game his success depends, and the conspicuous figures of industrial enterprise appear to be men who possess the quality of seeking their greatest economic gain to a very high degree.

Business Enterprise and the Ownership of Capital. — The enterpriser must secure land and equipment, which may cost a great deal of money. More often than not, probably, he has invested savings of his own in the business, but in many cases there is needed a larger supply of capital than can be met from his own resources, and in this case he borrows the savings of others. It is possible, and no doubt sometimes the case, that he may secure all of the funds for his business from other persons, but probably in most instances it will be found that the capital is owned partly by the enterpriser himself and partly by persons from whom he has borrowed it. Thus, the business man may perform at one and the same time the functions of both capitalist and enterpriser. He is an investor who has utilized his savings in the creation of remote-goods, and an organizer who employs land, labor, and equipment in the carrying out of an industrial project. But though these functions may thus be centered in the same person, they are economically of a different nature and must be thought of as distinct. The part which the enterpriser plays in furnishing savings is different from that which he plays in combining those savings with labor for production. In the complex forms of business enterprise which have developed in the twentieth century, the relation between the ownership of capital and the conduct of business enterprise has become somewhat confused, so that it is not always easy to separate the two functions. This presents some interesting problems which will be taken up in a later paragraph.

B. Forms of Business Organization

The Single Enterpriser. — The simplest form of business enterprise is that in which one individual alone assumes responsibility for the management of the business. Thus, the farmer employs his hired man, tools, and other equipment upon his land in the raising of agricultural produce. He is in business alone for himself. He is master of his own time and that of his men; he markets his own produce; the gains of the business are his, and the loss is borne by him, if there is any. This type of enterprise is found in many other comparatively simple businesses, such as that of the village garage, the hardware store of a country town, the small restaurant, etc. Professional men, such as physicians, lawyers, and writers, are usually independent enterprisers. In such cases as these, oftentimes little or no equipment is employed, and the activities of the individual partake mostly of the nature of labor, there being little necessity for the functions of management or superintendence. It is among the single enterprisers also that the functions of capitalist, enterpriser, and frequently laborer, are often centered all in one individual.

The Partnership. — Where the business is somewhat more complex, it is desirable for several individuals to combine their resources and abilities in a single enterprise. The simplest form of such association, as well as the earliest historically, is known as the *partnership*. This consists of *an association of two or more individuals for the conduct of an enterprise based upon an agreement or contract between them*. The quantity of capital which one individual can command, either from his own savings or by borrowing upon his personal credit, is relatively small, but by the association of several individuals into a partnership their resources can be pooled, and by their combined credit greater quantities can be borrowed. Usually each of the partners in such an enterprise shares in the management of the business, each one perhaps assuming the direction of a department. Sometimes, however, there are one or more silent partners, who simply invest their savings in the enterprise, leaving the management to the active partners. In this case the silent partners are to be looked upon as capitalists rather than as enterprisers.

Legally, the members of a partnership are liable jointly and severally for all the debts of the partnership. Suppose, for instance, that A, B, and C form an agreement to conduct a banking business together, and the firm goes into bankruptcy, it being found that it has incurred debts amounting to $100,000 above the assets of the business. Suit for any part or all of this sum may be brought by the creditors against A, B, or C, and the entire sum collected from any one of them. This one may then collect a share of the debt from the others, if they are able to meet it, but if their resources are inadequate, the burden may be his alone. This subjects the members of a partnership to a considerable degree of risk, so that it is essential that the partnership should be based upon mutual confidence and reliability of the members. Another legal characteristic of the partnership has been that it becomes dissolved upon the death or retirement of one of the members to the agreement. Both the unlimited liability and this feature, however, have been modified in some states by laws permitting some limitation upon the liability of the members and by provisions permitting a more permanent existence.

Where the amount of capital required in an industrial enterprise is small, where the organization is comparatively simple, so that it can readily be financed from the resources of a few individuals and so that the functions of management are capable of easy division among the parties to the agreement, the partnership is a very satisfactory and common form of organization. Thus, it is especially likely to be adopted in associations of enterprisers based primarily upon the skill, training, or reputation of a few individuals and calling for very little plant, such as among lawyers, physicians, accountants, architects, and other professional men.

The Corporation. — However, the development of the large industrial enterprises of the modern world, calling as they do for large plant and equipment and intricate organization, has led to the necessity for a form of business which would permit the accumulation of even greater quantities of capital and greater efficiency of organization. This is only possible by the combination of the resources of a larger number of individuals, coupled with a limitation upon their liability, which will lessen the property risk. At the same time, such a combination of persons will permit greater centralization of management than is afforded by the partnership. The result is that corporations have shown a tremendous growth in numbers since the advent of the Industrial Revolution, until they are today the dominant form of business organization in manufactures and large industries.

The corporation may be defined as an association of individuals (known as stockholders) acting, under a charter from the State, as a single person in the conduct of a business enterprise. It consists usually of not less than three persons, and many corporations are indeed limited to this number of members; but the typical case of greatest interest to the economist is that in which a large number of persons are stockholders, in some cases running into the hundreds of thousands. Each stockholder is limited in liability, usually to the amount he has invested in the business. Thus, if one has invested $10,000 in the stock of the United States Steel Corporation, in the event of the failure of this enterprise he may lose that which he has invested, but he cannot be assessed any further amount to make good the debts of the company. This feature lessens the risk of investment and makes it possible for the corporate organization to attract a greater amount of savings than would be possible under the partnership.

The management of a corporation, while resting nominally in the stockholders, is usually delegated to a Board of Directors. Finally, the death or retirement of a stockholder has no effect upon the life of the concern. His holdings can be transferred to another party by the simple sale of his stock, and the corporation meanwhile retains its entity and continues its operations, unaffected by the transfer. The essential features of the corporation as contrasted with the partnership are, then, (1) the greater number of individuals (usually) who partake in the enterprise, (2) the limited liability of the stockholders, (3) the delegation of management to the Board of Directors, (4) the transferability of ownership in the corporation, and (5) its perpetual life. The corporation is so important and significant a form of enterprise in the conduct of modern industry that some of its features call for more extended discussion.

The Organization of a Corporation. — The primary owners of a corporate business enterprise consist of the *stockholders*. These invest a certain quantity of savings in the enterprise, in return for which they receive shares of stock representing, nominally at least,[1] their investment in it. They are then owners of the business, and its ultimate direction and control is in their hands. In practice, however, especially where there is a large body of stockholders, it is impracticable for them to exercise this control directly. They elect, consequently, a *Board of Directors* from their number, to whom they delegate the powers of management. There is also a *President,* who may also act as chairman of the Board. The Board of Directors usually meets at regular intervals, and exercises a considerable degree of oversight regarding the

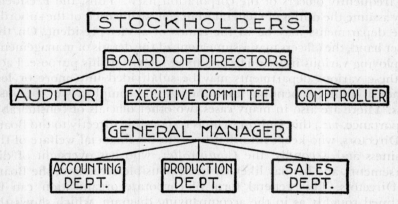

Figure 6. A Common Form of Corporate Organization.

conduct of the enterprise. In particular, it determines the general financial policy of the business and appoints the leading officials of the company. Oftentimes the directors elect from their membership a still smaller body, known as the *Executive Committee,* which is in closer touch with the affairs of the corporation and exercises a somewhat more detailed direction of the business, only those matters of greatest importance ever coming before the Board of Directors as a whole. But the actual direction of production is placed in the hands of a *General Manager* or Superintendent, appointed by the directors, and who is the chief executive of the business. He is assisted by a staff of subordinate officials and departmental heads, often expert engineers, who direct the various branches of the business.

Frequently the corporate enterprise will have three general departments, at the head of each of which is an important official of the

[1] Originally a share of stock represented an actual investment. Due to the practice of "stock-watering" (which is described below), this is no longer always the case; but a share of stock is nominally a certificate of investment in the corporation.

company. There is, first, what is known as the *Production Depart-ment,* by which is meant here the actual work of handling and work-ing up the raw material of the business into the product which is fin-ally turned out.[2] This work is in the hands of a *Production Manager.* Secondly, there is the *General Office,* in charge of an *Office Manager,* who has charge of the accounting, keeping records of costs, attending to the correspondence of the firm, looking after the financial and credit details of the business, etc. Finally, there is the *Selling Depart-ment,* in charge of a *Sales Manager,* who takes care of the advertising, sales force, shipping of the goods, etc. In practice these various officials are frequently officers of the corporation itself. Thus, the President may assume the duties of General Manager, while each of the subordi-nate departments may be in the hands of a Vice-president. On the other hand, the officers may assume none of the details of management, employing various individuals at a fixed salary for this purpose. Each of these various departments may be subdivided into more or less minor divisions, depending upon the size and complexity of the busi-ness. There are also in many cases two other officials of considerable importance, *viz.,* the *Auditor,* who is responsible directly to the Board of Directors, who keeps information as to the financial welfare of the business and, secondly, the *Comptroller,* who has oversight of dis-bursements, and he may likewise be responsible directly to the Board of Directors. This general form of corporate organization can be outlined roughly as in the accompanying diagram, which shows the chief units in the organization and the delegation of authority. This is only one of several possible forms of organization; the flexi-bility of the corporation is such that a variety of arrangements is pos-sible.

Ownership of Capital and the Direction of Corporate Enterprise. — The investors in the capital of a corporation may be and usually are divided into different classes, and their interests in the business are represented by correspondingly different classes of securities. Thus, the capital of a corporation may be represented in part by *bonds,* held by bondholders. These bonds are really the promissory notes of the corporation. They represent sums which it has borrowed and which it agrees to repay at a certain date, usually a number of years in the fu-ture. They are usually secured by some tangible form of property of the corporation, such as a mortgage on its real estate or similar asset. They bear a fixed rate of interest, the annual payment of which is guaranteed. Failure to meet this obligation may force the corporation

---

[2] Note that this is a different use of the word "production" from that which was de-fined in Chapter II.

into bankruptcy. Thus, the bonds of a well-established corporation represent a high grade security, the risk on which is not especially great. The bondholders are not members of the corporation and are not entitled to vote or have any share in its management. They are creditors. The next class of securities is known as *preferred stock*. This, like the bonds, bears a fixed rate of interest, but payment of this interest is not guaranteed and is only made when the profits of the corporation are sufficient to warrant it. Holders of preferred stock are members of the corporation, and may or may not be entitled to vote at the meetings of the stockholders. Finally, there is the *common stock*, which bears no fixed rate of interest. Purchasers or holders of common stock have a vote, in proportion to the number of shares of stock which they hold, but no return is paid them on their investment until after the dividends upon the preferred stock have been paid. Thus, they do not represent as high a degree of security and they involve a greater element of risk. While these three classes constitute the most usual forms of securities, each of them may be subdivided, and there are various intermediate types, so that there may be many different kinds of securities in a corporation; but it is not essential for us to go into these details.

Because of these differences in the nature of corporate securities, and because of the delegated character of the management, from stockholders to directors and from directors to executives, the functions of capitalist and enterpriser in corporations are difficult to distinguish and the line between them is vague and confused. The bondholders of a corporation, it has been pointed out, have no share in its management. They provide a part of its capital, often a major part, upon which they receive a guaranteed interest; but further than that they have no interest in the corporation. They are capitalists pure and simple. The stockholders, on the other hand, are the managers of the business, nominally at least, for they are the ultimate source from which all the authority in the conduct of the affairs of the corporation is drawn. In fact, however, a great many, if not a majority, of the stockholders in many large corporations are little or nothing more than capitalists, for they do not follow the affairs of the corporation closely and do not participate in the meetings of stockholders. Quite frequently their voting power is transferred to the officers or leading spirits in the corporation by means of proxies. Their activities consist simply in supplying a certain quantity of capital upon which they receive dividends from time to time.

In many corporations the actual power of control is in the hands of a few insiders, who own or control enough of the stock to determine

the policy of the corporation, and are its real directing heads.[3] Even
the majority stockholders and directors of a corporation may delegate
the actual work of management to a superintendent, to technical engineers or other experts, who assume control of the corporation's productive operations, being employed at a salary. In this case, however,
the responsibility for the business still rests on the owners, that is, the
stockholders. There is thus a tendency in the business world for the
functions of the capitalist to be separated from those of the enterpriser,
and for the functions of enterprise itself to be separated into two operations—the actual work of superintendence, done by the directing
heads of the plant, and the assumption of general responsibility, borne
by the stockholders.

Overcapitalization. — A share of stock usually represents, nominally at least, the investment of a certain amount, specified on its face,
in the capital of the corporation. This is its par value. The total par
value of all the outstanding securities of a corporation is said to be its
capitalization. A company which has issued stocks and bonds to the
amount of a million dollars, for instance, would be said to be capitalized at that figure. But this capitalization may be greater than the
amount of its actual assets. The practice of issuing securities whose
par value is in excess of the tangible wealth of the corporation is
known as *overcapitalization,* or stock-watering. This may be done in
a number of different ways and for different reasons.

Suppose that five competing electric companies in a large city have
plants whose actual cost was $100,000 each, and is represented by
shares of stock outstanding equal to that amount ($500,000). Certain
persons interested in the electric business in that city may conceive the
idea of amalgamating these five companies into one, thereby creating
a monopoly which, by the elimination of competition, will be able to
charge higher rates for its service than the separate companies are able
to charge, and thereby increase the profits. In order to induce the
present stockholders of the independent companies to consent to such
a consolidation, the promoters of the consolidation may issue, let us
say, $1,000,000 worth of stock in a new corporation, which we may
call the Amalgamated Electric Company, which stock they offer in exchange for the stock of the independent companies. Each holder of the
original stock, therefore, receives stock in the corporation to twice
the par value of his former holdings. We now have a corporation own-
ing all five plants. The plants represent no more real capital than before and no additions to them are made, but the nominal capitalization of these plants is $1,000,000, or twice their actual cost. In other

words, 100 per cent "water" has been introduced into the stock. There is no more real wealth there, but by printing pieces of paper which bear figures twice as high as the old ones, it has been made to appear that there is more wealth than before, and by virtue of the monopoly which has been created it is possible that the new company can earn profits which will pay just as high a rate of dividends on the new stock as was possible on the former stock of the independent concerns. Moreover, the holders of this watered stock will expect to receive such dividends. Hence, if the old corporations were paying 7 per cent on an investment of $500,000, the new concern will be expected to pay dividends amounting to 7 per cent on a capitalization of $1,000,000, which can only be accomplished by an increase in the prices which they charge for the current. The stockholders will now be receiving 14 per cent on their actual investment, but this high profit is concealed by the overcapitalization, which makes the return appear only half of that. This extra profit the consumers of the current will have to pay, and it is herein that one of the evils of overcapitalization rests. In nearly all consolidations of corporations in this country, in the organization of mergers and trusts and combinations of various sorts, overcapitalization has gone on and has been made the basis for charging higher and higher rates for the commodities and services sold to the public by these combines, so that the abuse has become widespread and has received a great deal of condemnation in public discussion.

Another way in which watered stock may be used is to make the sale of stock attractive to investors, making it appear that they are getting more than their money's worth. A common scheme, for instance, is to offer for sale a certain quantity of preferred stock at its par value but to give with it a bonus of common stock. Preferred stock in such a corporation represents cash actually paid in, while the common stock is simply so much paper issued to holders of the preferred stock to attract them to the proposition. Here again the excess stock may be used as a basis for charging higher prices to the public.

Overcapitalization or stock-watering is also sometimes resorted to by the promoters of an industrial scheme for the purpose of securing savings for the project from investors, while retaining the control in their own hands, without making any investment themselves, or only a relatively small one. Thus, a group of financiers may decide to establish an oil company. To secure the necessary funds for the drilling of wells and the erection of refineries, they may sell bonds or preferred stock to the public at large, at the same time issuing a large block of common stock to themselves gratis, giving them a voting control in the meetings of the stockholders. They are, then, equipped with the funds of others to be used as they see fit, and they will share in all the earnings of the corporation through the ownership of the stock which they have issued to themselves.

The abuses of overcapitalization have become so serious that laws prohibiting or restricting it have been passed in many states. The custom has also come into pretty general use of issuing stock of no par value. A corporation then has no nominal capitalization, the actual value of its capital being determined by the price at which its securities are selling in the market where such things are bought and sold. This is really what determines the value of the capital of a corporation anyhow, the nominal capitalization being of little significance when the enterprise has once been fully launched. There is, therefore, much reason for attaching no par value to shares of stock. Notwithstanding these measures, however, there is still a great deal of overcapitalization in industry.

Stock Dividends. — In addition to the cash dividends which corporations pay to their stockholders as their share in the earnings of the business, they sometimes issue what are known as *stock dividends*. These consist of additional shares of stock distributed gratis to the stockholders in proportion to their present holdings. Stock dividends of 25, 50, 100 per cent and even more are not at all uncommon in the case of successful enterprises. There is much popular misunderstanding about these stock dividends, it being felt that they are a species of abuse representative of exorbitant earnings on the part of the corporation. This attitude is not always justified.

Very frequently the directors of a corporation, instead of distributing the profits of the business each year to the stockholders, will reinvest all or a part of them in extending the company's plant or developing new branches of the business. When this occurs, the stockholders now own more capital than their present shares, which correspond to their original investment, represent. When this surplus of capital accumulated out of reinvested earnings amounts to a considerable fund, the directors declare a stock dividend; which simply means that they distribute to the stockholders new shares representing the new capital that their reinvested earnings have made possible. If the new shares do not exceed in par value the actual value of the extensions to equipment made possible by the reinvested earnings, there is no overcapitalization in this proceeding. If there is any abuse in it, it consists not in issuing shares of stock for capital actually invested, and which is not fully represented in the old shares outstanding, but rather in the fact that past earnings were so large as to make the accumulation of the extra capital possible. It is perfectly reasonable and proper that all the capital owned by the corporation should be represented by shares of stock. Whether or not it is proper that a corporation's profits should be so large as to make the accumulation of large funds of surplus capital out of reinvested earnings possible is another matter, into which we will not here enter.

If stock dividends are issued when there has been no increase in the corporation's capital above its original investment, there is, of course, overcapitalization. It might be argued, however, that if there has been an increase in the value of the original capital, without any increase in its amount, that stock dividends might be issued without causing any overcapitalization. Usually, however, stock dividends represent surpluses accumulated out of reinvested earnings, so that these questions do not generally enter into the matter.

Abuse of the Rights of Stockholders. — The securing of a majority control in the management of the affairs of a corporation by a relatively small group of promoters, or "insiders," places them in a position to benefit themselves at the expense of the minority stockholders, who have furnished a large part, often a majority, of the capital for the enterprise. Not only do these promoters share in the earnings of the corporation, which earnings are made possible by the capital put into the enterprise not by themselves but by the minority stockholders, but they may resort to other practices to secure their own gain at the expense of the latter. They can appoint themselves and their friends to lucrative offices in the corporation, perhaps at salaries so large as to take up all the profits of the business and leave no dividends for the stockholders. Or they may organize companies, of which they are the sole owners, to supply materials for the original corporation. By forcing the latter to pay excessive prices for these materials, they can make handsome profits for themselves, while these high prices raise costs for the original company to the point where no profits are available for its stockholders. They can, moreover, in order to "freeze out" the stockholders, so manipulate the affairs of the corporation as to make it appear that it is losing money for a time. The stockholders, frightened at the prospect of a total loss on their investment, will sell their stock at very low rates. The insiders, knowing that it is all a trick, may then buy up this stock, and having secured its possession, proceed to conduct the affairs of the corporation on a successful basis, bringing high earnings and greatly increasing the value of their stock, yielding them a handsome profit as a result of their activities. For example, a fruit grower in California started an orchard by the sale of stock to investors who knew very little about fruit growing. After securing the invested money, and knowing that it would be some years before the orchard would bear, he started on a deliberate campaign of frightening the investors by incurring huge expenses and levying assessments on the stock, until they, disgusted, attempted to dispose of it. He purchased it from them at a very low price, so that by the time the orchard began to bear he owned nearly all. The adventure proved a very profitable one, the orchard yielded handsome dividends upon the stock, greatly increasing its value, and the clever promoter reaped a profit.

Transferability of Shares of Stock. — Under the corporate form of business organization, it is very easy for the owners of the business to transfer their holdings, simply by selling their shares of stock. This transferability of ownership has promoted greatly the development of business enterprise, for it encourages investors to place their savings in permanent capital, secure in the knowledge that if they need the funds later for other purposes, they can convert their stock into cash by selling it. The same is true of bonds. Were it not for this transferability of corporate securities, investors might hesitate to tie up their savings in permanent form. The buying and selling of securities has led to the establishment of organized stock exchanges to facilitate such transactions. The value of securities in such a market varies with the success of the businesses they represent, so that there is much opportunity for speculation in stocks, and to a lesser degree, in bonds. Some of this speculation serves a useful purpose; but much of it also is more or less of a pure gambling nature, and, therefore, to be condemned. These matters will be discussed more fully in the next chapter.

The Corporation's Characteristics Summarized. — The corporation differs from the partnership in that it has usually a large number of members, it has limited instead of unlimited liability, it has delegated instead of direct management, and it has perpetual instead of limited life. Its great number of members has made possible the aggregation of very large amounts of capital in a single business organization, a feature which has rendered it well adapted to the needs of machine industry. Its easy transferability of ownership has promoted investment. Its delegated system of management has increased the possibilities of specialization and efficient business organization. The corporation has thus promoted industrial development ably. On the other hand, the ease with which it has lent itself to overcapitalization, and the power it has placed in the hands of those who control it to misuse the savings of stockholders, are abuses widely prevalent in the business world, and which present problems for the reformer to solve.

Coöperative Business Organizations. — In addition to corporations of the sort described, there is another kind of corporate organization, known as the *coöperative*. Coöperatives differ from other corporations in that the owners of the enterprise are at the same time either its customers or employees. Four types of such coöperative enterprise are fairly common.

Coöperative stores are organizations of consumers to secure supplies on better terms than they can purchase them from regular merchants. They are usually organized as corporations in which the stockholders are the intending purchasers of the store's merchandise. A record is kept of the purchases made by each member of the association (stockholder). When a dividend is declared it is paid to the members in proportion to the volume of their purchases during the period elapsed since the last distribution of profits. In this way the members in the long run obtain their goods cheaper than they could by patronizing ordinary establishments. A moderate rate of interest will usually be paid on the capital of the enterprise before a dividend is declared.

Coöperative producers' organizations are corporate enterprises, usually devoted to some sort of manufactures, in which the employees are the owners of the business. The capital may be supplied out of their own savings, or borrowed, but the workingmen are responsible for the direction of the business. They select the officials and determine the general policy. The voting is sometimes equal among all the members, sometimes proportional to their holdings of stock. In the former case each worker gets a single vote, regardless of how many shares of stock he may own; in the latter case each person has as many votes as he owns shares of stock, as in ordinary corporations. Coöperative producers' organizations have not usually been very successful, though this is not true of all.

Coöperative selling agencies are associations of producers of a certain commodity for the better standardization and marketing of their product. The association need not be a corporation. By selling all their goods through a single channel they can sell more advantageously than if they acted separately.

Coöperative credit associations are organizations of borrowers for the purpose of obtaining loans. They are really coöperative banks, in which the bank's customers are the stockholders. By putting their own savings in the business and using their joint credit to borrow from outsiders, they provide available funds to loan to their members. Building and loan associations, and farmers' rural credit societies, are examples.

Government Enterprises. — Some types of production are carried on by government agencies of one sort or another. The post office is an example of an important service carried on by the federal government. The production of electric power by the Tennessee Valley Authority is another. Many municipalities operate their own waterworks, and some run their own street railways. New York City operates its own subway system. Sometimes the commodities or services thus supplied by governments are sold in the market at a price, like the goods produced by private companies; at other times, they are supplied gratis to the citizens and paid for out of tax receipts. The latter is the case with highway facilities, fire and police protection. No general rule can be laid down concerning the form of these various government enterprises. Sometimes they are operated by departments of the executive branch. The post office department, for instance, is administered by the Postmaster General, who is a member of the President's Cabinet. Municipal waterworks may have a similar relation to the city government. At other times, special commissions may be created to direct the government enterprises. The Tennessee Valley Authority is headed by a three-man board of this kind. Again, a corporation may be set up, resembling the corporations of private enterprise, but differing from the latter in that their stock is all held by the government, instead of belonging to separate individual stockholders. There is some tendency for governments to embark on more ventures of this kind as time goes on, so that eventually such corporations may come to occupy a far more important place in our economic organization than they now do. At present much the greater part of production is carried on by private businesses.

Efficient Management. — With the growth of technical knowledge and scientific methods in human affairs generally, there has come a tendency to apply scientific methods within the field of industry in order to make possible the most economical and efficient production. This has resulted, in part, in the placing of the detailed conduct of a business, such as manufacturing methods, handling of labor, and the keeping of accounts, into the hands of salaried trained experts or technical engineers, the owners of the business confining their activities to broad matters of finance and general policy. In the hands of these technical men, business management is coming to be more and more a form of applied science. It is called scientific management.

It was formerly customary to assign a task to a given worker and to permit him to perform it in his own way, or according to the traditional methods of his trade. Careful students of production methods, however, have discovered that there is usually one way of doing each task best, and they go so far as to prescribe in detail the movements which should be undertaken by a worker in performing such a task; the prescribing of periods of rest at certain intervals, etc. In addition to this, the efficiency movement endeavors to select men with greater care, so that the proper individual is assigned to each task, and given the sort of work to do for which he is best fitted. This is coupled with proper training of workers, teaching them the best ways of accomplishing their work and developing a greater degree of skill, as well as looking after the human side—the payment of adequate wages, the reduction

alth and contentment of the worker,
s efficiency as a productive agent.
ethods can be applied to many other
e. Within the plant, for instance,
oper correlation of the work of dif-
hat no department is delayed by the
s needs; so that the whole concern
nost direct and economical attain-
em all, *viz.*, the production of cer-
much waste of materials and time is
establishment to find out wherein
nomical methods prevail. The ar-
o that there is no lost motion as the
s stages in the process of its manu-
arefully watched, so that there may
and so that the departments may
hich they need to go on with their
ways, every detail of the conduct
a careful study, so that the greatest
maintained. The rapid growth of
ized the last few years is due to the
dividual enterprisers of increasing
xpenses; but this movement is of
it is to the individual employer,
ste and inefficiency in production,
ncome.

USINESS OPERATIONS

In the last chapter we discovered
tablishment, a scale of operations
ts to a minimum. We called this
tput, and the corresponding aver-
n costs. In any one industry these
concern to another, because the
ewhat different equipment, and
quality, while they are managed
Among these differences there is
that is best suited to the condi-
production, and which is, on that
account, more efficient than any other. We call this most efficient organization the *optimum business unit* (or the *optimum firm*) for that in-

dustry. It may be defined as that type of business organization which, with prevailing technology and the existing market for its product, can produce at lowest average unit costs in the long run.

The optimum business unit depends upon a number of influences, which include the technical conditions of production affecting the industry concerned, the type of managerial work which is required for its supervision (and the availability of managers suited to those requirements), the size and character of the market for the product, the financial requirements necessary to provide it with the most suitable equipment, the kind of labor required to carry on the different operations of production, and other influences. To a considerable degree, the optimum form of organization centers in the question of the scale of operations, because the conditions named have to do mainly with the size of the establishment. Existing technology may require the use of very heavy plant and complicated expensive machinery in one industry, or small plants with relatively light and inexpensive equipment in another. The managerial problems may be complex, calling for a large supervisory staff and an expensive organization; or they may be simple, so that they can easily be supervised by one or two executives. The labor operations may be of such a character that they must be carried on by a few very highly skilled men, working mainly on their own initiative; or they may call for large numbers of unskilled men, working at routine tasks under organized supervision by a staff of foremen and other executives. The market may be national or international, and readily served by a few large producing establishments; or it may be local and restricted, calling for scattered small establishments, in close contact with consumers. The subsequent discussion will show in greater detail, by concrete illustration, how some of these influences work.

Where there is competition in industry, there is no doubt some tendency for the optimum form of business organization to dominate each branch of production. Those firms which are able to produce at lowest costs will be able to undersell their rivals, and, because of the greater cheapness of their product, will get the bulk of the business. The less efficient enterprises will be compelled to adopt the more efficient methods and more economical scale of operations of their more successful competitors, or be driven into bankruptcy. Therefore, the optimum business unit seems likely sooner or later to establish itself as the typical one in each industry. This does not mean that, if we survey a given branch of production at any one time, we will find all the establishments in it operating at the maximum level of efficiency, but it does mean that a continual process of weeding out will be going on, so that less efficient methods are being discarded and the optimum form or organization is tending to assert itself. Even where competition is restricted, something of the same tendency is probably at work, though less actively. A business firm which is protected against its competitors by monopoly power may be able to carry on with an inefficient organization, but if its managers are alert, it may be expected to seek the most economical methods of production that are available. As old machinery wears out, it will be replaced by improved devices, and when plants must be rebuilt, the company can be expected to look for the most efficient type of construction it can find; because anything it can do to reduce its unit costs will enable it to reap greater profits, and profit is the goal of its activities.

When we come to study how the prices of commodities are determined, we shall find that the concept of the optimum business unit is an important one; and it is also significant for an understanding of the organization of production.

The Growth of Large-Scale Business Organizations. — In many industries the size of the optimum business unit appears to have been growing ever larger over a period of several decades. Whereas production was formerly carried on in many small scattered shops, each employing but a few men and turning out a small quantity of product, today we are accustomed to huge manufacturing establishments, representing the aggregation of great quantities of capital, employing hundreds—in some cases thousands—of men, and with a very large output of goods. This phenomenon is known as large-scale production.

The reasons for this growth are to be found in economies, attendant upon large-scale methods of production, which make the optimum unit in the industries concerned a large one. There are a number of reasons why large-scale production results in such economies.

(1) *The proportion of fixed to variable costs.* In the last chapter it was explained that there are usually two kinds of costs in a business enterprise, known as fixed and variable. The fixed costs are chiefly those associated with maintenance of the plant, such as interest, depreciation, fire insurance, and real estate taxes. These run on pretty much the same from year to year regardless of the volume of business done, because the plant is permanent in character. The variable costs are chiefly those involved in the hiring of labor and the purchase of materials. They vary in rough correspondence with the volume of business, because more labor is hired and more materials are purchased when output expands. It was also explained that, since the costs of producing goods can usually be divided in this way, the cost of any *single unit* of goods produced consists likewise of two parts, one part the variable costs, which can be measured rather accurately

by estimating the quantity of raw material and the number of hours of labor actually put upon the unit; and a share of those fixed or overhead costs which, not being directly chargeable to each unit, must simply be divided among all the units proportionately. Hence, in many industries, especially where the ratio of fixed to variable expenses is very large, the expense of production per unit of product will decrease within the individual plant as the output of that plant is increased.

In a shoe factory, for instance, suppose that the fixed costs of interest, salaries of permanent staff, insurance, taxes, and the like, amount to $100,000 per year, and that the raw materials and manual labor that go into each pair of shoes represent an expense of $5 per pair, regardless of the number of shoes produced. If the total output of the factory is 100,000 pairs of shoes per year, there will be a fixed cost of $1 per pair chargeable to each pair of shoes, which, added to the variable cost of $5, brings the total cost of manufacturing to $6 per pair. Suppose, however, that 100,000 pairs do not represent the maximum capacity of that plant, and that, without any addition to its equipment or fixed costs, it can increase its production to 200,000 pairs per year. The variable costs will then be $5 per pair as before, but the share of fixed costs chargeable to each pair of shoes will be only 50 cents. Thus, the total cost of manufacture per pair will be $5.50, where formerly it was $6. Thus we see an economy in production results as the volume of output increases. This advantage of large-scale production is only significant where the fixed costs are large. This will include all businesses which work with elaborate plant, such as railroads, electric power plants, locomotive and automobile factories, and many others.

(2) *Use of machinery.* Because of the more economical distribution of the fixed costs associated with expensive equipment, establishments of large size are in a better position to utilize the economies which come from the use of machinery and power. Many of the mechanical devices of manufactures are very complicated and expensive pieces of mechanism. Because they cost so much, they are not economical to use unless the quantity of output is very great. The late Professor Taussig[4] cited the case of a machine used by the International Harvester Company for shaping the poles for wagons and harvesters. It cost the company $2,500. It saved them one cent per pole over the former method of making them, before the machine was introduced. It would not pay a small company to use so expensive a machine when the saving is so slight, but the International Harvester Company turns out poles by the hundreds of thousands yearly, and a saving of one cent

[4] *Principles of Economics,* Vol. I, p. 53.

per pole on such a large quantity amounts to a considerable sum in the aggregate. This is but one typical illustration of what must be equally true of a great deal of the machinery used in modern business. The remarkable development of mechanical methods which characterizes our industrial processes has inevitably been accomplished by a growth in the size of individual establishments and would not have been possible otherwise.

(3) *Economies of increased specialization.* Large-scale production makes possible a more minute division of labor than can be developed in small-sized plants, for it was shown in our discussion of the division of labor that a high degree of specialization on the part of workers is only possible where the quantity of output is great. It is impossible to keep one man at work upon the simple task of tacking the heels upon a shoe unless enough shoes can be produced daily in the establishment to keep that individual occupied all day long every day of the year at that single task. The greater the quantity of output, the more readily can the process of production be split into simple operations in this way. It has already been shown that this specialization brings with it many advantages and economies in production; consequently, the large-scale plant is more capable of the fullest utilization of such economies than the small one. All the advantages of specialization inure to the big establishment with greater force than to the small one.

(4) *Economies of buying and selling.* The large plant can take advantage of economies in the buying and selling of goods that are not possible for a smaller enterprise. In the buying of goods especially, it is usually possible to obtain a better price when materials are purchased in large lots than in small ones. Sears, Roebuck and Company, the great mail-order house, does so great a volume of business that it can purchase goods in huge quantities and in some cases may absorb the entire output of certain factories. The proprietors of such a factory, assured of a steady market for their goods and relieved of the trouble and expense of hunting for customers and shipping goods to various points, will naturally sell their produce to the mail-order firm at a lower figure than they could offer to smaller buyers, thus giving a considerable advantage to the former. Similar advantages occur in the selling of goods. Commissions to salesmen, advertising expenses, branch offices, and the other items incidental to the disposition of one's product, are less per unit of goods sold when they are sold in large quantities than where the output is smaller. Consider the single item of salesmen's commissions. If the salesman is selling a product for which there is a limited demand and which commonly is produced in small quantities, he will sell a relatively small number of these per

month, yet he will expect to receive as much pay for his efforts as the salesman of equal ability for another product for which there is an active and widespread demand, and of which a much greater number can be sold in a month's time. The first salesman, therefore, necessarily must be paid a higher rate of commission on his sales than the second, in order that his aggregate earnings may be as great.

(5) *Utilization of by-products.* A big company is in a better position to reap the economies that come from the utilization of by-products than a small one. By by-products is meant the production of certain side lines which are incidental to the main activities of a business. The main business of the great meat-packing houses of Chicago is the slaughtering of livestock and the preparation of the meat for human food. In the obtaining of this meat, however, many other products are derived from the carcass of the animal, such as hides, glue, fats, bone, and hair. Compare the small butcher in a country town with one of these huge Chicago enterprises. He too gets the materials for all of these by-products from the animals he kills, but he slaughters so few in a month's time that it would hardly pay him to develop the products. From the bones of animals, buttons and fertilizer can be prepared, but the country butcher would not have enough bones to set up a button factory or fertilizer plant. The large meat-packers can do so; hence they are able to utilize the by-products to a remarkable degree. It is this feature that has been one of the principle causes of their tremendous growth and success.

Another example is that of lignite coal. Here the main product is fuel, but in the process of obtaining it, it is possible to derive many important other commodities, such as coal-tar dyes, ammonium salts, lubricating oils, perfumes, and a great number of other commodities. Here, again, it will only be possible to develop these products in plants of sufficient size to produce them in quantities great enough to make their extraction commercially possible. Similar examples can be found in many other industries.

(6) *Experimentation and research.* Finally, a large-scale enterprise is in a better position to undertake experiments regarding the possibilities of developing new methods of production than a small one. Experimentation is costly, for the experimenters must be paid, and sometimes permitted to carry on expensive projects whose success is problematical, and which, during the period of experimentation, at least, in no way facilitate production in the industry and bring in no revenue. Small companies cannot afford to do this, but in large plants, where the volume of business transacted runs into the hundreds of thousands of dollars, a few thousands spent in experiments is a negligible item which can be carried on for years without serious financial

loss to the company, and which may result from time to time in important discoveries which eventually pay for the investment many times over. Large corporations, such as those operated by the Du Pont industries, maintain elaborate laboratories, where corps of chemists and scientists of various sorts are kept constantly employed, working out plans for the utilization of by-products of the business, such as the well-known Du Pont "Cellophane," developing processes of manufacturing dyes, and so on. Research work is becoming a very important feature of large industrial enterprises, but is not feasible for smaller concerns.

In these (and perhaps other) ways, large-scale production makes possible economies which mean lower costs and give to big establishments an advantage over their smaller competitors.

Influences Which Make for a Small Optimum Unit. — Notwithstanding these manifest advantages, there are sometimes conditions favorable to the smaller concerns, so that there has not yet appeared any wholesale elimination of the latter from the field of industry. Great industrial enterprises call for a high degree of managerial ability which is rarely found. Few persons possess the genius for organization and administration requisite for the smooth running of great industrial projects. Without such direction, these projects become unwieldy; their various parts do not work smoothly together; lack of coördination results in waste and inefficiency, which may more than counterbalance the savings. Hence, there is a limit to the possibilities of large-scale production, and vast industrial projects of giant size are comparatively few.

Certain industries, moreover, do not lend themselves to large-scale methods. Chief among these, perhaps, is agriculture. The introduction of large-scale production into agriculture can take place only by increasing the acreage under cultivation, and this entails a spreading out of the productive unit over a larger and larger area. It is difficult to take advantage of the economies of huge plants in such a case. Large quantities of workmen cannot be concentrated into a small space, and complicated machinery is not so readily introduced. Moreover, the processes of agriculture lack that degree of uniformity and routine which is essential to a high development of the division of labor and standardization. The processes of agriculture shift with the seasons and with weather conditions from day to day. Hence, the organization must be constantly changing to meet these conditions. That is more readily accomplished where there are only a few men at work in each separate agricultural enterprise than where there is a huge staff with its complex organization. While in some of our western states there have been some examples of large farms covering thousands of acres, in which advanced forms of complex equipment have been employed, this movement has not spread to farming operations as a whole, and the tendency seems to be for farms to become smaller in size rather than larger. In short, the optimum unit in agriculture is small.

There are other industries in which no great aggregations of equipment are necessary, and in these the advantages of large-scale production are not sufficient to cause it to develop. In the making of artistic products, for instance, where individuality and hand work are required, the large-scale method is not likely to appear. Specialties, the demand for which is limited, do not admit of production in great quantities.

Large-scale production is most manifest in manufacturing, transportation, and merchandising. In manufactures it is seen in the great plants that are typical of some of our well-known industrial enterprises, such as the automobile factories of Detroit, Michigan, where the business of turning out automobiles by the thousands has been systematized to a remarkable degree, and the great meat-packing plants of Chicago. In the transportation industries it is exemplified by some of our huge railway systems—such as the Pennsylvania, the New York Central, the Northern Pacific—and by some of our city transportation systems. In the merchandising industry, we find the great department stores of our big cities combining a multitude of retail shops under one roof and dispensing thousands of pieces of merchandise to customers daily. We find also the great mail-order houses, and the chain tobacco and grocery stores. In retail trading, however, especially in the case of such commodities as groceries and similar products which are purchased in small quantities daily by the various households, it is less easy to concentrate the business into large plants, for consumers expect these facilities to be near at hand, and in many cases they will patronize a small shop near their homes rather than a large establishment farther away. Hence, the large-scale enterprise in this field often takes the form of many small-scale stores under one management, instead of one big store, and the economies of large-scale methods must then be confined within narrower limits.

Notwithstanding the wide prevalence of large-scale enterprises in these fields of production, many small establishments continue to do business and are apparently not being forced out of the market by the competition of the larger concerns. In every case the little independent retail grocer flourishes alongside of the chain store, the men's haberdashery shops compete successfully with the department stores, small manufacturing plants continue in business despite their larger rivals. This is due probably to the difficulties of organizing the larger plants on a huge scale, and the lack of men of sufficient caliber to carry out such projects. It is to be considered, also, that in a small business there is a direct connection between effort and reward. The proprietor manages it himself, and his profits directly reflect the efficiency of his management. In the large-scale business, the connection between efficiency and reward is not so apparent. The managers are hired employees, working on a salary. The profits of superior efficiency go not to them, but to the owners—in a corporation, the stockholders. Hence, the managers have less incentive to do their best. While large-scale enterprises, therefore, are numerous, and will probably continue to increase, it is not apparent that the small producer is likely to be forced from the field.

The Reconciliation of Different Optimum Influences. — In many industries there may be some factors favorable to a large scale of operations, and others favorable to a smaller organization. For instance, in retail merchandising there is an advantage in having many small stores scattered in different localities close to the housewives who patronize them, rather than one huge emporium in a central location. On the other hand, the economies made possible by large-scale advertising, purchasing, and packaging of goods favor the single, unified organization. In the production of automobiles, some parts can be manufactured most cheaply in central, large-scale factories, which specialize on them alone, but the bulkiness of the finished product and the costs of shipping it over long distances may favor assembly in a few moderately large plants located in different sections of the country. In such cases as these, the flexibility of the corporate form of business organization makes it possible to adapt the structure of the enterprise to the varied requirements of the situation. The chain store plan solves the problems of the first illustration. It retains the advantages of centralized management, large-scale purchasing and packaging, with those of decentralized selling. The similar problem of the automobile industry is solved by having centralized parts establishments, with separate scattered assembly plants, all in one giant organization. In such ways as these, the form of business organization can be adapted to the special conditions with which business men in different branches of production are confronted, and the optimum form of organization can be worked out so as to develop the highest possible efficiency.

Combination. — Another characteristic of the industrial enterprises of the present time is the tendency toward combination. By this is meant the coming together under one management of a number of separate plants. An interesting example of this is to be found in the development of the electric lighting business in one of America's largest cities. Originally in this municipality the furnishing of electric current for lighting and power purposes was done by a number of independent companies located in various parts of the city. In order to reduce the competition between these rival concerns, they determined to combine under unified management. At first there was a consolidation of many scattered companies into four or five, and finally these few were united into a single corporation. While the plants which were actually engaged in producing the current remained separate, the management was eventually combined into one. Many examples of a similar sort are continually in the public eye throughout the United States. Our so-called trusts, such as the American Tobacco Company, the Standard Oil Company, the United States Steel Corporation, the unified street railway systems of many of our big cities, the great railway systems and chain stores which have already been alluded to, are examples of combination.

Combination is not the same as large-scale production. Plants may grow larger in size, employing greater numbers of men and quantities of capital, and turning out larger output, while retaining their separate, independent, competitive existence, and without any tendency toward unification of management. This is large-scale production without combination. On the other hand, there may be combination without large-scale production. This was the case of the electric company which has just been described, where many small plants were united under single corporate control but were still operated as separate establishments, no large-scale methods being introduced. In practice, however, the two generally go hand in hand; and indeed large-scale production is very likely to lead to combination, for where the economies of increasing plant are substantial, it is difficult for small competitors to maintain their position in the face of larger rivals, and they are thus led to combine with these big concerns, or are eventually bought out by them. The biggest combinations of modern times, the giant corporations which are a conspicuous feature of the American business world, have attained their position and continue to hold it partly by virtue of large-scale methods.

Horizontal, Vertical and Complex Combination. — There are three principal types of combination. Consider the tobacco business. We have seen that the processes of industry are divided into a number of stages which tend to be carried on as separate enterprises. In the tobacco business, therefore, we may find some producers who are growing tobacco, some who are dealers in raw tobacco, purchasing it from the farmers and selling it to the manufacturers, others who manufacture tobacco into cigars, cigarettes, and other forms, wholesale dealers in these products, and finally retailers who dispense them to consumers. If, now, a number of independent cigar manufacturers decide to combine their businesses into a single corporation for their mutual benefit, we have a type of combination which may be described as *horizontal,* because it is a union of different producers all engaged at the same stage or level in the industry. Similarly, there might be combinations of tobacco retailers, of tobacco wholesalers, and, conceivably, of tobacco growers. Each of these would be a horizontal combination. The typical trusts are combinations of this sort. They are unions of many plants all producing a like product and all engaged in the same stage of production. Thus, we have combinations of sugar refineries, of railroads, of retail stores, and many others.

Suppose, on the other hand, that our combined tobacco manufacturers, recognizing the advantages that come from unified control, and having built up a great organization which is carrying on a large volume of business, are desirous of increasing their power and progress still further by carrying out a combination of a more thoroughgoing sort. They may conclude that it is to their advantage to acquire tobacco plantations of their own, making them independent of many scattered tobacco growers and assuring them of a continual supply of their raw material, whose production is under their own control. They may also extend their operations into the selling field, organizing their own distributing centers and even opening up retail stores. This brings all the operations of tobacco production, from the growing of the leaf to its final disposition, into one great organization. Plantations, drying houses, cigar, cigarette, chewing tobacco, pipe tobacco, and snuff factories, wholesale and retail stores, all become part of one vast enterprise. Combination here has been extended not only horizontally to different plants within a single stage of production, but it has been extended vertically, so that all the stages are brought within the scope of one organization. This may be called *vertical combination.* Examples of this type of combination are numerous. The United States Steel Corporation has its own mines, its own railroads and manufacturing plants. The various Standard Oil Companies in some cases control all of the stages of oil production, from the extraction of the crude oil from the wells, through the processes of refining, shipping in pipe lines and tank cars, to the marketing of the product, not to mention the many by-products that they extract and dispose of. The beef packers of Chicago not only slaughter meat and prepare the by-products therefrom, but maintain their own lines of refrigerator cars and wholesale houses. Combinations of vertical type can become very powerful and can effect important economies by the elimination of middlemen and by similar means. Hence, some of our strongest corporations are combinations of this sort.

There is often found a kind of combination that cannot be classified as either horizontal or vertical; it is perhaps best described as *complex*. Here the business ramifies into various fields which are more or less loosely associated with its main activities. Take the case of General Motors Corporation, whose principal line of business is the manufacture of motor cars. In order to gather into its organization facilities for manufacturing its own electric parts (such as storage batteries), it found it advantageous to purchase the Delco business, which had the facilities that were needed; but this concern was already engaged in the manufacture of electric apparatus of other kinds, such as farm lighting equipment. So the General Motors Corporation entered into lines of business whose connection with automobile production was rather remote. The meat packers afford an illustration of this kind of combination also. In order to transport and market their meat products satisfactorily, they found it advantageous to own their own refrigerator cars, and to provide themselves with cold storage plants in different cities. But refrigerator cars and cold storage plants can be used to handle other goods than meat products; so, in order to make full use of these facilities, the packers branched out into handling various perishable commodities. In this particular case, the extension into other lines became so serious that the government became concerned, lest a general monopoly of food products be created; therefore, it interfered to restrict the operations of the meat packers. There are many other cases where business men find it advantageous to combine different types of industry in one organization, sometimes on a quite small scale. In many a small town, coal and ice are handled by the same merchant, in order that he may offset the slack season for one of these products by the active season for the other. This kind of "dovetailing," as it is often called, can be found in many types of industry.

The term *integration* is often used to denote the various forms of combination which have just been described. In some respects it is a more appropriate term, because what takes place is the bringing together into one organization of various steps which might conceivably be carried on by separate enterprises; and this need not take place through the combination of formerly independent business units— it may merely be due to the growth of a particular concern. There are, then, three types of integration—horizontal, vertical, and complex.

Monopoly. — With the growth of large-scale enterprise and of combinations, there comes a tendency to monopoly of production. It is but a step from small plant to large, from large enterprise to combination of a number of enterprises, and from combination to monopoly. *By monopoly is meant the single control of the sources of supply of a commodity.* Few monopolies are so perfect that they have control over all the sources of supply, but not infrequently a single organization may obtain command over the source of a sufficient amount of a goods to exercise a considerable degree of influence upon the market. Most monopolies are of this sort.

Monopolies may arise in a number of different ways. (1) In the first place, the supply of a commodity may be *limited by nature* to a few sources which can readily be brought under unified management. The great majority of the diamonds of the earth are to be found in the mines that lie within a comparatively small area in South Africa. It has not been difficult for one corporation to obtain possession of these mines and thereby effect a monopoly of the diamonds of the world. The anthracite coal of the United States is to be found almost exclusively within certain districts of Pennsylvania. Here there is a natural limitation of supply which makes possible monopoly. This supply being within the control of a very few railroads, it has not been difficult for them to work in such harmony with each other that there is said to be an effective monopoly of anthracite coal. The Standard Oil monopoly was built up in this way by obtaining control over the few oil fields which existed in this country at the time of its greatest power. In a sense, individuals sometimes are possessed of such talents that they may be said to have a sort of monopoly in their field. This is the case with great artists (whose work is of such character that it is subject to little or no competition), with great musicians, actors, and other geniuses.

(2) In the second place, monopolies may come about through the *economies of large-scale production.* It has been pointed out that in some industries, as the individual plant grows larger the economies of large-scale production, and the decreasing ratio of overhead to operating expenses, bring about a decreasing cost per unit of product. In such a case the most economical method of producing the needed supply of the goods turned out in that industry is for them to be produced in a single plant, for in such a plant the costs will be lowest. Hence, the large plant in such a business has an advantage over its rivals by which it can undersell them and gradually absorb their business. The larger it grows the stronger becomes its position, because its costs continue to decrease. The natural end of such a process is the eventual dominance of one producer in the field,—that is, the establishment of monopoly. Large-scale production does not always lead

to such a result, for it may be offset by counterbalancing tendencies before this point is reached; but it may tend to eventual monopoly. This is the principle which has brought about the growth of the great meat packers of Chicago and the eventual concentration of this business into the hands of a few packers. It is this principle, in part, coupled with the natural limitation of supply, that has helped to create such monopolies or partial monopolies as those of the United States Steel Corporation and the former Standard Oil Company.

(3) A third type of monopoly may be due simply to the *control of a huge amount of capital* by a single corporation or combination. Where the resources of an organization are sufficiently large, while there may be no natural limitation of supply and no tendency to decreasing costs, it can, nevertheless, by virtue of its financial power, prevent competitors from occupying the field, for it can afford to undersell these competitors even at a temporary loss to itself until the rivals are driven from the market, when the big corporation can recoup its losses from enhanced monopoly profits. Monopolies of this sort must depend upon cutthroat competition and often unfair methods to maintain their position.

(4) Monopolies may be based upon *secret processes*. Where an important product is manufactured by methods known only to one individual or group, and there is no other known way of producing it, the lucky possessor of the secret can use his power to monopolize the industry. The drug argyrol, widely used in the treatment of diseases of the throat, nose, and eyes, is manufactured by a secret process which chemists have been unable to discover. The result is that its production has been controlled by a single producer who has reaped a fortune from it. Other examples of this kind of monopoly can be found, but they are not numerous. Almost every industry has its trade secrets, but they seldom are vital enough to give the possessor a monopoly position.

(5) Finally, *monopolies are sometimes created by law* to serve the interests of public welfare. These are known as *legal monopolies*. Patents are a monopoly granted by the government to protect men in securing to themselves the profits of their own inventions and to encourage by this means progress in the arts of production. In at least one case, that of shoe-machinery manufacturing, the control of patents made possible the building up of the shoe-machinery trust, which has a large degree of control over the shoe-manufacturing business in this country today. Every patent is, of course, a monopoly; although few of them lead to such widespread domination over an important industry as in this case. Municipalities sometimes find it advantageous to grant the exclusive use of their streets to a single corporation for the building of street railway lines, the erection of electric wires, or the

laying of gas and water mains, on the principle that the most efficient service to the public is to be obtained by unified management. Such franchises confer monopoly privileges. They may be hedged about with such restrictions and degree of control over the corporation receiving the grant as to prevent them from taking an unfair advantage of their monopoly position, although municipalities have often failed to protect themselves in this respect.

Social Significance of Monopolies. — It is not within the scope of this book to enter into a full discussion of the monopoly problem. It is apparent, however, that the control over production of commodities that lies in monopoly may have important possibilities for the good or ill of society, especially where the product monopolized is one of the necessities of life. Monopoly power gives control over the price of goods. The degree to which this control can be exercised, and its effect upon the prices of commodities, will be discussed in later chapters, but the broader questions of social welfare involved in the monopoly problem must be left to the field of applied economics.

SUMMARY

A business enterpriser is one who is responsible for the direction of a business. He is also a kind of laborer, and he may be also a capitalist, or may borrow part or all of his capital from others.

The forms of business organization are: (1) the single enterpriser, where one individual conducts the business; (2) the partnership, an association of two or more individuals under an agreement; (3) the corporation, an association of stockholders acting under a state charter for the conduct of a business. The partnership is characterized usually by few members, small capital, unlimited liability, direct management, short life; the corporation usually by numerous members, larger capital, limited liability, delegated management, easier transferability of ownership, and perpetual life. The stockholders, owners of the corporation, delegate the broad conduct of the enterprise to a Board of Directors, who often act through an Executive Committee. Details of production are handled through the staff of officials, centered in the President or General Manager, with departments under him. The capital of the corporation is represented by three sets of subscribers: bondholders, preferred stockholders, and common stockholders. The corporation promotes investment, makes easier large capital with its attendant advantages, and is adaptable to efficient managerial organization. On the other hand, the practice of overcapitalization and abuse of stockholders by those in control have created social problems. Corporations often issue stock dividends, which usually represent surplus capital accumulated by the reinvestment of earnings. The transferability of ownership of corporate shares encourages investment; it also promotes speculation in securities. Coöperative business organizations differ from ordinary corporations in that the stockholders are usually either employees or customers of the enterprise. There are four common forms of coöperative enterprises: coöperative stores, coöperative producers' organizations, coöperative selling agencies, and coöperative credit associations. Some business enterprises are operated by government agencies. Production is being made more efficient by the application of scientific methods to the problems of management.

There is a tendency for the enterprises in each industry to adopt the form of the optimum business unit, which is that type of organization that can produce at the lowest average unit costs. In many industries the size of the optimum unit is increasing, because of the following economies which arise out of large-scale production: (1) apportionment of heavy fixed costs over a larger number of units of product, (2) better use of expensive machinery, (3) increased specialization, (4) economies of buying and selling, (5) utilization of by-products, (6) possibility of experimentation and research. Notwithstanding these economies, large-scale production has not eliminated small producers; the optimum unit is small in certain groups of industries, such as agriculture. It is large chiefly in manufactures, transportation, and merchandising.

Combination of enterprises under single management is another characteristic of modern business organization. Combinations are of three types: horizontal, where a number of plants at a given stage of production are united; vertical, where a number of different stages of production are united in a single organization; and complex, where the manufacture of by-products or side lines is undertaken by the parent concern. Combination often leads to monopoly. Monopolies may arise (1) by natural limitation of supply, (2) as a result of the economies of large-scale production, (3) by the competitive power of huge aggregations of capital, (4) by knowledge of secret processes, or (5) by legal grant. Monopolies present a social problem because of their power to control prices.

REFERENCES AND SUGGESTIONS FOR FURTHER READING

The "Dominant Tendencies of Business Organization" in the modern world are set forth with his characteristic completeness in Book II of Alfred Marshall's *Industry and Trade* (1921); and that whole volume has some bearing upon the subject of the present chapter. Good, concise discussions of business organization and development are to be found in Horace

Taylor's *Making Goods and Making Money* (1928)—especially Chapters 3 to 6, and E. A. G. Robinson's *The Structure of Competitive Industry* (1932), which develops very interestingly the factors which determine the optimum size of the business unit. On the technical problems which confront the business enterpriser see R. H. Lansburgh, *Industrial Management* (1923). I have found Chapters 4 and 6 of F. W. Taussig's *Principles of Economics* (4th edition, 1939) valuable in preparing the descriptions of large-scale production and combination for this chapter. A well worked-out theory of the enterpriser and his functions is contained in Maurice Dobb's *Capitalist Enterprise and Social Progress* (London, 1925).

The Temporary National Economic Committee (T.N.E.C.), appointed by Congress in 1938, has published a series of more or less exhaustive studies dealing with the growth of monopoly in this country and related problems. A complete list of these publications can be found in The American Economic Review, June 1941 (Vol. XXXI, pp. 347–350). An interpretation of the findings contained in the studies was published as a supplement to The American Economic Review for June, 1942.

Chapter VII

RISK IN INDUSTRY

A. The Nature and Incidence of Risks

The Prevalence of Risks. — Life itself is full of hazards, and economic life is no exception to this rule. The carrying on of production is fraught with numerous risks—risks of a personal nature and risks of loss of property. A great many of these risks arise out of the fact that, in the roundabout processes of modern industry, production is spread over time. We have seen that the first stages of production are carried out long in advance of their completion, requiring advances of savings, and waiting for a reward. Two possible sources of risk are inherent in this fact—the possibility that the production will not in the end be as great or of as good a quality as was anticipated, and the possibility that the market for it will not be satisfactory. We may call these technological risks and marketing risks, respectively.

The technical efficiency and final completion of production may be interfered with in a number of ways. One's factory may be destroyed by some unforeseen catastrophe, such as a fire, an earthquake, or a flood. Drought or excessive rains may spoil the farmer's crops. A workingmen's strike may force a plant to suspend operations. An important machine may break down and have to be scrapped. There is no end to the possible obstacles and losses that may prevent the successful consummation of production. There is probably no industry that is entirely free from these chances.

Even more important is the risk that when a thing is once produced, it may not be possible to sell it at a price that will cover its costs of production. Production is carried on in anticipation of demand. The retailer has to estimate the wants of his customers and lay in a corresponding stock of goods in advance. The wholesaler must keep on hand a sufficient supply to meet the needs of the retailers. The manufacturer must purchase his raw materials, employ labor, and make up his products in anticipation of sales to wholesalers. So it goes in every phase of industry. Only to a small extent is it possible to get orders in advance and then fill the orders. Consequently, almost every business man is called upon to study the future market for his product, and incur present expense in the expectation that his judgment will prove correct. His judgment may often be poor, however; and the market may change due to circumstances which he could not foresee. As a result, he may incur a loss. Demands change, competitors undersell or offer more attractive merchandise, prices rise or fall, and a thousand and one other contingencies may arise to ruin one's market. There is also the ebb and flow of business prosperity in recurring cycles (to be described in a later chapter), which may affect one's business adversely.

These circumstances involve mainly the risk of loss of property. There are also many personal risks in industry: risk of death, accident, unemployment, loss of reputation, decline in earning power, failing health, and so on. Risk is universal and takes a variety of forms.

Risks of the Enterpriser. — The fact that the enterpriser is responsible for the direction of a business causes the property risks of industry in their first instance to fall very largely on his shoulders. It is his task to look after the technical and marketing aspects of the business in such a way as to make it a success. He usually makes a contract with capitalists, from whom he has borrowed funds, to pay them a fixed amount of interest. Wages, also, show a certain amount of stability under ordinary business conditions, so that the amount he pays to his employees tends to lag behind the general movement of prices. Thus, his payments for interest and wages remain more or less constant, while the prices he pays for his materials and those which he gets for his products are subject to considerable fluctuations. If the efficiency of his plant is good, the market conditions favorable, and his judgment sound, he gains profit; if not, he suffers losses. So far as is possible, he guarantees his creditors against loss, and they expect him to bear the chief risks of his enterprise. If the risks are small, any slight losses that occur will affect only the enterpriser, by reducing his profits. If losses are large, however, the enterpriser can only make them good if he has property of his own which can be used to pay his debts. In fact, he usually does have savings invested in the business, and oftentimes he has other property which can be levied against. The limited liability feature of the corporations, however, limits the responsibility of stockholders to the amount they have invested, as we have seen. The enterpriser thus runs a risk in his capacity of capitalist, at least to the extent of his investment, and sometimes more. Important also is the risk of position and reputation which he bears. In his business he has at stake his personal prestige, his credit in the business world, his income-earning power, the comfort and happiness of himself and family. If his business judgment is sound, and conditions favorable, success in these respects, leading to the pinnacle of wealth and power, is possible; if he fails, his downfall is great.

It is a mistake to emphasize the risks of the enterpriser to the exclusion of those of other participants in industry, as some writers have done. Although most unfavorable developments in the conduct of a business strike the enterpriser first, there is often opportunity to shift the burden ultimately to someone else. For instance, there are insurance men and speculators whose business it is to assume risks for others in ways presently to be described. The enterpriser can transfer part of the burden of unfavorable business conditions to his employees by closing his factory and dismissing his workers until better times return. Finally, in case of complete failure, if the enterpriser has not enough property of his own to make good his debts, the creditors will have to pocket the losses. So we see that there are other classes in the community who run risks as a result of their participation in industry.

Risks of the Capitalist. — There is a hazard involved in the very ownership of wealth. It may be destroyed by fire or lost by theft. If loaned to others there is the chance that it will never be repaid. Most wealth is loaned to business enterprisers by investment. The degree of risk varies with the type of investment, but even in the safest it is not entirely absent. The bonds of a strong, stable government are usually regarded as almost certainly safe; yet that there is the possibility of loss even here is shown by the fact that the communists overthrew the Czar's rule in Russia and repudiated its debts; while the first World War made the Allied nations unable to pay interest on their debts to the United States. Both of these obligations may eventually be met by the governments concerned; but it is not at all probable. Bonds of a sound business enterprise, secured by a first mortgage upon its real estate, are usually a reasonably safe investment, but changes in industrial conditions or in the particular industry concerned may greatly reduce the value of its capital and cause the bondholder to suffer loss. Less well protected securities entail a correspondingly greater hazard. Moreover, the capitalist is oftentimes also an enterpriser; that is, he has not only made an investment in an enterprise, but assumes along with it a certain amount of responsibility for the direction of it. This is the case with the stockholders of a corporation. In such instances the capitalist runs all the risks to which enterprisers are subject.

Every creditor is a capitalist, although he may have made no permanent investment in his debtor's enterprise. If the business owes him money, he has invested funds, temporarily at least, in it. So long as the debt is unpaid there is a risk. If a wholesaler sells goods to a retailer, accepting his promissory note in lieu of payment, he takes a chance of loss through the inability of the retailer to redeem his note. Every business man and capitalist has certain "accounts receivable," which means that other persons are indebted to him. There is always a danger that these accounts may be uncollectable, causing the creditor loss.

Risks of the Laborer. — The risks run by the workingman in industry have often been slighted or ignored. Because they are of a more personal nature, involving the comfort and happiness of the great mass of our people, they are even more important than the property risks to which other classes of society are subject. Also, they have just as much economic significance. The laborer shares in the prosperity or reverses of his employer. If the business is good, he is steadily employed at good wages; if it is poor, he may be forced to work only part time, his wages may be reduced, or he may be laid off entirely. Every period of business depression is accompanied by wholesale unemployment which brings poverty and suffering to hundreds of thousands of families. Depressions in a particular trade or enterprise have similar effects on a smaller scale. We have already seen that the reduction of working time or the laying off of men is one way in which enterprisers shift part of the burden of their losses to their employees. The worker may also suffer a permanent decline in the demand for his skill due to some change in the methods of production or the state of the market of the industry in which he is employed. For instance, a harness-maker may find his occupation gone as the automobile replaces the horse; or the glass-blower may be replaced by a machine which does his work. A workman's skill may be the result of years of training and apprenticeship; it is to him a sort of capital; it is his chief reliance for means of support. When it becomes valueless, he has suffered a severe loss which greatly reduces his earning power. Such cases are very frequent, so that the worker's position is always a precarious one. Other risks run by employees in industry are those of accident and occupational disease. Many employments place the worker in danger of limb or life. Whirring machinery, heavy objects moving on cranes overhead, mine explosions, molten iron, frail supports at dizzy heights—these are but a few of the thousands of possibilities of being maimed or killed which daily face almost every manual laborer. Some occupations are peculiarly likely to lead to the development of certain diseases. Such are the deadly trachoma which attacks those who handle cattle; pneumonia, tuberculosis, and other ailments of the lungs, which may come to those who are exposed to severe changes of temperature, and dust- or moisture-laden atmosphere;

"phossy jaw," which results from the handling of white phosphorus in the making of certain kinds of matches, and so on. Then, finally, there is gradual failing of earning power through the coming on of old age, often induced prematurely by the excessive strain and fatigue of certain employments.

General Methods of Dealing with Risks. — There are, in general, three possible courses of action which a person who is confronted with a risk may follow. The most obvious is to ascertain the source of the danger, and, if possible, remove it. This we may call the method of *elimination*. Fires can be very much reduced by fire-proof building construction, and the provision of adequate facilities for extinguishing them before they do serious damage. Accidents to workmen can be lessened by the use of proper safeguards at the points of danger. Research into the causes of loss will often suggest means of avoiding them. Careful market analyses, for instance, in place of guesswork or crude estimates, will enable an enterpriser to ascertain with reasonable certainty the possible sales of his product. Business forecasting is a growing field whose purpose is, by keeping records of various indicators of business activity, such as the prices of stocks, the volume of bank loans and reserves, the volume of production, etc., to predict forthcoming booms or depressions in industry. Study of past business cycles reveals certain characteristics which afford the basis for such predictions. A number of agencies now exist for making business forecasts, which they sell to business men. The latter can then take advantage of the information so secured to accommodate their businesses to the expected developments. Business forecasting is not yet perfected by any means, but has developed sufficiently to enable the business man who uses such services intelligently to reduce his losses, in so far as they depend on general fluctuations of business. In these, and other ways, proper attention to the danger points in industry makes possible the total elimination or substantial reduction of many risks.

Another method of dealing with risks is to shift them to somebody else. This we may call the method of *transfer*. Certain classes of men make the bearing of risks their chief business, or at least an important part of it. They are specialists in risk-bearing. There are a number of ways in which risks can be transferred to such specialists. One of the most common is by means of *insurance*. The men who are in the business of insurance guarantee to their customers that they will make good any losses sustained by the latter as the result of certain occurrences, such as fire or shipwreck. The insured thereby transfers his risk to the insurer. How the insurer can give such a guarantee and make a profit from it will be shown presently. A risk can also be transferred to speculators by hedging or contracting out. A *hedging* deal can be illustrated by the case of a grain dealer, who, having purchased a quantity of wheat, is desirous of protecting himself against loss from a decline in its price while it is in his possession. He therefore makes a contract in the speculative produce exchange to sell wheat for future delivery at an agreed price. Now if a decline in the price of wheat forces him to sell his stock to the trade at a loss, he can make a corresponding gain on his "futures" transaction in the speculative market, for, presumably, the price of wheat will have declined there also, and he can now buy up the wheat necessary to fulfill his futures contract at a lower price than that at which he agreed to sell it. Thus his transaction in the speculative market acts very much like an insurance policy to protect his ordinary trade sales against market losses. He has transferred the risk to the speculators in wheat. The machinery of hedging will be described presently in greater detail.

Contracting out resembles hedging. A builder contracts to build a house at a certain price. Immediately he lets sub-contracts for the plumbing, heating, painting, plastering, mason-work, etc., by which the sub-contractors agree to supply their respective materials and labor for the house at an agreed price. The builder is now assured in part as to how much it will cost him to erect the house, and as to what he will get for it. He can count on a certain gain. While by this process he foregoes a possible greater profit which would accrue if the prices of materials or labor fell, he is also protected against the possible loss he would sustain if they rose. The builder has transferred his risks to the sub-contractors (who may in turn transfer them to others), and to the purchaser of the house. Another type of transfer of risks is that from other business classes to enterprisers. We have seen that the latter partly guarantee the payment of interest to capitalists, and make advance payments of wages to labor. Here both capitalists and laborers have shifted certain risks to the enterpriser. We have also seen that the enterpriser can in some circumstances shift certain of his risks to the capitalists or to the employees.

The transfer of risks to specialists and others is not always a certain guarantee against loss. An insurance company may fail and be unable to meet the obligations it has assumed, throwing them back upon the parties it has insured. Some of the parties in a hedging or contracting-out agreement may not make good. However, these methods of meeting risks are generally effective, and serve greatly to reduce the chances of loss to the individual who thus shifts the hazards on to the shoulders of others.

If a risk cannot be eliminated or transferred, it must be *assumed;* and the individual must fortify himself as best he can to meet it. In the long run, all risks that cannot be eliminated must be assumed by someone; for although one individual can transfer a risk to another, someone must bear it. Insurers, speculators, and to some extent, enterprisers, are professional risk-takers. It is their business to assume risks and take the gains and losses that result from them. We shall learn more about the enterprisers' part in this in the chapter on profits. Insurance and speculation will be dealt with here.

B. INSURANCE

Principles of Insurance. — It is seldom that an individual can predict just when his death may occur, his house burn down, or various other catastrophes take place. For some of such happenings, however, it is possible, by the use of accurate statistics, to know just how often they will take place on the average, if a large enough number of cases is taken. We do not know when we may die, but an actuary can tell us how long the average expectation of life for persons of our age, sex, and general condition is. No one can say whether or not his house will be destroyed by fire within the next twenty-four hours, but it can be ascertained with considerable accuracy just how many fires per day will occur out of a certain number of thousands of buildings of a certain type. In other words, when a large number of risks are consolidated, what is a great uncertainty for the individual case, becomes a certainty for the group. The occurrence of a single accident may ruin an individual, if not provided for. To lay up by himself sufficient funds to meet every possible risk would be so tremendously expensive that it would be out of the question. A large number of such persons, provided with statistics of the sort just mentioned, however, can pool their resources so as to meet these contingencies cheaply. If each of them pays in a small contribution to a common fund, enough can be accumulated to pay for the occasional losses that are sure to come to some members of the group. This is mutual risk-bearing.

Insurance companies take advantage of this principle. They issue policies to their customers which guarantee to make good the losses which the latter may sustain from certain occurrences. The premiums which the policy-holders pay in to the company are kept in a common fund to meet the losses of the various individuals as they occur. Knowing that, out of its large number of risks, a certain amount of losses can be counted upon on an average, the company is able to fix a definite price for its insurance, which will cover these losses, meet the administrative costs of carrying on the business, and provide a return to the owners of the enterprise. The insurance enables the policy-holder to substitute a small certain loss (the amount of the premium), for an uncertain, very great loss. The protection is well worth this relatively small cost.[1]

The principle of insurance can sometimes be applied without having recourse to an insurance company. If a business is large enough, so that it has a great many risks of a certain kind, the number will be great enough to admit of consolidation. That is, the losses will average a certain predictable amount annually, which can be carried as an ordinary business cost, paid out as an operating expense, saving the business the administrative and profit charges of the insurance company. Thus, a large employer of labor need not take out accident insurance to protect himself from loss arising out of damages due the workers for accidents sustained in his employment; he can count on a certain fairly constant amount of such losses annually among his large force of workers, and make the necessary provision of funds to meet it. Similarly, a great railroad need not insure its station buildings against loss from fire, since there are so many of them that a certain definite number of fires will occur annually on an average, entailing a predictable loss which the company can provide against regularly. Such insurance is known as self-insurance. Smaller businesses cannot count on averaging their risks in this way; they, therefore, consolidate their risks with those of other enterprises by using the services of an insurance company.

Not all risks can be provided for by insurance. The above discussion makes clear that, in order to be insurable, there must be a large enough number of independent risks to permit the operation of a fairly constant average. If there is such a large number, and it is possible to gather statistics of the average losses sustained among them, the element of uncertainty can be reduced to a certainty, and the principle of insurance is then applicable. As a practicable business proposition, certain other conditions are requisite to make it worth while for an insurance company to undertake protection; but the general principles already explained suffice for a general understanding of the matter, without going into these details. The method of statistics has been developed so far that the occurrence of various kinds of disasters can now be foretold with remarkable precision, and insured

---

[1] The insurance company, moreover, can protect itself against the occurrence of an unusual catastrophe, for which its ordinary resources would be insufficient, by reinsuring a part of its risks with some other company. Suppose, for instance, that a certain fire insurance company has a large number of policy-holders in a certain city. The premiums it charges may be adequate to cover all ordinary fire losses; but if a great conflagration should occur, like that which destroyed Baltimore some years ago, the company's losses may be so great as to ruin it unless provided for. It can meet this catastrophe hazard by distributing its losses above a certain amount among other companies, who, not having so many fire risks concentrated in the area concerned, could afford to take such reinsurance safely.

against. Some risks are insured which cannot be so predicted; in such a case the insurance contains a large element of speculation; but the great majority of the insurance business today is based on sound knowledge, and the element of chance has been almost eliminated.

Types of Insurance. — For convenience we may divide the types of insurance into three general classes: insurance against property losses, insurance against personal losses, and social insurance. The third of these is really a special form of the second, but presents certain characteristics which make it worth while to classify it separately.

Among the most important forms of *property insurance* is that against fire, which is highly developed, and very widely used. Fire risks are classified according to the combustibility of the buildings insured, their location with reference to fire-extinguishing facilities, the uses to which they are to be put, etc.; and a carefully graduated schedule of premiums based upon the hazard involved is charged. Marine insurance, both ocean and inland, protects owners against every conceivable loss incurred in transportation, such as shipwreck, piracy, theft and pilferage, fire or collision at sea, and damages to baggage, freight, etc., in railway, truck, or other transportation. Automobile insurance is rapidly growing in popularity. Various forms protect the car owner against loss from liability for damages to the property or person of others, from collision, from theft, and from fire. Other types of property insurance offer protection against losses from tornadoes or hail, from theft or burglary, from the failure of one's debtors, and so on.

Of *personal insurance* the most important is life insurance. This is really insurance against loss of earning power arising through death, giving protection to the family or other dependents of the insured. Life insurance has been developed very greatly, a wide variety of policies adapted to the needs of various individuals being available. A huge amount of such insurance is written annually. By careful selection and classification of risks through medical examinations, and by the use of carefully worked out mortality tables drawn from statistics of deaths among the population, classified according to age, sex, locality, occupation, etc., an insurance company can predict the losses very accurately and provide protection at the lowest possible cost. Insurance against accidents, particularly in travel, is also quite common. More difficult to conduct on scientific principles is health (sickness) insurance. Notwithstanding the fact that the element of uncertainty here is great, many companies are writing this kind of insurance, at rates which are rather high.

The hazards to which the average workingman is subjected in his employment are so great that much attention has been given by social workers and statesmen to the problem, in order to protect him, to some extent at least, from them. As a result, various forms of *social,* or *workingmen's insurance* have been developed. Among the contingencies provided for are accidents, sickness, old age, and sometimes unemployment. In the case of accidents, a fixed scale of compensations, according to the extent of the injury, is provided. In case of sickness, medical aid and a certain percentage of the worker's wage is paid to him during the period of his illness. Old age insurance provides a modest income for the rest of his life when he reaches a certain age. Unemployment insurance provides usually a part of the worker's normal wage during periods of involuntary idleness. It is somewhat difficult to administer, owing to the necessity of accompanying it with some machinery for finding the worker a job if one is procurable, in order to prevent him from purposely avoiding work and living on the insurance. For this reason it is still in an experimental stage, but has nevertheless been widely adopted. Social insurance differs from other forms, in that its cost is not usually paid for entirely by the beneficiary himself. The worker may contribute a part of the premiums out of his wages, but a part, or even all of it, is frequently borne by the employer, or by the state, or by both.

Social insurance against losses of employees caused by accidents in the course of their work has been provided in most of the states in this country for many years by Workmen's Compensation laws. These laws make it difficult for employers to defend themselves against suits brought by their employees for damages arising out of injuries sustained in their employment. To avoid these suits, the employers prefer to transfer the risks of accident compensation to state or private insurance companies. This is precisely the result that the laws are intended to accomplish, this roundabout method having been adopted to avoid constitutional difficulties. Other forms of social insurance were not generally adopted in the United States until the passage of the Social Security Act in 1935. This law brought into existence a comprehensive, nation-wide system of old age and unemployment insurance. The law provides retirement annuities for certain groups of workers after they reach the age of 65. Outright pensions are paid jointly by state and federal governments to those over 65 who cannot qualify for the annuities. There is also provision for state unemployment insurance funds. The cost of the old age annuities is met by a small tax on wages and employers, of the unemployment insurance by a tax on employers alone. The pensions are paid for out of general tax receipts. Similar national systems of social insurance were in effect throughout Europe long before the Social Security system was established here.

The Effect of Insurance on Prevention of Risks. — Insurance not only provides protection against losses from the hazards of industry, but it stimulates the adoption of measures tending to eliminate such hazards, in so far as they are preventable. Insurance companies often compel their policy-holders to inaugurate certain preventive measures as a condition to obtaining insurance. For instance, an employer may not be given liability insurance unless he installs certain protective devices on his machinery. The same result is secured by charging higher rates to poor risks than to good ones. Thus fire insurance is offered at lower premiums to owners of houses which are built of fireproof materials. By such means as these, insurance has led to a great deal of preventive activity tending to reduce the risks of industry.

Guaranty and Suretyship. — Similar in form to insurance, though somewhat different in principle, are the protections provided by some companies to guarantee the validity of real estate titles, the honesty of persons holding responsible positions of trust, the performance of contracts, etc. For example, real estate title insurance is not based solely on the principles of insurance. Instead of merely calculating the average losses on a large number of risks and charging a premium to cover these losses, the title insurance company makes a careful search of court records and satisfies itself that the title is clear. It issues a policy only when convinced that there is little risk. By this means a person who buys a piece of real estate or lends money on a mortgage can obtain a guarantee against loss through any defect in his title, by the payment of a moderate fee. Similarly, a surety company will guarantee an institution, such as a building and loan association, against loss through the dishonesty of its treasurer. The surety company makes a thorough investigation of the character and resources of the individual in question, and when it is satisfied that there is no great risk it gives the necessary bond. There are various types of bonds issued by surety companies, guaranteeing that certain obligations will be met, and thus protecting the guaranteed parties from loss.

C. Speculation

Speculation in Produce. — It was shown above that risks can be transferred to professional risk-takers by hedging in the speculative markets. This suggests that speculators may perform a useful function in our economy, notwithstanding a popular opinion to the contrary. There is no doubt that speculation is subject to serious abuses which warrant condemnation, but it is also true that the more honorable activities of speculators help to stabilize the supplies and prices of commodities which might otherwise fluctuate widely. Consider the following example.

Let us suppose that in a certain season there is a bountiful crop of corn, but that there is the prospect of a short crop in the coming season. With an abundant supply on the market, and demand no greater than usual, the tendency would naturally be for its price to be low, and because of its exceeding cheapness, for it to be freely and perhaps wastefully used. But the following season the reverse would likely be the case; corn being then scarce, its price would tend to be high, and there would be a dearth of corn products. Such would be the case if there were no speculative dealings in corn. But speculators, anticipating the future rise in the price of corn, would take advantage of the prevailing low price to buy up corn to be sold in the future. This has the effect of withholding corn from the present market and adding it to the market in the future. The consumption of corn is thus made more even throughout the year, both present waste and future scarcity are very much reduced, and consumers benefit. At the same time the price is stabilized, for the purchasing of corn by speculators in the present increases the immediate demand for it and prevents the price from falling as low as it otherwise would, while their sales of corn in the future increase the supply of it at that time and prevent the price from rising as high as it otherwise would, on account of the small crop. Speculation in produce, therefore, stabilizes both the supply and price of commodities over periods of time.

The stabilizing of the supply creates time utilities by saving produce from a time when it is too abundant to a time when it is more needed; the stabilization of price reduces the risk to which business men are subjected. Producers of corn would be subject to much more violent fluctuations in prices if there were no speculation in this commodity. Their business would then be subject to great uncertainties; while one year might bring great gains, another might bring such losses as to result in ruin. It is apparent, therefore, that the activities of speculators reduce the risks of industry.

To have this effect, however, the speculation must be intelligent. If it is badly done, it will increase the fluctuations in prices rather than reduce them. If speculators anticipate a fall in prices and sell, when in reality there is impending a rise of prices, their haste to dispose of current stocks depresses prices now, while the future shortage of goods is increased and prices rise even higher than they would have done. Unwise speculation is, therefore, as disastrous as wise speculation is beneficial. For this reason it is important that speculation be kept in the hands of those persons who are most competent for the work.

Whether or not our present machinery of speculation actually secures this is a question of some uncertainty. Without attempting to answer it positively, we can gain some light upon it by a consideration of the means by which speculation in produce is carried on.

While all business men are speculators to a considerable degree, we learned in an earlier part of this chapter that they shift many of their speculative risks to other persons. The machinery of speculation enables producers to transfer certain kinds of risks to professional speculators by means of dealing in futures and hedging. Thus speculation acts very much like insurance, providing a means by which the ordinary business man can to some extent obtain guarantees from others which will free him in part from some of his uninsurable risks. Let us look into this process.

Dealing in Futures. — This refers to the practice of buying and selling goods for future delivery at a price agreed upon some time in advance. It is the chief business of the speculator in produce to deal in futures. For instance, a wheat speculator may have reason to believe in July that the price of wheat the following September will be not more than $1.20. He, therefore, agrees to sell a certain quantity of it for September delivery for $1.30 (assuming that he has found a buyer at that price), expecting to buy it at the lower figure at that time. In other words, he is selling wheat which is not yet in his possession. This is known as a "short sale." If his expectations are realized, when the time comes to make delivery he can buy his wheat at the price he anticipated and fulfill his contract at a profit. If, however, the price of wheat in September proves to be higher than $1.30, he is forced to fulfill his contract at a loss.

Produce Exchanges. — The market for dealing in futures for many of the staple products is organized into produce exchanges. These are associations of dealers, speculators, and brokers who meet together for trading, primarily in future sales of certain commodities. Any commodity for which there is a large, general demand the year round, and which is capable of being standardized as to quality, so that one who buys a certain amount of it for future delivery can be sure of just what he is getting by specifying the grade (as *e.g.* No. 1 wheat, No. 2 wheat, etc.) can be dealt in on an exchange. Among the commodities handled in the various produce exchanges of the United States are wheat, corn, oats, rye, barley, flax, hayseed, cottonseed oil, butter and eggs, pork products, coffee, sugar, and others. Traders on the exchanges may be legitimate dealers, who actually handle the commodities they deal in; they may be speculators, who have no interest in the commodities other than to buy and sell orders with a view to making profits by successful anticipation of price changes; and most of them act also as brokers, handling orders for clients not members of the exchange, and charging a small commission for the service. The exchanges are provided with elaborate facilities for enabling their members to transact business quickly and without formality; they report immediately all sales and send out the price quotations over telegraph tickers so that they quickly become known throughout the business world; and they provide their members with information and services of various sorts. The traders make use of all available information, such as government crop reports, indices of trade conditions, prevailing price quotations, the behavior of their competitors, and so on, in their attempts to estimate the future trends of prices, and they conduct their speculations accordingly. There is much speculation in produce outside the exchanges, but the superior facilities of the latter make it much easier for speculation to be carried on in them. The exchanges are useful to the extent that speculation itself is useful, and they are likely to make speculation more intelligent by virtue of the greater publicity and information which they make available as a guide to traders. Against this, however, is to be set the disadvantage that the ease with which transactions can be made in the exchanges through brokers encourages many dabblers to speculate in produce who have no special knowledge or fitness for the work, with disastrous results to themselves and with disturbing effects on the market.

Contracting Out. — It is chiefly by means of the facilities offered by the produce exchanges that a business man is able to transfer certain of his market risks to speculators. Suppose that a miller has a contract for flour to be delivered at a certain date, the manufacture of which will require a thousand bushels of wheat, the price of the flour being agreed upon in advance. Not wishing to lay this wheat in stock at once, the miller desires to be assured of being able to obtain it later at a price which will enable him to fill his contract at a profit. He, therefore, buys futures in wheat on the produce exchange at the prevailing price. He is now protected against adverse price fluctuations, for he knows he can get the wheat when he needs it, and just what it will cost; he knows also he can sell his flour, and at just what price. He has transferred to the speculator, from whom he buys futures in wheat, any risk of loss from possible fluctuations in the price of that commodity; and he has transferred to the purchaser of the flour any possible loss from changes in the price of it. This is a simple futures transaction which takes the form of contracting out. It is sometimes regarded as a form of hedging. The typical hedging deal, however, is a more complex transaction, which will now be described.

Hedging. — Hedging consists in the making of a purchase and a sale at the same time, the one in the ordinary trade market, the other in the speculative (futures) market, in such a way that a loss from adverse price fluctuations on the one transaction will be offset by a corresponding gain from the other. Consider again the example of the miller. This time we will suppose that he has no contract for the sale of flour, but has laid in a supply of wheat, at a cost of one dollar per bushel, which he expects to convert into flour and sell at a price which will pay back his investment, plus the cost of milling the wheat, plus a manufacturer's profit of five cents per bushel on the wheat so converted into flour. If the price of wheat declines before he has sold the flour, the price of flour will probably fall correspondingly, and he may lose. To protect himself, he makes an agreement on the produce exchange, simultaneously with his purchase of wheat, to sell wheat for future delivery, at the prevailing futures price, which we will assume to be also one dollar per bushel. Now if the price of wheat declines ten cents, and flour correspondingly, it will wipe out the miller's five cent profit and cause him a five cent loss on his milling transaction; but he will gain ten cents on his futures transaction; for, having contracted to sell wheat at one dollar, he is able to fulfill his contract by buying it at ninety cents. The price fluctuation so adverse to his milling operations has been entirely offset, and he makes his five cent profit, as he had anticipated. If the price of wheat rose (and with it the price of flour), he would make an extra profit on his milling operation, but would lose a corresponding amount on the futures deal. He thus gives up a speculative chance of profit (or loss) for a manufacturer's normal trade profit. The hedging transaction serves as a kind of insurance by which he transfers his market risk to speculators on the produce exchange.

There are many possible hedging deals of this sort. In this case a trade transaction in a manufactured product (flour) is hedged against a speculative deal in its raw material (wheat). Similarly, cotton goods may be hedged with raw cotton, or wool yarn against wool. Or, a trade transaction in a raw material can be hedged against a speculative deal in the same material, as in the example cited earlier, where a grain dealer protected himself against a possible fall in the price of his stock of wheat by selling wheat futures in the produce exchange. Other examples of this would be the hedging of corn against corn, rye against rye, or cotton against cotton. It is also possible to hedge one commodity against a less closely related commodity, as, for instance, lard against cottonseed oil. Since these two commodities are to a considerable extent substitutes for each other, their prices may be expected to move upward or downward together; and trade transactions in the one can be balanced by futures deals in the other.

For a hedge to furnish perfect protection, it is essential that the two commodities vary in price in exact correspondence. If, for instance, the price of cotton goods varied independently of the price of raw cotton, a hedging deal between the two might not insure the dealer against loss from price fluctuations in one or the other. Of course two such commodities will vary independently of each other to some extent, but, in general, there is a close enough correspondence to make the protection afforded by hedging a fairly good one.

The Risk Reduction and Discounting Functions of Speculation. — Most economists hold the theory that dealing in futures and hedging, through the machinery of the produce exchanges, reduces the total risk in industry by transferring the burden of such risks from business men in general to a particular class of speculators who are specialists in risk-bearing. We have seen that intelligent speculation stabilizes prices and lessens uncertainty of market conditions. It is believed that professional speculators, with their facilities for obtaining information about conditions likely to affect the market, and with the judgment which is the fruit of experience, are more likely to speculate intelligently than are business men in general. Therefore, it is argued that the machinery of the produce exchanges, and speculators as a class, are useful adjuncts of industrial life. This is probably true of many speculators, and perhaps true of the machinery of speculation as a whole. It must not be forgotten, however, that produce exchanges enable many novices to take a plunge on the market, with evil results; we shall see, also, that some of the activities of professional speculators are of dubious value.

Some writers have laid considerable stress on what they call the *discounting* of price changes as a useful function of the speculative markets. By discounting they mean the anticipation, a considerable period in advance, of forces tending to cause a change in prices. For instance, it is said that if next season's cotton crop is going to be small, causing scarcity and high price of cotton, the best informed speculators will know this a long time ahead, and will begin to buy up cotton to hold it for the rise. This buying will cause prices to start upward slightly, and they will continue to rise gradually, so that when the shortage of cotton is actually upon the community, the price will not shoot precipitously upward, but will already have accommodated itself to the situation. In this way business men are protected from sharp fluctuations in prices. This emphasis on discounting is merely another way of explaining the general stabilizing effect of speculation on the supply and price of a commodity that has already been described.

Speculation in Stocks. — Speculation in the stocks and bonds of corporations, particularly stocks, is even more prevalent, and is much more in the public eye, than speculation in produce. As the earnings of a corporation rise and fall, ownership of its securities becomes more or less desirable, and their market prices fluctuate accordingly. In this fluctuation there is abundant opportunity for speculation. Sometimes the prices of stocks will change very rapidly, and fortunes can be made or lost in a few days by those who speculate in them. In order to facilitate dealings in securities, stock exchanges, very similar to the produce exchanges already described, have come into existence. Of these the New York exchange is by far the largest and most important. Only members may trade in the exchanges, and as membership is limited, it is highly prized in the more important exchanges, "seats" on the exchanges being bought and sold for large sums of money. Only approved securities of corporations already well established are admitted to transactions on the exchange; new enterprises and older ones of doubtful standing must find a market for their issues elsewhere, either through investment bankers and brokers or by direct appeal to the public. Some exchanges are less conservative than others. For instance, the New York Curb Exchange lists securities which are not accepted by the New York Stock Exchange. As in the case of produce, the buying and selling of securities is frequently handled by agents or brokers who utilize their membership in the exchange to make purchases or sales of stocks or bonds for their clients. For this service they charge a small commission. Speculation in securities is very active, and is facilitated by the financial news printed in newspapers and special news services, by the publicity of accounts required of corporations whose securities are listed on the exchanges, and by the elaborate system of telegraphic communication which has been developed, by which transactions in the exchanges and important bits of business news (as well as gossip) are quickly made known in brokers' offices throughout the country. It is not necessary here to enter into a detailed discussion of the nature of stock transactions or of the machinery for carrying them on; we are interested primarily in their functions and social significance.

Corporate securities are not like such commodities as cotton or wheat, which are produced in seasonal supplies of unequal volume which must be spread out more smoothly for their efficient utilization. Stock speculation does not, therefore, have the stabilizing function on supply which speculation in produce has. Nor does it provide facilities for the shifting of business risks to specialists by hedging and dealing in futures to the same extent as speculation in produce does, although there is some hedging of one type of security against another.

Two other useful social functions are claimed for it, however. The existence of an organized market, where securities can readily be turned into cash, is undoubtedly an encouragement and guide to investors. Persons would hesitate to invest their savings permanently in industrial capital if there were no assurance that they could withdraw them and use them in other ways if they so desired. The stock exchange enables them to do this, and it indicates also which securities are likely to prove the most sound investments. There are always speculators who stand ready to buy securities, and a variation of a few points in the prevailing price will bring out more buyers or more sellers who are willing to take a chance on a well-known stock or bond. Hence, the salability of listed securities is assured, and investment in them thereby attracted. The various brokers and bankers who deal in securities also maintain a market for the stocks and bonds not listed on the exchanges. This market is less well organized and the salability of such securities at favorable prices is not so certain, but to a considerable degree it performs the same function as the exchanges.

Another function claimed for the stock market is that of discounting changes in general business conditions or in the condition of individual enterprises, in much the same way that the produce exchanges discount changes in the demand or supply of produce. That is, it is said that such changes become known to "insiders" and speculators generally before they take place; speculators then seek to take advantage of their knowledge by buying or selling the securities likely to be affected favorably or adversely by the expected change. This buying and selling raises or lowers the price of the securities. When the event takes place, the price of the securities has already been adjusted to it, and the sudden change in their value which would otherwise occur is by this discounting prevented. To some extent this discounting makes it possible, by watching the trend of stock prices, to anticipate certain changes in business. This principle is utilized by the various agencies now engaged in business forecasting. The discounting is also of use to bankers and business men in their lending and borrowing operations, which are an important phase of business activities. Borrowers frequently pledge stocks or bonds to lenders as security for repayment of their loans. If these securities were subject to sudden large fluctuations in price, lenders would be liable to losses from which they are now protected. The daily quotations of the prices of securities listed on the stock exchanges enable banks to know at all times just how well protected their loans are; hence they prefer listed securities.

Against these advantages of the stock exchanges, however, must be set certain useless and wasteful features of their activity. There is much dabbling in stock speculation by ill-informed outsiders, which interferes with the proper functioning of the exchanges. There is downright gambling, in the form of betting on changes in the prices of stocks. Sometimes, too, there is manipulation of securities on the part of powerful interests who can buy or sell enough shares of certain stocks to raise or depress their prices for purposes of their own. Such manipulation deliberately creates price fluctuations which would not otherwise exist, and this must be offset against the stabilizing effect of more legitimate dealing. Because of these features, some of the activities of stock exchanges must be classed as unproductive.

In order to stop some of the more flagrant abuses of the speculative markets, the federal government in this country now has regulative machinery to supervise their activities. This consists of the Commodity Exchange Commission, to regulate the produce exchanges, and the Securities and Exchange Commission, to exercise control over stock exchanges and dealers in securities. While these agencies are doing good work, they can hardly be expected to stamp out all of the undesirable practices which crop into speculative dealings.

Speculation in Land. — The speculator in produce and securities depends for his gains on price changes over a relatively short period. Land speculators must make large, permanent investments and may wait a long time for their profit. In a growing country the increase in population tends gradually to raise land values; hence there is an almost certain gain and very little risk of loss involved in land ownership. Land in some localities may decline in value, but this is the exception and not the rule. The speculator must take a risk as to the rapidity of the rise, however, and there is always the chance that business development will not take the direction he anticipates. If the land does not increase in value fast enough, the gains may not be sufficient to pay interest on the investment during the period of waiting; but if, as is usually the case, the land is put to some productive use in the meantime, it can be made to pay the interest while the process of value accretion is going on. Land in and near fast-growing cities rises rapidly to fabulous values, and many great fortunes have been built up by the lucky owners of building sites in the heart of New York, Philadelphia, Chicago, and other industrial centers. Owners of farm lands and sites used for other purposes frequently carry on their enterprises for years at very moderate returns, depending on the rising value of their land to bring them more substantial profits. Land speculation is thus frequently associated with ordinary business undertakings.

Economists have usually regarded the land speculator as performing no socially advantageous function. He does not create the values by which he benefits, and his merely holding land does not produce any utility for others. Moreover, where he keeps land in idleness for speculative purposes, he is withdrawing from production a resource

that otherwise might be improved and productively employed. It has
been said in his defense, that if the land is not being used now because
the improvements which would have to be made on it for such use
would interfere with a more valuable use in the future, it is to the advantage of the community that it should be held for this more valuable
purpose. The argument is weak, however, for it is seldom that the productive use of land now would interfere with its still more productive
employment later. For the reasons which have been set forth, therefore, we must regard speculation in land as being very different in its
nature and functions from the other types of speculation which have
been described.

Speculation and Arbitrage. — Speculation is so often associated
with arbitrage that they are sometimes thought of as different phases
of the same thing. There is, however, an essential difference between
them. Speculation consists in buying at one time and selling at another, to take advantage of changes in prices in the interval; while
arbitrage consists in buying and selling the same commodity at the
same time, but in two different markets, to take advantage of differences in the price of the commodity in the two places at the same instant. The first helps to stabilize supplies of a commodity over a period
of time, thereby creating time utility, and to stabilize prices, thereby
reducing risks; the second helps to equalize the supplies of a commodity (relative to the demands for it) in different places, and thereby
creates place utility. Both operations are greatly facilitated by the
existence of organized produce and stock exchanges, and traders on
these exchanges engage in both sorts of transactions. In fact, both operations may be involved in a single deal. Suppose, for instance, that
the price of September wheat (in July) is higher in Boston than in
New York. A trader could then make a profit by buying wheat for
September delivery in New York and selling for delivery at the same
time in Boston (provided the difference in price would more than
cover transportation costs). Here both the time and place element is
involved. It is both a speculative and an arbitrage transaction.

Gambling. — At first thought it may seem that insurance and speculation are simply forms of gambling. When a company insures a house
against fire, is it not making a bet with the owner that the house will
not burn? When a speculator buys wheat on a futures contract, is he
not making a bet with the seller that the wheat will rise or fall in price,
as the case may be? While there is this superficial resemblance, gambling differs from these two types of transaction both in its nature and
in its social consequences. When two gamblers make a bet, what the
one gains the other must lose. There is thus a transfer of wealth which
is of no benefit to society, for it leaves it no richer than before. More-

over, by leading the gamblers to seek this apparently easy way of increasing their prosperity, it withdraws them from productive employment, thereby reducing the social income. The gamblers give up a certainty—their present wealth—for an uncertainty—the possibility of gain or loss. A new, avoidable risk is deliberately created. While there may be some exhilaration and enjoyment in this taking of a chance, the evils probably far outweigh this doubtful benefit.

Insurance is very different. Here there is a transfer of an unavoidable risk to a specialist, who, by consolidating a large number of risks, reduces the uncertainty to a practical certainty. For an unknown possible loss there is substituted a definite small cost. There is a transfer of wealth as in the case of gambling, to be sure; but it is accompanied by a reduction of uncertainty which facilitates the conduct of business and is a service to society. Some kinds of insurance do look like gambling, on the surface. When a firm like Lloyd's insures the promoters of a fair against loss from wet weather, or guarantees that a coronation will take place as scheduled, there is no way of calculating the exact hazard involved, so that the transaction looks very much like a wager between the company and the insured. Even in these cases, however, the risks are scattered in so many different directions that the losses in one will pretty surely be offset by the gains in another. Hence, the principle of pooling is applicable, after all.

Speculation, again, differs from gambling in its social consequences. A hedging contract makes possible the transfer of a business risk from an ordinary manufacturer, who is not well able to bear it, to a specialist, the speculator, who, by virtue of his specialization, is in a better position to do so. This not only facilitates the conduct of business, but it actually reduces the degree of uncertainty in industry as a whole, if speculators' expectations and actions are based on superior knowledge. But there are also types of speculation which are little more than gambling. When two speculators are dealing with each other, one selling in anticipation of a fall, the other buying in anticipation of a rise, the transaction is practically a bet between them as to the probable trend of the market. It merely transfers wealth from one to the other without performing any social service, except that it may be regarded as a necessary adjunct and incentive to the more beneficial activities of speculators. Dabblers in the markets, whose transactions are based on no sound knowledge of the commodities they deal in, and who perform no business service, are certainly to be classed as gamblers. Stock speculation is much in the nature of gambling; but it does perform indirectly the useful services that have been referred to. Bucket shops, where a mere pretense of stock selling and buying goes on, no securities actually being exchanged, are merely betting establishments. Their business is not properly to be dignified by the term speculation, but is gambling pure and simple. Such establishments are unlawful.

Summary

Our study in this chapter has shown that risks of many kinds are very prevalent in industry. In the first instance these risks fall in part upon enterprisers, because of their responsible position as directors of business operations. They also fall partly upon capitalists, and in part upon laborers. These individuals may deal with the risks in one of three general ways: (1) eliminating them by research and prevention; (2) transferring them to specialists by insurance, hedging, contracting out, or similar means; (3) assuming them themselves. In the long run, all non-preventable risks must be assumed by somebody.

In insurance, it is possible to substitute a small certain loss for a large uncertain one, if a large enough number of risks can be consolidated to permit the accurate computation of average losses. Thus an insurance company can guarantee the losses of its policy-holders without danger and make a profit at the business. Many forms of property, personal, and social insurance have been developed to meet a wide variety of risks. Guaranty and suretyship differ from insurance in that, instead of ascertaining a certain loss by pooling a large number of risks, the surety company assures itself by careful research that little risk exists before granting a policy.

Speculation in produce stabilizes the supply of commodities over periods of time, and reduces business risks by also stabilizing the price. Moreover, by means of hedging contracts, associated with dealings in futures in the well-organized produce exchanges, business men are able to transfer their risks in part to professional speculators. By hedging is meant making a purchase in the trade market coincidental with a sale in the futures market, so that a gain or loss on the one transaction is offset by the other. In this way speculation provides protection from losses due to market changes, much as insurance provides protection from other losses. It is claimed also that, since professional speculators are better informed concerning market conditions than is the average business man, the concentration of market risks in their hands actually reduces them, to the advantage of society. Speculation in stocks and bonds is very similar to speculation in produce, but there is no dealing in futures; hence its functions are different. There is no stabilizing effect on supply, but the market for securities which stock exchanges furnish promotes investment, and it is claimed the discounting function of the stock market smooths the fluctuations in the prices of securities, facilitates business forecasting, and reduces the risks of bankers in making loans on collateral. In this country both commodity and stock exchanges are now regulated by the federal government. Land speculation is different from either of the other types in that the general trend of values is usually upward, but requires a large investment and long waiting for gains. It is not usually regarded as performing any service to the community, the activities of land speculators being classed as unproductive.

Gambling differs from insurance and speculation in that it merely transfers wealth from one person to another without either the reduction of uncertainty or the social advantages of the latter two types of activity. There are forms of both insurance and speculation, however, which virtually amount to gambling, or near it.

REFERENCES AND SUGGESTIONS FOR FURTHER READING

The two volumes which have been of greatest assistance to me in writing this chapter are C. O. Hardy, *Risk and Risk Bearing* (1923) and F. H. Knight, *Risk, Uncertainty and Profit* (1921). The first is a comprehensive survey of the nature of business risks, and of the institutions of insurance and speculation which have developed to take care of them. The second, especially in Chapters 7 and 8, presents a more general statement of risks and the principles underlying risk-bearing, with less description of the technique of insurance and speculation. For a fuller discussion of insurance than that of Hardy consult R. Riegel and H. J. Loman, *Insurance Principles and Practices* (3d edition, 1923). A good analysis of the produce exchanges, and of futures trading, is to be found in J. G. Smith, *Organized Produce Markets* (1922). A thorough description of stock exchanges is that of S. S. Huebner, *The Stock Market* (revised edition, 1934).

The problems of social insurance, with an account of how they have been met in various countries, are discussed in Barbara Armstrong's *Insuring the Essentials* (1932). For a description of the American social insurance system, see Paul H. Douglas, *Social Security in the United States* (1936), or Eveline M. Burns, *Toward Social Security* (1936).

Chapter VIII

THE MONETARY SYSTEM

A. The Nature and Kinds of Money

The Functions of Money. — Under simple economic conditions, such as those which prevailed in the early American colonies, the interchange of products was accomplished largely by barter. The colonial trapper used to bring his furs to the trading post, where he exchanged them directly for the foodstuffs, clothing, and ammunition which he needed. As industry grew more complex, it became increasingly difficult to carry on the operations of exchange in this way. A barter system would be quite impossible today. How impossible it would be for a manufacturer of pins or toothpicks to trade his products directly for radios, automobiles, ocean voyages, and the various other goods which he uses in his daily life! Imagine a United States Steel Corporation which had to trade directly every steel rail, every coil of wire, every girder, for the various commodities needed by its stockholders! It has, therefore, been found convenient to accept some one thing as a medium of exchange. That which is used for this purpose is called money. *Money* may be defined, therefore, as *any generally accepted thing which serves as a medium of exchange.*

This definition indicates that it is the primary function of money to act as a medium of exchange. In this capacity, it aids immensely the operations of commerce. Our manufacturer of pins, who wants potatoes, radios, and pleasure trips, would find it awkward to trade his pins directly for these articles; but when he sells the pins for money, and with the money purchases the things he wants, the transactions are easy enough.

Money also serves as a unit of account by which to compare the values of the goods that enter into trade. This is needed in order to know how many eggs to exchange for a sack of flour, or how many pairs of shoes for a radio. When a common medium of exchange has been adopted, either by law or by general consent, it is possible to express the value of every good in terms of it. When the value of a good is thus expressed in terms of money, it is called a price. For instance, in the United States we have the dollar as our monetary unit. With such a unit the value of any good can be expressed in general terms, so that it can instantly be compared with any other good. Thus it is possible for the producer of eggs, or of shoes, to calculate his income in terms of general purchasing power, and so figure the amount of all other goods which he can obtain in exchange for his own product.

Money, then, has two primary functions—to serve as *a medium of exchange,* and as *a measure of values.* Two additional functions are sometimes stated. Money is used as *a standard of deferred payments,* in terms of which debts may be paid in the future. If one lends to another a thousand dollars today, these dollars constitute a unit for reckoning the amount to be repaid some time hence. Similarly, if an automobile is purchased, to be paid for in installments, the agreement of sale indicates, in terms of money, the amount to be paid in each succeeding month. Money is also used as *a store of purchasing power.* One may save a sum of money, to be used sometime in the future. This may take the form of a hoard (such as paper money stored in a safe deposit box) or of a deposit in one's bank. These last two functions of money are closely allied to its function as a measure of values, and may be regarded as a special case of the latter. Hence, they are secondary to the two primary functions mentioned above.

Commodity Money and Nominal Money. — The thing which is used as money may be some commodity which is so generally desired by the members of the community that they are glad to receive it in exchange for other goods. Examples of this are numerous. Pastoral folk frequently use cattle or sheep as money. Instances of exchanges made in terms of so many head of sheep are mentioned in the Bible. At one time the Romans used iron. Copper and bronze were much employed in former days. In modern times, however, the precious metals—gold and silver, especially the former—have been most widely used. Their general adoption was due mainly to their durability, their malleability (which made it easy to stamp them into coins), and their great value.

However, it is not necessary for money to consist of a commodity. It may be a merely nominal unit of account, which has no value apart from its monetary use. A British economist [1] cites the case of the island of Uap, whose savage inhabitants kept account of their wealth by making identifying marks on certain large, immovable rocks found there. Large sums were transferred from one islander to another by the

[1] D. H. Robertson, in *Money* (revised edition, 1929), p. 159.

simple process of shifting ownership of these rocks, indicated by changing the markings. Certain African tribes use a conventionalized type of throwing knife as their medium of exchange. The knives are made especially for monetary purposes, and are not suitable for cutting or throwing. The American Indians used wampum, consisting of strings or bands of beads, arranged in intricate patterns. The fact that beads were also used for ornamentation (though not in the form of wampum) may be said to give this money something of a commodity character, but it was largely nominal. Among modern peoples, paper money is much employed. Where (as is frequently the case) this paper is a form of promissory note, issued by banks or the government, entitling the holder to receive gold or silver in exchange for it, the money still retains a commodity basis; but situations sometimes arise in which the paper is not redeemable in metallic money, yet it continues to be used as the medium of exchange. In such cases it is nominal.

The distinction between commodity and nominal currencies has led to two opposing theories concerning the fundamental nature of money. The first of these, which may be called the commodity theory, holds that money originates in the frequent employment of some commodity which is well suited to be a medium of exchange, and that the money derives its value from that of the commodity on which it is based. Some support for this theory is to be found in the fact that until recently most monetary systems were based on gold or silver, other forms of money, such as paper, being redeemable therein. The second view, which may be called the nominalist theory, holds that money originates in the adoption of a certain medium of exchange either by the authority of the state, or by general business usage. Money is thus a mere claim, or sort of ticket, which derives its validity from the fact that custom and law have sanctioned its use. Its value is measured by what it will buy, and depends on the amount of it in relation to the goods for which it is exchanged.[2]

Historically, modern monetary systems appear to have begun on a commodity basis, but to be evolving towards a nominal currency. At the time of the Industrial Revolution, gold and silver money came into general use because those metals were a universally desired commodity that proved very suitable for monetary purposes. Gradually, however, there was increased use of paper money, and, in still more recent times, of checks drawn against bank deposits. We shall see that the connection between these last two forms of money and the gold and silver on which they are supposed to be based is growing

[2] See the further discussion of the value of money in Chapter X.

more and more tenuous, so that the time may not be far distant when commodity money will disappear entirely, and only nominal money remain.

Coinage. — When metals first came into use as money they were handled in bulk, and weighed out by the pennyweight, ounce, or other unit, as the occasion demanded. During the days of the gold rush in California the precious dust was carried about in bags, and payments were made with it by weight. Such a method is inconvenient, however, for it allows uncertainty as to the accuracy of the scales, or the purity of the metal, and it permits opportunity for deception. The use of stamped coins is much more satisfactory; hence it early became established. Where coinage is left in the hands of private parties or of governmental bodies which abuse their power, however, there is still the possibility of short-weight pieces or impure metals. For instance, in China coins used to be issued by many different authorities, much variety in kind and quality of the money existed, and the situation was very confusing. It has become customary, therefore, for national governments to assume a monopoly of coinage, prohibiting it entirely on the part of any other party. This makes possible the issuing of uniform, easily recognized, stamped coins, of guaranteed weight and fineness. The milled edge and stamped surface prevent chipping or "sweating" the pieces, and provide easy detection of worn or light money. Thus a satisfactory, generally accepted medium of exchange is provided.

Free coinage is said to exist when anyone who has a quantity of the standard money metal may bring it to the government mint and have it converted into coin (or exchanged for paper certificates, redeemable in metal, which may circulate in place of coin). This is equivalent to purchase, by the government, of all the standard metal offered to it, at a fixed price, known as the *mint price,* determined by the weight of metal in the standard monetary unit. In the United States, the standard dollar consists of $15\frac{5}{21}$ grains of gold nine tenths fine (containing, therefore 13.7 grains of pure gold). This weight is $\frac{1}{35}$ of an ounce; hence $35 can be made from each ounce of gold. The mint price of gold in this country is, therefore, $35 an ounce. Prior to 1934 there was free and unlimited coinage of gold in the United States, but in that year this policy was somewhat modified. Now only licensed persons may bring gold to the mints, and they receive in exchange for it neither gold coin nor gold certificates, but other forms of paper money, which will presently be explained.

Sometimes governments make a charge for coining metal. Where the charge is large enough to cover more than the cost of the coining operation, so that it brings a profit to the government, it is called a *seigniorage.* In former times seigniorage used to be a considerable source of revenue to princes and others who had the privilege of coining money. Today a large seigniorage is not often charged. Frequently, however, a small fee is exacted, sufficient to cover the cost of turning the metal into coin. This is known as a *brassage* fee. In other countries, no fee at all is charged; coinage is then said to be *gratuitous.* The United States government makes a charge for assaying and refining metal brought to the mints, and also a small brassage fee for exchanging money for gold or vice versa. There is a large seigniorage in the case of silver.

We now see one way in which money gets into circulation. Various individuals come into possession of gold or silver. They may be the proprietors of mines, who have the precious metal as the product of their business; or, they may be exporters or bankers, who have received it from abroad in payment for debts owed to them. They sell it to the government and receive newly issued gold or silver coin, or other forms of money, in exchange for it. They spend the money so received, and it thereby passes into general circulation. Governments may also initiate the circulation of money in other ways, by the purchase and coinage of silver or other monetary metals, or by the simple process of printing and spending paper notes, as we shall see. In the next chapter, it will be shown that banks likewise play an important part in the issuing of certain kinds of money.

Subsidiary Coinage. — To facilitate exchanges involving small sums, a system of petty currency is needed. Gold is so valuable that gold coins of small denominations are too tiny to be practicable. Paper money in small sums is likewise inconvenient, although it has sometimes been used. Ordinarily, however, coins of silver, copper, or bronze are provided for this purpose. These coins are generally overvalued, in the sense that the metal they contain is not worth, as metal, the face value represented by the coin. A silver half dollar does not contain fifty cents' worth of silver; the copper in a cent is not worth one hundredth of a dollar. Yet these coins circulate readily at their face value. They are accepted, firstly, because they are useful, and, as the government has a monopoly of coinage, no other token money is available. Secondly, the government will usually replace them with money of larger denominations if presented to it for redemption. In this country, the government will redeem subsidiary coins if offered in amounts of twenty dollars or multiples thereof. A fund is frequently maintained for this purpose. The redeemability of the coins, and the fact that they are limited in quantity to the amounts actually needed for petty transactions, are the principal reasons for their circulation at their face value.

Convertible Paper Money. — It has been pointed out that the use of paper substitutes for metallic money has become widespread in recent times. This paper money may be divided into two general classes: convertible and inconvertible. We shall consider the former first.

By *convertible paper money* is meant *paper that is redeemable in specie (i.e., metallic money) if the holder so desires.* This kind of money may be issued by a government, or by banks. Its convertibility is maintained by providing a specie reserve for the purpose of redeeming the bills. Convertible money may be issued because of its convenience, or as a source of profit. How it achieves these effects will be made clear by a consideration of some of the different kinds of it which are to be found.

The *gold and silver certificates* of the United States are a type of paper money issued because of their great convenience. Gold and silver money is heavy and bulky to carry about. It is subject to wear, so that it becomes light in weight. Our government, therefore, issues certificates in the form of paper which circulate instead of the coins themselves, the actual gold or silver which they represent being kept in the national treasury in the form of bullion (*i. e.*, stamped bars) or coin. The certificate states on its face: "This certifies that there have been deposited in the treasury of the United States of America ten dollars (or whatever the sum may be) in gold (or silver) coin, payable to the bearer on demand." [3]

Somewhat different are *government notes*. These are promises to pay on the part of the government, against which a redemption fund in coin or bullion is maintained, but it need not be to the full amount of the notes outstanding. The government relies upon the fact that so long as it is generally known that the notes are convertible, people will accept them freely at their face value, and will not often present them for payment. Since only a few are likely to be presented at a time, it needs only to hold a substantial sum in reserve to meet calls upon it when they arise. When the notes are presented for payment they can be reissued, and thus remain in circulation in undiminished volume. The issuing of notes of this kind is a source of profit to the government that makes use of them. It obtains the full purchasing power represented by the notes, and has to deposit only a portion of this amount as security. The difference between these two sums is a sort of loan it obtains free of interest, and without any cost other than that of engraving and printing the notes. Our government has had nearly $350,000,000 of such notes (known as United States Notes) out-

[3] Since the financial crisis of 1933 gold certificates have not been permitted to circulate generally, being held exclusively by Federal Reserve Banks, and they have been redeemable in gold only under certain restrictions. Silver certificates are still in general circulation.

standing since shortly after the Civil War. Against them it retains a redemption fund of about $150,000,000 in specie.

Banks issue bank notes in much the same manner. One of the chief purposes for which a bank exists is to lend money. If it can print its own notes, and get people to accept them as money, it can earn interest on the notes so loaned, and thereby derive profit. If people have confidence in the integrity of the bank, these notes will circulate freely like other money. In most countries the issuing of bank notes is regulated by law and the banks maintain a reserve of cash with which to redeem the notes when presented for payment; thus their security is amply provided for. Where not regulated by law, banks can abuse the privilege of issuing notes, flooding the country with worthless paper currency, as we found out by bitter experience in this country in the days of "wildcat" state banks. Where there are legal safeguards governing bank note issues, and ample security is required in the shape of cash reserves and other backing, the holders are protected against loss of the money represented by the notes, and they circulate freely. We shall learn more about them in the following chapter.

Inconvertible Paper Money. — Suppose a government is in need of funds which it cannot raise conveniently either by taxation or by the issuing of bonds. In time of war, for instance, it may become necessary to strain every available financial resource in order to secure means with which to purchase munitions and supplies. Under these circumstances governments frequently resort to the printing of paper money, which supplies them with the needed purchasing power. Such money is usually a kind of promissory note, pledging the credit of the nation to the payment of the sum specified on its face. Because of the circumstances under which the notes are issued, however, the government is not prepared to redeem them immediately. It may have the intention of exchanging them for specie at some time in the future, when its financial resources are stronger, but frequently they are never redeemed at all. Such money is called *inconvertible money*.

Inconvertible paper money is accepted by the people, and circulates readily in all kinds of business transactions, partly because the government makes it full legal tender, which means that creditors must accept it in payment for debts. It is, therefore, a kind of forced loan imposed upon the people. The holders of this paper are really creditors of the government; in accepting it they are making the government a loan, but they have no choice in the matter. Because it thus circulates by command, or fiat, of the state, it is often called *fiat money*. Furthermore, the people may have confidence in their government, and believe that the promise to redeem the notes in specie will eventually be carried out. However, if the notes have been issued in enormous amounts, as they sometimes are, it is apparent that they can never be redeemed; yet they continue to circulate. Indeed, there are cases where the paper no longer has even the form of a promise to pay specie, but is put out merely as a ticket, representing a certain number of units of currency. These cases reveal that the basic reason for the acceptance of paper money lies in the need for some kind of medium of exchange, and in the established habit of using paper, perhaps of the convertible kind, in the past. They are an instance of a purely nominal currency.

Bank Deposit Money. — In England during the seventeenth century, when gold and silver were much more used in actual monetary circulation than they now are, people of means had considerable stocks of monetary gold to take care of. Since the goldsmiths of that period had facilities for storage of the precious metals, many such people entrusted their gold to them for its protection, accepting a receipt as evidence that they had a certain amount of the metal on deposit. It then became the practice to make payments to others by writing out orders on the goldsmiths for the transfer to the payees of a certain amount of the gold so deposited. In many cases, the payees were content to leave the gold in the safe-keeping of the goldsmiths, transferring ownership thereof to other payees, by giving the latter, in turn, orders on the goldsmiths for payment. So, the gold lay safely in storage, while written orders for payment circulated in its stead. In the growth of this practice, an important step was taken away from a commodity money and towards a nominal one.

At first, the business of receiving gold deposits and transferring title thereto was merely a sideline to the goldsmiths' trade; but in time it became so important that special institutions were established to handle it. In this way banks of deposit came into existence. The orders, transferring title to deposits of gold, developed into bank checks. Today, the use of such checks has grown to the point where they exceed in importance all other forms of money. It is estimated that in the United States this means of payment is used in fully nine-tenths of all exchange transactions, instead of using specie or paper money. As a result, the banks have come to play a unique and significant rôle in our economy which merits very careful analysis. We shall make it the subject of a separate chapter, immediately following the present one.

It is convenient to have a terminology by which bank deposits can be distinguished from other kinds of money. For this purpose, we shall use the term *cash* to denote metallic and paper money, *deposit money* to denote bank deposits against which checks can be drawn.

The Distribution of Monetary Metals. — The purchasing power, or value, of money, is reflected in the prices of goods. When the supply of money increases, relatively to the goods for which it is to be exchanged, prices go up, because people in general have more money to offer for the things they purchase. Hence, each dollar (or other unit of money) will buy less than before—its value has decreased. Conversely, if the supply of money decreases in relation to goods, its value will rise, and prices will fall.

Now, when a commodity like gold is used as money, it has value as a commodity as well as in its monetary use. These two values may differ, temporarily. For instance, suppose that the output of gold is increasing, and that, for some reason, nearly all of this gold is going into monetary use, relatively little of it going into the jewelry industry. The increase in money will cause prices generally to rise, and the price of gold jewelry will go up correspondingly. Gold as money will then be falling in value, while gold used in jewelry will be getting more valuable, so that a profit can be made by turning monetary gold into jewelry. In this situation, some gold will be withdrawn from the monetary system and put into manufacturing. The supply of money will then decrease, causing prices to fall and the value of gold as money to rise. At the same time the supply of jewelry will increase, causing its price to fall until the value of gold in the two uses is equal. We may conclude that the supply of a commodity used as money tends to be distributed between its monetary and its commodity uses in such a way as to bring its value in both to equality.

Something similar takes place when the same commodity is used as money in more than one country. It will be recalled that gold has been so used throughout a large part of the world, and silver in a number of countries. Now the value of gold or silver, as reflected in the general levels of prices in two countries having a common monetary basis, may differ, temporarily. For instance, prices might be relatively higher in Great Britain than in the United States. Gold, when converted into money, would then be more valuable in this country than in Great Britain. There would be a tendency, therefore, for gold to be withdrawn from the monetary circulation in Great Britain and to be brought into this country where it would buy more; that is, British people would buy American goods, because of our low prices. As the supply of money thus became scarcer in Great Britain and more plentiful in the United States, prices would fall over there and rise here, until monetary gold had the same purchasing power in both countries. We may conclude that the supply of a monetary commodity tends to distribute itself among the various countries which use it as money in such a way as to bring its purchasing power in all of them to equality. It follows that prices move up and down together in countries whose monetary basis is gold, and there is a similar correspondence in the price movements of those countries whose monetary basis is silver.

Gresham's Law. — An important corollary, known as Gresham's law, follows from the principle just explained. Suppose that a great deal of paper money is issued in a country that has hitherto been using gold as money. The increase in the supply of money occasioned by the issue of paper will cause prices to rise, and the purchasing power of money to fall. This means that the value of gold, as money, will fall too; but its value in the arts (*i.e.,* for industrial uses, such as jewelry) and in other countries, will be no less than before. In such a situation, the paper money is said to be overvalued, because it is represented in the monetary system as being equal in value to gold (which it is not, in fact), and the gold money is said to be undervalued, because it is represented in the monetary system as being no more valuable than paper money (when, in fact, it is). The paper money is also said to be "cheap" money, and the gold "dear" money, because the former can be issued very cheaply, but the latter depends on the costly process of obtaining gold. Now, under the circumstances given, people who have gold metal will not bring it to the mint for coinage, because they can get more money for it by selling it to industrial users, or by importing goods from abroad (where prices are lower) and selling them here (where prices are higher). Likewise, people who have gold coin, or who can get it in exchange for paper money (if the latter is convertible) will find it profitable to melt down the coin and sell it as metal to jewelers, or export it abroad. If the issue of paper is great enough in volume, this may go on until all the gold disappears from monetary use.

The same thing can happen when two different commodity moneys, such as gold and silver, are used side by side. The two monetary units (*e.g.,* the gold and the silver dollar) may have the same face value, but the values of the metals contained in them, in the market where they are used as metal or in other parts of the world, may differ. One of the coins will then be overvalued, the other undervalued. The undervalued metal will tend to disappear from monetary use, since it will move toward that use where its value is greatest. This will be made clearer in the discussion of bimetallism, below.

The principle just explained is called Gresham's law, because it was first enunciated by Sir Thomas Gresham, a British merchant of the sixteenth century. It may be formally stated as follows: *overvalued money tends to drive undervalued money out of circulation.* Or, one may say, cheap money tends to drive dear money out of circulation.

B. Types of Monetary Systems

Standard Money. — Where a number of different kinds of money—gold, silver, paper, and bank checks—are used simultaneously, a chaotic situation is likely to develop, unless some provision is made to maintain parity between them. If the various moneys represent different units of value, prices for the same commodity may differ according to the particular unit in terms of which they are expressed, and, like the bank tellers of China, one would have to be an expert in all the various kinds of currency in use in order to transact business satisfactorily. To avoid such confusion, most countries have adopted by law a definite unit to serve as the standard in terms of which payments are to be made. In the United States this standard is the gold dollar, defined as a certain weight of gold, and all prices and exchange transactions are expressed in terms of it. Similarly, Great Britain has the pound sterling, France the franc, Germany the mark, and so on. To ensure actual use of the standard by the people, the government maintains a monopoly of, or strictly regulates, its issue, so that no rival medium of exchange can readily displace it. Furthermore, it is made full legal tender by the state, which means that payment of a debt in the standard money will be accepted as valid by the courts, so that the creditor must accept it. Custom also plays a part; when people once get accustomed to the use of a certain money unit, it comes to be taken by everyone, without much thought as to what it represents.

The Automatic Gold Standard. — Prior to the first World War, most of the nations of advance economic development had adopted a gold monetary unit as their standard. All other kinds of money in each country were kept at par with this standard by an undertaking, on the part of the government and the banks, to exchange them for gold at their face value on demand. Furthermore, gold was permitted to flow into or out of the monetary system at the will of the holder, without any restriction from the government. This allowed free play for the operation of the principles above explained, by which gold tends to distribute itself throughout the world in a manner that equalizes its value. Since all other forms of money were convertible into gold, the quantities of such moneys issued were somewhat limited by the amount of gold in each monetary system. Consequently, the whole monetary system was regulated by the movement of gold into and out of it. In all the gold standard countries, prices moved up and down together in rough correspondence. It is this automatic system that is commonly meant when the term *gold standard* is used.

Two conditions are essential to the maintenance of the gold standard in the sense of the self-regulating system just explained. The first of these is that gold must be permitted to enter freely into monetary circulation. Anyone who holds gold must be permitted to bring it to the mint in unlimited quantities, and have it converted into coin, or receive in exchange its equivalent in paper money. The second is the complete convertibility of all other forms of money. Holders of any kind of money must be able to obtain its face value in gold coin or bullion [4] and to remove this gold from the monetary system for other uses —for the arts, for exportation abroad, or for hoarding, as they desire. If these conditions prevail, the whole monetary system will be based upon gold, and the value of the money-unit will be equal to that of the gold in terms of which it is defined. This gives the currency something of a commodity basis, although the various other kinds of money erected thereon may be so much greater in quantity than the gold money that the connection may be, in fact, a rather tenuous one.

Where several nations have gold standard monetary systems, the movements of gold between them in payment for goods imported and exported have important repercussions which we shall need to consider when we come to the subject of international trade.

The Automatic Silver Standard. — A few nations of Asia and Latin America have based their monetary systems upon a standard silver unit, instead of gold. An automatic silver standard has identically the same characteristics as the gold standard, except that silver is used in place of gold.

The Managed Gold Standard. — Since the first World War, gold has come to occupy a less important place in the world's monetary systems. In order to meet the huge expenditures necessary to carry on that conflict, the governments of the warring powers found it necessary to issue paper money in such quantities that it was not possible to redeem it in gold upon demand. Therefore, the second of the above conditions for the maintenance of a gold standard (convertibility of all other moneys into gold) could not be met, and the gold standard was suspended. The standard money then became, in fact, a nominal paper unit.

Some of these countries afterwards returned to gold; but no nation in the world today (1941) maintains a genuinely automatic gold standard. They have considerable stocks of monetary gold, but the paper and bank deposit money which circulate cannot be redeemed in the

---

[4] A distinction is sometimes drawn between a *gold circulation standard,* in which other kinds of money are convertible into gold coin, which circulates from hand to hand, and a *gold bullion standard,* in which other kinds of money can be converted only into stamped bars, or ingots, of gold of guaranteed weight and fineness, known as bullion. These bars contain several thousand dollars worth of gold, so that money is convertible only when presented in large sums. The gold bullion system, nevertheless, preserves the parity of money with gold and meets all the essential conditions for an automatic gold standard.

yellow metal except under certain restrictions. The reason for these restrictions is that, under an automatic gold standard, fluctuations in the monetary circulation, with consequent repercussions on price movements, business activity, and the fiscal situation of a government, depend partly on what is going on in other gold standard countries. The political and economic conditions of many nations since the first World War have been so disturbed that each country has tried to isolate itself from disturbances initiated elsewhere by making its monetary system less responsive to gold. In this country it is no longer legal to own gold; it must all be sold to the government. But the government will release gold under special license to those who use it in the arts, or who need it to pay debts abroad. Thus, while our dollar is defined in terms of gold, and while there are huge reserves of gold back of our monetary system, there is not free convertibility of the currency, and our monetary system is not fully responsive to gold movements. It is a kind of "managed" gold standard.

The Gold Exchange Standard. — In the period following the first World War, some countries, wishing to attain a virtual gold standard monetary system, but desiring to avoid the expense of acquiring and maintaining large gold reserves, adopted a *gold exchange standard*. This is an arrangement by which the government undertakes to redeem its money, not in gold, but in drafts upon some country which maintains a genuine gold standard. India, for instance, had such a standard for a number of years. The holder of Indian rupees could secure from the Indian government orders for payment in London (known as London drafts), where gold could be obtained for them. In order to maintain such a system, the government must have funds on deposit in the gold standard country against which it can draw. It can secure these in any of three ways. Firstly, it may borrow from banks in the gold standard country. Secondly, it may purchase, in its own financial markets, securities of that country. These it can sell in the gold standard country if need be, and deposit the proceeds. Finally, it can purchase, again in its own financial markets, drafts drawn upon the gold standard country arising out of exports. In the case of India, for instance, Indian merchants usually sell more goods in Great Britain than they buy therefrom, so that they have excess claims upon British debtors, payable in London. These claims take the form of negotiable drafts, calling upon the debtors to make specified payments. The Indian government buys enough of these claims to meet demands for English drafts by holders of its currency. Thus it appears that the monetary reserves of the gold exchange system consist partly of deposits abroad, and partly of foreign securities and drafts in the possession of the government. There may also be small gold reserves.

The effect of this system is to keep the currency of the country which adopts it on a par with gold, the same as if a genuine automatic gold standard prevailed. It makes the gold reserves of the gold standard countries, in effect, reserves for the gold exchange countries as well. This is not altogether an advantage to the former, for it places their specie reserves somewhat at the mercy of conditions in the satellite countries.

Bimetallism. — At various times different countries have tried the experiment of having two standard moneys—gold and silver. This double standard monetary system is known as bimetallism. *Bimetallism is the free and unlimited coinage of both gold and silver, at a legally established ratio, with both made full legal tender.* This means that anyone who has either gold or silver bullion may bring it to the mint in unlimited quantities and have it coined. These coins are both recognized as standard money, which will be recognized as legal by the courts, and must be accepted by creditors in payment for debts.

Where bimetallism exists there must be established a definite ratio of value between the two metals when used for monetary purposes. The two metals, naturally, have different values. But if both are to be used as money it is desirable to have two standard coins which are interchangeable with each other. Thus if bimetallism existed in the United States (which it does not), there would be a standard silver dollar and a standard gold dollar, both of which would be recognized as of equivalent value in payment for debts. The government must decide what weights of their respective metals the two coins shall contain. In practice these weights should approximate the market value of the two metals as commodities. If gold is thirty times as valuable as silver, a silver dollar should contain thirty times as much silver as the gold dollar. The ratio thus established is known as the *mint ratio.* In the example we have chosen the mint ratio would be 30 to 1. This means that the government recognizes the value of gold as being thirty times that of silver for monetary purposes, and governs the weights of the two standard coins accordingly.

It will be observed that the mint ratio is based closely on the *market ratio,* that is, on the relative values of the two metals as commodities in the markets where precious metals are bought and sold for manufacturing purposes. If the monetary system is to have any stability, the mint ratio must be fixed permanently, or at least for a considerable period of time. Otherwise the weights of the coins would have to be changed frequently, causing coins of different weights to be circulating side by side and introducing hopeless confusion into the monetary system. But the market ratio is not stable. It fluctuates from day to day and from month to month, according to the ever-changing conditions of supply and demand for the two metals. In consequence, the mint price of the two metals is sure to overvalue one of them, and undervalue the other. This makes it practically impossible to maintain both standard coins in circulation. Let us see why this is so.

Suppose that bimetallism existed in the United States with the mint ratio 30 to 1 at a time when the market ratio was 25 to 1. Then anyone who possessed twenty-five ounces of silver could sell it in the market for an ounce of gold. This he could take to the mint and have converted into $35 in gold coin (assuming the weight of a gold dollar to be the same as now). If he took his twenty-five ounces of silver to the mint he would get less than $35 in silver coin, because at the prevailing mint ratio thirty ounces of silver would be required to produce as many dollars as one ounce of gold. Therefore, it would be more profitable for the holder of silver to exchange it for gold in the market, and bring the gold to the mint for coinage, than to have the silver itself coined. His silver brings a higher price in the market than at the mint. At the mint silver is undervalued. Gold is correspondingly overvalued. Under these conditions, no silver would be brought to the mint for coinage. Such silver coins as were already in circulation would tend to disappear. It would be profitable to melt them down and sell the metal for gold, or to ship them out of the country to pay foreign debts, if a good price for silver could be obtained in those countries. In time, only gold coins would remain, and the bimetallic standard would cease to exist in fact. Here we have an instance of the operation of Gresham's law, which was explained above.

Suppose that the market ratio were 35 to 1, instead of 25 to 1, the mint ratio being 30 to 1 as before. The situation is the opposite of that just described. Gold is now undervalued at the mint, and silver is overvalued. It will be profitable for holders of gold to exchange it in the market for silver, bringing the latter to the mint for coinage. For, an ounce of gold in the form of money is worth only $35; but this sum will buy thirty-five ounces of silver in the market, which silver will make more than $35 in coin (35/30 of $35, or $40.84), yielding a substantial profit. Under these circumstances gold coins will disappear from circulation, and only silver will remain.

In theory, if the divergence between the market and the mint ratios is very slight, the effect of bimetallism may be to stabilize the prices of the two metals. For if silver is overvalued, more of it will come to the mint, less of it will remain in the market, and its growing scarcity there will cause its market price to rise. At the same time, gold is disappearing from the mint and appearing in the market, its greater abundance there tending to cause its price to decline. This may go on until the price of silver rises sufficiently and that of gold falls sufficiently for the market ratio to be brought equal to the mint ratio. Thus the mint ratio has a controlling effect on the market ratio. In practice, however, the market ratio varies so far from the mint ratio that all of one of the metals disappears from circulation before the stabilizing effect is produced. The history of experiments with bimetallism in France, in the United States, and elsewhere, has shown that it results in the disappearance of one of the metals from the monetary system altogether. Some economists believe that if bimetallism were internationally adopted this would not occur, as the displaced metal could not disappear into other countries where bimetallism does not exist, and stabilization of the two metals at the mint ratio could be effected.

Silver Money in the United States. The "Limping" Standard. — A unique situation in the use of silver money has long existed in the United States. In several of our western states the mining of silver is an important industry. Therefore, there is strong pressure in Congress from these states for the issuing of overvalued silver money, so that the silver producers can get a higher price for silver from the mint than they could get for it from manufacturing users. Prior to 1896 there was persistent agitation for the adoption of bimetallism at a ratio of 16 to 1 (which would have greatly overvalued the silver) and this became the principal issue of the presidential campaign in that year. The bimetallists (led by William J. Bryan) were defeated, and the country became definitely committed to the gold standard. However, the pressure of the silverites continued strong enough to force Congress to enact legislation from time to time, providing for special purchases of silver at a high mint price and the coinage of this silver into "standard silver dollars," at the above mentioned ratio. The ratio has since become 27 to 1, through a change in the weight of the gold dollar which will presently be explained. In the Great Depression of the post-war period Congress was persuaded to go somewhat further, in the belief that some expansion of the currency, in the form of silver money, would help to stimulate more business activity by raising prices. Accordingly, the Treasury was instructed to buy silver, at specified prices far exceeding the then market ratio, until our stocks of monetary silver should amount to twenty-five per cent of our specie reserves. The government thereupon began buying silver in substantial quantities and issuing silver certificates based thereon, the silver itself being held in the Treasury's possession. A large number of these certificates are now (1941) in circulation.

Although they are designated as "standard" dollars, the situation does not amount to bimetallism, for there is not free and unlimited coinage of silver. It has sometimes been called a "limping" standard.

None of the silver purchase acts caused the issuing of enough silver money to displace the gold, and, prior to 1934 (following a policy laid down in the Gold Standard Act of 1900), our government maintained a gold standard in spite of them, by redeeming silver dollars in gold, at their face value, upon demand. This put the silver dollars, in effect, in the same status as subsidiary coinage. Since 1934, as above explained, none of our money is freely convertible into gold. So long as this policy prevails, the government can hold on to its gold reserves, no matter how much silver money may be issued. The silver policy is, however, generally regarded as a mistaken one by most monetary experts. It adds no element of strength to our monetary system, and it tends to raise prices unduly by making money more plentiful. It amounts to a special subsidy in favor of silver producers, who are paid for their silver more than it is worth, at the expense of the American people, who pay for this subsidy in the higher prices which prevail for commodities generally because of it.

Paper Money Standards. Inflation. — It was stated above that governments occasionally find it expedient to issue inconvertible paper money, especially in time of war. This amounts, in effect, to the abandonment of a specie standard and its replacement by a paper monetary unit of purely nominal character. There is no reason, in theory, why such a paper standard should not function satisfactorily, provided it is wisely managed. Indeed, there are reasons for believing that it is superior in some respects to a currency based on gold.

Hitherto, however, the use of inconvertible paper has been confined, for the most part, to times of financial stress which placed the issuing governments under a strong temptation to abuse it. At such times it is difficult to obtain sufficient funds by taxation or bond issues. It is easy to raise revenue by the simple process of printing "promises" to pay. The result is likely to be the flooding of the country with great issues of fiat currency. This is known as paper money inflation. Let us see what further consequences may follow. We may suppose that the United States government, having previously adhered to a gold standard monetary system, begins to issue large quantities of fiat paper dollars. As paper, these dollars will be practically worthless, but on their face each represents a sum of money equal to a gold dollar. Each will be legal tender for one dollar the same as gold, and the courts will not recognize any difference in their value. At first, moreover, the government may attempt to redeem them in gold upon demand. The paper dollars are overvalued in relation to gold, however, and will tend to drive gold out of circulation, in accordance with Gresham's law.

How the law operates in such a case was explained in an earlier paragraph. It was there shown that, as more paper money is put into circulation, prices rise, so that a dollar (including the gold dollar) will buy less than formerly. If there has been no inflation in foreign countries, however, gold will buy just as much in them as before. Holders of gold coin or bullion will therefore be likely to send it abroad, where it will buy more than here. Also, gold may be withdrawn from monetary to manufacturing uses. The overissue of paper will cause the prices of jewelry and gold leaf to rise along with other prices, so that it will pay holders of paper dollars to exchange them for gold dollars, convert the latter into high-priced gold products, and sell these for a much larger number of dollars. Finally, as gold becomes more scarce, and paper money continues to depreciate in value, holders of gold are likely to store it away for future use, when, they hope, the paper money may be redeemed, and more stable monetary conditions restored. It is to protect themselves against loss of their monetary gold in these ways that governments abandon specie payments and resort to an inconvertible paper standard.

Before the complete disappearance of gold from circulation, *a premium on gold* may arise. At this stage people will offer more than one paper dollar in exchange for a gold dollar, and two prices may be quoted for commodities—a gold price and a paper price. A gold dollar will then buy more than a paper dollar.

All these occurrences have disturbing effects upon business activity which may be very serious. They bring economic loss and discomfort to a great many persons, and may lead to a general business depression. This will be explained more fully in another place. The consequences will be more grave if the rise of prices is rapid and great. The effect of large overissues of paper, therefore, is disastrous to the community where it takes place.

Excessive inflation of the sort described took place in many European countries during and after the first World War. Beginning with small issues, the governments soon found themselves in a vicious circle of inflation; for, as prices rose, the purchasing power of the paper money declined and tax receipts likewise yielded less real income. Hence, the financial authorities were forced to issue still larger quantities of money in order to make up for the deficiency. The successive issues pushed the price level higher and higher, making still larger issues of paper money necessary. In some cases the quantities of money printed and put into circulation were tremendous. In Russia and Germany it passed all bounds, the paper rubles and marks put out running into trillions and quadrillions. Things reached the ridiculous stage where people who received money would run to the nearest store to buy goods with it as quickly as possible, for prices were going up by the hour. Money was so changeable a measure of value that prices were often quoted in terms of commodities, such as eggs, instead of marks or rubles. The situation was chaotic and ruinous to millions whose money incomes did not keep pace with rising prices.

Redemption, Repudiation, and Devaluation. — The results of excessive inflation are so obviously disastrous that, sooner or later, governments come to realize that it must be stopped and a sound and stable currency restored. Then arises a question as to what is the best method of bringing about such restoration. In the opinion of many, the only sound and ethical course for a government to pursue is to redeem its paper money issues in undepreciated money (usually gold). Government notes are nominal promises to pay such money, and failure to redeem these promises is regarded as an evidence of bad faith on the part of the government. Moreover, it is detrimental to the government's credit. If the inflation has not been very severe, this may be the wisest course. The United States succeeded in redeeming its currency, dollar for dollar, after the Civil War, and this greatly strengthened its credit and the world's confidence in the integrity of our government. England was able to do the same thing with its currency after the first World War.

However, the process of redemption is itself disturbing. The government must secure as much gold as possible by purchase, and it must withdraw from circulation such excess of the paper money as cannot be redeemed with whatever gold it is able to obtain. This means that it must borrow, and levy heavy taxes, for its receipts must exceed its expenses by the amount of money that is to be retired. These are difficult financial operations. Moreover, the reduction of the monetary circulation makes money more scarce, and thereby raises its value. There results a fall in prices to somewhere near their original level. This deflation may upset business even more than the inflation which preceded it.

Where the overissue of paper money has been very great, redemption may be quite impossible. The promise to redeem it must then be repudiated, in whole or in part. The discredited money may be outlawed entirely, allowing a new currency, backed by adequate gold reserves, or otherwise restricted in quantity, to take its place. The usual procedure, however, is to redeem the money, not at its face value, but at something like its depreciated value in terms of gold. The American government, after the Revolution, redeemed the paper money issued by the Continental Congress at about one cent on the dollar.

Such a stigma is attached to the term repudiation, however, that in recent monetary reconstruction policies a softer word, devaluation, has been used in its place. The term implies that the money is not repudiated, but is merely revalued in terms of gold, at somewhere near its actual market worth. In most of the European countries this was accomplished by establishing a new standard money unit with a new name, and then setting up a fixed ratio of exchange between the two moneys thus circulating side by side. In time this permitted the governments to replace all of the depreciated currency with the new money at the ratio so established. Devaluation by such methods accomplished the transition from a discredited to a sound currency with a minimum of disturbance.

The "Cheap" Money Fallacy. — The student should now be able to appreciate the importance of the distinction between paper money and wealth, which was emphasized in an earlier chapter. Failure to realize the difference between them is responsible for a great deal of fallacious thinking.

Some persons naïvely imagine that money creates wealth in some miraculous way, and that if the government were only to print enough paper money and distribute it abundantly to everyone we would all be rich. The unhappy experiences of post-war Russia, with its billions upon billions of paper rubles at the very time that its population was starving, is a striking refutation of this reasoning. Printing pieces of paper does not produce bread, build houses, or make clothes. Instead, it only makes those things higher in price, upsets business stability, and causes chaos.

Now it is true that rising prices increase business profits, and rising profits stimulate business activity. This probably justifies a moderate amount of monetary inflation to help bring about business recovery after a depression, for depressions are usually accompanied by a deflation of the currency which causes falling prices and business losses. A reversal of this deflation is merely a return to more normal conditions. But this must not be carried to the point where serious currency depreciation and a feverish rise in prices are likely to take place. Yet many quack reform proposals are based on the mistaken notion that if money can only be made to circulate fast enough, it will so greatly accelerate the pace of business as to bring about a Utopia of general prosperity. For instance, the Townsend old age pension plan, which attracted so much support during the third decade of the present century that it became a serious political movement, proposed that the government pay pensions of $200 a month to all persons over sixty-five years of age, on condition that they would not work, and that they would spend the entire $200 during the month in which it was received! The $200 was to be provided by an arrangement which would have made it virtually a fiat money issue. A very rosy picture of the wondrous results which would follow the adoption of this proposal was painted by its advocates. The truth, however, is that real incomes for the aged on the scale contemplated by this plan would have placed a very heavy burden on the working population. The goods sold to the pension recipients would have to be produced and paid for by the rest of the people. Inflationary money magic could not do away with this necessity and would only work a great deal of mischief.

The Townsend plan was merely one variant of the many monetary panaceas which are proposed from time to time. Others hope to make capital free by having the government lend paper money without interest, forgetful that money is not capital. Still others suppose that the people can escape the burden of taxation by paper money issues, forgetful that the burden of rising prices would be equally, or more, difficult. One cannot lift one's self by one's bootstraps, and this is as good a principle in economics as in physics. If the government needs goods, the people must pay, and no amount of juggling with the currency would suffice to avoid it.

The Monetary System of the United States. — In the foregoing paragraphs, most of the various kinds of money now used in the United States have been described incidentally. In concluding this chapter, however, it will be helpful to review these all together, so that we may have a picture of this country's monetary system as a whole.

Prior to 1933, the standard monetary unit of the United States for many years had been the *gold dollar,* which then consisted of 25.8 grains of gold nine-tenths fine (containing, therefore, 23.22 grains of pure gold). It was freely coined and full legal tender. In 1933 the President was given the power to reduce the weight of gold in the dollar, for the purpose of stimulating our exports (by making our dollar cheaper to foreigners) and of raising our prices. He accordingly reduced it (January, 1934) to $15\frac{5}{21}$ grains of gold nine-tenths fine. It now contains, therefore, 13.7 grains of pure gold. This makes the mint price of gold 35 dollars per ounce. The President is empowered to make further changes, within the limits of 50 to 60 per cent of the old content, at his discretion. In 1933, also, all holders of gold or gold certificates were ordered to surrender them in exchange for other kinds of money, which thereby became virtually inconvertible. The surplus gold released by the devaluation of the dollar was confiscated by the government partly to set up a "stabilization fund" for currency and foreign exchange operations,[5] and partly for other purposes. Although the law states that "all forms of money

[5] These will be described in Chapter XVIII.

issued or coined by the United States shall be maintained at a parity with this standard," we have, in fact, adopted a sort of managed currency. Gold bullion and coin are held by the United States Treasury, and gold certificates by the Federal Reserve Banks, but other kinds of currency cannot be freely exchanged for them. Even the gold certificates are not redeemable without restrictions. Licensed persons may, however, secure gold from the mints for use in the arts, under certain regulations, and the Treasury will also sell gold for export to foreign central banks.

We also have a considerable number of *standard silver dollars,* which have come into circulation through the various acts of purchase mentioned in a previous paragraph. These contain 412.5 grains of silver nine-tenths fine (containing 371.25 grains of fine silver). Their ratio to the present gold dollar is 27 to 1, approximately. They are greatly overvalued. We also have a *subsidiary coinage,* made up of the familiar silver half-dollar, quarter, and dime, the nickel five-cent piece, and the copper cent. All are overvalued, but redeemable at par in money of larger denominations.

The following kinds of paper money are also in existence here:

Gold certificates, secured, dollar for dollar, by gold held in the possession of the government. These certificates do not circulate actively, but are held in the reserves of our Federal Reserve Banks.

Silver certificates, secured, dollar for dollar, by silver held in the possession of the government.

Treasury Notes of 1890—a small remnant of a former issue of government notes, now secured dollar for dollar in silver, and, hence, substantially the same as silver certificates.

United States Notes—the unredeemed remnant of the "greenbacks" issued to help finance the Civil War. A specie reserve of slightly less than half their face value is held against them by the Treasury.

National Bank Notes and *Federal Reserve Bank Notes*—remnants of convertible note issues, secured by a five per cent gold reserve fund and United States government bonds, deposited with the Treasury. These notes are being retired; very few of them remain in circulation.

Federal Reserve Notes—notes issued by the Federal Reserve Banks in a manner to be described in the next chapter. They are secured by a forty per cent reserve of gold certificates and by certain other assets.

Since 1935 all the above kinds of money have been full legal tender.

In addition to these forms of cash, we have the bank deposit money which, as explained earlier, constitutes the bulk of the medium of exchange in this country today. This will be fully described and explained in the following chapter.

SUMMARY

Money is any generally accepted thing which is used as a medium of exchange. Its functions are: to act as a medium of exchange, as a measure of values, and (incidentally to the last) as a standard of deferred payments and a store of purchasing power. Money may consist of some generally acceptable commodity, or of a purely nominal thing, such as paper notes. Our economy is evolving away from a commodity money towards a nominal one. Coinage makes metallic money more convenient and reliable in use. Free coinage exists when anyone can have bullion in unlimited amounts exchanged for money at the mint. The amount of coin or other money that can be got for a given quantity of bullion is called its mint price. A seigniorage or brassage fee may be charged for coinage. Subsidiary coins are issued in small denominations for convenience. Although overvalued, they circulate at par because of their usefulness, limited quantity, and redeemability.

Convertible paper money is issued by governments or banks. When the monetary system is based on specie, such money can be exchanged for gold or silver coin or bullion from a redemption fund kept for that purpose. Inconvertible paper (or fiat) money is a form of government note not redeemable in specie—a nominal currency. Bank deposits, transferred from person to person by checks, constitute the most widely used form of money in modern economic systems.

The monetary metals tend to distribute themselves among the countries that use them, and between their monetary and manufacturing uses, so as to equalize their values everywhere. This tends to make prices move up and down together in those countries whose monetary basis is the same metal (gold or silver, as the case may be). According to Gresham's law, overvalued money tends to drive undervalued money out of circulation.

Standard money is a definite unit established as the legal medium for payment of debts. The automatic gold standard bases the entire monetary system upon a gold unit. To maintain it, there must be free (unlimited) coinage of gold and free convertibility of other forms of money for gold; in short, gold can be introduced into or withdrawn from monetary use at the will of the holder. The automatic silver standard is the same, except that silver is used in place of gold. Managed gold standards (more prevalent today) restrict the flow of gold from and into the monetary system so as to give the government more control. The system is then less responsive to gold movements. A gold exchange standard keeps the currency of a country on a par with gold by the readiness of the government at all times to exchange money for drafts on a gold standard country.

Bimetallism is a monetary system in which there is free (unlimited) coinage of both gold and silver at a legally established ratio. Deviation of the market ratio of the two metals from the mint ratio tends to cause displacement of one of the metals, in accordance with Gresham's law, making the system impossible to maintain, except by international agreement. In the United States a limited number of overvalued "standard" silver dollars have been introduced into the monetary system by special purchases from time to time—a situation sometimes called the "limping" standard.

Although a paper standard is theoretically workable, hitherto it has usually been adopted in times of financial stress which lead to over-issue. The resulting inflation causes the money to depreciate in value, leading to a rise in prices, a premium on gold, and the disappearance of gold from circulation. Sometimes, the money may eventually be redeemed at par (which causes a disturbing period of deflation); but more often the money must be repudiated by redemption in specie at way below its face value, or by devaluation through the issue of a new and more stable money unit, exchangeable for the depreciated currency at a fixed ratio. The idea that large issues of cheap money create wealth and bring other benefits is a mischievous fallacy, although moderate inflation in a period of deflation may be a wholesome influence.

The monetary system of the United States is based on a standard gold dollar, the weight of which is subject to change, within certain limits, by the President. It is a sort of managed gold standard in which other moneys are exchangeable for gold only under certain restrictions and at the will of the Treasury. Other forms of money in this country are: "standard" silver dollars, subsidiary coins, gold and silver certificates, Treasury Notes of 1890, United States Notes, National Bank Notes, Federal Reserve Bank Notes, Federal Reserve Notes and —most important of all—bank deposits.

REFERENCES AND SUGGESTIONS FOR FURTHER READING

D. H. Robertson's *Money* (revised edition, 1929), though brief, is an excellent survey of the subjects discussed in this and the following chapter, written in a very interesting style. For a more formal text, F. Cyril James' *The Economics of Money, Credit and Banking* (3d edition, 1940) may be consulted. Harold G. Moulton's *Financial Organization and the Economic System* (1938) gives a comprehensive description of financial institutions and their operation. The present writer is indebted to Howard S. Ellis for the discussion of the commodity and nominalist theories of money in his *German Monetary Theory* (1934).

The references cited at the close of the next three chapters also have a bearing upon the subject-matter of this one.

Chapter IX

THE BANKING SYSTEM

A. The Nature of Banking Operations

The Functions of Banks. — In the preceding chapter it was shown how our banks grew out of the deposit business which was carried on by the goldsmiths in seventeenth-century England. In the present chapter, we shall examine the operations of these banks in greater detail. We may begin by noting the various functions which banks now perform. There are two primary functions—a loan function and a monetary one.

The loan function can be briefly described as follows: In the carrying on of their operations, business men need to borrow funds with which to purchase the equipment which they require. The banks procure such funds, either from those who have savings to invest or out of their own resources, and lend them to business men. In its purest form, the loan function puts the bank in the position of an intermediary, which gathers together the voluntary savings of many individuals and transfers them to enterprisers, who invest them in equipment of one kind or another. We shall see, however, that the loan function of banks has become so intertwined with their monetary function that the funds supplied by banks do not come wholly from voluntary savings but are, in large part, evolved out of the lending process itself.

The monetary function was partly explained in the preceding chapter. It was there shown how there developed the practice of transferring title to gold deposits from person to person through written orders, which orders thereby became a part of the medium of exchange. The modern counterpart of this mechanism consists of bank deposits which are transferred from person to person by means of checks. We shall learn that these deposits do not necessarily consist of cash put into the banks for safe-keeping, but are a form of nominal money created by the banking system. This aspect of banking operations so overshadows all others that it justifies us in classifying the banks as a part of our monetary system. A considerable part of the present chapter will be devoted to a discussion of these monetary operations.

Aside from the two primary functions just stated, certain kinds of banks perform two other services of a less important sort. The first of these is to act as custodians for the safe-keeping of funds. Most persons do not have facilities for storing large amounts of cash where it will be protected against robbery or fire. Therefore they deposit it in banks which have such facilities. Also, most banks rent safety deposit boxes where valuable papers, jewelry, or other small objects can be safely preserved. The second minor function is a fiduciary one. Many banks will act as trustees for administering large sums of money. For instance, a wealthy man may die, leaving a valuable estate which he wants kept in trust, the income therefrom to be paid to certain beneficiaries named in his will. The bank will take charge of the estate, invest the principal and disburse the funds as directed. Likewise the bank may act as a guardian for the wealth of a minor person. This type of business has developed as a natural corollary of other banking operations because the banks, from their knowledge of investments and with their facilities for handling money, are in a logical position to do this work.

Kinds of Banks. — A certain degree of specialization has taken place in the development of institutions to perform the various functions above described. Accordingly there are several different kinds of banks, known as investment banks, savings banks, commercial banks, and trust companies, respectively.

Investment banks are businesses which provide funds for permanent investments. They supply funds to various enterprises for financing the purchases of durable equipment, such as buildings, machinery, and railway rolling stock. They secure the money for these purposes mostly from well-to-do investors who rely upon them for guidance in investing their savings.

Savings banks are also engaged in financing permanent investments, but they derive their funds mainly from the small savings of people of moderate means. The latter deposit their savings with the banks, which pay them a rather low rate of interest for the use of their savings. The banks then invest the savings in real estate mortgages, bonds, or high grade stocks at a somewhat higher rate of interest, thereby making a profit. The total amount of savings so collected and invested in this country is very large. As savings banks are entrusted with the savings of people to whom loss would be a serious calamity, the law usually limits their use of funds to the safer kinds of investments.

Commercial banks perform both loan and monetary functions. In the past, their loans were mostly for short periods of thirty, sixty, or ninety days. The sums loaned were used by the borrowers primarily to finance the purchase of more perishable forms of equipment, such as raw materials, fuel, and stocks of merchandise, all of which are soon turned into goods which can be sold for cash and thereby make possible repayment of the loans within the short periods indicated. Such loans were also used by business men for advancing wages to their workmen from week to week. This kind of loan still plays a prominent part in the operations of commercial banks, but, in recent years, the latter have used a considerable portion of their funds for long-time investment in ways that will presently be described. These banks also accept demand deposits, against which checks can be drawn. They thus provide the community with an important form of money, as we have already learned. Just how the business of deposit banking is related to the lending operations of commercial banks is a matter which we must examine in considerable detail, in subsequent paragraphs.

Trust companies, as their name implies, exist primarily to act as trustees for funds or other property left in their care for specified purposes. Hence they specialize in the fiduciary function above described, administering the estates of decedents, acting as financial guardians for orphans and minors, dealing in real estate, and so on.

While these various kinds of banks specialize mainly in the types of activity stated, they are not mutually exclusive. Investment and savings banks confine their operations almost entirely to long-time loans, but commercial banks and trust companies are more varied in their activities. Many commercial banks have trust and savings departments in which they carry on trust and investment banking operations. Most trust companies engage in all kinds of banking. Some of them are directly engaged in investment banking, and nearly all of them are also savings and commercial banks.

Investment Banks and Related Institutions. — We need not concern ourselves further with trust companies, but the other kinds, especially investment and commercial banks, must be more fully discussed. It was stated that investment banks confine their operations to the financing of long-time investments. Thus they perform a loan function. Their business can be described as that of dealing in stocks and bonds. They have a circle of clients who depend upon them for advice in the investment of their savings, and to whom the banks sell the securities in which they deal. When a corporation needs to finance the purchase of some durable equipment, it will take its problem to one of these banking firms. The latter will look into the financial standing of the business, its probable future earning capacity, and other matters pertaining to the proposed loan. The bank will then arrange with the corporation to buy an issue of its stocks or bonds, in the expectation that it can resell these to its customers at a profit. The process of undertaking to market an issue of securities for a business enterprise in this way is known as *underwriting*. It puts the bankers in the position of intermediaries between savers, who have surplus incomes to invest, and business enterprisers, who can utilize these savings to advantage in financing the time-consuming processes of production. Very frequently, particularly if the issue of securities is large, a syndicate of associated bankers in different cities will be formed to dispose of them. If their judgment has been wrong, and the public does not buy the securities at the price expected, the bankers may lose. A successful investment banker must be a good judge of business prospects in the branches of industry with which he deals. Since investors rely upon the advice of such bankers to a large extent, the latter exert a considerable influence upon the direction which business developments may take. The larger investment banking firms occasionally handle enormous projects, sometimes of an international character.

Investment banks also act as security brokers; that is, they provide a market through which owners of securities can sell them to other investors, in case the former desire to dispose of their holdings. They also are usually members of the stock exchanges in which securities are bought and sold. These exchanges do not deal in new issues of securities, but only in those which have already been underwritten and on the market for some time. The investment banks buy and sell in the exchanges for their clients. They also rely partly upon the prices of securities prevailing in the exchanges to guide them in determining which lines of business offer the most suitable channels for new investments.

Although they are not listed as banking institutions, insurance companies perform something of an investment banking function. In the course of their business, they accumulate large reserve funds to meet future contingencies that may arise. Endowment policies, for instance, call for the payment of certain lump sums to policy-holders, upon the attainment of certain ages. The insurance companies must gradually set aside sufficient funds to make these payments when they fall due. Hence, these companies are in a position to invest large sums of money in business undertakings. They do this, either directly (as, for instance, in the placing of mortgages on real estate) or indirectly, through brokers and investment bankers. However, insurance companies do not carry on an underwriting business; they invest their funds chiefly in real estate loans, and in stocks or bonds whose soundness has already been established.

Investment does not have to take place through the medium of investment bankers. Enterprisers may appeal directly to the savers of the country, by offering their securities for public subscription, through advertising, through solicitation by mail, and through salesmen. Those businesses which cannot secure financial support from investment bankers are more likely to resort to these methods. The fact that they do so is often, but not always, an indication that the enterprise is a hazardous one. Most of them fail, although many new ventures get their start to success in this way.

Well-established corporations, if successful, often accumulate profits which are not all distributed to their stockholders. The excess constitutes a surplus which may be invested. Frequently it is reinvested in the same business, providing the company with a new plant or other equipment. Here the board of directors of the corporation can be regarded as making a decision on behalf of the stockholders to save their earnings instead of consuming them. This might be described as saving by proxy.

Commercial Banking. — What investment and savings banks do for the long-time investment market, commercial banks do for the short-time market. The distinction between them, therefore, is partly a matter of time. If a business firm has to finance the purchase of expensive, durable equipment, the cost of which cannot be recovered from the proceeds of the business for a period of some years, it secures the funds from an investment bank through an issue of stocks or bonds; or, in the case of an individual borrower, he may mortgage his property to a savings bank or an insurance company. But if the need is for equipment the cost of which can be recovered in the course of a few weeks, the funds can be obtained by borrowing from a commercial bank on a promissory note. Such a loan would be appropriate for the purchase of raw materials, fuel, or stocks of merchandise, or for the payment of wages, where the expenditure will soon give rise to some salable product, receipts from which will be sufficient to repay the loan. Loans of this character ordinarily are for periods of thirty, sixty, or ninety days; but at their expiration they are frequently renewed. If renewed repeatedly, as they may be, the loans in effect run for much longer periods.

Within the present century a number of developments have been going on which blur the distinction between investment and savings banks, as suppliers of long-term loans, on the one hand, and commercial banks, as suppliers of short-term loans, on the other. The practice of renewing loans, just referred to, is one of these developments. There are others of greater importance. For instance, investment bankers, in order to purchase a block of securities for later sale to the investing public, may borrow the necessary funds on short-time loans from commercial banks. Commercial bank funds thus find their way into the long-time market, at least temporarily. So advantageous is this kind of business to both parties, that not a few commercial banks became closely affiliated with investment banks, through holding company or interlocking directorate arrangements, until recent legislation put a curb on such relationships. Moreover, commercial banks sometimes have funds available for which there is an insufficient demand in the short-term loan market. In that case, they find it advisable to invest these funds in securities, or in mortgages on real estate. This puts the funds directly into more or less permanent investments. Commercial banks in this country, however, are not permitted to underwrite new issues of securities. Since the Great Depression which followed the financial collapse of 1929, commercial bank holdings of securities (especially government bonds) have become their most important investments, exceeding in volume their loans to short-time borrowers. This is materially changing the character of commercial banking. The growth in security holdings appears to be due partly to the fact that, in the years of the depression, there was less demand on the part of business men for loans of the usual type, while there was a great demand for loans (secured through bond issues) on the part of state and federal governments for public works projects and relief expenditures. The banks therefore turned their lending power in that direction. Another factor has been the growing practice, on the part of corporations, of meeting their needs for short-time funds by drawing on their own surpluses, instead of by borrowing from banks.

From the foregoing discussion we may conclude that, in so far as their loan function is concerned, commercial banks differ from other banks mainly in the period of time for which loans are made, but that this difference is less sharp than it formerly was. It is in the performance of the monetary function that they differ most sharply from banks of other varieties. Investment and savings banks do not participate in the monetary function, because they do not have deposits subject to check. Investment banks receive funds only for the outright purchase of securities. Savings banks accept deposits, but the nature of these is such that the depositor cannot draw checks against them, payable on demand. He must give the bank notice, usually two weeks or a month in advance, before he can withdraw any part of his money.[1]

---

[1] Some savings banks permit their depositors to draw a limited number of checks in a given time period; but the checking privilege is too restricted, even in these cases, to make such deposits a significant part of the medium of exchange.

This makes it impossible to transfer such deposits freely from hand to hand, so that they cannot be used as money. Such deposits are known as *time deposits*. Commercial banks may have savings departments in which there are time deposits with the same restrictions as those of savings banks. The bulk of their deposit business, however, consists of *demand deposits,* against which checks can be freely drawn. These checks the bank is obligated to honor by immediate payment upon demand. Since the checks are freely negotiable by merely being endorsed upon the back, they can be passed from hand to hand and the deposits themselves can be transferred from person to person by being deducted from one account and credited to another on the books of the banks. It is in this way that commercial banks, unlike all others, provide the community with an important part of its medium of exchange. The nature of demand deposits, and their relation to the lending operations of commercial banks, must now be more fully explained.

Bank Credit. — It should now be clear to the student that business is carried on in large measure with borrowed funds—that is, on credit. In its broadest meaning, credit may be defined as a promise of payment in the future in lieu of immediate payment. We say of a person that "his credit is good" if his promises to pay are accepted by those with whom he has business dealings. When an individual buys an automobile "on time," obtaining immediate use of it by promising to pay for it in installments over a period of some months, his credit has been accepted by the dealer. In a more restricted sense, the term credit is used to denote the evidences of debt which arise out of credit transactions. It would be more accurate to call the latter "credit instruments," but the shorter word, "credit," is more often used. The installment buyer of an auto signs some kind of promissory note when he makes his purchase; the note is an instrument of credit. Many kinds of business documents, such as notes, drafts, and checks, which give evidence that sums of money are payable by one party to another, are likewise credit instruments.

Commercial banks are dealers in credit, in one form or another. *They sell their own credit to their customers*. Looked at from one point of view, their operations consist very largely in an exchange of bank credit for personal credit. An illustration will help to make this clear. Suppose that a wholesale dealer in dry goods sells a thousand dollars' worth of merchandise to a retailer. The latter may not have the funds to make immediate payment. The wholesaler, therefore, accepts his promissory note for the amount for two months, at which time the retailer expects to have sold the goods and will have funds from the proceeds with which to pay for them. The wholesaler now holds the retailer's note for one thousand dollars. This is a form of *personal credit*. Suppose that the wholesaler has debts to meet and does not care to wait until the retailer pays his note. He might pass the note on to his creditors; but the probabilities are that they would be reluctant to take it. They do not know the retailer, are doubtful about his ability or willingness to pay, and do not care to take the responsibility of collecting the thousand dollars from him. Besides, like the wholesaler, they may wish to use the money immediately and cannot wait until the note becomes due. In other words, personal credit is not sufficiently negotiable to be passed around freely; it does not circulate readily. Our wholesaler, therefore, takes the note to his bank. It is the business of the bank to deal in such "commercial paper," as it is called. The wholesaler endorses the note, thereby assuming obligation for its eventual payment by the retailer, and the bank *discounts* it. This means that the bank lends the wholesaler purchasing power to the amount of the note ($1,000), less interest thereon for the time the loan is to run. This deduction for interest is the discount. The purchasing power which the bank lends consists of its own credit. What the wholesaler wants is any form of money power which will be readily accepted in payment of his bills. He cares not whether it is gold, beads, or paper, so long as he can pass it on to his creditors in settlement of his debts. He cannot pass on the retailer's note in that way. But a bank is more or less of a public institution; it is so well known (and in most countries so well safeguarded by law) that people have confidence in it. Its promises to pay will be accepted by everyone without question. They will circulate as money. The bank, therefore, *lends its promise to pay* to the wholesaler. It has exchanged *bank credit* for the personal credit represented by the note. This bank credit is freely negotiable and is a medium of exchange as truly as gold coin. The credit which a bank lends in this way may take one of two forms —bank notes or bank deposits.

Bank Notes. — An important form of bank credit in most countries is the bank note. In the United States, however, it is less used than the bank deposit, and the latter is becoming more general elsewhere in recent years. We have already learned that bank notes are a form of paper money. They are simply the bank's promises to pay to the bearer the amount stipulated on their face. The bank finds it advantageous to lend them, rather than specie, to its customers, because it costs little to issue them, whereas gold and other kinds of money, as everyone knows, cannot be had (even by banks!) for the asking. By lending the notes out at interest the bank derives a profit. The notes circulate as money because of popular confidence in the institution that issues them. In most countries this confidence finds additional justification in the laws regulating banking which limit the amount and conditions of issue of the notes.

Like other promises to pay, bank notes are of value only when the promise is kept. Banks must be prepared to redeem their notes in the standard money of the country if it is demanded. If the standard be gold, holders of the notes may require the banks to exchange them for gold at any time. In practice most persons are satisfied with the paper, but occasionally they may desire gold to pay for goods imported from abroad, or for other purposes. Also, each bank, in the course of its business, receives the notes of other banks. These it is likely to send to the issuing banks for redemption, desiring to lend out only its own notes, on which its profit is greater, and desiring also to keep as large a supply of gold on hand as possible. Thus banks are faced with the necessity of redeeming their notes, and must keep on hand a reserve of specie for the purpose. Since, however, not all the notes will be presented for payment at one time, the reserve need be only a fraction of the total volume of notes outstanding. The reserve is provided out of the capital which the bank has invested in its business and from money deposited by its customers.

Since banks may be tempted to increase their profits by large note issues with small reserves, governments have found it wise to regulate them. Otherwise, the country may be flooded with an inflationary paper currency, with the disastrous results pictured briefly in the preceding chapter, and many banks may fail because of their inability to redeem their notes, thereby undermining popular confidence in banks generally. There was a time when state banks in this country, allowed to do business without adequate supervision, abused the note-issuing privilege in this way. Congress stopped the practice in 1863 by putting a prohibitive tax on note issues of state banks. National banks, however, were permitted to issue notes under suitable restrictions. Regulations along somewhat similar lines usually prevail in other countries. The growing use of checks as a means of payment has caused bank deposits to become the dominant form of bank credit in the past few decades, with a consequent decline in the importance of bank notes. This fact, coupled with certain technical difficulties associated with the national bank notes, caused our government to do away with them. Beginning in 1935, they were gradually retired, by being exchanged for other kinds of money, so that very few of them now remain in circulation. However, a special form of bank note, known as the Federal Reserve Note, still has some importance in our monetary system. It will be explained, in connection with a general description of the Federal Reserve System, in a later part of this chapter.

Demand Deposits. — A demand deposit is in some respects very similar to a bank note, the principal difference between the two being that, in the case of the note, the bank hands the borrower paper money of its own making, whereas, in the case of the deposit, it merely gives him a right to draw checks against it. In the previous example of the wholesaler who had a note discounted at his bank, we said that the bank lent him its credit in return for the note. If the credit took the form of a bank deposit, the bank would simply credit him with a deposit of one thousand dollars, less the discount. This would be recorded as a deposit in the accounts of both the bank and the wholesaler. The latter could then draw checks against this sum from time to time, as his needs required; and the bank, having assumed the obligation, would have to honor these checks for payment. Thus the deposit is a loan of the bank's credit to its customer. The bank derives profit from this transaction, in the form of interest on the loan, and the customer obtains the immediate use of deposit money, which he can use to pay his bills.

The word "deposit" suggests that some kind of cash has been put into the bank, and this is no doubt the conception of a bank deposit held by a great many persons. It should be clear from the above example, however, that a bank deposit does not necessarily have this character. It is merely a form of bank credit. A demand deposit may be defined as *a liability on the part of a bank to pay a certain sum of money on demand to a person known as a depositor*. The liability may arise in any of three ways: (1) Cash may have been left in the bank for safe-keeping, or for the greater convenience of being able to make payments by check. In this case, cash has merely been exchanged for deposit money, which circulates in its stead. There has been no net addition to the monetary circulation. (2) A check, drawn by some other depositor, may have been deposited to a customer's account. Here, the amount of the check is merely deducted from the account of one depositor and credited to that of another. A portion of the former's deposit has changed hands. In this case, also, the total quantity of money is unchanged. (3) The bank may have made a loan to the depositor on a note, in the manner above described. The great majority of bank deposits arise in this way. Now, in this case, the loan extended by the bank may merely take the place of a previous loan to the same or some other borrower which has just been paid off. If so, again there has been merely a transfer, to the new borrower, of money already in existence. But if (as may be the case) the loan represents an addition to the total of bank credit previously in existence, the volume of money has been increased. On the other hand, if loans are repaid by borrowers, and not replaced by others, the deposits built up on these loans pass out of existence, and the volume of money shrinks. Thus the total volume of bank deposits may expand or contract. This phenomenon will presently engage our attention. Prior thereto, however, it will be well to consider further the way in which bank deposits perform the functions of money.

The Circulation of Deposits. — A bank is under obligation to redeem its deposits in standard money (or in some form of cash, other than its own notes, that is convertible into the standard) upon demand. This means that depositors, or the payees of checks drawn against deposits, can demand payment in cash if they care to. In fact, however, they seldom do so. It is safer and more convenient to make payments by checks than by other forms of money, for a check can be made out for the exact sum that is needed, and it can be sent through the mail with very little risk. If lost, it can easily be replaced with another, and there is not much danger of theft, for it can be cashed only on the order of the payee, whose signature it must bear. Consequently, when a person receives a check in payment for something, he does not usually seek to convert it into cash; he merely deposits it to his own credit, and later draws new checks against this deposit. The bank, then, does not have to pay out cash; it merely transfers the sums drawn from the account of one individual to that of another on its books. In this way the deposit (or portions of it) changes hands, and does the work of money. Moreover, before it reaches the bank, the check itself may change hands one or more times, each time being used as a means of payment.

Let us look at an example of this process. Suppose "A" has had a note discounted at his bank for $5,000. He now has a deposit for that amount, less interest. He buys goods to the value of $2,000 from "B," and draws a check for this sum to the order of the latter. "B," in turn buys $2,000 worth of merchandise from "C," and endorses "A's" check over to him. "C" deposits it in the bank. The bank now simply deducts $2,000 from "A's" account and credits it to "C." Part of "A's" deposit has changed hands. *It has circulated.* Two distinct exchange transactions have taken place by means of it, yet no cash at all was used. "A" may go on drawing against his deposit to other persons, who likewise deposit the checks in the bank, until the entire amount has been transferred, without the bank having been called upon to produce any other money.

The Clearing of Checks. — It may happen, however, that the two parties to an exchange of this sort do not deal with the same bank. This is more often the case than not, particularly in large cities where there are many banks. A check may be drawn against one bank and deposited by the payee in a different bank. The latter must now collect payment on the check from the bank on which it was drawn. It can present the check to that bank, and receive cash for it; but the banks have worked out a method by which these payments can largely be done away with, through the cancellation of their mutual obligations to each other. In the course of a day's business every bank receives many checks drawn against other banks. To a very considerable extent these checks offset each other; that is, the claims received by one bank on its neighbors are balanced by counterclaims received by them. The banks of a community, therefore, get together in an institution known as the *clearing house*. Here their representatives meet daily and present the checks they have received drawn against other banks which are members of the clearing house association. The claims and counterclaims are canceled against each other, and the balances are paid in cash. The following is a very much simplified illustration of this procedure:

Suppose three banks, "A," "B," and "C," to be members of a clearing house. At the close of a day's operations their representatives meet and find that:

Bank "A" has checks totaling	$10,000	drawn against Bank "B"
" "A" " " "	6,000	" " " "C"
" "B" " " "	12,000	" " " "A"
" "B" " " "	9,000	" " " "C"
" "C" " " "	7,000	" " " "A"
" "C" " " "	11,000	" " " "B"

The balance sheet of the various banks would then look like this:

			Excess of	
Bank	Credits	Debits	Credits	Debits
"A"	$16,000	$19,000	None	$3,000
"B"	21,000	21,000	None	None
"C"	18,000	15,000	$3,000	None
Totals	$55,000	$55,000	$3,000	$3,000

In this case "A" would pay $3,000 in cash to the clearing house association, and the latter would pay a like amount over to "C." The remaining items entirely offset each other. With $3,000 in cash $55,000 of business has been transacted, and the banks have settled all their mutual indebtedness. Commercial banks in all the large cities clear their obligations to each other by this method of offsetting checks. In the New York Clearing House a tremendous volume of clearings takes place with a surprisingly small amount of cash. Banks not members of a clearing house association can clear their checks through other banks with which they have dealings, and which are members.

In this country there is a growing tendency for bank clearings to

be effected through the Federal Reserve Banks which are located in
twelve important financial centers. Nearly every bank has a deposit
account with one of these Federal Reserve Banks. Hence, checks in
the possession of one bank drawn upon another can be sent to the
Federal Reserve Bank and the amount credited to the deposit of the
bank presenting them. The Federal Reserve Bank then deducts a corresponding amount from the deposit of the bank against whom the
checks were drawn. The latter, in turn, probably has checks to be
credited to it and debited against other banks. So in the Federal Reserve Bank the various obligations of the individual banks to each
other are offset the same as in the clearing house.

Clearings can also be made between different cities through the
Federal Reserve Banks. Each Federal Reserve Bank keeps a deposit
of gold certificates in a Gold Settlement Fund at Washington. Claims
in New York against banks in other parts of the country, such as Chicago, are sent to the New York Federal Reserve Bank for collection.
Similarly, Chicago claims against New York find their way to the
Chicago Federal Reserve Bank. The claims are offset against each
other, and if any balance is due, let us say from Chicago to New York,
the amount is deducted from the Chicago bank's deposit in the Gold
Settlement Fund and credited to the account of the New York bank.
Not unless there is a steady flow of claims in one direction which cannot be settled in this way will there be any actual shipment of gold
certificates between the two cities. The same principle applies in dealings between other sections of the country.

The clearing house system makes it possible to carry on the business transactions of a nation very largely by a system of bookkeeping
entries. It is a marvelous mechanism of *circulating credit,* which makes
possible the processes of exchange with the least possible use of cash.
About nine-tenths of all the business done in this country is paid for
in this way. We see, then, that bank deposits constitute by far the
most important part of our medium of exchange.

Deposit Reserves. — In view of the fact that banks are not called
upon to meet very many of their deposit obligations in cash, they are
able to lend their credit to an amount greatly exceeding the quantity
of cash in their possession. Hence they commonly expand the volume
of their loans to many times the sum of their cash holdings. However,
any depositor has the right to claim a part or all of his deposit in cash,
and every bank constantly receives some such demands. People need
cash to carry in their pockets for small daily transactions; business
firms may pay their employees in cash; gold may be needed to meet
debts abroad, and so on. Therefore, the banks are compelled to keep
some cash reserve to meet such demands. Experience has shown that

about five or ten per cent of their total deposits is sufficient to meet all ordinary needs for this purpose.

If all depositors were to demand cash to the full amount of their deposits at one time, the banks could not supply it. The total of all the cash in the country does not begin to equal the total of bank deposits. Being unable to meet their debts, the banks would be legally insolvent, and forced to close their doors. So long as everything runs smoothly, however, this situation does not arise, for depositors have no occasion to ask for the cash. Ordinarily the banks can rely upon this fact with perfect safety. But if anything happens to upset the depositors' confidence in the banks, they may begin to demand cash. The failure of a large bank, or some similar circumstance, may precipitate such a situation. When large numbers of depositors begin to draw out their funds in cash, there is said to be a "run" on the bank. If the "run" spreads to other banks, their combined efforts may be unable to cope with the situation. They have not enough cash to meet the demands. A financial *panic* may be precipitated, in which everybody wants cash which is not to be had, and business is paralyzed for a time.

Because of the possibility of a panic, and because banks are tempted by the desire for profit to expand their loans beyond the limit of safety, deposit banking is strictly regulated by law. Confidence in the integrity of the banks must be maintained if panics are to be avoided. Banks must not be allowed to expand their deposits recklessly if depositors are to be protected from loss. Hence, legislation specifies the nature and amount of bank reserves that must be held against deposit liabilities, and to some extent the kind of loans that a bank can make. The deposit reserve provisions of the banking laws in the United States will be described in connection with the Federal Reserve System, below.

The Relation Between One Bank and Other Banks of the System. — We have seen that the various banks of a banking system have reciprocal obligations, caused by checks on each of them being deposited in others, which checks are commonly offset through the clearing process. However, if a bank owes more to other banks than they do to it, the balance cannot be offset, but must be paid in cash. Hence any bank which is continually in debt to other banks will steadily lose cash from its reserves. In order to maintain the cash reserves required by law and by good banking practice, it will be compelled to reduce the volume of its loans until the volume of its deposits shrinks to the point where checks drawn against it and deposited with others are offset by checks drawn against other banks and deposited with it. In this way, a general balance between all the banks in the banking system is maintained, the available cash being distributed among them in proportion to the demand for it in various localities, and the volume of deposits in each being adjusted to the cash reserves which it is able to maintain.

Now if, in such a balanced situation, one bank expands its loans independently of other banks, it will find itself in the position just described, where it is continually in debt to others; for the increased volume of checks drawn against the now enlarged volume of deposits will no longer be offset by checks held against other banks, and the difference must be paid in cash, impairing the expanding bank's reserves. It will presently be forced to protect its reserve by curtailing its loans, until it is in balance with the other banks once more. It is to be concluded that one bank cannot expand its loan deposits out of proportion to the deposits of other banks.

A similar proposition holds with respect to contraction of loans. If a single bank, having previously been in such balance with the other banks that its checks were just offset, so that it was neither losing nor gaining cash, reduces its loans (and hence its deposits), checks drawn against it and held by other banks will fall short of the checks drawn against other banks held by it. It will collect the difference in cash, causing its cash reserve to increase. Now this accretion of cash represents a potential source of profit, which can be utilized only if the bank can secure borrowers to utilize deposits built upon the new reserves. The bank is stimulated to seek new business and expand its deposits. At the same time, the loss of cash by the other banks is forcing them to refuse to extend credit, so that customers seeking loans are likely to be driven to the bank which has the excess of reserve. So, the deposits of the latter expand, until this bank is in balance with the rest once more. It is to be concluded that one bank is not likely to contract its loan deposits out of proportion to the deposits of other banks.

Expansion and Contraction of Bank Credit. — It is entirely possible, however, for the banks generally to expand or contract their loans simultaneously. If they are all expanding together, their mutual obligations will increase in rough correspondence. The increased checks drawn upon each can be offset by the increased checks drawn upon the others; so long as the movement is even, none need gain cash at the expense of the rest. However, with given legal reserve requirements, the amount of such expansion is limited by the total amount of cash reserves in the whole banking system. As we have seen, withdrawals of cash by depositors for the making of cash payments in their ordinary business transactions will tend to vary directly with the total volume of deposits, and will expand as the latter expands. If the loans are too great, the cash withdrawn will reduce the reserves below the amounts required by law and by the needs of banking practice. This will force the banks to reduce their loans until the necessary reserves are restored. The limit to contraction, on the other hand, is the volume of cash in the banks. Loans might be reduced to zero, theoretically, but deposits could not fall below the amount of cash left with the banks for safe-keeping. It appears, then, that the cash reserves constitute a sort of anchor, to which bank credit is tied, but that the cord which ties them is an elastic one, which can stretch up to a certain limit, or shrink to a minimum.

Within these limits, deposits do fluctuate considerably in magnitude, depending upon the demand of business men for loans. If business activity is great, more loans will be made, and bank credit may expand up to the maximum permitted by the reserves; if business is dull, fewer loans are likely, and bank deposits may shrink to a relatively small volume. In the latter case, bank reserves are said to be excessive, or partly idle. Thus, while over long periods of time the average volume of bank deposits will bear a fairly constant ratio to the average size of the reserves, over shorter periods the ratio is quite variable. These short-period fluctuations really constitute repeated inflations and deflations of money, the effects of which may be very disturbing to the economic process, as we shall see.

How Cash Increases and Decreases Affect the Banking Process. — What has just been said shows that there is a more or less definite average relation, over long periods, between the volume of bank credit and the size of the bank reserves. It follows that if more cash flows into the reserves, a corresponding expansion of bank deposits is likely to take place sooner or later, and that if the cash reserves shrink, there will be a corresponding contraction of credit. A closer examination of how this takes place will give a clearer understanding of the manner in which the banks collectively are able to build up a volume of deposits many times greater than the cash which they hold.

New cash may be introduced into the monetary system by the mining of new gold or silver which is sold to the government in exchange for paper money; or, gold or silver may be imported from abroad in payment for goods exported from this country; or, the government may issue some fiat paper money. The additional cash is deposited in a certain bank or group of banks. Let us suppose that the reserve of a large city bank is increased by $100,000 in this way. This will make possible some expansion of its loans, such loans taking the form of increased demand deposits. We have seen, however, that such an expansion will entail a considerable loss of cash to other banks on the part of the one which is expanding. The borrowers will draw checks against most of the new deposits with which they have been credited, and a considerable proportion of these checks will find their way into other banks. If the expanding bank has previously been in such balance with other banks that it was just able to offset the checks drawn against it, it will now be faced with an excess of debts to other banks which cannot be offset. Therefore, it must settle the claims against it by giving up some of the new cash which it has received. Experience indicates that, if a ten per cent reserve is to be held against the new loans, the total volume of the latter must not greatly exceed the initial amount of new cash on which they are based. In other words, if the bank lends $100,000, it will lose about $90,000 of cash to other banks. Of its original cash increase of $100,000, it will then have $10,000 remaining as reserve for the new loans. The $100,000 of new cash deposited supports loan deposits of an approximately equal amount *in the bank which first receives the cash.*

Now, if $90,000 of the new cash is lost to certain other banks, their reserves are temporarily increased by this amount, on which they, likewise, can build up an equal volume of loan deposits. We now have new deposits totaling $190,000 as a result of $100,000 of new cash entering the monetary system. But this is not all. Of the $90,000 added to the reserves of the second group of banks, ninety per cent, or $81,000, will in turn be lost to a third group, and will be used as the basis for a corresponding expansion of loans. This will go on from bank to bank, in a decreasing series, like this: $100,000 + $90,000 + $81,000 + $72,900 + . . . until the items approach a limit of zero. The total sum of this series is $1,000,000. So, if cash reserves of ten per cent are maintained, a given increase in cash will support deposits of ten times as much *in the banking system.* If reserves of twenty per cent are kept, the volume of loans supported can be five times the amount of the cash; if reserves of five per cent are maintained, the loan deposits can be twenty times as great.

A withdrawal of cash from the reserves of any bank starts a chain of contraction which is the converse of the expansion just described. With its reserves depleted, the bank first affected must reduce its loans by an approximately equal amount to the cash that has been withdrawn, provided its loans were previously at the maximum which its then reserves would support. This means that there will henceforth be fewer checks drawn against it to be offset in the clearing process; consequently, other banks will have to settle more of their obligations to it in cash. Their reserves will shrink by nine-tenths the amount of the original cash withdrawal, forcing an approximately equal shrinkage of loans. Other banks in turn will lose cash and reduce loans until, when the whole series is completed, the total reduction of deposits will be ten times the amount of the original cash withdrawal.

However, a bank is not compelled to expand its loans when its cash reserves are increased, and will not, unless business conditions at the time are favorable. Likewise, a bank is not compelled to contract its loans when its cash reserves are decreased, unless its reserves were previously at their minimum. Therefore, the processes of expansion and contraction described must be regarded as tendencies which will manifest themselves more or less, according to circumstances.

B. THE REGULATION OF BANKS

The Changing Objectives of Regulation. — The banking system plays so important a part in the economic processes of modern times that if it does not perform its functions well, serious disturbance to the business world may result. In order to prevent such disturbance, governments usually subject the banks to a considerable amount of regulation.

The objectives of this regulation in the United States have been slowly changing. In the beginning the result aimed at was chiefly the _safety_ of bank credit. Safety was interpreted as redeemability of bank notes or deposits in standard money. If a bank is unable to redeem its notes or deposits, it fails, and the note-holders or depositors lose part or all of the funds which they hold in these forms. If a considerable number of banks find themselves in this situation simultaneously, a panic is likely to occur; whereupon the whole structure of bank credit temporarily collapses. There is then not enough money with which to carry on exchange, and business activity is paralyzed. Therefore, early regulative legislation was designed to preserve the integrity of notes and deposits by requiring the banks to maintain adequate reserves, and by other measures.

As time went on, a second objective, which may be termed _elasticity_, was stressed. By elasticity is meant the ability of bank credit to expand and contract with the needs of business. It will be recalled that bank credit grows out of loans to business men. It was felt that when business men demanded more credit, the banking system should be in a position to supply it; but that when this demand fell off, the quantity of bank money should shrink correspondingly. Thus the volume of bank credit would respond automatically to the pace of economic activity. Since both bank notes and bank deposits are payable on demand, however, elasticity must not be allowed to impair redeemability. Too much expansion of credit might be at the expense of safety. To provide against this, _liquidity_ was insisted upon. By this was meant that the loans on which bank notes and bank deposits were based must be "liquid" (_i.e._, easily converted into cash). For instance, a loan is liquid if it is secured by stock exchange collateral (stocks or bonds which are listed on the stock exchange, pledged to the bank as security), because, if the borrower fails to meet his obligation when due, the banker can recover the funds loaned by selling the collateral on the exchange. Short-time loans are more liquid than long-time loans, because they must be paid off in cash by the borrowers in the relatively near future. If the banks are faced by growing demands for cash, they are more likely to be able to meet these demands if they can count on an inflow of payments from expiring loans. If a bank's investments are in the long-time market, its assets are more likely to be "frozen"—that is, not readily convertible into cash. Hence, such investments were considered dangerous for banks that issued demand notes or deposits.

The objectives of elasticity and liquidity have led to rather complicated legislation providing, among other things, for somewhat flexible minimum reserve requirements, for central banks to make loans to other banks faced with greater demands for credit than they can meet out of their own resources, and for certain requirements as to the kinds and qualities of loans that commercial banks are permitted to make.

The objectives of safety, elasticity, and liquidity are based on the idea that the primary function of banks is to lend money for business operations. We have learned, however, that contemporary monetary theorists hold that the most important function of commercial banks is to supply the community with deposit money. Recognition of this leads to a conception of the objectives toward which bank regulation should be aimed somewhat at variance with those which have already been stated. In practice, elasticity of bank credit causes a disproportionate expansion and contraction of deposit money, with disturbing effects upon prices. When the volume of bank credit increases, prices go up, profits increase, and business is stimulated; when credit contracts, prices go down, profits decline, and business activity is retarded. Recent investigations indicate that the elasticity of bank credit is partly to blame for upsetting the balance of industry and causing business depressions. Many economists now believe, therefore, that bank policy should be directed towards a new objective—*stability*. According to this view, bank credit should be manipulated so as to prevent any monetary influence tending to disturb prices, and so as to promote business stability.

The rise of this newer attitude has led to a division of opinion among experts in the field of banking. One group, which may be called *the commercial banking school,* emphasizes the loan function of commercial banks and believes that the object of bank regulation should be to make loans responsive to the needs of business, with adequate safeguards for bank solvency. Therefore they stress safety, elasticity, and liquidity as proper criteria for bank regulation. Most of the existing bank legislation in this country is based on these principles, and most of the practical bankers, as well as the regulating authorities, can be classed as adherents of this school of thought. The other group, which may be called *the monetary school*, stresses the monetary function of commercial banks and believes that the proper object of bank regulation should be control of the volume of bank credit in such a way as to promote business stability. The majority of academic monetary writers probably belongs to this group. Their influence is gradually coming to be felt in legislation and in the policy of the monetary authorities.

The National Banking System. — Bank regulation in the United States on a national scale began with the passage of the National Banking Act in 1863. Prior to that time there were no national banks, but many banks scattered throughout the country, acting under charters from the several states. The states did not regulate these banks sufficiently, with the result that bank notes were recklessly issued and many banks failed because of their inability to redeem the notes when called upon to do so. The period has been described as one of "wildcat" banking.

The new law was designed to correct these abuses. It provided that national banks might be incorporated by the federal government, subject to certain measures of regulation. There was required a certain minimum of capital (to prevent the incorporation of banks with inadequate resources), the accumulation of surplus in addition thereto, and the holding of certain minimum reserves against deposits. The banks were also required to make periodic reports to the Comptroller of the Currency, and to submit to thorough examination of their books by members of his staff at least twice a year. All these provisions are still in effect, although some of them have been modified in certain details.

The issuing of notes by state banks was effectively stopped by the placing of a ten per cent tax thereon. This gave a monopoly of note issue to the national banks under conditions set forth in the law, which were designed to maintain their convertibility.[2] State banks were still permitted to exist, however, and thousands of them now continue to

---

[2] Banks were required to purchase United States government bonds with a par or market value (whichever was lower) equal to the amount of note issues. These were deposited as security for the note issues with the Treasury of the United States. As additional security, the banks had to deposit with the Treasury lawful money equal to five per cent of the notes put into circulation (lawful money then consisted of gold or silver coin or certificates and United States notes. In 1934, all forms of cash in this country were made lawful). The United States government guaranteed the redemption of the notes and it maintained the five per cent reserve fund for this purpose.

do a commercial banking business. A large volume of national bank notes were issued under the prescribed conditions from time to time. They continued in circulation until 1935, in which year their gradual retirement was begun in order to remove from our currency a form of money which was judged to be too inelastic, and over the volume of which the government had little control.

It will be observed that the national banking system thus established was aimed primarily at safety, by providing a system of national banks with adequate capital and surplus, well-secured notes, and substantial deposit reserves. The results, however, were somewhat disappointing. In spite of this provision, panics occurred, and there were various other difficulties. It was concluded that the system was too rigid and that greater elasticity of credit, under governmental control, was needed. In foreign countries, such control had been exercised through the medium of central banks, closely affiliated with the government. These banks were bankers' banks, *i.e.*, they made loans to other banks, thereby making it possible for the latter to extend further credit to business men when the latter demanded more funds than the smaller banks could provide out of their own reserves. The central banks also had a monopoly of note issue. It was believed that a somewhat similar system might prove successful in the United States. Accordingly, in 1913 there was passed the Federal Reserve Act, which supplemented our decentralized system of national banks with some central banking machinery.

The Federal Reserve System. — The basis of the system rests in twelve central banks, known as Federal Reserve Banks, located in important cities in the various parts of the United States.[3] These are bankers' banks; that is, they do business with other banks, known as member banks. All national banks are required to become members; state banks may do so, and many of them have joined. Member banks must subscribe to the capital of the Federal Reserve Banks, and they have a voice in the management thereof, as well as a share in the profits. Of the nine directors of each Federal Reserve Bank, six are appointed by the member banks (three representing the banks, and three representing other business interests), and three by the Board of Governors of the system. The Federal Reserve Banks are thus semi-public, semi-private institutions. Owned and partly managed by private banks, they nevertheless exist for a public purpose, and are subject to a great deal of control by a central Board of Governors (commonly known as the Federal Reserve Board).

This Board consists of seven members, appointed by the President

[3] They are located at Boston, New York, Philadelphia, Cleveland, Richmond, Atlanta, Chicago, St. Louis, Minneapolis, Kansas City, Dallas, and San Francisco, with numerous branches in other cities.

of the United States. Its powers over the Federal Reserve Banks, and through them, over our entire banking system, are sweeping and important. In addition to appointing three of the directors of the Federal Reserve Banks, its approval is required for the selection of the presidents of these institutions, and it may also suspend or remove any of their officials at its discretion. It controls the issue of Federal Reserve Notes by the Federal Reserve Banks, and it has power to fix the rate of rediscount which they charge for loans. Within limits, it may also alter the reserves which member banks must hold against their deposits. The Board can compel one Federal Reserve Bank to rediscount the discounted commercial paper of other Federal Reserve Banks, if that seems necessary. Through its Open Market Committee, it has a major voice in directing certain open market operations, presently to be described. By means of the Board of Governors, the Federal Reserve System is centralized and coördinated into a unified whole. Its sweeping authority causes the success or failure of our banking system to rest very largely in its hands; hence its integrity and freedom from political influence are vital matters of public concern.

The relationships between Federal Reserve Banks and the other banks of the system center mainly in three things—rediscounting, the banking reserves, and open market operations. It is through these, for the most part, that the Board of Governors exerts its control. Incidentally, the Reserve Banks perform certain other functions. They supply the community with paper money, in the form of Federal Reserve Notes. They provide a means of clearing checks between member banks. They also act as custodians of funds, and as fiscal agents, for the federal government. The last of these activities is not of sufficient importance for the economic process at large to require our attention. The clearing operations have already been described. Rediscounting, the bank reserves, open market operations, and Federal Reserve Notes need some further explanation.

Rediscounting. — The Federal Reserve Banks do business with other banks; for the most part they do not have relations with the public at large. Chief among their operations is the making of loans to member banks through the process known as rediscounting. This process may be illustrated by an example. Let us suppose that a bank in Springfield, Illinois, has demands for loans from its customers which are greater than its present resources enable it to supply without overstepping the limits of the minimum reserves required by law. It desires to accommodate these customers. In the course of its ordinary business operations, this bank will have discounted many of its customers' notes. That is, it has granted loans to them (in the form of bank deposits) to the amount of their promissory notes, less interest thereon for the time the loans are to run. The bank holds these discounted notes—discounted commercial paper, it is called—as security for the loans. It can now take some of this commercial paper to its Federal Reserve Bank in Chicago and have it rediscounted; that is, the Federal Reserve Bank will issue a new loan to the Springfield bank, holding the already once-discounted paper as security. The member bank in Springfield now has a deposit with its Federal Reserve Bank to the amount of the commercial paper it has placed with it, less the rediscount. The deposit thereby created with the Federal Reserve Bank can be counted as part of the legal reserve of the member bank. With this additional credit at its disposal, it can increase its loans to the business men of Springfield and prevent the stringency of credit which otherwise would have been felt. If such rediscounting is going on pretty generally, there may be a nationwide expansion of credit.

The rate of rediscount is controlled by the Board of Governors. If it believes that credit expansion is needed, it can encourage such a development by lowering the rate, thus making it cheaper for member banks to borrow from the Federal Reserve Banks and making it more profitable for the former to lend to their customers. If the Board believes that contraction of credit is desirable, it can raise the rate of rediscount, thus discouraging loans by making them more expensive to the borrowing banks. The rediscounting process is supposed to give elasticity to bank credit, by permitting it to expand and contract with the needs of business; control of the rediscount rate is intended to prevent such expansion or contraction from going too far.

Deposit Reserve Provisions. — A further element of elasticity (without loss of safety) is supposed to be provided by the reserve requirements of the system. Under the National Banking System, the deposit reserves of the national banks were excessively high and rigid. Under the Federal Reserve System, they are lower and more flexible. As the law now stands (1941), the reserves must not be less than thirteen per cent for member banks in New York and Chicago (designated as "central reserve cities"), ten per cent in other large cities ("reserve cities"), and seven per cent in the smaller towns. Since 1935, however, the Board of Governors has had power to raise these requirements, at its discretion, up to amounts not exceeding twice these figures. By exercising this power it can check somewhat the tendency to credit expansion which is latent in large excess reserves; by lowering the requirements again when reserves grow smaller, it can offset contraction of credit somewhat. The Board of Governors has the further power, in times of emergency, to suspend the reserve requirements for thirty days and to renew the suspension for periods of fifteen days, but the banks whose loans exceed the amount that would be permitted by their reserves must then pay a tax on the excess thereof. On time deposits, where large reserves are less necessary, the law specifies minimum reserves of only three per cent.

The required reserves must be kept in the form of deposits with the Federal Reserve Bank of the appropriate district. This means that the member banks' reserves really consist of Federal Reserve Bank deposits, which, as we have seen, may be established through the process of rediscounting. The Federal Reserve Banks, in turn, must hold reserves of thirty-five per cent in lawful money against their deposits. Thus our deposit reserves (except gold and silver, which are now kept mostly in the federal Treasury) are concentrated in the Federal Reserve Banks. Expedience requires, however, that member banks keep

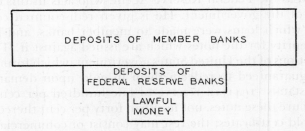

Figure 7. The Pyramiding of Deposits.

a small reserve of cash to provide for withdrawals by their depositors. The concentration of reserves in the Federal Reserve Banks provides much greater security than was possible when the reserves were scattered among the individual national banks of the country, even though the proportion of reserves to deposits is less than before. With the reserves concentrated in the Federal Reserve Bank of a given district, they can be used to extend credit to any member banks of the region, which may have need for it. The law also provides that, in case of need, the surplus reserves of one Federal Reserve Bank can be transferred temporarily to another district where the situation is acute.

It is noteworthy that the reserves of the member banks do not consist of cash, but of deposits in the Federal Reserve Banks. The latter, like any other demand deposits, are merely liabilities of the Federal Reserve Banks to pay cash on demand. The real cash reserves of the system, therefore, are those which the Federal Reserve Banks hold against their deposits. The resulting situation is sometimes described as the pyramiding of deposits, because a large superstructure of deposits is built upon a small reserve of cash, like an inverted pyramid.

This is illustrated in the drawing above (Figure 7). Since Reserve Bank deposits can be nearly three times the size of their cash reserves, and member bank deposits about five to ten times their reserves of Reserve Bank deposits (depending on the legal minimum), the total of member bank deposits can rise to some fifteen or thirty times as much as the cash reserve on which they are based. However, the Federal Reserve Banks can supply additional cash, if it is needed, in the form of Federal Reserve Notes.

Federal Reserve Notes. — If member banks desire to convert their Federal Reserve Bank deposits into cash, the Reserve Banks have the privilege (subject to approval by the Board of Governors) of supplying a form of paper money known as Federal Reserve Notes. These are issued to the Reserve Bank by a member of its board of directors, designated as the Federal Reserve Agent, who acts in this capacity as an agent of the government. He is given rediscounted commercial paper on which loans were made to member banks, and holds it as partial security for the notes which are issued against it. These notes are obligations of the United States government, which formerly (prior to 1933) guaranteed to redeem them in gold upon demand. As the law now stands (1941), a reserve of one hundred per cent must be held to secure these notes, not less than forty per cent thereof being in gold or gold certificates; the rest may consist of commercial paper or United States government securities. The notes are now legal tender, and they circulate readily because they are amply secured; (1) by the credit of the United States government; (2) by the credit of the business men upon whose rediscounted paper they were issued; (3) by the forty per cent reserve fund of gold certificates; (4) by the gold in our Treasury to secure these certificates; and (5) by the assets of the member banks, which are indebted to the Federal Reserve Banks to the amount of the loans out of which the Federal Reserve Notes arose.[4]

The Federal Reserve Notes were intended to be an elastic form of money. Through the issuing of the notes against rediscounted paper, currency was supposed to expand when the needs of business required it. Contraction of the notes was expected to take place as follows: when the business men whose rediscounted paper is held as security pay back to the member bank the amount of the loans which this paper represents, the member bank must repay its loan to the Federal Reserve Bank, and if it has no new paper to deposit as collateral for a

[4] Federal Reserve Notes must be carefully distinguished from Federal Reserve Bank Notes. Despite the similarity in name they are very different. Federal Reserve Bank Notes were formerly issued under conditions similar to those of National Bank Notes, and temporary issues under other circumstances have twice been made. However, they do not arise out of the rediscounting process, and they are not now an important part of our money system.

new deposit, the Federal Reserve Notes issued against the first loan must be withdrawn. However, an amendment to the Federal Reserve Act provides that when the loans behind the Federal Reserve Notes are repaid, in lieu of retiring them, the Reserve Banks may continue them in circulation by keeping a reserve of one hundred per cent in gold (or gold certificates) as security. During the first World War and after, huge quantities of gold came into this country in payment for our exports and loans abroad, and as this gold found its way into the Federal Reserve Banks, Federal Reserve Notes were allowed to circulate against it. Now this part of the Federal Reserve circulation is inelastic, for it depends in no wise upon the needs of business, and is contingent upon the somewhat arbitrary movement of gold reserves. Although the gold would no doubt have gotten into the monetary circulation in some form or other anyway, its use in this manner partially defeated the maintenance of elasticity of bank notes.

Open Market Operations. — The open market operations of the Federal Reserve Banks constitute a device by which the banking authorities can exert a strong influence on the volume of funds available for loans without being dependent upon the spontaneous process of rediscounting. These operations are under the control of an Open Market Committee, composed of seven members of the Board of Governors and five representatives of the Federal Reserve Banks, chosen so as to represent five different sections of the country. If a Federal Reserve Bank has surplus funds for which there is no demand from member banks, it may go into the financial market, under the direction of this committee, and purchase certain types of commercial paper, government bonds, and foreign bills of exchange. The money it pays out for these purchases will be deposited by its recipients in the commercial banks, thereby increasing their deposits. In this way the Federal Reserve authorities can stimulate some expansion of bank credit if they deem it advisable to do so. If, on the other hand, they desire to bring about a contraction, they can sell in the open market such commercial paper or government bonds as they may have on hand. The money they receive from these sales will be drawn out of the commercial banks in this way: The buyers draw checks against their deposits in member banks to the order of the Federal Reserve Banks, to whom the paper is sold. This obligates the member bank to the Federal Reserve Bank, which obligation is met by canceling part of the member bank deposit with the Reserve Bank. Since the member bank deposit constitutes its reserve against the deposits of its own customers, its capacity to extend credit to the latter is thereby reduced. Open market operations can also be used to transfer funds from Federal Reserve districts where there is a surplus to districts where there is a lack, and the purchase and sale of foreign drafts can be used to help stabilize fluctuating foreign exchange rates. This last operation will be explained in a later chapter.

The Insurance of Bank Deposits. — Notwithstanding the various regulations which are intended to provide safety of bank deposits, the number of bank failures in this country is very large. In the decade from 1923 to 1932 inclusive, 9,883 banks, with combined deposits of over four billion dollars, failed. There were four thousand failures in the single year 1933. Such failures represent losses of millions of dollars to depositors even in years of prosperity, while in times of business crises and depression the losses become enormous. The banking collapse of 1933 convinced Congress that something would have to be done to protect depositors henceforth from such losses. Therefore a plan to insure the depositor was adopted.

Under this plan a Federal Deposit Insurance Corporation was created. It is provided with a guarantee fund derived from the following sources: $150,000,000 was appropriated from the federal treasury; each Federal Reserve Bank was required to subscribe an amount equal to one-half of the surplus in its possession on January 1, 1933; and all other banks which participate in the plan are subjected to an annual assessment which amounts to about one-twelfth of one per cent of their average deposits. From this fund the corporation guarantees to reimburse all depositors in insured banks for losses of their deposits resulting from bank failures, up to a maximum of $5,000 each. All solvent member banks must enter into this arrangement, and non-member state banks may participate. Since the latter must compete with the member banks for customers, they are under strong pressure to join. All participating banks are subject to frequent examination by the examiners of the corporation for the purpose of checking unwise practices and protecting their solvency. One advantage of the plan is that it thus brings more state banks under federal supervision. If a bank should fail, the corporation takes charge and proceeds to liquidate it. Insured deposits are paid out of the guarantee fund, either through transfer of the deposit claim to a new bank organized in the same community to take over the business of the insolvent one, or to some already existing insured bank, or in such other manner as the Board of Directors of the Federal Deposit Insurance Corporation may prescribe.

SUMMARY

Banks have two primary functions, *viz.*, they make loans for financing the time element in production and they create money, in the form of bank deposits. They also act as custodians for the safe-keeping of money and as administrators of trust funds. The kinds of banks which specialize in the performance of these several functions are investment banks, savings banks, commercial banks, and trust companies. Insurance companies also supply funds for investment. Investment and savings banks act as intermediaries for gathering together the savings of individuals and placing them in permanent investments, thereby financing the construction of durable equipment. Commercial banks make short-time loans for business investments which result in quickly salable products; and recently they have also been putting funds into the long-time investment market. Their loans take the form of demand deposits subject to check. These banks exchange their own credit in the form of notes or deposits for the credit of business men by discounting the notes of the latter. Bank notes are paper money issued by commercial banks in the lending process, redeemable upon demand. Bank deposits represent the bank's promise to pay the depositor; they arise primarily out of loans. Through the transferring of deposit accounts by the process of clearing checks, these deposits circulate and perform the functions of money. To meet the demand for cash by depositors, money reserves are kept by the banks, according to law. Within the limits set by the reserve requirements, bank credit expands and contracts according to the demand of business men for loans.

The objectives of bank regulation are safety, elasticity, liquidity, and business stability—the evolution being from the first toward the last. Federal regulation began with the national banking system, which provided for the incorporation of national banks, with suitable restrictions as to note issues and cash reserves. Greater centralization of control was later provided by the Federal Reserve System. In this system, twelve Federal Reserve Banks engage in the activities of rediscounting commercial paper for member banks, holding deposit reserves, issuing Federal Reserve Notes, and carrying on open market operations. A central Board of Governors has sweeping powers of control. The system is directed mainly toward maintaining safety and elasticity of bank credit. To protect depositors from losses occasioned by bank failures, bank deposits are guaranteed by the Federal Deposit Insurance Corporation.

REFERENCES AND SUGGESTIONS FOR FURTHER READING

The subject of banking is so closely connected with that of money that the literature of the two is largely coextensive; hence the references mentioned at the close of the last chapter are also applicable to this one. The following are also especially pertinent to the topics discussed in the present chapter:

Lauchlin Currie, *The Supply and Control of Money in the United States* (2nd edition, 1935). This work develops the thesis that the primary function of commercial banks is a monetary one, and it discusses ways and means for controlling the amount of deposit money.

C. A. Phillips' *Bank Credit* (1920), gives a detailed description of banking operations, and is especially noteworthy for its analysis of bank credit expansion and contraction.

J. M. Keynes' elaborate and original *Treatise on Money* (1930) is one of the most significant of recent contributions to the subjects discussed in this and the next two chapters.

For clear, brief accounts of the Federal Reserve System see E. W. Kemmerer's *The A, B, C of the Federal Reserve System* (10th edition, 1936), and the Board of Governors' own pamphlet *The Federal Reserve System, its Purposes and Functions* (1939).

Chapter X

THE FLUCTUATING PRICE LEVEL

A. THE NATURE AND CONSEQUENCES OF PRICE LEVEL MOVEMENTS

Changes in the Price Level and Their Measurement. — In the last two chapters several references were made to the upward and downward movements of the price level brought about by monetary causes. Everyone who lived through the second and third decades of the present century became keenly aware of these movements. The first World War started a great rise in prices which culminated in 1920. At the end of this period, prices fell sharply for about a year, remained fairly steady until 1929, then fell steeply again until 1933, when they started upward once more. While general changes of this sort are clearly discernible, the prices of all goods do not move exactly in unison. Potatoes may be dear in a year when tomatoes are cheap; the price of building materials may be going up while that of coal is falling. Nevertheless an average of all individual fluctuations will usually show a movement upward or downward over a period of time. Such is the behavior of the general level of prices.

This general movement can be measured by a device known as an index number. The index of wholesale commodity prices computed by the United States Bureau of Labor Statistics will serve as an illustration. This bureau now keeps a weekly or monthly record of the wholesale prices of nearly a thousand representative commodities. From this record it is able to ascertain the average price of each commodity in any given year. To obtain the index of all the prices for that year, what may be described as a "weighted aggregate" is worked out. A simple sum of the prices of the many articles recorded would be unsatisfactory in making comparisons with other years, because a great change in the price of some relatively insignificant commodity might influence the total unduly. Each article is therefore given its due importance in the aggregate by "weighting" its price. That is, its average price for the year is multiplied by the estimated quantity of that article which was marketed in the year 1919, as shown by a census which was taken in the latter year. For instance, clover seed is a commodity very little used. Only 467,000 hundredweight of it were marketed in 1919. Changes in its price should, therefore, be minimized in computing the index of prices. On the other hand, granulated sugar is a staple product of very great importance; 7,884,900,000 pounds of it were marketed in 1919. Hence, changes in the price of this commodity should be given more weight in the index than those in the price of clover seed. By multiplying the two prices by the quantities given, this effect is obtained.

The sum of all the prices, so weighted, gives the aggregate for the year. This aggregate can then be compared with the similar aggre-

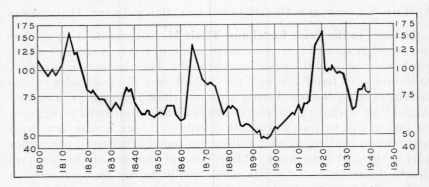

Figure 8. Wholesale Commodity Prices in the United States since 1800.
Base, 1926 = 100.

gate of prices in some other year which has been selected as the basis for comparison. Most recent index numbers take some year shortly before or after the first World War as the base, because the war period was one of abnormal price upheaval. The index number in any given year is shown as a certain percentage of the prices in the base year, which, in Figure 8, is 1926. For instance, the index for 1930, as there shown, was 86. This means that the aggregate of wholesale prices for that year, when divided by the aggregate for 1926, gave .86 as the quotient; and it shows that the level of prices in 1930 was 14 per cent lower than that of 1926.

A world comparison of index numbers shows that in every country the price level is subject to considerable fluctuation. At times the change may be gradual; again, it is erratic and extreme. Figure 8 shows in graphic form the movement of wholesale prices in this country since 1800.[1] It will be observed that, during this period, there were three violent upward movements, followed by similarly violent de-

[1] The figures are those of the United States Bureau of Labor Statistics.

clines. Even when prices are not behaving in so erratic a manner, there is continual change going on, such as the gradual rise shown in the chart from 1896 to 1910, with lesser oscillations from year to year. A chart of prices for any other nation would show very similar changes. These facts indicate that price levels in the present economic order are very unstable.

An Unstable Price Level Means an Unstable Dollar. — These changes in the general level of prices reveal corresponding changes in the value, or purchasing power, of money. When prices are high, the value of money is low (for it will buy less in commodities), and vice versa. By money prices we indicate changes in the values of commodities, but if money itself changes in value, prices expressed in terms of it are rather unreliable. Our dollar, instead of being a fixed unit of measurement, is a variable one. This lack of stability in our standard of value causes a great deal of inconvenience. Imagine us buying groceries, using as our standard of weight a flexible unit which varied from month to month and from year to year! In purchasing a pound of sugar we would never know just how much of it we would really receive, and there would be all sorts of opportunity for miscalculation and injustice, for at one time the grocer would be giving us less sugar to a pound than at another. Or, suppose we were accustomed to measuring cloth with a rubber yardstick, the length of which varied with the looseness or tightness with which it was stretched! In purchasing ten yards of material we would never know just how much we were getting. We are in exactly this situation when we deal in terms of dollars. When a wage-earner accepts employment at a wage of forty dollars per week, he has no way of knowing just what his real wage will be, for his forty dollars will not always purchase the same quantity of economic goods. If a man borrows a thousand dollars, agreeing to repay it at a later date, he cannot know just how great an obligation he has really assumed; for if the value of money changes, he will have to pay back more or less real purchasing power, as the case may be. In measuring weight, length, volume, temperature, the flow of electric current, the heat-giving capacity of foods, and the like, we no longer tolerate such uncertainty. We have devised invariable units, such as the pound, the foot, the cubic foot, the degree (of temperature), the ampere, the calory, and other standards which are fixed and invariable. But we have not yet achieved a fixed standard of value.

The Effects of Changing Price Levels on Debtors and Creditors. — One of the major difficulties of a fluctuating price level is its disturbing effects on debtors and creditors. Suppose that a corporation engaged in manufacturing milk bottles has borrowed $25,000 in bonds, bearing five per cent interest, which bonds mature in ten years. Suppose further that, when the bonds were issued, the company was doing business as follows:

Annual sales (5,000,000 bottles @ 1 cent each)	$50,000
Expenses (excluding interest on the bonds)	45,000
Net earnings	$ 5,000

If business continues at this rate, the company will have $5,000 annually out of which to pay the interest charges of $1,250, leaving it $3,750. It can lay aside $2,500 of this as an amortization fund, which will be sufficient to retire the bonds fully when they expire, and it will have a clear profit of $1,250 besides. Suppose, however, that there is a general fall of prices to half their former level. Presumably, the price of milk bottles will fall correspondingly. This will affect the company very disastrously, for, although many of its costs will fall along with prices, the interest and amortization charges on its debt will not. The new situation will be something like this:

Annual sales (5,000,000 bottles @ ½ cent each)	$25,000
Expenses (half former amount)	22,500
Net earnings (also half former amount)	$ 2,500

Now, after paying the yearly interest charges of $1,250, the company has only $1,250 remaining with which to pay for the retirement of its bonds. At this rate it cannot possibly redeem them when they fall due in ten years. Thus the company's financial security has been seriously impaired. A corporation whose indebtedness was very large, entailing heavy annual interest payments, might be unable to meet even the interest, and would be forced into bankruptcy.

Suppose, on the other hand, that prices rose to double their former level, instead of falling, the price of milk bottles increasing correspondingly. The sales of the corporation would then be $100,000, and its expenses (exclusive of interest) $90,000, leaving net earnings of $10,000. It could then pay its interest of $1,250 and amortization charges of $2,500 with ease, and have a clear profit of $6,250 besides. The company would be prosperous. In both these cases, the corporation feels the effects noted because it is a debtor. Its debts having been contracted in terms of money, it loses if the purchasing power of money rises, gains if it falls. Any other debtor would be affected similarly.

The effects on creditors are just the reverse. For instance, a bond-holder of the milk bottle corporation receives annually a fixed sum of money as interest on his bonds; and, he can look forward to the return of a fixed money principal at the end of ten years. If prices fall, neither his interest nor his principal decreases—he receives just as much as before; but this money will buy more goods, because the latter are cheaper. His standard of living rises. On the other hand, if prices rise, he loses. His interest and principal remain unchanged, but they will buy less goods. He feels keenly the pinch of the rising cost of living; his standard of living is reduced. All other creditors are in a similar position. If they depend mainly for their living on the fixed money income from their investments, they suffer a real hardship.

We will realize how far-reaching are these effects if we consider the enormous number of persons who are in either a creditor or a debtor position. When the price level rises, millions of debtors (such as enterprisers and stockholders—whose corporations are often doing business on borrowed funds) reap profits at the expense of millions of bondholders and other creditors. The creditors may be educational foundations, who now find the income from their endowments inadequate to meet the increased money expenses caused by a rising price level. They may be the recipients of insurance funds, painstakingly accumulated by someone through long years of saving, to provide what was expected to be an adequate income for helpless widows and children, or to care for the declining years of old age. The effect of the rising price level is equivalent to confiscation of part of the savings represented by these endowments and insurance policies. On the other hand, a falling price level makes it impossible for many debtors to meet their obligations. During the falling price level which accompanied the Great Depression of the 1930's, thousands of home-owners and farmers lost their homes and farms because of their inability to meet the interest on their debts. These debts consisted of mortgages couched in the form of fixed money sums, made at a time when prices, including the price of real estate, were high. When the fall in prices came, the money incomes of the mortgagors fell with them, until these incomes reached a point where it was no longer possible to pay the interest on the mortgages. Foreclosures followed, and the wealth of the unfortunate debtors passed into other hands. Falling prices also meant the bankruptcy of many business firms, with consequent stoppage of industrial activity and the creation of unemployment.

Other Effects of Changing Price Levels. — An unstable price level also has far-reaching effects upon the prosperity of wage-earners. The labor market is sluggish, and money wages cannot be adjusted immediately to every change in the general level of prices. This is especially true where wages are fixed by collective agreements which have several years to run. If prices rise and wages do not, the laborer loses; if prices fall, he gains. There is, in fact, some tendency for wages to lag behind in periods of rising prices; but the organization of labor unions has made this less true than it formerly was. The unions are often able to force wages up as fast as prices rise—sometimes even faster. Falling prices are almost certain to bring disaster upon the laboring class, because they lead to unemployment. However, for those laborers who continue to be employed, there is likely to be some gain, for their wages will not usually decline as rapidly as commodity prices.

Rising price levels usually lead to increasing business profits, for business enterprisers finance their operations very largely on money loans, the amount of which remains fixed, while the selling prices of their merchandise increase. They also gain, as employers, from the lag of money wages behind commodity prices. Finally, they gain from the fact that, as prices keep going up, the money value of the goods which they have purchased is continually rising while it is in their hands. By laying in stores of materials or merchandise in advance, and selling them later, when prices have risen, they reap a corresponding profit. When prices fall, however, the effects upon business men are very disastrous, for now the reverse of the conditions just described takes place. The prices of goods in producers' hands fall, so that there is loss on all stocks laid in in anticipation of future sales; wages fall more slowly than the prices at which commodities are sold; and money debts remain as great as before, while money incomes from business operations are declining.

Because of these effects, rising prices have a stimulating effect upon business, promoting activity and causing a sort of feverish prosperity. Falling prices, on the other hand, have a depressing effect, causing stagnation. Hence, business men favor rising prices, and are likely to favor some inflation of bank credit to bring this about. They forget that such prosperity is purchased at the expense of other members of the community, who suffer by rising prices, and that eventually it brings about a disastrous reaction, as we shall see. Stability of the price level, and an even tenor of business activity, would promote a more healthy condition of economic life, and is greatly to be desired. The failure of the existing monetary system to provide it is one of the great weaknesses of the present economic organization of society.

The Effects of Extreme Monetary Inflation and Deflation. — All these effects are most marked during those periods of extreme monetary inflation and deflation which were described in Chapter VIII. We can perhaps appreciate the enormity of the catastrophe involved in such inflation by considering how the wealth of thousands of people can be completely wiped out by it. Let us imagine the situation in Germany, following the first World War, when inflation in that country had passed all bounds. Thousands of investors had put their savings into mortgages on real estate, into the bonds of corporations, and into the bonds of the German government itself. In many cases these investments represented the entire fortunes of the investors. They

were debts contracted in terms of German marks, and they represented, at the time of the loans, large quantities of wealth. Then marks
began to depreciate and prices began to soar. When prices had increased so many times that every commodity sold brought into the
seller's hands thousands of times as many marks as it formerly had,
it was a comparatively simple matter for the debtor corporations to
pay off their bond issues and mortgages in the depreciated currency.
It was as though a debt of thousands of dollars could be paid off for a
few cents. In this way the debts of many corporations were easily
discharged—at the expense of the creditors. The latter received as
many marks as they had originally invested, to be sure; but these
marks were practically worthless. The fortunes of the investors were
gone. They had been defrauded of their wealth by the depreciation
of the currency. Even creditors of the German government, who
bought bonds in good faith, found the value of these bonds shrinking and shrinking, until they became so much worthless paper.

The results of sharp deflation are likewise very serious. All the effects of falling prices, described in the foregoing paragraphs, are
aggravated. Debts cannot be paid, so that debtors and creditors both
lose. Businesses fail by the thousands, factories close down, unemployment ensues. It is a time of general paralysis, accompanied by
much suffering.

It must not be supposed, however, that because the effects of fluctuating price levels are most pronounced in times of drastic monetary
inflation and deflation, they are not a serious problem at other times.
Any substantial change in prices creates disturbance. The problem is,
therefore, a perennial one.

B. THE CAUSES OF PRICE LEVEL MOVEMENTS

The Equation of Exchange. — Let us now proceed to consider the
causes of these fluctuations. Enough has been said already to suggest
that these causes are largely monetary. The problem is one of the
changing value of money. Like other values, this value is chiefly a
matter of demand and supply—the demand for and supply of money.
The demand for money consists of all the goods which are offered
in exchange for it; the supply is made up of all the means of payment actually used in the purchase of goods. Since nearly all the
goods produced are sold for money, and nearly all the money is used
to purchase goods, it is roughly true that the value of money, and
hence the price level, depends upon the ratio of money to goods.

The same proposition can be arrived at by another line of reasoning. If we give $4.00 of money for 10 pounds of coffee, the av-

erage price of the coffee is 40 cents per pound. That is, the average price of one unit of the goods is equal to the total quantity of money paid for them, divided by the number of units of the goods. If we let p equal the price of a unit of goods, m the money paid for them, and t the total of goods bought, then $p = \dfrac{m}{t}$. This is true of any transaction; it must, therefore, be true of all transactions put together. That is, the average of all prices must be equal to the sum of all the money paid for goods, divided by the total number of goods sold. This simple proposition needs some elaboration. Let us look more closely at the two things—money and goods.

The supply of money, we have learned, consists, firstly, of cash —gold and silver coin and bullion, government notes, bank notes, any other kind of paper money, and subsidiary coins. It consists, secondly, of bank deposits subject to check (demand deposits). However, some of this money may be used little or not at all, while other portions of it may be used a great deal. Most of our gold and silver coin and bullion is securely locked up in government strongholds; it does not circulate in exchange. So long as this money is not actually in circulation, it cannot enter into the determination of prices. It is likewise with demand deposits, carried on the books of the banks; unless checks are actually drawn against them, they do not enter into the price-determining process. On the other hand, the cash and bank deposits which actually do circulate may be used over and over again in the course of a few weeks or months. Every time they are used they help to determine a price. Therefore, the total supply of purchasing power which really enters into the determination of the price level consists of (a) the volume of money of all kinds in the community, and (b) the rapidity or velocity of circulation (i.e., the turnover) thereof.

The demand for money, we have seen, consists of all the goods which are offered in exchange for it. These goods include not only physical commodities, but the services of laborers, the making of loans, the renting of real estate, and so on. In fact, every time there is a business transaction of any kind in which any commodity or service is offered in exchange for any form of money payment, the price level is affected thereby. Furthermore, if a given article passes through several hands (as when it is sold by a manufacturer to a wholesaler, by a wholesaler to a retailer, and by a retailer to a final consumer), a price is established at each such transfer. Therefore, it enters into the price level several times. We find, then, that the demand for money consists of the total number of units of commodities and services that enter into exchange; or we may say, simply, it consists of the total number of exchange transactions that take place within a given period of time.

The relation between these various elements is most conveniently expressed in an algebraic formula, known as *the equation of exchange*. This equation may be written as follows: $P = \dfrac{MV}{T}$. Here P stands for the average, or general level, of prices. M represents the total stock of money, including both cash and demand deposits,[2] either in active circulation or in bank or government vaults. V indicates the velocity of circulation, or rate of turnover, of this money.[3] T is the total volume of trade, or the number of transfers of commodities and services entering into exchange. It will be observed that the value of P (the average, or general level, of prices) depends upon the ratio between the numerator and denominator of the fraction with which it is equated. The numerator of the fraction represents the circulation, or "flow," of money; the denominator represents goods. Any increase in the flow of money raises the value of the numerator and tends to increase the magnitude of P. Any increase in the volume of trade, on the other hand, raises the value of the denominator and tends to decrease the size of P. So, the equation is a convenient way of stating the truth, that the general level of prices varies directly with the flow of money and inversely with the flow of goods. It also indicates in some detail the various factors that are at work in determining the price level.

The Quantity Theory. — The relationships expressed in the equation of exchange are sometimes referred to as *the quantity theory of money*. This term is more accurately used, however, to describe a particular theory of prices which was once widely held by economists, and is still defended by a few. According to this particular theory, M (and especially that part of M which consists of cash) is supposed to be the most important item in the equation. In other words, the price level is said to be moved upwards or downwards by changes in the quantity of cash in the monetary system. To support this theory, it must be established that the other factors which we have noted are either passive, or are dependent upon the quantity of cash. The quantity theorists believe that, in a given state of industrial development, with established banking facilities and practices, the velocity of circulation of money is not actively changing;

---

[2] Some writers prefer to separate deposit money from cash in this equation. It is then written $P = \dfrac{MV + M'V'}{T}$, where M stands for cash and M' for demand deposits, V and V' for their respective velocities of circulation.

[3] The velocity of that money which is held in the vaults as reserve is, of course, zero; hence this money has no direct effect upon the value of P at all.

hence, it can be taken as given, and will not be a significant cause of changes in prices. They assert, further, that the volume of trade changes rather steadily and slowly. These two factors, therefore, are not thought to be important. There remain, then, only two factors—the volume of cash and the volume of deposit money. The amount of deposits is said to depend on the quantity of cash, because of the requirements concerning bank reserves. This is based on the fact, explained in the preceding chapter, that the amount of cash in the reserves sets a limit to the quantity of deposit money that the banks

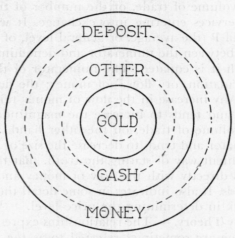

Figure 9. The Relation of Gold to
Other Forms of Money.

can issue. The quantity theorists admit that there may be some contraction and expansion of bank deposits within these limits, over short periods, but they argue that, over longer periods, the average volume of deposit money will bear a certain relation to the volume of cash reserves. Hence, if the quantity of cash increases, deposit money will expand in the same proportion; if it decreases, deposit money will contract correspondingly. They argue further, that, if a country maintains the gold standard, since all its paper money, as well as its deposits, must then be convertible into gold, the whole volume of the monetary circulation will depend on the quantity of gold in the system. This is illustrated in Figure 9. With a volume of gold of the size shown by the inner circle, an amount of paper money can be built up not exceeding the limit represented by the second circle, and deposit money not greater than the wider limit represented by the outermost circle. These limits change with the quantity of gold, as shown by the dotted lines. By this chain of reasoning it is sought to establish that cash, and particularly gold (in most cases), is the ultimately controlling factor in determining prices.

This theory has been subjected to so much criticism in recent years that few economists now hold it, except in a very qualified form. The critics point out that the velocity of circulation of cash and of deposits, the volume of deposit money itself, and the volume of trade, are all subject to independent fluctuations from causes having no connection with the quantity of cash or of gold; therefore, changes in the price level cannot be attributed solely, nor even mainly, to the latter. Moreover, in an economy where goods are sold today to be paid for sometime in the future, it is possible that changes in prices may be the cause of changes in the quantity of money (instead of the result); for, if business men obligate themselves to make certain payments in the future, they may go to the banks and borrow the funds needed to fulfill these obligations, thereby bringing deposit money into existence. The reply, sometimes made by quantity theorists to this objection, that these changes are confined to the short run, and that in the long run a certain average relation between the quantity of cash and the level of prices must hold, is beside the point. Short-run changes in prices may be just as significant as long-run changes; indeed, many of the most pressing problems of contemporary economic life are short-run problems. Therefore, a theory which ignores the short run, and explains only long-run phenomena, is inadequate. Moreover, not even all long-run changes in the level of prices can be attributed to changes in the quantity of cash. Customs and laws may be equally important. For instance, the growth of deposit banking over the past few decades has tended to increase the ratio of bank deposits to cash in the monetary system; and the passage of the Federal Reserve Act, in 1913, greatly increased the quantity of deposit money which a given volume of reserves could support. In this case, deposits were the important factor making for a rise in prices.

All this is not to deny that changes in the quantity of cash will exert an important influence on the price level. Under gold standard conditions, an increase in the world output of gold does tend to swell the cash reserves of countries whose monetary systems are based upon gold, and this does tend to increase the volume of deposit money, thereby exerting an upward influence upon the price level, in the manner set forth by the quantity theory. The steady upward rise of prices, which took place in this and other gold standard countries from 1896 up to the time of the first World War, was probably due to this cause, for this was a period in which new mining methods were greatly increasing the world output of gold. Also, a marked paper money inflation will undoubtedly raise prices sharply, as it did in most countries during and after the war. Subsequent deflation can produce a corresponding fall in prices. However, it is now fairly clear that changes in the price level cannot be attributed solely, nor even chiefly, to causes of this kind. Therefore the quantity theory, in its narrower form, cannot be upheld. It can be made tenable only by qualifying it so much that it loses most of its significance.

The Causes of Changes in the Price Level. — What generalization can we make, then, concerning the causes of changes in the general level of prices? Simply this, that *any* condition which affects *any* of the items in the equation of exchange is a potential cause of a change in the price level. Optimism on the part of business men, which causes them to anticipate higher prices, may cause such prices to be quoted, thus raising the value of P in the equation of exchange —and the flow of money may adjust itself to the new quotations. Pessimism may have the contrary result. An increase in the size of the specie reserves, either because of changes in the output of gold or silver, or because gold is flowing into a country in response to changing conditions of international trade, may affect M in the equation, and thereby change the level of prices. A change in the metallic content of the standard monetary unit may have similar effects. For instance, if the number of grains of gold in a standard dollar is reduced (as it was in 1933), more dollars can be circulated against a given volume of gold reserves, exerting an upward influence upon prices. The issue or retirement of paper money tends to raise or lower the magnitude of M in the equation, and it influences P correspondingly. The growth of banking facilities also tends to increase M, and thereby to raise prices. Expansion of bank loans, in response to more active demand on the part of business men, has a similar effect. Contraction of loans works in the opposite direction. If a bank crisis occurs, with a general loss of confidence in bank credit, there may be a rapid shrinkage in M, with a sharp drop in prices. Changes in the volume of production, through their effects on T, tend to raise or lower the price level. Changes in the structure of industry may also influence prices, through their effect on the number of exchange transactions. For instance, the vertical integration of business enterprises, by eliminating exchanges between the successive stages of production, decreases the size of T, and thereby tends to raise the price level. Finally, recent investigation has shown that the velocity of circulation of both cash and credit is subject to considerable fluctuation, so that these items, instead of being passive, are now regarded as important influences.

Not all of the factors above enumerated act independently; there are numerous interactions among them. Sometimes several factors reënforce each other in such a way as to induce a general upward or downward movement of prices. For instance, an inflow of gold from abroad, by increasing bank reserves, may cause the banks to lend money more freely, and this may cause business men to increase their borrowing; thus M' expands with M. The resultant rise in prices may stimulate increased business activity, which increases the volume of T. Increased activity, in turn, speeds up the circulation of money, V. On the other hand, a change in one of the items of the equation may sometimes be offset by a compensating change in one or more of the other items. The increased velocity of money which accompanies business expansion is partly offset by the increase in the size of T which results from increased production. In view of all these considerations, it can be appreciated that the causes determining the level of prices are very complex. The factors at work in any given case cannot be ascertained by *a priori* reasoning, but must be discovered by careful analysis of all the surrounding circumstances. The equation of exchange tells us where to look for the factors which are at work, but it does not tell us which influences are most active in the given situation. It is a tool of analysis, but not a complete explanation.

The Money Balance Form of the Equation of Exchange. — In the form in which we have been considering it, the equation of exchange lays stress on the velocity of circulation of money as an active element in determining the price level. The item V represents money in motion—in the act of being spent for goods. There is another form of the equation which is preferred by some writers, especially in Great Britain. It stresses the importance of money at rest—of money which is unspent for the time being. Each person who has any claim to a share in the proceeds of industry receives a certain amount of gross money income more or less regularly, from week to week or from month to month. He does not spend all of these receipts immediately; a part he prefers to hold in cash, or in the form of a balance at his bank. These holdings constitute his money balance, or his "unspent margin," as the economist Hawtrey has called it.

There is a close relation between these holdings and the velocity of circulation of money, for they are really two different aspects of the same thing. While money is being held in an unspent balance it is not circulating; therefore its velocity for the time being is zero. It has velocity only when it is in the act of being spent, at which time it leaves one person's balance, only to come to rest in another. In view of this relationship, it is possible to measure the two phenomena in similar terms. In the previous equation, we measured velocity by the average number of times that money is turned over in a given period (usually a year). So, now, we can measure people's holdings of money by the average length of the period in which money is held idle, before it is spent. If a person receives $3,000 each year, and holds an average money balance of $150, it is evident that his balance is $\frac{1}{20}$ of a year's money income. By the same method, we can ascertain the average fraction of a year's income which the whole community holds in the form of money. This fraction is denoted by the symbol K. The mathematical relationship between K and the symbol V is that the one is the reciprocal of the other. For example, if money is being held, on the average, for half a year before being spent, its velocity of circulation must be two times per year; therefore, in this case, $K = \frac{1}{2}$ and $V = 2$. If the money is held for three months, its velocity must be four times yearly; here $K = \frac{1}{4}$ and $V = 4$. So, in every case, $K = \frac{1}{V}$ and $V = \frac{1}{K}$.

This makes it possible to write the equation of exchange in another form, in which K appears in place of V. Since $V = \frac{1}{K}$, we can write $P = \frac{MV}{T} = \frac{\frac{M}{K}}{T}$. So, we derive the new equation, $P = \frac{M}{KT}$, or $M = KTP$.

Alleged Advantages of the Money Balance Approach. — It follows from this discussion that, in the money balance approach to the price level, the same fundamental factors are at work as in the earlier version, namely, the volume of money, its velocity of circulation (now represented as the average time period over which money is held unspent), and the volume of trade. However, those who prefer this second form of the equation do so largely because it focusses attention on certain monetary factors that might readily be overlooked when the other equation is used.

Let us trace some of these factors. There appear to be three reasons why people choose to hold part of their assets in money, instead of in goods. In the first place, money incomes are usually received at stated intervals—wages are paid once each week or fortnight, salaries are usually paid monthly, dividends once or twice a year. The receipts of business men are likewise somewhat periodic—bills may be collected monthly, or intermittently, as orders are delivered. On the other hand, a great many expenditures must be made from day to day. The housewife finds it convenient to do her shopping on several days of the week, even though her husband gets his pay envelope on Saturday, and the business man must pay his workers weekly, even though his customers pay him less often. Therefore, the recipient of money income cannot spend it all on the day he receives it; he must spread it out over the period that will elapse before his next receipts are to be expected. Following the terminology of the British writer Keynes, we may call this *the transactions motive* for holding money. In the second place, ordinary prudence makes it wise to hold a certain amount of money in reserve for contingencies. The wise man keeps a balance on hand to meet possible expenses caused by sickness or accident; the prudent business man holds a reserve against the breakdown of a machine which may require expensive repairs, and so on. This reason for holding money Keynes calls *the precautionary motive*. Finally, people may hold money from a *speculative motive*. For instance, if prices are expected to fall, one may postpone contemplated purchases of goods, in the hope that they will presently be cheaper; money will then be held in reserve for this eventuality. On the other hand, if prices are expected to rise, one is tempted to spend immediately, before things get dearer; in that case the amount held for speculative purposes will be reduced.

The size of K depends on the strength of these motives. If they are strong, K will be a relatively large fraction of a year; if they are weak, it will be a smaller fraction. How strong they will be depends, in turn, partly on the background of economic and social institutions prevailing, and partly on the other variables in the equation of exchange. The background of institutions is important, because such things as the abundance or scarcity of banking facilities, and their safety or riskiness, will affect the ease with which money can be held and disbursed, while such things as the methods of wage payment which happen to be customary (whether by the day, week, or fortnight) will affect the way in which money expenditures must be spread out. The other variables in the equation are important, because K is not an entirely independent factor—it is interrelated with P and T. This will appear in what follows.

A second advantage claimed for the form of the equation which we are now considering is, that it sets the demand for money directly over against the supply of it. Let us look again at the equation, in the form $M = KTP$. Here M is the total supply of money in the community, and KTP is the total demand for it, or the total of money balances. This demand depends on the three factors that make it up; that is, it depends on the average time period for which money is held (K), on the total volume of goods offered for sale (T), and on the average prices paid for those goods (P). The demand represented by these three factors must be equal to the supply of money (M), be-

cause all the money in existence must be held by somebody. Therefore, if there is a discrepancy between the amount of money in existence, and the quantity of it which people *wish to hold* in their
unspent balances, there will be readjustments in some or all of the
items in the equation until a stable equilibrium is established (that
is, until people are willing to hold all the money there is, so that
the demand for money is equal to the supply of it). For instance, suppose the supply of money to increase to the point where there is
more of it than people wish to hold. They will then spend money
somewhat faster than they formerly did (a decrease in K), and this
increased spending will cause prices to rise (an increase in P), until
the higher level of prices forces people to hold more money for transactions purposes (K increases again). There may be further repercussions in other directions (for instance production may be stimulated,
so that T increases, and there may be some tendency to invest money
in goods for speculative purposes, which tends to reduce K); but in
the end, a stable equilibrium tends to be worked out, at a higher
price level, where people are led to hold willingly all the new money
that has come into existence. If money decreases to the point where
there is less of it than people want to hold, all these influences will
work in the opposite direction. An initial increase or decrease in any
of the other items will have similar repercussions. The exact causal
sequence in each case depends upon the particular circumstances.

So the equation constitutes an effective tool for analysis of the
mutual relationships between money, prices and production. Some
writers have found it especially useful for investigating the problems
of economic instability, which will engage our attention in the next
two chapters. Its superiority for this purpose is not conceded by all
economists, however. It is not really necessary to have two equations so nearly alike. Therefore, we shall continue to use the equation $P = \dfrac{MV}{T}$, which is quite adequate for the purposes of our subsequent discussion.

SUMMARY

The general level of prices is subject to fluctuations, which can
be measured by means of index numbers. Such indexes indicate that
the price level (and hence the value of money) is very unstable. Rising prices benefit debtors and business enterprisers, injure creditors
and wage-earners; falling prices have the opposite effects. The instability of prices aggravates the ups and downs of business prosperity
and depressions. All these effects are much more severe when brought
about by extreme monetary inflation or deflation.

Changes in the general level of prices are effected through the items in the equation of exchange, $P = \dfrac{MV}{T}$. Another form of this equation, stressing people's demand for money, as reflected in their money balances, is $P = \dfrac{M}{KT}$, or $M = KTP$. According to the quantity theory, cash (and especially gold, where the gold standard prevails) is held to be the most important factor in this equation; but critics point out that any of the items may be causal. The real causes of changes in the price level lie in the various influences which may affect one or more of these items.

REFERENCES AND SUGGESTIONS FOR FURTHER READING

A clear and detailed analysis of the equation of exchange is set forth in Irving Fisher's *The Purchasing Power of Money* (1911). For a briefer statement of his ideas, see his *Elementary Principles of Economics* (1910), Chapters 8 to 12. Both forms of the equation of exchange are quite fully dealt with in Chapters II to IV of Lester V. Chandler's *An Introduction to Monetary Theory* (1940).

Both Fisher and Chandler support the quantity theory in a very qualified form. For arguments against the quantity theory, consult Wesley C. Mitchell's *Business Cycles: The Problem and its Setting* (1927), Chapter II, Part IV, sec. 5; and Chapter XXVI of J. S. Lawrence's *Stabilization of Prices* (1928).

Chapter XI

MONETARY ASPECTS OF ECONOMIC BALANCE

A. SAY'S LAW AND ITS IMPLICATIONS

Monetary Influences on the Volume and Direction of Economic Activity. — If the economic system is to function efficiently, it must accomplish two things—it must find work for all the productive agents whose employment is worth while for the community, and it must direct their use into the proper channels. In other words, an efficient economy maintains full employment, and balance. Full employment does not mean that every member of the population and every bit of capital must be working day and night; it means only that every able-bodied person who desires remunerative work must be able to find it, that savings shall be invested in productive equipment, and that equipment must not be forced to lie wholly or partly idle for want of a market for its products. Balance in the economy refers to that condition where the various branches of industry are nicely adjusted to each other, and the whole directed toward the wants of consumers in such a way that there is a smoothly flowing stream of raw materials, partly finished and finished goods, moving from forest, field, and mine, through the factories, warehouses, and shops to the consumers. If industry is to be properly balanced, there must be produced just the right quantity of clothing, foodstuffs, houses, automobiles, books, musical instruments, and other consumers' goods to conform to the desires and money incomes of the people, and there must be just enough raw materials, skilled and unskilled labor of each type, equipment of the proper sorts, and so on, to supply the wherewithal for these consumable goods. In order to meet the needs of consumers for clothing, retailers and wholesalers must have laid in just the right stock of it, manufacturers must have made up just enough to supply these dealers, just enough wool and cotton must have been grown to supply the manufacturers with materials for the clothing, there must be

enough coal to operate their furnaces, just the right quantity of
railroad cars, locomotives, and men to haul the coal, cotton, wool,
and finished suits to the places where they are needed, and so on.
Similarly, there must be just the right quantities of potatoes, corn,
wheat, and other foodstuffs, and of fertilizers, agricultural implements, farm labor, and transportation facilities to make this possible.

It should be the function of money to facilitate, but not to interfere with, this process. It was shown in the previous chapter, however, that the vagaries of the monetary system exert disturbing effects
upon the economy. In that chapter, our attention was focused upon
the fortunes of debtors, creditors, wage-earners, and enterprisers.
However, the disturbances which an erratic medium of exchange
can cause are not confined to the gains and losses which occur to
these several classes of persons. The phenomena of money ramify
deeply into every aspect of economic life; therefore, monetary
changes are capable of influencing both the volume and direction
of economic activity. There are times when expansion of the currency, by raising prices and thus boosting profits, stimulates business
to very high levels of activity. There are other times when deflation
of the currency lowers prices and reduces profits, causing (or ag-
gravating) a general decline in activity. Also, the entrance of new
money (especially bank credit) into circulation at this or that point
in the system will induce an expansion in the affected sections of
industry which throws the economic process out of balance. Withdrawal of money, by causing contraction at the points where it passes
out of circulation, can be equally upsetting.

We must investigate these things. In the present chapter, therefore, we shall consider some of the factors upon which the maintenance of full and balanced activity depends, with special reference
to the effects of monetary disturbances.

Say's Law. — One of the most fundamental propositions concerning the level of economic activity was first clearly stated more than
a century ago by the French economist, J. B. Say. He pointed out
that practically all the goods produced within a country are exchanged for each other.[1] In a system of specialization, each producer
is making goods in the expectation of selling them—that is, of exchanging them for other goods. He is offering to buy the goods of
other producers with his own products. Therefore, every product
is a demand for, and a means of purchasing other products. The

---

[1] The fact that many goods are exported to other countries does not alter the essential truth of this statement; for sooner or later there is imported in exchange for
them an equivalent quantity of foreign goods which enter into domestic trade the same
as if the goods exported had been retained here. The truth of this will be made evident in the chapters on international trade.

whole of economic activity resolves itself into one vast mutual interchange of goods. The aggregate demand for all the products taken together, therefore, is—those products. *The total demand for goods is the total of goods produced.* This is known as *Say's law of markets,* or, more often, simply as *Say's law.*

The law can be made clearer by the aid of the diagram in Figure 10. We here suppose a community all of whose people are engaged in producing the few staple commodities represented in the circles of the drawing. The manufacturer who makes clothing does so be-

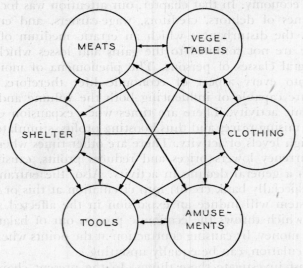

Figure 10. The Identity of Total Demand and Total Supply.

cause he believes the other members of the community will desire it, and that they will take it in exchange for their products. His offer of clothing, therefore, constitutes a demand for meats, vegetables, shelter, tools, and the like. Each of the other members of the community, in turn, expects to exchange a part of his goods for clothing. The part of their products which they offer for this purpose constitutes the demand for clothing. The exchange of the clothing for the other goods is indicated by the connecting lines. Similarly, each other product is offered for a part of all the others. The sum of the individual products, therefore, constitutes the total of offers, and makes up the aggregate demand. We therefore see that the aggregate demand and supply of the goods in the community are one and the same thing. All the goods are exchanged for each other.

The Circuit Flow of Money. — In this explanation of Say's law, goods have been represented as being exchanged directly for other goods. We know, however, that exchange takes place in this way only under conditions of barter. In modern economies, goods are first exchanged for money and the money is then used to purchase other goods. The introduction of money does not alter the fact that goods are produced in the expectation of exchanging them for other goods, nor does it alter the fundamental truth that the total supply of goods is, in the last analysis, the total demand, but it does complicate the relationship, and it creates possibilities of maladjustment that would not arise under barter conditions. Let us first translate Say's law into money terms; we shall then consider some of the maladjustments.

The monetary equivalent of Say's law can be stated as follows: the money incomes of the members of the community are equal to the money costs of production—in fact, they are identical. Money costs consist of payments of money made by enterprisers to those who participate in production—wages to labor, interest or rent for the use of equipment, and possibly profit to enterprisers.[2] Payments for materials purchased become wages, interest, and rent for labor and equipment employed in producing those materials. Wages, interest, rent, and profits are incomes to their recipients; therefore it is impossible for the total of money incomes to be any less than the total of money costs. Furthermore, unless new money is created they cannot be any greater, for the only source from which money income can be obtained will be either directly from enterprisers in return for productive services rendered, or by transfer (a gift, for instance) from someone who has been so paid. It follows that if there is any deficiency of total demand for goods relative to the total supply of them, it cannot arise from inadequacy of income. The money incomes of consumers should suffice to buy the goods which enterprisers produce, without loss to the latter.

The identity of money incomes and money costs can be more clearly visualized by Figure 11, which pictures the flow of money from income recipients, through industry, back to the income recipients again. This cycle is often referred to as the circuit flow of money.[3] Looking at the left side of the diagram, we observe that

[2] For the purpose of this analysis, profits must be treated as costs, for whatever an enterpriser receives for his goods is cost to the person who buys them from him.

[3] The rate at which money passes through this cycle is known as the *circuit velocity* of money (also called *income velocity*). This differs somewhat from the exchange velocity described in the last chapter. In computing exchange velocity, money is counted every time it passes from one person to another in the purchase of goods; in computing circuit velocity, it is counted only each time that it completes the circuit from consumers, through the various stages of industry, back to consumers again. For example: If, in a given time period, a person spends a dollar for groceries, and the grocer turns it over to a wholesaler in the purchase of supplies, and the wholesaler pays it in wages to an

the money spent by income recipients in consumption goes to purchase near-goods, and is paid out by the sellers thereof to the agents of production used in producing them, which agents, in their capacity as income recipients return it into the flow again. Thus it goes round and round the circle perpetually, unless destroyed or withdrawn in ways which are not yet apparent. At first thought, it might seem that money saved would be withdrawn from the flow, thereby causing the total monetary demand to fall short of money costs. However, this is true only if the savings are hoarded, which is not

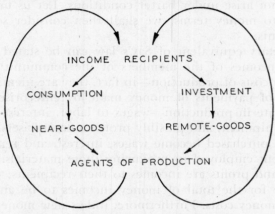

Figure 11. The Circuit Flow of Money.

usually the case. Ordinarily savings are invested, in which event the money saved is used to purchase remote-goods, and is passed on to agents of production by the sellers thereof, the same as when it is spent for near-goods. Thus money saved and invested likewise goes round and round the circle repeatedly. This is shown by the right side of the diagram. The diagram shows clearly the identity of money incomes with money costs. It follows that the total monetary demand for goods should be equal to the total costs of supplying them, provided all the money received by the members of the community is either spent or invested.

The Assumptions Underlying Say's Law. — The proviso just stated suggests that conditions may arise in which the identity of money demand with money costs may be destroyed. Say's law, in its monetary form, rests upon the assumption that the circuit flow of money will not be broken. Unfortunately this assumption does not

employee (who, as a consumer, will subsequently use it to buy goods for his own consumption), its exchange velocity in that period is three, but its circuit velocity is only one.

always hold. Circumstances may arise in which part of the money received by the agents of production will be hoarded, either in the form of stores of cash or in the form of unused bank deposits, so that the total money demand for goods falls short of money costs. The goods cannot then be sold without loss to producers, and a partial stoppage of production is likely to result. Again, money may pass out of existence through the liquidation of bank loans and a consequent reduction in the volume of bank deposits. This may also cause the amount of money demand to fall short of money costs. Both the conditions here described have occurred from time to time, causing serious disturbance of the balance of industry.

It is likewise possible for new money to be introduced into the circuit flow as a result of increased production of specie, the issuing of new paper currency, or the expansion of bank credit. The effects of this will depend partly on the point in the circuit at which the new money first appears. We shall see that this also is likely to disturb the balance of industry and bring about unfavorable repercussions.

Another assumption underlying Say's law is that the various kinds of goods will be produced in proportions that correspond to the several demands for them. Suppose that consumers are trying to spend 30 per cent of their incomes on foods and 20 per cent on clothing, but that only 20 per cent of enterprisers' expenditures in production is going into foodstuffs, while 30 per cent is going into clothing; then the demand for foodstuffs will exceed the supply of them, while the demand for clothing will fall short of the supply. This will destroy the identity between the total demand for all goods taken collectively and the total supply, because consumers will have surplus incomes which are not being spent, and producers will have surplus goods which they cannot sell.

Our economic system depends upon the movement of prices to correct such a condition of unbalance. The excess supply of clothing will cause its price to fall below its money costs, while the excess demand for foods will cause their prices to rise above their costs. The high price of foodstuffs will encourage more of them to be produced, while the low price of clothing will bring about curtailment in that industry until balance is restored. In the long run, therefore, the identity of total demand with total supply will be maintained, provided the price system does its work. But this involves the further assumption that a flexible price system prevails, in which the prices of goods are free to move up and down in response to the influence of demand and supply. Not only must the prices of commodities be flexible but so also must be the prices

of the agents of production (wages, interest, and rent) so that labor
and equipment may move into the industries where they are demanded. If any of these prices are rigidly held at fixed points, this
adjustment will be interfered with and a condition of maladjustment
may result. Unfortunately there are tendencies to rigidity in the
present economy which makes for an inflexible price system and
which, therefore, tends to unbalance the economic process.

Of the two basic assumptions just explained which are requisite
to the validity of Say's law, the first is monetary, the second non-
monetary. The disturbances to the economy which result from the
failure of these assumptions always to hold true are accordingly due
partly to monetary and partly to other causes.

General Overproduction versus Misdirected Production. — If
widespread maladjustments of the sort above described occur, a condition of business depression is likely to prevail. Business men cannot make profits; accordingly, they reduce their outputs or close their
plants entirely and dismiss many of their employees, so that there
is a great deal of unemployment, loss of earning power, and priva-
tion. At such times the notion is likely to prevail that too much has
been produced. General overproduction is often put forward as an
explanation of business depressions by the ill-informed. At such
times various proposals are strongly advocated, which have, as their
general object, the checking of production in the future, so that
the alleged glut of merchandise will not occur again. The proposals
may take the form of a demand for reduced working hours which
will curtail the output of labor; or they may be directed at establishing maximum production quotas for each industry. The foregoing
analysis reveals that this diagnosis is faulty and that such remedies
are ill-advised. An understanding of Say's law should make it clear
that the trouble cannot lie in an excess of total production. Production can never outrun demand so long as goods are produced in
the right proportion and so long as the circuit flow of money is not
disturbed.

It is remotely conceivable that a time may come when the people
of society will have so many goods that they will desire no more.
This time is so far distant, however, that it is not a matter of practical moment. To all intents and purposes the desires of contemporary peoples, and hence their willingness to consume goods, will long
remain far in excess of their capacity to produce them. There can
be no general overproduction, then, in the sense of production in
excess of desires. Given an uninterrupted circuit flow of money,
there can be no aggregate production in excess of purchasing power,
for the money incomes of consumers must then always be equal to

the money costs of production. This is the fundamental truth of Say's law. Hence, if a condition of *apparent* overproduction exists, it must be due to one of two general types of difficulties—either the circuit flow of money must have been interrupted, or goods must have been produced in the wrong proportions. In either case, the remedy is not to produce a smaller aggregate volume of goods. If the difficulty is of the first sort, monetary correctives are indicated. If it is of the second sort, the guidance of production by prices is at fault; either improvement of the pricing mechanism is needed or some other method of directing production must be sought. An all-around restriction of production will not remedy either condition; it will simply make the community poorer in real income.

When goods have been produced in unbalanced proportions it is quite correct to say that there has been overproduction in particular branches of industry. By the same token, there has been underproduction in other branches. The general condition is one of *misdirected production*. The remedy is to direct production into the proper channels. Provided the monetary system is not functioning badly, it will then be found there is plenty of purchasing power to buy all that is produced at prices which will cover their costs.

History confirms the general reasoning of Say's law. The Industrial Revolution, with its specialized labor and its power-driven machinery, greatly increased the production of goods in the western world. Yet this did not cause any general glut of products. The various populations found plenty of use for all the goods and plenty of purchasing power to buy them with. Industry has been subject to ups and downs, to be sure, but this does not alter the fact that, on the average, we produce and find the means to pay for many times as much product as the people of a century or two ago. The occasional breakdowns which occur are not due to excessive production, but to other difficulties which have already been partly indicated and which our subsequent analysis will reveal more fully.

"Lump of Labor" and "Make Work" Policies. — Very similar to the general overproduction fallacy is the belief that there is only a certain amount of work to be done in the community, and that, therefore, it is good policy to set up otherwise wasteful or extravagant work projects to keep people occupied, or to oppose any method of saving labor because it will lessen the amount of employment, or to spread every productive operation over as long a period as possible. Workingmen are particularly prone to these notions, and most people hold to one or more of them. It is a common practice for workingmen to oppose efficiency methods in industry, and deliberately to "soldier," or shirk their work. Trade unions often have rules prohibiting their members from doing more than a certain amount of work per day—a policy known as limitation of output. Immigration is sometimes opposed on the ground that it will lessen the opportunities for employment of people already established in this country. It is sometimes thought that women should not enter into industry because it will then be more difficult for men to secure jobs. And disasters, such as hurricanes or blizzards, may be hailed as a blessing in disguise, because it is thought that they will make work for laborers who will be hired to repair the damage or to shovel away the snow.

Now there are special circumstances, of not uncommon occurrence, where this kind of reasoning has some validity. Our discussion of the assumptions underlying Say's law brought out the fact that conditions may arise in which the circuit flow of money has been interrupted, so that the total amount of expenditure is lessened, whereupon prices fall, business men incur losses, and the volume of industrial activity is reduced; also, that the various branches of industry may be so out of balance with each other that the operations of production and exchange are interrupted for the time being. In such situations, it is true that the demand for labor is temporarily limited, and there may actually not be enough work to go around among all the people who are seeking employment. This being the case, the more work each person does, or the greater the number of new immigrants or other persons entering into industry, the less will be the opportunities for employment of others; and the introduction into industry of labor-saving methods or devices at such a time will aggravate the prevailing unemployment. In these circumstances, a policy of limiting the output of those who are employed, and of opposing the adoption of labor-saving methods in industry, may be justified for the time being. The reduction of hours of work for everyone at this time, in order that what work is available may be spread more evenly among all the workers who are seeking employment, may then be reasonably defended.

Furthermore, the creation of work projects by the government, if financed by new money issued for the purpose, or by loans which draw into circulation funds which would otherwise be hoarded, can restore the circuit flow of money to its previous volume, and thereby enable industry to resume its normal functioning. This is the justification for the policy of "pump priming" which has been so popular in the United States during recent periods of business depressions.

There is also a partial justification for the policy of limiting output, so commonly practiced by labor, in the fact that employers are prone to overwork their men. In the early days of the factory system the customary working hours were from sunrise to sunset. Such a working day was entirely too long, so that labor can hardly be blamed for fighting to reduce it. These long hours seldom prevail nowadays, but the pace of industry has been quickened so that workers are likely to be overdriven if they do not defend themselves. In view of this fact the practice of limiting both hours and output is not unreasonable, provided it is not carried past the point where it is needed to protect the health and happiness of the wage-earning classes.

However, all these are special circumstances which justify the "making" of work and the limiting of output only under the given conditions and to a limited degree. In the long run, policies of this sort, if generally practiced, will reduce the real income of the community without bringing any compensating advantages. Provided the various branches of industry are properly balanced and the circuit flow of money is not interrupted, there is no limit to the demand for labor. According to Say's law, every product offered in exchange constitutes a demand for other products. It follows that the addition to production made by each worker constitutes a demand for the products of other workers. Therefore, the demand for labor grows as fast as its supply; in the long run, the one can be neither greater nor less than the other. Every addition to the labor force of a community gives previously established laborers work to do in providing for the needs of the newcomers, while the latter can find employment catering to the ungratified desires of those who were already employed. It is in this way that we have been able to absorb millions of immigrants into our country's industry. In a similar manner we should always be able to find employment for any labor that is released from its former occupation by improvements in the efficiency of industry or by labor-saving inventions which reduce the amount of labor needed in established enterprises.

Illustrations of the Lump of Labor and Make Work Fallacies. — This reasoning will be more convincing if we consider some specific cases in greater detail. Suppose that a great snowstorm occurs. Many laborers will be hired to clean the streets and shovel the sidewalks. Here, it seems, is work created. Provided industry was formerly in balance and the circuit flow of money was running on continuously, however, an equal number of laborers would have been employed if the snowstorm had not occurred. This must be so, for the laborers who shoveled the sidewalks had to be paid for their work by the persons who hired them. Had there been no snowstorm, these persons would have spent their money for something else which they must now do without. Laborers would have been employed to make these other things. The snowstorm, then, has caused less labor to be devoted to producing the latter, and has put men to work at shoveling snow instead. It has changed the *direction* of the demand for labor, but has not increased its *amount*. Society, however, is poorer; for had the snowstorm not occurred, just as much labor would have been employed, and new goods would have been produced; as it is, the new goods are lacking, the productive power that would have created them having been dissipated in getting rid of the troublesome snow. Of course the snow-shovelers gain, but at the expense of the other laborers who would have been employed, and at the expense of society, which has less real income than it might have had.

Or, take the case of the trade union which limits the output of its members below the point necessary to protect them against overdriving. Now it is true that, if the limitations were removed and every laborer did as much work as he could reasonably be expected to do, there might not be needed as many men in that trade as formerly; but the principle of Say's law tells us that the surplus of unneeded workers would be set at new production which would give them ample employment. This would come about in the following way: Since it would now take less labor than before to turn out a given amount of product, that product would cost less. The employers would have more money to spend for other things; or, if the price of the product were reduced, its consumers would have more. They would, therefore, be able to purchase other commodities which they could not formerly buy. The demand for these commodities being thus increased, more labor would be needed to supply the additional output. Thus, new employment would be offered equivalent to that displaced from the industry first considered. Thus there would be just as large a volume of employment as before, and society would have more goods, if these policies were not practiced. By producing less than they reasonably might, workers injure themselves in the long run, for they make goods scarcer and more expensive. Since laborers and their families are the greatest consumers of goods, they are thus cutting off their own noses, as it were.

Temporarily, such practices as limitation of output may have the effect of providing employment or increasing the demand for certain types of labor, but not for labor as a whole. If carpenters do less work than they are capable of doing, it will take more carpenters to accomplish a given task. If people need this work done badly enough there will be a demand for more carpenters, and the latter may be able to get more wages or more employment. But this means that there will be less demand for the labor of other workers because people, having to spend more for carpenters' products than they otherwise would, must spend less for other things. If carpenters are the only group practicing this sort of thing, they benefit at the expense of other labor and of the consuming public. But the practice is almost universal. The carpenter makes the bricklayer pay more for carpenter work than is necessary, and the bricklayer treats the carpenter in like manner, while all the other working groups in the great circle of exchange play the same game. With each trying so to gain at the expense of the rest, they defeat each other's purposes, and there is no gain to anyone, only a loss of real income to all.

Let us take one more case, that of labor-saving machinery, the introduction of which into industry has generally been bitterly opposed by organized labor because of the belief that it displaces labor and causes unemployment. It is true that this effect does result temporarily; permanently, however, such devices do not lessen the amount of employment. Labor-saving machinery makes it possible to produce goods with less labor than formerly. There results a saving in wage costs which will either be passed on to consumers in lower prices or will accrue to the enterprisers in increased profit. If the consumer gets the benefit, he will need less of his money income than before to buy the now cheaper commodities. He will use the money thus released either to buy more of those same commodities, or to purchase other goods of which he was formerly deprived. If the producer gets the saving, he will presumably spend his increased profit, either for new equipment or to increase his consumption. In any case, unless the money is hoarded (which is not the usual situation), there is an increased demand for goods and, hence, an increased demand for labor with which to produce them. In this way the displaced workers are reabsorbed into industry. A good example of this is afforded by the linotype machine, the invention of which made it possible to set up the type for a newspaper with much less labor than had formerly been required. But it brought the price of newspapers down so low that everybody could buy them freely. The newspaper industry grew by leaps and bounds until it required more employees than ever. The thousands of labor-saving inventions that have been introduced into the world within the last century have not lessened the total volume of employment. On the contrary, they have vastly increased our goods, while we keep gainfully employed a larger population than ever before.

The Short and the Long Run. — The foregoing discussion reveals a conflict between certain long-run factors which tend towards a balanced adjustment and a full level of activity in industry, and certain short-run disturbances which disrupt the balance and reduce the level of activity. Say's law holds true in the long run, but its operation is impeded by the interfering influences of the short run. Now men live, for the most part, in the short run; they are governed largely by short-run considerations because the immediate situation which confronts them is always a short-run situation. Hence the policies which are most likely to be followed are those which are calculated to protect the individual from temporary disaster or abuse, even though they may be at the expense of the long-run welfare of society. We can hardly blame the workman for loafing on his job when he has no certainty that he, as an individual, will immediately find other employment when his present task is completed. We can hardly blame the skilled artisan for opposing the introduction of a machine which will eliminate the demand for his particular kind of skill and throw him, at least temporarily, into the ranks of the unemployed. It is small consolation for him to be told that society will benefit from the reduced costs brought about by the machine, and that some workers, somewhere, will be hired by the funds released from this saving in costs. Unless he can see some immediate benefit to himself, he is certain to look upon the new device as his enemy, and to act accordingly. People cannot be expected to behave on long-run principles until their short-run needs are taken care of. Therefore, if society is to enjoy the benefit of full labor productivity, efficient industrial methods, and mechanical devices, it must find a way to take care of the individuals who are temporarily injured by these things; and if the full possibilities of Say's law are to be realized, interruptions to the circuit flow of money must be prevented, and balance between the various branches of industry must be maintained. The development of a program to accomplish this is a problem of applied economics, which goes beyond the scope of this volume.

B. Saving, Investment, and Interest

Saving, Investment, and the Circuit Flow of Money. — In Chapter IV, we gave some consideration to the phenomena of saving and investment. We there learned that savings, when invested, cause equipment to be created, thereby adding to the wealth of society and to the productive capacity of industry. This could not be described completely, however, until the functioning of the monetary system had been explained. Now that this has been done, we can return to the former problem and examine the monetary aspects of saving and investment. We shall find that this has an important bearing upon the volume and direction of business activity, which is the subject of our present concern.

Heretofore, we have regarded saving and investment as two different aspects of the same thing. However, they are not identical, and they are not always linked together. Saving has both a monetary, or nominal, and a non-monetary, or real, aspect. In its monetary aspect, it consists in the withdrawal of money income from expenditure for immediately consumable goods (near-goods) to be held in reserve or invested. In its non-monetary aspect, it consists in the diversion of production from near- to remote-goods. Nominal savings become real savings through investment, that is, through the expenditure of money savings for remote-goods. Investment does not necessarily follow from money savings, however, for the money may be hoarded instead. Also, it is possible for investment to take place without having been preceded by money saving, if money is newly created for the purpose. The saving and investment of money are thus two different things which, though normally associated, may sometimes be quite distinct from each other. Furthermore, the two operations are commonly carried on by two different sets of persons. A large proportion of the recipients of money income save more or less of what they receive. These savings are usually entrusted to bankers, who act as middlemen by turning the saved funds over to enterprisers who perform the actual process of investment. It is the enterprisers who really spend the money for equipment of one kind or another. Money savings thus constitute a supply of investible funds, the demand for which comes from business enterprisers.

The relation between the demand and supply of these funds has an important bearing upon the balance of industry, because of its effects upon the circuit flow of money. If money savings do not flow into investment, a part of the money income stream is diverted into hoards of cash or idle bank balances, and the circuit flow of money is thereby interrupted. Indeed, if the money saved is used to pay off bank loans, so that the aggregate of deposits is reduced in amount, deposit money actually passes out of existence. In this case, monetary deflation occurs, which causes a disparity between the amount of money received by enterprisers in payment for goods, and the amount of money they have previously paid out for agents of production in producing those goods. Because the money paid out does not all return, costs exceed receipts, losses are suffered, businesses fail, and the volume of economic activity is reduced. On the other hand, if new money is created for investment through the expansion of bank loans, a monetary inflation is generated. Since the money has not come from savings accumulated by income recipients, the circuit flow is augmented at the investment stage. Not only does this cause a rise in prices, with a consequently stimulating effect upon business activity, but it diverts production away from near-goods toward remote-goods, and thereby disturbs the adjustment between the various branches and stages of industry. Only if money savings flow regularly into investment, and if investment is financed solely out of money savings, can constancy of the circuit flow of money be preserved, and upsetting effects upon the balance of industry from this source be avoided. It is important, therefore, to ascertain the conditions upon which equality between money savings and investment depends.

The Function of Interest. — People save money for a variety of reasons—to meet possible contingencies, such as sickness or accident; to provide for their old age; to take care of their widows and children in case of death; to enjoy the power and prestige which comes with the ownership of great wealth; and so on. All of these objectives can be attained in some measure by merely hoarding the savings, without investing them. Then later, when the contingencies arise for which the savings were made, they can be drawn upon, and used up. If the savings are to be invested, there must be some inducement; for investment usually involves some risk of loss which savers would be reluctant to face unless it was counterbalanced by the prospect of gain. There is such a prospect in the fact that investments in productive equipment yield future income, as explained in Chapter IV. Out of this yield, borrowers can pay interest for the use of loanable funds. This prospective interest encourages the savers to entrust their funds to the borrowers; or, if the former prefer, they can invest in equipment of their own and obtain directly a yield of income which is the equivalent of interest. Interest, thus conceived as the income derived from the use of equipment, constitutes the principal incentive for investment. It is also an incentive for saving itself, for people will presumably save more if their savings can be made to yield interest than if no interest were obtainable.

Interest is commonly reckoned as a percentage of the sum invested, so that, if one thousand dollars will yield an income of fifty dollars yearly, the rate of interest is said to be five per cent. If the yield is sixty dollars, interest is six per cent; and so on. Since interest is an incentive for saving and investment, it is logical to infer that these will fluctuate with the rate—more will be saved and invested when interest is high, less when it is low. Also, more savings will ordinarily be hoarded when interest is low than when it is high. Thus the rate constitutes a sort of governor, which helps to control the relation between saving, hoarding, and investment.

The analysis of a previous paragraph has made it clear that this relationship, through its influence upon the circuit flow of money, has a great deal to do with the level and balance of economic activity. Furthermore, as we go on it will be shown that the relationship between what is invested, on the one hand, and what is consumed, on the other, also affects the level and balance. The regulative function of the interest rate, therefore, is a very important one, on which the smooth adjustment of the economy depends.

The Equilibrium Rate of Interest and the Bank Rate. — This is not the place to consider in detail the influences which determine the rate of interest. That is best taken up in connection with the analysis of how the social income is apportioned, which constitutes the subject-matter of some later chapters.[4] It will suffice here to outline briefly those aspects of the matter which are most relevant to the present problem. The subject is one which is clouded with some uncertainty, and about which there is considerable difference of opinion among economists. The following is, however, a widely held view, which seems to the present writer to be generally valid, although perhaps needing more refinement and clarification.

Every business man knows that there are many different rates of interest, depending on the particular type of investment. For instance, the rate on short-time loans fluctuates more widely than that on long-time loans, and risky investments offer the inducement of a higher prospective yield than safer investments. Among the many prevailing rates, however, two are considered of paramount importance for the problem of economic balance. One of these is known as the "true," "normal," or "equilibrium" rate of interest. The other is the "bank" rate, sometimes called the "market" rate. For the present, we shall use the terms *equilibrium rate* and *bank rate,* respectively, because these most clearly suggest the part which they play in the economic process.

The equilibrium rate of interest is the one which, if it actually prevailed in the loan market, would preserve balance in the relations between consumption, saving, and investment, thus permitting a full level of economic activity. This rate depends upon the supply of savings offered for investment, on the one hand, and the demand for them from enterprisers desiring to finance the purchase of equipment, on the other. What rate the enterprisers can offer depends upon how much the equipment is expected to earn. The greater the volume of investment, the less the prospective earnings will be; for more investment means more equipment, without any corresponding increase in the land or labor with which it must be used. Hence the equipment will be used at an increasing disadvantage which will cause its earnings to decline. It follows that, as the supply

4 See especially Chapter XXI.

of investible funds increases, the rate of interest that can be obtained for them goes down. Looking at this the other way around, a high rate of interest reduces the amounts that will be borrowed, a low rate of interest increases it.

The supply of savings offered for investment works in just the opposite direction. A high rate of interest encourages people to save more, or at least to invest more (and hoard less) of what they do save. A low rate of interest tends to discourage saving, or at least to discourage investment (people will hoard more of what they do save). Hence, the supply of funds offered for investment tends to rise as interest rises and to fall as interest falls.

If we bring these two influences together, we get a picture of what would happen in the loan market if there were no interference from the banks. A high rate of interest would cause a large amount of funds to be offered for investment, but a small amount to be taken. Holders of the unused funds would offer them for less, rather than let them be idle, and this would drive the rate down. It would presumably continue falling until borrowers' demand was sufficiently stimulated and the supply sufficiently reduced to bring the two to equality. The loan market would then be balanced. On the other hand, if the rate were too low, borrowers' demand for funds would be greater than the supply; some borrowers would be disappointed. Rather than forego the opportunities for profitable use of equipment, the latter would offer slightly more to obtain the funds they seek, and the rate would be driven upward. As it rose, lenders would be induced to offer more funds for investment, so that supply would increase to meet the demand. This would presumably go on until the two were equal.

From all this it appears that there is a tendency for a rate of interest to be reached where the amount of funds taken by borrowers exactly equals the sums offered for investment by savers. This is the equilibrium rate.

The bank rate of interest is the rate charged by commercial banks for loans. If the funds loaned by these banks were derived exclusively from savings placed in them by their stockholders and depositors, this rate would be in close correspondence with the equilibrium rate just described, for the banks in that case would merely be intermediaries through which the natural influences of the loan market would exert their balancing effects. However, we know, from the description of banking operations in the second preceding chapter, that funds for bank loans do not have to come out of money savings; they can be created by the banking system itself through the process of discounting. Therefore, the supply of such funds is limited, not by the amount of money placed in the banks by their stockholders and depositors, but by the size of the bank reserves. If the reserves are large in relation to the demand of borrowers, banks will lower their rate of interest in order to encourage expansion of their deposits. If the reserves are low in relation to borrowers' demand, the banks will raise their rate in order to profit by the scarcity of funds. The result is that the bank rate of interest fluctuates independently of the equilibrium rate, sometimes rising above and at other times falling below it. This deviation has disturbing effects upon the economy, for it upsets the balance between savings and investment.

Involuntary Saving and Overinvestment. — Let us suppose that bank reserves have become relatively large for one reason or another. Possibly new cash has been flowing into the banks in payment for goods sold abroad, causing the reserves to expand, or perhaps business activity has been at a low ebb, during which there has been but little borrowing, so that deposits are small in relation to existing reserves. Under these circumstances, the banks will seek to encourage increased use of their lending facilities. They will offer loans at attractively low rates of interest. The bank rate may thus be pushed down below the prospective earnings of equipment, so that it is lower than the equilibrium rate. Since prospective earnings now exceed the cost of obtaining funds for investment, business men will be stimulated to borrow. The funds obtained by them will not be taken from the previously accumulated savings of the people, but will be created by bank credit expansion. The result is that investment now runs ahead of money savings, and the normal balance between saving and investment is destroyed. The condition can be described as one of *overinvestment*.

This process of credit expansion puts money into the hands of business men, by means of which they are able to compete with consumers for the products of industry. More money is offered in exchange for goods than before, causing prices generally to rise. At the outset of this process, however, consumers' money incomes have not been increased. Confronted with rising prices, the consumers find that they cannot buy as much goods as previously. Their consumption is forcibly curtailed. Business men, however, have more money than before, thanks to the banks. They use this money to buy equipment. The decline in consumer purchases is offset by an increase in producer purchases. Industry is thus diverted somewhat from the production of near-goods to the production of remote-goods. Consumers have been forced to give up some consumable products in order that industry may have more equipment. The real savings of the community have increased without the saving of money by the recipients of income. This is known as forced or *involuntary saving*.

The reverse of this situation can occur if, for any reason, bank reserves become relatively too small, from the banks' standpoint. Perhaps cash has been drawn out of the reserves in payment of a foreign trade balance, or bank credit may have been expanded to the point where the percentage of reserves to deposits is at its minimum limit. In these circumstances, the banks are likely to force a contraction of loans by raising their rate of discount above the equilibrium rate, so that the cost of loans to borrowers now exceeds the prospective yield of investments. Business men therefore reduce their loans, and the volume of deposits shrinks. The circulation of money is reduced and prices fall. The curtailment of loans first affects the money incomes of business men rather than those of consumers, so that, for a time, the latter benefit by the fall in prices— they can buy more consumable goods with a given amount of income than before. Business men, however, having less bank credit at their disposal, can buy less equipment. Production is thus diverted from remote- to near-goods; there is a sort of involuntary increase in consumption.

Vertical Maladjustment of Industry. — These influences are disturbing to the smooth functioning of the economic process. Consider the fact that industry is arranged in a series of stages, beginning with those remotest from, and culminating with those nearest to, their ultimate end in consumption. In Chapter IV this succession of stages was called the *vertical structure* of industry. The expansion of credit, by diverting production from near to remote stages, unbalances this vertical structure. Too much of industry is devoted to the making of equipment, not enough to satisfying the immediate needs of consumers.

The difficulty caused by this distortion of normal relationships is illustrated by the drawing of Figure 12, which pictures its effects upon the circuit flow of money. Here the flow of money as it would be in the absence of interference from the banks is represented by the solid lines. The dotted lines picture the injection of new money into the system through the process of bank credit expansion. Observe that this new money enters the flow on the investment side, thereby giving a stimulus to the production of remote-goods. If there are idle resources in the community, some increase in the production of remote-goods may conceivably take place without any diminution in the output of the near-goods industries, but if the credit expansion continues, there is bound to be a diversion of productive agents from near- to remote-goods, and the resulting scarcity of near-goods will cause their prices to rise, along with the prices of remote-goods. But, since the newly created bank money goes first of all to enterprisers, before it is passed on to the other productive agents, consumers' money incomes are not increased until after some rise in prices has taken place. It is this lag of consumers' incomes behind prices which forces the public to curtail its consumption, and places it in the position of saving involuntarily.

The new money which was injected into the investment side of the circuit does not stay there. Let us trace it further, according

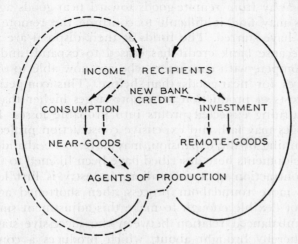

Figure 12. Distortion of the Circuit
Flow by Bank Credit Expansion.

to the dotted lines of the drawing. In the process of producing remote-goods this money is paid out to the agents of production employed in producing them. It is thus transformed into money income in the hands of the general public. Now since the people did not curtail their consumption voluntarily, they will try to use this addition to their money incomes to buy the consumable goods of which they had been deprived. Therefore the new money returns to the circuit flow mostly on the near-goods side, tending to pull the vertical structure of industry back to its former arrangement. This will make it impossible for the increased production of remote-goods to be continued unless financed by further bank credit expansion. But this is exactly what usually happens. The banks go on pumping new credit into the investment side of the circuit, so that the business men are enabled to keep one jump ahead of consumers, and the vertical structure of industry is progressively lengthened.

But this process has its limits. Bank credit is not indefinitely expansible; the reserve requirements will eventually bring it to a halt. Moreover, as remote-goods become more plentiful and near-goods more scarce, the prospects for profitable use of the former will become relatively less attractive than those for profitable production of the latter. Hence, borrowing for investment will be retarded. When those two circumstances cause the expansion of credit to cease, consumers' incomes will catch up with those of enterprisers, and the former will resume their former mode of consumption. This pulls production away from remote-goods toward near-goods again. Now enterprisers may find it difficult to continue the remote processes which they have started. The funds at their disposal are no longer growing, because bank credit has ceased to expand, and they are forced to compete with consumers who are now able to offer much higher prices for near-goods than before. This competition may make the costs of production at remote stages higher than was anticipated, turning expected profits into probable losses. Businesses at these stages may fail, and expensive construction projects, begun at the beginning of the expansion, may have to be abandoned.

The developments here described have been likened to the expansion and contraction of an accordion. Industry is first lengthened out into a more roundabout process, then shortened again. The system is not flexible enough to make this adjustment smoothly. A generally unbalanced relation between the successive stages of industry is thereby brought about, which produces a condition of business depression.

Horizontal Maladjustment of Industry. — The structure of industry has a horizontal as well as a vertical pattern, which can be visualized with the aid of the following scheme:

Foods	Textiles	Furniture	Chemicals	Automobiles
Stages	very	near to	the	ultimate	consumer
Stages	less	near to	the	ultimate	consumer
Stages	rather	remote from	the	ultimate	consumer
Stages	very	remote from	the	ultimate	consumer

If we read across this scheme from left to right, we find several branches of industry running parallel to each other, such as foods, textiles, and furniture. This is the horizontal structure. If we read down the scheme from top to bottom, we see the successive stages from near- to remote-goods. In the case of textiles, for instance, cotton clothing manufacture might represent a stage of production very near to the ultimate consumer; the making of cotton cloth, the construction of machinery for weaving the cloth, the conversion of iron into steel for the machinery, and the mining of iron to be converted into steel, would constitute stages successively more remote.

Economic balance requires that both types of industrial structure shall be correctly proportioned. Either or both of them can become unbalanced, and so interrupt the smooth functioning of industry. If the several stages of production do not fit, so that iron and steel production, or perhaps building construction, are overdeveloped in relation to the near stages, such as the manufacture of finished clothing or food products, there is a vertical maladjustment. If the several parallel branches of production are unbalanced in relation to consumers' demands, automobiles and chemical products being overdeveloped in relation to clothing and foods, for instance, the maladjustment is horizontal. This type of maladjustment is identical with the misdirected production which was described in connection with the discussion of Say's law, earlier in this chapter.

We have seen that vertical maladjustment is closely connected with malfunctioning of the monetary system, because the expansion and contraction of bank credit are most likely to inject money into and withdraw it from the circuit flow at stages more or less remote from the consumer. Horizontal maladjustment is less likely to be of monetary origin; it is due to faulty anticipation of demand in particular industries. It is capable of generating a process of monetary contraction, however; for the interdependence of all industry is such that, if one branch of production is in serious difficulties it may affect other branches, causing a general reduction of business activity, with monetary repercussions. This cumulative process will be more fully described in the following chapter.

Hoarding as a Cause of Maladjustment. — In analyzing the relation between saving and investment, we have hitherto tacitly assumed that savings will be invested in productive equipment so long as the latter can be made to yield interest. This assumption must now be examined critically. We know, from the discussion of the money-balance theory of prices in the last chapter, that people usually hold some money in reserve to carry them over from one installment of money income to the next, to make various expenditures from day to day, to pay their debts as they fall due, to provide for possible contingencies, and for speculative purposes. A certain amount of such withholding is normal, and does not disturb the economy. So long as the quantity of money so held in idleness is constant, the circuit flow will be even, and the money flowing into payments for goods (either near or remote) at one end of the circuit will be equal to the money paid out to agents of production, as costs, at the other. However, if people begin to hoard their money, instead of spending or investing it, there will be a reduction in the stream of money flowing down from the top of the circuit. This is shown in Figure 13. The conditions necessary for the operation of Say's law will not then be fulfilled. Prices will fall, the money receipts of enterprisers will be less than the costs they have paid out, and losses will result. This may precipitate a condition of reduced business activity—perhaps a severe business depression. It is the remote-goods

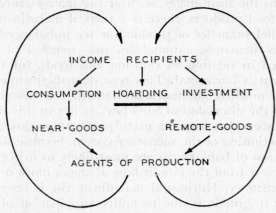

Figure 13. Stoppage of the Circuit Flow
by Hoarding.

side of the circuit that is most affected by hoarding, for people are most likely to hoard the funds which they would otherwise invest, not those which they would ordinarily spend in consumption.

There are three important situations in which a tendency to hoard money, instead of invest it, may arise. The first of these has to do with speculation. If, for any reason, prices begin to fall and there is a prospect that they may continue falling, people who have money in excess of their immediate needs are likely to figure that if they invest it in goods now, those goods will presently be worth less, in money terms, than they now are, and that if, on the other hand, they hold the money until prices have fallen further, it will then buy more goods. They will therefore hoard it for the time being. This reduces the circuit flow and forces prices to fall even more than they otherwise would, which encourages still more hoarding, and so on, so that the situation may become progressively worse. Such a movement is likely to run its course sooner or later, but in the meantime the consequences may be serious. We shall hear more of this in the following chapter.

The second cause which may give rise to hoarding is political. In times of revolutionary upheaval or impending military defeat, people may feel that the safety of investments is threatened. They will then seek to accumulate as much cash as possible in some safe place, thereby withdrawing it from circulation. Excessive taxes or onerous regulations which hamper business men or which darken their prospects for profits will also check investment.

Finally, if investment is too great, so that there is an oversupply of equipment, the interest yielded therefrom may be so low that it is insufficient to attract investors. Rather than run the risks of loss which are always attendant upon investment, savers may prefer to hold their surplus in the form of money. Economists have hitherto supposed that this condition would bring its own remedy, through the functioning of the interest rate, as described in an earlier paragraph. That is, the low interest rate should make it possible for business men to utilize forms of equipment that would not otherwise be profitable, so that the demand for investible funds would grow. At the same time the low rate should discourage saving, so that people would spend more and save less, thereby reducing the excess supply of funds to the amount which could be absorbed by this expanded demand. But what if the supply of savings is not responsive to the interest rate? What if people persist in saving in spite of a lack of suitable opportunities to invest all of the savings profitably? Then there will indeed be trouble.

Keynes' Theory of Employment. — This is precisely the situation which is pictured by the British economist Keynes, as now confronting the countries of western civilization. His argument runs somewhat as follows: [5] He believes that the volume of money savings grows larger as incomes increase, regardless of the rate of interest; hence, in those countries where technical efficiency is high and where real incomes are correspondingly great, the volume of savings will grow progressively larger. These savings cannot be invested unless profitable opportunity for the use of more equipment exists. Such opportunities are more and more difficult to find, he believes, because there are fewer and fewer frontier regions to be developed, and population is not growing as fast as it formerly did, so that the demand for consumers' goods is no longer increasing very rapidly. There might be sufficient demand for all the savings if the rate of

---

[5] The argument is here stated in my own terminology, not in that of Keynes, whose use of terms is somewhat unusual. This theory is further explained in Chapter XXI.

interest could fall low enough to permit enterprisers to obtain loans cheaply; but this cannot happen, for one thing, because people will hoard, rather than invest, if the interest yield does not suffice to off-set the risks of investment. Besides, he believes that people have become so accustomed to prevailing interest rates that there is a psychological obstacle to their reduction. The result is that not all of the money savings can be invested, and so they are hoarded instead. This breaks the circuit flow of money and starts a deflationary fall in prices which has unfavorable repercussions on business activity. The volume of production is thereby reduced and, with it, the amount of employment. As production declines, real income is reduced, leading to a decrease in the volume of saving. This goes on until money savings have fallen to the point where they no longer exceed the possibilities for profitable investment. Hoarding will then cease, the circuit flow of money will be continuous, and the economy will be in equilibrium. However, it will be an equilibrium in which the level of activity is so low that labor is not fully employed.

Keynes' theory thus makes investment the determiner of the level of economic activity and of the volume of employment. Only if current investment can be kept equal to the flow of money savings can full employment be maintained, and this will not occur automatically in a world confronted with disappearing frontiers and a relatively stationary population. Observe that this amounts to a denial that Say's law can operate under present conditions, for Say's law holds that total demand tends to equal total production. Keynes argues that total demand depends upon investment, and that this is a limited quantity. Say's law takes it for granted that money saved will be invested and the circuit flow thereby maintained; Keynes holds that not all the money saved will be invested and, therefore, the circuit flow will be broken.

So pessimistic a theory should not be accepted until it has been critically examined and tested. Convincing evidence has not yet been presented to establish Keynes' belief that opportunities for profitable investment of savings are declining. There are still many regions of the world whose resources are not fully exploited, and which offer boundless opportunities for development. All that is needed is the establishment of more stable government and the spread of more progressive ideas among the inhabitants of those regions. The outlook for new industries, made possible by the progress of science and invention, is very good. The development, within the past few decades, of such products as airplanes, radios, talking pictures, rayon, and plastic materials, may be followed by many others equally revolutionary. Moreover, it has not been demonstrated that rates of interest cannot fall below those which have hitherto prevailed. Taking all these things into consideration, it does not appear that Keynes has said the last word upon this subject.

SUMMARY

In this chapter we have considered the conditions upon which the maintenance of full and balanced economic activity depends. Monetary influences have a special bearing upon this problem.

According to Say's law, the total demand for goods is identical with the total supply; hence, a full level of activity is not prevented by lack of sufficient demand for the products of industry. The circuit flow of money, from income recipients, through consumption and investment, to agents of production, and thence to income recipients once more, demonstrates Say's law for a money economy, by showing the identity of money incomes with money costs. However, the working out of the law depends upon fulfillment of two assumptions: namely, that money savings will be invested (not hoarded), and that the several branches of industry will be in balanced adjustment with each other. Conditions may arise in which these assumptions do not hold true. It follows from Say's law that there cannot be general overproduction of goods; but there may be misdirected production. It also follows that the demand for labor will be equal to the supply of it; therefore, in the long run, limitation of output and the making of useless work are unnecessary to the maintenance of full employment. Labor can hardly be blamed for advocating such policies, however, in view of the temporary maladjustments which frequently limit their opportunities for employment.

The continuity of the circuit flow of money and, hence, the maintenance of a full level of activity, depends upon the investment of money savings. It is the function of interest to keep investment in balance with savings; if savings exceed investment, the rate of interest falls, tending to reduce saving and stimulate investment; if savings fall short of investment demand, the rate rises, saving is encouraged and borrowing is reduced, until they are equal. There is thus an equilibrium rate of interest which tends to preserve the balance of industry. The bank rate of interest, however, is based on the relative size of bank reserves and is different from the equilibrium rate. If it is below the latter, investment exceeds voluntary saving, the excess being financed by bank credit expansion. Consumers are thereby forced into involuntary saving, because, prices having risen faster than their money incomes, they cannot buy as much as before. A bank rate above the equilibrium rate has the opposite effect.

Credit expansion with involuntary saving causes a vertical maladjustment of industry, by stimulating production at remote stages out of proportion to production at stages nearer the consumer. Industry may also be maladjusted horizontally, by unbalanced development of the various branches of industry through faulty anticipation of demand. Vertical maladjustment is largely of monetary origin; horizontal is not, but it may start a chain of monetary contraction. Such contraction will also be brought about if savings are hoarded instead of invested—a condition which may be precipitated by an incipient decline of prices, by political conditions unfavorable to investors, or by a reduced yield resulting from an oversupply of equipment. Keynes believes that highly developed countries offer increasingly limited opportunities for investment, with a high level of incomes which leads to excessive savings. The surplus savings are hoarded, so that prices fall, activity declines, and real incomes are reduced, until the excessive saving no longer occurs. There results an equilibrium in which the level of activity is low and in which there is unemployment. The truth of this theory is not yet established.

REFERENCES AND SUGGESTIONS FOR FURTHER READING

J. B. Say's own statement of his law of markets is to be found in his *Treatise on Political Economy*, Book I, Chapter XV (3d American edition, 1827). This is reprinted in S. H. Patterson's *Readings in the History of Economic Thought* (1932), pp. 66–72. A more modern discussion of this law and its implications is contained in Chapters XIV to XVI of F. M. Taylor's *Principles of Economics* (1921). The concept of the circuit flow of money here presented is a simplified form of the more elaborate description contained in *Money*, by W. T. Foster and W. Catchings (1923).

The theory of the effects upon the economy of deviations of the bank rate of interest from the equilibrium rate is largely the work of the Swedish economist, K. Wicksell. See Volume II of his *Lectures on Political Economy* (English translation, 1935). Further references on the subject of interest will be found at the end of Chapter XXI of the present work. For a description of the way in which vertical and horizontal maladjustments occur, and of their effects upon the course of business activity, see G. von Haberler's *Prosperity and Depression* (revised edition, Geneva, 1939). Keynes' theory is expounded at length in his *The General Theory of Employment, Interest, and Money* (1936). His treatment is so ponderous that the average reader will find it more profitable to read the simpler and more lucid interpretation of his views given by Joan Robinson in her *Introduction to the Theory of Employment* (London, 1938). See also the last two chapters of Lester V. Chandler's *Introduction to Monetary Theory* (1940).

Chapter XII

BUSINESS CYCLES

A. The Nature and Course of Business Cycles

Cyclical Fluctuations of Business Activity. — The discussion of Say's law in the last chapter indicated that in a well-balanced economic system a high level of activity may prevail—a level in which labor and capital are relatively fully employed, and in which there is, consequently, a large volume of production. But the discussion also showed that there are maladjustments, which may interfere with the attainment of such a prosperous state and lead to a generally reduced level of business activity. As a matter of fact, neither of these conditions is continuously maintained in our society; we have neither permanent prosperity nor chronic stagnation. Instead, the business world is characterized by alternating waves of prosperity and depression.

In the alternations, there is a fairly well-marked series of changes, which recur in a more or less rhythmical manner. Because of this recurring character, these movements are commonly called *business cycles,* although the more general term, *economic fluctuations,* is also sometimes used. The cycles are closely associated with the monetary phenomena which have been the subject of the last four chapters. Their influence is far-reaching. They affect not only production, prices, and trade, but they extend into the lives of the people, through their effects upon wages and unemployment. It seems that they cause the whole life of man to pulsate in a social rhythm of ascent and decline. Even such apparently unrelated things as the prevalence of crime, the rate of marriage, and the number of births and deaths, are subject to this influence.

Phases of the Business Cycle. — Four phases of this cyclical movement are usually recognized. These phases are: prosperity, crisis (or recession), depression, and revival. Each of these will now be described in turn.

If we analyze the conditions prevailing during a period which promotes increasing business activity, and which business men describe as prosperous, we will find a number of distinctive characteristics. These are the earmarks of what we may call the period of *prosperity*. In this phase of the cycle, prices are found to be rising, and, with them, interest rates and (more slowly) wages. Business activity is brisk: new investments are freely made, old establishments are enlarging their plants, building construction is increasing, factories and other shops are operating at or near full capacity, and there is but little unemployment. There is a ready market for securities. Stocks sell at high prices, favoring the launching of new enterprises. Banks are very busy; their deposits are large, and the ratio of money reserves to deposits is low. Among business men there prevails a tone of pronounced optimism, which leads them to undertake risks boldly. All these conditions are cumulative; they become progressively more pronounced, until sooner or later a reaction sets in, and the next phase of the business cycle is begun.

The onset of reaction is called a *crisis*, or *recession*. It is primarily financial in its nature. At this stage the cumulating prosperity has gone so far that it has produced a marked inflation of credit. Prices are at their peak; interest rates have risen so high as to discourage further borrowing; plants have been extended as far as, or farther than, the demand for products warrants; many persons' credit has been badly strained. A few firms that have invested too boldly may fail. The banks have permitted inflation of their deposits to go as far as possible; they are now forced to curtail further loans and put pressure upon business men to get their affairs more nearly on a cash basis. The precarious situation of the more reckless enterprises has produced a feeling of uneasiness and doubt as to the soundness of loans, leading both bankers and other business men to be cautious about further borrowings and lendings. The interest rate becomes prohibitive. Inasmuch as business has been carried on by the free extension of credit, the new situation causes tenseness and puts a check to business enterprise. Business men go through a period of liquidation, in which they reduce their borrowings and lendings and bring their affairs out of speculative uncertainty onto a more careful and more nearly cash basis. During this phase the stock market is adversely affected, the prices of stocks declining sharply. Business failures are numerous. Prices begin to fall.

The crisis, if severe, may take the form of a *financial panic*. If one or two great industrial enterprises fail, possibly causing the failure of the banks which supported them, business men may become frightened as to the safety of their bank deposits. Knowing that their continued business activity and reputation depend upon their ability to pay their debts, and fearing that they will be unable to obtain either cash or credit, they hasten to draw out their deposits and turn every asset into cash. We know there is not enough cash in the community to carry on the normal operations of business, since about 90 per cent of business transactions are settled with deposit money. But the deposits rest on confidence, and, when that is destroyed, runs upon the banks begin, and all the depositors demand cash simultaneously. Not having the cash, the banks are unable to meet the demands, and are forced to close their doors. The result is financial chaos. There is a wild scramble for cash; a premium on cash payments appears. Securities are dumped on the stock exchanges and sold at great losses. The rate of interest on call loans soars. Business activity in the financial centers is paralyzed. There is simply not enough money available to do the work of exchange.

After passing through a crisis, business is subject to a more or less prolonged *depression.* Activity having been checked by the critical period of liquidation, recovery is slow. Conditions are now almost the exact reverse of those prevailing during the period of prosperity. Business is "dull." There is a little buying and selling. Stocks of merchandise have accumulated in warehouses and on dealers' shelves. Prices, wages, and interest rates are low. Factories are closed or running on part time, and thousands or millions of persons are unemployed, often suffering severely from the resulting poverty. Borrowings are few; credit is reduced in volume; the ratio of bank reserves to deposits is large. New issues of stock are hard to "float," old issues are low in price. A tone of pessimism prevails among business men; they are very cautious, and hesitate to expand or take risks.

The depression may last for several months or even years, but sooner or later a *recovery* ensues. The necessity for replenishing depleted stocks of merchandise, and for repairing or replacing worn-out equipment, causes some resumption of buying. The low rates of wages, interest, and other costs, which have prevailed during the depression, make it possible to carry on operations at low prices. The prospect of being able to resume production profitably encourages a growth in investment. Business men are more willing to borrow from the banks. Credit expands, and the circuit flow of money is increased. Resumption of wage payments causes more consumer spending. So, in these and in other ways, unemployed labor and idle factories are brought back into production, and a new wave of expansion is begun. As it proceeds, it develops gradually into the phase of prosperity, and the cycle repeats itself.

No two cycles are exactly alike. They differ in duration, in intensity, and in many other details, but all exhibit the same general sequence of events. We shall describe these phenomena in greater detail as we proceed.

Indexes of Business Activity. — Within comparatively recent years, economists have worked out techniques by which the movements of business activity can be measured with a fair degree of accuracy. The business cycle shows itself in many fields, and, by gathering data indicative of activity in these fields, a very good view of its development can be obtained. Among the indexes used for this purpose are statistics of production, especially those showing the output of pig-iron, coal, and other fundamental raw materials. The production of basic manufactured goods—such as iron and steel products, textiles and food products, and the volume of building and other construction, are also used. Since prices move upwards and downwards with the cycle, index numbers of the price level are likewise helpful. The banks are even more responsive to the cyclical movement. Consequently, statistics of bank deposits and of reserves, loans, and discounts, are widely used. The best index would be one showing fluctuations in the volume of trade itself; that is, the actual transactions taking place in the business world. This is not easy to measure, but it is rather clearly reflected in such items as checks cleared through the banks, the shipment of goods over railways and other common carriers, and the volume of wholesale and retail sales of merchandise. Still other data which can be employed are wages, interest rates, unemployment, and business profits.

Statistical Measurements of the Business Cycle. — Unrefined statistics showing the movements of these various indexes, however, do not reveal the course of business cycles accurately, because the cyclical pattern is obscured by other changes, not cyclical in nature, to which business is subject. The actual movements of business activity result from a mixture of interacting causes, which must be separated if the cycle is to be distinguished. This is illustrated by Figure 14, which shows the movements of bank clearings outside New York City during the years 1918 to 1929, inclusive. Since most business transactions involve payments by check, these clearings constitute a fairly sensitive barometer of general business activity. Bank clearings inside New York City are excluded, because the financial transactions of the great metropolis are so largely dominated by speculation that they are not truly representative of the general trend of business, and are of sufficient volume to distort the picture. The solid jagged line of the graph represents the actual clearings as they occurred from month to month during the period studied. On analysis, it is possible to discern three separate kinds of movement in this line. To begin with, it is to be noted that it has a generally upward direction from left to right, indicated by the straight line AB. This corresponds to the gradual expansion of industry which goes on over a period of years in any progressive community, and which may be thought of as its normal growth.[1] During the period of prosperity this growth is more rapid, while during depression it is slowed up, or temporarily reversed. Hence, the graph takes the form of a line moving upward and downward, but usually rising higher than it was in the corresponding period before. The general direction of this

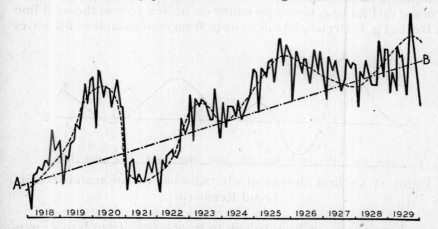

| 1918 | 1919 | 1920 | 1921 | 1922 | 1923 | 1924 | 1925 | 1926 | 1927 | 1928 | 1929 |

Figure 14. Seasonal Variation, Cyclical Movement, and Secular Trend.

ascent (from A to B) is known to statisticians as the *secular trend.* The broad deviations above and below this line, which are indicated by the curved line in the drawing, represent the *cyclical movement.* But industry is also subject to *seasonal changes,* some months in the year being more conducive to certain types of activity than others. In our illustration, for example, there is a sharp drop in bank clearings every February and a marked rise every October and December. These seasonal variations take the form of lesser fluctuations in the curve. In our figure they are the zigzag waves of the solid line, above and below the curved line representing the cyclical movement. There are also usually some sporadic, or random, movements, less regular in nature, which may arise from such phenomena as strikes, the vicissitudes of the weather, and a variety of other causes.

By appropriate methods, it has been found possible to correct the statistical data so that the secular trend can be removed; and, if it is

---

[1] Curves for new industries which are expanding rapidly will slope upward more steeply. On the other hand, the slope for declining industries will be downward. In a country that is moving backward industrially, it may even slope downward for business generally. Also, it may rise for a period of years and then fall, or vice versa.

found desirable, the seasonal variations can be eliminated also. A graph can then be plotted from the corrected figures which will show the cyclical fluctuations as movements, like so many waves, above and below a horizontal straight line. Figure 15 is an approximate picture of how our original graph of bank clearings would look after being corrected for both items. The secular trend has been reduced to the horizontal line A'B', and the seasonal and random variations have been smoothed out. What remains is our former curved cyclical line, now represented on its new base as the solid line a b c d e f g. Each complete movement from crest to crest of the waves

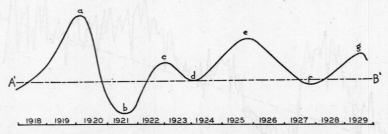

Figure 15. Cyclical Movement with Seasonal Variation and Secular Trend Removed.

(*e.g.*, from a to c), or from trough to trough (*e.g.*, from b to d), represents one cycle. Observe that the three cycles here shown differ from each other somewhat in both duration and magnitude. This is typical of such movements.

To be fully accurate, our illustration would need a further correction. In the chapter on the price level we learned that, when the statistician deals with items expressed in terms of money, he must allow for changes in the purchasing power of the dollar. Our figures, showing the dollar volume of bank clearings outside New York City, reflect not only changes in the actual volume of bank transactions due to general business conditions, but also changes in the value of money during the period considered. Were the figures to be corrected by an index number of prices, so that the volume of clearings could be shown in terms of the price level as of a certain date, any changes then remaining in the data would be changes in the actual volume of bank transactions.

With the data made available from such sources as have been previously indicated, and with the necessary correction for secular trend, seasonal variation, and the price level, a very good index of the general business cycle can be obtained. It may consist of a composite figure, including a number of indicative items, or of a single item, known to be sensitive to changes in general activity. One of the most suitable items for such a purpose, in addition to the volume of bank clearings outside of New York City which we have used, is the volume of production.

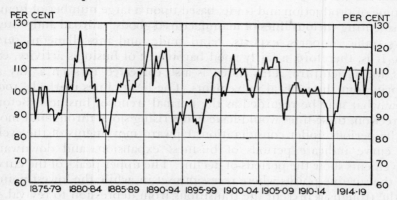

Figure 16. Bank Clearings Index of Business in the United States, 1875–1919.

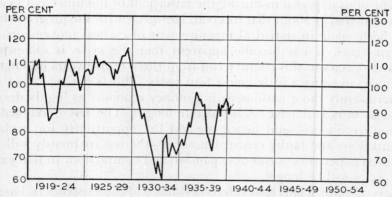

Figure 17. Production and Trade in the United States, 1919–1940.

An Index of Business Cycles in the United States. — In Figures 16 and 17 there are given, in graphical form, two indexes, one showing movements of the business cycle in the United States from 1875 to the end of 1919, the other from 1919 to 1940.[2] The first of these indexes is based upon bank clearings outside of New York, corrected for changes in the price level, seasonal variations, and secular trend.

[2] Both indexes are based upon figures published from time to time by the Federal Reserve Bank of New York.

Therefore, it shows truly the cyclical movements, except for random, sporadic fluctuations which occur from time to time. This index was discontinued some years ago; therefore, it has been supplemented by the second index, which is a composite, weighted measure of the volume of production and trade, based upon a large number of items, representing various lines of manufactured goods, railroad and waterways traffic, imports, exports, retail trade, and miscellaneous services. It is, therefore, a fairly good barometer of business activity, except for agriculture. This index is also corrected in such a way as to bring out the cyclical movements. The heavy lines marked "100" show what may be regarded as the normal trend of business. Before correction, these lines would have had a rising slope throughout most of the periods under consideration. Upward movements of the cyclical curve indicate periods of business expansion, and downward movements show the periods of decline. The upper peaks of the curve are the turning points where recessions set in, while the lowest points in the troughs represent the transitions from depression to revival.

The Duration of Business Cycles. — It was formerly believed that business depressions recurred rather regularly every eight to ten years. Economists were led to this belief by the fact that a number of conspicuous depressions during the latter half of the nineteenth century occurred at about that interval. However, with the progress that has been made in statistical measurement of cyclical movements in recent years, it has become apparent that the cycle is somewhat shorter. Cycles in this country run from three to five years in length, the average being a little below four years. This is not typical of all nations. Only those nations with a money economy as highly developed as ours will have cycles of our length. The less developed a nation's economy—and hence the less the opportunity for broken circuit flows and faulty credit structures—the less frequently will its business experience waves of expansion and contraction. In that case, the cycles will be longer.

Several statisticians have offered evidence of the existence of longer cycles, existing along with the short cycles just referred to. Some still contend that business cycles of eight to ten years' duration can be detected; others hold that there are cyclical movements as much as fifty years in length. It is quite possible that there may be several wave-like movements intertwined. So, the accepted four-year cycles may fluctuate about a wave-like movement of fifty years or thereabouts, in the same way that seasonal variations fluctuate about the course of the business cycle. But there is some question about the existence of these longer wave-like movements. If their reality is once fully proved, we shall have to interpret the phases of prosperity, crisis, depression, and revival with reference to the longer waves of which they are a part. A prosperity in the trough of a long wave will not represent as high a level of activity as one on the crest of the longer movement, and a depression in the trough of a long wave will be much more severe than one on the upper part of it. An analogy may make this clearer. Let us think of a day as analogous to prosperity and a night as comparable to depression. We may then see that, while all days have common characteristics, as do all nights, the position of the earth, as it revolves about the sun, makes considerable difference in the duration and intensity of both day and night. The position of the earth in its orbit makes the summer days longer and warmer than the winter days. A summer night, conversely, is shorter and less cold than a winter night. One point that lends some support to the belief in the existence of long wave-like movements, about which ordinary cycles fluctuate, is the nature of cycles in the decade immediately following 1929. The graph of that period in Figure 17 reveals a wave-crest in 1936–37 high enough to mark it, by comparison with the depression, as a period of prosperity, but the level of the entire period, including this relative prosperity, is low. Therefore, advocates of the long-wave theory would contend that the 1936–37 prosperity was seated in the trough of a long depression. On the other hand, there is still room to argue, as some economists have done, that these long waves are not cycles at all, because it is said that they lack the rhythmical pattern which is essential to the cycle concept. They may be merely accidental shifts in secular trends, the result of fortuitous events.

The Magnitude of Business Cycles. — We have said that cyclical fluctuations appear most frequently in highly developed money economies. Such nations depend partly upon foreign trade, so that they are influenced very considerably by conditions abroad. A depression in England, for example, means that we will sell less goods to England, and reciprocally we will have less foreign exchange with which to buy from England. The curtailment of our imports means still less income for the English with which to buy our goods. Our foreign trade therefore declines still further. Our domestic trade must also fall when our total national income dwindles. So, there is a cumulative chain of reactions which causes the depression to spread to this country.

Economic interactions of this sort are world-wide, existing wherever there is trade. But the less developed a nation is in a monetary direction, and hence, the less of a trader it is, the less it will be influenced by outside circumstances. Moreover, as we have already noted, it will be less frequently subjected to cyclical ups and downs. Such cycles as do develop will be mild in amplitude.

The United States has a highly evolved money economy which permits cyclical movements of great magnitude; but they vary in severity. A visual picture of the extent and variation of the movements can be obtained from observation of the graphs in Figures 16 and 17. A statistical average of a number of business cycle indexes indicates that, in this country, the average drop from prosperity to depression, and the average rise from depression to prosperity, is about twenty-five per cent. Occasionally the rise or fall is far greater. The unprecedented collapse that followed the crash of 1929 was more than double the average.

B. Explanations of Business Cycles

External and Internal Causes. — If we think of the economic process as consisting primarily of monetary and price transactions, it is apparent that important events occurring outside of that process may exert great influence on it. Some writers regard business cycles as the result of repercussions in the economic process from such external occurrences. For instance, there are said to be cyclical movements in natural phenomena, such as temperature and rainfall, which are supposed to cause variations in the yield of agricultural crops. Since agriculture is an important branch of production, fluctuations in it may upset the balance of industry, and thereby affect business conditions generally. Other economists have stressed the influence of such cataclysmic events as earthquakes and wars, which may seriously disturb the economic balance of a nation or a whole group of nations. A number of writers have emphasized the importance of new discoveries and inventions as factors which give an impetus to industry, and thereby start an expansive movement which eventually spins itself out, until some new impelling occurrence comes along to stimulate another expansion.

There is no denying that external forces of this kind may have powerful stimulative or depressing effects upon economic activity; but it is hard to see how the sporadic occurrence of a war or an earthquake can explain the rather uniform, rhythmical, sequence of phases which is characteristic of busines cycles. The theory that alternations of crop activity are the basic cause is a somewhat more satisfactory explanation in this respect, but it has not yet been proved that climatic and crop cycles are correlated closely enough with business cycles to account for the occurrence of the latter. Although no two business cycles are alike, the fact that they have a generally similar pattern suggests that there must be something in the nature of the economic process itself (*e.g.*, a monetary disturbance) which is responsible for such movements. Even though a war or the opening up of a new territory might start an expansion, we have still to look within the economic process for the forces which cause the expansion to take the particular form that it does, and eventually to bring about a reaction which culminates in a depression.

Some students of the problem believe that there are enough internal causes to account for all the cyclical phenomena commonly observed, without the necessity of introducing any external causes into the explanation. Others say that external factors provide the impulse which starts a movement of business, while internal factors explain the cumulative and rhythmical effects of action and reaction which follow after the impulse has taken effect. Perhaps the most reasonable attitude is to regard certain factors in the economic process as making for a condition of inherent instability, of such a nature that any disturbing force, either from within or without the system, can set in motion an expansion or contraction which is cumulative and rhythmical in character. The analysis of the preceding chapter suggests that there are such destabilizing factors, tending to upset the balancing factors which make for stability. How these two sets of influences can react upon each other in such a way as to produce a cyclical pattern of events will be developed at a later point in our analysis.

Psychological Waves of Optimism and Pessimism. — Another group of students believes that business cycles are the result of waves of feeling which sweep over the business world from time to time. According to this view, the phase of prosperity is one in which business men are unduly optimistic, and this begets unwise and reckless adventures. There is a process of cumulative error, resulting from an exaggerated estimate of the possibilities of expansion. The errors are presently revealed when market realizations do not come up to expectations, and profits are succeeded by losses. The resulting disasters cause a feeling of worry and anxiety, often of actual fear, which permeates the world of finance and is partly responsible for the collapse of credit. This is succeeded by a tone of pronounced pessimism, which helps to continue the depression and prevent a speedy recovery.

Psychological influences undoubtedly have something to do with business cycles. Too much stress is laid on these factors, however, when sole responsibility for the cycles is laid at the door of social psychology. There must be underlying economic causes for the changing mental attitudes of business men. Hence, it seems probable that waves of optimism and pessimism accompany, accentuate, and perhaps prolong prosperity and depression, but are not the primary causes.

The Underconsumption Theory. — A very popular theory, especially in the United States, may be summed up in the words *oversaving* and *underconsumption*. According to this view, too much monetary income is poured into the remote-goods side of the circuit flow, not enough into the near-goods side. The excessive saving leads to an increase in equipment, which eventually increases the output of near-goods. But, since there is a deficiency of consumptive expenditure, these goods cannot be sold at prices which will cover the costs of producing them. As a result, prices fall, producers suffer losses, business failures occur, and a depression is begun. The halting of production stops or reduces the excessive flow of near-goods into the market; meanwhile accumulated stocks of unsold merchandise are disposed of at low prices. When the supply of near-goods has been reduced to the point where it no longer exceeds consumptive demand, prices go up to profitable levels again, and a revival of business activity sets in. As this develops into prosperity, saving is resumed, and again becomes excessive. The cycle is then repeated.

According to socialistic writers, who have long been the chief supporters of this theory, deficiency of consumers' demand is only the symptom of a deeper, more basic maladjustment. The fundamental difficulty is that incomes are too unequally divided. The rich property-owners get so much that they cannot consume it all, so they invest the surplus in equipment, which is used to produce goods for sale to the masses. But the wage-earning masses are too poor to buy the goods at profitable prices. So, the capitalistic system breaks down at intervals, because of its chronic inequality.

Other economists say that the source of the difficulty rests in the fact that wages do not go up as fast as commodity prices in periods of technological progress or cyclical boom. The resulting lag of costs behind selling prices gives rise to excessive profits, which profits are reinvested, so that productive capacity and output increase at a more rapid rate than expenditures for consumption. There may also be some lag in farmers' incomes; this likewise slows up demand for consumers' goods, for manufacturing industries rely to a considerable extent upon farmers to buy their output.

Recall now what was said about saving, investment, and the interest rate, in the preceding chapter. It was there pointed out that there can be too much saving, in relation to what is spent for consumption, but that this ought to be corrected automatically, through the working of the interest rate. If too much is invested in equipment, interest should fall, so that further saving would be discouraged and more of the people's incomes would be spent. There is some question, however, about the responsiveness of saving and consumption to the interest rate. And even if there is such a response, it may be that it does not work delicately enough to maintain a balanced adjustment. It is possible that oversaving may go so far, before the corrective process can take effect, that a critical readjustment is unavoidable. Perhaps the ups and downs of prosperity and depression are but the symptoms of a regulative mechanism which works clumsily and jerkily. These considerations give to the underconsumption theory some plausibility.

There is no reason to suppose, however, that underconsumption is a necessary result of inequality. The rich do not have to invest any more of their incomes in industry than they care to. There are plenty of opportunities for spendthrift consumption, as well as for constructive philanthropy. If the prospective rate of interest did not offer them a sufficient inducement to make investment seem worth while to them, it is reasonable to assume that they would turn to these other alternatives. The trouble, then, lies not so much with the existence of inequality as with faulty anticipation of earnings and the faulty behavior of the interest rate. It might well be, however, that a rapid change in the distribution of incomes, such as the increase in profits in relation to wages stressed by some proponents of the oversaving theory, might cause an increase in saving too rapid to be corrected by a fall in the interest rate. This is at least a tenable hypothesis; but we must not accept it too hastily, for there are considerations which weigh against it, and there is another theory which is even more plausible.

For many years the underconsumption theory was confined to socialistic circles, and was generally rejected by competent economists; but since about 1930 it has been supported, in one form or another, by some economists of standing, especially in the United States. The majority of careful students of the business cycle, however, are more inclined to the overinvestment theory, mentioned in the last chapter, and presently to be set forth more fully.

The Alleged "Dilemma of Thrift." — What has just been said about the tenability of the underconsumption theory must not be taken as a defense of the view, put forth by certain writers, that *any* saving *necessarily* involves the economic process in difficulty, because, they say, saving withdraws money income from demand at the same time that it increases the supply of goods. The goods cannot then be sold without a fall of prices, which destroys profits. Society is thus confronted with a dilemma: if it does not save, it cannot make progress; if it does save, it is plunged into a depression. This naïve view is clearly untenable. We know, from the circuit flow analysis, that savings, if invested, do not withdraw money from the demand for goods; they merely divert it into new channels. Money saved and invested is paid out for remote-goods instead of near-goods. But, money spent in the purchase of remote-goods is just as truly a demand for commodities as if it had been spent for clothing or food. If a community, having an income of one hundred million dollars in a given period, saves ten per cent of it, there is a demand for ten million dollars worth of equipment and ninety million dollars worth of immediately consumable goods in that period. If the industries of that community will produce near- and remote-goods in those proportions, there will be no overproduction of either, for the time being, and demand and supply will be in balance.

But will they also be in balance in the long run? According to the dilemma of thrift philosophy, they cannot be, because, *if there is any saving whatever, beyond what is necessary to replace existing equipment as it wears out,* there will be an increase in productive equipment which must sooner or later increase the output of near-goods. This means that the prices of these goods must eventually fall, thereby causing a decline in profits, and leading to a depression. Observe that this line of reasoning does not stop with the admittedly undeniable statement, that saving *can* be out of balance with consumption; it asserts that *any* saving which increases the output of goods *must* lead to disaster.

Against this extreme view there are two things to be said. In the first place, prices need not fall merely because the output of goods is increasing; for there may be at the same time an increase in money incomes. It would be natural to expect some increase in the monetary circulation parallel with productive expansion. In the second place, even if prices do fall as a result of an increase in equipment, this need not cause business losses, for there should be a concomitant decline in costs of production. The extra output made possible by the growth of saving is accomplished without any addition to costs other than interest; for the investment of savings does not involve the employment of more agents in production (except for saving or waiting); it requires only that the existing agents be used in a more roundabout process.[3] This process is more productive than the shorter process which would be employed if there were less saving; hence the costs *per unit of output* are less. There is one exception to this

[3] Recall the discussion of this in Chapter IV.

statement. Since more waiting is involved, the interest charges may conceivably be greater; but if the lengthening of the process is due to an increased supply of savings (as the theory assumes), the rate of interest should be lower, which should offset the increased cost of waiting, at least in part. There is likely to be a further decline in unit costs, resulting from progress in the arts. If the increase in saving and investment takes place steadily and gradually, we may expect improvements in the technique of production to keep pace with it—especially in a progressive country like the United States. These considerations lead us to conclude that saving (in excess of what is needed for equipment replacements) need not *necessarily* cause business losses, nor plunge industry into a depression. Only if saving is *excessive* in relation to consumption need there be any disturbance. This last is possible, but not inevitable. It will not occur if the interest rate performs smoothly the functions attributed to it.

Monetary Inflation and Deflation. — The explanation of business cycles offered by the underconsumption theory lays very little stress on the behavior of the monetary system. Yet it is clear that monetary factors cannot be left out of the picture. The cycle is a phenomenon peculiar to those economies which have a highly developed system of credit. Many of its characteristics, in fact, are definitely monetary in character. The period of revival and prosperity is one of monetary inflation, when an increase in production is financed by expanding bank credit, and accompanied by a consequent increase in the general price level. The crisis, if at all severe, is conspicuously a time of financial strain, when credit is hard to obtain, loans are being called, and everybody is seeking to make his position as "liquid" as possible, by converting his assets into cash. Credit then shrinks noticeably in volume, hoards of cash are accumulated, and bank balances are allowed to lie idle. Thus the circulating medium shrinks in volume, constituting a deflation which continues during the depression, accompanied by a fall in prices due to the reduced flow of currency.

These facts lead some economists to attribute business cycles primarily to monetary causes. The medium of exchange on which the modern economy depends is an intangible and precarious structure of credit, based on very small reserves of cash, and dependent for its continued existence on the solvency of most business men and the general preservation of confidence. Through the power which the banking system has to extend new loans when demand for them is brisk, the volume of credit is easily expanded; but the amount of such expansion is limited, and the reaching (or even approaching) of its limit may cause serious trouble. Moreover, since the whole structure is based upon loans, its integrity depends upon the ability of borrowers to pay their loans when due, so that if anything happens to weaken the security of debts, the structure of credit may readily collapse.

These occurrences are so obviously a feature of business prosperity and depression that no explanation that does not take them into account can be entirely satisfactory. On the other hand, it is too much to attribute cycles to monetary causes alone. To be sure, the vagaries of the monetary system can have important effects upon the operations of industry, so that it is not unreasonable to think of monetary phenomena as a cause of economic disturbance; but the monetary system is also responsive to changes in the underlying industrial process, so that it is just as reasonable to suppose that industrial unbalance is a cause of monetary repercussions. The best explanations of business cycles, therefore, are those which run in terms of interactions between the structure of industry and the monetary system.

The Monetary Overinvestment Theory. — The monetary theory of overinvestment, set forth in the last chapter, affords the basis for such an explanation. This theory emphasizes the distortion of the vertical structure of industry—a maladjustment brought about by banking operations. When the banks have excess reserves, they encourage business men to borrow, by offering loans at less than the equilibrium rate of interest. There follows the creation of new credit, which is pumped into the investment side of the circuit flow of money. This raises prices before the money has been passed on to the consuming public, so that the latter are forced into involuntary saving. So long as the credit expansion continues, consumers' incomes lag behind the upward movement of prices, and the involuntary saving continues. Business is very active, however, because of the new investments promoted by the expanding bank credit. This activity constitutes the prosperous phase of the cycle. It is a false prosperity, however, because investment is running ahead of voluntary saving, thereby altering the vertical structure of production in a way that cannot be maintained after the credit expansion ceases.

The crisis comes when the bank reserves will not support any further extension of credit. Funds for investment, no longer swelled by expanding bank loans, must henceforth come from voluntary savings. But these do not suffice to finance the equipment programs already under way. Some of these have to be abandoned. Also, investment banks which have borrowed money in order to underwrite new issues of stocks and bonds, expecting presently to sell them to the investing public, will find the market for their securities less than was anticipated. The volume of voluntary savings falls short of the amount of securities offered. The investment banks are then caught, and may be unable to pay their debts.

These difficulties are complicated by the fact that there is now a sharp shift in demand from remote- to near-goods. Consumers' incomes, which lag behind the price level as long as credit expansion is going on, catch up with it when the expansion ceases. When the new purchasing power created by the banks has all been passed on to consumers, they resume the mode of expenditure to which they had been accustomed before involuntary saving was forced upon them. So, the demand for near-goods is increased. This will not affect adversely those industries whose roundabout processes, growing progressively longer during the expansion period, have attained a stage of completion where they can now deliver finished goods by the new processes directly to consumers; but it will be disastrous for those industries which are caught with their new projects unfinished.

Let us illustrate the distinction presented in this last sentence. Suppose that, during the boom, an important railroad system, hitherto operated by steam locomotives, embarks on a program of electrification which requires several years to complete. The industries which furnish the necessary electric generators, poles, wires, and other supplies, likewise embark on projects of expansion, which involve, in turn, construction of new equipment on the part of industries located at stages still more remote from the railroad. Now, if all this has been completed before the crisis occurs, the newly electrified railroad need not be embarrassed by the shift in demand to near-goods that takes place at this stage. It can utilize its new equipment to move such goods rapidly and efficiently from farms and factories to consumers. But if the electrification is incomplete, not only the railroad, but the industries which are auxiliary to its electrification program, may face disaster. The railroad is called upon to deliver to consumptive markets immediately a greatly increased volume of goods. It must carry on by the old process for the time being, mustering all the steam power facilities at its command to handle its traffic. Funds available for investment (which are now scarcer than they were) must be diverted from the electrification project to the quick repair of locomotives which were soon to have gone to the scrap heap, and for putting every available facility into condition for the immediate handling of goods. The manufacture of electric locomotives and related equipment must wait. The industries which supply electrical equipment for the railroad are faced with canceled orders, or at least with the absence of new ones which they had anticipated and prepared for. They have borrowed money with which to purchase equipment in order that they might meet these orders, expecting to meet the loan charges out of receipts from new business which is now not forthcoming. Unable to meet their debt charges, they fail.

Meanwhile, the whole electrification project is beginning to look more and more dubious. It was begun at a time when the prices of materials were low and funds could be borrowed at low rates of interest. A margin of earnings above the expected costs was visible—a margin more than sufficient to meet the interest and amortization charges, and thereby to justify the investment. Now the rising costs reduce this margin to the point where a loss on the investment appears probable. It may have to be abandoned. All that has been done on it to date, not only in the railroad itself, but in the antecedent industries, will then be a total loss. Business failures may occur all along the line.

At every crisis, many industries find themselves in positions similar to this. Overexpanded during the period of prosperity, they are caught with incompleted and prospectively unprofitable projects on their hands when the expansion of credit ceases. Lacking the stimulus of repeated injections of new credit, they are unable to carry on. Industries at stages near the consumer are supported by the shift of demand to near-goods, but those at remote stages are hard hit, and many are unable to weather the storm. So, the boom, started by the expansion of credit, collapses. There ensues a general process of liquidation, in which business men, hard pressed for funds with which to pay their debts, dump their goods on the market for whatever they will bring.

Loans are paid off, or written off by the creditors as a loss, so that a deflationary contraction of credit takes place. The forced sales of goods and the shrinkage of credit forces the price level downward.

At this stage, investment falls short of voluntary saving, for new projects do not look very attractive. Unexpended surpluses are accumulated as idle bank balances, and there is some hoarding of cash. As loans shrink, bank reserves become larger in relation to deposits, a condition which leads the banks to lower their interest charges below the equilibrium point, in order to attract borrowers. This makes credit cheap enough to make loans look profitable again, which tends to promote a revival of investment. Eventually it does revive. Then a new expansion begins, and the cycle is repeated.

Overinvestment and Underconsumption Contrasted. — At this point, it may be well to draw a brief contrast between the overinvestment and the underconsumption theories, for the two are in some respects so similar that they are sometimes confused; yet there are sharp differences between them. The similarity consists in the fact that they both stress the importance of excessive investment in the remote-goods industries; but there the likeness ceases. The underconsumptionists view the excess of investment as the result of too much voluntary saving, arising out of inequalities of income; the overinvestment theorists view the excess of investment as the result of involuntary saving, arising out of the power of the banking system to expand the volume of credit. To the underconsumptionists, the difficulty created by the excessive investment is that consumptive demand is too small to buy the goods resulting from the excessive investment; to the overinvestment theorists, the difficulty is that consumptive demand is too great, after the expansion of credit ceases, to permit the investment projects to be completed—agents have to be shifted from remote- to near-goods in order to satisfy customers.

The following table will throw these distinctions into sharp relief:

	Basic weakness causing maladjustment.	Nature of the maladjustment.	Immediate cause of collapse.
Underconsumption theory.	Inequality of incomes—insufficient purchasing power of the masses.	Too much voluntary saving and investment; too little spent in consumption.	A glut of products, in relation to an insufficient consumptive demand, leading to a fall in prices.
Overinvestment theory.	Power of the banking system to expand credit.	Investment in excess of voluntary saving, financed by expanding bank credit, stimulated by a too low rate of interest.	Insufficiency of voluntary savings to complete investment projects after credit expansion ceases; redirection of production to near-goods to meet increase of consumptive demand when consumer incomes catch up with rising prices.

Of the two theories, the overinvestment one appears to account more fully for the observed phenomena of the cycle than does its rival. It probably has more adherents among competent economists than any other. However, taken alone, it is hardly a complete explanation. It needs to be supplemented by certain other factors. In particular, we need to consider two other explanations which have some bearing on our problem, before attempting to bring together all the influences which are requisite to a complete explanation.

Magnified Fluctuations in Demand for Durable Goods. — It has repeatedly been noticed that those industries which are engaged in the production of durable equipment such as buildings, industrial plants, railroads and railway rolling stock, shipyards, and the like, are the ones which suffer the most extreme fluctuations in the different phases of the business cycle. This is also true of those industries producing durable consumers' goods, such as automobiles and dwelling houses. Both the underconsumption and overinvestment theories offer an explanation of this, in attributing the cause of the cycle to too much investment. There has also been developed a theory, sometimes called the "principle of acceleration," but perhaps best described as *the principle of magnified demand*. From time to time there are shifts in consumers' demand which result from new inventions or changes in habits. These changes lead to derived changes in the demand for the equipment which is used in the production of near-goods; but the demand for equipment necessarily fluctuates much more violently than the demand for the near-goods on which it depends.

The reason for this can be explained by a simple illustration. Suppose that a small garment factory is equipped with ten sewing machines, each capable of stitching 10,000 garments per year. The output of the factory, when working at capacity, will then be 100,000 garments annually. Suppose, further, that each of these machines wears out in ten years of use, so that it has to be replaced at the end of that time. There will then be ten new machines to be bought in each ten-year period. It is not likely that all of these will be bought at one time; if the proprietor is a good manager, he will try to arrange his affairs so that he discards one old machine and buys one new one each year. This will spread out the cost of the machines so as to constitute a moderate annual expense. So long as his output remains the same, the manufacturer of sewing machines can count on selling him one machine yearly. Now suppose that the demand for garments increases ten per cent, so that the garment manufacturer finds it possible to sell an output of 110,000 garments yearly. Since each sewing machine produces 10,000 garments, he will now need eleven such machines, instead of ten. This means that this year he must buy two new machines, instead of his usual one—one new one to replace the machine which is worn out this year, and one to take care of the increased production. Therefore, his demand for new sewing machines has *doubled*, although the increase in the demand for his garments was only ten per cent.

Now suppose that the demand for garments had fallen off ten per cent, instead of increasing. The manufacturer could then have sold only 90,000 garments, for which nine sewing machines would suffice. Hence, he could have discarded one sewing machine that year without needing to replace it. His demand for the machines would have fallen to *zero,* although the decline in demand for his product was only ten per cent!

If we multiply this illustration to cover the whole garment industry, we obtain a moving-picture of what happens to the sewing machine industry when the demand for garments fluctuates. So long as sales of garments continue at a fairly even rate, there will be a reasonably steady demand for machines to replace worn-out equipment, but if there is only a moderate shift in the demand for garments, the demand for sewing machines will move upwards or downwards violently, presenting a difficult problem for the sewing machine industry.

The illustration is typical of what happens to the equipment-producing industries generally, when the demand for near-goods changes. The precise amount of fluctuation will vary in different cases, depending on the amount of equipment in use, relative to the normal output of the industry, and on the life of the equipment; but, in any case, the variations in demand for equipment will exceed the variations in the demand for its product.

Even if there were not this arithmetical relationship between demand for end-products and demand for equipment, the durable goods industries would nevertheless fluctuate more than those producing raw materials and perishable products. If production is to go on, new fuel and materials must be purchased more or less regularly to keep the factories running; but an old machine can usually be made to go on a while longer, so that its replacement can be postponed. The result is, that purchases of equipment are likely to be concentrated in periods of prosperity.

This also holds true of durable consumers' goods. Consumer purchases of such perishable products as food and clothing do not vary greatly from year to year, for people must eat and dress in order to live, and as these goods are rapidly used up, they must be continually replaced. But this is not the case with such things as houses, furniture, and automobiles. If consumers' incomes are shrinking, repairs to their homes can be postponed, the old furniture can be kept in service, and the old car can be run for another year or two; therefore, expenditures in these directions are drastically curtailed. When consumer incomes increase, on the other hand, there is not much occasion to spend more on clothing or food, so the surplus is used to repair homes, buy new furniture, and purchase new cars.

The development of science and invention causes similar fluctuations in the durable goods industries. When a new kind of product or a new mechanical device is invented, much equipment in the industries affected may be rendered obsolete. There will be an enormous demand for the equipment until the obsolete capital has been replaced, after which the demand will decline to a fraction of its former level.

This theory will explain why the durable goods industries are more seriously affected by cyclical fluctuations than other industries; but, standing by itself, it does not constitute a complete theory of business cycles, for it does not explain the expansion and shrinkage of *total* monetary demand which is characteristic of the alternations of prosperity and depression. According to Say's law, an increase in the demand for sewing machines would necessarily be offset by a decrease in the demand for something else, so that total demand would remain the same as before, unless there was a change in the monetary circulation. If, however, the machine expansion is the result of newly created credit (the involuntary savings process of the overinvestment theory), there need be no shrinkage of money demand elsewhere, and a general expansion might be initiated. Likewise, with a decline in the demand for sewing machines, in the absence of a shrinkage of currency, the money not spent in the sewing machine industry would find its way into other channels, so that the total demand would remain the same as before; but if the reduced investment in the machine industry is used to pay off debts, or is hoarded, so that there is a decrease in the monetary circulation, a general contraction might be initiated. These observations lead to the conclusion that the theory under discussion is best regarded as supplementary to some of the other theories which have been explained; but it does elucidate one link in the chain of business cycle causation.

The Uneven Movement of Costs and Prices. — We have seen that the ups and downs of business activity are accompanied by a rising and falling general level of prices. However, these prices do not all move in exact correspondence. Some are much more responsive to inflationary or deflationary influences than others. In particular, the prices of public utility services, such as railway and electric power rates, which are controlled by governmental regulation, and the prices of commodities controlled by monopolies, are relatively inflexible. The same is true of wage rates, especially in organized trades where labor unions have enough power to resist wage reductions, and where employers' associations can resist wage advances. Interest on fixed money indebtedness, and amortization charges for the same, likewise do not change during the life of the particular loan involved. In the case of bonds this may be a long period. On the other hand, there are some prices which change rather freely. This is true in competitive industries generally, including most agricultural products and a great many raw materials. Short-time interest rates are also easily readjusted at frequent intervals.

These disparities in price movements are undoubtedly significant in accentuating the movements of the business cycle. The relative stability of wages and long-term interest rates is particularly important. When commodity prices begin to rise, as a result of some expansionary impulse in the economic system, the lag of wages and interest causes a widening spread between costs and selling prices, which spread is a source of increasing profits to business men. These profits encourage further expansion, aided by the banks, which becomes cumulative. As the upward movement proceeds, unemployed labor, unused plant capacity, and hoarded savings, are gradually drawn into industry, until they become increasingly scarce. In an attempt to continue the expansion, enterprisers now bid up the prices of these factors, so that at this stage they rise faster than the increase in the prices of finished products. Profits now begin to shrink, and may easily be converted into losses. Those industries which have the greatest difficulty in raising the prices of their products will be hardest hit by the increase in costs, and may be forced into bankruptcy. The expansion comes to a halt, and recession sets in. In the ensuing deflation, the flexible prices fall faster than the inflexible ones, and, in particular, the selling prices of commodities drop more rapidly than such factor costs as wages and interest. This accentuates the deflation. As unemployment becomes extensive and hoarded funds excessive, wages and interest rates slowly decline, until eventually they reach a point low enough to permit a revival. Here, again, is a theory which explains some of the factors which aggravate the movements of the business cycle, but, like most of the other theories we have examined, it must draw partly on the monetary theory for its explanation. It is helpful, but not a complete analysis.

An Eclectic View. — The phenomena of business cycles are so varied and complex, that we can hardly expect to explain them by any one simple theory. The weakness of all the explanations we have been considering is that they try to do just that. Yet all (or most) of them do reveal important links in the chain of causation. A satisfactory explanation must be eclectic; it must choose from all of the several explanations those elements which, when put together, give a logical and coherent account that accords with the known facts. Thus is derived a composite explanation which gives due weight to each causal factor. It must recognize the occurrence of external events which impinge upon the economic process, and of conditions within that process which cause it to react rhythmically to such stimuli. It must take cognizance of both monetary and non-monetary repercussions, and of both vertical and horizontal maladjustments in the structure of industry. So, by drawing together the threads of various theories, we may get a pretty clear idea of how the business cycle runs its course. The description must be in general terms, and we must remember that each cycle exhibits differences of detail; but something like the following sequence of events usually takes place.

How Prosperity is Generated. — Let us begin with the assumption that a depression prevails, and then trace the factors which start a revival and lead on into a period of prosperity. In the depression, there is unemployed labor and unused plant capacity. Hoards of money exist, in the form of idle bank balances and large bank reserves. As a consequence of these things, prices, wages, and interest rates are low. Moreover, the banks are in a position to supply ample credit to any borrowers who have a reasonable prospect of meeting their obligations. So, the business situation is one in which any stimulus can readily start a general expansionary process. Such a stimulus may come from internal sources. Stocks of merchandise may have become exhausted to the point where production must be increased in order to meet current demand, or equipment may be so worn out that replacements are urgently needed. Or, some external event may give the needed impetus, such as a war, with its tremendous demand for munitions of all kinds, a new invention, giving rise to a new industry, or an increased demand from abroad, due to a change in the international trade balance.

From one or another of these stimuli, a few progressive business men are led to make new investments, drawing on their idle balances in the banks, or possibly making new loans for the purpose. They are encouraged by the banks to borrow, by a rate of interest lower than the equilibrium rate. The sums so invested are paid out to the owners of the agents of production employed in the new ventures, and are spent by the recipients, mainly for near-goods. This increases the demand for the latter, and leads to expansion in the industries producing them. These industries, in turn, increase their production, drawing funds from hoards or loans, and make further payments to productive agents. So, the expansion spreads from industry to industry, in an endless chain. As it gets under way, selling prices rise faster than costs, leading to profits, in the manner described in a preceding paragraph. This leads to a general return of confidence, which encourages further expansion. The process is cumulative, the monetary circulation necessary for continued expansion being supplied by bank credit inflation. Confidence grows to optimism and optimism develops into enthusiasm. Before long, a wave of prosperity is in full swing. Labor and resources are relatively fully employed.

prices are high, and profits are good. This prosperity may continue for some months or years, depending on the strength of the stimuli at work and on the particular form that the development takes. Let us now see what happens to bring it to an end.

The Crisis or Recession. — In the process of expansion just described, all of the several factors which have been analyzed in the foregoing explanations of business cycles have been at work. There are the initial stimuli from external events and internal developments. The psychology of optimism, tending to errors of overanticipation, is present. Monetary inflation is going on. As a result of this last, investment is running ahead of savings. The demand for durable goods is being magnified. Productive capacity is increasing faster than consumption, and selling prices are running ahead of costs.

All of these tend to generate, in the economic process, strains which must, sooner or later, reveal fundamental weaknesses in the situation. Particularly serious is the fact that remote-goods have been stimulated at the expense of near-goods. As newly created money gets into consumers' hands, they try to keep up their customary level of consumption by increased expenditures for near-goods. So long as unused plant capacity, unemployed labor, and ample reserves of credit, are available, these weaknesses may not appear to be serious, but when production approaches the point where existing resources are fully utilized, and credit is near the limit of expansion which existing bank reserves permit, further expansion becomes increasingly difficult. Even if credit is still available, the growing scarcity of productive resources means that further monetary inflation will only increase prices, without any substantial increase in the output of goods. In the exuberance of the boom, construction projects may have been begun on the assumption of a continued increase in demand, which projects now come to a halt for lack of finances with which to continue them; or, the total volume of undertakings which have been contracted for may exceed the capacity of industry to produce. Frenzied bidding for the scarce agents of production ensues in order to complete these contracts. This raises the prices of the productive agents to the point where costs rise above actual or prospective earnings. Costs have also been increased by the growing inefficiency which characterizes a period of active business. In a revival, the most efficient labor is first employed, then, when it becomes scarce, less efficient workers are hired; moreover, in the general process of speeding up, supervision gets more lax and quality suffers. Meanwhile, credit is increasingly difficult to obtain, the banks becoming uneasy because of their shrinking reserves and the increasingly precarious position of many business enterprises. The banks refuse new loans, and scrutinize with unusual care applications for the renewal of old ones. Under these conditions, it would not take much to start a downward movement.

Recession sets in when some important industry, or group of industries, incurs such losses that it cannot meet its obligations. Some large businesses fail, and, in failing, may cause failure of the banks which financed them. This, in turn, causes difficulties for other concerns which depended upon those banks for credit. There now starts a process of progressive contraction which is just the reverse of the expansion previously described. The industries which are first to curtail dismiss their employees, stop paying dividends, and may not even pay interest on their bonds. This reduces the income of wage-earners and property-owners, who are thereby forced to curtail their expenditures. Thus there is a decline in demand for products of other industries, which, in turn, are forced to contract, dismissing more employees and reducing dividends and interest payments to other security-holders, and perhaps embarrassing other banking institutions. The contraction spreads by this process from industry to industry. Optimism turns to such pessimism that everyone, including the banks, is afraid to extend credit to anyone else. So there is pressure to pay off one's debts by converting every possible asset into cash. There ensues a general process of liquidation, in which commodities and securities are thrown on to the markets for such prices as they will bring. Prices fall, but costs fall less rapidly, causing further losses and accelerating the general downward movement. The process of contraction gathers momentum, until production and employment are reduced to a low level. In the process of liquidation, there is a general deflation of currency. Part of the money actually disappears, through the reduction of bank deposits which comes from the paying off of loans. Another part is hoarded, in the form of idle bank balances or actual cash. This shrinkage in the currency is the vehicle for the shrinkage in prices.

If the crisis is very acute, it may degenerate into a panic. Fear concerning the credit structure seizes the business community, and all depositors rush to the banks in an effort to withdraw their funds. Reserves of cash being insufficient to meet these demands, the banks are forced to close their doors. This collapse of credit paralyzes business. Failures take place in great numbers and the business world is in chaos. Panics do not accompany every recession. They occur only in crises of unusual severity.

The Ensuing Depression. — The fall in prices necessitated by liquidation sounds the death knell to business profits, and without the prospect of profits business activity does not go on. When everybody is trying to sell and get rid of reserve stocks, there is very little demand for further production. Then ensues a time of industrial stagnation. Industrial plants close down or continue to operate at less than normal capacity. Thousands, even millions of employees are laid off. Wages drop. Poverty is widespread. It is a time of great suffering for the workingman. No new construction is undertaken.

The period of stagnation, in which business is now plunged, may be more or less severe and more or less prolonged, according to circumstances. Usually, the more feverish the preceding period of prosperity has been, the more drastic the recession and the more prolonged the depression. But it cannot go on forever, for existing stocks of merchandise become depleted, the populace must still be fed and clothed, and more commodities must be produced. Conditions are now ripe for revival, as explained in the beginning of this analysis. Business gradually resumes, and the cycle is repeated once more.

The Control of Business Cycles. — At this point there is a temptation to embark upon a discussion of the various ways and means that have been suggested for doing away with depressions, but such a discussion exceeds the scope of this volume. Our task is to describe existing institutions and processes; the prescription of remedies must be reserved for another place. Let it here suffice to say that, in so far as cycles are due to expansions and contractions of credit, it is apparent that any action designed to control business cycles must include adequate monetary and banking regulations. Such measures alone will not eliminate cycles, but they will mitigate them. Reforms of this sort are entirely practicable, and could be put into effect without drastic change in the basic institutions of our economy.

The maintenance of perfect balance and stability in industry would require control of the non-monetary causes, whose rôle in cyclical phenomena must not be minimized. For the time being, these are not so amenable to control as are the monetary factors. To cope with them, we would probably have to institute some form of central economic planning. So long as we rely on spontaneous processes for the guidance of industry, we must expect some ups and downs to continue.

SUMMARY

Economic activity is subject to rhythmical fluctuations, which are known as business cycles. These cycles pass through four phases: prosperity, crisis (or recession), depression, and revival. From statistical data of representative business activities, indexes of business cycle movements can be computed, and charted in the form of graphs. The crude figures must be corrected so as to eliminate seasonal variations, secular trends, and changes in the price level. Cycles in this country usually run from three to five years in length. Some students believe that there are several cycles intertwined, the longest of these having a duration of about fifty years. The average amplitude of the fluctuations in this country is about twenty-five per cent. The international relations which prevail between highly developed modern nations make the cycles international in scope.

Although economic disturbances may be initiated by causes external to the system of money and prices, the rhythmical character of business cycles is to be attributed to internal influences which make the system unstable. Psychological waves of optimism and pessimism aggravate the cyclical movement, but can hardly be viewed as their primary cause. The underconsumption theory, which attributes depressions to too much saving in relation to spending, resulting in production of near-goods in excess of consumptive demand, is logically tenable, because of the possibility that the interest rate may fail to work smoothly in adjusting the balance between saving, investment, and spending; but this is not necessarily the case, and the view that underconsumption is the inevitable result of inequality is very questionable. Also, the theory that saving withdraws money income from demand, at the same time that it increases the supply of goods, and thereby precipitates depression by causing a fall in prices, is unsound; for the fall in prices may be prevented by increased monetary circulation, and, even if not, the falling prices need not cause business losses, for costs may be correspondingly reduced by the more roundabout methods and falling interest rates that go along with increased saving and investment.

The most satisfactory explanations of business cycles emphasize the influence of monetary inflation and deflation. According to the overinvestment theory, expanding bank credit permits investment in remote-goods to exceed voluntary saving; after credit expansion ceases, voluntary savings are insufficient to complete the investment projects that have been started, and there is a further difficulty because production has to be redirected into near-goods, to meet the increase in consumptive demand which takes place when the newly created money passes into consumers' hands. Deviations of the bank rate of interest from the equilibrium rate initiate credit expansion and contraction, which is an important factor in the foregoing sequence of events. Cyclical fluctuations are felt most severely in durable goods industries, partly because small fluctuations in consumers' demand cause large fluctuations in the demand for productive equipment. Another theory of business cycles attributes them to the uneven movement of costs and prices; wages and interest lag behind commodity prices, leading to profits and business expansion, then later these relationships are reversed.

By combining the best elements in the several foregoing theories, a step-by-step picture of the sequence of events through which prosperity is generated, crisis occurs, depression ensues, and recovery takes place, can be developed. Monetary controls can probably do much to reduce the severity of cyclical movements, but it is doubtful if they can be completely eliminated without some kind of central economic planning.

REFERENCES AND SUGGESTIONS FOR FURTHER READING

The study of business cycles has been approached by both empirical investigation and theoretical analysis. The literature of each kind is too extensive to be dealt with at all adequately here, but the following selections are fairly representative.

The leading empirical investigators have been Wesley C. Mitchell and his colleagues on the staff of the National Bureau of Economic Research. Mitchell's *Business Cycles* (1913), and *Business Cycles: The Problem and its Setting* (1927), are outstanding in this field. W. L. Thorp has compiled a useful historical account of business cycles throughout the world in *Business Annals* (1926). For a study of the statistical measurement of business cycles, in addition to Mitchell's second book mentioned above, Carl Snyder's *Business Cycles and Business Measurements* (1927) may be consulted.

Of the theoretical works, I have found G. von Haberler's lucidly written *Prosperity and Depression* (revised edition, Geneva, 1939) most helpful. I have relied on it considerably in writing some portions of this chapter. A. H. Hansen's *Business Cycle Theory* (1927) is another convenient summary, which synthesizes the theories of various writers into a coherent explanation.

Mention should also be made of J. M. Clark's *Strategic Factors in Business Cycles* (1934), which attempts a theoretical interpretation based on the statistical findings made at the National Bureau of Economic Research under Mitchell's direction, and of Joseph A. Schumpeter's monumental work, *Business Cycles* (2 volumes, 1939), which covers the subject historically, statistically, and theoretically.

Chapter XIII

INDIVIDUAL PRICES: THE DAY-TO-DAY MARKET

A. Basic Concepts and Assumptions of Price Analysis

Individual Price Movements. — In the chapter dealing with the price level we saw how the prices of the many commodities which enter into trade are continually changing. Some are rising and some are falling, while others remain almost unchanged for considerable periods of time. Our concern in that chapter was to study the general trend of such movements, taken as a whole. We found that there was such a trend, which could be measured and charted, and our analysis led to the conclusion that this mass movement was a reflection of changes in the value of money. However, if money alone were the only factor causing prices to change, they would all rise or fall to the same degree. Since they do not move in this way, we must conclude that there are forces at work which affect different commodities unequally, that each commodity has certain characteristics which determine its price to some extent independently of other prices.

In Figure 18, the heavy, irregular line indicates the changes which took place in the general level of wholesale prices in the United States from 1896 to 1913; the other lines show changes in the prices of four separate commodities during the same period.[1] The prices shown are relative prices; that is, they are expressed in percentages, instead of in dollars and cents. The year 1896 is taken as a basis of comparison, the price of each commodity in that year being represented by 100, and subsequent changes by the appropriate fraction or multiple thereof. For instance, in 1911 the curve for rosin stood at 380, while that for wood alcohol stood at 59. This means that the price of rosin in 1911 was 380 per cent of what it had been in 1896 (almost a fourfold increase), while the price of wood alcohol was 59 per cent of what it had been (a decrease of almost one-half). The

[1] This graph is adapted from a somewhat similar drawing in Frederick C. Mills' *The Behavior of Prices* (1927), p. 65.

other curves are to be interpreted in like manner. If we were to record the relative prices of several hundred commodities in this fashion, the graph would become a jumble of intersecting lines, but it would reveal the same characteristics. Some prices would be moving upward, others downward, and yet others now upward now downward, irregularly, all about the general average or central tendency.

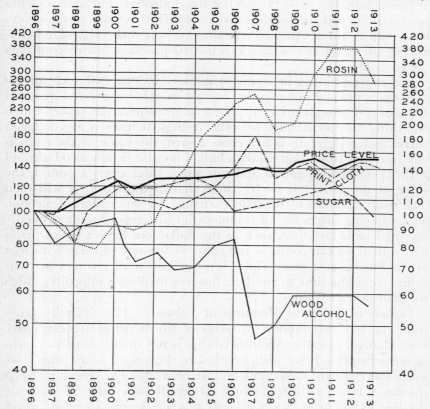

Figure 18. Some Individual Price Movements, 1896–1913.

Values and Prices. — Such price movements reveal changes in the *values* of the different commodities. By *value* is meant *the power of a good to command other goods in exchange.* This needs some explanation. At many points in our study we have observed that a constant interchange of goods is going on in the business world. Men are producing commodities to be exchanged for other commodities. In fact, exchange may be regarded as the central process in which all economic forces come to a focus. The manufacturer of rosin is not making it for his own use, but for sale. With the proceeds of that sale he will buy other products which he consumes in his daily life, including print cloth, sugar, and wood alcohol (for, if he does not use these materials in their pure form, he probably buys things in which they are important ingredients). His prosperity depends largely on how much of other things he can get in exchange for his rosin— that is, on the value of rosin. It is the same with the manufacturers of print cloth, of raw sugar, and of wood alcohol. The values of the products they sell, and of the products which they must buy, are very important to them. An understanding of how such values are determined, therefore, is one of the principal problems which confronts the economist.

We express values in terms of money, and we call such an expression a price. *Price* may be defined as *value expressed in terms of money.* Through prices we can easily compare the power which one thing has to exchange for other things. If rosin is five dollars a barrel and print cloth is five cents a yard, the value of the rosin is one hundred times that of the cloth. Likewise, when wood alcohol is thirty-six cents a gallon and raw sugar three cents a pound, the value of the former is twelve times that of the latter; it will then take twelve pounds of sugar to exchange for one gallon of alcohol. So, by having prices for all commodities in terms of some generally accepted monetary unit, such as the dollar, we have a set of prices with which we can compare the value of any one of them with that of the others, at a given time. We can also trace changes in their values from one time to another; but this involves a difficulty, which we shall now consider.

Defects of Prices as Measures of Values. — The difficulty arises from the fact that money, in terms of which prices are expressed, itself changes in value. Such variability is not usually found in units of measurement. If we wish to measure the weight of an object, we use as our standard the pound, and we know that our pound is always the same. If we wish to measure the length of a body, we may use the foot as our unit, and we know that the length of a foot never changes. Consequently, if a person at ten years of age is four feet tall, and five years later is five feet tall, we know that he has grown one fourth in height during that period. We can be certain of it, because our unit of length is fixed and invariable. But if we find that the price of a pound of sugar is five cents at one time, and ten cents five years later, it does not follow that the value of sugar has doubled. It depends on what has happened in the meantime to the purchasing power of money.

From our previous analysis of price levels we know that, if the purchasing power of money is falling, prices in general, in addition to the price of sugar, will be rising. Hence, the higher price of sugar may not mean that sugar is increasing in value; it may be merely a reflection of the lowered value of money. If the price of other commodities has risen in like proportion to that of sugar, its power to command other commodities in exchange will be no greater than before. For instance, if, while sugar is rising from five to ten cents, flour is rising from four to eight cents, the ratio of exchange between them is the same as it was (5 : 4 = 10 : 8). Conversely, if the purchasing power of money is rising, prices in general will fall; but this cannot be taken as indicating that there has been a corresponding decline in values. Indeed, all values cannot possibly rise or fall simultaneously, for the value of any good is, by definition, its power to exchange for other goods; therefore, if a good will command more of others in exchange than it formerly did, they must, by inexorable logic, command less of it. So, as the values of some things rise, that of others must fall. Hence, a general rise or fall of prices merely indicates a change in the value of money; it does not indicate corresponding changes in the relative powers of exchange of different goods.

Correcting for Price Level Changes. — How, then, are we to use prices as a means of measuring changes in the values of goods from month to month or from year to year? The problem is like that of the navigator, who must determine the direction of his ship by a magnetic needle which is continually changing its own direction. Knowing the deviation of the needle from the true north in different parts of the ocean, he obtains a corrected reading by making allowance for this divergence. In much the same way the economist, knowing, from an index number, the variations in the purchasing power of money, must make allowance for them in comparing the prices of commodities at different times. He can thereby arrive at a correct measure of changes in values.

To illustrate this, we may again refer to the data of Figure 18. According to those data, the price level in 1913 stood at 150 (as compared with 100 in 1896), indicating a decrease in the purchasing power of money. Had there been no changes in the values of commodities during this period, their prices would have risen correspondingly, so that in 1913 their relative prices would also have stood at 150.[2] But, as we have already observed, there was no such equality in the price movements. By measuring the disparity, we

---

[2] The correspondence would not, in fact, be so exact, for money does not spread its effects equally at all points in the price system (see the discussion of "The Influence of Money on Individual Prices" at the end of the second chapter following); but any failure of prices to rise or fall in the same proportion does indicate changes in their values. The method of correction here employed is, therefore, valid.

can calculate the changes in commodity values. Take rosin, for instance. Since its price rose to 276 (in 1913) while the average of all prices was rising to only 150, its power to exchange for other commodities must, on the average, have increased in the ratio of 276 to 150. Its value, then, was $\frac{276}{150}$, or 184 per cent, of what it had been. The price of wood alcohol, on the other hand, fell to 56 during the same period. Since its price was declining while the prices of other things were generally rising, its value must have fallen even more than its price. Its value, in fact, was only $\frac{56}{150}$, or 37.3 per cent, of what it formerly was. The price of print cloth, however, moved in closer agreement with the average of all prices. Its relative price in 1913 was 146, almost the same as the all-commodity index. Its power to exchange for other commodities, therefore, was almost the same as in 1896, showing a slight decline of only 3 per cent ($\frac{146}{150} = 97$). From these examples, it should be apparent that we can always compute the change in value of a given commodity from one time to another by dividing its relative price by the price index of all commodities.

Since our present concern is with individual prices, not with the price level, we may assume, for the rest of our discussion, that we are dealing with corrected prices. That is, we shall speak of prices and individual price movements as though they were always true measures of commodity values. With this explanation, let us proceed with our problem, which is to explain why individual prices behave as they do, and what part their behavior plays in the economic process.

The Rôle of Prices in Our Economy. — We can better appreciate the importance of this problem when we consider the part which prices play in our lives and in the world of business. Practically every product is produced in the expectation of a sale at a price. The business man secures his labor and equipment, including raw materials, by purchasing them at certain prices. He relies upon prices to guide his policies. If the price of his product rises in relation to his costs, so that he makes a profit, he takes that as an indication that more of his goods are demanded, and he expands his output accordingly. If he finds his prices falling in relation to his costs, so that his profits are declining, or he is incurring losses, it conveys to him the implication that his goods are too plentiful in relation to demand, and he therefore reduces his output. Investors offer their savings for loan where the highest interest rates (a form of price) are offered. Laborers move from place to place, or from industry to industry, as higher or lower prices (in the form of wages) are offered for their services. In this way, prices guide the whole economic process. The incomes of the farmer, the manufacturer, the merchant, and the professional man are all determined by the prices paid to them for the commodities and services which they offer for sale in the market place. The incomes of the wage-earners and investors in industry are derived from the same source. Even the income of the housewife, who receives an allowance from her husband, or of the college student, whose bills are paid by his father, are derived from what the husband and father can earn in industry, which, in turn, depends on the prices of his products. We convert money into real income by purchasing goods—that is, through price exchanges. Indeed, we live in a world of prices, where all our daily activities take the form of price transactions. The behavior of prices is, therefore, of vital importance to every individual.

Prices Reflect Conditions of Demand and Supply. — We can get some insight into the factors which influence the behavior of individual prices by looking at a single price transaction. Let us suppose that a soap manufacturer purchases one hundred barrels of rosin to be made into laundry soap, for which rosin he pays five dollars a barrel. There are two immediate parties to this transaction—the manufacturer who buys the rosin, and the dealer who sells it to him. If we look at the rosin market as a whole, we will see that in each transaction there is a buyer and a seller, so that we have a number of buyers on the one hand, and a number of sellers on the other. In common parlance, the buyers *demand* rosin and the sellers *supply* it. The price at which rosin is sold is somehow or other the result of agreement between these two groups. It must be worth five dollars to the buyers, or they would not purchase it, and five dollars must be a price which the sellers are willing to take, or they would not sell it. It is conceivable that there might be a shortage of rosin which would make it difficult for soap manufacturers to get all that they need, in which case they might compete with each other to obtain it by offering more than five dollars. Under such circumstances, the price would go higher. It is equally possible that dealers might find themselves overstocked with rosin, through some miscalculation of the needs of buyers. They might then lower the price in order to encourage more sales.

So, the price depends on the conditions of demand and supply. On the demand side of the market are not only soap manufacturers, who have use for rosin as a raw material, but behind them, laundry operators and housewives, who have clothes to wash. So, we have two

or more interconnected groups of buyers, stretching from soap manufacturers through dealers to ultimate consumers, all of whom have
something to do with the price. On the other side of the market
we have dealers in rosin and producers thereof, which takes us back
to the evergreen forests in various parts of the world. If we would
understand what influences the price of rosin and causes it to change,
we must analyze these demand and supply influences. We must find
out what makes ultimate consumers willing to pay more or less for
soap and, in turn, how that affects the willingness of soap manufacturers and dealers to buy. We must find out, also, what determines
the conditions under which people are willing to devote their labor
to and invest their savings in the extraction and preparation of rosin;
for it is in these conditions that we will find the forces making for
prices on the supply side of the problem. We see, then, that prices
reflect the conditions of demand and supply for commodities.

Some Basic Assumptions for Price Analysis. — The influences
through which prices are established are so many and complex that
we cannot grasp them all at once in their entirety. It is necessary to
simplify the problem by breaking it into its elements and analyzing,
one at a time, the various factors which play their part in the pricing
process. Therefore, we shall begin our analysis by making certain
assumptions which will reduce the problem to its simplest terms.
Then we may proceed to the complexities, so that at the end we will
have a fairly complete picture of the whole process.

Our first assumption is that we are dealing with prices which are
not interfered with by changes in the value of money. In other words,
we assume that the price level is free from fluctuations, so that
changes in the prices of individual commodities are the result of
changing conditions of demand and supply for them, and not of any
vagaries of the monetary system. We have already dealt with this
assumption in an earlier paragraph when we said, "Since our present concern is with individual prices, not with the price level, we
may assume for the rest of our discussion that we are dealing with
corrected prices. That is, we shall speak of prices and individual price
movements as though they were always true measures of commodity
values." After the analysis is complete, however, we must qualify
our conclusions, in recognition of the fact that monetary influences
may, in fact, affect the prices of commodities unevenly, and so cause
changes in their values.

We shall also assume, at the outset, that the price of a commodity
can be studied as a thing apart, as though it were determined irre-
spectively of the prices of other commodities. This will enable us to
examine in detail the forces which operate upon any one price in a

world of prices; but it is somewhat artificial, because prices are so interrelated, in fact, that each one depends more or less upon the others. Indeed, the whole complex of prices constitutes an interdependent system, a complete picture of which can best be shown in the form of a series of simultaneous equations. But the one price approach is the simplest, as well as the most practical, for the great majority of price problems which arise in the actual world are concerned with the prices of particular commodities, rather than with all prices taken together. Therefore, we shall begin with typical examples of individual prices and will later introduce cases of interdependent price relationships and of the price system as a whole.

We must also make certain assumptions about the state of competition in the markets where prices are established. In actual markets, various degrees of monopoly and competition can be found, but seldom a perfect case of either unmixed with the other. Rarely is there a monopoly so absolute that it does not have to take account of at least potential competitors, or to reckon with legislative interference; not often is there a competitive situation so perfect that some sellers do not have a preferred position in relation to their rivals. Yet if we are to discover the elements out of which actual price situations are made, we must proceed on the assumption that we are dealing with pure monopoly or pure competition (as the case may be), before passing on to those hybrid situations which can be described as monopolistic competition. In this way we will equip ourselves with analytical tools which can be applied in appropriate proportions to any given price problem in the world of reality.

The Influence of Prices Upon Conduct. — Finally, we must make certain assumptions concerning the behavior of human beings in respect to prices. For, since prices result from exchange transactions between persons, their determination is largely a matter of conduct. In a price transaction there is a converging of decisions in which price considerations play a part. This part is an important one. We cannot here discuss all the matters of instinct, habit, social customs, styles, and personal taste which lead people to buy the things that they do—that will be reserved for a later chapter; but whatever be the motives which actuate consumers, the prices of the goods they buy will affect their choices. Since our incomes are limited and our desires are vast, we want to get as much as we can for our money, and, therefore, we tend to buy where goods are cheapest, all other things being equal. The same desire, to get as much as possible for a given expenditure, leads producers to seek as high a price as possible for their merchandise. Consequently, they will ordinarily offer their goods for sale where the best prices can be obtained for them, other things being equal. The prices actually reached represent a resultant, or balancing, of these two sets of influences.

Some economists have pictured the human being as an *economic man* who is dominated exclusively by motives of loss and gain. He is represented as a kind of calculating machine, who measures all his actions in dollars and is governed by no other consideration. At least, he is so visualized by his critics. A truly economic man would budget his income in the most economical manner possible, so that he would always get the greatest possible value for his money and would never spend a dollar for one thing if he could get more utility by spending it for something else. Other things being equal, he would always buy every commodity at the lowest price for which it could be secured. As a business man, he would hire labor at the lowest possible wages and drive an equally hard bargain with all of those from whom he purchased materials or borrowed capital. He would produce those goods whose prices were highest, in proportion to the labor and capital employed, and would sell them to those who offered the highest prices. It is easy to criticize a theory of pricing based upon such a concept. It is obvious that other than pecuniary motives influence the conduct of human beings. Love, hate, pride, ambition, greed, and mere caprice affect our behavior, and they at times may make us act in ways that run counter to our economic interests. We must not base our theory on a contrary assumption.

Fortunately, we do not need to assume that men are economic in the extreme sense of that term; but it will be admitted that price is *one* of the influences which shapes our conduct. Therefore, when prices change, our reaction to a given situation will be affected *somewhat* thereby. For instance, a housewife may patronize a certain grocer, even though his prices are somewhat higher than those of the chain stores nearby, because she gets more individual attention and has a more cordial personal feeling toward him. The difference between his prices and those of the competing concern is not sufficient to induce her to withdraw her patronage. Were she actuated by pecuniary motives alone she would go to the chain grocer, but she considers the extra service and friendly atmosphere of her favorite merchant worth the extra prices which she must pay him. Let his price rise still higher, however, and she may have to reconsider the situation. A little difference between the two dealers does not cause her to patronize the chain store, but if the difference becomes great enough she is likely to do so. This is characteristic of consumers in general. Since it is so, we may confidently assume that a rise or fall in the price of a commodity tends to affect the sale of it. Take another case: An employee may stick to an employer for motives of loyalty or congenial surroundings, even though his wage be less than he might obtain in some other employment. Let the difference in wages become more pronounced, however, and he is likely to yield to the inducement of a larger income. So, we may take it for granted that in all business relations changes in price will affect the behavior of buyers and sellers, that buyers will take more goods when prices are reduced and sellers will offer more goods when prices are raised. This does not mean that people are completely dominated by motives of loss and gain. It merely means that, in a given situation, a sufficient change in the price stimulus will produce a change in their behavior.

Business men are probably more responsive to price incentives than consumers or laborers. This is not because business men are any less susceptible to ordinary human emotions than other people, but the immediate objective of every business enterprise is to make profits, and all the activities of business are means to this end. It is a little bit like a football game. The players may find in it an outlet for many emotions. Some play the game for love of combat, others to gain prestige in the eyes of their fellows, and yet others get intellectual enjoyment from the strategy of the contest; but, whatever be the actual motive, the activities of all are centered upon getting the ball across their opponent's goal line, for that is the accepted object to which the game is directed. Similarly, men may be in business to win wealth, power, fame, love, prestige, or for any combination of reasons; but the one recognized objective by which success in business is measured is monetary gain; to that goal their efforts are, therefore, directed. So, in deciding upon policies in the employment of men and in the marketing of their products, pecuniary loss or gain will be the most important and deciding factor, and they will buy where goods can be had at lowest prices and sell where they get the highest prices, all other things considered. Except in retail markets, where goods are sold to ultimate consumers, and in the labor market, where services are sold by individual workers, business men are the active parties on both sides of most price transactions. We will not be far wrong in assuming, therefore, that, in such cases, considerations of loss and gain will have a predominant influence. When we come to retail prices and wages we must make more allowance for other influences.

The Abstract Method. — Critics of economic theory argue that the various assumptions which we have made depart so far from the facts of economic life as to render the analysis valueless. They argue that the economist pictures an abstract world conjured up by his imagination, instead of the actual world we live in, and that consequently his conclusions have little or no bearing upon the world of reality. These critics fail to realize that the happenings of our world are too complex to be comprehended in their entirety, that the limitations of the human mind make it necessary to break them down into simpler elements, so that we can study one phase of them at a time. They forget, too, that the method of science is always one of abstraction from reality. When a physicist seeks to study how the force of gravity affects a falling body, he does not drop an object from a high precipice to the floor of the valley beneath it, for its motion under such circumstances would be complicated by too many other forces besides the one with which he is for the moment concerned. The resistance of the air would impede its passage, a strong wind could deflect it from its course, and it might become caught on the roots or branches of a projecting bush. Therefore, he constructs in his laboratory a long vacuum tube, in which none of these confusing factors is present to disturb his observations. He then discovers that *under these ideal conditions* all bodies fall at exactly the same rate of speed, regardless of their size and shape. On the basis of this observation, he formulates the well-known law of falling bodies, which says that a body tends to fall sixteen feet the first second, thirty-two feet the second second, and so forth. Except in the physics laboratory no body falls in exactly that way, but we accept the law as a scientific truth which helps us to understand how bodies do fall under ordinary conditions.

Similarly, the biologist, in studying the laws of heredity, may place white mice under artificial living conditions, where disturbing influences of the environment will not interfere with the observations. And the chemist, in observing the properties of an element, abstracts it from the other elements with which it is commonly combined, so that he may observe it in its pure state. Many other examples could be cited to show that, even in the more exact sciences, the phenomena observed are studied under ideal conditions artificially created for the purposes of experiment; yet we do not question the validity of conclusions reached by these methods.

The economist cannot conduct laboratory experiments. Human beings cannot be put into vacuum tubes or cages; their behavior can only be observed as we find it in the world about us. However, we can follow a method somewhat analogous to that of the physical and natural sciences by conceiving in our minds ideal conditions under which disturbing conditions are imagined to be absent. This is the significance of the phrase "other things being equal," which we employ from time to time. We can then proceed by a series of logical deductions to trace the chain of causation involved in the phenomena which we are investigating. This is the method which we shall follow in our analysis of prices. But though we begin with simple assumptions and rather abstract conditions, we shall move on step by step to more complicated situations which approximate those of the actual world about us.

B. Market Prices

The Nature of a Market. — Wherever buyers and sellers meet for the exchange of goods, there is said to be a *market*. The meeting need not be face to face, for a market is not a place, but a set of contacts. The contacts may be made in a building devoted to that purpose, such as the produce exchanges of our large cities; but market relationships can also be established by mail, telephone, or telegraph. To constitute a market for a given commodity, it is only essential that all the sellers of it be in actual or potential contact with all the buyers. If there are a million persons using a certain product and ten thousand selling it, and if any one of the million may become a customer of any one of the ten thousand, then they are all in the same market for that commodity, regardless of where they may be. The same individuals may be in different markets for different commodities, but the market for any one product is as broad as the connections which exist between the buyers and sellers thereof.

Geographically, the market may extend over a large territory or be limited to a small region. If the commodity is widely used and is one that can be transported cheaply far from the place where it is produced, the market will be very large. The market for wheat is international; buyers for it can be found throughout the world, and wheat produced in the United States, Argentina, Australia, or Ukrainia can be shipped to Liverpool, Paris, or Chicago. If the product is one which is used only in a limited region, or if it is so perishable or of such a character that it cannot readily be transported over long distances, the market will be local. Certain species of snails, for instance, which are considered a table delicacy in France, cannot be sold in the United States because our people are not accustomed to eating them. Gas, which is used for cooking, heating, and lighting, is difficult to put in a form to be shipped economically to distant points; it must, therefore, usually be sold near the natural deposits or gasworks where it is obtained. Modern transportation facilities, such as refrigerator cars and fast freight trains, have greatly widened the markets for perishable commodities, so that there may now be said to be one great national (and to some extent international) market for such things as eggs, meat, and fresh fruits, where formerly there were many independent local markets.

A *market,* then, may be defined as *a group of buyers and sellers in such contact with each other as to make possible the purchase and sale of one or more kinds of goods.* In a perfectly competitive market, all the buyers would be in actual or potential contact with all the sellers; every buyer would know the price being asked by every seller, and every seller would know the prices being offered by every buyer. Perfect markets are not found in the actual world, but something approaching them exists in the organized produce exchanges which were described in an earlier chapter. We shall, therefore, choose a commodity traded on such an exchange to illustrate the competitive price-making process. Cotton is such a commodity. Its market is well organized, and international in scope.

The Law of One Price. — On March 25, 1937, the price of raw cotton for immediate delivery in various cities of the United States was as follows: New York, 14.55 cents per pound; Galveston, 14.12 cents; New Orleans, 14.29 cents; Savannah, 14.59 cents; Memphis, 13.85 cents; Augusta, 14.82 cents. Several thousand bales of cotton were sold at these prices on that day. At the same time, the price in Liverpool, England, was 7.95 pence, which at that time was equivalent to about 16 cents in our money. It is significant that the price in all these cities was approximately the same, except for Liverpool. The reason for this similarity is that all these places are really in one market, and, where competition is present, *the price of a given commodity throughout the whole of a given market tends to be the same, except for differences in transportation costs.* This is known as *the law of one price.* If, in one market, some dealers ask higher prices than others, most buyers will patronize only those asking the lowest prices. This will force the others to reduce their prices to the same figure. For instance, if cotton is dearer in New York than in Memphis, dealers will place orders in Memphis and start selling in New York. The increased orders in Memphis will raise the price slightly there, and the decrease of orders in New York will lower the price in that city. Thus, through a process of arbitrage, the price tends to equality in both places. However, where one place is farther from the source of production than another, the price of the commodity will be a little higher in the first place than in the second because of the differences in the cost of transporting the product to the more distant point. This will explain why the price of cotton in New York is slightly higher than in Memphis, and why the price in Liverpool is higher than that in New York. Hence the qualification, "except for differences in transportation costs," in our statement of the law.

Where there are several local markets for the same commodity, as in the case of fuel gas, there will be a single price in each market for the good, but different prices may prevail in each of the different markets. Gas rates differ greatly from city to city. Often, however, even where markets appear to be local, there are connections between them which keep their prices in rough corrspondence. Fresh milk, for instance, is sold in many local markets; but in any of them the milk can be condensed, or dried into powder, or converted into cheese, or its cream churned into butter. All of these products are readily transported, and sold in a wide market where one price tends to prevail. If fresh milk is worth more in a given local market than it would be if converted into milk products and sold in a wider market, less of it will be put into the latter, and more into the former, reducing the local market price; but if the local price of fresh milk is so low that it is worth less than it would be if converted into milk products and sold in the general market, less will be offered locally, causing the local price to rise. In this way the wide market for milk products establishes a connection between the separate fresh milk markets and maintains an approximate equality in the price of fresh milk between them. Indirect connections of this sort are frequently found for other commodities.

It is to be observed that the law of one price, like many other economic laws, is stated as a *tendency*. This is done because we recognize that the conditions we have assumed for the problems of price study are imperfectly realized in the actual world; hence the law of one price will be approximated, but there will be some discrepancies. The word "tends" in the law means that, in so far as competition prevails, and in so far as people obey their economic interests in their buying and selling, it will hold true. Where competition is restricted, or where people do not buy and sell as economically as they might, it will not work out exactly. Business men, in their buying and selling, have a keener eye to prices than consumers, and are better informed on market conditions. Therefore, wholesale prices follow the law of one price more closely than do retail prices. In the case of the latter, considerable differences in the prices asked by different dealers in a single market may exist; but even here the tendency to one price is at work, setting limits beyond which the deviations cannot go; for extreme price differences would sooner or later cause a shift of patronage from high-priced to low-priced dealers, which would force a reduction upon the former.

Characteristics of Commodity Price Movements. — In a well-organized competitive market, the price of a commodity does not usually remain at the same point very long; it varies from day to day, or even from hour to hour. This is shown in the case of cotton by Figure 19, which traces the daily movements of the price of that commodity for the month of July, 1937. Most commodities traded at wholesale exhibit similar fluctuations. Retail prices move less frequently, but they, too, change from time to time.

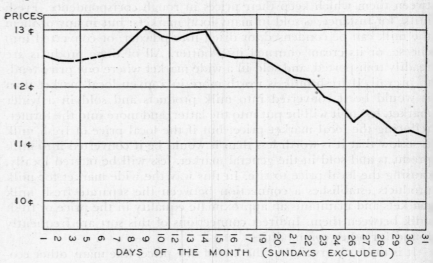

Figure 19. Daily Prices of Spot Cotton in New York during the Month of July, 1937.

The level of these fluctuations is not the same for different products. This is to be seen in the following table, which gives the highest and lowest prices which were quoted in New York for a number of staple commodities during the first six months of 1937:

Commodity	Highest Price	Lowest Price
Cotton (per pound)	.1525	.1236
Wheat (per bushel)	1.61	1.34
Cocoa (per pound)	.1320	.0695
Pork (per 200 lb. bbl.)	32.37	27.00
Beef (per 200 lb. bbl.)	24.00	17.00
Iron (per ton)	25.76	22.76
Copper (per pound)	.17	.12
Standard Tin (per pound)	.6575	.4955
Rubber (per pound)	.2694	.1848

Observe that cotton prices moved within a range of 12 to 16 cents, wheat between $1.34 and $1.61, tin between 49 and 66 cents. Each product appears to have its characteristic level, about which its price oscillates.

If we examine price movements over a longer period, we find that these levels themselves are changing, sometimes rather rapidly, at other times more slowly. We have already seen this to be true of rosin, print cloth, sugar, and wood alcohol, whose relative prices were charted in Figure 18. It is shown for cotton in Figure 20, which plots the average monthly prices of that commodity for the season

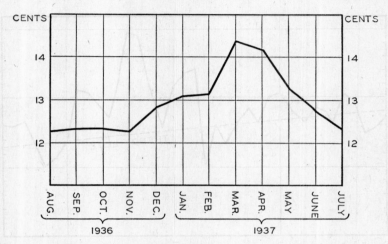

Figure 20. Average Monthly Prices of Spot
Cotton in New York, 1936–1937.

of 1936–37, and in Figure 21, which plots the average yearly prices from 1900 to 1936. The last-named quotations are corrected for changes in the price level, so that they show changes in the value of cotton, after allowance has been made for changes in the value of money. Although the movements pictured on this chart show considerable irregularity from month to month, a general downward trend is to be noted, interrupted by a marked rise during and after the first World War.

Market Prices and Normal Prices. — In these price movements we can discern at least two different types of price-making influences. On the one hand, there must be certain deep, underlying causes for the different levels about which the prices of different commodities fluctuate. Something must be at work which keeps the price of cotton somewhere between 12 and 16 cents, while it keeps the price of tin within the range of 49 to 66 cents. These causes are not fixed in their action, for the level of price movement for each commodity

shifts from year to year; but they change slowly. On the other hand
there must be other forces, less potent and less constant in character, which cause the lesser day-to-day variations of prices about their
general level or average position. The actual price prevailing at a
given moment is evidently the combined result of both sets of causes
working simultaneously. The case is not unlike that of a floating
bottle, which tends to rest on the water in a certain position, determined by its buoyancy and shape, but which is continually bob-

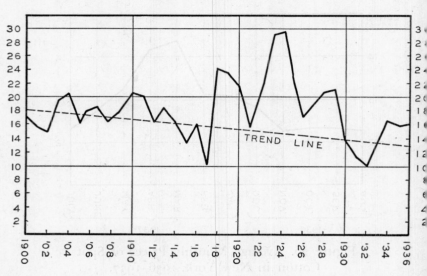

Figure 21. Average Yearly Prices of Spot Cotton in New York, 1900-
1936, Corrected to the Price Level of 1926.

bing up and down and here and there because it is disturbed by currents, tides, winds, and waves.

Recognizing these two aspects of price phenomena, economists
commonly distinguish between *market prices* and *normal prices.*
Market prices are *the prices which actually exist,* with all their erratic irregularities. They are comparable to the actual motion of
the bottle. *Normal prices* are *the prices which would exist in a state
of equilibrium,* if all the disturbing influences which are continually
interfering with stable price adjustments could be removed. They
are comparable to the bottle as it would rest, if there were no currents or winds or tides to disturb its position. Thus, they are somewhat of an abstraction; yet they have reality, in the sense that they
constitute the focal point about which market prices actually fluctu-

ate. Since market prices fluctuate within a general area or range that is fairly well defined, we can conceive of them as in oscillation about a definite center, or norm, which itself is slowly moving. That center, or norm, in competitive markets, is the normal price.

The concept of market and normal prices is a useful device by which we make, in our analysis, the distinction we have observed in actual data between those price-making influences which are superficial and those which are more fundamental. This suggests a mode of procedure in which we first examine the mechanism of demand and supply as it manifests itself in the day-to-day market, and then endeavor to probe more deeply into the underlying determinants. In short, we begin with market prices and go on to normal prices.

The Demand Schedule and Curve. — We are now ready to examine the influences acting upon the market price of cotton, which cause it to be approximately 14 cents on a given day. We know, from what has already been said, that this price is, in some way or other, a result of the conditions of demand and supply for the commodity. We shall consider the demand first.

In its broadest sense, demand refers to readiness to buy. This implies a desire for the good in question, coupled with some means of payment, on the part of possible purchasers. Readiness to buy will not lead to actual purchases, however, unless the commodity is obtainable at a price which buyers are willing and able to pay. That is, demand may be only potential; but when the price is within the range of buyers' offers, a part of the demand, at least, becomes effective. *Effective demand* may be defined as *the quantity of a good which purchasers will buy at a given price*. The qualifying phrase "at a given price" is important, for the quantity which buyers will take is not rigidly fixed; it depends upon the price prevailing. Had the price of cotton on the day which we have chosen for our example been 16 cents, instead of 14 cents, fewer bales would have been purchased. Had it been 12 cents, on the other hand, a larger quantity would have been bought; for buyers tend to hold back when prices are high and to buy more freely when prices are low. This is an almost universal characteristic of demand, the reason for which will presently be explained. For the moment, we can take it as a fact of general observation. Therefore, if we had sufficient information about the attitude of buyers toward cotton on a particular day, we could draw up a table showing the quantities which they would purchase at each price within the probable range of the market.

Let us construct such a table for cotton. In the absence of exact knowledge, our figures must be hypothetical, but they will suffice to illustrate the principle. Suppose, then, that the following represents the actual conditions in the market for cotton on the given date:

If the price is:			The effective demand will be:
20¢	per pound		10,000 bales
19¢	"	"	12,250 "
18¢	"	"	15,000 "
17¢	"	"	20,000 "
16¢	"	"	25,000 "
15¢	"	"	30,000 "
14¢	"	"	40,000 "
13¢	"	"	50,000 "
12¢	"	"	60,000 "
11¢	"	"	70,000 "
10¢	"	"	80,000 "

Such a table, showing the quantities of a commodity which will be purchased at a corresponding series of prices, is known as a *demand schedule*.

A more convenient way of representing it is by means of a drawing, such as that of Figure 22. In this drawing, vertical distances along the line OY measure prices, horizontal distances on the line

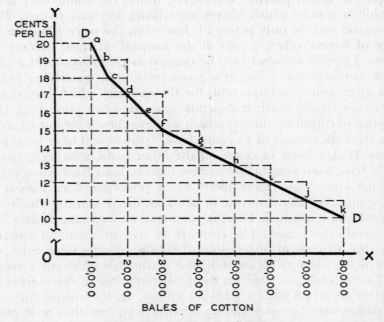

Figure 22. A Demand Curve.

OX measure quantities, in this case bales of cotton.[3] The curve D
is a *demand curve,* which gives us a graphic picture of the demand
for cotton. It is constructed in such a way that, if, from any point
on it, we draw a horizontal line to the OY axis, and a vertical line
to the OX axis, it will show the quantity which buyers will take at
the corresponding price. For instance, a horizontal line drawn from
the point f intersects the OY axis at 15, and a vertical line from f
intersects the OX axis at 30,000. This means that, if the price is 15
cents, buyers will take 30,000 bales. The points $a, b, c, d, e, f, g, h,$
$i, j,$ and k correspond to the prices and quantities given in our
hypothetical demand schedule, a indicating purchases of 10,000 at
20 cents, $b,$ 12,250 at 19 cents, and so on. The curve can also be
used to show (what the schedule does not) quantities that will be
purchased at prices which involve fractional parts of a cent. For instance, at 11.5 cents, 65,000 bales would be taken. Since diagrams
similar to this one are commonly used in explaining the determination of prices, the student should study it with care and familiarize
himself with its every detail, in order that he may understand the
other graphs which will follow as we go on.

The Supply Schedule and Curve. — Let us now look at the supply
side of the problem. In its broadest sense, the word supply denotes
readiness to sell. This depends on the existence, actual or prospective, of a stock of the good in question and a willingness on the part
of the holders thereof to dispose of some or all of it for a price. Not
all of the existing stock will necessarily be offered for sale at any
one time. How much will be offered depends on whether existing
prices are adequate to persuade sellers to dispose of their wares.
Hence, the supply may be either potential or effective, depending on
the price prevailing. *Effective supply* may be defined as *the quantity
of a good that will be offered for sale at a given price.* Just as we
constructed a demand schedule, showing the quantities of cotton
which purchasers will take at each of several different prices, so we
can construct a *supply schedule,* showing the quantities which sellers
will offer at the same prices. This schedule will move in an opposite
direction to that of demand, for, whereas a high price deters buyers
and a low price encourages them, a high price will attract sellers and
a low price will repel them. The supply schedule for cotton, therefore, may be something like this:

[3] To be strictly accurate, equal distances on the line OY should measure equal price
amounts; this would bring the figure 10 in the cents column ten spaces above the base
line OX, instead of close to it, as here shown. Since it suffices for our purpose to consider only the range of prices from ten to twenty cents, we secure a more compact
diagram by omitting the prices from 1 cent to 9 cents. The omission is indicated by a
break in the line OY.

At a price of:	The effective supply will be:
10¢ per pound	5,000 bales
11¢ " "	20,000 "
12¢ " "	30,000 "
13¢ " "	35,000 "
14¢ " "	40,000 "
15¢ " "	45,000 "
16¢ " "	50,000 "
17¢ " "	55,000 "
18¢ " "	60,000 "
19¢ " "	62,250 "
20¢ " "	65,000 "

We can now construct a *supply curve,* just as we did for demand. Such a curve is shown by the line S in Figure 23. Here, as before, prices are measured on OY and quantities on OX, any point on the curve denoting, by reference to its two axes, the number of bales of cotton which sellers will offer (*i.e.,* the effective supply) at the corresponding price.

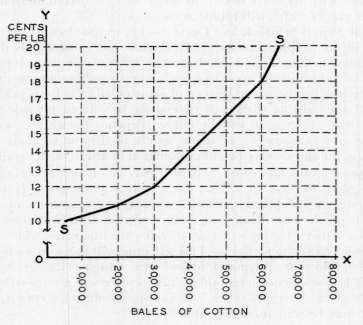

Figure 23. A Supply Curve.

Increase and Decrease of Demand or Supply. — In our subsequent discussion, we shall sometimes have occasion to speak of increasing or decreasing demand, and increasing or decreasing supply. As the concepts of changing demand and supply are beclouded with some ambiguity, it is necessary to clarify them.

Consider the heavy curve D in Figure 24, which is exactly the same demand curve as the one we have already examined in Figure 22. Suppose that the price of cotton, having been at 15 cents, falls for some reason to 12 cents. According to the curve, there will be an increase in sales from 30,000 to 60,000 bales. Does this indicate an increase in the demand? In one sense, it does, for the effective de-

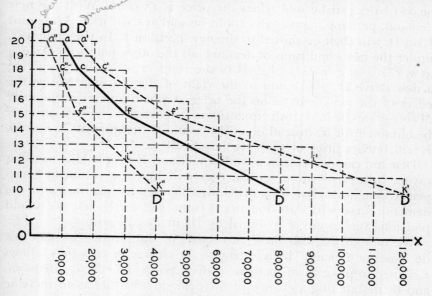

Figure 24. Increase and Decrease of Demand.

mand is clearly greater at the lower price than at the higher. In the same sense, there will be a decrease in demand if the price is raised, for in that case a smaller quantity will be purchased. For instance, if the price goes up from 15 cents to 18 cents, sales will shrink from 30,000 to 15,000. In neither of these cases, however, has there been any fundamental change in the attitude of buyers, as reflected in the demand schedule. The demand curve itself is unaltered. What has really happened is that some change in the price (which may have originated on the supply side of the market) has made effective a demand that was formerly only potential. That demand was already existing, but was not expressed. In this case, the change in price was the cause, and the change in demand was the effect.

It is possible, however, for the attitudes of buyers toward a good to change in such a way as to alter the whole demand schedule. We will then have a change in the demand which is not the effect of a change in a price, but a cause of it.[4] Suppose fashion decrees that more cotton dresses shall be worn next year. Buyers of cotton goods will then want more cotton than before, even at the old prices. A new demand schedule will come into existence, indicating the greater quantities of cotton that can now be sold at each of the possible prices. To represent this graphically, a new demand curve must be drawn, as follows: We have assumed an original demand in which 30,000 bales can be sold when the price is 15 cents. With the new demand, perhaps 45,000 bales could be sold at that price. The point *f*, on D, will then be shifted to the new position *f'*. In the same way, under the new conditions of demand, all the other points on D, such as *a, c, i,* and *k,* will be shifted to the right (*a', c', i',* and *k'*) giving a new curve D', above and to the right of the old one. Notice the effect of the new demand on the price at which any given quantity of cotton can be sold. If the quantity is 30,000 bales, 17 cents can now be obtained for it, instead of 15 cents, and if the quantity is 60,000, it will fetch a price of 14 cents, instead of 12.

Demand can decrease in a similar manner. If people take to using rayon, instead of cotton goods, they will buy less cotton at given prices than formerly. The demand schedule will decline, and the demand curve will shift downward from, and to the left of, its old position. Such a curve is shown by D" in the diagram.

We may distinguish these two senses of the phrase "increase (or decrease) of demand" by referring to the change in sales that follows a change in price as an increase or decrease *in the effective demand,* and by designating a change in the demand schedule as an increase or decrease *in the schedule of demand.*

Changes in effective demand refer to shifting points on an unchanging demand curve; changes in the demand schedule refer to shifts in the position of the curve itself. When the demand schedule changes, more (or less) of the commodity can be sold *at a given* price than before; or (what amounts to the same thing) the same quantity can be sold for a higher (or lower) price than formerly; but, when there is merely a change in the effective demand, the quantity which can be sold at any given price (or the price that can be got for any given quantity) remains the same as it was. Thus changes in the demand schedule are more fundamental. Usually one can distinguish

---

[4] However, a *prospective* change in prices may cause a change in demand in the sense here explained; for if buyers expect prices in the future to be higher than they now are, they are likely to want to buy more at present prices, so that demand schedules will move upward; and if prices are expected to fall, they are likely to buy less now, so that schedules will move downward.

from the context in which sense a change in demand is meant in any given case, but if there is the slightest chance of ambiguity, it is wise to be explicit.

All that has been said of changes in demand is equally applicable to supply. By an increase (or decrease) in supply, we may mean an increase (or decrease) in the quantities of a good offered for sale by sellers as a result of a raising (or lowering) of the price, or we may mean an offering of larger (or smaller) quantities than formerly *at any given price.* The former is an increase (or decrease) *in the ef-*

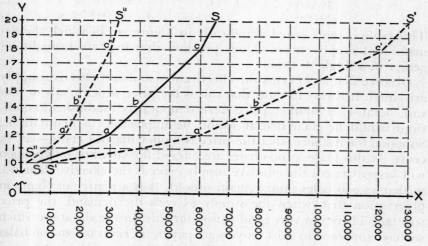

Figure 25. Increase and Decrease of Supply.

fective supply, and is indicated by different points on an unchanging supply curve (such as *a, b,* and *c* on the curve S in Figure 21). The latter is an increase (or decrease) *in the schedule of supply,* and is indicated by a shift of the supply curve to the right (or left) of its old position. In Figure 25, for instance, if S is the original supply curve, S' portrays an increase in the schedule such that, at each of the several prices, double the former quantities will be offered for sale. S'', on the other hand, shows a decrease to half the original quantities.

Temporary Equilibrium of Demand and Supply. — By bringing the demand and supply schedules together, we can see how they react upon each other to establish a market price. The following table, constructed from the demand and supply schedules previously given, shows the effective demand and supply at each possible price from 20 to 10 cents:

Effective Demand	Price	Effective Supply
10,000	20	65,000
12,250	19	62,250
15,000	18	60,000
20,000	17	55,000
25,000	16	50,000
30,000	15	45,000
40,000	14	40,000
50,000	13	35,000
60,000	12	30,000
70,000	11	20,000
80,000	10	5,000

This table is represented graphically in Figure 26, in which the demand and supply curves of our previous drawings are brought together in a single diagram.

Observe that at 14 cents the effective demand and effective supply are equal. It is easy to show that this is the price which tends to prevail, because, if another price were temporarily established, conditions would be such that it would be impossible to maintain it. Suppose, for instance, that the price is higher than 14 cents—say 15 cents. At this price 45,000 bales are offered for sale, but only 30,000 will be purchased; the effective supply exceeds the effective demand, so that 15,000 bales must remain unsold. It is a matter of common observation that, when the supply exceeds the demand, the price will fall. There is a very good reason for this. In the situation which we have supposed to exist, buyers are paying 15 cents for 30,000 bales of cotton which they might readily enough have obtained for 12 cents, for sellers are willing to dispose of that quantity at the lower figure. Buyers have but to seek out those sellers who are willing to take less than 15 cents to force a drop in the price. Competition among sellers will accomplish the same result, for, since, not all who would like to sell at the higher price are able to do so, many will offer their cotton for less, attracting buyers away from the high-priced sellers. In either case, the price must fall; but it cannot fall below 14 cents without causing an opposite reaction. Suppose the price to be 13 cents. Here there is an effective demand for 50,000 bales, but an effective supply of only 35,000. The demand now exceeds the supply. In this situation sellers are very foolish if they do not raise their price, for, since all those who wish to purchase at 13 cents are unable to do so, many will pay more rather than go without. Indeed, the demand schedule shows that 40,000 bales can be sold if the price is raised to 14 cents. Sellers will therefore raise it; and if they do not, buyers, unable to get the supplies of cotton which they need at 13 cents, will offer more in order to obtain them. Therefore, the price is bound to rise.

By similar reasoning, it can be demonstrated that any price above or below 14 cents is bound to create an excess of effective supply or demand, which will cause the price to return to that figure. At 14 cents, however, the market is stable, for there is just enough cotton supplied at that price to meet the demand of those who wish to buy.

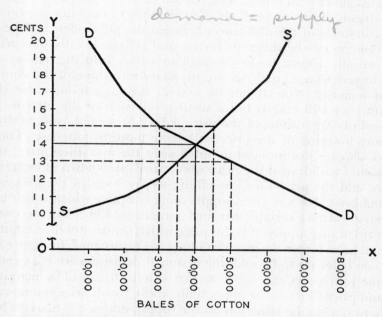

Figure 26. Market Equilibrium of Demand and Supply.

So long as the demand and supply schedules remain as we have shown them, the price tends to stay at that figure. When effective demand and supply are thus equal, they are said to be in equilibrium. However, it is a very temporary one at that, for the demand and supply schedules of the day-to-day market are continually changing, and, with them, the equilibrium price.

The Law of Demand and Supply. — We have now established a general principle with respect to prices. This principle is known as *the law of demand and supply*. A simple statement of it is that *the price of an economic good tends toward the point where the effective demand for it equals the effective supply*. The law is an important one—so important, indeed, that it has been said one could make an economist out of a parrot by teaching him to repeat it. The mere statement of the law, however, gives but a superficial picture of the price-making process. Before we are through with it, we will find that it would be a very remarkable parrot indeed who could understand it thoroughly.

Marginal Demand-Price and Marginal Supply-Price. — The price which prevails in a state of equilibrium is the same for everyone, although some buyers are willing to pay more than others and some sellers ask more than others. The reasons for this uniformity of price have already been set forth. It is interesting to consider, however, the significance of the differences between the price offers and price requirements of the different buyers and sellers. If only one price is to prevail, it must be low enough to attract into the market all those buyers whose purchases are necessary to dispose of the equilibrium quantity. Not all can be sold to the high bidders, for the amount they will take is but a small proportion of the total to be disposed of. Any raising of the price will cause some buyers to drop out; any lowering of the price will cause more to purchase. Those buyers who are just induced to purchase at the prevailing price, and who would withdraw if the price were raised, are known as *marginal buyers,* and the price they are willing to pay is called the *marginal demand-price.* For any given supply there is a price which is just low enough to attract certain marginal purchases, which are necessary to get rid of that supply. It is this price which constitutes the marginal demand-price under the given conditions. For instance, in Figure 26, if 50,000 bales are to be sold, the marginal demand-price is 13 cents. If some purchasers can get it at that price, all can. The marginal demand-price thus sets the upper limit, above which price cannot rise.

There is a similar situation on the supply side of the market. Not all the sellers of a given good hold out for the same price. Some are willing to sell for less than others. However, if a given supply is to become effective, the price must be high enough to attract into the market all the sellers whose offerings are necessary to make up the given quantity. There are always some sellers who are on the verge of withholding all or a part of their stocks, and who would withdraw from the market if the price were any lower. These are known as *marginal sellers,* and the price which just induces them to sell is known as the *marginal supply-price.* In Figure 26, if 50,000 bales are to be offered for sale, the marginal supply-price for that quantity is 16 cents. Although there are some sellers who would offer their cotton for less, there would not be 50,000 bales at any lower figure. To attract the fifty-thousandth bale onto the market, the price must be 16 cents. If some sellers can get that price, all can get it. Hence, the marginal supply-price is controlling.

We have already learned that price tends to be established at the point where the effective demand equals the effective supply. It is equally correct to say that it tends to settle at the point where the marginal demand-price equals the marginal supply-price. These are merely two different ways of looking at the same phenomenon. In the first case our attention is focused on the quantities of the good purchased and offered for sale at different prices; in the second, we are looking at the prices offered by buyers and asked by sellers for different quantities of the good. Equilibrium of effective demand and supply occurs when equality of marginal demand-price with marginal supply-price is reached. In Figure 26, marginal demand-price equals marginal supply-price at 14 cents, and effective demand equals effective supply at the same price.

The Case of Fixed Supply. — The supply curve which we have drawn for the wholesale cotton market takes it for granted that not all of the stock of cotton in existence on a given day is to be sold immediately; dealers may withhold a part or all of it until they are convinced that prevailing prices warrant its sale. There are some commodities which are of so perishable a nature that this withholding is not feasible (although the development of cold storage facilities is making these cases less numerous than they formerly were). When a carload (or several carloads) of perishable fruit reaches a city produce market, it may be necessary or expedient to sell all of it on the day of its arrival. In that case, the supply is fixed for the time being, and must be sold for whatever it will bring. In these circumstances, not a single crate must be left unsold; therefore, the price must be low enough to secure the marginal purchase which is just necessary to dispose of every crate available. This means that the marginal demand-price governs the market, for there is no marginal supply-price to set against it.

The case is illustrated by Figure 27. Here the supply, instead of being represented by a gradually rising curve, as in our previous illustrations, is pictured as the vertical straight line S, indicating that there are just 1000 crates of strawberries to be sold, no more and no less, regardless of the price prevailing. The demand curve (D) has the characteristic slope which we have already observed in our previous illustrations. This curve indicates that some strawberries could be sold at as high a price as $2, and a larger quantity at a $1.50, but the marginal crates can only be disposed of if the price comes down to $1. Since only one price can prevail in a market, this is the price which tends to be established, and at which all of the strawberries will presumably be sold. It is not likely, however, that the market would reach this price immediately, for the buyers and sellers do not have so accurate a picture of the demand and supply conditions as to know the exact price which will just barely effect the sale

of every crate of strawberries. It is likely that there will be some
bidding, at which the first crates will go at a price somewhat higher
than a dollar, and it is conceivable that when this price does not
move the entire stock on hand, dealers may lower the price for some
buyers to less than a dollar. One dollar nevertheless represents approximately the point at which the strawberries are likely to be sold.

A somewhat similar situation may arise in the case of style goods
toward the end of a season. Styles change so rapidly that certain types
of clothing cannot readily be sold if held over to another season, be-

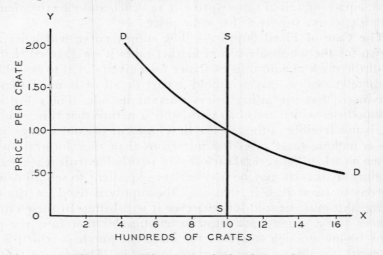

Figure 27. The Case of Fixed Supply.

cause they will no longer be fashionable. Dealers will then hold special sales, at which their remaining stocks of such goods are offered
at sacrifice prices, in order to get rid of them before they lose their
value entirely. Prices are presumably set just low enough to dispose
of existing stocks, but, of course, the method is a crude one which
does not reach the exact equilibrium price.

**The Relation of Middlemen's Schedules to Consumer and Producer
Schedules.** — So far, we have taken demand and supply schedules
pretty much for granted, as observed facts of the market; but a
thorough explanation of prices must tell us why they have the characteristics which they possess, what determines their general positions, and what may cause them to change. Therefore, let us look at
the buyers and sellers in the wholesale cotton market, to see if we
can find out what influences their decisions as to the prices they are
willing to pay or to take. The buyers are not the ultimate users of
cotton, nor are the sellers the farmers who grew it. They are dealers

(who buy and stock cotton for later sale to manufacturers), exporters (who buy for resale to foreign customers), speculators (who buy "long" or sell "short" in the hope of making a profit from price fluctuations), and brokers (who act as agents for other persons, buying and selling on a commission). Since these are all middlemen, the prices they ask, and the prices they are willing to pay, must be based on some sort of estimate as to what ultimate consumers will pay for cotton products, and as to what planters will accept for their crops. In short, the demand and supply schedules of the organized commodity markets are derived from the more fundamental demand schedules of consumers and supply schedules of producers.

However, the relation between the demand and supply schedules of the wholesale market and ultimate demand and supply schedules is a somewhat loose one, because of the lapse of time which ensues between the production of commodities and their ultimate sale to consumers. The wholesale market stands between cotton growers and cotton manufacturers, on the one hand, and consumers of cotton goods, on the other. The dealers of that market must estimate, to the best of their ability, the probable quantities of cotton which will be forthcoming from growers, and the quantities which the manufacturers of cotton goods will require to meet the demands of consumers. Professional speculators play a very active part in this process. The estimates of all those who participate in the market will be very much influenced by the stocks of cotton known to be already available, by the forecasts as to the probable yield of the coming crop, and by the expected needs of consumers. If the government Department of Agriculture forecasts a bumper crop, so that a large quantity of cotton is to be anticipated, the price will drop sharply on the day of such announcement, for buyers and sellers alike, expecting a fall in the price of cotton products, will revise their schedules downward. If news reaches the market that women's styles will emphasize cotton dresses in the coming season, an increase in consumers' demand is to be expected; buyers and sellers on the cotton exchange will revise their schedules upward, and the price will rise. So, the wholesale price is responsive both to present conditions and to the visible future, but always it goes back to the underlying conditions of production and consumption.

Market Prices in Less Well-organized Markets. — Every commodity (and every service) has its market price, but the market is not always organized into formal produce exchanges, so that in many cases the vacillating influences of demand and supply do not have so free a play, and the response of prices to changing conditions is not so quick as in our example. In the wholesaling and retailing of groceries, for instance, there is no general meeting place where all the buyers and sellers can keep in close touch with each other and with market conditions. Custom, good will, and established habits have more influence. Such cases depart from the state of perfect competition on which our analysis for the present is based; they belong rather to the conditions of imperfect competition, which will be considered later. The general principles which have already been outlined, as to the relation between wholesale prices and the underlying conditions of production and consumption, nevertheless apply. All prices, in the last analysis, go back to consumers' demands, on the one hand, and to producers' supplies, on the other. The future course of our investigation, therefore, lies in that direction.

SUMMARY

Prices of individual commodities exhibit differences in their movements. These differences reveal changes in their values, that is, in their power to command other goods in exchange. Prices are values expressed in terms of money. However, since money itself changes in value, we must correct price readings by an index of the general price level if we want to compare the values of goods from one time to another. Our present concern is with such corrected individual prices. Prices play an important rôle in our economy because nearly every economic process involves an exchange transaction at a price.

In studying prices we shall assume: (1) that commodity prices are not distorted by changes in the price level, (2) that some prices are determined under conditions of pure competition, some under pure monopoly, and some under imperfect competition, (3) that the price of one commodity can be studied in isolation from that of other commodities. We shall also assume that human choices are influenced (but not completely dominated) by price considerations. We shall proceed from these simple assumptions to more complex conditions approaching those of reality. This abstract method is roughly analogous to the method of the natural sciences.

Prices are established in a market, defined as a group of buyers and sellers of a given good in such contact with each other as to make possible the purchase and sale of one or more kinds of goods. According to the law of one price, the price of a given commodity tends to be the same throughout the whole of such a market, except for differences in transportation costs. Prices follow this law more accurately in wholesale than in retail markets. Observation of market price movements reveals that they fluctuate about a certain level which slowly changes. Economists, therefore, distinguish between market (actual) and the normal (stable, equilibrium) prices, about which the former fluctuate.

The forces determining prices are revealed by an analysis of demand and supply. Effective demand denotes the quantity of a good which purchasers will buy at a given price. The demand schedule shows the different quantities which they will buy at a corresponding series of prices; it is represented graphically by a demand curve. Effective supply denotes the quantity of a good which will be offered for sale at a given price. Analogous to the corresponding concepts of demand, we have the supply schedule and the supply curve. The terms increase and decrease of demand or supply may refer to a change in the effective demand or supply, without any alteration of the schedules (a shifting point on a single demand or supply curve), or they may refer to a change in the schedule itself (a shifting of the demand or supply curve to a new position). According to the law of demand and supply, the market supply of a good tends to the point where the effective demand for it equals the effective supply. Another way of putting this is to say that price tends to a point where the marginal demand-price and marginal supply-price are equal. Where supply is fixed, the price will equal the marginal demand-price for the given stock. Prices are more responsive to changing conditions of demand and supply, and they reach a more perfect equilibrium, in organized produce exchanges than in less well-organized markets.

REFERENCES AND SUGGESTIONS FOR FURTHER READING

The literature dealing with individual prices (the theory of value) is vast. The suggestions here (and following the next three chapters) can indicate only a few of the more outstanding works. Most writers on the subject, including the present author, are deeply indebted to Alfred Marshall's *Principles of Economics* (5th or later edition); Book I, Chapter 3 of this work, and Appendices C and D of the same, deal essentially with the underlying assumptions and methods of price analysis. Lionel Robbins deals brilliantly with this theme in Chapters 4 and 5 of his *Essay on the Nature and Significance of Economic Science* (2nd edition, London, 1935). See also Chapter 1 of F. H. Knight's *Risk, Uncertainty and Profit* (1921). A simple little book, presenting the theory of value in an interesting and suggestive way, with special emphasis on the functions of prices in guiding the economic process, is H. D. Henderson's *Supply and Demand* (1922), especially Chapters 1 to 5.

H. J. Davenport, in Chapters 2 and 3 of his *Economics of Enterprise* (1913), emphasizes prices as the central problem of economics. For an elaborate statistical study of price movements, see Frederick C. Mills' *The Behavior of Prices* (1927).

Chapter XIV

THE BACKGROUND OF DEMAND AND
SUPPLY. MONOPOLY PRICE

A. Fundamental Characteristics of Demand

Consumers' Choices. — We know that the basis of all economic activity rests in the fact that goods are scarce in relation to our desires. To the individual, the scarcity takes the form of a limited money income. Although a very few lucky people have incomes which are very large, rare indeed is the person who has enough to buy everything which he desires. Therefore, each consumer is compelled to choose which desires shall take precedence over others. So, consciously or unconsciously, he compares the different directions which his expenditures may take, and spends his money accordingly. In making these decisions, the prevailing prices for the various goods among which he must choose play an important part. If the price of a silk shirt is twice that of a cotton one, he may decide that, in view of the other things which he would like to do with his money, the silk is not worth the difference. He will buy the cotton shirt and do without the other. His reaction, together with that of all other shirt-wearing men, determines the effective demand for shirts at the price prevailing. If, at this price, the demand over a period of time is just sufficient to take off the market the shirts which manufacturers find it worth while to produce at that price, the market has established an equilibrium between the underlying conditions of demand and supply, and the price tends to remain where it is. But if the rate at which consumers are buying shirts is greater or less than the rate at which they are being produced, there is not an equilibrium of the underlying forces, and hence the market price cannot then be long maintained. It will change in the direction necessary to bring about a better balance. It is the same with every other commodity. So, market prices are trial balloons, put out to test the underlying conditions of demand and supply. It is these basic conditions which determine, ultimately, what prices will prevail. To understand the price-making process, we must know what are the fundamental determinants of demand and supply.

Our immediate concern is with the demand aspect of this problem. After we have cleared that up, we shall go on to the supply aspect. Then, by putting the two sets of factors together, we will have a complete picture of the forces making for normal prices. We shall not here attempt to describe the complex reactions of the mind which lead human beings to prefer one thing to another. That is primarily a problem for the psychologist. For our present purpose, we can take people's choices for granted. We do need to know more, however, about how consumers will behave in respect to the price of a particular good. This behavior reflects itself in consumers' demand.

The Law of Demand. — In constructing a demand schedule for raw cotton in the day-to-day market, we observed that more cotton would be purchased when the price was low than when it was high. This is a characteristic feature of all demand schedules. It is true of consumers' demand, and hence of the demand of manufacturers and dealers also; for the demand of the latter, it will be remembered, is derived from that of the former, and follows the same general pattern. Accordingly, it may be stated that, *the greater the amount of a given commodity to be sold in a given market at a given time, the lower must be the price.* Or, to put it more concisely, the lower the price, the greater the effective demand. This is known as the *law of demand.* There are four reasons for the operation of this law:

(1) In the first place, although human wants in general seem to be capable of indefinite expansion, our desire for any one thing can be completely satisfied, at least for the time being. Satisfaction does not occur all at once, but develops gradually as more of the commodity is consumed. For instance, the first taste of a delicious fruit may whet the appetite for more, but if we consume several of them in succession, we have soon had enough. In civilized society, the possession of at least one shirt is so important that a man would give up a good deal to secure it; additional shirts are desirable, but not quite so necessary; and after one has a dozen or so, a further addition to his stock adds very little to his satisfaction. This principle is known as the *law of diminishing utility,* which may be stated as follows: *After a certain point has been reached, the intensity of one's desire for additional units of goods diminishes as the stock pos-*

sessed increases.[1] This is true of all goods, with one qualification. It is assumed that, after the first units of a good are consumed, enough time has not elapsed to allow the gratification derived from them to pass away. After one has worn out a shirt and thrown it away, a new one may have as much utility as its predecessor, or even more; but, already possessing some which are still serviceable, additional ones will add less to the satisfaction of the user. The significance of this for prices is that, if, in a given time period, the quantity of goods to be sold is more than enough to meet the first and most pressing desires of consumers, the price will have to be lowered in order to induce them to increase their consumption.

(2) The second reason for the law of demand lies in the fact that many commodities have different uses, some of which are more important than others. Cotton is used for various products in the home, including clothing, sheets and pillow cases, turkish towels and wash-cloths, handkerchiefs, laundry bags, draperies, and chair covers. In some of these uses it has greater utility than in others. We would be very uncomfortable without clothing, but we could get along well enough without laundry bags. Likewise with water. Our very lives depend on it for drinking, and we need it rather urgently for bathing and dish-washing, but for lawn sprinkling it is merely a dispensable luxury. Similar instances could be multiplied many times. We may call this *the principle of different uses*. It contributes to the law of demand in this way: If the price of a commodity is high, its use will be restricted to those purposes for which the purchasers consider it most important, and the effective demand will then be relatively small; but if the price is low, consumers will employ it for less important uses, and the effective demand will then be greater.

(3) The fact that people differ in their requirements, situations, and tastes also contributes to the law of demand. People in cold climates need more wool and less cotton than people in warm climates. The demand for these products in the two regions differs ac-

---

[1] The principle of diminishing utility explains the apparently paradoxical fact that things of very great usefulness sometimes have very little value. We may call the sum total of satisfactions derived from all the units of a commodity which are consumed its *total utility*. Because of diminishing utility, the total utility does not increase proportionately if more of the commodity is consumed. If our stock of such things as bread and water is very large, we attach very little importance to a single loaf of the former or a single bucket of the latter; because, were we to lose either, we would still have plenty left, and our total utility would not be very much reduced. The importance attaching to such a single unit of the stock of a good is called its *marginal utility*. The marginal utility of a commodity is less to an individual, the more of it he possesses. How much he can be induced to pay for that commodity will depend on its marginal, rather than upon its total, utility to him. Hence, if the quantity of any good is so great that everyone in the community is well supplied with it, so that its marginal utility to everybody is small or nothing, the value of that good, and its price, will be correspondingly small or zero, as the case may be—no matter how great its total utility.

cordingly. Some people are passionately fond of grand opera, others enjoy it only moderately, while still others find it boring. Those who derive extreme pleasure from it will pay well for opera seats rather than go without; hence, if the quantity of tickets is limited, they can all be sold to the opera-lovers at fairly high prices. Those whose desire for it is less will not pay so much; hence, if their demand is to be added to that of the others, the price must be lowered. This we may call *the principle of different desires*. It is applicable to most commodities.

(4) Finally, the fact that personal incomes are unequal gives further force to the law of demand. The rich man has so much purchasing power that he can outbid the poor man, although his desires may be no more urgent than those of the latter. Consequently, if the quantity of a commodity is small, it can all be sold to the well-to-do, who can pay a high price for it; but if the quantity is greater, some of it must be sold to consumers of more moderate means, in which case the price must be lower. We may call this *the principle of different incomes*.

Elasticity of Demand. — The law of demand tells us that, as the effective supply of a good increases, the price that consumers will pay for it falls. But this fall does not always take place at the same rate for different goods. In the case of some commodities, an increase in the amount to be sold will depress the price rapidly. With other commodities, the descent will be more gradual. Looking at the matter a little differently, a change in the price of some commodities will cause a relatively great change in the effective demand; with other commodities, the change in demand will be relatively small. The sensitivity of effective demand to changes in price is known as *elasticity of demand*. All demands have some elasticity, but some have more than others. A demand that is quite sensitive to changes in price is said to be *elastic*. One that is only slightly sensitive is said to be *inelastic*.

Elasticity of demand can be measured mathematically by comparing the percentage of drop in price with the percentage of increase in purchases; or (what amounts to the same thing) by observing the effect of price changes upon the total receipts from sales. This is illustrated by the two demand curves shown in Figure 28 (on page 324), and by the adjacent table, which is calculated from those curves. Here, total receipts are computed by multiplying the price in each case by the effective demand. If a drop in price is compensated by a corresponding increase in effective demand, so that the total receipts remain the same, the demand is said to have an *elasticity of unity*. For instance, a fifty per cent drop in price may result in a one hun-

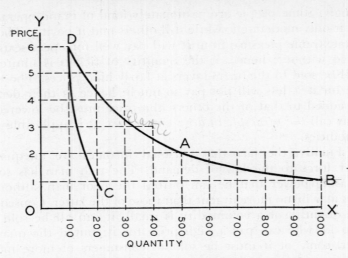

Figure 28. Elastic and Inelastic Demand.

| | Schedule DAB | | | Schedule DC | |
Price	Effective Demand	Total Receipts	Price	Effective Demand	Total Receipts
6¢	100	$ 6.00	6¢	100	$6.00
5¢	150	7.50	5¢	105	5.25
4¢	225	9.00	4¢	110	4.40
3¢	325	9.75	3¢	130	3.90
2¢	500	10.00	2¢	150	3.00
1¢	1000	10.00	1¢	200	2.00

dred per cent increase in the number of units bought. This is the case with the demand schedule DAB at its lower extreme; when the price falls from two cents to one cent, the effective demand increases from 500 units to 1,000, so that the total receipts are $10.00 in both cases. This demand, therefore, has an elasticity of unity in the lower part of its range. However, in the upper part of the schedule, its elasticity is *greater than unity*, by which is meant that a given decrease in the price is offset by a relatively greater increase in the amounts purchased, so that total receipts grow greater with successive price declines. Observe that as the price falls successively from six cents to five, four, and then three cents, the receipts increase from $6.00 to $7.50, $9.00, and $9.75, respectively. In the drawing, that part of the curve from D to A has an elasticity greater than unity, that part from A to B an elasticity of unity. Demand schedules with an elasticity of unity or greater may be classed as elastic.

When the elasticity is less than unity, the demand may be classed as inelastic. This means that the successive decreases in price are not offset by a proportionate increase in purchases; hence, the total receipts decline. This is the case with the demand schedule DC. The figures of the table indicate that, as the price falls by successive steps from six cents to one cent, the receipts decline gradually from $6.00 to $2.00.

Demand schedules need not be as consistent in their behavior as the two cases we have considered. They may be elastic in a part of their range, and inelastic in another part. They are likely to be more elastic at high prices than at low ones. The curve DAB, in fact, is more elastic from D to A than from A to B.

What Determines the Elasticity of Demand. — The degree of elasticity which characterizes a demand depends largely on the urgency of consumers' need for the commodity in question. In the case of luxuries, such as works of art or automobiles, demand is usually pretty elastic. These are things which we can do without; consequently, when they become more expensive, we curtail our purchases of them. Conversely, when they become cheaper, we buy them more freely. The demand for necessities, on the other hand, is usually more or less inelastic. For instance, if the price of bread were doubled, purchases would not decrease very greatly. Consumers would feel that they must have their usual quantity of bread, even at the high price. Rather than be deprived of it, they would go without other things that they considered less essential.

Demand is also inelastic in the case of commodities which are very low in price, but for a different reason. Such things as matches, salt, or spool cotton, which cost but a few cents, represent so small a percentage of our total expenditures that we buy all we desire of them, without much thought of economy. Lower the price, and very few more will be bought, for everyone has already all that he needs. Raise the price to even double what it was, still the amount is so small that consumers will not greatly curtail their purchases. However, if the price were raised ten or a hundredfold, this would no longer be true, and a considerable reduction in consumption might be expected. The same principles hold true where the price of a good is an insignificant part of the total cost of some larger article, such as doorknobs in a house.

The extent to which substitutes for a given commodity are available also has much to do with elasticity of demand. Take the case of butter and oleomargarine for illustration. Butter is a food so important that, if there were no substitute for it, people would buy a good deal of it even if the price were pretty high, and the demand would then be rather inelastic; but so long as oleomargarine is available, some people will resort to it if butter becomes very expensive. This makes the demand for butter elastic. We may conclude that demand is more elastic when there are substitutes than when there are not.

Every demand schedule must be elastic in the extreme upper part of its range. Otherwise the price of a commodity might go to infinity if it were scarce enough, and there would still be purchasers; but this is impossible, for no one has an infinite amount of money to spend. Therefore there must always be a price at which sales will fall to zero, and as this point is approached, total receipts must begin to decline. When the decline sets in, demand is elastic. Likewise, every demand schedule must be inelastic in the extreme lower part of its range; for if the price were to fall to zero, total receipts would likewise become zero; therefore, total receipts must decline as this point is approached. When this tendency sets in, demand is inelastic.

Marginal Receipts. — What has now been said about elasticity of demand makes it clear that, as the price of a commodity is changed, the total receipts from its sale may change also. The amount of change in receipts which results from a slight change in the price is known as *marginal receipts*.

We can gain an understanding of the behavior of marginal receipts by studying the following table, which may be supposed to represent the situation that confronts a rug merchant in a town of moderate size. Let the prices be those which he might charge for rugs of a certain quality, and let the quantities be the number of rugs sold per day:

1 Price per Rug	2 Quantity Sold	3 Total Receipts (Col. 1 x Col. 2)	4 Marginal Receipts (Computed from Col. 3)
$100	1	$100	$100
75	2	150	50
60	3	180	30
50	4	200	20
42	5	210	10
35	6	210	0
30	7	210	0
25	8	200	−10

This demand is elastic in the upper part of its range; therefore the total receipts (shown in Column 3) increase as the price is lowered successively from $100 to $75, then to $60, and so on. When the price falls from $100 to $75, receipts increase from $100 to $150; therefore the marginal receipts in this case are $50. When the price falls from $75 to $60, receipts grow to $180, an increase of $30 over the former figure; hence, the marginal receipts are now $30. Marginal receipts for each further decrease in price, calculated in the same way, are shown in Column 4. Notice that they grow steadily less, until they become zero at $35, and remain zero at $30. This is where total receipts do not increase at all, the elasticity of demand being unity at these points. When the price is reduced still further, the demand becomes inelastic, so that total receipts shrink. Observe that, when the price is $25, receipts are only $200, which is $10 less than when the price is $30. Here, then, the marginal receipts are a negative quantity (— $10).

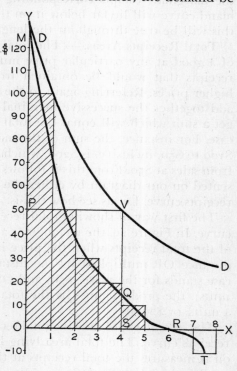

Figure 29. Marginal and Total Receipts.

It is possible to construct curves showing marginal receipts, just as we drew curves portraying schedules of demand. This is done, for the case just set forth, in Figure 29. Here the curve D represents the demand schedule given in Column 1 of the table. The blocks with the diagonal cross lines indicate the successive marginal receipts, resulting from successive decreases in the price. These are plotted from Column 4 of the table. There are no blocks between the quantities 5 and 7 on the base line because here the marginal receipts are zero. The block from 7 to 8 is placed below the base line, to show that here the marginal receipts are negative. Now, by drawing the curve MQRT through these blocks, we have a marginal receipts curve, which shows the amount of extra receipts that could be expected to result from each possible reduction of price.

A marginal receipts curve will usually lie below the demand curve from which it is derived,[2] for the following reason: if a man can sell ten pairs of shoes at $5.00 a pair, and eleven pairs at $4.75, the sale of the eleventh pair does not add $4.75 to the total receipts, for there is a reduction in receipts of 25 cents each from the other ten pairs, which are now sold at a lower price. Total receipts increase only from $50.00 to $52.25, making the marginal receipts $2.25. In other words, the marginal receipts for the eleventh pair of shoes are much less than the price which is obtained for them. Hence, on a diagram, the marginal receipts corresponding to the point $4.75 on the demand curve will lie far below it on the marginal receipts curve, and this will be true throughout the length of the two curves.

Total Receipts Areas. — The total receipts derived from the sales of a good at any particular price must be the sum of the marginal receipts that would be obtained from successive reductions from higher prices. Referring again to the table above, if the student will add together the successive marginal receipts in Column 4, he will get a sum which will equal the total receipts corresponding in each case. For instance, the sum of the marginal receipts at the prices of $100 to $50, inclusive, is $200, which is the same as the total receipts from sales at $50. From this it follows that total receipts can be represented on our diagram by either the demand curve or the marginal receipts curve. Let us see how this is.

The first way of showing total receipts is by means of the demand curve. In Figure 29, the rectangular area OPVS indicates the amount of the total receipts when the price is OP. This area is equal to the distance OP multiplied by the distance OS, and since OP in this case stands for the price ($50) and OS for the quantity purchased (4 units), the product must be the total receipts (price per unit times 4 units, or $200).

The second way of showing total receipts is by means of the marginal receipts curve. The total area lying beneath that curve at any point on it measures the total receipts at the corresponding price. For example, when the price is $50, 4 units are sold. The successive marginal receipts up to 4 units are represented by the first four blocks (or by the area OMQS). Therefore these blocks (or that area) must indicate the total receipts, for it has just been demonstrated that the sum of the increments equals the total.

It follows that the combined areas of the first four blocks must be

[2] In the following chapter we shall find that there is an important class of exceptions to this rule.

equal to the rectangular area OPVS, since both indicate the same volume of total receipts. Therefore, OMQS must also equal OPVS, since *it is so drawn as to enclose areas equal to the blocks through which it passes.* From any other point on the demand curve, an area similar to OPVS can be drawn, which will show total receipts at the given price, and a corresponding equal area, similar to OMQS, will be described by the marginal receipts curve.[3]

Having now surveyed the general characteristics of demand, we must turn to a similar survey of the underlying conditions of supply. We will then be in a position to bring our knowledge of the two together in one picture, which will show us how prices are fundamentally determined.

B. Fundamental Characteristics of Supply

Scarcity and Costs. — Our analysis of the law of demand indicates that, when a commodity is plentiful, its value is less than when there is not so much of it. Therefore, scarcity is a fundamental factor in determining the prices of goods.

A few commodities are scarce because they exist only in definite quantities and cannot be reproduced. Such are the paintings of old masters, genuine antique furniture, rare postage stamps, and certain jewels. If the entire stock of these were offered simultaneously in the market, their prices would be determined as in the case of fixed supply, which was explained in the preceding chapter. However, most rare articles with a value to collectors are sold one at a time, either in an auction, at the price offered by the highest bidder, or in an individual transaction, where the price is reached by bargaining between the buyer and the seller. Under these circumstances the price may vary within wide limits.

Most goods, however, result from current production. They are scarce, not because more of them cannot be had, but because the agents of production, through the use of which they are secured, are limited in quantity and capacity. Production requires labor; but laborers are limited in numbers, and their productivity is limited by their strength, their intelligence, and their willingness to exert themselves. Production also requires land; but this is limited in area, and the productivity of every piece of it is restricted by its fertility, its mineral deposits, or its accessibility. Modern productive operations

---

[3] The fact that, at every possible price, the area beneath the marginal receipts curve must equal the corresponding total receipts area on the demand curve, defines the geometrical relationship between the two curves, and leads to a rule for deriving one of them from the other. For a discussion of this see Joan Robinson's *Economics of Imperfect Competition,* Chapter II, especially paragraphs 3 and 4.

require elaborate equipment, which means that there must be saving and waiting; but the amount of saving is restricted to whatever surplus of income above present necessities may be available, and by the thrift of the people. Managers are required to direct the processes of production; but there is a natural scarcity of men with the requisite ability to perform this function. Also, the carrying on of industry entails risks, and not everyone is willing to hazard life, limb, or property in operations that place these in jeopardy. All these are resistances growing out of scarcity of the agents of production. In the case of reproducible goods, therefore, it is scarcity of productive agents that makes for scarcity of products, and it is scarcity of products that gives the latter their value. Because the products are valuable, the agents of production are valuable, too. Having value, both products and agents command a price. So, the use of these agents in production must be paid for. *The payments so made in bringing forth the various products of industry are known as costs of production.*

The Basic Elements of Costs. — If we ask any business man what are his costs, his answer will not sound much like the language of the foregoing paragraph. More than likely he will give a list of the items which he carries in his accounts as business expenses. Among them will be wages for labor employed, salaries and commissions to executives and salesmen, interest on borrowed funds, rent for real estate leased from others, depreciation reserves laid aside to replace worn-out or obsolete equipment, outlays for materials, advertising, insurance, freight or express charges, taxes, lawyers' fees, and certain other items. Many of these expenses are composite and overlapping; they can be reduced to simpler elements. Salaries, for instance, do not differ fundamentally from wages; both are payments for labor, though it may be labor of different kinds. Payments for raw materials can be broken down into wages for labor, interest on borrowed funds, and other payments involved in producing those materials at earlier stages of production. Depreciation is a device for charging up to current production its share of the original cost (in wages, interest, and so on) of providing the equipment now employed in the industry. In like manner, advertising, insurance, transportation, taxes,[4] and other expenses can be broken down into more elemental items. In this way we can resolve all the costs of producing

---

[4] Taxes may be resolved into the expenses for labor, saving, etc., of running the government. However, the amount of these expenses entering into the cost of production of a particular commodity does not arise naturally out of the production process itself, as do the other costs mentioned, but is levied upon the industry by the government on very different principles, into which we need not enter here. It suffices for our present purpose to point out that taxes frequently exercise an effect on the prices of commodities, similar to the other costs here described.

any commodity into payments for the agents of production employed in making it. Roughly, these agents can be designated as labor (including labor of management), saving, and land.

However, the amount of costs does not depend merely on the *quantity* of the agents employed. The wages paid to labor, for instance, do not depend merely on the number of hours or days worked, but also on the *kind* of labor. Therefore, wages can be broken down into payments for labor-effort and payments for ability, and, in the case of dangerous labor, payments for risk. The payment for saving is interest, but interest is not only a compensation for saving as such—it also includes some return for the risks of the investor. Rents paid for real estate may include returns for the effort, ability, saving, and risk involved in constructing and maintaining the buildings, plus payment for the use of the land itself, on which the buildings are situated. Payments for land may include a price for the natural materials it contains (such as fertility or mineral deposits) and, perhaps, compensation for some natural advantage of location which makes it particularly desirable as a business site.

In the last analysis, then, costs can be resolved into payments for the following factors: (1) effort, (2) ability, (3) saving, (4) land space, (5) natural materials, (6) risk-bearing. These are the basic elements of costs which will appear in production under competitive conditions. It should be pointed out, also, that if any of the agents of production affecting a particular commodity at any stage of the production process are controlled by a monopoly, an element of monopoly profit may be introduced which will reflect itself in a higher price at the stage of production where it occurs. This monopoly profit will then raise the costs of production of those enterprisers who come after, and the cost to the ultimate consumer. If we call the action of a monopolist in controlling the supply of a commodity *withholding,* we can list withholding as a seventh element of costs.

Physical Costs and Pecuniary Costs. — What any article costs to produce will depend on two factors. In the first place, it will depend on the amounts of effort, ability, saving, land space, natural materials, risks and withholding of various kinds involved in its production, from its initial stages, through all the processes intervening, up to the stage at which its price is being considered, and, in the case of consumption goods, up to their delivery to the consumer. Within broad limits these amounts are determined by the technical conditions of production. We may call them the *physical costs.* Some writers call them *real costs.*[5] In the second place, it will

[5] The classical economists, and some moderns with classical leanings, identify *real costs* with human efforts and sacrifices (disutilities), which are alleged to consist of

depend upon the prices of these things. The quantities of agents employed (physical costs), multiplied by their prices, give us the *pecuniary costs*. It is these which are active in determining the supply-prices of producers.

Differences Between the Economic and the Business Concepts of Cost. — Although we have succeeded in reducing the items of cost listed by the business man to those regarded as fundamental by the economist, it is yet to be noted that the latter includes in the term costs certain elements not always recognized as such by the former. These elements are three in number. Firstly, costs, in the economic sense of that term, include not only interest on *borrowed* savings, but also interest on savings *owned by the enterpriser* himself. Very frequently the enterpriser regards interest on his own savings as a part of his profits, rather than as one of his costs of production. Yet the economist cannot fail to regard this as a cost, for it is a necessary payment which must be made, and recovered from the price of the commodity, if production of the latter is to continue. If a business does not yield the current rate of interest on the savings invested in its equipment, no matter who owns it, there is not sufficient inducement for any further investment in that business, and there is good reason for putting the savings already there to some other use, if that be possible; or if not, to allow the equipment to wear out without replacement (for the amount required to replace it could be put to more remunerative use elsewhere). Therefore, if the price of the products of that business does not permit the payment of interest on the enterpriser's investment, in the long run those products will disappear from the market. This shows that such interest is one of the costs of production that enter into the determination of prices.

Secondly, costs include a remuneration to the business enterpriser for the time and energy he expends in directing and managing the business. This we may call his *wages of management*. It is a sort of salary paid to himself for his labors as superintendent of the enterprise. It may seem strange to consider this an item of cost, since the business man very frequently regards it as a surplus or profit left over after the costs of the business are paid. As in the preceding case, however, it is not truly a surplus, but a necessary charge which must

---

labor-effort and the supposed "pain" of waiting and saving. They believe that all costs can ultimately be resolved into those two elements. There is some validity to this concept of costs *for philosophic purposes*. There is a sense in which it is convenient to speak of what it costs mankind in toil and trouble to secure goods. In the view of many, however, including the present writer, this concept of real costs is not tenable *as an explanation of prices*. Prices conform to the pecuniary costs of the market place, and these cannot be resolved into disutilities. Differences in wages, for instance, do not correspond to differences in the efforts put forth by the different classes of labor. See the discussion of wage differences in Chapter XX.

be recovered from the selling price of the product if its production is to be continued; for the business man will not give his labor for nothing, and if a certain industry does not yield to its enterprisers as much as they might earn as wages if employed by other persons, they are likely to withdraw from it sooner or later. Certainly new enterprisers will not be attracted into it, and those already established must eventually die, even if they do not presently fail, or go into other businesses. Wages of management, therefore, are one of the costs that enter into the values of commodities.

Finally, there are certain enterprisers' risks involved in production, payment for which must be regarded as a cost. Some payments for risk are included in ordinary wages and interest, and others in insurance premiums, all three of which appear on the books of the business man as costs; but enterprisers usually look to their profits to compensate them for their own risks, and do not regard such compensation as a cost. Yet this is a cost from the economic point of view; for if a business does not offer prospect of sufficient reward to the enterpriser to induce him to subject himself to such risk, he will not carry on the business, and the goods in question will not be produced. Compensation for enterprisers' risks, therefore, is a necessary cost which must be obtained from the price of the commodity if its production is to be carried on.[6]

To some extent there is a recent tendency among business men and accountants to include in their costs the first two of the items just discussed. Corporations, for instance, usually pay salaries to their executives for the managerial work of the latter; and even individual business men in some cases pay salaries to themselves from month to month, which salaries are carried on the books as costs, to be deducted before profits are computed. There is also some tendency for accountants to treat interest in a similar manner. Whether these items are so handled in the accounts of the business or not, there is no real inconsistency between business practice and the usage of economists. The business man's concept of costs is based on his need for some criterion by which to estimate the success of his business. That success is measured by the net returns he derives from his investment and his labor. He may, therefore, find it useful to regard all of this return as a profit, and none of it as a part of his costs. The economist, however, is concerned with costs as elements entering into prices, and, therefore, as determinants of values. As a social scientist, he looks at the problem from the community point of view, rather than from that of the individual enterpriser. Since the community must pay interest on enterprisers' savings, wages of manage-

6 But see what is said on this question in Chapter XXIII.

ment, and a reward for risk, in the prices of the commodities it buys, these things are costs to it. There is no essential contradiction between the two concepts, but merely a difference in the point of view from which the phenomena are regarded.

Opportunity Costs. — The definite determination of pecuniary costs—that is, the process through which the prices of the agents of production are fixed—is very much complicated by two circumstances. In the first place, a number of different productive agents are combined in the making of every product. For instance, in the making of a cotton sheet, there are employed agricultural and building land, labor of various occupations and degrees of skill, divers buildings and machines, and other agents. In some way, the price obtainable for the finished sheet must be apportioned among all these different agents which contribute to it. A complete explanation of costs necessitates an investigation of this. This leads us into the problem of income sharing, which has to do with the division of the income of society into shares which are paid to the owners of the various agents of production. Since this will be outlined in some later chapters, the discussion of it may conveniently be deferred for the present. We must bear in mind, however, that it is an essential part of the problem of costs which we must eventually clear up.

In the second place, each of the productive agents is used, not for a single product only, but for a great many. A given type of labor, for instance, may be employed in a score of different industries. Its wage, then, must depend simultaneously on all the products of those industries. A complete explanation of costs must give an account of this also. To this problem we will now turn our attention.

In certain parts of southern United States there is land suitable for the production of both cotton and peanuts. Since the land is scarce, and since both products cannot be grown upon it at the same time, the quantity that can be produced of either crop is limited by the other, and farmers must make a choice between them. Every acre of land devoted to cotton reduces the size of the peanut crop; and the more peanuts there are grown the less there will be of cotton. In such a case there arise two opposing demands for the land, cotton and peanut growers competing with each other to obtain it. The cotton growers must pay as much as the peanut growers, or they cannot get land for their purpose; whatever the land is worth when used for the peanut crop, therefore, will constitute a cost of production to cotton growers. By the same reasoning, whatever the land is worth when used for cotton raising will be a cost of production to the peanut producers.

The same principle holds for labor. In some of the regions immediately adjacent to the cotton fields of the South tobacco is grown. Cotton and tobacco planters compete with each other for the available workers. We may suppose that 30,000 workers in these regions are available for employment in the two industries. In Figure 30, let AB represent the value of these workers to the tobacco growers, and CD their value to the cotton growers. In other words, AB and CD are the demand curves for tobacco and cotton labor, respectively. The figures on OY indicate the prices (wages) per day which employers are able to pay for various quantities of labor, taking into consideration the demands for their products. As more workers are employed, their wages decline, because as more cotton or

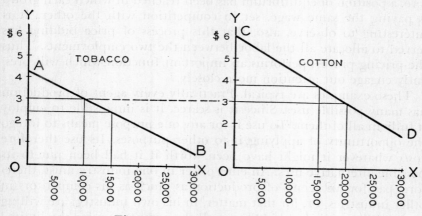

Figure 30. Opportunity Costs.

tobacco is grown by using the extra workers, the prices thereof will fall, in accordance with the law of demand. Now suppose that the laborers are evenly divided, 15,000 being employed in each industry. According to the drawings, those employed in the tobacco industry will be worth only about $2.35 per day, while those in the cotton fields will be worth $3.75. Since the tobacco growers cannot afford to pay more than $2.35, cotton planters can make a profit by offering somewhat better pay, say $2.50, to attract labor away from the tobacco fields. More men will then be employed in cotton, and more cotton will be grown, as a consequence of which it will be no longer worth quite so much; while less will be employed in tobacco, as a consequence of which less of it will be grown, and it will be worth somewhat more. Tobacco growers can then bid against the cotton growers to hold their men.

As the value of labor rises in the tobacco industry and falls in the cotton industry, there will come a point where it will be equal in both. In our illustration this occurs when 10,000 men are employed at tobacco growing and 20,000 in the cotton fields. Labor is then worth $3 in each employment, and wages will tend to be at that figure, for competition between the two sets of employers to hire all the men it is worth their while to have will prevent them from falling any lower. It will not pay the cotton growers to attract any more workers away from the tobacco industry, for if more than 20,000 are employed at cotton they will be worth less than $3; but they are worth $3 to the tobacco employers, who would not let them go for less. By a similar line of reasoning, it can be shown that tobacco growers will not employ more than the 10,000 they now have. Therefore, a position of equilibrium has been reached in which each group is paying the same wage, set in competition with the other. It is interesting to observe, also, that this process of price bidding has served to allocate all the labor between the two employments. Thus the pricing process performs an important function which will presently engage our attention more closely.

These examples are typical. Practically every agent of production has many possible uses. Since it is scarce, it is impossible to employ it fully in all of them. To use it for any one purpose means to forego the opportunity of applying it to other purposes. Its use therefore *costs* whatever it might have been worth if it had been put to its possible alternative uses. An enterpriser in one industry must, therefore, pay for his agents of production as much as his competitors in other industries (or, for that matter, in his own industry) are willing to pay. The combined bidding of all the competitors for the limited supply of the agents of production thus establishes prices for them which, as we now know, constitute the costs of production. This is known as *the principle of opportunity costs*. It may be stated as follows: *The use of any agent in production involves a cost which is determined by the prices offered for that agent in its possible alternative uses.* The full significance of this principle will be made clearer when we come to consider the functions of the price system, in Chapter XVI.

Costs in the Individual Enterprise. — Our immediate problem is to trace the relationship between costs of production, determined as above, and the supply schedules of producers, on which commodity prices ultimately depend. To do this, we must know how costs behave in the individual producing establishment, and the influence of this behavior on the policies of the enterpriser.

Some insight into this problem can be gained by reviewing the principles set forth in Chapter V, where the effects upon costs occasioned by varying the combination of productive agents in a business establishment were examined. In that chapter it was explained that there are two general kinds of costs—fixed and variable. The fixed costs are those associated mainly with the maintenance of industrial plant, such as interest, depreciation, fire insurance, and real estate taxes. These run on pretty much the same from year to year, whether the plant is operated at full capacity, at partial capacity, or not at all. The effect of this is that the fixed costs *per unit of product* will be large if they have to be charged to a relatively small output, and will be less, the greater the number of products over which they can be distributed. The variable costs are chiefly those associated with labor and materials used in operating the plant. Since more labor and materials must be used to produce a large output than a small one, these costs vary with the amount of production. But they do not vary in exact proportion with output, because of the principle of diminishing productivity. This principle, it will be remembered, tells us that, when variable agents of production are added to a fixed agent, there will at first be a progressively larger increase in the product, until the point of diminishing marginal productivity is reached, after which the increments of extra product will grow smaller, until finally a point is reached where production is at its maximum, and no further increase is possible with the existing plant. This means that increasing expenditures on labor and materials will yield progressively more product so long as the plant is not operated past the point of diminishing productivity, and variable costs *per unit of output* will therefore grow less; but such expenditures will yield progressively less product after that point has been passed, so that eventually the variable costs per unit of output will begin to rise.

Average, Marginal, and Total Costs. — It will be remembered, further, that the *average costs* of production, per unit of product, depend on the joint action of these two kinds of costs. As production in a plant is expanded from nothing, the tendency of both fixed and variable costs is to pull the unit costs downward, but sometime after the point of diminishing productivity is reached, the rising variable costs counteract the downward pull of the fixed costs, so that average costs begin to rise, and rise more and more steeply as the maximum capacity of the plant is approached. If we plot this in the form of a graph, as we did in Chapter V, we get a more or less U-shaped curve, such as CQA in Figure 31. The exact shape of this curve will vary with the nature of the particular enterprise. In those industries where there is a great deal of elaborate equipment, and where relatively little labor and materials are employed, the downward slope will be long and gradual, and the upward slope may be abrupt and

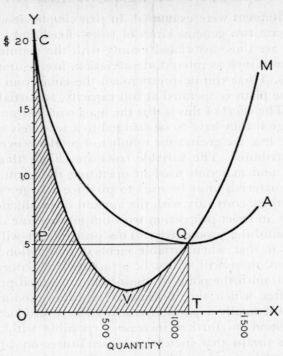

Figure 31. Average, Marginal, and Total
Costs in an Individual Enterprise.

steep; in industries where these conditions are reversed, the descent
of the curve may be sharper and the rise more gradual; but these are
differences of detail—the general character of the curves is the same.

There is a certain point in the operation of a plant where the average costs are lower than at any other point. This is at the bottom
of the average cost curve, at the point Q in the diagram. In Chapter
V this was referred to as the point of *optimum costs,* or the point
of *optimum capacity.* This marks the output at which the plant can
produce goods most cheaply. We shall find this to be of significance
when we come to consider how prices are determined under conditions of pure competition.

It is possible to show *total costs* by means of the average cost
curve, just as we showed total receipts by means of the demand
curve in an earlier paragraph of this chapter. For instance, in Figure
31, the rectangular area OPQT represents total costs of $5,500 when
the output is 1,100 units, for this area is the product of QT (which
measures average costs of $5 per unit), multiplied by OT (which

represents the number of units produced, or 1,100). The total costs for any other output can be represented by a similar rectangle drawn from any point on the average cost curve.

In Chapter V there was also developed the concept (and curve) of *marginal costs,* which are defined as the extra costs occasioned by the production of an extra increment of product. The relationship between marginal costs and average costs is similar to that between marginal receipts and the schedule of demand. Just as marginal receipts show the change in total receipts resulting from the sale of additional goods at a lower price, so marginal costs show the change in total costs resulting from a slight increase in output. These costs consist of a relatively large increment of fixed costs (associated with the plant) which must be met before even the first unit of output can be had, followed by successive increments of variable costs, resulting from the employment of labor and materials. We already know that the successive increments of variable costs decline until the point of diminishing productivity is reached, and thereafter rise with increasing steepness. This gives us a marginal cost curve of the general type illustrated by CVQM in Figure 31. It falls and rises more steeply than the average cost curve because all of the fixed costs are charged up to the first increment of output, instead of being averaged in with all the succeeding increments. It will be remembered that the marginal cost curve crosses the average cost curve at its lowest point (Q in the diagram), because so long as each increment of cost is lower than the preceding average, it must pull the average down, but as soon as the added increment of cost exceeds the preceding average, it must pull the average up; therefore, the average curve turns upward at precisely the point where the marginal curve crosses it.

It is possible to show total costs by means of the marginal cost curve, just as we were able to show total receipts by means of the marginal receipts curve. In fact, the relation between the curve of marginal costs and that of average costs is precisely the same as the relation between a curve of demand and one of marginal receipts.[7] Since total costs must be the sum of all the increments of marginal costs, it must be equivalent to the total area lying beneath the marginal cost curve at any given point. Therefore, the shaded area OCVQT in Figure 31 represents the total cost for an output of 1,100 units. This means that this area must be equal to the rectangular area OPQT, which also represents the total costs for this same output.

---

[7] Hence, the geometrical relationship between a marginal cost curve and a curve of average costs is the same as that between a marginal receipts curve and a curve of demand. See page 329 above, footnote 3.

The same equality will hold for any other corresponding areas on the two curves.

The General Rule of Policy. — Now that we have an understanding of the fundamental characteristics of demand and the nature of costs, it is our next task to see how these two groups of influences affect the policies of business men, for it is upon these policies that the actual production of goods depends. Since the primary goal of a business enterprise is to make profits, we must expect decisions to be made with that end in view. This means that the business man will try to adjust his production to the conditions of demand which confront him in such a way as to keep his profits at a maximum, or his losses at a minimum (if he is forced to endure losses for the time being). The general principle which fulfills this condition is that *marginal receipts must be equal to marginal costs.* We can see this most clearly if we will think of marginal receipts as extra receipts and marginal costs as extra costs. If a business man is making some profit already, he can always increase that profit by selling some extra goods, so long as the addition to his receipts resulting from their sale exceeds the extra cost of producing them. If he is suffering losses, he can reduce those losses by the same procedure. However, because marginal receipts fall and marginal costs rise (sooner or later) as output is increased, a stage will presently be reached where the margin between extra costs and extra receipts gets progressively smaller. At the point where this margin disappears, profits have reached their maximum, or losses have reached their minimum. Beyond this point, marginal costs will exceed marginal receipts, and the taking on of extra business will then involve a loss. Our general conclusion is, therefore, that the most profitable scale of operations for an enterprise is to be found at that point where marginal costs and marginal receipts are equal.

It may be objected that business men usually do not keep their accounts in such a way as to reveal accurately their marginal receipts and marginal costs. This is probably true of the majority of business men, although it is not true of all. Some of the more intelligent firms do look at their marginal receipts and marginal costs pretty carefully, although they may not use these terms. But whether accounts are kept deliberately with this end in view or not, nearly every business man is called upon to decide, with more or less frequency, whether it will be worth his while to fill a certain order for merchandise in addition to the business he is already doing. In making this decision, he is likely to ask himself and his accountant, Will this extra business be profitable to me? In so doing, he is asking himself, in fact, Will the extra receipts exceed the extra costs of filling the order? Moreover, in the absence of careful accounts, business men may be presumed to grope, by a process of trial and error, toward the policy that will yield them the greatest profit. To the extent that they are successful in doing this, they will, in fact, work towards a position in which their marginal receipts are equal to their marginal costs, for it has already been demonstrated that this is the position in which their profits will be maximized.

The truth of this proposition can be more clearly established by analyzing in detail the circumstances of a business enterprise when confronted by given schedules of demand and costs. This will, at the same time, enable us to see how the underlying conditions of demand and supply interact in such a way as to determine the price of a commodity. The simplest illustration of this interaction is that of a monopoly, where we have only one business establishment to consider. We shall, therefore, begin with the case of pure monopoly price before going on to the more complicated situations in which many different enterprisers compete in the market.

C. Prices under Conditions of Pure Monopoly

Monopoly Price. — A pure monopoly exists when the entire supply of a commodity is controlled by a single seller, or by a group of sellers acting in concert. For instance, there may be only one manufacturer of a given product, or there may be several who agree to market all their output through one selling agency. How will prices be determined under these conditions?

Let us suppose that someone has developed a new chemical product with properties which make it extremely useful in the household. Let him be fully protected against competition by patents covering the basic process of manufacturing it. Now, if the producer is bent on exploiting his discovery to the limit, what conditions will determine the price which he will charge? This case presents the problem of monopoly price in its clearest form. For the present we will postpone consideration of those more complicated cases where elements of monopoly are mixed with competition.

The first thing that our monopolist will have to reckon with is the demand for his product. To be sure, he can fix the price at any figure he chooses, and the public must pay that price or go without; but there is a limit to the quantity which can be sold at any given price, and this limit grows narrower as the price is raised; for, although a monopolist, like any other business man, may strengthen the demand for his product by advertising, he cannot set aside the law of demand. Therefore, he is confronted with the fact that, the higher the price he sets, the less he will sell. The second thing which he must take into consideration is his costs of production. In accordance with the principles developed in the last few paragraphs, the cost per unit will vary with the number of units produced, depending on the type of plant he constructs and how fully its productive capacity is utilized. If he has made a careful analysis of his market, he will have a rough idea of the demand schedule for his chemical, and he will presumably build one or more plants of the optimum size

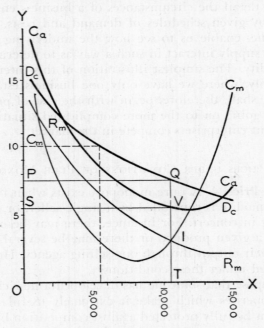

Figure 32. Monopoly Price.

for the output which his market calls for. Once having established such a plant, he will find himself confronted with a situation similar to that represented in Figure 32.

The supposed schedule of demand is represented by the curve D_c in the drawing. This is not the temporary, day-to-day demand of dealers and speculators, but the somewhat more settled demand of consumers. It indicates the number of pounds of the commodity which consumers will buy for their own use at each of the several prices; hence we denote it by the subscript c. We may think of this demand as a *schedule of consumption*. Since the habits of consumers do not change greatly from day to day, this schedule presumably has some permanence. Therefore we can think of it as indicating the rates of consumption over a given period of time at each of the several prices. We can then interpret the figures as sales of so many pounds per week or per month. The schedule has the characteristics which the discussion of demand in the first part of this chapter would lead us to expect: sales are small at the highest prices shown on the line OY, and increase with considerable elasticity as the price is lowered.

The average costs are shown for the various possible outputs by the curve C_a (the subscript a being used to differentiate the curve from the curve of marginal costs, C_m). To be comparable with our figures for demand, these outputs must also be construed as indicating the rate of production, per week or per month. Observe that this schedule has the features which our previous analysis has shown to be characteristic of costs: the average cost per unit is high when output is very small, it drops to a minimum of about $5.00 when the output is at its optimum of 12,000 pounds, and then it rises again.

If the monopolist wishes to exploit to the limit the advantages of his exclusive patent, he will seek to find the price which will yield him the greatest possible profit. The general rule of policy developed in a preceding paragraph was that profits are greatest when marginal costs and marginal receipts are equal. On our diagram this occurs at the point I, where the curves of marginal receipts and marginal costs intersect. If we erect a line vertically upward from this intersection to the point Q, on the demand curve, and downward to T, on the base line, it shows what price and what output will be most advantageous for the monopolist. By this reckoning, he should fix his price at $7.50, and restrict his output to 10,500 units.

This enables us to compute his profits. Since his sales at $7.50 are 10,500, his total receipts at that price must be $7.50 × 10,500 = $78,750. From the point V, on the average cost curve, we know that his average unit costs for an output of 10,500 are $5.50; therefore, his total costs must be $5.50 × 10,500 = $57,750. Subtracting total costs from total receipts, we get $78,750 − $57,750 = $21,000, which is the amount of his total profits. These profits are represented on the diagram by the area SPQV, for this represents the difference between the total receipts area (OPQT) and the total cost area (OSVT).

Profits must be greater at $7.50 than at any other figure, because, at any higher price, marginal receipts will exceed marginal costs (the line QT will be to the left of its position in the drawing), and so long as this situation prevails, an extra increment of output, sold at a slightly lower price, will always add something to the profits. At any lower price, marginal costs will exceed marginal receipts (QT will be further to the right) causing a loss on the marginal increments of output. Hence, we conclude that the monopolist, if he seeks his greatest advantage, will set his price at the figure indicated.

Some Limits to Monopoly Price. — How high a monopoly price will be depends partly on the elasticity of its demand and cost schedules. Where the elasticity is low, as in the case of necessary commodities for which no satisfactory substitutes are available, total receipts will be greater at high than at low prices, so that it may pay the monopolist to raise his price to a very high figure. Where demand is very elastic, on the other hand, he must reckon with the fact that, with every rise in price his total receipts fall off considerably, while his unit costs are likely to rise. Therefore, it pays him to keep his price moderately low in order that he may take advantage of lower unit costs and a larger volume of sales. The shape of the average cost curve has much to do with this. If it is nearly horizontal, he can curtail his output without much increase in unit costs, and his price may then be high; but if the curve falls sharply, as it does in our illustration, there is an inducement for him to keep the price low enough to take advantage of the lower unit costs which come with increased output.

Moreover, a monopolist may find it inexpedient to take full advantage of his economic power. Where profits are known to be high, there is an incentive for others to enter the field, and there is always a possibility that some enterprising competitor may gain a foothold in the industry, a circumstance which will weaken the monopoly's exclusive control. High prices are also likely to provoke legislative interference. Consumers resent being exploited; therefore, when monopolies become ruthless, anti-trust laws are passed and regulatory commissions are created which step in to curb the abuse of monopoly power. It may be, also, that a monopolist may have enough altruism to give a good product to the public at a reasonable price, rather than to amass riches by a policy of extortion. Cases are not unknown, for instance, where the discoverers of valuable devices and medicines have chosen to allow their manufacture by anyone, under competitive conditions, rather than to exploit their inventions for their own benefit. All these things may combine to make monopoly prices in a given case moderate. In general, however, it is to be expected that monopoly prices will be somewhat higher than competitive prices, for the next chapter will show that the latter are ordinarily held down by conditions that do not affect monopolies.

SUMMARY

All demands are derived ultimately from the demands of consumers. These are characterized by the law of demand, which states that, the greater the amount of a given commodity to be sold in a given market at a given time, the lower must be the price. This law is true because of four influences, *viz.*: (1) The law of diminishing utility, which states that after a certain point has been reached, the utility of any unit of one's stock of economic goods diminishes as the stock possessed increases; (2) the principle of different uses, which states that some uses of a good are more important than others; (3) the principle of different desires, which states that some people have greater desires for different goods than others; and (4) the principle of different incomes, which states that some consumers have more income with which to buy goods than others. When we put these principles together, we see that goods must be sold at lower prices when their quantity increases, because additional units will have less utility to those who already have some stock on hand, and because the extra units must be sold for uses of lesser importance and to people who have less desire and less income with which to buy.

Demand is elastic when its sensitivity to changes in price is equal to or greater than unity, and inelastic when its sensitiveness is less than unity. The demand for luxury goods and for goods that have substitutes is usually quite elastic, while the demand for necessities for which there are no substitutes, and for goods which are very low in price, is usually somewhat inelastic. The amount of change in total receipts which results from a slight change in the price is known as marginal receipts. Marginal receipts curves lie below the demand curves to which they are related, and are drawn in such a way that the total area lying beneath them measures total receipts. Total receipts for any given price can also be shown by means of a rectangle drawn from the corresponding point on the demand curve.

The supply of goods depends ultimately on the agents of production. Because these agents are scarce, they command prices which constitute the costs of production. The costs appearing in business accounts can be resolved into payments for effort, ability, saving, land-space, natural materials, and risk-bearing. So, the cost of producing a good depends on the quantity of these elements required for its production (physical, or real costs), and on the prices thereof (pecuniary costs). Costs, as construed by the economist, include wages of management, interest, and some compensation for enterprisers' risks. According to the principle of opportunity costs, pecuniary costs are determined in a process of competitive bidding, so that each agent receives a price equal to what is bid for it in its possible alternative uses.

Costs in the individual enterprise can be calculated as either average or marginal. A curve of average costs is approximately U-shaped, its lowest point denoting the optimum costs and the optimum capacity of the plant. The curve of marginal costs is more steeply U-shaped, falling considerably lower than the average cost curve, then rising sharply, crossing the average curve at its lowest point. Total costs can be represented either by the area of a rectangle drawn from the average cost curve, or by the total area at any point lying below the marginal cost curve.

The general rule of business policy is to maximize profits or minimize losses. This requires that the output of an establishment be adjusted to demand in such a way that the marginal costs equal the marginal receipts. If accounts are not accurate enough to permit such a calculation, it can be approximated by a process of trial and error. The working of this principle is clearly revealed by the case of pure monopoly, where the entire supply of a commodity is controlled by a single seller, or by a group of sellers acting in concert. A study of the demand and cost schedules for a typical case of such a monopoly demonstrated that its profits were greatest when the marginal receipts and marginal costs were equal. In actual practice a monopoly may be restrained from taking full advantage of its position by the fear of potential competition or of government interference.

REFERENCES AND SUGGESTIONS FOR FURTHER READING

The analysis of demand in the foregoing chapter departs from the usual treatment in some respects. Most writers lay great stress on marginal utility, but this seems to me to be open to the objection that it is not realistic; and it is quite unnecessary. The marginal utility approach can be found in Alfred Marshall's *Principles of Economics* (5th or later edition), Book III, especially Chapters 3 and 6. The doctrine of opportunity costs herein set forth is more fully elaborated in my article on *The Nature and Fundamental Elements of Cost,* which appeared in the *Quarterly Journal of Economics* for November, 1936, pp. 30–62. It is developed from the work of several earlier writers, notably H. J. Davenport, in Chapters 6 and 8 of his *Economics of Enterprise* (1913), and Gustav Cassel, in his *The Theory of Social Economy* (English translation, 1923), Book I.

The analysis of marginal receipts and marginal costs in their relation to prices (though partly anticipated by others, so far as marginal costs is concerned) is mainly the work of two recent writers, *viz.,* Edward Chamberlin, in his *Theory of Monopolistic Competition* (1933), especially Chapter 2, and Joan Robinson, in *The Economics of Imperfect Competition* (1933), especially Chapters 2 and 3. My presentation of the theory of monopoly price is also based on their treatment of this problem.

Chapter XV

PRICES UNDER PURE AND MONOPOLISTIC COMPETITION

A. The Case of Pure Competition

The Course of the Analysis. — Let us look now at the main outlines of the analysis which we are making, in order to refresh our memories as to the ground we have already covered, and to visualize the problems which lie ahead.

We began our study of the pricing process by observing the action of demand and supply in the day-to-day wholesale market. We found that, behind the schedules of buyers and sellers in that market, there was a background of consumers' demand and producers' supply which needed to be investigated. We traced consumers' demand to its source in consumers' choices and incomes, and we traced producers' supply to its source in the scarce agents of production. We found that the use of these agents involves costs which have a characteristic behavior in each individual enterprise. With this background, we were able to develop the general rule of policy, that a business enterpriser will find it to his advantage to expand his output to the point where his marginal costs equal his marginal receipts. The application of this rule showed us how price tends to be fixed when the supply is controlled by a monopoly.

Our next task is to see what determines fundamental prices in conditions of pure competition. We shall then proceed to those more complicated cases in which there is a mixture of competitive and monopolistic influences. In all of this, our ultimate purpose is to find the normal prices which underlie the temporary, fluctuating prices of the day-to-day market.

Pure Competition. — *Pure competition* is said to exist when: *(1) the sellers all offer an identical good; and (2) there are so many sellers that the amount offered by any one of them is too small a portion of the total supply to have any appreciable influence on the price.* This is fairly well exemplified by the case of cotton. It is a standardized, graded commodity. Its world production runs to some twenty or thirty millions of bales yearly. The output of even the largest plantation is so insignificant a part of this enormous total that its effect upon the price is insignificant. If the output of any one plantation were doubled, or if it were destroyed, it would make no difference. The market would not be sensitive enough to take note of so small a change in the available quantity. Cotton will, therefore, afford a useful illustration of the competitive price-making forces. This will enable us to carry on the analysis in terms of the same commodity that we used for our example of market prices.

Our problem is to find out how production in the whole cotton industry is adjusted to the total demand (in the absence of deliberate interference by any governmental program of crop control). In this way we can discover the normal equilibrium of demand and supply which lies behind the actual prices of the day-to-day market in purely competitive conditions.

Some Further Cost Problems. — We now know that the costs of the various producers will play an important part in the ultimate adjustment of supply to demand. But the process of this adjustment will not be so simple as it was in the case of monopoly, where we had only one producer to reckon with. The presence of a great many competitors in the market complicates the problem. One such complication arises from the fact that costs are not the same for all the producers engaged in an industry. Enterprisers vary in the excellence of their organization, the efficiency of their equipment, the quality of their labor force, the shrewdness with which they purchase materials, and in other respects. Whose costs are most significant? On which costs do normal prices depend? Then, as we have already learned, costs in each enterprise vary with the amount of output. This is significant for the industry as a whole. At a given time, an industry has at its disposal a certain amount of land and equipment which are adapted or readily adaptable to its needs, and a certain number of workers, trained to do its work, who look to it for their livelihood. These resources are capable of a certain maximum production, but they may not, and usually will not, be utilized to their full capacity. Since the efficiency of production depends, among other things, on the amount of pressure which is being exerted on existing facilities, costs will vary accordingly. Moreover, these facilities can be increased or decreased, if given time enough, by the construction of new equipment and the recruiting and training of new labor, or by the wearing out of old equipment and the retirement of workers. Such changes may be expected to follow any permanent alteration in the schedule of demand for a product. They will have some effects upon costs. We must, then, analyze further than we have yet done the relation between costs, output, and productive capacity. Finally, costs may change as the result of population growth, the development of new techniques, and other dynamic influences. We must pay some attention to these. In all of these problems, our purpose is to find the relation between costs and supply-prices, in order that we may see how supply is ultimately adjusted to demand.

The questions here raised are too complex to be answered by any simple formula. The analysis must therefore be broken up into several parts. (1) We shall begin by considering how the individual producer reacts to the market situation which confronts him. In this we shall be on ground that is already familiar, for the most part. (2) With that as a background, we can build up a picture of the cost schedule for a whole industry, (a) first, on the assumption that production must be adjusted to demand within the limits of capacity afforded by existing facilities, (b) then, on the assumption that the industry will in time be able to expand or contract those facilities, if necessary. (3) This will enable us to see how an industry adapts itself to changing schedules of demand. (4) Finally, we shall survey the effects upon prices of technological and other changes which alter the costs of production in an industry. In pursuance of this plan, consider now the position of a particular enterprise in a competitive business situation.

The Position of the Individual Producer. — It has already been stated that the individual producer under conditions of pure competition has no appreciable influence upon the price. This presents him with a problem considerably different from that of the monopolist, who can manipulate the price upward or downward to suit his convenience. The competitive producer must take the prevailing price as a fixed datum for his calculations, and adjust his production accordingly. We must expect him to follow the general rule of regulating his output so that his marginal costs will be equal to his marginal receipts; but the marginal receipts behave very differently in his case from their behavior in a case of monopoly. No matter whether he produces much or little, the price he gets for his product will be the same. Therefore, although the demand schedule *for the whole market* will follow the law of demand (and can be represented by the usual type of demand curve), the demand schedule *for the output of the individual producer* will be such that the same price can be obtained from buyers, no matter what portion of his output he offers for sale. This means that *his* demand curve, as he sees it, will be a horizontal straight line, the height of which is fixed by the average price prevailing in the market during a given season (for he is more likely to make his calculations with reference to the average price over a period of time than with reference to the price on any one day). Such a curve (if we may call it that) is shown by the line dd in Figure 33. Here we are supposed to be dealing with a producer, the maximum output of whose plantation is 100,000 pounds of cotton in an average season. The prevailing price is assumed to be 13 cents. The demand line indicates that the producer can sell

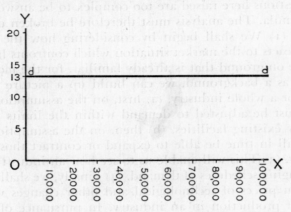

Figure 33. Demand and Marginal Receipts for an Individual Seller Under Conditions of Pure Competition.

any amount of cotton he produces, from nothing up to his maximum of 100,000 pounds, at this same price.

Since the grower can sell increasing amounts without any diminution of the price, his marginal receipts do not fall as his volume of sales increases. Every additional pound of cotton he offers for sale adds 13 cents to his total receipts. Therefore, his curve of marginal receipts is likewise a horizontal straight line at the prevailing price. This makes it coincident with the demand line—the two curves are identical. This is always true for the individual seller under conditions of pure competition.

Now, if our producer follows the rule of regulating his output so that his marginal costs equal his marginal receipts, he will simply produce up to the point where marginal costs are equal to the price, for price and marginal receipts are in this case the same. This, then, is the special application of our general rule of policy for the case of pure competition—marginal costs must equal selling price. If our reasoning has been correct, our cotton producer will find his profits greatest, or his losses least, if he obeys this principle.

Let us see how this works out in a particular case. We may suppose that the curves C_a and C_m, in Figure 34, represent the average and marginal costs, respectively, for different outputs on the plantation of our imaginary cotton grower. These curves are the same in all three parts of the drawing. Now look at part A of the drawing. It is here supposed that the price is 13 cents (OP). If our farmer follows the rule, he will produce 65,000 pounds of cotton, for at that output his marginal costs (RQ) are just equal to the price. He is

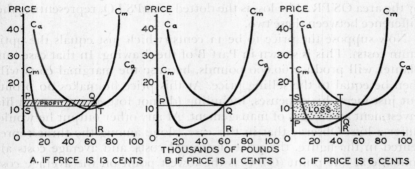

Figure 34. Adjustment of the Individual Producer to the Price Situation in Pure Competition.

making a profit (represented by the shaded area SPQT), because the selling price (OP) exceeds his average unit costs (RT, or OS). This profit area represents profit per unit (QT) times number of units produced (OR, or ST); also, it represents the difference between total receipts (OPQR) and total costs (OSTR). The reasoning by which the general rule of policy was developed demonstrates conclusively that, so long as the price remains at 13 cents, profits must be greater for the output shown (65,000 pounds) than for any other.

Suppose the price were very much lower, say only 6 cents. This is shown in Part C of the drawing. Now our farmer must suffer losses, for the price is below even his optimum costs. At first thought one might conclude that it would be better for him to give up the business entirely, but this is too hasty a judgment. It is true that he cannot go on indefinitely producing at a loss, but he may be better off if he continues producing for a time than if he stops altogether. He has an establishment on his hands which entails fixed costs which he must meet as long as he is able, whether he produces or not. If the price yields him anything over the variable costs, the excess will reduce his losses on the fixed costs by the amount of the excess. By so minimizing his losses, he may be able to tide himself over one or two lean seasons in the hope that the price will later rise again. The price being 6 cents, what output will bring his losses to a minimum? The answer is the same as in the preceding case: He should produce up to, but not beyond, the point where his marginal costs equal the price.

Part C of Figure 34 shows the resulting situation. Here C_a and C_m are the curves of average and marginal costs, respectively, as before. Price is 6 cents (OP) and output is somewhat in excess of 40,000 (OR). Total receipts are measured by the area OPQR and total costs by the area OSTR. The loss is the dotted area PSTQ, representing the difference between these two.

Now suppose the price to be 11 cents (which just equals the optimum costs). This is shown in Part B of the drawing. In that case our planter will produce 60,000 pounds, because the marginal costs will then be equal to the selling price. At this price he makes no profit, but just meets his expenses, including (do not forget) interest on his investment and wages of management. At any other output he would suffer a loss. Observe that in this case, alone among the three represented in the figure, the price, marginal costs, and average costs all coincide at one point (Q). Q is the lowest point on the average cost curve; hence it marks the optimum. Total receipts (OPQR) are the same as total costs (OPQR); hence there is no area of profit or loss.

Short-Period Equilibrium of Demand and Supply—The Case of Fixed Capacity. — Our cotton producer is only one of thousands who contribute to the whole supply of cotton. Each of these has a farm or plantation with a certain maximum capacity, within which he can vary his output. The combined capacity of all these enterprises constitutes the maximum capacity of the industry, for the time being. Given time enough, this capacity could be increased or decreased: more land could be brought into cotton cultivation; more equipment for ginning, baling, storing, and transporting cotton could be constructed; more labor could be persuaded to move into the cotton growing districts and (for those occupations where special skill is required) trained for the work of cotton production. Or, land now used for growing cotton could be diverted to other crops; existing equipment could wear out and some of it not be replaced; labor now employed in the industry could withdraw therefrom. However, these changes cannot take place quickly, and would probably not be made at all unless the demand for cotton were strong enough over a fairly long period to encourage permanent expansion of existing facilities, or weak enough to force permanent contraction. For short periods of time, therefore, cotton will have to be produced with whatever land, equipment, and labor are already existent in the industry. Its capacity is fixed, but within the upper limit set by that capacity the output can be varied.

Now, each of the many cotton growers will be governed by calculations similar to those of the hypothetical plantation which we have already examined. Each will endeavor to maximize his gains or minimize his losses, by pushing his output up to the point where his marginal costs are equal to the price prevailing. So, although their average costs will differ from one to another, their marginal costs will all be brought to the same level. By adding up the total of all the amounts which each would produce at each of the several prices which might conceivably prevail, we will have a supply schedule which is simply a schedule of marginal costs. For instance, the schedule of the cotton grower whose costs we have just been considering would be as shown for producer A in the following table:

| Price | Output of Typical Producers | | | Total Offerings of These Producers |
	A	B	C	
.05	35,000	10,000	50,000	95,000
.10	55,000	17,000	65,000	137,000
.15	70,000	30,000	75,000	175,000
.20	75,000	32,000	83,000	190,000
.25	80,000	35,000	90,000	205,000
.30	82,000	36,000	95,000	213,000
.35	83,000	37,000	97,000	217,000

In each case the output shown for this producer is derived from the marginal cost curve in Figure 34. The schedules of producers B and C are supposed to represent marginal cost calculations for two other cotton growers whose output and cost situations are different. The totals shown in the last column are the sums of the outputs of the three producers at each of the several prices. If we were to add together, in the same way, the outputs which each producer in the industry would offer at the various prices, we would then have the total supply schedule for cotton. It would show what the effective supply would be at every possible price. From this schedule we could construct a supply curve.

Let S_m in Figure 35 be such a curve (the subscript m being used to denote that the supply schedule in this case is based on marginal costs). This curve indicates that an average of 10 million pounds of cotton will be produced and sold yearly when the price is 7 cents, 15 million pounds when the price is 11 cents, 17 million pounds when it is 13 cents, and so on, up to 25 million pounds, which is assumed to be the maximum capacity of the industry with its present facilities. Beyond this point the curve would rise vertically, indicating that, within a short period of time, no increase in price could cause any further increase in production.

If a demand schedule be now set against this schedule of marginal costs, we can readily see how the demand and supply interact for short periods to establish an equilibrium price. Let the heavy demand curve of Figure 35 represent the schedule of demand for cotton. It differs from the market demand curves we have previously

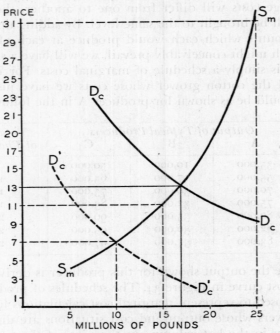

Figure 35. Short-Period Equilibrium—
The Case of Fixed Capacity.

dealt with in that it is free from the vicissitudes and distortions of the day-to-day market. It is based on the fundamental reactions of consumers, as they were described in the preceding chapter. Therefore, it indicates the average quantities of cotton which will be purchased *for consumption* each year (in the form of cotton products), so long as the present habits of consumers in respect to cotton goods continue. In the discussion of monopoly price, we called such a schedule of demand a consumption schedule, and we designated it by the notation D_c. All the demand curves which we shall deal with from now on will be of this type. Consumption schedules may be shown equally well in terms of average quantities per day, per week or per month, provided they be assumed to continue in the same position for a period of time long enough for production to be adjusted to them.

From the intersection of the demand and supply curves it is clear that equilibrium will prevail only when the price is 13 cents. At this price there is an effective demand (consumption) of 17 million pounds, and an effective supply (production) of the same amount. At any higher price, more would be produced but less would be purchased, leaving an unsold surplus to be disposed of; this surplus would force the price down. At any lower price, less would be produced but more would be demanded for consumption, causing a shortage; this shortage would force the price up. For the time being, then, the only price which will keep consumption and production in balance is 13 cents. This may be called the *short-period price*. It is also called, by some writers, the *short-period normal price*. So long as the situation pictured continues to prevail, market prices may be expected to fluctuate in the neighborhood of this figure, and the annual output of cotton, averaging the bad years with the good, should approximate 17 million pounds. Were the demand very much smaller, such as is represented by the dotted curve D_c', the short-period price would be only 7 cents, and the output of cotton would be only 10 million pounds.

Variable Capacity and the Influence of Optimum Costs. — The equilibrium just described is not permanently stable. Our analysis of a particular firm showed that, when its marginal costs are equal to the selling price, it may be making either profits or losses. In the market as a whole the same is true. If the demand is strong in relation to existing capacity, short-period price will be high enough to induce producers to push their output to a point where marginal costs exceed optimum costs—at least for some firms. Profits in excess of interest on invested savings and ordinary wages of management will result. Wages for hired labor are also likely to rise above what is being paid elsewhere. If this situation bids fair to continue, investors will be led to put more funds into cotton-producing equipment, and new workers will be attracted into the industry. So, capacity is no longer fixed; it begins to expand. When this new capacity becomes effective, the schedule of supply, based on marginal costs, will increase (the supply curve will move to the right), and price will tend to fall.

On the other hand, if demand is weak in relation to existing capacity, short-period price will be below the optimum costs—at least for some producers, and there will be losses. Wages will also be low and there may not be full-time employment for cotton workers. If these conditions are long continued, investors will be discouraged from putting more funds into cotton-producing equipment, and new labor will not be attracted into the industry. So, as existing equipment wears out and workers grow old and retire, neither will be fully replaced. Capacity is thereby reduced. As a result of this reduction, the schedule of supply, based on marginal costs, will decrease (the supply curve will shift to the left), and price will tend to rise. So, in the long run, the capacity of an industry is not fixed, but variable; and a price based on fixed capacity is only temporary. Diagrams to illustrate these conditions will be offered presently.

What, then, is a position of *stable* equilibrium? It is one in which the price is just equal to the optimum costs of production, so that there are neither profits nor losses, and hence, no reason for either expansion or contraction. However, since the optimum costs of production for different producers are unequal, a price which just covers the costs of one may bring profits or losses to others. So long as these differences persist, price instability must continue, for those who are making profits will be likely to seek additional customers by underselling their less successful rivals. Equilibrium could never be stable until the optimum costs of all were equal. Needless to say, such equality is never attained in reality; but there is a tendency toward it, through the leveling effects of competition. In Chapter VI it was pointed out that in each industry there is a size of plant and a method of organization which is most efficient for that industry. An enterprise with such a plant and organization was said to be an optimum firm. We may now designate the optimum costs of such a firm as *the optimum costs for the industry*. The influence of competition tends to bring the costs of all producers toward this optimum, for if those whose costs are higher do not bring them down by adopting the methods of the leaders, sooner or later they are likely to be driven from the industry. It is to optimum costs in this sense, then, that prices in the long run tend to conform. *This is the normal price, about which all other prices fluctuate.*

It follows that, in a position of normal equilibrium, the situation of the individual enterprise in respect to price will be as it is shown in Part B of Figure 34 above. Observe that the price line PQ (which is both the line of demand and of marginal receipts for the individual seller) is tangent to the average cost curve at its lowest point, where it is intersected by the marginal cost curve. This is the point of optimum costs. There is no profit or loss area.

Since it is the object of business men to make profits, the conclusion that prices tend to be equal to costs of production may seem questionable. The layman might be inclined to argue that prices must be far enough above costs to allow some margin of profit. However, it must be borne in mind that we include in the term costs a wage of management to the enterprisers and interest on the savings invested by enterprisers in their own businesses. The wage is equivalent to the salary which they would be able to obtain if employed by others, and which, therefore, may be said to be the value of their labor of direction and superintendence. The interest included is equivalent to the earnings which they might expect from their capital if invested in businesses with the same degree of risk as the ones in which they are now engaged. Business men presumably would not remain in business if they did not get these returns; but most persons would rather be earning these returns as independent enterprisers than as employees or inactive investors; therefore, wages of management and interest on investment should be sufficient to keep them in business. They will take more than this if they can get it, of course, but there are always so many eager to take advantage of any opportunity to make surplus gains that if any line of business is offering such a surplus, more producers will come into that field, until the increase in production that results from this influx forces the price of the commodity in question to the point where it no longer affords any extra inducement to enterprisers. At this point, the industry is in a position of equilibrium.

We have now reached the center of the competitive price-making process. We now know, not only what constitutes a normal price, but also what is the normal capacity and the normal output of an industry. A plant is working at its normal output when its average costs are at their optimum; the capacity of an industry is normal when its plants are all producing their normal output; and the price is normal when their combined normal outputs are in such a relation to the demand that the price just equals the optimum costs.

Long-Period Equilibrium. Normal Price. — Let us try to picture this situation in terms of demand and supply curves. This will enable us to see graphically how the short-period equilibrium represented in Figure 35 would be modified by the long-period influence of varying capacity. The problem is to find out how optimum costs behave in a whole industry, and what is their relation to the marginal cost schedules on which production at any given time depends.

We know, from the behavior of costs in an individual enterprise, that optimum costs lie somewhere between the upper and lower extremes of marginal costs, for a marginal cost curve always crosses the average cost curve at the optimum point. This suggests that we can represent production at optimum cost by a line cutting through the marginal cost curve somewhere between its two ends. Consider Figure 36, for instance. Here the curves D_c and S_m are the same as the corresponding curves of Figure 35, except that their upper ends have been omitted because we do not need them—they are too far removed from the position of equilibrium to be relevant to our problem. The short-period price is 13 cents, as before, and the output, based on the capacity assumed to exist for the time being, is 17 million pounds. The optimum costs are represented by the dotted line S_o. Like the curve of marginal costs, this line is a picture of a

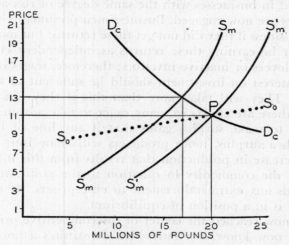

Figure 36. Expansion of Capacity to a Position of Normal Equilibrium.

supply schedule, the schedule of the average unit costs at which different quantities of cotton could supposedly be produced, if each plantation were of the optimum size and efficiency, and if it were producing its optimum output.

Observe that this line slopes upward to the right, but much less steeply than the short-period supply curve. This implies that the optimum costs will be higher if the industry has developed the capacity for a very large output than if its capacity were less. This will not always be the case, but it is typical of certain types of industry. Therefore we can accept it for the moment, and postpone for a little while further discussion of the point, as well as the consideration of other cases, where the optimum supply schedule has different characteristics. Taking the given schedule for granted, how does it exert its influence upon the price situation we have pictured? Notice that the short-period price of 13 cents is well above the optimum costs. This means that producers are enjoying unusually good profits. The equilibrium is therefore unstable, for there is an inducement to expand the facilities for cotton production. As this expansion takes place, the short-period supply schedule will increase (causing S_m to shift to the right); for, with more capacity in the industry, a larger supply will now be effective at any given level of marginal costs. With the increase in production, price will fall, so that profits will no longer be as high as before. When expansion has proceeded to the point where the short-period curve occupies the position S_m', price will have fallen to the level of optimum costs (11 cents), so that there is no further stimulus to increase. A position of stable equilibrium has now been reached, where marginal demand-price, marginal costs and optimum costs all coincide. Observe that the three curves intersect at the same point (P). Effective demand and supply are in equilibrium at 20 million pounds, the price being 11 cents. In the absence of some change in the schedule of demand or in the technology of production, there is no reason why this price should be disturbed. Here, then, is a permanent or long-period equilibrium. Here is the normal price.

Figure 37 shows the opposite situation, where demand is so weak in relation to existing capacity that the short-period price is below the optimum costs, causing losses to producers. S_m is the original curve of marginal costs, the same as S_m in the previous drawing. With demand as shown, the price is temporarily only 7 cents, and the output of cotton 10 million pounds. Because of the losses which growers sustain at this price, cotton-producing facilities would be gradually diminished, causing the marginal cost curve to recede, until it occupied the position S_m'. With this shrinkage in production, price would rise to 9 cents (at P), where stable equilibrium would be reached.

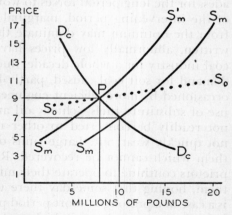

Figure 37. Contraction of Capacity to a Position of Long-Period Equilibrium.

This would then be the new normal price. Normal output would be 8 million pounds.

The Relative Character of Short and Long Periods. — The concepts of the short and the long period, which play so important a part in this explanation of prices, cannot be defined in terms of months or years, for they differ from industry to industry. What is a long period for one branch of production may be a short period for another. It all depends on the quickness with which equipment and labor in the particular case can respond to changing conditions of demand.

In industries where the equipment employed is of a simple and not very durable character, and the labor not too skilled, adaptation may take place rather rapidly. Here the long period may be only a matter of a few weeks or months. In the making of certain simple garments, such as aprons or cheap cotton dresses, for instance, small establishments can be quickly set up by the renting of vacant floor space, the purchase of a few sewing machines, and the hiring of women who require very little skill to operate them. Such a business can be promptly disbanded if unsuccessful. In cases of this sort, the influence of optimum costs is fairly direct, and deviations of market and short-period prices from normal prices will not ordinarily be very great, nor persist for very long.

On the other hand, in industries which require a great deal of elaborate and durable equipment and which employ highly skilled labor, such as railroads or coal mines, it may take years, or even decades, for the long-period forces to work out their effects. In the whole of the intervening period, marginal costs which differ considerably from the optimum may dominate the situation. At the time this is written, abnormally low prices have prevailed in the bituminous coal industry for a whole decade, due to a decline in the schedule of demand for soft coal caused, partly by economies in the use of coal occasioned by more efficient engineering, and partly by the growing use of substitute fuels—chiefly oil and natural gas. Coal mines cannot readily be converted to other uses, and their equipment does not quickly wear out. Large sums of money have been invested in them which cannot be recovered. Rather than lose all of this, proprietors continue to operate their mines for what they can get out of them, hoping that some day there will be a turn for the better. It is a case of a prolonged short-period price!

In the cotton industry, which we have used mainly for illustration, the short period is again a relatively long one. A large geographical area has adjusted itself so thoroughly to this one crop that its whole economy—its railroads, even its cities and towns—are based upon it. To adjust all the institutions of our Southern states to a drastic change in the demand for cotton would require an economic and social upheaval of vast proportions. Also, in this, as in most agricultural industries, the vicissitudes of the weather have so important an effect on the production from one year to the next that all calculations have to be based on averages over several years. Hence, the short period is of considerable duration, and the influence of optimum costs less immediate. In such cases, the deviations of market prices from normal prices may be marked and prolonged, and even the influence of the short-period factors—of marginal costs—will not be as apparent as it is in manufactures. Nevertheless, both the short- and long-period forces are at work, helping to establish the prices which do prevail.

Industries of Increasing, Decreasing, and Constant Costs. — In discussing the long-period adjustment of supply to demand, the schedule of optimum costs has so far been represented as rising gradually with any expansion of production. Accordingly, the line of optimum costs was pictured as having an upward slope. This will often be the situation, but in other cases the line may slope downward, or even be horizontal. Let us consider the factors on which this depends.

The expansion of any industry is held somewhat in check by the fact that the productive agents which it requires are limited in quantity. In the course of decades, more land may be made available by exploration and settlement, more labor may be provided by population growth, and more savings may be accumulated; but these cannot be counted on, especially in these days of disappearing frontiers and declining birth rates. Hence, an increase in the output of any one branch of production may have to be accomplished by drawing some of the productive agents away from other branches or by the more intensive use of the agents already employed, or by bringing into use poorer land or labor, that it has not been considered worth while to employ hitherto. All of these are likely to occur, and all tend to raise the costs of production, for the following reasons: If agents have to be drawn away from other uses, higher prices will have to be bid for them, so that the cost of employing these agents is increased. If land, labor, or equipment have to be used more intensively, the law of diminishing productivity is brought into play, so that less product is obtained per unit of agents employed, and unit costs are correspondingly higher. If poorer agents are brought into use, there is again a lower product per unit, with a correspondingly higher unit cost. Therefore, unless these influences are offset by some counteracting influence, the expansion of the industry in question will involve a rise in its optimum costs. The line will then have an upward slope.

However, the expansion of an industry may be the means of effecting more economical methods of production, that could not be employed if the industry were smaller. We are familiar with the principle that a single enterprise can sometimes produce more cheaply when operating on a large than on a small scale. Something analogous can happen to a whole industry when it is organized to produce in greater volume. Even though (as the theory of competition supposes) each separate establishment is of the optimum size before expansion begins, there may be certain economies associated with the growth of the industry which are shared by all who are engaged in it, and which reduce the costs of doing business for all of them. For instance, when automobile manufacture first began, each manufacturer had to make his own parts in small quantities. As the work was unfamiliar, labor had to be specially trained for it, and costly experiments had to be made. Many factors of this sort contributed to make expenses high. In time the industry grew to the point where it became possible for special businesses to be established for the manufacture on a large scale of such parts as storage batteries, starters, distributors, carburetors, gears, and bodies. Every maker of automobiles could obtain these parts more cheaply as a result of this specialization. In addition, the quality of labor was improved by the training of the workers to the particular skills needed by the industry. Many developments of this sort made available to manufacturers economies that would not have been possible were it not for the enormous growth of the industry. As a result, each producer enjoyed lower costs, so that now one can buy an excellent automobile at a price much lower than one would have had to pay twenty years ago for a car not nearly as good. Economies of the sort here described are known as *external economies,* because they arise in the industry at large, and are shared alike by all those engaged in the trade.

This will distinguish them from those economies which arise only in those establishments which, because of their great size, are possessed of advantages of large-scale organization not available to their smaller competitors. Economies of this second sort are known as *internal economies.* Internal economies may also play a part in the reduction of costs which comes from the expansion of an industry, if that expansion makes possible the use of known devices and processes which could not be employed if the industry were smaller. An example of this is assembly belts, on which automobiles by the score are moved along while workmen attach the various parts to the chassis, resulting in much more efficient production. These belts could not have been used in the earlier stages of the industry when not even the largest manufacturer could find sale for as many cars as are produced in a single plant of Chrysler or General Motors today.

Where economies of these kinds predominate, expansion of the industry will result in a decline in its optimum costs, so that the optimum cost line will have a downward slope.

In most industries, probably, tendencies to both rising and falling costs are at work, so that the net effect depends upon which set of tendencies is strong enough to outweigh the other. If the rising cost factors prevail, the branch of production concerned is said to be an *industry of increasing costs;* if the falling cost factors prevail, it is said to be an *industry of decreasing costs.* In some cases the two sets of influences may be so nicely balanced that production may expand or contract without any change in optimum costs, in which case the curve of optimum costs would be a horizontal straight line. We then have an *industry of constant costs.* Tendencies to increasing costs are most likely to prevail in extractive industries, such as mining, quarrying, and agriculture, where scarcity of mineral deposits and of suitable land is an important limiting factor that predominates over the economies of large-scale operation. Decreasing costs are most likely to be found in manufacturing, where economies of both the external and internal sort are most effective. Constant costs are most nearly approached in handicraft industries, where skilled labor is the principal agent of production employed, and natural resources and economies of machine processes are of little significance.

B. Price Adjustment to Changes in the Underlying Conditions of Demand or Supply

The Adjustment of Production to Changing Schedules of Demand. — Although the price-making influences which have so far been described are based in part on hypothetical assumptions which are never fully realized (for instance, the assumption that the costs of all producers are equal), they offer a very helpful approach to an understanding of the behavior of prices in the actual world. This will be more fully appreciated if we trace the sequence of events by which prices react to changing conditions of demand or supply.

Let us assume a situation in which, the price of a commodity having been somewhere near its normal, an increase in the demand occurs to disturb the approximate equilibrium. We may suppose that the cotton industry is in the position of equilibrium (P) shown in Figure 38. Production and consumption average 20 million pounds yearly, and the market price fluctuates around a normal of 11 cents, varying with the vagaries of the weather and other temporary influences, but always about that focal position. The industry is supposed to be one of increasing costs, so that the optimum line has an upward slope. Now let us imagine a marked increase in the schedule of demand for cotton. Such an increase might be brought about by the increasing use of automobiles, for whose tires and upholstery great quantities of cotton are required. It will cause the original demand curve, represented by D_c in the drawing, to shift upward to the right, occupying some such position as D_c'.

The first effect of such an increase will be to raise the market price to a point where considerable profits are to be made in the cotton

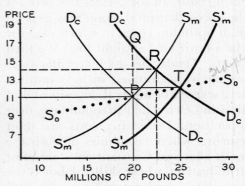

growing industry. (We can think of the new price as lying somewhere along the upper part of the new demand curve, in the vicinity of Q.) Planters will then be stimulated to grow more cotton. Existing facilities will be worked more intensively and marginal costs will rise (as shown by the curve S_m). Meanwhile, the increasing supply will cause the market price of cotton to fall somewhat (along the line D_c') until it meets the rising costs. Here a new equilibrium be

Figure 38. Adjustment of Supply to Changing Schedule of Demand in an Industry of Increasing Costs.

tween the demand and supply is established for a short period. In the diagram this occurs at R, the output being then 22½ million pounds and the price 14 cents. It will not pay producers to tax their present productive capacity any further, for it has now been pushed to its most profitable level. However, this price is above the optimum costs (indicated by S_o). Therefore, if the increase in the schedule of demand is permanent, the high profits prevailing will provide an incentive for an increase of capacity. New facilities for the growing and handling of cotton will be created, causing a shift of the marginal cost curve to the right. As a result of these developments, there will be a further decline in the price, until it reaches a new position of stable equilibrium where marginal demand-price, marginal costs, and optimum costs again coincide. In the drawing this is at T, output being 25 million pounds and the price being 12 cents. Observe that the new normal price is higher than the old, because the industry is one of increasing costs. Market prices and yearly production should fluctuate about this new normal. Observe that the price moves successively from P, to Q, to R, and then to T, where it tends to remain until disturbed by some new development in the underlying conditions of demand or supply.

Were the industry one of decreasing costs, the first effects would be the same as in the example just considered (market and short-period price would rise); but the ultimate effect would be different, for the new normal price would be lower than the old, because the expansion of the industry induced by the increased demand would make possible economies that would reduce the optimum cost. And if the industry were one of constant costs, the new normal price would be the same as the old, because in such an industry the optimum cost is the same for a large output as for a small one. Both these cases are illustrated by Figure 39, which should be self-explanatory. The movement of prices in each case is from P, to Q, to R, and then to T—the position of new long-period equilibrium.

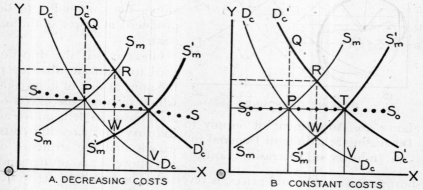

Figure 39. Adjustment of Supply to Increasing Schedules of Demand in Industries of Decreasing and Constant Costs.

An industry will adjust itself to a decrease in the schedule of demand in a very similar manner. Referring to Figure 40, let D_c represent the original schedule of demand, and S_o the line of optimum costs, as in previous cases. This time we start with equilibrium at T, price being 12 cents and output 25 million pounds. Now, if the schedule of demand declines to the position D_c', production continuing temporarily at its old rate, the market price will fall to the vicinity of V, so that producers will suffer losses. They will minimize these losses by curtailing their output, thereby reducing their marginal costs (along the line S_m). As output declines, the market price will rise again, until it coincides with marginal costs at W, where a short-period equilibrium is reached. The price is now about 9 cents, and output is 22½ million pounds. If this situation continues for a long period, there will be a decrease in capacity in the industry, for equipment will not be replaced as it wears out, and new labor will not appear to fill the thinning ranks of those already established there.

The marginal cost curve will then shift to the new position, S_m'. Production will decline and price will rise, until a new stable equilibrium is established at P. The normal price will then be 11 cents and the normal output 20 million pounds. Market prices and actual production should average not far from these figures. Observe that the new normal price is lower than the old, because the shrinkage of the

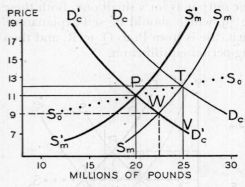

industry has relieved the pressure on the scarce agents of production and reduced somewhat the force of the law of diminishing productivity, enabling the commodity to be produced at lower optimum costs.

Figure 40. Adjustment of Supply to Decreasing Schedules of Demand in an Industry of Increasing Costs.

Observe that the drawing used to illustrate this case is the same as that of Figure 38, which pictured the effects of an increase in demand for an industry of increasing costs, except that the sequence of the movements of demand, short-period supply, and prices, is reversed. The first drawing would have illustrated the case of a decreasing schedule of demand just as well as the second, if we had read it backward.[1] Therefore, we do not need to draw new diagrams to show how supply adjusts itself to decreasing schedules of demand in industries of decreasing and constant costs—we can use the drawings of Figure 39. We now suppose that D_c' represents the original demand in both cases, and D_c the new (decreased) demand. S_m' is the original marginal cost curve and S_m the new curve, after supply is adjusted to the new demand. Normal equilibrium at the beginning of the problem is at T. When the schedule of demand decreases, market prices drop to the vicinity of V. Producers then curtail their output, so that the short-period price settles at W. Eventually capacity is reduced, so that the short-period supply curve shifts to the left, until a new normal price is established at P. In both these cases, then, the sequence of prices is from T, to V, to W, and then to P. Observe that in the case of constant costs, the new normal price is

[1] However, it will not always be possible to read backwards a line of increasing optimum costs; for, in an extractive industry like petroleum or mining, mineral deposits once removed from the soil can never be replaced. Therefore, if costs have risen with the growth of the industry through the years, due to the exhaustion of the richer and more accessible deposits, a decline in the schedule of demand may not bring the costs back to the low figures that formerly prevailed. This case is difficult to distinguish from the case of an upward shifting line of optimum costs, shown in Figure 41.

the same as before, because optimum costs have not changed; but in the case of decreasing costs, the new normal price is higher than the old, because, now that the industry is smaller than it was, the economies *which were dependent on the large scale of operations which the industry had reached* can no longer be maintained, so that optimum costs will be higher than before.

It is interesting to note that the *first* effect of an increase in the schedule of demand in every industry is always to raise the price, and of a decrease in the schedule of demand to lower it; but in an industry of decreasing costs, an increased demand tends *ultimately* to lower the price, and a decreased demand tends ultimately to raise it.

The Effects of Changes in the Basic Conditions of Production. — The foregoing section shows how prices will be affected when, *the underlying conditions of supply being given,* production is adjusted to changing schedules of demand. We have so far been concerned only with those changes in supply schedules which are induced by changes in demand. In all these cases, the schedule of optimum costs has been assumed to be fixed. But the underlying conditions of supply can change, irrespective of the state of the demand, and in this event optimum cost schedules will shift, while schedules of demand remain fixed. Let us consider some of these possibilities, and trace their effects upon prices.

The most important single influence which may alter the underlying conditions of supply is a change in the arts of production. In a progressive economy the general effect of this factor is to exert a downward pressure upon costs. Scientific research is continually revealing new processes, new ways of doing things which are more economical than the old. Synthetic products which can be cheaply produced may be substituted for expensive natural raw materials. Chemical discoveries may improve the efficiency with which metals can be extracted from their ores. Improved design may permit lighter and hence less costly construction (*e.g.,* of automobiles). New fuels may be developed. Mechanical inventions may be devised which greatly increase output, per unit of labor and other productive agents employed. As these changes become effective in an industry, marginal and average cost schedules both move downward (regardless of what is happening to demand) and a new optimum cost schedule is established, lower than the old. Normal price accordingly falls.

Another circumstance tending to reduce optimum cost schedules may be a decrease in the price of an agent of production used in a given industry. For instance, an influx of immigrants into a country may lower the wages of unskilled labor, and so reduce costs of those branches of production where much common labor is employed. A permanent fall in the rate of interest would lower costs appreciably for those industries in which much expensive equipment is used.

These cases are illustrated by Figure 41. Here D_c represents the schedule of demand, which is assumed to remain unchanged throughout the period under consideration. S_o is the original curve of op-

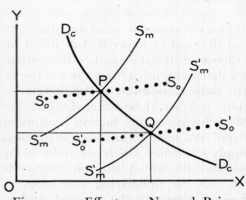

timum costs, and S_o' the new curve.[2] The marginal cost curve S_m (here sketched in lightly in order to emphasize the controlling influence of optimum costs) likewise moves downward to S_m'. Normal price decreases from P to Q.

This case is often confused with the case of decreasing costs which we previously discussed, and which was pictured in Figure 39, Part A. There we were concerned with a tendency for opti-

Figure 41. Effect on Normal Price of a Shift in the Schedule of Optimum Costs.

mum costs to decline because of economies made possible by the expansion of an industry. These economies were not the result of new scientific discoveries or inventions, but came about because, with a larger output, the industry could make use of techniques *already known,* but which could not be employed so long as the industry had to operate on a smaller scale. These economies would be lost if the industry had to contract. They were thus dependent on the strength of the schedule of demand. Because they represented the lower supply-prices which would prevail for large outputs, they could be represented as shifting points on a single optimum cost curve. The reduction in costs with which we are now concerned is not dependent on the scale of operation of the industry, nor on the state of the demand. It consists in a shifting of the whole schedule of optimum costs brought about by a change in industrial knowledge. The cheaper methods will not be lost if the industry has to contract. Hence they must be pictured by a shifting of the optimum cost curve to a lower level. The first case involves an increase in the effective supply, without any change in the long-run supply schedule; the second case involves a change in the schedule.

---

[2] This curve may slope upward, downward, or be horizontal. In each case the general reasoning is the same.

It is also possible for the schedule of optimum costs to shift upward, thereby raising normal price; but in a progressive economy this is less likely to happen than the case we have just considered. We do not often lose the advantages of scientific discoveries and new inventions, once they have become part of our civilization. However, events may happen which will raise the prices of certain agents of production, and so force optimum costs upward in particular industries. The prohibition of child labor no doubt increased the costs of manufacture in the cotton mills of the South, where a great deal of child labor was formerly employed. A permanent rise in the rate of interest would increase the cost of obtaining equipment, and so tend to force optimum costs upward in manufacturing industries. Other examples will no doubt occur to the reader.

These cases can also be represented by Figure 41, if it be read in reverse order. Let S_0' now represent the original schedule of optimum costs, which is then forced upward to the position S_0. Marginal costs move with it from S_m' to S_m. Normal price, which was at Q, rises to P.

Market, Short- and Long-Period Price Movements Combined. — Early in the second chapter preceding, certain characteristics of commodity price movements were described. The prices of a number of products, including cotton, wheat, cocoa, iron, rubber, and other common raw materials, were there observed to be constantly changing, but changing within a more or less clearly defined area, the general position of which was itself seen in each case to be moving slowly over a period of years. Our subsequent analysis revealed the basic causes of this behavior. It showed that some of these causes are slow in working out their effects, others more rapid. Therefore the competitive price-making process was divided into three parts, which were designated as market equilibrium, short-period equilibrium, and long-period (or normal) equilibrium, respectively. The long-period, or normal, price depends on the adjustment of productive capacity to demand; but since capacity cannot be altered quickly enough to keep pace with the eddying currents of our dynamic world, the adjustment is seldom, if ever perfect. This being the case, supply must be adjusted to demand temporarily on the basis of what capacity there is. So, the price moves for short periods, now above, now below, the normal, guided by marginal costs. But even this adjustment requires changes in the output of producing establishments which are not rapid enough to respond instantly to the vagaries of the day-to-day market. Therefore, market prices move up and down around the position of short-period equilibrium, depending on the relation of the day's demand to the stock of the commodity already in existence or nearly ready for the market—that is, on the supply which is "visible," or "in sight." So, market prices fluctuate about short-period prices, and the latter, in turn, fluctuate about long-period or normal prices. The last-named are thus the center, or focus, about which all other prices move—and this center itself in each case is slowly moving, as the various influences of shifting consumption and production schedules exert their effects through the years. Since all of these influences are constantly operating, the price actually prevailing for any commodity at a given moment is a resultant of all of them. The location of the general area within which its price moves is determined by the long-period forces, but the range of its movement, and its actual position within that area, depend on the short-period and market factors.

The Influence of Costs is Prospective, Not Retrospective. — In all the foregoing analysis, a great deal of emphasis has been placed on the influence of production costs upon prices. It must not be inferred from this that current prices depend mainly on past costs. The influence of costs upon prices works forward into the future rather than backward into the past. Enterprisers base their policies on the prices they expect to get and the costs they expect to incur, rather than on the prices and costs that formerly prevailed. Hence, the maintenance of a correspondence between prices and costs depends upon the correctness of these forecasts. If the forecasts have been faulty, the prices may be out of line with the costs; for when a commodity has once been produced, it must be sold for what it will bring on the market, regardless of what it may have cost to produce it. This is one of the chief reasons for the deviation of market from normal prices. However, in determining their future policy, producers are guided by their past experiences. If prices have recently been running below costs, in the absence of any reason to suppose that demand will increase or costs will fall, enterprisers will produce less in the immediate future, so that supply and demand may be brought into closer correspondence; prices will then rise until costs are met. Or, if prices have been above costs, and producers have reason to believe that this condition will continue, they are likely to increase their output of the affected commodities until prices fall to costs again. It is in this way, by constant trial and error, that the influence of costs upon prices is effected.

In spite of the abstract assumptions with which the analysis began, we have now developed a dynamic explanation of prices which takes account of the ever-changing character of economic life, and which makes it possible to account for most types of price behavior that are likely to occur in competitive markets. We have yet to consider, however, what happens when a mixture of monopolistic and competitive conditions prevails, and we have still to introduce certain refinements to allow for the connections that may exist between the prices of different commodities. These problems will constitute the subject-matter of what follows.

C. THE CASE OF MONOPOLISTIC COMPETITION

Monopolistic Competition Distinguished from Pure Monopoly and Pure Competition. — We have now considered two broad types of price situation—pure monopoly and pure competition. While conditions approximating these two types of cases can be identified in the actual world, there is very often a situation which lies somewhere between them. In this no-man's-land of pricing, there are two or more producers competing with each other (so that it is not a case of pure monopoly), but the conditions necessary for the maintenance of pure competition are not fully realized. Those conditions were set forth at the beginning of this chapter, where it was stated that pure competition exists "when there are so many sellers of an identical commodity that the entire amount contributed to the supply by any one of them is too small a portion of the total to have any appreciable influence on the price." According to this statement, there are two criteria of pure competition: (1) There must be so many sellers that no one of them controls a portion of the supply large enough to have any significant influence on the price, and (2) they must all be offering identically the same commodity. It follows that pure competition is departed from: (1) if the number of sellers is small enough so that the output of any one of them does have an appreciable influence on the price, or (2) if they are producing similar, but not identical, commodities. The term *monopolistic competition* is used to cover both of these cases. Some writers prefer the term *imperfect competition*.

Oligopoly and Product Differentiation. — Monopolistic competition is subdivided into two general classes, depending on which of the two conditions just mentioned prevails.

The first of these is known as *oligopoly*. This may be defined as *the condition in which a good is supplied by a small number of producers, but without definite agreement concerning prices or outputs.* (If there is definite agreement, the case is one of pure monopoly.) This is a not infrequent state of affairs. In the manufacture of steel rails, gasoline, and raw copper, for instance, a few large producers dominate the scene. The same is true of many mineral products, such as pitchblende and certain varieties of marble, which can only be obtained from a few natural deposits. In cases of this kind, although there may be no monopolistic agreement among the several producers, the position of each is very different from that of a small farmer who contributes only a few bales of cotton or bushels of grain to a total crop of many millions. Each of the oligopolists knows that his policy will have some effect on the price of the product and on the actions of his competitors; hence his calculations will not be the same as those of the farmer. We will consider this case more fully in the following section.

The second type of monopolistic competition is known as *product differentiation*. It arises when, though there may be many producers, there is some difference in the products or services contributed by each, so that customers may prefer the one to the other. Safety razors, for instance, are pretty much alike, yet each has some little feature of its own which makes it slightly different from the others. Some users prefer this brand, some that. There are many similar instances of manufactured goods which contribute to the same purpose and are therefore competitive, yet which differ in details of construction, so that the competition is modified by the fact that one is supposedly or actually better adapted to the needs of users than another. Typewriters, fountain pens, cameras, and electric refrigerators are further illustrations. Sometimes the differences rest on patents (*e.g.,* noiseless typewriters), so that the superior qualities of the one cannot be imitated by its competitors. Or, advertising of the "accept no other" variety may build up in the minds of customers a belief that products of one brand are better than those of another, thus giving the advertiser a slightly more favorable position than his competitors. The protection of trademarks given by our government encourages this type of differentiation. Sometimes certain sellers will offer special inducements not offered by their competitors. The retail store that has a liberal credit policy, which permits its customers to carry charge accounts and defer their payments, may enjoy an advantage over the cash merchant. The store which delivers its goods to the homes of its customers may have a similar advantage over the one which does not. Mere reputation for fair dealing and good merchandise may build up that intangible asset, known as "good will," to such an extent that it gives the favored merchant a price advantage. All these cases are described as product differentiation, because the products or services of the supposed competitors differ sufficiently to make possible some differences in the prices charged, and often prices somewhat higher than would prevail under conditions of more perfect competition. We shall consider this case more fully after the analysis of oligopoly.

Product differentiation and oligopoly often go hand in hand, causing a situation which may be described as *differential oligopoly*. Most modern manufacturing requires rather large-scale establishments. The result is that relatively few enterprises—a dozen, a score, or perhaps a hundred—suffice to meet the demands for the goods. The market is not great enough to require the hundreds or thousands of establishments which would make the industry purely competitive. For instance, according to the Census of Manufactures, there were in this country in 1937 only 3 linoleum factories, 12 locomotive-building establishments, 25 smoking-pipe factories, 34 cigarette factories, 38 piano factories, 55 wool carpet and rug mills, and a long list of other industries, the number of establishments in which did not exceed 100. In all of these there is, therefore, a situation of oligopoly. Yet in all of them there is also product differentiation. There are differences in the composition and patterns of the linoleums produced by different manufacturers, in the qualities of the pianos made in different factories, in the tobacco mixtures used in different cigarettes, and so on. Therefore, in interpreting the price situations which may be met with in such industries, the student must realize that the principles of both oligopoly and product differentiation, which are about to be explained, may have to be brought to bear upon the problem.

Having now discussed the nature of monopolistic competition in general terms, let us proceed to the details of price-fixing under the conditions described.

Prices Under Conditions of Oligopoly. — Let us suppose that a new and exquisite gem has been discovered, of which there is at first only one known deposit, so that its owner enjoys a complete monopoly of its production. We may assume that, by experimentation, he finds that he reaps his greatest profit when he prices his precious stones at $500 per carat, and that the price is held at this figure, although his average costs are only $100. Now let another deposit of this gem be discovered, which is controlled by a competing producer. The case will then be an oligopoly of two sellers (or *duopoly*, as this case is sometimes called). To simplify the problem, we may suppose that the average costs of the new producer are also $100. What will determine the price under these conditions?

The case is illustrated by Figure 42. Here D_c represents the schedule of consumptive demand for the gems, RC_a the average costs per carat for both producers. These are assumed to be constant, regardless of output, in order to avoid unnecessary complexity. We start with the price at $500, the quantity sold being 5,000 carats annually. The profit at this price is $400 per carat, or $2,000,000 in all; this is represented by the shaded area SPQR. So long as there is only one producer, he enjoys this profit alone, but this situation is altered by the entrance of the second producer. Suppose that the latter accepts the prevailing price, and sells his gems, too, at $500. Then total sales will remain at 5,000, and the profit will be divided between them. If each obtains an equal share of the business, each will be selling 2,500 carats, and making profits of $1,000,000. This is shown by the vertical dashed line, dividing the profit area into two parts. But now it will pay either one of the producers to cut the price, hoping thereby to draw customers away from his rival and increase his total profits. For instance, if one of them offers the gems at $400

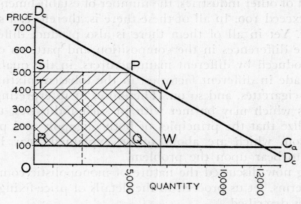

Figure 42. An Oligopoly Price Situation.

(the other keeping his temporarily at $500), all the buyers will presumably give their patronage to the price cutter. According to the diagram, he will sell about 6,500 carats, reaping a profit of $300 per carat, or $1,950,000 in all—nearly twice as much as he, individually, was making before. This is shown by the shaded area TVWR. But this is a game at which two can play. The first producer will not sit idly by and let all the business go to his competitor. He is likely to retaliate by cutting his price below $400. Then all the business will go to him, at the expense of the original price cutter.

It is possible for this process of competitive price cutting to go on until the price has fallen to $100, where profits disappear for both of them. It may go even lower, if one of them feels that his financial resources are strong enough for him to endure losses for a time, in the hope of putting his rival out of business. But if the two producers are nearly equal in strength, they may decide that there is no sense in continuing the competition, and will come to an agreement. The case is then no longer one of oligopoly—it has become a pure monopoly. Or, without any formal agreement, each may decide, independently, that his wisest course is to pursue a policy of "live and let live," by refraining from price competition. The resulting price is likely to be somewhat close to the pure monopoly figure.

The general conclusion to be reached from this analysis is, that the price prevailing under oligopoly conditions may vary anywhere from the point which might be expected under pure competition to that which would prevail under pure monopoly. Unlike the theories of pure monopoly and pure competitive price, which give a definite point at which the market forces come to a focus, the theory of oligopoly price gives us the two extremes within which the price may be expected to lie. Which extreme is more likely to be approached depends, in considerable degree, upon the number of sellers there are in the industry. If there are only a few producers, each is apt to be more conscious of the policies of the others, and to be more fearful of the consequences of retaliation, than if there are many. Not infrequently, there will be one large producer who stands out among his smaller competitors as the acknowledged leader of the industry. In this case, it may be the general policy to allow him to set the price, and the others will adhere to it. Each will then adjust his output to the price fixed by the leader so as to maximize his profits, following the general rule of policy with which we are already familiar. The price set by the leader will usually be high enough to allow profits for all those who are already established, but it may fall short of the pure monopoly price, for fear of attracting new competitors into the industry. On the other hand, where the number of producers is fairly large, these restraints are less likely to be operative, and conditions more nearly resembling those of pure competition are likely to prevail. The oligopoly price will then be at or near the competitive level.

Prices under Conditions of Product Differentiation. — Where there are some differences in the products of different producers, each seller has a clientèle which prefers his goods to those of his competitors. Nevertheless, he has to reckon with the fact that there are other products very much like his, to which his customers may turn if they have sufficient incentive to do so. Too high a price for his goods may constitute such an incentive. Their preference for his product may be strong enough for him to get a little more than his competitors, but not much more. Thus, while his position is somewhat like that of a monopolist, in that he is the sole producer of the exact product which he offers for sale, it differs from that of the monopolist, in that the demand for his product is so extremely elastic that the limits within which he may vary his price are rather narrow. His position resembles the purely competitive one also in that his demand curve is nearly horizontal, but it differs in that it slopes slightly (as in Figure 43).

Let us take the case of safety razors for illustration. Although there is some competition among the producers of different makes of this article, each has certain patented features and exclusive designs which cannot be exactly duplicated by any of the others, and which are represented in advertising as very advantageous. Customers, influenced partly by this advertising, or perhaps by their own expe-

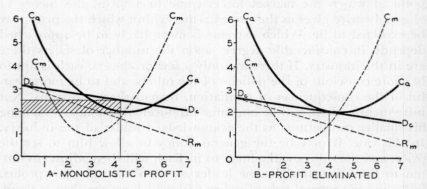

Figure 43. Price Under Conditions of Product Differentiation.

rience, have their particular preferences. Let the situation of one manufacturer be represented by Figure 43. We may suppose that his position at a particular time is that shown in Part A of the drawing. Here C_a denotes his average costs of production. These are at their minimum of $1.90 when his output is about 4,500 units. We know that, under conditions of pure competition, his demand curve would be a horizontal straight line tangent to the cost curve at this point, and the price would normally be at that figure. However, the demand schedule (D_c) for his razors is tipped slightly away from the horizontal, and lies somewhat above the average cost curve for part of its length. Following the general rule of policy, that his greatest advantage is obtained by fixing the price at the point where his marginal receipts equal his marginal costs, he charges $2.50 for his razors and produces and sells only 4,200. Thereby he reaps a fairly good profit, represented by the shaded area.

If the razors of this manufacturer have advantages which cannot be met by his competitors, this profit may continue. The case is then almost the same as pure monopoly. However, other makers of razors will do all they can to encroach on his position, by improving their products or by clever advertising. If they succeed, he will lose business to them, and his demand schedule will shift downward. It tends to approach the position shown in Part B of the drawing, where it has come to rest just tangent to the cost curve. Here he sells only 4,000 razors, getting a price of only $2.00, which just covers his costs for that output. If competition is keen enough, all producers may be driven into a similar position. The industry is then in a sort of equilibrium, where there are no profits to attract newcomers, and no losses to drive out present producers. But few industries remain so stabilized; the picture is ever changing, with some making profits, while others are less fortunate.

It is to be observed in the drawing that the firm is operating at less than optimum capacity, and its costs are above the optimum. This is due to the fact that competition tends to force the demand curve towards its point of tangency with the average cost curve, and so long as the demand curve is sloping, this point must lie somewhat to the left of the optimum. Price therefore remains slightly higher than it would be under pure competition, even though producers are making no profit.

From all this we may conclude that, under conditions of monopolistic competition with product differentiation, prices may differ slightly among the several producers, and the latter may or may not receive an element of monopolistic profit; prices may exceed or be equal to costs; they will be lower than under pure monopoly and higher than under pure competition.

Pure Monopoly, Pure Competition, and Monopolistic Competition Contrasted. — It will be instructive at this point to compare the three broad types of price determination which we have so far considered, namely: pure monopoly, pure competition, and monopolistic competition. We can do this best by contrasting the position of the individual firm in each of the three cases. Such a contrast is presented in Figure 44. Part A represents the case of pure monop-

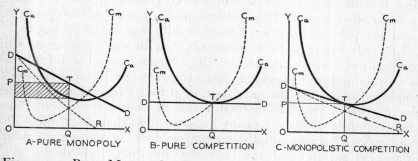

Figure 44. Pure Monopoly, Pure Competition, and Monopolistic Competition.

oly, Part B that of pure competition, and Part C that of monopolistic
competition where there is product differentiation. The average and
marginal cost curves in the three drawings are identical, because it
is not in respect to costs that these three cases differ, but in respect
to the demand schedules for the products of the individual producers.
Therefore, the demand curves are different. In the case of pure
monopoly, the demand curve has considerable slope and lies well
above the cost curve in part of its length, thereby affording a substantial profit (shown by the shaded area) to the monopolist. Output
is considerably below the optimum, and costs somewhat above the
optimum level. In the case of pure competition, the demand curve
is a horizontal straight line, tangent to the curve of average costs
at its optimum point, and it is identical with the marginal receipts
curve. The plant is operated at its optimum output, and the price
is equal to optimum costs. There are no profits. In the case of
monopolistic competition, the demand curve is tipped slightly away
from the horizontal, and it tends toward a position of tangency to
the curve of average costs, although it might lie slightly above it.
Price is equal to, or somewhat above, average costs, but slightly
higher than optimum costs, and output is slightly less than optimum.
These three cases sum up concisely the basic elements of the pricing
process.

Class Price. — It will be recalled that a demand schedule is made
up of a series of price offers of different buyers. There are always
some who are willing to pay more for a given article than others.
Where pure competition prevails they nevertheless all pay the same,
according to the law of one price. However, if competition is impure, or complete monopoly prevails, it is possible to charge different prices to different buyers. This enables the seller to take advantage of the high prices that a few customers will pay, at the same
time that he reaps the benefit of a large volume of sales at a lower
price to other buyers. This phenomenon is known as *class price*, because the price charged is adjusted to different classes of buyers.

Not only where there is monopoly, but in some cases even with
competition, class prices can prevail, if buyers are not well informed
as to products and prevailing market prices, or if a clever ruse is
employed to deceive the purchaser, or if long custom has sanctioned
the practice. A few examples will make the matter more clear. Physicians commonly charge wealthy patients more than poor ones. This
can be done because usually one patron does not know the amount
of another patron's bill, and because custom has established it as an
approved policy. The publisher of a copyrighted book, such as a
popular novel, first puts it on the market at a high price, until as

many eager buyers as can be induced to pay this figure have bought it; then a later edition is sold at a much lower sum, and further sales result. The first edition brings in a handsome profit; the second a more moderate return. In this case the class price is made possible by the fact that the two editions are sold at different times. Occasionally, two different prices for a good may be charged at the same time by disguising the higher-priced article so as to make it seem more desirable. For instance, the same grade of candy, put up in an elaborate package, may be made to appear of much higher quality than when offered in less attractive form, and will bring a higher price.

Figure 45 illustrates this phenomenon in diagram form. We may suppose this to represent the case of a handsomely illustrated book which can be sold at a high price to a limited number of buyers, but which could be marketed in much larger quantities if the price were sufficiently low. If the publisher fixes the price at $4.00, he can sell only 10,000 copies, bringing in a gross return of $40,000. His average costs for this output would be $1.80 per copy, making his total costs

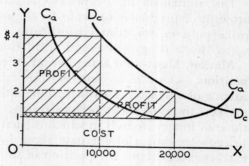

Figure 45. Class Price.

$18,000. His gross profit would then be $22,000. On the other hand, if he fixes a price of $2.00, his sales will be 20,000 copies, and he will have the advantage of lower unit costs, for at 20,000 his costs reach their optimum of $1.00. But this policy would not be as profitable as the other, for the difference between total costs ($20,000) and total receipts ($40,000) would be only $20,000, which is less than before. He decides to take advantage of the high price at which some copies can be sold by offering a de luxe edition at $4.00, and at the same time to reach the wider market by offering a popular-priced edition at $2.00. In this way he is able to reduce his unit costs for both editions to $1.00 (plus 20 cents extra for the superior paper and binding of the de luxe edition, represented by the double shaded area in the diagram). He sells 10,000 of the higher-priced volumes at a profit of $2.80 per volume, or $28,000 in all, and another 10,000 of the popular-priced edition at a profit of $1.00 per volume, bringing the grand total of profits to $38,000. These profits are shown by the lightly shaded areas in the drawing.

The phenomenon of class price must be added to the exceptions to the law of one price, which were mentioned in a preceding chapter. Here we are making another departure from the rigorous assumptions with which our analysis of prices began. While this departure makes the explanation of prices less precise, it is in closer accordance with reality. It has already been pointed out that exceptions to the law are more likely to occur in retail than in wholesale markets. Nevertheless, there are limits to the deviations which the circumstances of economic life permit. If the normal price of a pound of candy of a certain grade is 80 cents, the actual price to some customers may be 60 cents and to others one dollar, according to the type of package and the circumstances of its sale, but the range is not likely to be so great as from 25 cents to 10 dollars.

Discrimination in the prices charged to different buyers, in the attempt of producers to profit by the opportunities offered by class-price policies, sometimes constitutes a serious problem of justice, which leads to governmental regulation.

Market, Short- and Long-Period Prices under Monopolistic Competition. — Our discussion of competitive prices revealed the existence of three types of price fluctuations—those of the day-to-day market, those of short periods during which capacity is fixed, and those of longer periods in which capacity can be varied. Short-period prices were shown to fluctuate about long-period normal prices, and market prices about the position of short-period equilibrium. Somewhat similar considerations apply to prices fixed under conditions of pure monopoly and monopolistic competition; but they apply only in part, because, while schedules of demand may shift just as readily in the one case as in the other, the response of sellers to these changes is not so spontaneous when monopolistic elements are present. Prices are less likely to move up and down irregularly from day to day; they are more likely to be held at fixed points for considerable periods of time. However, permanent shifts in the underlying conditions of demand or supply must eventually bring responsive changes in prices, and these changes will be governed by the same fundamental factors that work under competitive conditions. That is, if demand schedules rise, marginal receipts curves will rise with them, and producers will find it advantageous to seek the new point of equality between marginal receipts and marginal costs. Sooner or later, therefore, a price readjustment is likely to be brought about. If the prices of factors of production change, or technological improvements bring a lowering of schedules of costs, these too will bring price readjustments. And it will also be true that changes in schedules of demand must necessarily be met for short periods by increasing output within the limits of existing capacity, whereas, in the long run, capacity is likely to be increased or decreased, as the case may be. In all of these adjustments, the general rule of policy, that producers tend to equate their marginal costs with their marginal receipts, may be expected to hold. Moreover, it seems probable that, in the long run, there is a tendency for monopolistic enterprises to develop plants of the optimum size for their industry. This would be only common sense for a pure monopolist, because, if he has occasion to build a new plant at all, he will naturally want to build the most efficient one that is possible, and where conditions of monopolistic competition prevail, there may be enough of the competitive element to compel it. Unlike the case of pure competition, however, there is no tendency for prices in the long run to come to equality with optimum costs. Under conditions of either pure monopoly or monopolistic competition, prices must always be expected to lie somewhat above the optimum cost figure.

The diagrams which we have used to illustrate monopolistic competition are based on the assumption that we are dealing with given schedules of demand and given plant capacities, whether of the optimum size or not. The student should now be sufficiently at ease in the use of demand and supply curves to be able to work out for himself the changes in price that might be expected to result from alterations in these schedules of demand and of costs. Therefore, it is not necessary to develop these cases in further detail.

Summary

In this chapter we have considered the process of price determination under conditions of pure competition and of monopolistic competition.

Pure competition exists when there are so many sellers of an identical commodity that the entire amount contributed to the supply by any one of them is too small a portion of the total to have any appreciable influence on the price. Under this condition the demand schedule for the output of an individual producer is a horizontal straight line, fixed at the level of the prevailing price, and the marginal receipts curve is coincident with this line. Hence, the general rule of policy (that it is advantageous to equate marginal receipts and marginal costs) means, in this case, that each producer will control his output so that his marginal costs equal the prevailing price. Since each producer follows this practice, the supply schedule for the whole market, over short periods during which capacity is fixed, will be based upon marginal costs. If a schedule of consumptive demand is set against this schedule of marginal costs, an equilibrium price is found at their point of intersection, where effective demand and effective supply are equal. This point marks the·short-period price. Over longer periods, if price is above (or below) the optimum costs of an optimum firm, productive capacity will be increased by expansion (or decreased by contraction) of equipment and labor in the affected industry. This causes schedules of marginal costs to shift until a position of equilibrium is reached where curves of consumptive demand, marginal costs, and optimum costs all coincide. This is the point of long-period equilibrium, or normal price. The short and long periods here referred to are purely relative; what is a short period for one industry may be a long period for another. How long these changes require depends on the nature of the particular industry in question. Schedules (and curves) of marginal costs always have an upward slope, but optimum cost schedules may have an upward, horizontal, or downward slope, depending on whether the industry is one of increasing, constant, or decreasing costs.

An increase in the schedule of demand for a commodity tends to cause a sharp rise in its market price, followed for a short period by a decline to the position of equilibrium between the new schedule of demand and the schedule of marginal costs; in the long run, capacity will expand until price falls to the position of optimum costs. A decrease in the schedule of demand leads to a fall in the market price, followed for a short period by a rise to the new position of equilibrium between demand and marginal costs; in the long run, decreasing capacity will cause the price to rise to the new level of optimum costs. In both of these cases, the new long-period price may be higher or lower than the original price, depending on whether the industry is one of increasing, decreasing, or constant costs. Where schedules of optimum costs are lowered by improvements of technology or by a decline in the prices of productive agents, new (and lower) normal prices are established at the new point of equilibrium between schedules of demand, marginal and optimum costs. Increases in optimum costs are less usual, but when they occur will work in the opposite direction. The behavior of any price in competitive markets is a resultant of all the forces which have been described; market prices fluctuate about the point of short-period equilibrium, and this point, in turn, fluctuates about the position of long-period, or normal, equilibrium. In all of this analysis, the influence of costs is prospective, rather than retrospective; past costs are significant only as a basis for future expectations.

Monopolistic competition prevails either where the number of sellers is so small that the output of each one of them has an appreciable influence on the price (oligopoly), or where there is a difference among the products of the competitors, so that consumers may prefer one to another (product differentiation). Where there is oligopoly, the price may lie anywhere between the normal price of pure competition and the maximum price of pure monopoly, depending on whether the number of oligopolists is relatively many or few. Where there is product differentiation, each seller adjusts his output to the demand for his individual product on the same principle as a monopoly, but since the demand curve is not tipped very far from the horizontal, the price will usually be not far above that which would prevail under pure competition. If the competitive influences are strong enough, the demand curve for a particular seller may be forced to a position of tangency to his curve of average costs, at a point somewhat above the optimum; price will then be equal to costs, and there will be no monopolistic profit. Some monopolistic conditions permit producers to charge different prices for the same commodity in the same market by making slight variations in the quality or appearance of the product. This is known as class price. There are some differences between market, short- and long-period prices in cases of monopoly and monopolistic competition, but prices may not fluctuate as much as under conditions of pure competition.

REFERENCES AND SUGGESTIONS FOR FURTHER READING

The analysis of short- and long-period equilibrium developed in this chapter follows in a general way the masterly work of Alfred Marshall, although departing from it in some respects. See his *Principles of Economics,* Book V, especially Chapters 3, 5, 8, and 9 (5th or later edition, 1907). Marshall's approach is here supplemented by, and blended with, the individual firm analysis of Chamberlin and Robinson. See Edward Chamberlin's *The Theory of Monopolistic Competition* (1933) and Joan Robinson's *The Economics of Imperfect Competition* (1933). I have also relied mainly on Chamberlin for the discussion of monopolistic competition. A good discussion of the dynamics of competitive prices, resembling slightly the analysis here presented, can be found in Chapters 13 and 14 of F. B. Garver's and A. H. Hansen's *Principles of Economics* (rev. ed., 1937). There is an ingenious development of the theories of oligopoly and product differentiation, with illuminating comment on the applications of the theories to current pricing practices, in Chapter 27 of Kenneth E. Boulding's *Economic Analysis* (1941). G. J. Stigler's *The Theory of Competitive Price* (1942) is a concise, rigorous and elegant treatment of the subject suggested by its title.

Chapter XVI

INTERRELATED PRICES AND THE PRICE SYSTEM

A. INTERRELATED PRICES

Prices are Interrelated. — So far we have confined our analysis of the pricing process to one price at a time, as though the price of a given commodity were determined independently of all other commodities, so that it might be viewed as an isolated phenomenon. It was stated in Chapter XIII, however, that this is an oversimplification of the real world, that we must eventually take account of the fact that prices are interrelated. Sometimes there is an especially close relationship between the prices of certain commodities or groups of commodities. This is most likely to be true when they are joined together in use (as in the case of newsprint paper and printer's ink), or where they are produced together (as in the case of lamb legs and lamb chops). But even where the connections are not so close, there is a more general relationship, arising out of the fact that people's incomes are limited, so that the more they spend in one direction the less they can spend in another, and also out of the fact that all production draws to some extent on the same resources, so that when productive agents are employed in one industry the development of other industries is somewhat affected. In the last analysis, indeed, all prices are related to each other in one complex, interrelated system. Therefore it behooves us to investigate these relationships. We shall consider first those cases in which the connections between different prices are very close, then we shall proceed to the broader relationships which pervade the price system as a whole.

Derived Demand. — We have seen that all demands for goods arise ultimately from consumers' desires. Many goods, however, are used not directly by consumers, but at some stage of production more or less remote from them. To revert to the case of cotton, most people do not use this commodity in its raw form. They want cotton shirts, underclothing, and towels. Their demand for these articles leads to a derived demand for cotton yarn, and this in turn to a further derived demand for raw cotton, and indirectly also for machinery to be used in growing, ginning, spinning, and weaving it. At every stage of cotton goods production there is likewise a derived demand for such fundamental agents of production as labor, land, and saving. This is typical of production in every field. Always the consumers' demand for finished goods leads to derived demand for equipment, raw materials, and primary agents with which to produce those goods. We may define *derived demand* as *a demand for commodities or services one or more stages removed from final consumers.*

Since the costs of production at every stage must eventually be covered by the price which the consumer pays, the demand-prices at successive stages must be less than consumers' demand-prices by the amount of the intervening costs. In terms of our diagrams, the derived demand curve at any stage will lie below the consumers' demand curve by an amount equal to the costs which will be required to complete the good into a finished consumers' product. The demand-price of cotton yarn will be less than the demand-price of cotton shirts, for which it is to be used, by the cost of working up the yarn into cloth and the cloth into shirts, as well as by the cost of marketing the shirts through the wholesale and retail establishments by which it reaches the wearer. A drawing to illustrate a case of this kind is presented in the Appendix at the close of this chapter.

The demand for all productive equipment, partly-finished goods, raw materials, and agents of production is a derived demand, except in those few cases where consumers buy such goods directly for their own use.

Joint Demand. — Frequently two or more goods are wanted together for a single purpose. The game of tennis requires rackets, balls, nets, and a court. None of these things is of much use without the others; hence, there is not a separate demand for each of these articles, but one demand for all of them taken together. In such cases demand is said to be joint. *Joint demand* may be defined as *a single demand for two or more goods which are complementary to each other.* Joint demand is often associated with derived demand. For example, in the building of a house, there is a derived, joint demand for lumber, stone, brick, plaster, cement, and other materials. In the production of most commodities, a similar situation is found. However, joint demand should not be confused with derived demand. Derived demand arises from the fact that goods at more or less remote stages of production are needed by the final consumer. It refers to *the successive stages* of production. Joint demand refers to the fact that several articles may be demanded simultaneously *at* *any one stage,* or by the consumer himself. The distinction between the two, then, rests in the difference between succession and simultaneity.

Examples of joint demand are numerous. Automobile manufacture involves a joint demand for rubber, leather, steel, and other materials. The user of the auto demands jointly gasoline, oil, and tires. Fountain pens, ink, and paper are demanded jointly by students. Land, labor, fertilizer, and agricultural implements are demanded jointly by the farmer. Lumber, stone, bricks, and plaster are demanded jointly by the building contractor. The various raw materials and agents of production are nearly always demanded jointly in combinations of one sort or another.

Where the purchaser of the several commodities which are to be used together can vary the proportions in which they are to be combined, it is possible to estimate the importance of each, independently of the others. For instance, in growing cotton, the farmer should be able to reckon how many more, or less, pounds of cotton he will obtain by the use of a certain quantity more, or less, of fertilizer. From such a calculation he can determine what the fertilizer is worth to him. Therefore, it is possible to construct a separate demand for fertilizer, in spite of the fact that it is used in combination with other things. In such circumstances we really have a case of simple derived demand, and not a true case of joint demand at all. It is, therefore, possible to treat it as a problem of isolated price by comparing separate demand and cost schedules, as we have done in previous examples. The demand for agents of production is usually of this sort; that is, the technology in a given industry generally permits some elasticity in the methods of production to be employed, so that it is possible to compare the productivity of alternative methods. From this the extra yield of a little more or less of any given agent can be computed and a demand schedule based thereon. We shall make use of this principle when we come to the problem of sharing the product of industry, which will be the theme of several succeeding chapters.

The real problem of joint demand arises when the proportions in which complementary goods are employed are fixed by technical considerations which permit no variation, so that it is impossible to separate the demand for one of the goods from that of the other. In the making of pencils, for instance, there must be a certain amount of lead and a certain amount of wood—neither more nor less. Likewise, in making an automobile tire of the first quality, considerations of strength and durability require that a certain amount of rubber and of cotton cord fabric be used in its construction. In such a case, how does the manufacturer know how much he can afford to offer for each? How can he derive, from the consumers' demand for the finished tire, separate demand-prices for the two ingredients? He cannot, in fact, make such a separation; but he does know how many tires he can sell at a given price, and there is a separate cost of producing the fabric and rubber necessary to make these tires. The normal price of the tires, therefore should be at that point where their marginal demand-price coincides with the combined optimum costs of the rubber and fabric. This leads to the general principle that, in the case of joint demand, the combined prices of the articles tend to the point where their combined costs of production coincide with their joint marginal demand-price, and their individual prices will be equal to their respective costs. This principle is also developed in diagram form in the Appendix which follows this chapter.

The demand for a good which is demanded jointly with other goods will usually be somewhat more inelastic because of that fact. Suppose $100 worth of window panes are required for a $10,000 house. A doubling of the cost of the panes would only raise the cost of building the house to $10,100. The 100 per cent increase in the price of glass makes only a one per cent increase in the total cost of the building. This is too slight to reduce the effective demand for houses very seriously; therefore, almost, if not quite, as many window panes would be sold as before. Likewise, a marked decrease in the price of the glass would not cause much more of it to be sold. But if the schedule of demand for houses increases or decreases, the schedule of demand for all the commodities demanded jointly with them (and derived from them), will be correspondingly increased or diminished (provided they are used for that purpose alone), and their prices will be affected accordingly. Also, if all the commodities of which houses are built rise or fall in cost *together,* the effective demand for houses will be influenced accordingly.

Composite Demand. — Consider cotton once more. It is desired for many different purposes: to furnish cord fabric for auto tires; yarn for sheeting, towels, clothing, and other textiles; padding for mattresses and upholstered furniture; rope for clotheslines; string for tying packages; gauze for bandages; and for various other needs. Hence the demand for it is quite complex. In cases of this kind, *where a good is demanded for two or more different uses, the demand is said to be composite.* Other illustrations can easily be found. The demands for practically all raw materials, such as iron, silver, copper, leather, coal, and wool, are composite. The same is true of the agents of production—skilled and unskilled labor, land, and saving.

Where the demand for a good is composite, its total demand schedule (and, therefore, its demand curve) will be the sum of the demand schedules for it in all the different uses to which it is put. For instance, at each price on the demand schedule for cotton, a certain quantity of it will be bought for manufacture into sheeting, a certain additional quantity to be made into toweling, a certain additional quantity for automobile tire fabric, and so on. The sum of these quantities constitutes the total effective demand at each price. This will give us a consumptive demand curve of the usual type, which can be plotted against cost of production supply curves the same as in more simple price problems. The normal price will be at that point where the total effective demand, so computed, equals the total effective supply, and in pure competition will tend to equal the optimum costs of production, as in the case of simple demand.

In the case of composite demand, because the total demand for the commodity is made up of so many separate demands, a change in any one of the component demand schedules will have only a slight effect on the price. An increase in the demand for gauze bandages will have very little effect upon the price of raw cotton, because only an infinitesimally small portion of the total demand for cotton is derived from that for bandages. On the other hand, a change in the conditions of supply for a commodity whose demand is composite may affect greatly the prices of all the products in which it is used. For instance, an increase in the cost of ginning cotton would raise the cost of manufacturing sheets, string, towels, shirts, bandages, tires, and all other cotton products, and cause their prices to increase.

There is a sense in which all demands are composite, for they are composed of the demands of all individuals who purchase the goods in question. That is, every demand schedule is the sum of the demand schedules of all the buyers (actual and potential) in the market. We could, if we chose, begin the analysis of consumers' demand with the demand schedule of a single individual, and then represent the demand schedule of the entire market as a summation of such individual schedules.[1]

Joint Supply, or Joint Costs. — Often, in the production of one commodity, others are obtained simultaneously with it. From the ginning of cotton there results, not only the cotton fiber, but also the seed, from which a valuable oil can be extracted. Copper and silver are frequently found in the same ore, so that in the refining

[1] An illustration of this has been worked out by Irving Fisher. See pages 278–281 of his *Elementary Principles of Economics* (1912). He has done the same thing for supply schedules on pages 303–305 of the same work.

of one, the other is produced at the same time. Nature has stored up in crude petroleum a variety of products, such as benzine, gasoline, kerosene, lubricating oils, and certain chemicals, many of which can be drawn off separately in one process of distillation by simply raising the temperature of the flame. In the meat-packing industry, hams, bacon, hides, blood, bone, hair, glue, fats, gut, and other useful raw materials are produced more or less together. All cases of so-called by-products fall in the same category. In these cases we have just the opposite of joint demand. Instead of several articles derived from separate sources being combined in use and therefore demanded jointly, we have several articles which are separately demanded but which are combined in production and, therefore, supplied jointly. This case is known as *joint supply*. It may be defined as *that relation where two or more products are obtained at the same time, in a single production process*. It is also called *joint costs*, because, where two or more commodities are produced together, their costs of production cannot be entirely separated. When copper and silver are found in the same ore, how can one say what part of the cost of mining the ore is the cost of producing copper and what part the cost of producing silver? When cotton-seed and cotton fiber result from one process of ginning, how are the costs of growing cotton and bringing it to the gin to be divided among these two products?

In most cases of joint or by-products, there are some costs which are associated with only one of them. For instance, in the refining of petroleum, it is possible, by the use of a "cracking process" which requires special machinery, to increase the proportion of gasoline that can be obtained from the crude oil. The extra cost of this machinery is clearly a separate one, which can be charged up to the extra gasoline thereby produced. The costs of producing cotton fiber and cotton-seed are inseparable up until the cotton is brought to the gin, but from there on they are separate. The oil must be pressed from the seed and refined, or it cannot be used. Clearly the cost of this process must be charged up to cotton-seed oil alone. If the demand-price for the oil is not sufficient to cover this cost, it will not pay to extract the oil. The seed would then be thrown away as a waste product and no problem of joint costs would arise. The entire cost of growing and ginning cotton would have to be charged up to the fiber, and only as much cotton would be grown as could be sold at a price sufficient to cover that cost. However, if the demand-price for the oil is more than sufficient to cover the cost of extracting it, it may be possible for the seed to command a price which will help to defray the expense of growing the cotton. The real problem of joint costs then arises. After the separable costs are deducted, what will be the normal relation between the joint costs of producing the two or more products and their separate demands? This case is the reverse of joint demand, and is governed by corresponding principles.

Under such circumstances, the combined prices of the products tend to equal the joint costs of their manufacture, and the price of each of the separate products will be equal to its marginal demand-price. Equilibrium is reached where the sum of the marginal demand-prices for the several products equals their joint costs of production. The nature of this equilibrium is shown diagrammatically in the Appendix at the close of this chapter.

Since the joint costs are apportioned among the joint products according to the relative demands for them, those of the products for which the demand is greatest will be made to bear the larger part of the costs, and will sell at a higher price than the others. A bale of cotton sells for a little more than a ton of cotton-seed, because the marginal demand-price for the former is greater. It cannot be said that either of them costs any more to produce than the other. Where the demand for a by-product is small, the commodity may sell for a price which covers but a very small part of the joint costs. Paraffin, a by-product of certain types of petroleum refining, is so cheap that its price only slightly exceeds the cost of filtering, casting it into cakes, and packing it. The burden of the joint costs is borne mainly by the gasoline, lubricating oils, and other valuable products.

In case the schedule of demand for any one of two or more joint products increases, its price will rise, and the prices of the other commodities produced jointly with it may be expected to fall. For instance, if the schedule of demand for cotton goods increases, the price of cotton fiber will rise, bringing profits to cotton growers. This profit will stimulate an increase in the cotton crop. With the increased output of cotton, there is an increase in the production of cotton-seed. Since there has been no change in the schedule of demand for seed, its price must fall. A decrease in the schedule of demand would have the converse effect. That is, if the demand for cotton were to fall as a result of the increased popularity of rayon, the price of cotton would decline, causing losses to producers, until less of it was grown. This would curtail the output of cotton-seed, causing its price to rise, until a new equilibrium was reached, with a lower price for cotton and a higher price for seed than that formerly prevailing. An interesting illustration of this is afforded by gasoline and kerosene, jointly produced in the refining of petroleum. Some decades ago, kerosene was in great demand for illuminating purposes, while there was little use for gasoline. At that time kerosene sold for a higher price per gallon than gasoline. With the coming of the electric light and automobile, the demand for kerosene decreased, while that for gasoline increased tremendously. As a result, the price of kerosene fell, while that of gasoline rose.

Composite Supply. — Sometimes the supply of a commodity is derived from more than one source. We have already discovered that a vegetable oil is derived from cotton-seed. This oil is useful as a food product in making salad dressings, for cooking, and in certain butter substitutes. Similar oils, equally good for these purposes, are obtained from other vegetable products, including peanuts and corn. Such a case is known as *composite supply*, which may be defined as *two or more products which are good substitutes for each other*. The term *alternative demand* is also used sometimes to denote this condition, because, where it exists, buyers have the alternative of changing from one substitute to the other. The case is the opposite of composite demand. In composite demand we have one product used for two or more purposes. In composite supply we have two or more products used for one purpose.

Perfect cases of composite supply are rare, for it is not often that one commodity is a perfect substitute for another. Usually there are slight differences which make one of them better adapted to certain uses than its competitor. In some cases, however, the differences are negligible. Beet sugar and cane sugar are so nearly the same that the average consumer cannot tell them apart, although they are produced from different sources by quite different methods. In such a case the two sources are combined into one supply schedule, made up of the several quantities of each of the two substitute products that will be offered at each of a series of corresponding prices. That is, at one price a certain quantity of beet sugar and a certain quantity of cane sugar will be produced; the sum of these constitutes the effective supply at that price, and so on for every possible price. Production of the two substitute commodities will be carried to the point where their marginal costs are the same, and the price will be that which equates the marginal demand-price with this cost.

Where commodities are approximate, but not perfect, substitutes for each other, there is not a true case of composite supply. Nevertheless, the price of each will affect that of the other, and their prices may be expected to move up and down together. Most people prefer butter to oleomargarine, yet the latter can often be used in place of the former. Hence, if the price of butter rises, some consumers are likely to switch to oleomargarine, causing its price to rise also. If the price of butter declines, consumers who have been using oleomargarine for reasons of economy will feel that they can now afford butter, and the schedule of demand for margarine will decline, causing its price to fall. So, we may usually expect the price of butter to be above that of oleomargarine by a fairly definite amount, and their two prices will move upward and downward in such a way as to maintain approximately this same differential. The presence of substitute commodities, to which consumers may turn for the relief of their pocketbooks, when the price of the commodity they have been accustomed to using goes too high, will usually make the demand more elastic than it might otherwise be.

Wherever there is more than one seller in a market, the supply is composite in a sense, for it is made up of the goods offered by each of the sellers who contributes his wares. A supply schedule is thus the sum of the individual schedules of the sellers who together compose it, just as the supply of beet and cane sugar is the sum of the supplies offered by the two groups of sugar producers.

B. The Price System

All Prices are Interrelated. — By this time it must be apparent that the relations between different prices in the economic world are rather complex. We see that the price of a good is not the result of isolated factors of demand and supply for it alone, but of a multitude of interrelated factors in which the prices of many other goods are involved. We may consider once more the case of cotton, which we have used so often for an illustration of the price-making forces.

The demand for it is derived from that of intermediate products, such as yarn and cloth, which in turn are derived from the demand for products higher up in the chain of processes, until finally we reach the demand of ultimate consumers for cotton goods. So here we have a vertical succession of interrelated prices. In addition to that, its demand is composite, for it is needed for many different purposes, such as automobile tires, upholstery fabrics, sheeting, shirts, dresses, and others too numerous to mention, as we have seen. Moreover, it is often demanded jointly with other commodities, such as rubber (in the case of tires), buttons (in the case of shirts), dyes (in the case of fabrics), to mention only a few instances. There is a further relation between its price and that of substitute products, such as linen, silk, wool, and rayon; for consumers are continually comparing the advantages of these different materials in relation to their prices, and governing their expenditures accordingly. All these relationships arise out of interlinked demands. There are similar linkages in respect to supply. Cotton is supplied jointly with cottonseed, from which are derived not only cotton-seed oil, but also cotton-seed meal (which is used in feeding cattle). Also, there is a situation resembling composite supply, in that linen, silk, wool, and rayon can be used as substitutes for cotton. Moreover, the production of cotton leads to a derived supply of the various products in which cotton is used. As a result of all these relationships, a change in the demand for any single cotton product may have an effect on the prices of all other goods in which cotton is used, as well as on the goods for which it may be substituted; and a change in the conditions of supply for cotton may have similar repercussions in the prices of all things with which cotton stands in derived, joint, or composite relationship.

The relationships among prices are not confined to such obvious cases as these. Every price is related to every other price, for the simple reason that the money incomes of consumers are limited, as are also the means of production. In other words, the interdependence of all prices goes back to the fundamental fact of scarcity, which underlies all things economic. If a man spends part of his income for one thing, he cannot spend it for another; for he cannot eat his cake and have the penny too. Each of us is, perforce, compelled to decide how to spend what money we have, and our decisions will affect the prices of all the things we buy. If we decide that we need more recreation and, therefore, spend more on golf, or theaters, or travel, than we previously did, we must curtail our purchases of clothing, or furniture, or something else. By so doing, we add to the demand for commodities of the former sort and tend to raise their prices, while we subtract from the demand for those in the second group and tend to depress their prices. Mass changes in consumption habits may shift the direction of demand so as to affect prices strongly and lead to rearrangements of whole industries, and any significant shifting of demand is pretty certain to cause far-reaching price adjustments. Some prices will be affected much more strongly than others, of course, and some remote from the scene of the disturbance may not show any appreciable change at all, just as the ripples in a pond will be very pronounced near the point where a stone strikes the water but will be too small to be noticeable on the shore a hundred yards away. The price of a bottle of ink is hardly likely to be changed because of a decline in the housewife's demand for pork chops, yet there is a remote connection even between the prices of such apparently unrelated things as ink and pork.

We can see this by considering the fact that, in the production of all commodities, land, labor, and savings are employed. These agents are limited in quantity. Therefore, if more of them is to be used in one branch of production, less must be used in another.[2] For example, in recent years, there has been a marked increase in certain branches of production, such as automobiles and chemical products (cellophane, rayon, plastics, etc.). The plants devoted to the manufacture of these goods occupy land and use savings and labor which would otherwise be employed in making other things—perhaps houses or carpets. The fact that they are used for autos and chemicals restricts the supply of agents available for other products and so keeps the prices of the latter higher than they might otherwise be. This action is reciprocal, the use of resources for houses and carpets restricting the supply of agents available for automobiles and chemicals. An adjustment has to be worked out between them, so that each industry employs as much of the available agents as is justified by the demand for its products. It is through prices that this is accomplished. Thus the prices of all the commodities concerned, and of the agents of production, are connected with each other. In fact, the principle of opportunity costs tells us that any agent of production can be used in a particular branch of industry only on condition that the price which business men in that industry can offer for it is equal to what is offered in other directions. So, whether we look at the problem from the standpoint of demand or supply, we find that prices are not isolated facts, but that they are part of an elaborate, coherent whole. It is this organic unity which justifies us in designating it as *the price system*.

When we combine this picture of interlinked prices with our previous description of the relations between market, short-period and long-period price equilibria, and with the analysis of prices under conditions of pure monopoly, pure competition, and monopolistic competition, we can appreciate the fact that prices do indeed constitute an intricate, closely knit, sensitive, ever-changing system. It is a system of such complete interdependence that a change in the price of any good necessarily has some effects on the prices of many others, and conceivably of all others.

The Guiding Function of Prices. — What is the inner significance of this network of prices? To answer this question we must go back

---

[2] At a given time (*e.g.*, during business depression), there may be unemployed resources which will permit expansion of one industry without forcing contraction upon any other, but this cannot be the case in the long run. There will come a time (*e.g.*, in prosperity) when the scarcity of resources must make itself felt in such a way that the growth of one branch of production involves encroachment upon other branches. It is also true that, in a progressive economy, technological progress is continually releasing agents of production for new uses; but if they are employed to accomplish expansion in one direction, this must be at the expense of expansion somewhere else. We cannot escape from the fact that productive agents are scarce, in relation to our wants, and therefore, that, in the long run, we can satisfy any particular want only by sacrificing some other satisfaction.

to the very basis of economic activity. In the very first chapter of this book we found that basis in the conflict between desires and scarcity. We there visualized our complex industrial system as an organization which has grown up in the effort of man to make the scarce means of production satisfy his desires more completely. However, technical efficiency in production cannot by itself fulfill the purposes of that organization. When industry is carried on by thousands of separate establishments, each specializing on one or a few products, it is necessary to coördinate the many parts into an articulated whole. Without such coördination there would be chaos. There must be direction and guidance if the different enterprises are to coöperate in producing the goods which men desire. We subsequently learned how direction and coördination are achieved within the individual business enterprise; but no business man can visualize the economic system as a whole; and in our industrial system there is no central planning body whose task it is to direct the economy in its broad outlines. What is it then, which guides the process and preserves such a measure of coördination and order as it does achieve? It is the price system.

The price system provides a mechanism for recording the collective judgment of all who participate in economic life. By spending their incomes according to their desires for this or that, consumers record their choices in demands. These demands are reflected in prices, which guide enterprisers in deciding what things to produce and how much of each. The enterprisers estimate how much consumers will pay for this product or that, and they proceed accordingly. Through them, consumers' demands become demands for materials, labor, land, and equipment, and are reflected in the prices of those things. Since those who are employed in industry are generally seeking the highest prices which they can obtain, production is thereby drawn into the channels where demand is greatest; for where demand is strong prices will be relatively high. Therefore, the farmer devotes his land to those crops for which he can get the best prices, in proportion to the land, labor, and materials he must use; the investor of savings puts them into those forms of equipment which will yield products whose price is greatest, in proportion to the amount of savings invested; and even laborers, skilled and unskilled, tend to select those occupations which offer the most wages for labor of their grade,—which means that they will be employed in those industries whose products command the highest prices, in proportion to the labor required. So, the price system constitutes the central, directing mechanism of an exchange economy. Working automatically, as it were, it records the choices and judgments of millions of persons and thousands of business men, and causes production to be directed accordingly.

The Price System Not a Perfect Guide. — At this point, a word of caution is needed. Some economists, lost in admiration of the way in which the price system spontaneously guides the economic process without the control of any central authority, have exaggerated its virtues and represented it as a perfect device for the attainment of maximum economy in industry. We have but to follow the guidance of prices, they hold, to approach the millennium of economic well-being. This is too optimistic an attitude. The price system would be a perfect guide for industry only if the following conditions could be fulfilled: (1) Demands would have to be an accurate indication of human needs; otherwise production would be misguided into wrong channels. (2) There would have to be no obstacles to the free movement of resources into the channels indicated by demands; otherwise resources would be prevented from being used most economically. (3) Enterprisers would have to be always correct in anticipating what the demands for their products would be; for if they exaggerated the demand, some resources would have been wasted through overproduction, while if some demands were underestimated, needs that should have been fulfilled would go unsatisfied. (4) The responses of production to changed conditions of demand would have to be prompt enough so that market prices would never deviate very far from normal prices; for wide departure of market from normal prices is an evidence that supply is badly adjusted to demand, and hence that production has been misdirected. (5) Finally, the price system would have to be free from interference caused by vagaries of the monetary system.

These conditions are very far from being realized in the price system as it now functions. (1) Demand does not register human needs, partly because people often spend their incomes very unwisely, causing production to be directed towards things which contribute little to their general well-being, at the expense of things which, from an ethical point of view, are far more important. Moreover, there are such inequalities of income in our present society that production is far more responsive to the wants, and even the whims, of the very rich, than it is to the most urgent needs of the very poor. (2) There is so much immobility of resources in our economy that they do not move freely into new directions as the channels of demand shift. Equipment is often so highly specialized that it cannot be easily converted from one purpose to another, and laborers trained to particular occupations have difficulty in shifting to new ones. Moreover, workers with established homes do not readily migrate from places where demand for them is slack to places where demand is greater. (3) Enterprisers' forecasts of demands are very often faulty; hence we get overdevelopment in certain branches of production, underdevelopment in others. The mistakes made are sometimes very costly, leading whole branches of industry into financial difficulties and causing idle plants and unemployed workers. (4) The response of production to changes in demand is sluggish, so that market prices frequently deviate far from normal prices, and may continue at variance over fairly long periods of time. Moreover, there are so many monopolistic elements in our economy that prices are often considerably above the normal prices of pure competition. Such prices are evidence that not enough production is going into the industries where the high prices prevail, and therefore that too much is being produced in other directions. (5) Our study of the monetary system showed that it does, in fact, interfere seriously with the functioning of the price system, thereby interfering with the rôle of prices as guides to industry.

The fact that we have poverty in the midst of plenty, idle workers and factories in the midst of want, and recurrent periods of business depression, when the whole economic process bogs down to a low level of efficiency, is sufficient evidence that the guidance of the economic process afforded by the price system under present conditions is far from perfect. Even if prices could always be kept at their normals, some of the difficulties above referred to would still prevail. Therefore, we cannot conclude that the spontaneous guidance of the economy by prices is necessarily the best that could be conceived.

The Concept of General Equilibrium. — Bearing in mind that all prices are interdependent, and that it is their function to direct and coördinate the economic process, we can conceive of a set of price relationships that would keep the entire economy in balanced adjustment. Among the conditions of such adjustment would be that all the land that was worth using would be used, that there would be no idle savings or equipment, and that every worker would be fully employed. If these conditions were not met, the adjustment would be incomplete, for, so long as any land, equipment, or labor was unemployed, it would tend to disturb the adjustment, by altering the existing price relationships. In most circumstances, a capitalist will permit his land or equipment to be used for a low price rather than not to be used at all, and a worker will accept a low wage rather than remain unemployed.[3] Therefore, incomplete employment of any

---

[3] This will not always be true. Labor may refuse to work for a wage it considers too low if it has sufficient political power to compel the government to pay unemployment relief.

agent of production tends to cause a fall in the price of that agent until it is worth someone's while to employ it. Only when all that can be productively used is employed is there no tendency for prices to fall further.

Moreover, a balanced adjustment would be one in which the productive agents would be used only to produce those things for which the demand was greatest. For instance, suppose that too much labor is employed in the manufacture of hats, in proportion to the demand for such clothing, and too little labor in the production of shoes, in view of the existing demand for them. In that case, the price of hats will be relatively low and that for shoes will be relatively high. Then labor could presumably earn more if it were withdrawn from the hat industry and put into shoe manufacturing. As less hats were produced and more shoes were made, the price of the former would rise somewhat, while that of the latter would fall, until nothing was to be gained by a further transfer. Then, and not until then, would there be balance between the two prices. Labor would then be adjusted between the two employments exactly in accordance with the demand for it. From this illustration it appears that, so long as production is not correctly adjusted to demand, price discrepancies will arise which tend to correct the difficulty. When production throughout the economic system was in perfect consonance with the demand, there would be no further tendency for prices to change, unless some new factor (such as a change in consumers' tastes, or a new invention, or a different productive technique) were introduced into the situation. Any changes of this character would necessitate some readjustment in the existing price structure. It would cause changes in the prices of the things most closely affected by it, and these changes would, in turn, cause repercussions elsewhere, until all prices were in complete adjustment to the changed conditions. So we see that there is a tendency for prices to coördinate all parts of the economic process, and to correct unbalance when it appears.

The set of price relationships which would provide such a coördination is frequently referred to in economic literature as a condition of *general equilibrium*. The term is derived from analogy with the equilibrium of forces in physics. We are all familiar with the fact that, when a number of different containers of varying sizes and shapes are connected with each other by several pipes, if we pour water into one of them, it will flow into the others until it stands at an equal height in all (see Figure 46). At this point it is said to be in equilibrium. Now, if water is again poured into any one or more of the containers, the equilibrium will be disturbed—the level will be higher in the vessels into which the water is first poured. If there are no obstructions in the connecting pipes, however, the water will again distribute itself throughout the containers until it reaches a new position of equilibrium. Such is the action of gravity.

Something similar to this takes place in the distribution of resources in our economy; but, in this case, disturbances are so frequent and interfering obstacles so strong, that perfect equilibrium is never attained, and the system is always in maladjustment. It is a little bit like the atmosphere, in which an area of high pressure tends to flow toward one of low pressure so as to equalize both, but the irregularities of the earth's surface, the changes in its temperature, and the constant motion of the earth itself, are such that the

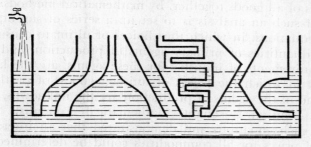

Figure 46. An Illustration of Equilibrium.

pressure here and there is always being disturbed, so that we have winds and storms, which are evidences of continuing efforts to effect an equilibrium. In like manner, there are in the economic process continual changes in prices, in response to the changed conditions of demand and supply; but always there is some tendency for the changes to be in the direction which will promote a more balanced adjustment. Only if we had an economic world in which no disturbing changes took place, or in which there was such perfect flexibility that adjustments to change could be made instantaneously throughout the system, would there be a true equilibrium. Economic theorists have sometimes conceived of such an unchanging or frictionless world, as a pure abstraction. They call it *the stationary state* or *the static state*. Such a conception is useful for theorizing about the ultimate tendencies of prices, but we must not make the mistake of assuming that any such perfect balance characterizes the world we live in. There is a tendency to it, but it is a tendency very much interfered with by counteracting influences.

The disturbing factors are sometimes more obvious than the balancing tendencies. A changing world like ours is continually upsetting established relationships. Every change in consuming habits, in incomes, in productive technique, in institutions, in governmental policies, or in population, is likely to have repercussions in the price system. The opening up of new frontiers, the migration of peoples from one part of the world to another, military conflicts, all kinds of social upheaval,—these react upon economic institutions and alter the price structure. What we have is a set of prices always moving toward mutual adjustments which tend to bring the whole economic system into equilibrium, but always being disturbed so that the adjustments can never be carried out to their final conclusion—a continuous effort at adaptation to continually changing circumstances.

The Equations of General Equilibrium. — It is possible to depict the general equilibrium of prices, and the forces which determine the prices of all goods together, by mathematical methods. The procedure of such an analysis is to set up a series of simultaneous algebraic equations, in which the choices of ultimate consumers, the existing quantities of primary agents of production, and the technical requirements of industry for these agents, are the known factors, and in which the prices of finished goods, of partly finished goods, and of the agents of production are the unknowns, for whose values a solution is sought. Mathematical economists have constructed such equations and demonstrated that an interdependent system of prices for all commodities could be determined theoretically by such means. Needless to say, the analysis is very abstract, and although it gives one a very illuminating conception of the interdependence of all prices, it is more appropriate for an advanced treatise than for an introductory text. We shall, therefore, not go into it.

Is the Particular Price Approach Theoretically Sound? — Recognition of the interdependence of prices raises some question about the validity of the customary approach to the problems of price determination. If the price of a commodity depends, not on an isolated demand and supply schedule for it alone, but on the demand and supply schedules of all other commodities as well, how can we maintain that its price is a resultant of *its* demand and supply schedules, as we have done for the most part in our analysis? Critics have, indeed, urged this objection against the method we have employed. It can be met in two ways.

In the first place, if we start with the supposition that a general equilibrium does exist, we may reasonably proceed to inquire what would be the effect, on any one price in that system, of a change in the conditions of demand or supply for the particular good to which it is attached, recognizing that other prices will also be changed, but not pushing the analysis into those changes because they are not the object of our immediate concern. For instance, we

may want to know what would be the effects of an unusual boll
weevil plague upon the price of cotton, assuming that this is the
only disturbing factor in the whole system of prices for the time
being. We would then have a new supply schedule for cotton, which
we may assume to be the schedule that would result in a new condition of general equilibrium in which the prices of all other commodities are likewise being adjusted to the change in the conditions
of cotton production. Similarly, we could trace the effects on the
price of cotton of a change in the demand for cotton products. Such
an analysis does not make the untenable assumption that the price
of cotton is determined independently of other prices; it merely
abstracts from the picture the demand and supply schedules of cotton in two possible positions of general equilibrium (namely, before
and after the change), as being the object of our immediate interest,
just as a biologist may remove the heart of a frog from its body for
separate study of its activity, although he understands well that its
functioning in the body depends upon the whole physiology of the
animal.

In the second place, there is some ground for believing that a
change in the price of one commodity will not affect *all* other prices
to an appreciable degree. The ravages of the boll weevil, by making
cotton scarce, would raise its price, and this would materially affect
the prices of those commodities closely associated with cotton in
such relations as those of joint or composite supply and joint or
composite demand, but the general effects of these ravages on other
prices would be diffused over so great a number of commodities that
the influence on any one of them would be negligible. We could,
therefore, safely ignore these more remote effects.

The individual price approach is the most useful one for practical
purposes. Most price problems have to do with the prices of particular commodities. Such questions arise as, what is a "fair" price
for electricity, or for aluminum, or for wheat, as the case may be.
To answer such questions, and to guide price-regulating authorities
in making decisions about them, we need to analyze the conditions
of demand and supply for the particular commodity concerned. This
does not mean that price problems may not sometimes arise in which
some attention needs to be paid to the general interdependence of
prices. Failure to recognize this interdependence may lead to mistakes.
Usually, however, analysis of the conditions of demand and supply
for a single commodity, and for those commodities whose prices are
most closely related to it, will suffice for practical problems.

The Influence of Money on Individual Prices. — We began our
analysis of price determination with such simple assumptions as the

existence of pure monopoly or pure competition, the maintenance of a single price throughout the market, the separation of the influences affecting the prices of different commodities, the existence of a stable general level of prices. One by one, we have had to relax these abstract assumptions in order to bring our picture of the price-making process into closer conformity with reality. However, we have continued to adhere to the assumption that the price level itself is unchanging. We did this in order to distinguish those influences on prices which arise out of the conditions of demand and supply for particular commodities from those influences which are to be attributed to money; yet we know, from the discussion in an earlier chapter, that monetary factors do affect the prices of goods. Therefore, we must now inquire how changes in the monetary aspects of our economy affect the price relationships of different commodities and services.

If the effects of a change in the circulation of money were diffused instantly and evenly throughout the economic system, all prices would move upwards and downwards together in exactly the same proportion, and there would be no effect on the relative prices (that is, on the values) of different goods. If the prices of cotton, iron, petroleum, hats, shoes, beefsteaks, etc., and of labor, land, and savings, all rose or fell in exactly the same degree, their values would remain exactly as they were, and the change in the level of prices would be of no consequence. It would be almost the same as if we woke up some morning to find the world and everything in it, including ourselves, exactly twice as large or half as large as it had been before. The change would be of no consequence; indeed, it is doubtful if we would be aware that it had even occurred—except, perhaps, by comparison with heavenly bodies outside the world.

But changes in the level of prices do not occur in so uniform a manner. If the flow of money is increasing or decreasing, the incidence of this change falls first upon those points in the system of prices which lie closest to the source of the change, and the full effects are transmitted slowly, through a succession of transactions, to other parts of the system, until they become generally diffused. If banks expand their loans, the new credit is put first at the disposal of business men who borrow for purposes of business expansion. Prices will rise first for those commodities which these business men buy. This will affect the prices of materials used in the production of those commodities, and the wages of labor and the rewards of other agents employed therein. The rise in the prices of materials, labor, etc., will lead to a further rise somewhere else, and so on in endless succession, until all prices in the system eventually feel the effects. Hence, during the transition period between the first impact of the change in the flow of money and its ultimate diffusion throughout the system, particular prices will rise or fall in relation to the prices of other goods, depending on the circumstances of the time and place. In the long run, changes of this character tend to cancel out as all prices rise or fall in response to the change in the flow of money; so that, in the absence of further disturbance, the long-run effects of such monetary changes on relative prices (that is, on values) would be small. However, in a dynamic world where money reserves fluctuate, and where expansion and contraction of credit are always going on, such changes, with their resultant effects on particular prices, are never absent. Therefore, our general conclusion about individual prices is that they are the result of the demand and supply influences analyzed in this and the preceding three chapters, as modified by the incidence of changes in the circulation of money.

SUMMARY

The prices of certain groups of commodities are more or less closely connected through derived, joint, or composite relationships. Where demand is derived (that is, removed one stage or more in production from final sale to consumers), the demand schedule will lie below the schedule of consumers' demand by the amount of the intervening costs. Where two or more goods are demanded jointly, normal equilibrium is at the point where the sum of their separate optimum costs is equal to their joint marginal demand-price, and the demand for any one of them is likely to be inelastic. Where a good is demanded by several groups of users for different purposes, the demand is said to be composite, in which case the total demand schedule consists of the sum of the separate effective demands at each of the possible prices. Where two or more goods are produced in one process, there is a condition of joint supply or joint costs, in which case price tends to an equilibrium where the sum of the marginal demand-prices for the separate products equals their joint optimum cost of production. In this case, an increase (or decrease) in the schedule of demand for one of the products will lower (or raise) the price of the other. Where two or more different commodities are perfect substitutes for each other, supply is said to be composite, and their prices will be the same. Where the substitutes are imperfect, the prices may differ, but will move upward and downward together.

The prices of all goods are so interrelated that they constitute a generally interdependent system, tending towards an equilibrium where all would be in balance. This can be shown by mathematical equations. Notwithstanding this interdependence, analysis of particular prices by individual demand and supply schedules is tenable and useful. Owing to the uneven incidence of its effects, changes in the circulation of money alter individual price relationships. The function of the price system is to guide and coördinate the economic process, tending towards a position of balanced adjustment. However, this does not mean that the guidance is ethically ideal.

REFERENCES AND SUGGESTIONS FOR FURTHER READING

Alfred Marshall analyzes the problems of derived, joint, and composite demand and supply with his usual depth of understanding in Book V, Chapter VI, of his *Principles of Economics* (5th edition, 1907, or later editions). There is also an illuminating discussion of mutually related prices in Chapter XVIII of Irving Fisher's *Elementary Principles of Economics* (1912). For a more detailed treatment of composite demand and joint supply than that here attempted, see my article entitled *Composite Demand and Joint Supply in Relation to Public Utility Rates* in pp. 40–62 of *The Quarterly Journal of Economics* for November, 1929.

A clear presentation of the general equilibrium theory of prices is to be found in Chapter IV of Gustav Cassel's *The Theory of Social Economy* (English translation, 1923). See also the equations in Berthil Ohlin's *Interregional and International Trade* (1933), Appendix I. Illuminating discussions of the functions of the price system are to be found in Cassel's work, and also scattered through H. D. Henderson's pleasant little book, *Supply and Demand* (1922) and Edwin Cannan's *Wealth* (London, 1914), to all three of which I am indebted for suggestive ideas.

Appendix to Chapter XVI

DIAGRAMMATIC ANALYSIS OF JOINT DEMAND, DERIVED DEMAND, AND JOINT SUPPLY

Joint Demand. — The problem of price determination where two or more commodities are demanded jointly can be solved by means of demand and supply curves of the usual type. Let us take for illustration the case of eye-glasses, the demand for which gives rise to a joint demand for frames and lenses. What we want to know is, how can we set the single demand for glasses against the two different supply (cost) curves for frames and lenses in such a way as to find separate equilibrium prices for each of the latter commodities? This case is represented in Figure 47. In Part A of this drawing, let the curve s_f repre-

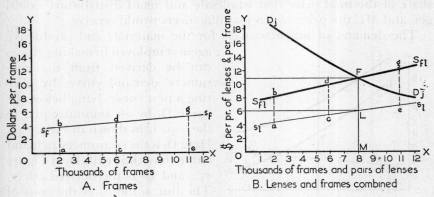

Figure 47. Joint Demand.

sent the optimum costs of manufacturing the frames. Let s_l, in Part B, represent the costs of producing the lenses. Since two lenses are used with each frame, the unit quantities shown on the base line OX in this case indicate *pairs* of lenses, and the prices shown are per pair, not per single lens.

We must now combine these curves in order to ascertain the combined costs of the two products in the finished glasses. We do this by superimposing the curve s_f upon the curve s_l in Part B, in such a way that the former lies above the latter by an amount exactly equal to its distance from the base line OX in Part A, so that s_l becomes the base line on which s_f is plotted. If this is done correctly, the distances ab, cd, and eg in Part B will be exactly the same as the corresponding distances in Part A. S_{f1} is then the combined cost (and supply) curve for the two constituents of the glasses. Now let D_j be the joint demand for the two products in the finished glasses. It intersects the supply curve at F. Therefore, at the price MF ($11), demand and supply are in equilibrium. The price for lenses should then be ML ($6) per pair (or $3 a piece), and for the frames, LF ($5).

Derived Demand. — The pricing problem presented by derived demand is really the same as that of joint demand, for it is simply a case of setting the demand curve for a finished product against the separate supply curves for the materials or agents of production that go into it at successive stages. The same drawing as above can be used to explain this problem, by changing the things for which the curves stand. For instance, let s_l now represent the cost of manufacturing the glasses, and s_f the cost of their wholesale and retail distribution. D_j would then be the consumers' demand for glasses at retail, and S_{f1} the total cost of supplying them to consumers. FL would represent the share of the total price that wholesale and retail distributors would get, and ML the price which manufacturers would receive.

The demand of manufacturers for the materials and productive agents employed in making glasses can be derived from the consumers' demand curve, by plotting a new curve, lying below the curve D_j by an amount equal to the costs s_f, as shown in Figure 48. Here D_j is the consumers' demand curve (identical with D_j in Figure 47), and D_f is the derived curve. The line s_f indicates the costs of distribution which intervene between factory and consumer. The

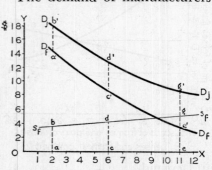

Figure 48. Derived Demand.

distances $a'b'$, $c'd'$, and $e'g'$ are equal to the distances ab, cd, and eg, respectively. The significance of this is, that manufacturers can offer, for the materials and services they use, whatever ultimate consumers will pay for the final product, less the costs which are incurred in stages which succeed the stage of manufacturing. The same principle will hold for any stage of production—the derived demand at that stage is the difference between consumers' demand and the costs that must be met at all subsequent stages.

Joint Costs, or Joint Supply. — The equilibrium price situation for a case of joint costs is shown in Figure 49, which is based on principles very similar to Figure 47. The case is supposed to be that of cotton-seed. C_j represents the optimum cost of producing the two commodities jointly. We have separate demand schedules for the two products, indicated by d_f (for the fiber) and d_s (for the seed). The combined demand schedules for the two products can be shown by super-

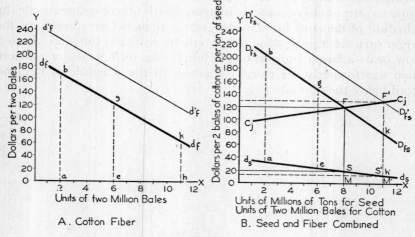

Figure 49. Joint Costs, or Joint Supply.

imposing d_f on d_s, using the latter as its base line, giving us the combined demand curve D_{fs}, in Part B of the drawing. The construction of this last curve is such that any distance between it and d_s, such as *ab*, *eg*, or *hk*, is exactly equal to the corresponding distances between d_f and the line OX in Part A. As in the case of joint demand, a unit of distance along the base line OX represents different quantities with respect to the several curves plotted against it. Since, for every two bales of cotton produced, there is obtained about one ton of cotton-seed, each unit space for the line OX indicates two bales of cotton (or multiples of two), and one ton of seed (or multiples of one); and the prices shown, therefore, are the prices per two bales in the first case and per ton in the second. Equilibrium is reached when the quantity OM of cotton and cotton-seed, respectively, is produced; for at that point their respective effective demands are equal to their effective supplies. The price of the seed will, therefore, be MS (or $20) per ton, and the price of the cotton will be SF (or $100) per two bales ($50 per bale). Observe that the costs are divided between the two products in proportion to their marginal demand-prices.

Now suppose the schedule of demand for cotton to increase to the position d'_f (in Part A), the schedule of demand for the seed (d_s in Part B) remaining unchanged. Superimposing the new curve on d_s, as before, we get the curve D'_{ts} (in Part B). A new position of equilibrium is reached where the output is OM'. The increased demand for cotton has caused an increase in the amount of cotton produced. The price of cotton has risen to S'F' (about \$110, or \$55 per bale) which is higher than before. But the price of seed has fallen to M'S' (\$17), because its output has necessarily increased with that of cotton, while the schedule of demand for it is no greater than before; therefore, the larger quantity can be disposed of only by reducing the price. Cotton now bears a larger portion of the joint costs, seed a smaller portion, than was formerly the case. A decrease in the schedule of demand would have the opposite effects.

Chapter XVII

THE MECHANISM OF INTERNATIONAL TRADE

A. FOREIGN EXCHANGE

The Growth of International Trade. — In the discussion of money and prices in the past nine chapters, we were concerned, for the most part, with exchange transactions within a single country, throughout which there was tacitly assumed to prevail a uniform monetary system and a fairly homogeneous price structure. If we are to have a complete picture of economic life in the modern world, we must now supplement this discussion by an analysis of the complications which arise when there is trade between nations with different monetary systems and different price structures.

These problems are of increasing importance because of the growth of international commerce. In the simple economic conditions which prevailed two centuries or more ago, trade was primarily local. That is, buying and selling took place within a small area; goods were consumed near where they were produced. They were not often shipped over very great distances, and seldom crossed national boundary lines. Some trade with the Orient, from which spices, silks, and other luxuries were imported to Europe, was carried on; and other merchandise found its way into international commerce; but the vast foreign trade of today is a comparatively recent development. Efficient means of inland and ocean transportation and communication have extended the paths of industry across seas and continents to the furthest ends of the earth. Nowadays we are so accustomed to selling cereals, meats, steel rails, machinery, and various other goods in England, France, Europe, Asia, or South America, and consuming daily the products of far-distant lands to the north, south, east, or west, that we scarcely give the matter a moment's thought. Yet this great volume of international trade involves a whole network of institutions and facilities of sufficient complexity to require considerable study in order to understand them. The theory and technique of international trade, in fact, constitute a branch of economics which has become a distinct field for specialists, who devote themselves exclusively to its study.

Bills of Exchange. — We may begin our discussion of this subject by considering a simple foreign trade transaction. Let us suppose that an exporter in New York, whom we shall call *A,* has sold cotton to the value of £1,000 to an English importer, whom we may call *B. A* must collect payment for his goods, and presumably he wants it in dollars, rather than in pounds; for he will want to spend it in this country for goods whose sellers will not accept English currency. How is this to be managed? How can a sum of foreign money, payable on the other side of the Atlantic, be converted into United States dollars, available for purchases here?

The usual procedure in a case of this kind is for *A* to draw an order against *B* for £1,000, calling upon him to pay that sum upon presentation, or at the expiration of a certain period, such as thirty or sixty days. This is a foreign *bill of exchange,* which is simply a negotiable draft, drawn by a creditor upon someone in a foreign country who owes him money. There are several forms of such bills, and they may arise in a number of different ways. They may be drawn by exporters of commodities, by sellers of securities in foreign markets, by bankers, or by any other persons who have money owing to them from abroad. In our present example, the draft is called a *commercial bill,* because it is drawn by a person whose claim arises out of a sale of goods. If it were drawn by a banker, against funds on deposit to his credit abroad, it would be a *banker's bill.* We shall presently consider a case in which a banker's bill is used; but for the moment, let us follow *A's* commercial bill somewhat further.

. How is *A* to obtain his money? It is conceivable that he could send his bill to an agent in London, collect it from *B* in English pound notes, present the notes to the British government for redemption in gold, bring the gold to the United States, and surrender it to the American government in exchange for an equivalent number of United States dollars. This would always be possible where a genuine gold standard prevailed; it would sometimes be possible under a managed gold standard, for some governments will redeem their currencies in gold to enable their debtors to meet foreign payments, when they will not do it for other purposes. But in the absence of any kind of gold standard, it would not be possible to get gold for British pounds at all; and, anyway, this is a somewhat unsatisfactory procedure, because of the expense involved. *A* would have to wait for the bill to be mailed to England, then for the gold to be shipped to this country, while he would have to pay freight and insurance charges on the shipment, besides losing interest on his money during the period of transit, plus a small loss of gold from abrasion. There is usually a better way by which most of this expense can be avoided.

Creditors, with payments to collect from abroad, are not the only persons engaged in international trade. There are also debtors, who have payments to make to foreign countries, for one reason or another. There are also foreign exchange brokers, whose business it is to bring these two parties together, collecting a small fee for the service. Through such a broker, A can probably find someone to buy his bill. There may be, for instance, an importer, $C,$ who has bought English cutlery to the value of £1,000. This sum he must pay to the Englishman from whom he purchased it, and whom we shall call D.

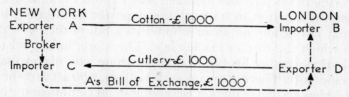

Figure 50. A Simple Foreign Exchange Transaction.

A's draft is an order for the amount C needs, and is payable in England, where C wishes to send the money. C, therefore, buys the bill from $A,$ paying him its equivalent worth in dollars. C sends it to his creditor, D. D collects payment on it from B, against whom it was drawn, and all the transactions are closed. A receives the money for his cotton when he sells his bill of exchange to $C;$ D receives payment for his cutlery when he collects the amount of the draft from B. Both debts are paid, and it is unnecessary to ship any gold across the Atlantic. The bills of exchange act as a kind of international currency, clearing payments between the two nations. The process is illustrated graphically in Figure 50.

In the diagram the movement of merchandise is indicated by the solid lines, the movement of the bill of exchange by the dotted lines, the direction of the movements being shown by the arrows. It will be observed that, in effect, there has been an exchange of cotton for cutlery, the one paying for the other. The bill of exchange is the medium by which this exchange was effected, making money unnecessary to the process. The diagram shows these facts very clearly.

The transaction described is a typical one. In the large markets of the world there are hundreds of persons who have debts to pay or credits to collect in foreign lands. Whether these debts and credits have arisen out of sales of merchandise, investments in securities, the carrying and insuring of goods, or in other ways, is unimportant. They are all handled by the same mechanism. The creditors have bills of exchange which they sell for domestic currency, thereby obtaining payment; the debtors buy the bills of exchange, which they send to the countries upon which they are drawn, thereby paying their debts. Thus the nations of the world carry on a vast interchange of commodities and services, these being made to offset each other through the use of bills of exchange, somewhat like the clearing of checks in domestic banking.

The Rôle of Dealers in Foreign Exchange. — We have seen that our exporter established contact with the importer, who bought his bill of exchange through the services of a broker, whose business it was to bring the two parties together. The exporter does not have the time nor the facilities to hunt up the importer for himself; besides, there may not be any importer who wants a bill of the exact denomination which the former has for sale. Therefore, he is glad to turn the task of marketing his bill over to someone who makes that business his specialty. There are many such brokers, who act as go-betweens in the foreign exchange market, receiving small commissions for their services. There are also bankers and other dealers, who buy and sell bills of exchange outright, on their own account. These dealers have business relations with correspondent banks in foreign countries, with whom they carry deposits. The deposits are established by buying bills of exchange and remitting them to the correspondents; the latter collect the sums due from the drawees, and hold them at the disposal of the dealers. The dealers or bankers can then draw new bills (the *bankers' bills* mentioned above) against these deposits, and sell them to buyers of exchange in whatever sums the latter may need. The dealer makes a profit by buying the bills for a slightly lower price than that at which he sells them.

Figure 51 illustrates graphically a foreign exchange transaction of this kind. Again we have an exporter, *A*, who sells cotton in London. In this case, instead of selling his draft directly to the importer, he sells it to a banker who deals in foreign exchange. The banker pays him slightly less than £1,000 for it, and *A* is willing to accept this, for the accommodation. The bank now transmits the bill to its correspondent bank in London, which collects it from the English importer, *B*, against whom it was drawn. In this way, the New York banker, by the purchase of many foreign bills, builds up a deposit in the London bank, against which he can draw bankers' bills of his own making. Now, just to vary the illustration, let us suppose that *E* is a well-to-do American, who wishes to spend some time traveling in England, and that he expects to spend £1,000 during his stay there. He goes to the New York banker, who draws a bill (or letter of credit) against his London correspondent, and sells it to *E*. *E* now has a means of paying for his expenses in England. He presents his draft to the London bank, and secures British money with which to meet his hotel bills, railway fares, and so on. The effect is the same as in our original illustration, only this time American cotton has been exchanged for English travel facilities, instead of cutlery. As before, the two transactions are set off against each other by means of bills of exchange. The banker has entered into and facilitated the process, but has not changed its essential nature.

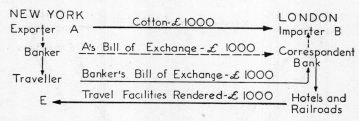

Figure 51. The Use of Banker's Bills in Foreign Exchange.

Triangular Exchange. — In these first illustrations, only two countries have been involved—England and the United States. It was assumed that an American exporter who had a bill of exchange on London could find an American importer of English goods (or some other person needing to transmit payments to England) to buy his draft. However, this may not always be the case, for it often happens that the trade between two nations is not evenly balanced. For instance, the United States commonly sells more goods to England than it buys from that country. In this case there are not enough persons here having remittances to make to English creditors to purchase all the London exchange offered for sale.

The mechanism of foreign exchange has adapted itself to this situation. While we may sell more to England than we buy from her, there may be another country which sells to us more than we sell to it, and which at the same time buys more from England than it sells to her. Suppose, for instance, that we buy a great deal of coffee from Brazil, but sell her few goods in exchange, and that Brazil buys great quantities of manufactured products from England, but sends back insufficient goods to make payment. There is then a balance of payments due the United States from England which cannot be directly offset by corresponding payments due in the other direction, a similar balance of payments due Brazil from the United States, and a similar balance of payments due England from Brazil. In such a situation, the seller of London exchange, unable to find purchasers for his bills who must make payments directly to England, can sell them to persons who owe creditors in Brazil. A bill of exchange on London or New York is good the world over, and freely acceptable in settlement of debts. The merchant in Brazil who sold coffee to an American importer will gladly accept a draft on London in payment thereof. This draft he can sell to a Brazilian importer who owes money to England. The latter can send it to his London creditor, who will present it to the person upon whom it was drawn, and receive payment of the amount represented by it. Thus, there is effected a three-cornered offsetting

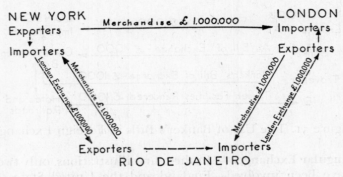

Figure 52. Triangular Exchange.

of debts by which the mutual interchange of goods between three nations is accomplished without the shipment of specie. This procedure is known as *triangular exchange*.

The process can be illustrated by a diagram (Figure 52) similar to that which we have already employed. Let us make the extreme supposition that merchants in the United States sell annually to England one million pounds' worth of merchandise, but buy nothing from that country in return; that Englishmen sell goods of equal amount to Brazilians; and that Brazilians sell goods of equal amount to persons in the United States. Then the American exporters, by drawing upon their London debtors, can provide exchange for the settlement of all the payments involved in these transactions, without the necessity of resorting to the use of gold or silver.

Again our illustration oversimplifies the process. In actual exchange operations, there would usually be middlemen acting between the exporters and importers in each country, transmitting to their London correspondents the exchange they buy from the exporters, and selling to the importers their own bills, drawn against the London deposits so created. The essence of all this is that the United States receives, in exchange for the goods it sells to England, other goods obtained from Brazil; and Brazil receives, in exchange for the goods it sends to us, merchandise imported from England. Thus there is a mutual interchange of products; behind the surface phenomena of drafts and financial negotiations is the international exchange of goods for goods.

Prior to the first World War, London was by common consent the world's clearing house. London exchange was the international currency by which the mutual obligations of the nations, in their commerce with each other, were offset. In recent years, New York exchange has assumed a similar function, though London is still important, partly because there is there (in times of peace) an open market where gold is bought and sold like any other commodity.

Rates of Exchange Under the Gold Standard. — A bill of exchange drawn upon a debtor in a foreign country is an order for the payment of a certain sum in the money of that country. Now, although the genuine (automatic) gold standard has been generally abandoned (or at least suspended) throughout the world, it still remains true that the standard monetary unit of many countries is defined in terms of gold; and, in some of these countries (for instance, the United States), money will still be redeemed in gold for the purpose of settling balances abroad. Therefore, a bill of exchange represents nominally— and sometimes actually—a claim to a definite amount of the yellow metal. This affords a basis for calculating the nominal equivalent of one nation's money in terms of another's. For example, in 1934 a draft for 10,000 guilders on Amsterdam was nominally an order for the payment in Holland of 93,242.2 grains of gold, for a guilder contained one ten-thousandth of that amount of the precious metal. This was equal in weight to 6,806 United States gold dollars; so that, if 10,000 guilders were converted into gold, then brought to this country and surrendered to our government for paper money, 6,806 dollars could be obtained for it. A French gold franc in the same year contained as much gold as .066 of a dollar; therefore, a draft on Paris for 1,000 francs represented the equivalent of 66 dollars. The equivalent gold content of the standard money of one country in terms of that of another fixes what is known as the *mint par value* of the two moneys. When a Dutch guilder contains .68 as much fine gold as a United States gold dollar, the par value of the guilder is 68 cents. The par value of the money of any two gold standard countries can be found in the same way, by comparing the pure-gold content of their standard coins.

Just because a draft on Amsterdam for 10,000 guilders is an order for the payment of the equivalent of $6,806 in American gold coin, however, it does not follow that the holder of such a draft could sell it for that sum. He might have to sell it for less; he might be able to get more. The price at which foreign bills of exchange can be bought and sold in the markets which deal in them is known as *the rate of exchange*. When bills of exchange on a certain country are selling for more than par, that country's exchange is said to be at a *premium;* when they are selling for less than par, exchange is said to be at a *discount.* Due to the close watch kept by dealers in foreign exchange upon the market, the rate of exchange between two countries will be in close correspondence in the markets of each of them. When Dutch exchange sells in New York at a premium, New York exchange will sell at a corresponding discount in Amsterdam; when Dutch exchange is selling at a discount in New York, dollar exchange will be at a premium in Holland.

The rate of exchange depends upon the relative demand for and supply of bills. We have seen that, out of the numerous transactions involved in international trade, there are always some individuals who have payments to collect from foreign countries. These have foreign exchange to sell. There are others who have payments to make to foreign countries. They wish to buy foreign exchange. From these two sources there arises a supply of and a demand for foreign bills. At any one time, however, the amount supplied and the amount demanded may not be equal. Let us suppose that more bills are offered for sale than buyers are in need of. To import the excess in gold would involve costs due to: (1) Charges for freight and insurance, (2) loss of interest on the money while in transit, (3) loss from abrasion of the soft metal in handling, and (4) brassage or other fees at either end for exchanging money for gold or vice versa. To avoid these costs, the holder of a bill will be willing to sell it for a little less than par. The low rate stimulates the sale of the bills to dealers who buy them in the hope that the situation will change so as to cause a rise in their value. If, on the other hand, the demand for bills exceeds the supply of them, buyers will be willing to pay a little more than par, rather than go to the expense of shipping specie to their creditors. Foreign exchange will then rise to a premium. In this way the price of exchange fluctuates now above, and now below par, according to circumstances.

The Gold-Shipping Points. — So long as any excess of demand for or supply of bills of exchange is only temporary, the premium or discount on foreign exchange will be small, and will tend soon to return to par. If, however, the condition is permanent, the premium will rise so high, or the discount fall so low, that it is cheaper to ship specie out of or into the country than to pay more or accept less for the drafts, as the case may be. If an exporter has to sell his bill of exchange at a price so low that he loses more than the cost of importing the gold which it can command abroad, he will ordinarily choose the latter course. The cost of importing gold, therefore, marks the point below which the discount on foreign exchange cannot fall, so long as the gold standard is adhered to. This point is known as the *gold-importing point*. When a nation's credits abroad are not offset even by the processes of triangular exchange, foreign bills will fall to this price, and gold will begin to flow in. Similarly, if the premium on foreign exchange rises so high that it equals the cost of exporting the gold necessary to settle American debts abroad, the gold will flow out, and exchange will rise no further. This is called the *gold-exporting point*. The two points are known collectively as the *gold-shipping points*, or simply the *gold points*. It will be noted that they are determined by the cost of shipping gold, and they mark the limits beyond which the premium or discount of exchange cannot go, so long as both countries are on a gold standard. This cost is small. It costs less than a cent to ship a dollar's worth of gold across the Atlantic. Hence, fluctuations in exchange rates between gold standard countries are normally slight.

Exchange Rates Under the Silver Standard. — All that has been said about rates of exchange between two countries, both of which have a gold standard, will apply with equal force to two countries which have a silver standard. The par of exchange between two such countries will be determined by the relative amounts of pure silver in their standard monetary units, and market rates of exchange will fluctuate about this par within the limits of *the silver-shipping points,* which will be determined by the cost of shipping silver, in the manner explained for gold.

Between two countries, one of which has a gold money standard, the other a silver standard, somewhat different principles apply. In this case the rate of exchange depends largely on the relative values of gold and silver. A bill of exchange on the silver standard country is worth to the holder (in the gold standard country) only what he can obtain in gold for the silver which it represents. This might be called the par of exchange, but it is not a stable ratio, for the price of bills in this case will fluctuate directly with the price of silver. If silver goes up in the metal market, the rate of exchange on the silver standard will rise; if silver goes down, the rate of exchange will fall. The converse will be the case with exchange upon the gold standard country, offered for sale in the country with the silver standard. In addition to the effects of the changing price of silver, exchange rates in these cases will be subject to all the other influences which ordinarily affect the demand and supply of foreign drafts.

Exchange Rates Under Nominal Money Standards. Purchasing Power Parity. — The foregoing principles were formerly of world-wide application, for, until recently, gold standard monetary systems were effective almost everywhere, except for a few countries in the Orient and Latin-America, whose currencies were based upon silver. However, with the evolution of monetary systems away from commodity standards towards nominal standards, the influence of gold and silver upon rates of foreign exchange is waning.

We can get at the influences which determine rates of exchange under nominal monetary standards by considering the case of two countries, each of which is assumed to have a paper standard, but in which the monetary system is so managed as to maintain reasonable stability of the price level, avoiding any inflation of the currency. Let us suppose that these two countries are the United States and England, having, as their standard monetary units, a paper dollar and a paper pound, respectively, both units being entirely unrelated to any metallic base. Under these conditions, a bill of exchange on London would represent a claim to paper pounds which would not be generally accepted in payment for goods outside of England. Therefore, their only value to a foreign holder would be derived from the goods which they might purchase in Great Britain. The value in American money of the English goods it would buy would then afford a rough basis on which to compute the value of the bill itself. If, for instance, £1,000 would buy goods in England which would be worth $3,000 in this country, £1 ought to be worth $3.00, less the cost of transporting the goods. Similarly, the value in London of a bill of exchange on New York ought to be worth approximately as much as the value, in England, of the goods which the American dollar would buy in this country. This is the reciprocal of the previous case (that is, $1.00 = £⅓); for if the goods purchaseable with £1 in England will bring $3.00 here, the goods purchasable with $1.00 in the United States will bring only £⅓ in England (less transportation costs in both cases). From this it would appear that the normal value of the two moneys in terms of each other would be determined by the ratio between the average prices in the two countries of those commodities which enter into international trade. This point will be further explained.

We learned in a previous chapter that there is a general level of prices which can be measured by means of index numbers. A similar index can be constructed in each country to measure the average prices in it of international goods—that is, of those goods which enter into international trade. According to the reasoning just developed, the value of one paper monetary unit in terms of another would normally be equal to the ratio between these two indexes. In other words, if the average price of a representative group of international goods in the United States, measured in dollars, is three times as high as the index of international commodity prices in England, measured in pounds, the normal rate of exchange between the two countries should be £1 = $3.00. A similar calculation would give the normal ratio between the currencies of any other two countries with nominal monetary standards. This norm is usually called the *purchasing power par* of exchange.

Just as market rates of exchange under gold standard conditions fluctuate about their gold pars, so will market rates under nominal standards fluctuate about their purchasing power pars. For instance, increases in demand for London exchange, from any cause (*e.g.*, from increasing imports), will tend to pull the rate up; decreases in demand (*e.g.*, from declining imports) to pull it down. This case differs from the case of specie standards in that there are no gold- or silver-shipping points to limit the extent of the fluctuations; therefore, deviations from purchasing power par may be quite wide. We shall learn presently, however, that such deviations tend to be corrected in time, for they bring reactions in the international movement of goods which pull the rates back toward their normals.

If the paper monetary system in one or both countries is not well managed, so that inflation is going on, a new and very uncertain factor is introduced into the exchange market. A bill of exchange on a country which is inflating its currency is a claim of somewhat dubious nature, for it is one which is likely to depreciate considerably in value before it can be collected and exchanged for foreign merchandise. The prospective purchaser of such a bill has no way of knowing how much it will depreciate, because the progress of inflation is usually erratic. Furthermore, there is always the possibility that, after inflation has run its course, it may be followed by a deflation which will cause the claim to appreciate considerably. There is even the possibility that the inflating country will presently tire of the vicissitudes of a badly managed paper currency, and return to a specie standard. Under these conditions, the market for foreign exchange is dominated by speculative factors. These overshadow all other influences so greatly that the stabilizing effect of purchasing power parity is not apparent, and the foreign exchange market is chaotic. Heretofore in the world's history, paper standards have usually been resorted to only under inflationary conditions; therefore, our experience with foreign exchange under nominal standards has mostly been of the erratic character here described. However, there is no reason, in principle, why paper monetary systems could not be managed in such a way as to maintain a fairly stable level of prices. Were this done, exchange rates with nominal standards would fluctuate only moderately about their purchasing power parities. In the future, we are likely to see a development in this direction.

Speculation and Arbitrage in Foreign Exchange. — It has been pointed out that dealers in foreign exchange perform important functions as middlemen, who facilitate the exchange of goods for goods between countries. We have seen that they make a profit by selling their bills for a slightly higher price than they pay for them. They are also speculators, who attempt to forecast future changes in exchange rates and to make a gain therefrom. For instance, if they think that the rate of exchange on any country is going to rise, they will buy up as many bills on that country as their judgment and resources determine, remit them to their foreign correspondents, and keep the funds so collected on deposit there. They are then in a position to supply bills on that country at the higher rate which comes to prevail later, if their expectations are realized. So, like the speculators in commodity markets, they profit from price fluctuations. There is a further opportunity to make gains by transferring funds from countries where low rates of interest prevail, temporarily, to countries where higher interest can be obtained. Funds are frequently transferred from one part of the world to another to take advantage of such conditions, thus tending to equalize interest rates from one financial center to another. They also profit by differences in exchange rates which may be quoted simultaneously in different countries. For instance, if British exchange is at a discount in New York at the same time that it is selling at a premium in Brazil, foreign exchange dealers can buy up British bills in this country, and sell London drafts on the same day (by cable) in Rio de Janeiro. The bills bought here, when transmitted to London, will provide funds to meet the drafts sold in Rio de Janeiro. In so doing, they not only make a profit for themselves, but they facilitate the triangular exchange of goods which was described in an earlier paragraph. This process of making a purchase in one market simultaneously with a sale in another is known as *arbitrage*. Since very slight inconsistencies in the rates prevailing in different financial centers are sufficient to give rise to arbitrage transactions of this kind, the inconsistencies are corrected before they become great. As a result, exchange quotations throughout the world are kept in close correspondence.

Dealing in foreign exchange has come to be a very specialized business, requiring great shrewdness and skill. Those who are engaged in it watch very closely the rates of exchange and interest which are prevailing throughout the world, and they shape their operations accordingly. They have complete sources of information which give them exchange quotations all over the globe, and they have facilities for transferring funds quickly by cable. They make their profits from very small fluctuations in exchange and interest rates. It is a very speculative business, which calls for great cleverness. These dealers perform a useful function in our industrial system by aiding in the international exchange of goods.

B. THE BALANCE OF INTERNATIONAL TRADE

The Items of Trade. — The commerce that goes on between the nations of the earth is very varied in character. We have already considered one example, in which a commodity (cotton) was exchanged for another commodity (cutlery), and a second, in which a commodity (cotton) was exchanged for a service (hotel and railway facilities). There are many other transactions involving either commodities or services, and others which belong in separate categories. All these transactions are generally classified into two broad groups, known as *visible items* and *invisible items,* respectively. These can be further subdivided as follows:

A. Visible items.
    (1) Commodities.
    (2) Monetary metals.
B. Invisible items.
    (1) Services.
    (2) Investments, and the earnings therefrom.
    (3) Other monetary transfers not in payment for goods.

The visible items consist primarily of *commodity exports and imports.* Every nation of advanced development has coming into its ports or across its borders, daily, a continuous flow of foreign products, and is sending out various domestic products to be sold abroad. The United States imports coffee, tea, rubber, silks, woolens, and many other products; it exports wheat, cotton, automobiles, agricultural implements, etc. Similarly, throughout the world there is going on a steady interchange of commodities. These items are called visible because their tangible character makes them easily counted and measured, so that their movements can be readily followed and recorded. A cargo of merchandise cannot easily be brought into a port without its presence becoming known. Usually there are customs officials whose business it is to follow such cargoes for the purpose of levying duties, particularly in the case of imports. Hence, official statistics of commodity movements in international trade are available so that we can know with considerable accuracy their nature and amounts.

Imports and exports of the precious metals (gold and silver), while included in the visible items, are listed separately because of the importance which they have in monetary use. They are exported and imported not solely for use as commodities, but chiefly to pay international balances where there is not a complete offsetting of goods against goods.

The invisible items are so called because they are less tangible in character and not so easily traced as the visible items. The *services* which are listed under this heading consist partly of *freight and shipping charges* for carriage of merchandise. For instance, a Scandinavian steamer may bring a cargo of French cosmetics to an American importer. Here is a service performed by the foreign shipowners for the American business men. For this the shipowners must be paid. Freight charges will then appear in the foreign trade account of the two countries concerned. This is an item of considerable magnitude to countries with a large merchant marine, such as Great Britain, Norway, Sweden, and the United States. Another important service consists of *traveling expenses*. Americans do a great deal of traveling in other parts of the world. In the course of their journeys they must purchase steamship and railway tickets, hotel accommodations, the services of guides, souvenirs, and what not. These expenses are items in our international trade similar to the purchase of commodities; we must pay the foreigners for the traveling facilities which we buy from them. Wherever there is travel between two different nations, items of this sort will appear. *Insurance* is another invisible service. Insurance companies have customers in foreign countries; marine insurance, in particular, is of an international character. Such concerns as the famous Lloyds, in England, have built up great businesses throughout the world. These insurance companies receive payment of premiums from foreign clients, and they pay benefits to foreigners who sustain losses. *Bankers' and brokers' commissions* for services performed for foreign customers must also be mentioned.

One of the most important invisible items consists of *foreign investments and the earnings therefrom*. Persons of wealth frequently find it advantageous to invest some of their savings in the stocks and bonds of foreign corporations, or in the bonds of foreign governments. They must make payments abroad for these purchases. If their investments are profitable, these persons will subsequently receive payments of *interest and dividends* on the foreign securities they hold. So, payments become receivable from foreign corporations and governments.

In addition to these items, there may be *other transfers of a monetary character*. The most important of these will be *personal remittances* to foreign lands. In the United States, the presence of great numbers of immigrants makes this item of considerable volume. Many of the aliens who come to our shores are thrifty. They save a considerable portion of what they earn and send funds home—perhaps to pay passage for bringing their families over here, or, maybe, to establish a nest egg with which to retire in later years, when they may expect to go back to their native countries. Since immigration to this country is now greatly restricted, this item is dwindling in importance. On the other hand, there is another item of a similar nature which is increasing. With disturbed economic and political conditions abroad, many people find it advantageous to transfer their funds from foreign countries to the United States. This means that they have assets abroad which they wish to sell for drafts on America, which drafts they will convert into assets in this country. These transactions, which are known as a "flight of capital," will presently be described more fully. Finally, *philanthropic contributions* sometimes constitute important items in international finance. At the time of the great earthquake in Japan, we sent a substantial sum to that country to assist them in the work of reconstruction. After the first World War, we sent huge sums to Europe to help feed starving people in the war-torn countries, and to assist in the work of reconstruction.

Every one of these items gives rise to either a supply of, or a demand for, foreign bills of exchange. Whenever people in this country have claims on foreign debtors—for commodities, services, or securities sold to them, or for any other reason—there will arise, either a supply of foreign bills in this country, or (what amounts to the same thing) a demand for American bills in foreign countries. Whenever Americans have payments to make to creditors abroad, for any reason, there will arise, either a demand for foreign bills in this country, or (what amounts to the same thing) a supply of American bills in foreign countries. It follows that every one of the items above listed exercises an influence on exchange rates. Just how these influences work will become clearer as we proceed.

The International Balance Sheet. — As a result of all these operations, business men in each country are continually entering into transactions, some of which give rise to incoming, others to outgoing, payments. The sums which are receivable from these transactions may be regarded as credits, and the sums payable as debits. It is possible to draw up an account of these credits and debits in the form of a balance sheet, which will show the state of a country's foreign trade during any particular period of time. Such a balance sheet for the United States is shown on the following page. The classification of items differs in some details from that given in the paragraph above, but has been made to conform to it as closely as the official figures permit.

The balance sheet shows very nicely how the business of international trade is carried on with a minimum amount of cash. The total exports and imports of gold, silver, and paper money combined were only a little over four billion dollars; yet the total transactions

The United States in Account with the Rest of the World (1939) [1]

Visible Items	Credits	Debits	Net Credits
	(in millions of dollars)		or Debits
Commodity exports and imports	$3,241	$2,362	+ 879
Gold movements	535	3,575	− 3,040
Silver movements	14	85	− 71
Invisible Items			
Services			
Freight and shipping charges	125	249	− 124
Travel expenditures	170	469	− 299
Government transactions	32	96	− 64
Miscellaneous services	147	59	+ 88
Investments, and earnings therefrom			
Long-term investments	1,624	1,510	+ 114
Short-term banking funds (net)	1,116		+ 1,116
Interest, dividends, etc.	531	211	+ 320
Miscellaneous capital accounts	69		+ 69
Paper currency movements	130	13	+ 117
Other monetary transfers			
Personal remittances	45	144	− 99
Institutional contributions		43	− 43
Residual balance	1,037		+ 1,037
Totals	$8,816	$8,816	

[1] The figures are adapted from the report of the United States Department of Commerce, entitled *The Balance of International Payments of the United States in 1939.* The meaning of most of the items has been made clear by the preceding discussion, but the following additional explanations may be helpful.

Government transactions include payments and receipts on account of armed forces, diplomatic and consular agents abroad, Panama Canal tolls, and a few other items.

Miscellaneous services include insurance payments, motion picture royalties, cable charges, patent fees, etc.

Long-term investments represent chiefly (on the credit side) foreign purchases of American stocks and bonds (constituting new foreign investments in this country), and repayment of principal by foreigners on their past borrowings (*e.g.,* sales of bonds) here. On the debit side they represent new American investments abroad (purchases here of foreign securities), return to foreigners of their past lendings here (maturing bonds), and resales in this country of American securities formerly held by foreign investors. Sales and purchases of properties not represented by security issues (*e.g.,* real estate) are also entered under this item.

Short-term banking funds represent, in considerable part, bank deposits transferred to this country to escape disturbed political and economic conditions abroad (see the paragraph on "The Flight of Capital" later in this chapter). They also represent funds transferred to take advantage of higher interest rates in the country to which they go, for speculation, or for other purposes, and short term credits extended to importers by exporters, who accept the promissory notes of the former in lieu of immediate payment for goods

Paper currency movements consist primarily of American paper money taken abroad to be hoarded in countries where disturbed political and monetary conditions make local investments or bank deposits unsafe. Foreigners put their assets into United States

carried on in this year exceed fifteen billions. The commodity and service items alone amounted to nearly seven billions. This was accomplished by the offsetting of debits against credits, through the use of bills of exchange. The account serves also to demonstrate a very fundamental and much misunderstood truth. It is that a *nation pays for the goods it buys by means of the goods it sells.* To reverse the statement, a nation receives payment for the goods it sells in the form of the goods it buys. International trade is a mutual exchange of commodities and services, the nations of the world simply trading products with each other, through the mechanism of foreign exchange.

It will be noted that all items on the credit side of the ledger, both visible and invisible, tend to cause money payments to be made to the United States. This is as true of such things as freights or interest receivable as it is of commodity exports. For this reason all the invisible credits are sometimes referred to as *invisible exports,* because they are analogous to commodity exports. Similarly, the invisible debit items are sometimes referred to as *invisible imports,* because, like commodity imports, they tend to cause money payments to be made from the United States to foreign countries.

Factors Affecting the Rate of Exchange. — We are now able to see in detail what are the factors which determine prevailing rates of exchange between two countries. Every item on the credit side of the above balance sheet represents claims by persons in this country against parties located in foreign countries; hence, it results either in a supply of foreign bills offered for sale in the United States, or a demand for American bills in some foreign country. Every item on the debit side of the account represents a claim on the part of someone abroad against someone in this country; therefore, it causes either a demand for foreign exchange here, or a supply of American exchange abroad. If the credits exceed the debits, the supply of foreign exchange here will exceed the demand for it, and rates of foreign exchange will fall to a discount; if the debits exceed the credits, the demand for foreign bills will exceed the supply, and rates of foreign exchange will rise to a premium. How far the rates will move depends upon how great is the discrepancy, and how long it lasts. If the deviations are moderate and temporary, speculators in foreign exchange may take care of the excess or deficiency, and their activities may exert a

---

currency so as to hold something of stable value. This item also includes paper money brought into the United States by refugees.

Personal remittances comprise funds brought here by immigrants and returning Americans, and sums sent abroad by immigrants and resident aliens.

Institutional contributions consist of sums spent in relief work abroad, missionary expenditures, etc.

The *residual balance* comprises a substantial volume of unidentified loan transactions, as well as the net result of possible errors and omissions in the other estimates.

stabilizing influence on the market; if the discrepancy is great or of long duration, rates of exchange may move to the specie-shipping point, if a specie standard prevails, or may fluctuate more widely, if a nominal monetary system is in effect.

Back of the items in this balance sheet lie more fundamental factors. Behind the commodity and service transactions are the underlying conditions of supply and demand for goods—the world distribution of resources and the demand in each country for the products of other countries. Behind the investment items lie the distribution of savings throughout the world, and the prospects for profitable investment in the different nations. The rate of interest prevailing from country to country is an important barometer of these two factors. In the last analysis, it is such fundamental things as these that determine the transactions of international trade, and it is these transactions which determine the rates of exchange. We shall learn more about these basic influences as we go on, particularly in the following chapter.

The Long-Run Balance of Trade under Nominal Money Standards. — In the international balance sheet for any particular year, there will not be a perfect offsetting of debits against credits, except as a trick of bookkeeping. Of course, the two sides of the account can always be made to look in balance, by entering any excess of credits as accounts receivable, or any excess of debits as accounts payable. In the balance sheet given above, the "short-term banking funds" and "residual balance" were resorted to for this purpose. But the essential fact is that total sales of commodities, services, securities, etc., may not be completely offset in any one year by total purchases, and the difference may not be immediately settled by payments in specie.

Over longer periods of time, however, there is a tendency for the accounts to balance; for, except on those occasions when we prefer to give goods away (as we sometimes do for foreign relief work), we expect to receive payment in one form or another for what we sell or lend, and, by the same token, we expect to make payment for what we buy or borrow. Therefore, if there is any excess of credits or debits for the time being, the balance must eventually be settled somehow.

The difference can conceivably be paid in money, if there is any (such as gold) which is internationally acceptable; but in the long run it will not be, for reasons which will presently be explained. And if there is no international monetary standard (which will be the case with inconvertible paper) it cannot be settled in this way. How, then, can equilibrium of trade be effected?

The sequence of causation is simplest in the case of nominal monetary standards; therefore, let us begin with those. Let us suppose that the United States has a managed paper currency, without any specie basis, and that it has an excess of credits over debits in its international accounts. We then have a net excess of claims receivable from abroad which cannot be offset by claims of foreigners against us. Under these conditions, foreign exchange will fall to a discount in this country, and American exchange will rise to a premium abroad. This means that Americans can buy more British pounds, French francs, or other foreign moneys, for a given number of dollars, than they formerly could. With prices abroad at given levels, it will now be possible to buy more foreign goods for a given expenditure in dollars than could be bought before. Foreign merchandise being cheaper, in terms of our currency, our effective demand for it will increase, and our imports will therefore expand. To the foreigner, however, American money is dearer than before, because American exchange has risen to a premium in foreign markets. British pounds or French francs will buy fewer American dollars, and so, fewer American goods. Since American goods are now dearer to foreign buyers, their effective demand for our products will be less, and our exports will decline. Our growing imports increase our debits, while our declining exports reduce our credits, until the excess of the latter disappears. Credits and debits will then balance, and trade between this country and abroad be in equilibrium. Exchange rates now return to their purchasing power parity, and nothing further is to be gained or lost by further trade adjustments.

If we have an excess of debits, instead of credits, exactly the opposite sequence of events will take place. There will be a demand for foreign bills in excess of their supply; foreign exchange in this country will rise to a premium, and American exchange will be at a discount in foreign countries. This will make foreign goods dearer to Americans, and American goods cheaper to foreigners. We will buy less of foreign goods, foreign countries will buy more of our goods; hence, our debits will decline and our credits will increase, until balance is achieved.

From this reasoning it follows that an excess of credits or debits sets in motion forces which tend to wipe it out. Therefore, we may conclude that the credits and debits of a nation tend toward equality. This reinforces the statement, previously made, that we pay for the goods we buy by means of the goods we sell; or, to put it somewhat more accurately, we pay for the goods we buy and the sums we borrow by means of the goods we sell and the sums we loan. International trade is reciprocal.

The Long-Run Balance of Trade Under Specie Standards. — If a gold or silver monetary standard prevails, the same result will be attained, but in a less direct manner. Let us begin, as before, with the assumption that our country has a continuing net balance of accounts receivable, and with the added condition that automatic gold standards prevail in the trading countries. (The same principles would apply in the case of silver standards.) Because of our excess of credits, the supply of bills on the countries with which we deal will exceed the demand for them, and rates of exchange will fall to our gold import point. For the time being we will be paid in gold for the balance due us. This gold will go into our monetary reserves. We know, from the analysis of the automatic gold standard in an earlier chapter, that this increase in the reserves will be likely to increase the price level here, sooner or later; for it will encourage an expansion of bank deposits, and so raise the value of MV, in the equation of exchange $(P = \dfrac{MV}{T})$.

Meanwhile, the outflow of gold from the countries which are sending it to us is likely to cause a fall in prices there. With prices rising here and falling elsewhere, we become a poor country in which to buy and a good one in which to sell. Hence, our exports begin to decline and our imports to increase. If undisturbed by other factors, this will go on until exchange is brought back to par and specie no longer flows into this country. A balanced state of trade has been produced once more, so that our sales abroad just equal our purchases.

If we had a continuing excess of debits instead of credits, the chain of events would be in the opposite direction. The demand for foreign exchange in this country with which to settle our adverse balance would force the rate up to our gold export point, and gold would flow out of this country into the countries where the balances were due. Our price level would fall and their price levels would rise. As our goods became cheaper, they would buy more from us, and, as their goods became dearer, we would buy less from them. So, our exports would increase and our imports would decline, until a balance of debit and credit items was restored.

These effects may not be immediate. If gold happens to flow into this country in a period of business recession, prices may not rise at first, because it may take more than an increase in our gold reserves to turn a down-swing of business into an upward movement. If conditions are not ripe for business expansion, the mere fact that a larger monetary base is available will not suffice to produce an expansion of bank deposits. Likewise, an outflow of gold in a period of prosperity might not lead to an immediate fall in prices; the expansionary movement of business would not necessarily be checked, unless it had reached the point where the outstanding volume of credit had reduced the ratio of bank reserves to almost its minimum. In the long

run, however, a continuing excess of debits or credits in the international trade balance would almost certainly work out as indicated,
for, under an automatic gold standard, the average monetary circulation over a period of years does respond to the size of the gold reserves upon which the monetary structure is built.[2]

It is not quite so clear how the effects of gold movements would
work out under the kind of managed monetary systems which now
prevail throughout most of the world. However, even under these
circumstances, it seems probable that a continuing credit or debit balance must sooner or later lead to the same results as in the two cases
we have already examined. Suppose, for instance, that we have a credit
balance which brings gold into the United States, but that the government does not wish to allow this gold to influence the price level.
This is indeed a condition which has prevailed in recent years. In
such a case, the government must be prepared to buy up all the gold
brought in from abroad, and, if it does not propose to issue money
against it, it must pay for it out of receipts from taxes or loans. This
would be a very costly policy to continue indefinitely. It is, therefore, only a temporary expedient. If the government does not wish to
do this, it can exclude the gold from the monetary system by refusing
to purchase it at all. This would destroy the gold pars of exchange
(which rest on the convertibility of the gold currency of one country
into that of another) and so bring into play the influence of widely
fluctuating exchange rates, which, in turn, would permit the opera-

---

[2] Certain qualifications to the above analysis must be made:

(1) Where a nation has gold mines of its own, gold may become one of its regularly
exported products. The continual addition of gold to its monetary reserves tends to
lower the purchasing power of the metal there, causing higher prices. Having greater
purchasing power abroad, the gold is shipped out of the country in purchase of goods.
Such a nation will normally have an excess of imports over exports (of goods other than
gold), exporting the gold to make up the difference.

(2) Temporary settlement of international balances is sometimes effected by the shipment of securities, instead of gold. If the United States has an excess of credits in its
relations with England, British bankers or governmental authorities (desiring to protect their monetary reserves against loss of gold) may decide to settle the balance by
buying up American securities held in England and sending them to this country for
sale, instead of sending gold here. The effect is to create an offsetting item on the
international account which may restore the balance of payments. The securities which
are sold on the American market give the British American currency with which to
settle their obligations here.

(3) If, for some reason, foreign importers are having difficulty in settling their obligations to American exporters (or vice versa), the latter, rather than see their sales
abroad decline, may decide to sell to the foreigners on credit, accepting promissory
notes in lieu of payment. This creates a debit item on our account (short-time loans
abroad) which balances the trade for the time being. However, this cannot offset a
long continuing excess of credits; for, as the loans become due, unless they are renewed indefinitely, some way of paying for the goods bought must be found.

(4) Finally, an item on one side of the account (e.g., a loan) may sometimes give rise
to an offsetting item (e.g., commodity exports) directly, without the movement of exchange rates or the shipment of gold. This will be explained more fully in a later
paragraph.

tion of the balancing mechanism which was described for nominal monetary standards. The writer does not know of any case where governments with managed gold currencies have refused to accept gold into their monetary systems; but the opposite case, of refusing to allow gold to be shipped out in payment of debit balances, has frequently been resorted to in recent years. To the extent that this is done, it again upsets the gold pars of exchange and permits wide fluctuations of exchange rates to operate. We shall have more to say about the machinery of exchange control in the following chapter.

The Effects of Long-Term Investments. — The making of long-term investments abroad has interesting and important effects upon the international balance of payments. When capitalists in one country invest in stocks, bonds, or mortgages in another country, the effect on the trade balance of the former is the same as though goods had been imported—the investors must make payments abroad for the securities they have bought. For instance, if English investors purchase United States Steel common stock, they must put London funds at the disposal of the seller, and so create a supply of British exchange in the United States, or they must buy American exchange in London with which to make payment. So, the transaction becomes a credit one for the United States and a debit one for England, for the time being. Later, if the investments prove profitable, the debit and credit relations will be reversed; for, if dividends are declared on the stock, payments must be made by the United States to the English investors, and this creates a demand for British exchange in this country, or a supply of American exchange in England. Likewise, if the Britishers have bought bonds instead of stocks, the bonds expire in time, so that they must eventually be repaid. This will constitute a debit item on our trade account, creating a demand for British exchange in this country. If the investments were made by Americans in British securities, the entire chain of events would be in the opposite direction. From this it appears that international investments first create debits for the investing country and credits for the country which is receiving funds, but later bring about a reversal of these results.

In the total investment account of any nation at a given time, there will be a balance one way or the other which has important effects upon its other items of trade; for we know that an excess of credits or debits for any one item or set of items tends to produce offsetting transactions in some other aspect of its trade relations. In connection with investment accounts, four cases (or stages) can be distinguished, which are commonly known as *the immature debtor stage, the mature debtor stage, the immature creditor stage,* and *the mature creditor stage,* respectively. These can be illustrated by the history of the United States.

In the first few decades of our existence as an independent nation, we had few manufacturing establishments and not much financial resources with which to establish them. On the other hand, our potentialities for future industrial development were so good that foreign capitalists were glad to invest in our young enterprises. Hence, European (especially British) funds were offered freely in purchase of American securities. The aggregate was so large as to constitute an important credit item on our international balance sheet, which persisted for some decades. This credit balance (through the mechanism described above) made it advantageous for us to purchase foreign goods, which we did in corresponding quantity. As a result, during this period we had an excess of merchandise imports over exports. In other words, the foreign investments actually took the form of commodities and services supplied to this country. The nation which thus has a large credit balance on its investment account, arising out of funds currently being invested in it from abroad, is said to be an *immature debtor nation*—immature, because it is not yet paying back enough in the way of interest, dividends, or maturing principal to outweigh its receipts of new investment funds.

Our country remained in this position until 1873. By that time the volume of interest, dividends, and maturing principal, due to foreign capitalists for their previous investments here, had grown so large that it now exceeded the sums receivable from new investments made by foreigners in our industries. A country in this stage is said to be a *mature debtor nation,* because it is now paying back more than it is currently borrowing. These return payments constitute a debit item on its balance sheet, which gives the foreign creditors claims on this country. These claims give rise to offsetting credit items, which are most likely to take the form of commodities or services sold abroad. Therefore, such a nation usually exports more commodities and services than it imports. If the student has followed the above explanation of the mechanism by which the balance of international payments is attained, he will understand how this is brought about. It is interesting to note that in 1873 our commodity exports exceeded our imports for the first time, and we continued to have a surplus of exports for many decades thereafter.

At the time of the first World War we became an *immature creditor nation.* Our capitalists had now grown so wealthy that they could help meet the needs of the Allied countries in Europe for funds with which to finance the conflict. American investors bought heavily of Allied government bonds; and, following the war, they continued to invest in European securities, because foreign governments and enterprises could not finance the work of reconstruction from their own resources, and were glad to avail themselves of American savings. These investments put at the disposal of the foreign borrowers claims on American funds, which constituted a large debit item on our balance sheet. To offset this there was an expansion of other items on the credit side. These took the form of a continuing excess of commodity exports. In 1941 we were still in the immature creditor position, our loans abroad exceeding current receipts from past investments. It will be observed that this is the exact opposite of the immature debtor position.

If we ever receive the returns of interest, dividends, and maturing principal which would normally be expected to accrue from our huge foreign investments (but which may never be forthcoming) we would then pass into the *mature creditor stage,* where incoming receipts on investment accounts would exceed outgoing payments for current new investments. We would then presumably experience a reversal of the other items in our balance sheet, particularly an excess of commodity imports over commodity exports. The only reason this has not already occurred is that the European governments defaulted on their debts to us. An example of a mature creditor nation is afforded by Great Britain, which for many decades prior to the first World War had a large excess of imports over exports because of its previous foreign investments. Her return on these investments came to her in the form of foodstuffs and raw materials received from her colonies and other foreign countries.

We see, then, that immature debtor nations and mature creditor nations both tend to have an import balance of goods, while mature debtors and immature creditors tend to have an export balance.

"Favorable" and "Unfavorable" Balance of Trade. — During the latter part of the eighteenth century, there prevailed in Europe an economic philosophy known as Mercantilism, which held it to be good policy for a nation to encourage exports and discourage imports, so that it might have a credit balance which would be paid in gold or silver. The Mercantilists believed that this was advantageous, because they considered the precious metals more important than other forms of wealth—partly because they had confused notions about wealth and money, and partly because the period was one in which money was becoming increasingly important, for it was a time when local self-sufficiency was giving way to national and international commerce. As a result of this philosophy, a balance of commodity exports over imports was termed "favorable," and a balance of imports over exports was called "unfavorable."

We now know that an excess of commodity exports does not necessarily bring in money, for it may be offset by invisible items on the opposite side of the balance sheet; in fact, this is more often the case than not. We also know that, under present circumstances, it is usually of no particular advantage to a country to have large quantities of money—increasing quantities of money inflate the currency, raise prices, and promote business disturbances. Hence, the philosophy of Mercantilism is no longer adhered to by well-informed persons; but the phrase "favorable" balance of trade still persists to describe that situation in which a nation's credits exceed its debits, and "unfavorable" balance when the reverse situation prevails. Sometimes the phrases are applied only to the commodity items; but at other times they are used with reference to the balance of payments as a whole.

So general is this usage that the terms are commonly employed even by economists. However, the student should be on his guard against misinterpreting them; he must not assume that a so-called "favorable" balance is in fact any more advantageous to a country than an "unfavorable" one. In this book the confusion has been avoided by using the terms *credit balance* and *debit balance,* respectively.

Further Observations on the Balance of Payments. — The discussion of the foregoing paragraphs has established the principle that the credit and debit items in a country's balance of international payments tend in the long run to be equal. It follows that a permanent change in any one of the items of trade tends to provoke repercussions which bring about a compensating change in one or more of the other items. For instance, we saw that when the United States changed from an immature debtor to a mature debtor position, its excess of commodity imports gave way to an excess of commodity exports. In the past, writers on international trade have been very much inclined to emphasize the commodity items as the ones which are most likely to be affected by these influences. However, this is not necessarily the case. All that we can say for certain is that a change on one side of the account tends to produce an offsetting change *somewhere* on the other side. Where the compensating change takes place depends on the state of reciprocal demand between the countries concerned—that is, on the relative demands in each country for the goods offered by the others. For instance, if, after the termination of the present war, the governments of Europe should begin to make substantial payments to the United States on their loan accounts, there are a number of possible ways in which our balance of trade might be affected. The payments would make supplies of foreign exchange available in the American market. Our citizens might take advantage of this exchange either to buy foreign commodities, or to do more traveling in Europe, or to make more use of European shipping facilities. Hence, our credits on account of loans might be offset by increased commodity imports, by tourist expenditures, or by freight charges. Among the various items on the two sides of the international account, a considerable number of combinations is possible, and the exact one that will prevail in any given case is not definitely predictable.

Moreover, more than one sequence of causation is possible. In the paragraphs above, the compensating adjustment was represented as taking place through movements in exchange rates and (in the case of specie standards) price levels, but it may sometimes be otherwise. For instance, when the British government needed to borrow funds in the United States to finance the purchase of war materials for use against Germany, it desired not merely American exchange, but American commodities. Hence, the funds were used directly to buy American products, and the exportation of these products took place as a direct result of the loans, not as an indirect result of the movement of exchange rates or the shipment of specie. Sometimes funds are loaned to foreign borrowers with the expressed stipulation that the funds will be used to make purchases in the lending country; here again the connection between the loans and the exports is direct and immediate.

Sometimes, the process of compensation may take place through a coincidence. For example, it is possible that an increased demand for American products abroad might occur at the same time as an entirely independent increase in American tourist travel to Europe. The one might offset the other without any disturbance of exchange rates. Our increase of commodity exports would thus pay for the increased travel facilities enjoyed by our tourists. Coincidences of this sort are not at all unusual. The pattern of international trade is always changing and many forces are brought to bear upon it at the same time. This makes it difficult to trace in isolation the effects of any one influence upon the balance as a whole.

The "Flight of Capital." — Disturbed economic or political conditions in any part of the world frequently give rise to a temporary movement of funds, which is called the "flight of capital." For instance, during and after the first World War, currency inflation and deflation, business depression, and political revolution made many of the financial centers of Europe very unsafe places in which to hold wealth or claims to wealth in any form. Assets held in money were likely to be depreciated by changing currencies. Securities or more tangible property were likely to shrink in value or to be confiscated by tyrannical governments. Hence, many persons of wealth endeavored to escape these disasters by transferring funds to safer places, especially to the United States. The procedure in such a case is for the European capitalist to exchange his assets for drafts on New York, with which he can create bank balances in this country. He may sell his real estate or securities in the European market for what they will bring, thereby securing funds with which to buy American bills of exchange, which bills can be used to build up bank balances here. This causes a great increase in the demand for American bills and raises the rate of exchange to our gold-importing point. This phenomenon reached such proportions in the decade or two following the first World War that enormous quantities of gold were shipped into the United States, until we held a very large proportion of the world's total stock of monetary gold. A large movement of this sort can take place in a period of time so short that there is no opportunity for a new long-run balance of trade to be worked out. It is typically a short-period phenomenon, and one which may be very erratic. As disturbed conditions spread from one capital to another there may be a "flight" of funds from city to city, tending eventually toward one or two places in the world that may still retain some semblance of stability. With the restoration of stable conditions in the countries from which the flight took place, the movement may be quickly reversed. Its erratic and temporary character makes it a disturbing element, which greatly interferes with the smooth flow of international trade relationships.

SUMMARY

The growth of world commerce makes the principles of international trade increasingly important. International payments are effected by foreign bills of exchange, which consist of drafts drawn by creditors in one country against their debtors abroad. Through the intermediary services of brokers and dealers, creditors are able to sell these drafts to debtors who must make payments abroad. This machinery causes international debits and credits to be offset in such a way that goods pay for goods, and the shipment of gold or other money from nation to nation is reduced to a minimum. By means of triangular exchange, international debts to one nation can be paid by drawing upon credits with another nation, drafts on London or New York performing the services of an international currency.

The rate of exchange varies with the demand for and supply of bills. Where gold standards prevail, exchange is at par when bills sell for their equivalent in gold. The rate may fluctuate above and below par, within the limits set by the gold-shipping points, which are determined by the cost of shipping gold. The same principles hold between two silver standard countries. Between a gold standard and a silver standard country, the rate fluctuates with the market price of silver in terms of gold, as well as with the other usual influences. Under nominal monetary standards, the par of exchange depends on the relative purchasing powers of the two currencies, as determined by their respective price levels. The rate may deviate greatly from this par, and may be very erratic when there is currency inflation or deflation. Dealing in foreign exchange is a specialized business, characterized by speculative and arbitrage transactions.

The transactions of international trade may be classified into (1) visible items, consisting of exports and imports of commodities and of monetary metals, and (2) invisible items, consisting of services, investments and the earnings therefrom, and other monetary transfers not in payment for goods. These items can be classified as credits or debits, and drawn up into a balance sheet showing amounts receivable and payable. It is these items which determine the rate of exchange, the credits giving rise to a supply of bills and the debits to a demand for them. In the long run, the credits and debits tend to balance, for if there is an excess of either, it will provoke reactions tending to promote an offsetting item on the opposite side of the account. Under nominal monetary standards, if a nation has an excess of credits, exchange rates will move so that its currency is dear in terms of foreign currencies, making foreign goods cheap; therefore, it buys more of foreign goods and foreigners buy less of its goods; until balance is attained. Under gold standard conditions, an excess of credits causes foreign exchange to fall to the gold import point, and the resulting inflow of gold causes a rise of prices which reduces exports, while in foreign countries the outflow of gold causes a fall of prices, which encourages exports there, until balance is attained.

There are four cases in the international investment relations among nations: (1) the immature debtor stage, in which current receipts from new investments exceed outgoing payments of interest, dividends, and maturing principal; (2) the mature debtor stage, where payments of interest, dividends, and principal on past borrowings exceed current receipts from new investments; (3) the immature creditor stage, where current investments abroad exceed receipts from past investments; (4) the mature creditor stage, where receipts from past investments abroad exceed current new investments. The immature debtor and mature creditor stages tend to cause an excess of imports over exports, and the mature debtor and immature creditor stages an excess of exports over imports.

An excess of exports over imports is sometimes called a "favorable" balance of trade, and an excess of imports over exports an "unfavorable" balance, but these terms are misleading. While changes in one item of a nation's trade balance tend to cause some offsetting change in other items, it is impossible to say which items will do the compensating, nor by exactly what sequence it will be brought about, for there are a number of possible combinations. Temporary "flights of capital," caused by disturbed financial or political conditions, lead to large temporary transfers of funds from one financial center to another, an influence which tends to disturb exchange rates and trade relationships, and to cause large movements of gold.

REFERENCES AND SUGGESTIONS FOR FURTHER READING

G. J. G. Goshen's *The Theory of the Foreign Exchanges* (16th edition, London, 1894) is the basis of most modern thinking on this subject. A compact little book, clear and concise, is F. Escher's *Foreign Exchange* (9th edition, 1920). A fuller, more recent, treatment by the same author is entitled, *Modern Foreign Exchange: An Elementary Treatise for the Lay Reader* (1932). More elaborate and technical treatises are I. B. Cross' *Domestic and Foreign Exchange* (1933); E. S. Furniss' *Foreign Exchange* (1922); and A. C. Whitaker's *Foreign Exchange* (2nd edition, 1933).

A satisfactory, brief explanation of foreign exchange and the balance of international payments is presented by F. W. Taussig in Chapter 31 of his *Principles of Economics* (4th edition, 1939). For a detailed discussion of some of the problems arising out of the disturbed exchange markets of recent years, consult S. E. Harris' *Exchange Depreciation: Its Theory and Its History 1931–1935* (1936).

These topics are also discussed in the more general works, dealing with the broader aspects of international trade, which are cited at the close of the next chapter.

Chapter XVIII

THE ECONOMY OF INTERNATIONAL TRADE

A. THE BASIS OF INTERNATIONAL TRADE

The Problem Stated. — We have seen how the wheels go round in the machinery of international trade, but we have yet to learn what is the motive power that drives it, and what, in the end, is accomplished by it. Therefore, it is our next task to inquire what basic forces generate and direct the commerce of the world, and what effects this commerce has upon the countries that engage in it. Since we know that the economic process is guided by the price system, we must expect to find the answer to the first of these inquiries in price relationships. The answer to the second will follow readily when we have gained an understanding of the first.

The World Distribution of Resources. — The basic fact underlying international trade is that facilities for the production of goods are unequally distributed throughout the world. Mineral deposits constitute a striking illustration of this. Diamonds are found chiefly in South Africa, gold in South Africa, California, Alaska, and a few other places, petroleum in the United States, Mexico, Rumania, and Russia, tin in the Malay States, Dutch East Indies, and Bolivia, and so on. There are likewise differences of soil and climate which cause differences in the products for which each country is best adapted. Conditions are especially favorable for ivory in Africa, for rubber in India, for rice in China, for silk in Japan, for coffee in Brazil, for lumber in Canada, for cotton in Southern United States, and for sugar in Cuba. There are also differences in the characters and cultures of the various peoples of the world which make for differences in their productive capacities. In some countries the people are poorly educated or lacking in mechanical aptitude—they can best devote themselves to unskilled pursuits, such as agriculture; elsewhere, the people are educated and possessed of mechanical ability—they tend to develop manufactures and products calling for highly skilled labor. Some peoples have a genius for music, others for organization, others for science and invention; each is best adapted to producing the kinds of goods which call for its particular talents.

Not only do the resources of the various countries differ in kind, but there are differences in the proportions in which productive agents of the same kind are found. For example, Puerto Rico is an island with a very dense population crowded into a limited area; in it, therefore, unskilled labor is relatively abundant and land is relatively scarce. In Canada, the opposite situation prevails; there the people are scattered pretty sparsely over a vast territory, so that there is an abundance of land in relation to labor. The result is that Puerto Rico is well adapted for the production of hand-made goods in which labor is the most important factor (such as laces), while Canada is better adapted for goods whose production requires much land but relatively little labor, such as lumber and wheat. Some countries which enjoy a very good income, such as the United States, are able to accumulate a large amount of savings, and thereby to provide themselves with an abundance of productive equipment for manufacturing industries. Others, less prosperous, such as Mexico, are unable to save so much, and therefore cannot readily possess extensive manufacturing facilities; they are better adapted to agriculture. In the case of these two countries, also, the existence of a greater proportion of skilled labor in the United States and of unskilled labor in Mexico further qualifies our country for manufacturing pursuits and Mexico for agrarian industry.

Comparative Cost and Price Structures. — The differences in the resources with which the various nations are endowed make for differences in the relative costs of producing different kinds of goods. Each country can produce at relatively low cost those kinds of goods for which its resources are best adapted, and will have high costs of production for those kinds of goods for which it is ill adapted. If there were no international trade, these differences in costs would cause wide differences in the prices of goods from country to country. In those countries which were best suited to the development of manufactures, manufactured goods would be relatively low in price and agricultural products would be dear, while in those countries which lacked the facilities for manufactures, but which were adapted to agriculture, farm products would be relatively low in price and manufactured goods would be dear. This can be illustrated by the following table, which we may suppose to represent the cost and price structures which would exist in the United States and China, respectively, if there were no trade between them:

United States		Products	China	
Output per $100	Cost (& price) per unit		Output per 100 yuans	Cost (& price) per unit
1,000	$.10	Steel	100	Y 1.00
400	.25	Cotton	200	.50
200	.50	Beans	400	.25
100	1.00	Silk	1,000	.10

The case is purely hypothetical, but will serve nicely to bring out the principles of trade. United States prices are expressed in terms of dollars and Chinese prices in terms of yuans (the Chinese monetary unit), the two monetary systems being supposed to be entirely independent. Observe that, with an expenditure of $100 in the United States, relatively much steel or cotton can be produced and relatively little of beans or silk, but with an expenditure of 100 yuans in China the exact opposite is the case. As a result, steel and cotton are relatively cheap in the United States and dear in China, while beans and silk are relatively dear in the United States and cheap in China.

In these differences of price structures, there is the basis for a profitable exchange of products. If trade is now opened up between the two countries, an American merchant could take $100 worth of steel (1,000 units) to China and sell it in that country for 1,000 yuans, for in China steel is worth one yuan per unit. With the 1,000 yuans he could buy 10,000 units of silk (for silk sells in China for .10 yuans a unit), which will sell for $1 per unit in this country, yielding him a gross return of $10,000. With an investment of $100 he has obtained a return of $10,000, which, even after allowing for transportation costs, is a profit of nearly a hundredfold! Likewise, a trader in China with 100 yuans could buy 1,000 units of silk, which would sell in the United States for $1,000; with this $1,000 he could purchase 10,-000 units of steel, which would sell in China for 10,000 yuans, giving him also a profit of almost a hundredfold. Very good profits could also be made both ways by exporting cotton from the United States in exchange for silk or beans and by exporting beans from China in exchange for cotton or steel, although the gains in this case would not be quite as great as in the former example, because the differences in the relative prices of cotton and beans in the two countries are not so extreme as in the case of steel and silk.

The profits cited may seem so extreme as to make the illustrations absurd, but they are not at all beyond the bounds of possibility. When trade is begun between two parts of the world which have not formerly had commercial relations, very handsome fortunes can be made on very small investments, simply because of the wide differences in the scales of prices which prevail in the two countries. The first American merchants in China did frequently become rich in that way, and it is well known that the early traders in Africa were able, with a small investment in 5-and-10-cent-store trinkets, to bring back very valuable ivory which could be sold in this country for many times the cost of the trinkets.

As a result of these opportunities for profit, there would soon be established a general process of exchange between the two countries. The United States would export steel and cotton to China and import silk and beans therefrom. Businesses would be built up specializing in each of these products, and middlemen would enter into the business of buying and selling American and Chinese exchange, in the manner explained in the preceding chapter.

The Law of Comparative Costs. — This illustration reveals that the business of international trade rests in the relative differences in prices which exist from nation to nation; and the differences in price structures, in turn, rest chiefly in the differences in the world distribution of resources which has been described. If the price structure in each country were identical, there would be no profit in exchanging products, and no trade between them would develop.

The principle which is at work here can be summed up in a general statement which is known as the *law of comparative costs*. This law can be stated as follows: *A nation tends to export those goods which it can produce at relatively low costs and to import those goods in which its costs of production are relatively high.*

The Equalization of Cost and Price Structures. — So far, we have dealt with price structures existing before the beginning of trade. After trade is once established, these price structures would be modified. In the case of China and the United States, the importation of Chinese silk and beans into this country would increase the supply of those products here, and cause their prices to decline. At the same time, the addition of the Chinese demand for our steel and cotton to the domestic demand for these products would cause their prices to rise. Just the opposite effects would take place in China. Their imports of our steel and cotton would lower the price of those products in that country, while our demand for their silk and beans would cause the Chinese prices of these goods to rise. The combined result of these forces would be to bring the price structures in the two countries nearer to equality with each other. Steel and cotton would no longer be so cheap in the United States, nor beans and silk so dear; beans and silk would no longer be so cheap in China, nor steel and cotton so dear. This process would go on until the price structures in both countries were the same, except for transportation costs; because, so long as the differences in the price structures exceeded the costs of transportation, there would be opportunities for expanding trade, according to the principle of our first illustration.

When the price structures had reached equality, there would be no further opportunities for abnormal profits from increasing the exports or imports of any particular commodity. The agents of production in each country would then be receiving their normal returns, but no more; trade would be in equilibrium. At the end of the process of readjustment, the price structures might look something like this:

United States prices (in dollars)	Products	Chinese prices (in yuans)
.50	Steel	.55
.35	Cotton	.38
.38	Beans	.35
.55	Silk	.50

Observe that steel and cotton are about 10 per cent higher in China than in the United States; beans and silk 10 per cent higher in the United States than in China. It is assumed that these differences just equal the cost of transporting the commodities concerned. Except for these transportation costs, the price structures of the two countries are the same. This is the result normally to be expected when international trade is in balance.[1]

The Gains from Trade. — While this equalization of cost and price structures is taking place, the horizontal structure of production in the two countries is also changing. The importation into China of cheap steel and cotton from the United States forces the price of these commodities below the Chinese cost of production, so that the steel and cotton industries in that country decline, and may pass completely out of existence. On the other hand, the new export market for Chinese silk and beans causes those industries to grow. The productive agents displaced from the declining industries are absorbed into those which are expanding. So, China gives up the production of steel and cotton and becomes a specialist in silk and beans. A similar shifting of production takes place in the United States. The importation of cheap Chinese silk and beans forces a contraction of the silk and bean industry in this country, the displaced agents being drawn

[1] Prices in yuans are here made substantially the same as those in dollars in order to simplify the illustration; actually, prices in yuans would be about three times as high, for one yuan is equivalent to about ⅓ of a dollar. This simplification does not affect the validity of the illustration, for we must remember that it is relative prices, not absolute prices, that are significant for international trade.

into our expanding cotton and steel production. We become specialists in the latter products.

In this redirection of production, there is clearly a gain to both countries. International trade permits the advantages of geographical specialization to develop, by allowing the people of each country to concentrate on the production of those goods for which their resources are best adapted, obtaining, in exchange, the products of other nations for which the resources of the latter are superior. The United States, by specializing on cotton and steel, and trading its surplus of these commodities for imports from China, obtains more silk and beans than could have been produced here. In the same way, China gets more steel and cotton than it could have produced out of its own resources. The advantage does not differ in principle from the gains which are obtained by specialization between individuals within a country. Just as it pays one person in the United States to specialize in shoe-making, and to buy his hats from another specialist, so it pays America generally to specialize in producing steel and cotton, and to buy our silk and beans from specialists in China. The mere fact that political boundary lines lie between the specialists does not, in itself, alter the economic advantage.

These principles apply to all the trade which naturally arises between nations. The United States specializes generally in the production of such products as cotton, wheat, iron and steel manufactures, automobiles, and many other goods, importing from foreign countries such things as bananas, silk, tea, coffee, and rubber. We get more of the latter products in exchange for our exports than we could have produced for ourselves, with the same expenditure of productive effort. The other countries, in turn, get more of the goods they import from us than they could have produced for themselves. So, the real incomes of all the countries that engage in trade are made greater thereby.

The gains are not equally distributed among all classes of the population. If there were no trade, the owners of those agents of production which were most scarce, in each country, would get very high prices for their goods, to the disadvantage of the owners of those agents which were more plentiful. In each country, the decline of the high cost industries, and the expansion of those which can produce more cheaply, weakens the preferred position of the owners of the scarce agents, and strengthens the position of those which are more abundant. But this has to do only with the relative status of different classes; it does not alter the fact that the average well-being of the population as a whole is improved by the increased real income which results from international trade.

Absolute and Comparative Advantages in Trade. — In developing the law of comparative costs, we have stressed the differences in pecuniary costs which result from the uneven distribution of world resources. We know, from the explanation of the background of supply in Chapter XIV, that these costs depend upon the physical quantities of agents used in the production of different commodities, and on the prices which those agents can command in the alternative opportunities which are open to them. It is illuminating to look at the operation of these two factors in international trade—the physical aspect of costs, and the alternative opportunities.

From the physical point of view, a nation may have either of two kinds of advantage in its trade with other nations. These are known as *absolute advantage* and *comparative advantage,* respectively.

An *absolute advantage* exists when, with equal quantities of productive agents, one nation can produce more of a given product than another. Let us imagine an experiment, designed to compare the efficiency of productive agents in the United States and Cuba in producing coal and bananas. We may suppose that in each country we have ten unskilled workers, under the direction of a manager of representative ability, working on one hundred acres of the land in each country that is best suited for the respective products, and equipped with equal kinds and amounts of tools. We would find a great difference in the yield of the two products in the two countries. The result might look something like this:

Output in the United States	Product	Output in Cuba
100	Bananas	100,000
100,000	Coal	100

The output of coal would be very much greater in the United States than in Cuba, but Cuba would produce more bananas. Under these circumstances, our country would have an absolute advantage over Cuba in coal, and Cuba an absolute advantage over us in bananas. It would clearly be advantageous for us to produce coal instead of bananas, obtaining our bananas from Cuba in exchange for our surplus coal.

A great deal of international trade rests in advantages of this kind. The tropical countries in general have such an advantage over the United States in the production of such commodities as coffee, rubber, spices, and certain fruits. Their climate and vegetation are suitable to the growth of these things, and their people adapted to the kind of labor it requires. Our climate and resources are not adapted to such industries. Undoubtedly, if we were to go to great expense to create artificially an environment in which tropical products would grow, we could produce some of them. We could raise our own bananas or rubber trees if we were to erect hot-houses and devote the necessary care to it. But this would require so much labor and capital that it would be a very expensive process. It is cheaper to import the foreign product. On the other hand, the United States has an absolute advantage over other countries in the production of certain goods. The climate, soil, and Negro labor of our South enable us to raise cotton more readily than in most other parts of the world, while our natural resources of iron, coal, and copper, coupled with the inventive genius of our people, give us an advantage in the production of manufactured goods equaled by few other nations. In all these cases the nature of climate, resources, or people—or a combination of them—makes it possible for one country to produce physically more of its particular products *per unit of labor, land, and savings* expended, than other countries. That is the essence of absolute advantage.

It may be possible, however, that a country may be less well adapted physically to the production of a certain product than some other country, and yet be able to export it to that country and find a ready market there. While it has no absolute advantage in the production of the commodity, it can have a *comparative advantage*. Let us imagine another comparison between the United States and Cuba, this time in cotton and sugar. We may suppose that the labor and other resources of Cuba are less efficient in the production of both commodities than the labor and resources of our country, but that our superiority in cotton is much greater than our superiority in sugar. This being the case, the output of the two products (from equal combinations of productive agents, as before) might be something like this:

Output in the United States	*Product*	*Output in Cuba*
100	Cotton	20
50	Sugar	40

Now it might seem that, since the *physical* costs of both products are higher in Cuba than in the United States, it would not be to our advantage to import either from Cuba; but this conclusion is erroneous, for trade rests upon relative, not absolute, costs, and, under the conditions of this illustration, sugar will be relatively cheaper in Cuba than in the United States. Let us restate the relationships in pecuniary terms. We may suppose that our representative group of agents in the United States costs $100 in wages, land rent, and interest, while the corresponding units in Cuba cost 100 pesos. Then, dividing these total costs by the number of units of output in each case, we will get the following costs per unit for the two products in the two countries:

Price in the United States	Product	Price in Cuba
$1.00	Cotton	P 5.00
$2.00	Sugar	P 2.50

Observe that in the United States sugar is twice as dear as cotton, while in Cuba cotton is twice as dear as sugar. It is clear that we have here the same kind of price relationships that we encountered in our previous illustration of trade between the United States and China. By the same kind of reasoning as we there employed, it can be demonstrated that a good profit can be realized by exporting cotton from the United States and importing sugar from Cuba. It will also pay Cuban merchants to export sugar to the United States and import cotton in exchange.

Here Cuba is said to have a comparative advantage over the United States in the production of sugar, in spite of its inferior physical efficiency. The United States has a comparative advantage over Cuba in the production of cotton, but it has a disadvantage in the production of sugar, in spite of its superior physical efficiency.

It is interesting to note that, even if the trading countries have the same monetary units, the country which is less efficient in physical terms will nevertheless produce the commodity in which it has a comparative advantage at a lower pecuniary cost than the more efficient country. The gold peso of Cuba has the same weight as the gold dollar of the United States; therefore, under gold standard conditions, and with unrestricted trade between the two countries, the prices of international goods would tend to the same level in each of them. Yet Cuba would be able to produce sugar at lower costs (measured in gold) than the United States, because, under the conditions given, productive agents in Cuba will not be worth as much (in terms of gold) as in the United States. This is due to the fact that our agents have superior opportunities in other directions which make them worth more. We may assume that the relative world demands for cotton and sugar, respectively, make the 100 units of cotton which our agents can produce worth more than the 50 units of sugar which we could produce with the same agents. The high value of the cotton crop causes the agents of production to command a high price, which is reflected in a high cost for producing sugar. But, in our example, Cuba's efficiency in cotton production is so low that this alternative is not as good for her as sugar. Therefore, her agents of production are worth only as much as they can get in the sugar industry, which will be less than our agents can get. So, for lack of superior opportunities, Cuban agents are priced low enough to enable her to sell sugar at lower gold prices than we.

This shows that the principle of opportunity costs is very important in international trade. The value of agents of production in each country depends upon the opportunities open to them in the world market. Each country specializes on the products for which its agents are most valuable. The high prices they can command in these industries make for a high level of costs in disadvantageous industries, forcing the latter to give way. So, each country enjoys a comparative advantage in those industries which offer it its best opportunities.

Some Further Bases of Trade. — In addition to advantages in trade which a country may derive from the quality of its labor and natural resources, there may be others of a more artificial character. For example, one country may have happened to establish a certain industry before others have done so. It usually takes some years of development to bring an industry to its greatest efficiency; hence the country in which it has gotten an early start may have an advantage over other countries where it is not yet established. It is difficult for the industry to gain a foothold elsewhere. The country of first origin then becomes an exporter of the commodity concerned. In this case we might say that the basis for trade rests in the momentum of an early start.[2]

A closely related situation arises when the nature of an industry is such that its optimum business unit is a very large one. The optimum unit may be so big, in relation to the world demand for the product, that there is room for only a small number of optimum establishments in the world. If this is the case, an advantage in the industry concerned will be held by those countries where the optimum units are first developed. Since the market is not large enough to permit the development of more optimum units elsewhere, other countries cannot compete. Locomotive building might constitute an industry of this sort. Locomotives can only be made economically in very large establishments, and the world market is probably too small to support many establishments of the necessary size. Therefore, only a few countries are likely to have locomotive factories; they will export their product to the countries which lack them.

Finally, political conditions may affect the course of trade. Where governments are unstable and revolutionary disturbances are likely to arise which make property rights insecure, capitalists hesitate to invest large sums of money in industrial equipment. Hence, politically

[2] *Cf.*, the discussion of tariff protection for infant industries in a later paragraph of this chapter.

unstable countries may be prevented from developing their resources to the fullest, and will lack industries which would otherwise prosper there. Countries where more stable conditions prevail will be able to develop their resources more effectively, and will enjoy an advantage in trade because of that. China and Mexico are good illustrations of this principle. Both have resources for the development of large industrial projects, such as petroleum (in the case of Mexico) and manufactures (in the case of China); but unstable political conditions have retarded the development of these industries. Countries like England and the United States, where long-established political stability makes the property rights of investors secure, enjoy advantages over them in this respect.

Interregional Trade. — Trade between different parts of a country rests on the same principles as trade between different countries. In the United States, New England specializes in manufactures, the Southern States in cotton and tobacco, the Middle West in cereal crops, the Northwest in lumber and fisheries, and southern California in citrus fruits, garden vegetables, and nuts. Each region exchanges its specialties for the specialties of the others. It is the same as though they were different countries, each exporting its own products, and receiving imports in exchange. This trade rests on differences in the distribution of resources, and resulting differences in price structures, just the same as in the case of international trade. The several regions enjoy absolute or comparative advantages because of the particular productive agents with which they are favored.

Differences in the productive resources of different regions within a country may give rise to a situation in which a product may be partly imported and partly produced at home. This will be due to the fact that one region of the country has a comparative advantage for the particular product, but cannot produce enough of it to meet the total national demand. For instance, we produce some cane sugar in Louisiana, in addition to what we import from Cuba and the Philippines. This indicates that Louisiana has the same kind of comparative advantage for sugar production as Cuba and the Philippines; but the total output of Louisiana sugar is not sufficient to meet the American demand, and other regions of the country, where sugar cannot be produced, cannot compete with these imports, either because their resources are unsuited to sugar cane cultivation or because their agents are so much more valuable for other products that they would be too costly to use in the sugar industry, in competition with Cuba and the Philippines. Cases of this kind are quite common. We produce most of our own meat, but import some from Argentina; we produce a great deal of lumber and wood pulp, but import much o both from Canada; we have our own oilfields, but we import Mexican and South American petroleum.

B. GOVERNMENTAL TRADE RESTRICTIONS

The Prevalence of Trade Restrictions. — In all that has been said about international trade up to this point (including the preceding chapter), it has been tacitly assumed that exchange rates, the balance of payments, and the flow of goods would be permitted to follow their natural courses, without interference from governmental authorities. The truth is, however, that notwithstanding the apparent advantages of unrestricted international trade, governments have found it expedient, for one reason or another, to regulate the foreign exchanges and the importation and exportation of goods, in various ways. We must now take account of these regulations, in order that we may discover what modifications they make necessary in the principles of trade that have so far been stated, and how they affect the gain from trade that has been explained.

Trade restrictions are of two general types. One type consists of measures designed to promote the growth of domestic industries, or to free the country from dependence upon foreign industries, or to prevent the loss (through exportation) of products whose retention is deemed essential for the national welfare. This type of restriction includes protective tariffs, subsidies, and embargoes on exports. A second type consists of measures designed to protect monetary systems from difficulties which may be caused by debit trade balances. These measures include, principally, import quotas, blocked accounts, exchange stabilization funds, bilateral trade agreements, and currency depreciation. Each of these measures will be discussed in the paragraphs to follow.

Some of these restrictive devices have prevailed pretty generally in much of the world for a long period of time. This is especially true of restrictions of the first type. Import duties to protect home industries against the competition of goods imported from abroad have been especially popular. However, in the past, the restrictions were not generally serious enough to prevent a very extensive flow of commerce between nations. Since the first World War, interference with trade has become much more serious, as a result of which the world's commerce has been very greatly reduced. The growth of trade barriers in the post-war period is due chiefly to three factors. In the first place, the Treaty of Versailles created in Europe a number of small, independent states, which had formerly been portions of larger political entities. The creation of these separate nations, coupled with the general development of patriotic feeling during the war itself, promoted an intense spirit of nationalistic sentiment, which led to a clamor for freedom from economic dependence on other countries, and a desire to develop as many domestic industries as possible. Hence, each state tried to restrict the importation of commodities from abroad, in the hope of building up its own industries. In the second place, the war left a good many countries with large debts payable to other countries. Germany was obliged to make huge reparation payments to the victorious Allies; some of the smaller states owed considerable sums to Great Britain and France, for advances made to them in order to help them finance their share of the conflict; and most of the Allied governments (including England and France) owed similar debts to the United States. Efforts to make these payments tended to produce marked disturbances in rates of exchange, and drastic alterations of pre-war trade balances. There was a terrific increase in the demand for foreign exchanges, which tended to force rates of exchange up to the gold-exporting points of the debtor nations. The debtors could not possibly hope that these outgoing payments would be offset by an expansion of their exports, because the expansion required would have been too great to have been accomplished in less than several decades. Moreover, the readjustments would have caused such serious changes in established trade relations throughout the world that all sorts of restrictions would have been set up to prevent it; therefore, the payments would have had to be made in gold. The outflow of gold threatened to drain the gold reserves from the monetary systems of the debtors; therefore, the latter sought to gain control over the foreign exchange markets in such a way as to prevent it. In the third place, during the war and post-war periods, most of the nations engaged had resorted to a certain amount of monetary inflation in order to finance the conflict. The effect of this inflation on their prices in itself tended to prevent the carrying on of normal trade relations, because, as we have seen, the importing and exporting of goods is greatly influenced by prevailing price levels. Moreover, each government desired to replace its depreciated currency by a more stable monetary system. According to all precedent, this meant the restoration of a gold standard. Hence, each country was attempting to get hold of as much gold as possible for monetary purposes, at the very time when the debt situation threatened to drain the gold out of the country. This aggravated the tendency toward restrictive policies. As a result of all these influences, governments throughout the world resorted to use of one or more of the various regulatory devices that are about to be described.

Protective Tariffs. — A favorite device of trade restriction takes the form of import duties designed to discourage the importation of certain products. These duties consist of a tax collected by the government on all importations of the commodity in question. Such duties are known as *protective tariffs*,[3] because they are designed to promote the prosperity of a domestic industry by protecting it from the competition of foreign producers. The policy is based on the belief that the industries so fostered result in some economic, political, military, or other advantage to the nation. The United States has pursued the policy of tariff protection for a great many years.

The immediate effect of protective tariffs is to prevent the full operation of the law of comparative costs. Suppose that woolen goods can be manufactured in England more cheaply than in the United States. This may hamper, or make entirely impossible, the manufacture of such goods in this country. The government may then place a duty on imports of woolens sufficient to raise the cost to the importer, to (or exceeding) what it costs to produce similar goods in this country. The importer cannot then sell the goods at a lower price than domestic manufacturers. This makes it possible for American producers to find a market for their wares, in spite of the lower costs of the English competitors.

This policy entails an economic loss to the country that practices it. It encourages the employment of labor and resources in disadvantageous, and therefore uneconomical, industries. The country loses the advantage of geographical specialization, by stopping up the natural channels of international trade. In the case assumed, the loss is evidenced by the fact that American consumers would have to pay more for woolen goods than if they could be imported freely. This increases the cost of living, leaves them less to spend in other directions, and so lessens their real incomes. Protection raises prices and reduces the real income of a nation.

Some Protectionist Fallacies. — On the surface, however, it appears that persons employed in the woolen industry are benefited by the tariff. To the superficial reasoner, it seems that protection creates an industry in the country that would not otherwise exist there; which, he concludes, is a net addition to the business of the nation, causing a greater demand for labor and capital than would exist without the tariff, and thereby increasing the volume of employment, the wages of labor, and the prosperity of business men. From this it is an

---

[3] A protective tariff should be distinguished from a revenue tariff. When duties are protective, they are designed to restrict imports by heavy taxation. If really effective for their purpose, they keep imports out and yield but little revenue. Duties levied for the purpose of raising revenue are designed not to prevent imports. They are best laid on commodities that of necessity must be imported in large quantities, like coffee. They do not seriously restrict the freedom of international trade.

easy step to the conclusion that a general policy of protection increases industry, raises wages, and stimulates general business prosperity.

This reasoning is entirely erroneous. It proceeds from the assumption that protection increases the volume of industry. If this were true, all the beneficent results mentioned would follow; but it is not true. The error lies in the fact that those who advance this argument fail to appreciate the truth, explained in Chapter XVII, that a nation pays for its imports by means of its exports. We have seen that, through the operation of the forces controlling the balance of international trade, if we buy goods from other nations, the other nations must make payment for them, and they do this by purchasing goods from us in exchange. If, by a policy of protection, we refuse to buy goods from foreigners, they will have no means of paying us for goods they would otherwise buy from us. By shutting our doors to imports, therefore, we are at the same time isolating ourselves from markets for our exports. It is an axiom of foreign commerce that a nation cannot sell if it will not buy; because, if sales exceed purchases, the credit balance so created raises our exchange rate, in terms of foreign currencies, and so makes our goods more expensive to foreigners, until our exports decline to the point where the excess over imports disappears.[4]

Protection, then, in building up new industries here, does not create *additional* industries; it merely diverts labor and capital from industries which would otherwise be exporting goods to the production of goods we would otherwise be importing. The total volume of business activity is neither greater nor less, the amount of employment is no larger, and real wages no higher, than if the tariff were not in effect. But the nation is poorer, for its labor and resources have been shifted from advantageous to disadvantageous industries, and it has lost the benefits of international division of labor. Less goods are produced; prices are higher; real income is smaller. Even the persons employed in the woolen (or other protected) industry are no better off. If there were no tariff, we would buy the cheaper English woolens, it is true, and our domestic woolen industry would decline. But our purchases of foreign wool would give foreigners increased purchasing power with which to buy our products. As the protected industry died out, an export industry would grow in its place. As much labor and capital would be employed as before, and that displaced from the disadvantageous industry would be utilized elsewhere in more advantageous employment. The policy of tariff protection, therefore,

---

[4] Or, under gold standard conditions, the credit balance causes an inflow of gold, until our price level rises to the point where our goods become too expensive for foreigners to buy.

cannot be regarded as anything other than an economic loss to the country which practices it.

In showing this, we have already exposed another naïve popular misconception regarding protection. Many persons fail to appreciate the mutual nature of international trade. The Mercantilistic notion still persists that, if a nation can export more than it imports, and receive the balance in money, it reaps a corresponding gain. It cannot be doubted that this belief is partly responsible for the maintenance of protective tariffs in many parts of the world. After what has preceded, it should hardly be necessary to point out the absurdity of this position. No nation can long continue to maintain a "favorable" balance and receive payment for it in money. Rising prices would soon check its exports. Nor would it be desirable, as we have already learned. There is no peculiar virtue in money. Great quantities of it in a country are not beneficial. It only makes prices high. Money is meant to be spent. It does a country no good to receive it unless it spends it, by buying back commodities from other nations. The real benefit of international trade comes from a mutual exchange of products, a natural balance between exports and imports, both visible and invisible.

Some Valid Arguments for Protection. — The foregoing reasoning leads to the conclusion, that tariff protection is uneconomical, causing a loss in *real* income to the nation that practices it. Nevertheless it does not follow that it is never wise for a government to impose such tariffs. It sometimes happens that, even though a thing costs us something, it may be worth the price. It is important to realize that protection does cost something; it lessens national income. But there may be considerations which make it worth while to incur this cost. We may consider some of the possible gains which may be derived from a policy of protection.

Protection of infant industries may result in economic gain in the long run, though for the time being it is a loss. In the early days of the American nation, we were largely dependent upon England for manufactured products. We had the resources and the labor for manufactures of our own, but it was difficult for such industries to get a start, owing to the competition of the older established and better developed English producers. In other words, we had the potentialities of advantageous manufactures here, but foreign imports prevented the ready development of these potentialities. Our government inaugurated protective tariffs to meet the situation. These tariffs may have been a helpful factor in developing manufacturing industries that are now as economical as those of England, and that are able to meet competitors throughout the world. Where an infant industry gives promise of eventually becoming an advantageous one, able to produce as cheaply as foreign competitors, temporary protection may not be unwise. But if it is an industry which will be permanently disadvantageous, with costs always above those of foreign producers, it is an uneconomical industry to foster. It would require permanent protection. Such protection would be unwise, so far as economic considerations go.

Protection is sometimes supported because it promotes *economic diversity* and *independence*. Some writers feel that a nation too highly specialized—as, for example, one whose industry is devoted exclusively to manufactures, or to agriculture—is likely to be one-sided and socially maladjusted. If a manufacturing nation, it has too much city life, causing congestion, slums, crime, etc. If exclusively agricultural, it is likely to be backward, unprogressive, lacking in refinement and culture. Protection, by preventing too narrow specialization, develops a well-rounded industrial life. Moreover, diversity makes a nation independent of other nations, and promotes national pride and unity. Just how much weight is to be attached to these considerations is a matter of individual judgment. Whether or not these are real advantages, and whether they outweigh the disadvantage of the economic cost entailed by protection, cannot be positively determined.

Finally, some persons advocate protection as a measure of *military preparedness*. In time of war, a nation's foreign commerce may be cut off. If it is dependent upon other nations for important supplies, such an occurrence may be disastrous. The United States was seriously inconvenienced in the first World War by being unable to get German chemicals and optical goods. Protection of *key industries* (*viz.,* those of peculiar military importance) may develop enough basic industries in a country to make it better prepared to stand an interruption of its foreign commerce in case of war. Here, again, the importance to be attached to this consideration will depend upon the abundance or lack of important basic industries in the nation concerned, upon the individual's judgment, as to just how serious interruptions of this sort are, as to the likelihood of war, and so on.

Subsidies. — The encouragement given to a domestic industry by tariff protection is indirect; the tariff policy relies upon freedom from foreign competition to permit the industry to grow of its own accord. A more direct method is for the state to pay an outright bounty or subsidy to an industry whose expansion it desires to foster. For instance, our government for years has paid such subsidies, in one form or another, to American merchant ships, in order to encourage the development of our merchant marine. This is done because a large merchant fleet is considered a valuable accessory to the navy in case of war. Often the subsidy is concealed in the form of liberal payments for the carrying of mail, payments which exceed the actual cost of the mail service. Our government has greatly promoted the development of commercial aviation in this country by that means.

The effects of such subsidies are substantially the same as those of protective tariffs. They tend to encourage the growth of industries for which the subsidizing country is not adapted. Hence there is a loss of the economic advantages which would be enjoyed if the goods so fostered were purchased from foreigners—a loss which may or may not be counterbalanced by the gain in military security or other advantages which the subsidized industry is supposed to bring.

Embargoes. — Protective tariffs and subsidies are designed to hamper or prevent the purchase of goods from abroad. The embargo is a device whose purpose is exactly the opposite, namely, to prevent the sale of goods abroad. Therefore, instead of curtailing imports, it reduces the quantity of exports. The purpose of such a measure is usually to conserve the domestic supply of certain goods, considered vitally important for national defense, or to prevent certain goods, usually of a military nature, from getting into the hands of foreign governments, for some political or military reason. If the United States was at war, exports of important war materials, such as gasoline, might well be expected to be embargoed. In 1940, an embargo of scrap iron shipments to Japan was decreed, in order to hamper the Japanese government in pursuing its war against China.

We know that, in the long run, imports and exports tend to balance. Therefore, if we reduce our exports permanently by embargoes, our imports could be expected to decline to an equal degree. Here, again, is a barrier to the free movement of international trade which deprives the nation of the economic advantages of specialization, for a presumed gain of a political or military kind.

Import Quotas, Blocked Accounts, and Bilateral Trade Agreements. — Let us turn now to various devices adopted by governments in the post-war period to prevent the loss of gold which was threatened by the debt situations mentioned above. These various measures may be grouped collectively under the general heading of *exchange controls*. Their general purpose is to prevent private purchases of foreign exchange from pushing exchange rates up to the point where governments might be embarrassed in making debt payments, or where large quantities of gold might have to be shipped out to settle adverse balances.

An import quota is a measure which limits the amounts of specified commodities which may be imported into a country. It may be accomplished by requiring each importer to procure a license before importing the designated goods, so that the total amount brought in can be controlled by the government. In this way the demand for foreign exchange can be limited; for, as we know, imports are one of the chief sources from which such a demand arises.

The blocked account can be explained by means of the following illustration: Let us suppose that a German importer has purchased oil from a Rumanian petroleum company, for which oil it owes the latter 10,000 marks. The German government, not wishing to allow the development of an adverse trade balance, stipulates that the importer may not make this payment by the purchase of Rumanian exchange (for this would affect the rate of exchange which the government is trying to control). Instead, he is only permitted to deposit the 10,000 marks to the credit of the Rumanians in the German Reichsbank. The Rumanian creditor can then use this deposit inside Germany for certain purposes specified by the government (for instance, the purchase of designated German goods), but he cannot sell his credits outside of Germany. The Rumanian oil company is then faced with certain alternatives: it may purchase the specified German goods; it may sell its claim (in Germany) to someone else who desires to purchase such goods; or, it can invest the money in Germany. Thus, this device insures that credits and debits will be offset so that no debit balance can arise. It has been much employed by Germany in its trade dealings with other countries.

Bilateral trade agreements have much the same effect. Such an agreement is in the form of a treaty between two countries, by which one party agrees to import a certain amount of goods from the other in return for the latter's agreement to take an equivalent quantity of exports from the former. Thus trade between the two countries is made to balance. It is evident that this prevents any triangular adjustment.

The effect of all these devices is to reduce the total flow of international commerce. Their widespread use causes an economic loss that is felt by nations everywhere. It is not only the controlling country that is affected; since the controls limit the imports of the countries that use them, they necessarily limit the exports of countries from which the exports would naturally come.

Exchange Stabilization Funds. — Another device, which is used to prevent adverse movements of foreign exchange rates and to stabilize the foreign exchange market, is the exchange stabilization fund. This has recently been employed as an instrument of policy by the governments of Great Britain and the United States, as well as by other countries. By this scheme, a considerable measure of control over foreign exchange rates is given to the Treasuries of the countries concerned, by placing in their hands a huge sum of money for the purchase and sale of foreign bills. Suppose that the rate of dollar exchange is rising in relation to the British pound, so that pounds are becoming cheaper in terms of dollars. Our Treasury can then use some of its stabilization fund to buy up British bills of exchange, which it may hold temporarily, or use to build up deposits in London for use in later stabilization operations. These purchases increase the demand for British bills and thereby prevent them from falling as much as they otherwise would, thus stabilizing the relation between the pound and the dollar. Now suppose that, for some reason or other, the movement of the exchanges is reverse, so that the American dollar begins falling in term of pounds. Our Treasury can then make drafts against its British deposits and sell them on the foreign exchange market. The additional supply of London drafts checks the tendency of British exchange to rise. Or the Treasury can accomplish the same result by using its London deposits to buy American exchange in England, thereby raising the dollar in terms of the pound. Even if it has no credits in London at the moment, it might borrow the necessary funds in the London market and carry out the same operation.

The operations of such a fund are usually carried out in secrecy. This is done in order to prevent speculators from taking advantage of the situation to make profits at the expense of the government. If it were known that the American Treasury was selling British exchange to prevent a fall in the dollar, speculators might sell British drafts short at a discount, later fulfilling their contracts by buying up drafts offered for sale by the Treasury. The activities of speculators working against the objectives aimed at by the Treasury might defeat the purpose of the operations. In the case of Great Britain and the United States, the two funds have been operated in close collaboration, with the single purpose of stabilizing the relation between the pound and the dollar.

Such operations as these may succeed in preventing erratic and speculative fluctuations of exchange rates, but they could hardly be expected to prevent fundamental, long-run shifts in exchange and trade relations arising out of basic conditions of trade. For example, if the prevailing balance of trade were altered by large debt payments due the United States from Great Britain, stabilization fund purchases of British exchange would hardly suffice to prevent American exchange from rising to Britain's gold export point. The rise could only be stopped if the stabilization fund was prepared to buy British exchange (or sell American exchange) in value equal to the amount of the debt payments to be made. The effect, of course, would be to offset the debt payment entirely by an increasing debt in the other direction; for sufficient American exchange to meet the payments could only be provided by placing a sum equivalent to the debt at the disposal of British creditors. It would be rather absurd for our government thus to nullify the British debt payment; if payment of the debt was for some reason not desired, it would be simpler to cancel it outright. The offsetting of a fundamental shift in imports or exports, arising out of changing conditions of international demand and supply of goods, would be equally difficult to accomplish. Therefore, our conclusion is, that exchange stabilization fund operations are effective only in controlling minor, short-period movements of exchange rates.

Competitive Currency Depreciation. — We have seen that the first World War and post-war periods were times of monetary inflation. Such inflation usually has the effect of forcing downward the rate of exchange on the inflating country. For instance, as German marks increased in quantity, their price in terms of dollars fell. Ever-increasing quantities of marks could be bought for a dollar. We know that there is also a tendency for prices to rise in the inflating country; but prices do not usually go up as fast as exchange rates go down, for dealers in foreign exchange anticipate the coming rise of prices by selling exchange at a discount in advance. This lag of prices behind the movement of exchange rates makes it temporarily profitable for foreigners to buy goods in the inflating country. If more German marks can be bought for an American dollar, and the prices of German goods have not risen by a corresponding amount, more German goods can be bought with an American dollar than before. Hence, it is profitable to turn dollars into marks, turn the marks into goods, and import the goods into this country. So, the temporary effect of currency depreciation is to stimulate the exportation of goods from the country where the depreciation is taking place.

This effect is only temporary, because, when prices in the inflating country catch up with the movement of exchange rates, there will no longer be any advantage in such a transaction as has been described. The decline in marks will be exactly offset by the higher prices of German goods, so that no more goods can be bought with a dollar than before. When this happens the stimulus to German exports has ceased. However, just as long as the process of inflation continues, exchange rates are likely to move ahead of prices, so that the stimulation of exports will be progressive.

This increase in exports has a certain buoyant effect on the industries of the exporting country, tending to produce a cyclical up-swing there. We can readily see, also, that it might prove advantageous to a country which is faced with the problem of making heavy debt payments abroad. The extra exports provide it with foreign exchange with which to make those payments. Hence, in the post-war period a number of the debtor countries deliberately depreciated their currencies for this reason. They did this by reducing the gold content of their standard money units. Their money immediately fell in the foreign exchange markets by the amount of the reduction.

Consider now how such a policy would affect other countries. The latter would find themselves faced with an unaccustomed flow of imports from the depreciating countries. These imports would not be the result of natural trade conditions, but purely the result of the monetary policies of the foreign governments. They would affect adversely the balance of payments of the countries which were receiving the goods, and they would arouse the hostility of local producers who had to compete with low-priced foreign goods—low priced, not because of cheaper methods of production abroad, but artificially reduced by the monetary policies of the foreign governments. These effects would naturally lead to retaliation, so that the receiving countries would depreciate their currencies, in turn, in order to counteract the effects of the policies that had been pursued by the foreign governments. So, in the post-war years, there occurred a series of competitive currency depreciations, spreading from one country to another like a pestilence. Even the United States did not escape the contagion. In 1933, the gold content of our dollar was reduced about 40 per cent, to meet the depreciation of other currencies. The result of such a situation is monetary chaos throughout the world, and a general disruption of trade relationships. Eventually it is likely to lead to some kind of truce or formal agreement among the competing countries, by which they consent to the maintenance of certain established ratios between their several currencies.

The Broad Effects of Trade Restrictions. — The net effect of the various trade restrictions which have been discussed is a world reduction of trade and a loss of real incomes resulting therefrom. These losses were severely felt in the post-war period referred to, and were a large factor in the generally depressed condition of economic life during that period. They are the joint result of political rivalries, misguided nationalism, and shortsighted economic policies which failed to distinguish between temporary gains and long-run advantages.

SUMMARY

The basis of world trade rests in the unequal distribution of resources among the different countries. As a result of these inequalities, cost and price structures for different kinds of goods differ from country to country. According to the law of comparative costs, each country tends to export those goods which it can produce at relatively low costs, and to import those goods in which its costs are relatively high. These exports and imports so change the demand and supply of commodities in the trading countries as to bring price structures therein to equality, except for differences in transportation costs. Each country reaps a gain of real income from this trade, because of the advantages of geographical specialization. Each concentrates on those things for which it is most efficient, exchanging its surplus for goods which other nations can produce more efficiently.

A country enjoys an absolute advantage in trade if it can produce more of a given product with a given quantity of productive agents than other countries; it has a comparative advantage when a given quantity of its productive agents is relatively more effective (or less ineffective) in the production of one commodity than another. Additional bases for trading are found in the momentum of an early start, the possession of large optimum business units in the face of a limited world demand, and in political conditions that favor investment. Trade between regions of a country follows substantially the same principle as international trade.

International trade is restricted by tariffs and controls of various kinds. Contrary to popular beliefs, protective tariffs do not add to the volume of industry or employment, for, in checking imports, they indirectly check exports also, through the operation of the balance of trade; they merely divert industry from advantageous to disadvantageous channels. However, protection of infant industries might lead to the development of advantageous production, and protection may be defended as promoting the economic independence and military preparedness of a nation. Some domestic industries are fostered directly, by government subsidies, instead of by tariff protection. Embargoes limit or prevent the exportation of certain goods for military or political reasons. Import quotas restrict the importation of certain goods to prevent debit trade balances. Blocked accounts achieve a similar effect by forcing foreign creditors, from whom goods are purchased, to use the proceeds of such sales for the purchase of specified goods, or for making investments, in the importing country. Bilateral trade agreements restrict the volume of goods bought from the other party to the agreement, to what can be exported to that country in exchange. Temporary stability of exchange rates between certain countries can be maintained by the manipulation of exchange stabilization funds, which enable the government to buy or sell foreign exchange in order to offset undesired fluctuations. Currency depreciation temporarily stimulates exports from the depreciating country, because its exchange rates fall faster abroad than its internal prices rise. The broad effects of these various restrictions has been a general disruption of world trade and a loss of the economic advantages which would otherwise have resulted therefrom.

REFERENCES AND SUGGESTIONS FOR FURTHER READING

There are three general types of theory concerning the basic conditions of international trade. The older, classical theory stresses differences in labor costs, and the principles of absolute and comparative advantage; it is carefully developed by F. W. Taussig, in his *International Trade* (1927). A more recent view, stressing the differences in price structures resulting from the unequal distribution of productive agents throughout the world, is set forth in Bertil Ohlin's *Interregional and International Trade* (1933). The third approach emphasizes the principle of opportunity costs. An exposition of this is to be found in Gottfried von Haberler's *The Theory of International Trade* (1936). The theories of Taussig and Ohlin are conveniently summarized in P. T. Ellsworth's *International Economics* (1938), which also deals comprehensively with the whole field of international trade principles and policies.

On the controversy over protection and free trade, consult F. W. Taussig's *Free Trade, the Tariff and Reciprocity* (1920), and the briefer discussion in Chapters 36 and 37 of his *Principles of Economics* (4th edition, 1939).

Chapter XIX

THE SHARING OF INCOME

The Nature of Income Sharing. Distribution. — The economic activities of mankind are devoted primarily to production. From the labor of millions of workers, the operation of countless machines, the everlasting bustle of commerce, and all the other myriad processes of the business world, there flows a continuous stream of commodities and services for the gratification of the desires of men. These goods are produced, not for the use of the identical persons who made them, but to be offered for sale in the markets of the world. We may think of these markets as one great central market place into which the stream of newly created goods is continually being poured. The patrons of this huge market are the members of society, who come there to obtain from the common stream the products of which they are in need. The transactions are effected through the processes of exchange, and with the aid of money. For the goods which he delivers to the market, each producer receives a sum of money. This sum of money we can think of as a kind of warehouse receipt for his products. By presenting this receipt (*i.e.*, by offering money for goods), he is able to withdraw from the market a supply of commodities and services for his own use. The same individuals appear in the proceedings in two different capacities. They contribute goods to the market as producers; they take out a corresponding amount of goods as consumers. The bringing of the stream of goods into being and the delivering of it to the market place is production. The stream of products resulting from this process is the real income of the people. The division of the product among the claimants who come to the market place for it is *the sharing of income*.

Only those who put labor or capital into industry have a direct claim upon the product, for only by offering something which contributes to production can they obtain "receipts" (money) to bring to the market in exchange for goods. It follows that the social income goes in the first instance to business enterprisers, capitalists, and wage-

462

earners who put themselves or their wealth into the business of production. After they get their shares of income, they may pass some of it on to others. The husband hands some of it to his wife to buy the family food and clothing, the father gives his son an allowance to meet his college expenses, and so on; but the wife and son derive their shares indirectly, according to family custom or paternal generosity, and it is clear that their share must depend on the amount that the head of the family is able to claim for his contribution to production. Hence, if we would understand how the income of society is apportioned, we must look at the payments which are made in industry to the several productive agents. Accordingly, for our present purpose, we may define *income sharing* as *the apportionment of the social income among the agents of production.*

Most economists use the word *distribution* to designate this process. This usage is confusing, because the word is differently employed in the language of business men and in everyday speech. In the business world, "distribution" usually means the process of getting commodities from the places where they are produced to consumers in other localities. For example, cotton is "distributed" from our Southern States throughout the civilized world, and anthracite coal, mined in Pennsylvania, is "distributed" through the Middle Atlantic and New England States. In this sense, "distribution" includes the whole process of transporting and marketing merchandise. To avoid the confusion caused by these two uses of the word, we shall in this text always use the term *income sharing* to denote the process of apportioning the product of industry; but, in reading the works of other economists, the student must be on his guard against misunderstanding, for he will usually find the term *distribution* used instead of income sharing, and not used in the popular sense at all.

The Shares of Income. — It has already been said that the first recipients of income are those who contribute in some way to production. Some persons are workers—skilled mechanics, unskilled laborers, clerks, foremen, salesmen, etc.—who receive some sort of wages or commissions for their services. Others are owners of capital, of one sort or another, which is employed in industry. Whether they are personally engaged in any productive activities or not, they are able to obtain a payment for the use of this capital, because of its value in production. Still others are enterprisers—directors of businesses of their own—who reap gains from their operations, if successful. These three cases represent three general sources of incomes, to which we shall devote the next four chapters. The revenue derived from each one of these sources constitutes a *share of income,* and has its appropriate name. Income from labor is called wages. Income from capital is called interest or rent, as the case may be. Income from business enterprise is called profits.

We shall find, as we proceed, that these three forms of income are not simple, but are composed of a number of elements. Economists are particularly prone to distinguish between that part of the income from capital which is derived from land ownership, and that part which is derived from other wealth. Profits consist partly of a reward for the labor of the enterpriser, partly of a payment for the capital he owns, and partly of other items. Wages can likewise be split up into a number of factors, although they are not so clear-cut as in the other two cases.

Moreover, the income of any particular individual may be a mixture of two or three of the income shares. A business man may be at the same time both enterpriser and capitalist; the net proceeds of his business then include both interest and profits. Although he may not differentiate them in his accounts, it is nevertheless true that the separate forms of income are really there, one arising out of his invested savings, the other out of his management. Also, the stockholder of a corporation is both capitalist and enterpriser, his dividends containing elements of both interest and profits, which are difficult to separate. The net income of a farmer who labors in his own fields includes both profits and wages; and if he owns the farm, it includes interest as well. Notwithstanding these instances, where the productive functions and forms of incomes are merged, a correct analysis must trace each income to its source and break it into its elements, which may conveniently be classified into the shares which have been named.

The economist seeks to discover what determines the amounts of these various shares. On what principles are rates of wages established? What determines how much interest an investment will yield? How is the annual rent of a piece of real estate fixed? What forces govern the size of business profits? These are the questions that the next few chapters will seek to answer. Before considering them in detail, however, we may consider some general principles which apply to them all.

Costs and Income Shares. — In our analysis of commodity prices it was pointed out that the costs of production involved in bringing any commodity to the market resolve themselves into prices paid for the various scarce agents of production employed in the process. The shares which constitute the primary sources of individual incomes are also resolvable into the prices of the agents of production. We shall learn, as we proceed, that the incomes received by laborers, by the owners of capital, and by business enterprisers, consist of payments made to them for labor, for the use of land, for saving and waiting, for business ability, and for risk. Hence the shares of income are made up of identically the same elements as the costs of production. In fact, the shares of income are costs of production looked at from a different point of view. Our analysis of the circuit flow of money showed us that every cost paid out by an enterpriser in the process of production must be income to someone. If the costs are in the form of wages, those wages are income to the laborers who receive them. If the costs consist of payments for interest on borrowed capital, that interest is income to the person who made the loan. It is the same with every other cost. Hence the analysis of income sharing merely continues and completes the discussion of prices begun in earlier chapters.

The relation between commodity prices and the prices of the agents of production is illustrated by Figure 53. Here the letters A, B, C, D, and E, are meant to represent five different commodities which are typical of commodities generally, and the agents of production are grouped into the categories—labor, land, and savings. Business enterprise is reserved for separate treatment, for reasons which will

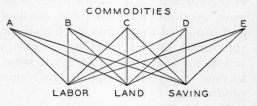

Figure 53. Commodity Prices and the Prices of the Agents of Production.

presently appear. The diagram pictures for us a dual relationship. On the one hand, from each of the several commodities, a demand for all three kinds of productive agents arises; this is illustrated by the lines which radiate downward from each of the points A, B, C, D, and E, to the three kinds of agents. On the other hand, the supply of each agent is divided among all of the products; this is shown by the lines radiating upward from labor, land, and savings, respectively, to each of the five commodities. The pricing problem involved in this relationship is a correspondingly twofold one. On the one hand, we have to ask ourselves the question, how is the price of each agent used in the production of commodity A related to its price when used for commodities B, C, D, and E? This question we have already answered in our analysis of commodity prices, by means of the principle of opportunity costs. That principle told us that, if an agent is to be used for the production of commodity A, the producer will have to pay just as much for it as will be bid by competing enterprisers who expect to use it for other commodities; therefore, the price of each of the three kinds of agents will be equalized in all of its various uses.

But this solution assumes that the producers of each commodity know what they can afford to bid for each of the agents they employ. This begs a very important question, namely—How can the producer of a given commodity know what to bid? He may know the price at which he can sell his product, but how does he know what part of that price he can afford to offer for labor, what part for land, and what for savings? In short, how can separate demands for the agents of production be derived from the demand for the various products in which they are jointly used? The shares of income which the owners of the various agents can command depend upon the answer to this question. Therefore, we must investigate this problem if we are to understand the income sharing process.

It should now be clear that the problem of income sharing is fundamentally a problem of pricing. This means that it requires a two-sided analysis—one of demand and one of supply. Since the shares of income are made up of the prices of the agents of production, we must ascertain how those prices are fixed, by studying the demand for and supply of the agents. Such a study will complete our analysis of the pricing process, by giving us a full account of the nature and determination of costs, while at the same time it will show us how the income of society is apportioned among those who participate in production.

Variable Proportions and Diminishing Productivity. — To explain the demand for the agents of production, we must go back to certain basic principles which were established much earlier in our studies, in the chapter entitled "Combining the Agents of Production." If the student's recollection of this chapter is somewhat hazy, he would do well to review it at this point before going any further. In that chapter, it was shown that, within the limits set by existing technology, an enterpriser can vary the proportions in which the several agents of production are combined. He can farm extensively, using much land with relatively little labor and machinery, or intensively, using less land and relatively more labor and equipment. If he is a manufacturer, with a plant already equipped, he can vary his output by using more or less labor and raw materials; and if he is building a new plant, he can vary the arrangement in such a way as to use much or little equipment, in relation to the labor force which he expects to employ. This means that, in the long run, wide variation is possible in the combination of production agents employed in industry. Productive techniques can be adapted to the relative abundance or scarcity of the several agents of production which are available.

The discussion in the chapter referred to established also the fact that, in this process of variation, a tendency to diminishing productivity is encountered. If a farmer, in the cultivation of a given quantity of land, employs more and more labor, tools, and machinery, each additional input of these added agents will at first increase the output by progressively larger amounts, but, after a certain point has been reached, the increments of output begin to decline, and thenceforth they become progressively smaller. To the increment of output obtained from one additional input of a variable agent we gave the term *marginal output,* or *marginal product.* The important fact for our present analysis is that marginal products eventually decline as the inputs of a particular agent of production increase. We may see how this is significant for the problem of income sharing by considering an illustration.

The General Principle of Demand for Productive Agents. — Suppose that a certain farmer has a large quantity of land at his disposal, which he desires to devote, in the most advantageous manner, to the growing of cotton. He cannot utilize this land effectively without employing labor and equipment. Therefore, he might bid a pretty high price to secure a small quantity of these agents, if compelled to do so. If the supply of them at his command was so small that the point of diminishing productivity had not been reached, each additional unit of labor and equipment would add very greatly to his crop, and would, therefore, be quite valuable to him. How much could he afford to pay for them? The answer to this question will reveal the general principle on which the demand for productive agents depends.

In our analysis of the pricing process, we learned that there is a general rule of policy, which it is advantageous for enterprisers to follow, in deciding how much of their product to produce. The rule was that it pays to increase output so long as the receipts from the sale of each additional increment exceed the extra cost of obtaining them. This principle is applicable to the present problem. It will be worth our farmer's while to employ additional workers and tools, so long as the extra products which they make possible can be sold for a price which is not less than the price he must pay for the extra agents. This means that his bid for those agents is limited by the price he can obtain for the marginal increments of produce which they yield. Our conclusion is that the demand of an enterpriser for the use of an agent of production is based upon the value of its marginal product.

Suppose, for instance, that the anticipated market price of cotton is 10 cents a pound, and that the marginal product obtainable from increasing inputs of labor on each acre is as follows:

Inputs of Labor (in weeks)	Total Product	Marginal Product (in lbs.)	Value of Marginal Product
1	60	60	$6.00
2	130	70	7.00
3	210	80	8.00
4	300	90	9.00
5	400	100	10.00
6	490	90	9.00
7	570	80	8.00
8	640	70	7.00
9	700	60	6.00
10	750	50	5.00

Then it would pay him to offer up to, but not beyond, the figures shown in the last column of the table, for the quantities of labor indicated in the first column. Putting the figures the other way around, if wages are $9.00, it will pay him to employ 6 weeks of labor, if wages are $7.00, he would employ 8 weeks, and so on.[1] If he stops short of employing the number of workers that will equalize the value of the marginal product with the wage, he will forego a possible chance of profit, for, so long as an additional input of labor will add to output a value in excess of its wage, profit will be increased by employing it. Not until the price obtainable from the output of the marginal labor just equals the wage that must be paid to get it, will the opportunities for profit be exhausted. This is in accord with the reasoning which was developed in our discussion of the general rule of policy.

It appears, then, that our farmer's schedule of demand for labor is based on the value of the marginal product of labor, and is represented by the first and fourth columns of the table. If we were to add to this the schedules of demand of all other employers of this kind of labor, calculated in the same manner, we would have the total demand schedule of the entire market in which such labor was employed. The schedule of demand for each of the other agents of production could be calculated in a similar way. So, we have now discovered the general principle on which the demand for productive agents is based: the demand for an agent of production is determined by the value of its marginal product.

This analysis applies not only to labor as a whole and to capital as a whole, but to each kind of the several agents of production. Every

[1] From the table it might seem that, with wages at $9.00, he might employ either 4 or 6 weeks of labor; but he would not stop at 4 weeks, because a fifth input of labor would add $10.00 to his product, at a cost of only $9.00, yielding a profit of $1.00. At this wage it would be a matter of indifference to him whether he employed the sixth input or not; therefore, this marks the limit to his effective demand at that wage. From this reasoning it follows that the really significant part of the demand schedule is the portion which comes after the point of diminishing productivity.

grade of skilled and unskilled labor, of land, and of equipment, has its own price. Each of these is established by the same market process. All are subject to the law of diminishing productivity, and the employment of each tends to be pushed down to that point where its price equals the value of its marginal product. We may conclude, therefore, that the demands for the various agents of production that are used in the making of commodities are derived from the demand for the commodities in proportion to their respective marginal products.

The combined values of these marginal products tend to equal the total value of the commodities. If it were not so, there would be a divergence between the costs of production of the commodities and their prices. Such a divergence cannot long be maintained if there is competition among enterprisers in production; for we learned in the discussion of prices that, if the market price is either above or below the costs of production, there tends to be an increase or decrease in the output, as the case may be, which pushes them towards equality.[2]

The Law of Demand for Productive Agents. — What will be the characteristic feature of demand schedules based on this principle? What will be the nature of the corresponding demand curves? Will they follow the same law as commodity demand schedules and curves, or will they follow a different law? Consider once more the producers of cotton. They are faced with two conditions. In the first place, as they employ more and more labor, in proportion to land and equip-

---

[2] This is the price aspect of a physical law, that the sum of the marginal products is equal to the total product. The following example, suggested by a similar one in J. M. Clark's *Economics of Overhead Costs,* illustrates this: Suppose that, with 10 men working on 50 acres of land, we get 500 bushels of product, which is an average of 10 bushels per acre. If we are working well past the point of diminishing productivity, the addition of more land will increase the yield by less than this average. Accordingly, we may suppose that, with 55 acres, and the same number of men as before, we get 530 bushels. The extra 5 acres of land have added 30 bushels to the product; hence the marginal product of the land in this case is 6 bushels per acre. Now suppose that we continue to use 55 acres of land, but increase the working force to 11 men. Observe that we now have the same number of men per acre (1 to 5) that we had in the beginning; therefore, the product ought to average the same as before (10 bushels per acre). Total product, then, should now be 550 bushels. Comparing this with the yield when we had 10 men and 55 acres, it appears that the eleventh man has added 20 bushels to the product. The marginal product of labor in this case is 20 bushels per man. It thus appears that, when 11 men are working on 55 acres of land, their marginal products are 20 bushels and 6 bushels, respectively. Multiplying the number of units of each agent by its marginal product, we get the following calculation:

	Marginal Product of Agent		Number of Units of Agent		Sum of Marginal Products
Land	6	×	55	=	330
Labor	20	×	11	=	220
			Total product		550

It follows that, if each agent is paid per unit a sum equal to the value (selling price) of its marginal product, the total paid to the agents will equal the proceeds from the sale of the product. This accords with the rule that the price of a commodity tends to equal its costs of production.

ment, or more and more of the latter in proportion to the former, and thereby increase the output of cotton, the price of cotton will fall, because of the law of demand for commodities. This makes the additional agents less and less valuable to enterprisers as more and more of them are employed. In the second place, increasing employment of any one agent brings into play the tendency to diminishing productivity, so that the marginal product grows progressively less as more and more of it is brought into use. This also tends to reduce its value to enterprisers. Therefore, it follows that the demand prices offered for any productive agent tend to decline as its effective supply increases. In other words, the demand for productive agents follows the same law as the demand for commodities: The greater the quantity of any agent offered for employment on the market, the lower will be the price at which the whole of it can be employed. In view of this, the demand curve for productive agents will have the same general slope (downward to the right) that is characteristic of commodity demand curves. We can draw the further conclusion, that those agents which are relatively scarce will command higher prices than those which are relatively more abundant. This last principle will presently be somewhat more fully developed.

The Equalization of Marginal Products. — We have not yet completed the analysis of the demand for the agents of production; for we have been considering only the use of these agents in the production of a single commodity (cotton); whereas, in reality, every agent is employed in the production of many things, and its price is determined by the combined demand for it in all its uses. The principle of opportunity costs supplies the missing link. We know from the previous discussion of that principle that the producers of cotton must compete with the producers of other commodities for the supply of the agents of production, and must pay the same price for the latter that competitors are willing to pay. In the production of all the commodities for which an agent of production is used, enterprisers seek to push the use of that agent as far as profitably can be; hence there is established an equilibrium in each employment where the price paid for the agent equals the value of its marginal product. This margin tends to be brought to equality in every employment, because of the competition between all producers. If one industry is offering more for a given type of labor than another, some workers will be attracted from the latter to the former. This will cause the marginal productivity of labor in the latter employment to rise, and in the former to fall, until their values are equal. It is the same with land or equipment. So there is established throughout all industries a common margin for each agent, such that its price is uniform throughout a given market; and such that the entire available supply of it is utilized. We may say, therefore, that *the price of any agent of production tends to equal the value of the marginal product of the entire supply of that agent.* It follows that the income of society is apportioned among the owners of the various agents of production in proportion to the respective marginal productivities of those agents.

The Supply of the Agents of Production. — The principle of marginal productivity gives us a general formula for the demand for any agent of production, but it tells us nothing about the supply. We have observed that the marginal product of an agent will vary with its quantity; therefore, an analysis of the factors determining the supply of the various agents of production is necessary to a complete description of the sharing of income. If an agent of production is very abundant, its marginal productivity and its price will be low; the income obtained from it by those who contribute it to production will be correspondingly small. If an agent of production is very scarce, its marginal productivity and its price will be high; the income derived from it will be correspondingly great.

The scarcity or abundance of the agents of production does not rest on any one general principle; on the contrary, the supply of each is determined by its own peculiar circumstances. A full discussion of these must be deferred to the next four chapters. However, a brief indication of the general lines which that discussion will take may be given here. The supply of labor is governed by the size of the population, the proportion of it gainfully employed, the number of persons capable of doing the various kinds of work, the willingness of people to work, and the desirability or unattractiveness of the work itself; so we must investigate the biological, psychological, and social factors which affect these things. So far as the income from capital is concerned, we shall find that some kinds of it (especially land) are practically fixed in quantity, but that other forms of capital are not. The income from land, therefore, is determined by the demand for it in much the same way as the values of commodities in cases of fixed supply, but the existence of great differences in the advantages of different pieces of land presents peculiarities which will require careful study. Other forms of capital can be produced by man, but their use in production requires saving, waiting, and risk, so that their supply is not unlimited. We shall need to examine, therefore, the conditions under which people are willing to save and wait and accept the risks of investment. Finally, the supply of business enterprisers depends on the percentage of managing ability in the population, and their willingness to accept risks.

Normal and Market Shares of Income. Competition and Mo-

nopoly. — The demand and supply of productive agents tends to reach an equilibrium in the same way as the demand and supply of commodities. Just as the price of a commodity tends to settle at the point where the effective demand and effective supply are equal, so does that of labor, of savings, and of land. And, just as there are long-period normal prices for commodities, about which short-period and market prices fluctuate, so there are normal prices of agents, about which actual prices move up and down from time to time. The fluctuations are not likely to be so rapid in the case of agents as they are in the case of commodities at wholesale; but, for this very reason, the deviations of actual from normal prices may be considerably prolonged. So, while in this part of our study we need not be much concerned with day-to-day movements of prices, we must recognize the fact that there may be substantial departures of wages, interest rates, and rents from their normals, which departures may persist for some time. We shall give our major attention to normal income shares, for these mark the center about which the fluctuations move, but we must not lose sight of the fact that the deviations are ever present.

The normal prices with which we shall deal are competitive prices, for the most part. So far as land is concerned, there is good reason to believe that there is usually active competition on both sides of the market. There is some monopoly or oligopoly in the ownership of particular kinds of land, especially those which contain deposits of rare minerals, but these are exceptional cases which need not require much discussion. The typical cases are those in which there are many competing landowners and many competing land users. As to savings, certainly no one has a monopoly of the demand for them, because there are thousands of enterprisers actively seeking funds for investment in their businesses; and there are millions of separate individuals seeking profitable channels for the investment of their savings. In the market for labor, however, monopolistic elements are much more often found. The supply of certain kinds of labor is frequently dominated by labor unions which practice restrictive policies, and the hiring of certain kinds of labor is sometimes dominated by associations of employers acting as a unit. Therefore, we shall have to give more attention to non-competitive influences in discussing the wages of labor.

An Illustration of the Income Sharing Process. — In order to appreciate the relation between the supply of the various agents of production, their marginal productivity, and the incomes derived by the various classes who play a part in the productive process, a typical illustration may be of use. Suppose such a situation as that which prevailed in the early American colonies, when land was abundant, but equipment and labor were scarce. Under such circumstances, it is easy for enterprisers to get land, but if they employ large quantities of it in proportion to their equipment and labor, it does not add much more to their production than if less of it were used. It is well known that extensive cultivation (which is the case here) does not yield as large a product per acre as intensive cultivation. This is because the application of land to other agents is carried so far beyond the point of diminishing productivity that its marginal product is small. In this case, a more effective way to increase production would be to employ additional labor and tools; for, since less of these are in use, the principle of diminishing productivity will not yet apply very seriously to them. But labor and tools are scarce. These are, therefore, the factors that set limits most sharply to production. It is always the short factors that are the limiting ones. Their scarcity places obstacles in the way of increasing production. Consequently, each employer will seek to obtain as large a share of the available labor and equipment as he can get, and each will offer as high a price for hiring labor and borrowing savings as he can afford. We have learned that he can afford to pay whatever the marginal product of the scarce agents is worth. In this case they will be worth a great deal, and the income derived from labor and savings will be relatively high.

Suppose the population grows, and increased savings make available a much larger fund of equipment than was to be had before; but that the quantity of land has not increased. We now have a situation more typical of advanced societies. In this case the principle of diminishing productivity becomes more sharply operative as regards labor and savings, and their marginal product is relatively small. Land is now the short factor whose scarcity is an obstacle to increased production. Those enterprisers who can obtain more land will avoid the tendency to diminishing productivity that results from employing too much labor and equipment in relation to land. All will therefore seek to obtain the scarce land, offering a good price to landowners for its use. They will pay as much as they can afford, and again this will be determined by what the value of the marginal product of the land happens to be. Since in this case that value will be high, landowners will receive handsome incomes, and the incomes of other classes in the community will be relatively small.

Thus, it is in accordance with the relative scarcity of the various agents of production, working along with the principle of diminishing productivity, that the income of society is apportioned.

Business Profits and the Marginal Productivity Theory. — In the foregoing discussion, attention has been focused on the shares of income paid to laborers and the owners of capital, but very little has been said about the profits of business enterprisers. The business enterpriser is an agent of production working in combination with other agents, and therefore the principle of diminishing productivity applies to him also. He, too, has his marginal productivity, the value of which indicates his productive worth. Because of his peculiar functions as the one who assumes responsibility for the direction of business, however, his income is more likely to vary from the value of his marginal product than in the case of other income shares. Hence the analysis of business profits is best considered apart from that of other incomes.

The Economy of the Income Sharing Process. — It is a significant fact, that, by this process of sharing the social income, each person who contributes his labor or his capital to production is rewarded in accordance with the productive importance of that labor or capital. If land is scarce, land is the thing which sets limits to production. Judged from a productive standpoint, therefore, it is more important than other agents. If savings are small in quantity, it is scarcity of equipment which limits production, and which is consequently more important. If labor as a whole, or any particular kind of labor, is scarce, that is the limiting factor, and hence the one most important to production. This importance is indicated by the high marginal productivity of the scarce agent in each case, and that marginal productivity is the true measure of its productive value. So the marginal productivity principle apportions income according to the significance which the various agents have for production.

This method of paying for the productive agents effects a sort of rough economy in their use. By setting a high price on the scarce factors and a low price on the plentiful ones, it induces enterprisers to use the scarce agents as sparingly as possible, and to substitute a cheaper for a more expensive one when this can be done. For instance, a wise enterpriser would never permit a skilled workman to do unskilled work, because his time is too valuable to be wasted in that manner when a laborer at much lower wages can be obtained for it. So the scarce agents are reserved only for their most important uses. The high price of the scarce agents, moreover, stimulates men to increase their supply, thereby adding to the productivity of industry. For instance, if savings to finance the construction of industrial plants are scarce, investments in such projects will bring in large incomes. This encourages people to save for the sake of this income, making available a larger supply of such industrial equipment. If a certain type of skilled mechanics is scarce, they will obtain high wages. This is a notice to workingmen that more mechanics of that sort are needed. More persons are thereby persuaded to learn that trade, with the result that the lack of such workers is remedied. These principles are but a further application of the function of prices in guiding production, which was described in an earlier chapter.

We must not fail to keep in mind, however, the significant fact there also pointed out, that the controlling influence in fixing demands, and, therefore, in deciding the prices of the productive agents, is not alone the desires of consumers, but their ability to back up their desires with purchasing power. Those whose incomes are small must be content to have many of their desires remain impotent in the markets. Hence, the economy of the process which apportions the productive agents according to the values of their marginal products is not a perfect one from the standpoint of human needs. It only effects an economical utilization of our productive resources from the standpoint of effective demands.

The Marginal Productivity Theory Not a Justification of the Present Shares of Income. — Since the present system of income sharing tends to pay each agent of production in accordance with its productive importance, one might easily jump to the conclusion that it is a just system. This would tend to justify all of our present inequality, with its attendant contrast between the very rich and the very poor. Some economists, indeed, have followed this line of reasoning. But we must be slow to accept it; for it does not follow so clearly from the premises as it appears to at first sight. To begin with, we must realize that market prices of the agents of production may deviate considerably from their normal prices. But even if they did not, we could not argue that incomes were divided in an ethically ideal manner. It is one thing to say that labor is paid in proportion to its importance in production. It is another thing to say that it is paid justly. Suppose that labor is so abundant that its importance happens to be very small—so small, in fact, that starvation wages result. We must then ask ourselves the question, Which is more important for social welfare—the maintenance of a productivity standard of income sharing, or the well-being of this mass of humanity? Or, consider another case. We may pay to the owners of land a price that measures accurately the importance of that *land* in production; but does it follow that the *landowners* ought to receive this income? The whole question of the justice or injustice of private property in land is involved. Therefore, when we say that for each agent used in production a price is paid which accurately measures its importance, we are using the word in a purely economic, and not in an ethical sense. We do not mean to imply that the system of income sharing based on this principle is the one that makes for the greatest human happiness. We are not here prepared to say whether it is or is not. It would be interesting to inquire whether a better scheme for dividing up the income of society might be found; but such a task does not fall within the scope of this volume. We must be content at present to describe the economic structure of society as it is, leaving the question of its improvement to other studies.

Marginal Productivity Does Not Imply Separate Productivity of the Agents of Production. — In all productive operations there are several—usually many—agents of production, coöperating in the making of the product. In the simplest conceivable occupation we have man, working with land and tools. Since they work together, it is clearly impossible to say how much of their product was produced by any one of them. If a farmer, with his tools, and a hundred acres of land, grows a thousand bushels of wheat, we cannot say that the farmer produced a certain number of bushels, the tools a certain additional number, and the land a third number. There is no product separately attributable to each one of them; the entire crop is their *combined* product. Some writers, who have not clearly comprehended the marginal productivity theory, have erroneously supposed that it implied some such separation of the products of the various agents. Such is not the case. If a farmer has three hired men, and finds that with them he obtains 100 more bushels of grain than he could with only two laborers, 100 bushels is the marginal product of the three men; and if the grain is worth one dollar a bushel it would pay the farmer to pay $100 each to retain all three of the men rather than let any one of them go. This, however, does not mean that a third man actually produces one hundred bushels; for he is working with land and tools as well as the others, and the product is the combined product of all three. The marginal product, therefore, is not the separate product of the agent measured; it merely indicates what the agent in question is worth to the enterpriser.

The marginal product of an agent of production has sometimes been called its "specific" product, and the marginal productivity theory of income sharing has been styled the "specific" productivity theory. These terms, however, are misleading; for they imply that separate demarcation of the products of the various agents which has just been shown to be impossible. It is preferable, therefore, to use the expressions marginal product and marginal productivity, which have no such implication.

SUMMARY

Income sharing is the apportionment of the income of society among those who participate (or whose capital participates) in production.

The income shares are wages (derived from labor), interest or rent (derived from capital), and profits (derived from the management of business enterprise). These forms of income correspond to the costs of production; hence the determination of the income shares is a special problem of pricing, requiring an analysis of the demand for and supply of the agents of production.

Within the limits set by existing technology, an enterpriser can vary the proportions in which he combines the productive agents. However, in increasing the amount of any one agent, relatively to the others, the principle of diminishing productivity is encountered. Because of it, an agent is worth less to an enterpriser, the more of it he employs. It pays him to carry the use of any one agent only to the point where the value of its marginal product equals the price he must pay for it. Competition among enterprisers for available supplies of agents forces their prices up to the values of their marginal products. Demand for agents is thus based on their marginal productivity. This demand is characterized by the same law as the demand for commodities, so that demand curves for productive agents slope downwards to the right. The value of the marginal product of an agent tends to be equal in all of its uses.

Since the marginal product depends on the quantity of the agent available, the conditions governing the supply of the various agents play an important part in income sharing. Those agents which are most scarce, in relation to the others, command the best prices. Market prices of productive agents deviate from their normal prices similarly to the way that market commodity prices fluctuate about their normals. The market for land and savings is mainly characterized by competition, but there are elements of monopoly in the market for labor.

The method of income sharing here outlined effects a certain economy in the use of the scarce agents of production, inasmuch as it causes them to be devoted only to those employments for which there is the greatest demand; and it leads enterprisers to use sparingly those agents which are scarcest, while at the same time encouraging an increase in their supply. This does not necessarily mean, however, that the agents are used for those things for which there is the greatest human need. Neither is it a justification for the present system of income sharing, with its great inequality. The marginal productivity theory does not purport to show what the separate product of any agent of production is, standing by itself, for there is no such separate productivity; it merely seeks to show how the importance of any agent can be determined in a given state of its abundance or scarcity, relative to other agents.

REFERENCES AND SUGGESTIONS FOR FURTHER READING

A clear, comprehensive, yet compact presentation of the modern theory of income sharing is that of T. N. Carver in *The Distribution of Wealth* (1904), which is well worth reading in connection with this and the next four chapters. A less lucid, but thoughtful analysis is that of Alfred Marshall, in Book VI of his *Principles of Economics* (5th edition, 1907, or later), Chapters 1, 2, and 11 of which bear particularly on the subject-matter of the present chapter. The theory of income sharing given in the present text, and followed generally by economists, owes much to J. B. Clark, whose *Distribution of Wealth* (1899) has greatly shaped economic thought. In it the idea of diminishing productivity and marginal (called by Clark *specific*) product is clearly presented; but the analysis is abstract, and incomplete, in that it ignores the conditions determining the supply of the productive agents. Much material, both deductive and inductive, on the marginal productivity theory is also to be found in Paul H. Douglas' *The Theory of Wages* (1934), the scope of which is considerably broader than its title indicates.

An attempt to develop an entirely different theory of distribution from that commonly held is to be found in J. A. Hobson, *The Industrial System* (London, 1910). While suggestive in certain respects, it is in others quite unsatisfactory.

Chapter XX

THE WAGES OF LABOR

A. The Nature of Wages, and the Demand for Labor

The Nature of Wages. — In everyday language the word wages is used to denote the payments made by employers to those of their employees who are paid by the hour, day, or week. These are usually manual workers, such as mechanics, artisans, operators of machines, farm-hands and day-laborers, or such persons as sales-girls, whose work, though not strictly manual, is of a rather routine character. These are the types of people that we have in mind when we speak of "the wage-earners." The earnings of those employees who are paid by the month or year, and who work with their brains rather than with their hands, are commonly dignified by more high-sounding terms, such as the "salaries" of clerks and executives, the "commissions" of salesmen, and the "fees" of lawyers and physicians. In economics, however, all these kinds of workers are included in the general term labor, and the payments they receive are likewise lumped together as a single form of income, which is called wages. By *wages,* as used by economists, therefore, is meant not the earnings of manual workers only, but *a price paid for the services of labor of any kind.*

Some writers speak of "the general rate of wages," as if there was a single price to which the earnings of all types of workers tended to conform; but such a general rate exists only in the imagination. In the real world of industry, as everyone knows, there are many kinds of laborers who receive very different rewards for their services. The executive of a great corporation is paid a handsome salary, the skilled mechanic is fairly well but much more moderately rewarded, while the day-laborer very frequently obtains scarcely enough to keep himself and his family in decency. To be realistic, we must recognize that the labor of a community is made up of different classes, having different characteristics and abilities. We may think of the workers as being grouped on a number of different levels, each of which has its own prevailing rate of wages. It is the forces determining this rate on each level that we are now seeking to find. We will discover that, notwithstanding the great differences in the earnings of the various groups, all the wages are established according to the same general principles. The problem of wages in this respect is not unlike the problem of the prices of commodities. Although each commodity has its separate price, these prices are observed to be fixed by the same laws of demand and supply. Similarly, the nature of the demand for all the different kinds of labor can be stated as a general law, and certain broad influences may be found operating to determine the supply on each level. Before setting forth these general laws of wages, however, it will be well to consider more carefully just what the wage earned by a worker is, and how it is to be measured, since this is important in making comparisons between the earnings of different groups.

Kinds of Wages. — Wages may take a number of different forms. These we may classify as time wages, piece-work wages, commissions, fees, wages in kind, and extra wages. Where time wages prevail, the basis of payment is the length of time worked by the employee, who is paid a certain rate per hour, per day, per week, per month, or per year, as the case may be. For instance, one may hire a housemaid, at perhaps three dollars per day, a bookkeeper at 150 dollars per month, or a factory superintendent at 5,000 dollars per year. Where piece-work wages prevail, the basis of payment is the number of units of product completed by the employee, instead of the length of time he is occupied. A paper-hanger, for instance, may be employed to paper a house at a certain sum per roll of paper hung, and coal miners are usually paid a certain price for each car of coal they mine. Piece-work wages are possible only where the work is uniform, so that the worker's product is easily measured; a plumber doing general repair work which took him from house to house at first one job and then another could hardly be paid by the piece because his work is so varied. Piece-work wages reward the worker according to his individual efficiency. The more he produces the more he will earn; hence this method encourages him to do his best. Time wages, on the other hand, do not establish so close a relation between earnings and output; they, therefore, make it easier for the worker to shirk. Under the piece-work system, also, different workers at the same occupation may earn very different wages; but under the time system, although the better employees may be paid at a higher rate than the less efficient, the wages in a given occupation are more nearly uniform. Where wages are paid by the piece, the worker may become careless and turn out work of poor quality in order to increase his speed, necessitating careful inspection of his product by the employer in order to maintain high standards. Where time wages are paid, there is less temptation to carelessness but more opportunity to loaf, requiring careful supervision of the employees to keep them steadily at their tasks. Employers generally favor piece-work wages where it is possible to introduce them, for by this method they get more product in proportion to the wages paid; but employees usually favor time wages, because the piece-work system may be used to drive the workers to excessive exertion. Trade unions also oppose payment by the piece because it makes for such differences in the wages of different individuals that they do not feel their common interest and the necessity for collective bargaining as they would if all earned the same amount.

Commissions are really a form of piece-work wages, but instead of being a fixed money sum paid the employee for each unit of product, they take the form of a percentage of the value of the business he handles for his employer. Commissions are most often used in the case of salesmen. Such persons are usually paid a certain proportion of each dollar's worth of goods they sell. An insurance agent, for instance, will receive as his commission a percentage of the premiums paid in by the customers to whom he sells insurance policies. An automobile salesman receives a certain part of the purchase price of every car which he disposes of. Fees are also very similar to piece-work wages, but in this case the product is usually a non-material service instead of a tangible commodity. A lawyer or physician is paid fees for his advice, which fees are a form of wages—at least in part. Wages in kind consist in payments to the worker not in the form of money, but in a share of the goods which he helps to produce. This form of wages is to be found in such cases as those of farm-hands who are hired on the understanding that they will receive a certain proportion of the season's crops, and domestic servants who receive board and lodging in addition to their money wages. Extra wages include bonuses, shares in the profits of a business, insurance purchased for his employees by an employer, gifts of shares of stock in the business in which one is employed, and so on. While not usually thought of as wages, it is clear that these extra payments constitute a part of the remuneration which the worker receives for his labor.

Wage Measurements for Purposes of Comparison. — In comparing the wages of one worker or group of workers with those of another, these various forms of wage payment must be reduced to some common basis. One cannot compare the price per hour paid to an automobile mechanic with the price per car paid to a coal miner. Neither will a comparison of per cent of commission earned by a book agent with the share of the crop obtained by a farm-hand be of any value. To be of any real use, we must know what are the average yearly earnings of the employees in question. To get this in the case of a piece-worker there is needed not only the price per piece he receives, but how many pieces he can produce per day, on an average, and how many days per year he can find employment at his occupation. Similarly, in the case of a worker paid by the hour or day, one must ascertain how many days in the year there is opportunity for work at his trade. A high daily wage in a very irregular line of work, such as coal mining or farming, may be much less than a lower daily wage in a steadier occupation, such as that of street-car conductors. Account must be taken also of all the forms of wages that are included in the earnings of the workers in question. A salesman may be paid both a salary and a commission, a mechanic may receive a weekly wage and an annual share in the profits of his employer. These are properly a part of the wage. In other cases a deduction may be necessary from the nominal wage to allow for necessary expenses in connection with his employment which the worker must incur. A coal miner must provide his own tools and explosives; his money wages are not, therefore, net.

Furthermore, in comparing wages at one time or in one community with those prevailing at another time or in another community, an allowance must be made for differences in the purchasing power of money at the two times or in the two places. Here a distinction may be drawn between money wages, which refer to the money sum the worker is paid, and real wages, by which is meant the goods he is able to buy with his money wages. This corresponds to the distinction between money income and real income made in Chapter II. If an electrician in the city of New York is paid more money than one in a small town, it does not follow that the real wage of the former is larger than that of the latter; prices in New York may be so much higher as entirely to offset the difference. If a bricklayer earns very much more money in 1941 than he did in 1931 it cannot be concluded at once that his real wage has increased; the cost of living (in money) may have gone up so much in those ten years that his present money wages buy him no more goods than before. Only by translating the monetary figures into terms of purchasing power can we obtain results of any value by such comparisons.

The foregoing considerations make clear what is meant by *a rate of wages*. The term refers not to money payments per piece, per hour, per day, or per week, nor to nominal wages only; it refers to *average total yearly real earnings*. It is rates of wages in this sense that will be discussed in the remainder of this chapter. Our problem is to find the forces which establish such rates.

The Nature of the Demand for Labor. — Like other productive agents, labor is wanted for its product. The demand for any particular kind of labor, therefore, depends upon the value of its product to consumers. What, then, is the product of labor?

Where a single laborer produces alone the whole of any good, his product is easy to define. It is the good itself. If an Indian goes out into the fields and gathers grass and reeds, which he then weaves into a useful basket, the entire basket is his product. Whatever he can sell it for to summer tourists who pass his way determines his wage. The entire value of the article belongs to him. A similar principle is involved where persons are employed in performing some service directly for consumers, as in the case of a valet. The wages of all such workers are determined, like the price of any commodity, by the marginal demand-price offered by consumers of their product. The greater the utility of that product, the greater the incomes of the purchasers, or the scarcer the type of labor available for the work in question, the higher will be the wage; and the less the utility of the product, the lower the incomes of consumers, or the more plentiful the labor, the lower will be the wage. If Indian baskets are greatly prized by tourists, if these tourists have plenty of money, and if Indians who know how to weave them are scarce, the baskets will command a good price, and the Indians will earn good wages; but if the baskets do not appeal to travelers, or if the latter are poor, or if there are so many Indians seeking to sell that the baskets are very numerous, their price will be low, and the earnings of the Indians will be small. This is the simplest possible case of wages. It is also the most unusual.

In the complicated productive processes of modern times, one worker seldom makes the whole of any product. Most persons are employed in large establishments where they work with fellow employees of different kinds, and with capital in many forms. Here the product of one man cannot be demarcated from that of another. All are producing the same commodities jointly. We are again faced with the problem raised in the last chapter, how to apportion the value of the total product among the various agents which contribute to it, and in particular, what part of it will be paid as wages to each of the various kinds of labor employed. The case does not differ greatly in principle from the simple one just presented. The demand for each kind of labor will depend—not on its specific product, for that is impossible to find—but on the importance of its use in production. As in the simpler case, this importance will be greater or less, the scarcer or the more abundant the labor. Just how this importance can be estimated is explained by the principle of marginal productivity, with which the student is already familiar.

The Marginal Productivity of Labor Determines the Normal Wage. — Let us think of the manager of a large automobile factory, and consider what wage he would be willing to pay to his unskilled laborers. A certain amount of such labor would be absolutely essential to the operation of his plant. There would be heavy objects to be moved, sweeping and cleaning to be done, freight cars to be loaded and unloaded, and so on. Some of this could be done by machinery, of course; but some hard manual labor to be performed by human hands would be indispensable. If unskilled labor were very scarce, therefore, the employer would be willing to pay very high wages in order to continue to operate his plant. The wages might go so high, in fact, that it would pay to use skilled workers to do unskilled work. If more unskilled labor was available, it could be utilized in the plant, but the additional workers would be less important. It might be found, for instance, that under present methods the motor was assembled by skilled men, but that by dividing the operation into a number of simple stages, each could be performed by an unskilled worker, thereby releasing the skilled men for more important tasks in some other part of the manufacturing process. The gain in product so brought about would be due to the additional unskilled workers employed; and whatever this product was worth would determine the value of those workers to the employer. It might be found, too, that if plenty of unskilled labor was to be had, expensive machinery, such as moving cranes and belt conveyors, could be dispensed with, human muscles being substituted for them. This would release savings for other purposes, and it could be put to work elsewhere in the business where it could be utilized to advantage. Again there would be a gain in product, the value of which would measure what it would be worth to the employer to secure the extra laborers. So, here and there throughout the factory, more unskilled workers could be employed in ways that would increase the productivity of the enterprise; but as more and more of them were introduced, the gains would become correspondingly less, for the possibilities of such substitutions as have been described are not endless. After the most productive ways of using the men were exhausted, more of them could be employed only by setting them to work at tasks which would yield smaller increases in product. It will be recognized that in this situation we have an illustration of the declining marginal productivity of unskilled labor. The illustration indicates also that the value of this marginal product tends to determine what price an employer would be willing to bid to add more men to his labor force.

Other employers of labor are in a similar position. They, too, will urgently need a certain minimum number of unskilled workers to operate their plants, and can use a greater number in ways which will increase their product, but at a diminishing rate. These employers will be in competition with each other to obtain as many as possible of the available laborers. They will always be willing to employ extra workers if they can get them at a wage which will be less than the value of the extra product which their employment makes possible, for the difference will be so much clear gain added to the profits of the business. If any employer is paying his workers less than the value of their marginal product, it will pay some other employer to offer them more to entice them away from their present positions. This will force the present employer to raise the wages in order to retain them. So, the market rate of wages for unskilled labor hovers about the value of its marginal product. That is the focal point which constitutes the normal wage. Competition among workers for the available positions tends to prevent any worker from getting more than this; for although those workers who are employed at tasks above the margin are more important to their employers than the marginal laborers, it is all unskilled work which any of them could do, and if any of them is receiving more than another, competition among them for the better paid positions exerts a pressure towards equality. The law of one price which applies to the market for commodities governs also that for labor; so in a well-organized labor market only one rate of wages for a given kind of labor tends to prevail.[1] The only rate which will maintain an equilibrium in the labor market is one which makes wages equal to the value of the marginal product of the kind of labor in question. If wages are less than this, there is a profit in the employment of every additional worker which will start competition among employers for the available supply, until the wages rise high enough to wipe out that profit; and if wages are more than this, not all the workers can be employed, for their product will not be worth their wage; hence, the competition of the unemployed for positions would bring the wage down until all could be taken care of.

This analysis of the demand for unskilled labor is equally applicable to the various grades of skilled labor, clerks, executives, salesmen, and so on. Employers are continually on the alert to secure opportunities for profit in their businesses. They compare the possibilities of employing a skilled worker here, an additional foreman there, fewer clerks at another place, and so on. They figure the productivity of one kind of labor as compared with another, and as compared with this or that machine. There is always competition among enterprisers to

---

[1] It will be shown presently, however, that the labor market is not well organized, and that competition between laborers especially is not perfect; as a result this principle is not completely effective.

secure more of the available supply of each kind of labor so long as the extra workers taken on add to their production more in value than employers are compelled to pay in wages. There is competition among the workers of each grade to secure the highest remuneration that employers can be induced to pay. As a result of these two sets of forces a wage tends to be established for each kind of labor such that it equals the value of its marginal product.

The Marginal Productivity of Different Labor Groups. — That marginal product itself depends on the number of laborers of each kind that are available for employment. We know from the preceding chapter that those agents of production are most important which are scarcest, in relation to other agents. The marginal productivity of those labor groups whose members are few, in relation to the quantity of capital and to other labor groups, will be high, and the persons fortunate enough to be members of such scarce groups will receive correspondingly high wages. The marginal productivity of those labor groups whose members are numerous will be low, and the persons who are unfortunate enough to be included in those groups will receive low wages. If incomes from capital are large as compared with incomes from labor, it is because savings and land are scarce, in relation to the needs of industry, while human beings are more plentiful. If wages of some kinds of labor are much higher than those of other kinds, it is because there are not enough workers of the first sort, and too many of the second, relatively to the demand for them. The conditions governing the supply of workers on each labor level are, therefore, important in determining their wages. Hence it is appropriate now to ascertain what these conditions are.

B. The Supply of Labor

General Conditions Governing the Supply of Labor. — In general, the quantity of labor that is available for production depends upon two circumstances: the size of the population, and the proportion of it that is gainfully employed. The first of these rests upon the proportion of births to deaths among the people, and upon immigration; and the second upon custom, the technique of production, the financial circumstances of the various classes among the people, the laws governing the labor of women and children, and similar considerations. Both of these sets of influences will have effects upon wages. If population multiplies so rapidly that it presses upon the means of subsistence, wages in general will be low; if preventive checks to population prevail, wages will be higher. If labor legislation prohibits the employment of children in industry, wages in the employments affected will tend to rise; if new social and economic conditions cause increasing numbers of women to seek employment in industry, wages will tend to fall. If immigration is encouraged, there will be more workers in some occupations, tending to depress wages; and if immigration is restricted, wages in those occupations will be higher.

The relation of the supply of labor to wages, however, necessitates an analysis of the conditions governing the number of workers available *in particular occupations;* for, as already explained, there is not one general rate of wages, but there are many different rates, each of which depends upon the demand for and supply of labor of a particular kind. What we need to know, therefore, is not what determines the size of the working population as a whole, but how and why that population is divided into groups of different sorts of labor, different in their abilities and in their numbers. It will be found that the number of laborers available for a particular occupation will depend upon: (1) the stratification of the population into levels or classes, known as non-competing groups; (2) the growth of population in those groups, as affected by their standards of living; and (3) the relative disutilities of the various occupations open to the members of any one group. Each of these influences will now be considered in turn.

The Stratification of the Population into Non-Competing Groups. — Human beings are very different in their characteristics and abilities, persons of some types being more plentiful than those of other types. Not every one has the talent to become a musician. Others have neither the mental capacity nor the training for such professions as the law. Some are able to do only manual work of the grossest kind. These differences in the natures of men cause differences in the supplies of labor that are available for different tasks. The differences are attributable to two groups of influences.

On the one hand, there are *differences in inborn capacities.* Biology teaches that heredity is one of the most important factors in shaping human destinies. We are born into the world with a certain innate endowment of natural faculties, which constitute the raw material out of which our achievements are made. This equipment of inborn traits sets limits beyond which the attainments of the individual cannot go. It makes possible to one the heights of success, and it limits another to a more lowly sphere. This does not mean that biology alone determines our performance; but it does set limits to it. The hereditary talents one possesses may not be cultivated, and may go to waste; but they mark the utmost possibility which the individual can hope to achieve. These statements are reënforced by recent developments of psychology which show that different minds have different capacities. Mental tests have been devised by which it is possible to classify the population according to levels of intelligence. They show that some persons are feeble-minded, yet of sufficiently high grade to do the crudest kinds of work and to earn a living at some simple occupation. Others are of average mentality, still others of superior ability, and some few, of course, geniuses. The wholesale application of these tests to the men drafted for the United States army during the first World War showed that the proportion of persons of low intelligence among our people is much greater than was commonly realized. While these tests are not yet entirely perfected, they are of sufficient reliability to support the general principle here advanced, *viz.*, that the innate capacities of different individuals differ considerably. Hence, the supply of labor available for any occupation is limited by the number of persons in the population of sufficient caliber to perform the type of work it calls for.

Similar differences in the industrial quality of individuals arise from *different environmental influences*. Some persons receive more adequate schooling than others. Large numbers of the people never get beyond the grammar grades. A small percentage receive high school training, and a still smaller number obtain the advantages of a college or university education. Capacity for high grade work depends also on the home influences in which a child is reared. Here are cultivated habits of thrift, sobriety, honesty, perseverance, and ambition, or those of shiftlessness, intemperance, dishonesty, unsteadiness, and indifference. The type of work for which one will be fitted will be governed accordingly.

These differences, both hereditary and environmental, are cumulative in their effects from one generation to another. Persons with inferior inborn qualities are likely, in marrying, to select mates of similar mediocrity. In turn, the children born of such a union inherit poor qualities of health, intelligence, and character. On the other hand, persons of superior ability are likely to marry people of high grade endowments, and to transmit the same or similar desirable characteristics to their children. The influences which surround the offspring of both types after birth tend to reinforce their heredity. Those who are born in homes where low standards of living and character prevail grow up without ideals or superior habits and are likely to establish similar homes. Persons reared in better surroundings maintain higher standards themselves and bring up their children to equally high standards. Thus the effects are cumulative.

So it is that society can be said to be stratified into levels. Without attempting an accurate classification, the economic stratification may for convenience be grouped somewhat as follows:

Unskilled manual workers.

Semi-skilled manual workers and low grade clerical workers.

Skilled manual, common clerical workers, school teachers, etc.

High grade mental workers, such as administrators and professional men.

Very talented workers—artistic and literary geniuses, "captains of industry," etc.

These groups are called *non-competing,* because a person located in one of them is not able to enter one of the occupations of the groups above him. Hence there is no competition between them. No matter how highly paid a factory superintendent may be, the presence of a plentiful supply of unskilled workers will not tend to lower his wage, for the common laborers, being unable to do such work, will not flock into superintendents' positions to compete with those already there. The lines between the groups are not sharply drawn, and there are always some individuals who, as the result of accidental ability or some fortunate combination of circumstances, succeed in rising from lower into higher groups. There are others who fall from higher into lower ranks. But such cases as these are exceptional, as compared with the great mass of persons. On the whole, each group tends to perpetuate itself. Each stratum constitutes, therefore, a separate supply of labor for certain types of work; and the wages of each group are separately determined by its marginal productivity.

The Relative Sizes of the Various Groups. — If we were to take a census of the population, classified according to the groups which have just been described, it would be found that a large number would fall within the unskilled and semi-skilled levels, and a progressively smaller number as we ascend the scale to the higher grades. This has sometimes been expressed by saying that society is pyramidal in form. A large majority of the population is able to do only work of simple quality, calling for little training and no very great degree of intelligence. There are comparatively few persons with the superior intelligence and training necessary for the occupations of the higher levels.

Herein lies the explanation of the great differences in the wages of the various kinds of labor. The marginal productivity of those workers who are most numerous is low, and their earnings are correspondingly small; the marginal productivity of those who are less numerous is high, and their wages are large in consequence. It is primarily a question of numbers, of scarcity. Because there are plenty of persons who are capable of doing ordinary manual work they are of little value in the labor market; because there are few who are capable of doing the more difficult work of the executive, the professional man, and the great artist, their value is great. It is not that the one group is "superior" to the other in any absolute or universal sense; it is a question of plentifulness or scarcity of supply. If our nation were composed of a race of puny men, with frail physique and weak muscles, but with great mental ability, the situation would be reversed. Those capable of doing the heavier sorts of manual work would be few, while persons qualified for the tasks requiring capable minds would be plentiful. In this situation the wages of what is now called unskilled labor would be high, and the earnings of mental ability would be low. The pyramid which we have imagined as representing society would be reversed.

Originally, no doubt, the reason for the scarcity of mental ability and the greater plenty of muscular strength in the population was that mental development came later in the scale of biological evolution, so that the race was well developed physically before happy combinations of hereditary factors caused individuals of better mentality to occur here and there. Nature tries her experiments on a few at a time; then if the experiments prove a success, those few thrive better than their fellows, and gradually increase their kind. Probably this evolution will always go on, and we may expect to find a small group of advanced types in our midst whose useful variations make them greatly in demand, and cause them to receive higher pecuniary rewards than the great mass of common humanity.

The Influence of Standards of Living upon the Non-Competing Groups. — The scarcity of some sorts of labor and the abundance of others, however, does not appear to be wholly a trick of nature. There seem to be certain economic influences at work controlling the growth of population. These operate through the influence of standards of living upon reproduction. In the discussion of the Malthusian law of population in Chapter V, there was occasion to emphasize the strength of the reproductive instinct among men, which is so powerful that if unrestrained it would soon cause so rapid a growth in numbers as to outstrip the means of subsistence. Among civilized peoples, however, there are certain preventive checks which keep down the birth rate and prevent such an excessive pressure of population. These checks do not operate with equal force among all classes of people. They are most pronounced among those classes which have the highest standards of living, and least pronounced among those classes which have the lowest standards. When a family has once become accustomed to a certain standard of living, it will endeavor to maintain that standard with the greatest tenacity. People who have become habituated to luxuries and leisure and the other comforts of wealth will not willingly give them up. A large number of children is incompatible with such a standard. Parenthood calls for much sacrifice of leisure and enjoyments on the part of the mother who must devote her time to their care and training, and the expense of maintaining them makes it difficult to purchase the luxuries that the parents desire. The result is that among the well-to-do classes married couples deliberately control the size of their families, and do not bring into the world more children than they feel they can support and educate properly without reducing their standard of comfort. In such groups, also, the maintenance of a wife and home is so expensive that marriage is deferred until the young men have completed a long education and have attained a position which brings in sufficient income to satisfy their requirements and those of their wives. These later marriages are likely to prove less fertile than earlier ones. So it comes about that there are fewer persons in the upper strata of society.

Among the manual working classes, on the other hand, and particularly among the unskilled and immigrant populations, large families are the rule. These people are not accustomed to a high standard of living. They have, therefore, less incentive to restrict the numbers of their children. They marry early, exercise little thought about the begetting of offspring, and their progeny is large. In the lowest groups, in fact, the pressure of population is so great that the wages fall very low, until they are just barely able to support the people at a minimum standard of living. Wages are then said to be at a subsistence level. Lower than this they cannot permanently go, for if they do so temporarily, many of the people will die, children will not grow up to maturity, and the laborers of this type will then become scarcer until their wages rise to a subsistence level once more. They are not likely to go permanently higher than this, either, for if they do so temporarily, the growth of numbers resulting from large families will be so rapid that unskilled labor will become more plentiful, until its wages fall to their former point.

Some writers believe that the relation of wages to the standard of living is so close, that the earnings of any particular group of workers will tend to remain at the point where they just suffice to maintain the families of the group at the level of existence to which they have become accustomed. Suppose, for instance, that skilled manual workers of the better grade have habituated themselves to a standard of living such that it costs the average family in the group three thousand dollars per year to maintain it. Then, according to this theory, the wages prevailing among those gainfully employed in that group will tend to average three thousand dollars per family. If they are less than that young men and women will find it so difficult to set up the kind of homes they desire that they will marry late, and will have but few children. The numbers of the group will decline, their marginal productivity will correspondingly increase, and the wages will rise until they reach three thousand dollars again. If they are more than that, young couples will find it easier to marry and establish a family, and they will have more children. The numbers of the group will then increase, their marginal productivity will fall, and the wages will decline until they have reached the former figure. So the supply of labor in each non-competing group is believed to adjust itself roughly to the demand for it in such a way as to keep the wage at about the cost of maintaining the standard of living deemed essential by the members of that group. This standard will range from mere subsistence among common unskilled laborers, up to the extreme luxury of the most prosperous stratum. There is probably an element of truth in this theory; but it must not be supposed that the adjustment of the wage to the cost of maintaining the standard is very close. It can be only a very rough approximation. Neither is it to be assumed that the standards of living of the various groups are fixed and unchangeable. Education of the poorer classes, and emulation by them of their more fortunate neighbors, may lead them deliberately to seek higher standards, and by late marriages and control of the birth rate to attain them. Also, if some chance circumstances, such as a sudden increase in the demand for a certain type of labor, or a shortage of the supply, should cause the wages of a group to rise above the accustomed level for a time, the group might become so wedded to the greater prosperity that their good fortune enabled them to enjoy that they would endeavor to perpetuate it through control of their numbers. The new standard would then be well established, and a permanently higher level of wages for the group might be maintained.

The presence of a large number of immigrants in this country has important effects upon the supply of labor, and upon the relative proportions in the various non-competing groups. Most of the foreigners who come here are unskilled workers. The large annual influx of such persons tends to increase the supply of that kind of labor, reducing their marginal productivity and depressing their wages. This has undoubtedly been a factor in the earnings of unskilled laborers in the United States. The restrictive immigration laws now in effect should, therefore, have the result of keeping the wages of this class higher than they would otherwise be. It is entirely possible, however, that the growth of numbers among the unskilled laborers already established here may be sufficient to prevent the wages from rising above subsistence. The children of immigrants do not necessarily remain in the same group as their parents. They are not necessarily of poor hereditary stock, and the advantages of American education, together with the stimulus of a new environment of superior opportunities, may enable them to rise into higher levels. In that case, of course, they affect the wages of native workers already established on those levels.

The Effects on the Supply of Labor of the Different Disutilities of Different Occupations. — Although some labor is pleasurable, most of it involves a certain amount of disutility which people naturally seek to avoid. Consequently, if an individual has his choice of two occupations, one of which involves more disutility than the other, and which are equal in all other respects, he will choose the one which involves the less. Putting the same proposition in another way, we may say that where one is at liberty to choose the occupation he shall enter, he will naturally select the one which presents the greatest net advantages to him. If some employments seem less advantageous than others, men will not be forthcoming in such large numbers to offer their services in those employments. Scarcity of supply means high marginal productivity, and high marginal productivity means high wages. The services of the laborers in the undesirable occupations will therefore command a better price than those in the more desirable ones. It will be necessary for employers to compensate for the disadvantages of the trade by offering higher wages to the persons employed in it. Only by this means can an adequate supply of labor for such occupations be obtained. Consequently, *where there is freedom of choice between occupations,* wages will vary directly with the disutility (or inversely with the net advantages) of those occupations. Let us consider some of the factors which make for greater or less disutility or disadvantage.

There are *differences in the pleasurability of work* in different occupations. The work of college professors, for instance, provides ample opportunity for congenial tasks, creative activity, short hours, long vacations, and many other advantages. Because of these features, those employed in this profession are usually paid a lower salary than the same type of skill and ability is able to command in other callings, such as those of the physician or engineer. This case is typical of many. In the various levels of society, there are choices between employments which offer short or long hours, day work or night work, pleasant and wholesome or foul and disagreeable surroundings, interesting or uninteresting activity, variety or monotony, or which are in some other respects more or less pleasurable. Whenever there are such choices, the disadvantageous employment can only attract recruits by the inducement of a higher wage.

Differences in risks will cause some occupations to pay higher wages than prevail in other employments which are less hazardous. Two painters of equal skill may be employed, one in ordinary house-painting and similar work, the other in such dangerous tasks as the painting of church steeples, tall towers, and so on. The latter is likely to receive a higher wage than the former, because there are fewer people willing to risk their lives in this way. Other examples of dangerous trades leading to higher wages are diving, mining, manufacturing explosives, and so on. The extra pay received in such cases can be looked upon as a reward for risk, similar to other risk costs that must be paid in the process of production.

Other occupations are unattractive because of the *long period of training* or apprenticeship required for entrance into them. This training necessitates a considerable expense, and the postponement of earnings during a period of months or years. In some of the professions today it is almost impossible for a young man to complete his course until he becomes 25 or even 30 years of age. Not everyone can afford the expense of such an education, nor have all the patience to wait so long a time for entrance into their life work. The supply of labor for such employments is therefore more limited than that for other occupations. It is necessary that there be the inducement of higher wages in prospect for the young man contemplating his career to make him willing to undergo the long period of waiting and expense required for entering such callings. Hence they yield higher incomes than others.

A consideration which offers some offset to the one just described arises from the *great esteem* in which some occupations are held. This is conspicuously the case with high public office, and with certain of the professions. The dignity attaching to the mayor of a large city, the governor of a state, or the member of a legislative body, is a lure which makes a large number of candidates available for such positions; and the result is that they can be secured for lower rates of pay than would prevail for similar ability in other lines of work. Many a successful business man or lawyer has given up a large income to accept public office in which he was paid a much lower salary. The same attraction brings a large army of recruits into such professions as medicine and the law, notwithstanding the long period of training which these require.

Similar to this factor in its influence is the *opportunity for advancement,* or the chances of conspicuous success offered by an occupation. The law is often the stepping-stone to a judgeship or some high official position. Also successful lawyers can make a great deal of money. Hence this profession has always been overcrowded. Consequently, while a few make large fortunes in it, there are always many lesser fry whose earnings are very low. Some employments offer little or no prospect of advancement. In these a compensating higher wage is to be expected.

Ordinarily an occupation which offers great *regularity of employment* will yield lower wages by the hour, day, or week than a similar one which is more irregular. Bricklayers are commonly supposed to receive higher wages than carpenters for this reason. This is a factor, too, probably, in the higher wages earned by coal miners. This is in line with what was said at the beginning of this chapter about the measurement of wages for purposes of comparing the earnings of different workers. The earnings per day or per piece will be higher in those trades which do not offer full employment throughout the year than in those which do, but the earnings per year should be the same, all other things being equal.

Compensating Differences. — Some economists make a distinction between real income, with which we are already familiar, and *psychic income,* by which they mean enjoyments or satisfactions obtained from economic activity. In one sense, wages consist of the goods which the laborer gets for his services; but his psychic income consists of the net satisfactions or utilities derived from his occupation. If the work is dangerous, fatiguing, or otherwise disagreeable, there is a disutility which must be subtracted from the utility afforded by the goods he buys with his money wages. If the work is creative, congenial, and otherwise pleasurable, there is a utility in the labor itself which must be added to the utility derived from the nominal wages. So far as individuals have freedom of choice in their selection of an occupation, they will select the work which offers the greatest net gratifications or psychic income. This causes a scarcity of labor for the more hazardous, irregular, unpleasant, and otherwise disadvantageous trades, which makes it necessary to pay higher wages in order to secure labor for them. It causes a plentiful supply in the more pleasurable callings, which reduces the marginal productivity of the labor employed in them and causes it to receive a lower wage. These differences in wages thus serve to equalize the psychic income or net advantage of the occupations. For this reason they may be called *compensating differences.* It should be remembered that it is through the adjustment of the supply of labor in the different occupations, according to the free choice of the individual, that these effects on wages are brought about.

Compensating differences in wages will not apply *between* noncompeting groups, but only *within* each group. It will not necessarily be true, for instance, that an occupation in a higher group, which offers greater advantages than one in a lower group, will be paid a lower wage in consequence; for here there is no freedom of choice on the part of the laborer in the lower group as to whether or not he shall take the more attractive position. He is not eligible to the better employment. Consequently, many of the most disagreeable, the most dangerous, and the most undesirable trades, such as that of the garbage man, the employee in a foul-smelling fertilizer factory, the domestic servant, etc., are among the lowest paid; while some of the most attractive occupations, such as that of the administrator, the executive, are among the highest paid. But as between occupations *within a single group* compensating differences will be found to operate. If, of two trades requiring equal grades of skill, one is more difficult, dangerous, or distasteful than the other, it will command a higher wage.

Irregularities of the Labor Market. — The principles of wages, as they have been set forth up to this point, represent tendencies which would work out with perfect accuracy and completeness only in a perfect market, where there was perfect freedom of contact between all the employers and all the laborers, and where there was active and unrestrained competition on both sides. Actually, however, such conditions do not obtain. There are certain peculiarities about the supply of labor which cause irregularities in the labor market, with consequent deviations in wages.

Most of these peculiarities have to do with the immobility of labor, which interferes with its freedom to move from place to place and from occupation to occupation even within one of the noncompeting groups. Most laborers are none too well educated and not well informed about the market for their services. They depend on a few employers in their immediate locality for positions, and the only way they can learn of opportunities elsewhere, is through the somewhat uncertain medium of the classified newspaper advertisements and the gossip of their friends, unless an agent from some great industrial plant seeking hands happens to cross their path. Even if they know of better opportunities elsewhere, it is difficult to pack up their belongings and move. Perhaps they have started to purchase the house they live in, and have money invested in it which cannot readily be removed. Possibly other members of the family are established in steady employment which they are reluctant to give up. The expense of transporting persons and belongings may be prohibitive. All this interferes with their geographical mobility.

There is a still greater obstacle to shifting from one occupation to another. An unskilled worker can be employed in any industry with equal facility; but a skilled man is trained to do only a particular kind of work. This was commented on in the discussion of specialization, where it was shown that his dependence upon a particular trade for a livelihood places the worker at the mercy of fluctuations in the demand in the industry where he is employed. If that demand declines, his wages may fall far below that of persons employed in other occupations within his non-competing group; yet he cannot enter those trades, because he is not skilled in them, and is perhaps too old to learn. Similarly, if the demand for skilled workers of a particular sort increases, wages may rise considerably above those of workers of the same grade in other occupations; yet there will be no sudden influx of new labor into the trade, for it takes time to learn it, and the old men do not possess the flexibility to do so. The greater the period of training required for an occupation, the more important does this immobility of labor as to trades become. It means that the supply of labor in such occupations will respond but slowly to the demand for it; meanwhile the wages may be all out of proportion to wages for other work of equal quality. In time, however, there will be a response on the part of the supply. Young men and women choosing their careers will shun those in which earnings have been depressed, and will be attracted to those where they are unusually high, until both return to normal.

In these respects labor is quite different from material commodities. If the price of potatoes is much higher in Chicago than in New York, sellers will quickly ship the vegetable from the latter to the former market until the prices are brought to equality; but if higher wages prevail for bricklayers in Chicago than in New York, there will be no such rapid adjustment, and the differences may prevail for a considerable period before enough workmen are induced to move to the point of greater demand. So also, if the medical profession is overcrowded, depressing the earnings of physicians, and electrical engineers are so scarce that they command high salaries, it will take a period of years for enough students to be attracted into engineering schools and discouraged from entering medical schools to bring the earnings of the two professions more closely into line. The upshot of all this is that, in the labor market, the deviations of market from normal prices can be wide, and they may continue over fairly long periods of time. The corrective, or normative influences, do not operate as freely as in commodity markets.

Some writers hold that wage deviations are more likely to work in a downward than an upward direction, so that market wages tend to be depressed below their normals in the majority of cases. This is attributed largely to the fact that wage-earners, as individuals, are likely to be less adept in bargaining than their employers—they are not as quick to sense new opportunities, and to take advantage of them. There are, without doubt, some "sweated" occupations, which are overcrowded with workers of very little skill, who get wages lower than is obtained by labor of similar quality in other industries or other localities. Yet the underpaid workers do not shift into these other markets because of their ignorance and helplessness. These conditions are most likely to prevail where immigrant labor is employed, especially in the case of women workers. The lack of knowledge of our language and customs makes these people easily victimized. Native labor may be in a similar predicament where the complex of social and economic forces has reduced the people to hopelessness and inertia. However, it is not so certain that actual wages in the wider labor market are below normal rates most of the time. It seems rather to be true that wage adjustments lag behind the influences which tend to pull the price of labor upward or downward, so that market rates are somewhat below their normals in periods of rising prices or of increasing demand for labor, and above them in periods of falling prices or of decreasing demand. We observed this to be the case in connection with business cycle movements, and it is very likely true also of the movement of particular wage rates, in response to changing conditions of demand or supply.

In view of these considerations, the principle that there is only one rate of wages for a given kind of labor in a given market, and the doctrine that within each non-competing group only such differences in wages can prevail as will just suffice to equalize the net advantages of the various occupations, must not be taken too literally. These are slow-moving, long-run forces. They are real tendencies, but tendencies to which the peculiarities of the labor supply present certain obstacles which obscure their effects. They work out only approximately, and considerable departures from them are frequently to be found.

The Effects of Labor Unions on Wages. — There are also important exceptions to the assumption, hitherto implicit in our reasoning, that the labor market consists of many individual employers, competing with each other for the available labor, and many individual workers, competing with each other for jobs. The fact is that in a considerable number of occupations labor is organized into unions which bargain collectively with their employers, so that the competition among individual laborers is very much reduced. In some cases, the employers are similarly banded together into associations to bargain collectively with the unions of labor. We are not here concerned with all the activities of labor organizations. Their efforts to obtain shorter hours and better working conditions; the beneficiary insurance funds which they maintain to assist workers and their families in meeting the hazards of unemployment, strikes, death, etc.; their pressure for legislation favorable to labor; their educational and recreational work—these do not bear directly upon wages. But one of the chief reasons for the existence of unions is to secure better wages for their members. This we must examine.

It is clear that, by bargaining collectively with their employers through union representatives, workers can escape from the disadvantages of individual bargaining which were set forth in the preceding paragraph. The combined resources of the union make it possible to employ leaders who are forceful and well informed regarding the wage market, so that they can bargain with employers (or combinations of employers) on a plane of equality. The threat of a strike, if the employer does not meet the union terms, is a serious one, which may often compel the employer to offer the very best wages which he can afford. So, if it is true (as the writers above referred to hold), that wages under individual bargaining are likely to be depressed below their normals, it seems likely that this condition would be corrected where labor is organized. However, this does not mean that the effect of union pressure is always (or even usually) to bring market wages into closer conformity with normal wages. What is more likely is, that they make market wages respond more quickly to favorable influences, but less quickly to unfavorable ones. In our study of business cycles we found that wages tend to lag somewhat behind the movement of prices, both in prosperity and depression, so that market wages would be somewhat below their normals in the up-swing of the cycle, and perhaps above their normals in the down-swing. Labor unions would be likely to correct the first part of this lag, but to aggravate the second; union leaders would press vigorously for wage increases during periods of business expansion and resist the efforts of employers to reduce wages during periods of contraction. So, market wages would move in fairly close correspondence with changes in normal wages during periods of rising prices, but would be held above their normals in periods of falling prices. The second of these effects no doubt tends to aggravate and prolong business depressions, by reducing enterprisers' profits. These are short-run effects.

What about the long run? Can the pressure of unions for higher wages raise the wages of labor permanently, or for long periods of time? We must realize that the schedule of demand for labor (as for all agents of production) has some elasticity. Enterprisers do not have to employ a fixed number of workers; they will employ more or less, depending on what they have to pay for them. The effective demand will not be as great when wages are high as when they are low. Hence, if unions make labor more expensive, less of it will be employed. This is illustrated by Figure 54, which may be supposed to represent the long-run schedule of demand for carpenters. According to the curve, 20,000 carpenters will be employed when the wage is $4.00 per day, only 14,000 when the wage is $6.00. We must remember that, as more carpenters are employed, their marginal product falls. The marginal workers are not worth more than $4.00 to their employers. Therefore, if the wage is higher, some way will be found to dispense with those carpenters who are not worth their hire at the new price. Methods of building construction will be employed in which not as much carpentry work is required. Perhaps mechanical wood-working machinery will be used to a greater extent, or possibly more masonry and less lumber will be used. In one way or another, the number of carpenters will be reduced, until the

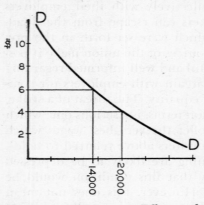

Figure 54. Long-run Effects of Union Demands for Higher Wages.

value of the marginal product of the smaller number of men has risen to $6.00 In our drawing, this is supposed to take place when 14,000 carpenters are employed. Now suppose that the normal wage of carpenters, in the absence of union activity, has been $4.00, and that approximately 20,000 men have been employed; then let the carpenters organize themselves into a union which demands an increase in wages to $6.00, threatening to go on strike if the demand is not granted. Their employers cannot compel them to work, and if the union is strong enough, it may be able to prevent strike-breakers from being introduced into the trade. It is entirely possible that the employers may be forced to pay the wage demanded. However, employers will henceforth hire only 14,000 carpenters, instead of 20,000. The increase in wages would cost some 6,000 carpenters their jobs. This would make an oversupply of carpenters on the market, and the competition of those who were out of work would make it difficult for the union to resist the pressure for a reduction of wages. Nevertheless, if it were strongly enough organized to resist this pressure, the unemployed carpenters would have to move to another market or another occupation, increasing the supply of labor elsewhere, and reducing the wages there.

This analysis indicates, firstly, that a union can ordinarily raise wages for its members only by reducing the number of workers in the trade. Hence, those unions are likely to be most successful in their efforts to obtain high wages which, by strict membership rules, high initiation fees, requirements of long membership, and similar devices, restrict the number of workers in their occupation, thereby causing a scarcity of their kind of workers. Unions in the skilled trades are often successful in accomplishing this. This is simply a case of a labor monopoly, which, like any commodity monopoly, obtains a higher price for its product by restricting the supply of it. Secondly, it shows that, where a union is successful in obtaining higher wages for its members, it does so at the expense of some other labor group whose wages are correspondingly depressed. For a union cannot compel an employer to hire, at higher wages, as many workers in a given trade as he previously hired at lower wages. Hence, if the high wage is maintained, the numbers in the trade will be smaller than they otherwise would have been, and there will be more persons seeking employment in some other occupation. This will reduce the marginal productivity, and with it the wages, of the latter.

If a great majority of all workers were organized, and all of them exerting enough pressure to compel employers to pay high wages, the effective demand for men would fall short of the effective supply, and there would be a great deal of unemployment. This may well be an important cause contributing to the unemployment problem which has confronted the United States in recent years.

There is a possibility that unions may contribute *indirectly* to higher real wages, by bringing about conditions that raise the productivity of industry. If unions make labor more efficient, or if they induce employers to improve their management and to set their establishments in better order (either for the sake of avoiding labor troubles, or out of desperation, as a means of meeting demands for higher wages), some of the increase in productivity is pretty sure to inure to the benefit of the workers. It is sometimes claimed that unions do have these effects. However, we must offset against this the fact that many union practices tend to reduce the product of labor. Nearly all unions have rules limiting the amount of work which their members are permitted to do and tending to prevent the more efficient workers from producing as much as they are capable of doing. How these influences work out on balance it is impossible to say.

The foregoing must not be interpreted as evidence that the author is opposed to unions. On the contrary, he favors them. Many of their activities are beneficial. But friendship for labor should not blind us to their mistakes, and nothing is to be gained by refusing to recognize the economic influences which limit their powers.

The Effects of Minimum Wage Laws. — Efforts are sometimes made to raise the wages of labor by laws forbidding the payment of wages below a certain minimum. It would be a happy circumstance if the problem of low wages could be solved by the simple device of making it illegal to pay them; but the possibilities in this direction are limited by the same conditions which restrict the power of unions to obtain high wages. Laws cannot compel employers to pay more to labor than the value of its marginal product. If minimum wages are fixed at a figure which is above the marginal product of unskilled labor, employers will find that some of their unskilled workers are not worth their hire, and will dismiss them. The minimum wage will then have been made effective at the expense of the unemployment of those who cannot earn it. Figure 54 will illustrate this case, as well as the case of union wages, for the underlying principles are identical. Let the law prohibit wages of less than $6.00, and it will throw 6,000 workers out of employment. This is not to say that minimum wage laws are never desirable. In the case of exploited, badly underpaid workers, who are unable to obtain a wage sufficient to meet the barest necessities of living, it may be better to regard them as public charges, to be supported out of relief funds as an act of charity, than to permit them to work long hours under bad conditions for a mere pittance. Furthermore, we have already noted that there are a few groups of "sweated" workers who, because of ignorance and lack of mobility, are not getting all that they might get under better conditions of bargaining. A minimum wage law which does not set too high a figure may compel employers to pay such workers all that they are really worth, and thus end the exploitation to which they were formerly subjected. Such laws may sometimes stimulate employers to devise methods that will make possible payment of the minimum wages without reducing their labor forces. However, it would certainly be quite impossible to force a general increase in wages for labor as a whole merely by forbidding employers to pay less than a certain minimum.

Wages as the Discounted Marginal Product of Labor. — Some writers present a theory of wages which, superficially, appears to differ in one respect from the explanation that has been offered in this chapter. They represent the demand for labor as being determined by the *discounted* marginal product of labor, instead of simply by the value of the marginal product. The use of the word "discounted" calls attention to the fact, developed in Chapter IV, that most wages are paid in advance; that is, labor is paid today, or this week, for a product which will not be sold until sometime in the future. In the case of those workers who are employed at very remote stages, the final sale of goods to ultimate consumers may not take place until long afterward. Therefore, the capitalists who make the advances must be paid interest on the sums so advanced, and this interest will be deducted from the proceeds which are ultimately realized from the sale of the product. This explanation does not differ essentially from that of this chapter. When we say that labor is paid the value of its marginal product, we mean, simply, that it is paid its *present* value, not the value that it will have at the end of the succession of productive processes. It is understood that a share of the ultimate value will go to the capitalist, as interest for savings used in financing the time-consuming production process. Labor will get the present value of its marginal product, that is, the ultimate value, less interest on the sums invested in wages, for the period of time that must elapse before the *ultimate* sale.

SUMMARY

Wages are defined as a price paid for the services of labor of any kind. They may take the form of time wages, piece-work wages, commissions, fees, payments in kind, or extra wages. All these can be resolved into average real earnings per year; and, in making comparisons between wages in different occupations or at different times, they must be reduced to this basis if error is to be avoided. Like other prices, wages are determined by certain general forces of demand and supply.

Labor is wanted for its contribution to production, and, where employed with other productive agents, this is valued according to the marginal productivity of the workers. Employers estimate the possible gains to be derived from employing a little more of this or that kind of labor in their enterprises, and they determine their demand for labor accordingly. Competition among employers and workers establishes the wages of each kind of labor at the value of its marginal product as thus determined. The marginal productivity (and hence, the wages) of those workers who are most numerous is low; the marginal productivity of those who are scarcer is greater, and their wages correspondingly higher.

The supply of laborers available for these different kinds of work depends upon the stratification of the population into non-competing groups, the growth of numbers in those groups (as affected by their standards of living), and the relative disutilities of the various occupations within a single group. The population is stratified into a number of different levels or classes as a result of differences in the heredity and environment of the people, which differences are cumulative from generation to generation. The more well-to-do classes are scarcer, partly because of natural differences in the distribution of ability, partly because of their deliberate efforts to maintain high standards of living by limiting the size of their families. Rapid increase in numbers, supplemented until recently by immigration, keeps the wages of unskilled workers at or near a subsistence level.

Within each non-competing group wages tend to equality, except for compensating differences, which are just sufficient to equalize the net advantages of the different occupations open to its members. This is because the greater disutility of those occupations which are unpleasant, dangerous, which require long training, which are not held in great esteem or which offer no opportunity for advancement, causes people to prefer callings which possess greater advantages, so that they can only be persuaded to enter the less attractive positions under the stimulus of a higher wage. This compensating principle does not affect wages between different non-competing groups, however.

Because of the ignorance of labor, its difficulty of moving from place to place, and the difficulty and length of time involved in learning new trades or professions, it is rather immobile in regard to both place and occupation. Hence the tendencies for labor of a given kind to command only one price in a given market, and for differences in wages within a non-competing group just to equalize the net advantages of different occupations, are considerably impeded, so that they work only slowly, and attain but approximate results.

Labor unions, through the power of collective bargaining, can cause wage increases to respond more promptly to conditions tending to increase the normal price of labor, and can retard somewhat the operation of influences tending in a downward direction. Also, unions which restrict their membership can obtain higher wages for workers in particular occupations, but this forces more workers into other occupations or markets, tending to depress wages there. Minimum wage laws can prevent the depression of market wages below their normals by labor exploiters, but cannot force wages for labor generally to higher levels, except at the expense of creating unemployment for those workers whose marginal product is not worth the wage established.

Wages are sometimes said to be determined by the discounted marginal product of labor. This merely emphasizes the fact that workers are paid for the present value of their product, a deduction of interest being made from the future value to reimburse the capitalists who advance wages before sale of the final product.

REFERENCES AND SUGGESTIONS FOR FURTHER READING

T. N. Carver, in Chapter IV of *The Distribution of Wealth* (1904), gives a brief, but fairly comprehensive, account of the demand and supply factors governing wages. A much fuller development of wage theory and related problems, including a discussion of union influences and wage regulation, is contained in J. R. Hicks' *The Theory of Wages* (London, 1932). A concise treatment of the institutions of the labor market, and of wage theory and policy, is to be found in M. Dobbs' *Wages* (1928). The best analysis of differences in wages with which I am familiar is that of F. W. Taussig, in Chapter 52 of his *Principles of Economics* (4th edition, 1940), from which I have obtained valuable suggestions for the present chapter. Much light on this question is also shed by Alfred Marshall in his *Principles of Economics* (5th edition, 1907, or later), Book VI, Chapters 3, 4, and 5.

Those who are interested in a statistical and mathematical approach to wages should consult Paul H. Douglas' *The Theory of Wages* (1934), which won the Hart, Schaffner and Marx prize for the best presentation of this subject.

Chapter XXI

INTEREST

A. The Income from Capital

Durable Capital as a Source of Income. — When wealth is of a temporary or transient nature, the utilities embodied in it are fleeting, and consumed immediately, or in a very short period of time. Ice cream lasts but a few hours; a ton of coal is burned up in a few days or weeks. Wealth of a more durable sort, however, is capable of yielding utilities for a considerable period of time—sometimes for an extremely long one. A dwelling house or a farm is a sort of permanent store of utilities, the benefits of which are released gradually to the user for many days or years. Much of the capital employed in production is of this sort; and some forms of consumers' capital, such as residences, are also. This capital is a permanent source of income to the community. The income consists of the goods—the commodities or services—that are derived, directly or indirectly, from it. A dwelling yields income annually in the form of shelter and comfort; a wheat field yields it in the form of the crops which are raised upon it; a railroad yields it in the form of transportation to passengers and freight. The permanent capital of the nation is one of its sources of income.

In the processes of exchange, this income is given a pecuniary value distinct from the value of the capital itself. The use of the dwelling house can be sold for a year at a given price; so can the use of the railroad or the farm. Many persons derive a part or all of their income from the durable capital which they own, whose benefits they either use directly, or sell to someone else in exchange for money with which to obtain income in some other form. It is with the *value* of the income from such capital that we are now concerned; for, upon the value of the real income from the capital which they own, the share of the nation's income received by all who possess income-bearing wealth depends. The problem of this chapter and the next is to analyze the forces which determine the value of the income from capital.

This income, expressed in price terms, commonly goes by either o two different names—rent or interest. Each of these terms refers to income from capital, the difference between them being not so much in the nature of the income itself, as in the point of view from which it is regarded.

Rent. — When a form of durable wealth is leased or let by one person to another for a consideration, it is said to be rented. A farmer can rent an acre of agricultural land, a family can rent a residence in which to live, or a college professor can rent a typewriter for his use. In this case the rent is expressed as a certain sum of money per day, per month, or per year, paid for the use of the good in question. In using the term rent, the actual article of wealth from which the income is derived is always kept in mind. The rent is thought of in relation to the physical capital-good, and is expressed in terms of a certain price for its use. A house may rent for fifty dollars per month; a fancy dress costume for two dollars per day; a farm for ten dollars an acre per year. Any durable article, such as a piece of real estate, a piano, an automobile, or even a dress suit, can be rented; but always there is such an article of wealth—we do not speak of renting a sum of money. We may define *rent,* therefore, as *income from capital viewed with reference to the particular article of capital from which it is derived.*

Where there is a definite leasing contract between an owner and a renter, in which a stipulated sum for the use of the rented wealth is payable, the rent is said to be *explicit;* but there may be *implicit* rent, even where there is no such contract. When an individual uses his own capital, and does not lease it to another party, he receives the income from it; only in this case he gets it in the form of direct benefits from the wealth itself, instead of in the form of a money payment with which to buy other utilities. For instance, if a man owns the house in which he resides, he receives income from it in the form of the shelter and comfort it affords him. If we think of these direct benefits in terms of their value, they can be regarded as rent received by the owner for his property just the same as if he had leased it. It is in this case that the rent can be called implicit. The essence of rent, then, is not that it is a price paid, but that it is income received, from a durable good. All capital can be thought of as yielding rent in this sense. It is not usually necessary to use the terms explicit or implicit rent. The word rent, alone, includes them both, and is sufficient for most purposes.

Interest. — The income from capital is also called interest. For instance, when a bank makes a loan to a customer, it obtains from him interest payments for the use of the amount borrowed. When an investor buys the bonds of a corporation, they yield him annual money income, which consists of interest payments by the corporation for the use of the investor's wealth. Suppose the amount of each of these loans is $1,000, and the amount of the interest $60. What has really been loaned in these cases is command over capital; the borrower has been given purchasing power with which to obtain $1,000 worth of wealth, which the lender might have possessed if he had kept the money for his own use. The $60 of interest, therefore, is really a payment for the use of this capital, just the same as if the capital had been rented by the lender to the borrower. But since there has been no direct transfer of goods between the parties to the transactions, each thinks of the deal in money terms, and the payment for the use of the capital is regarded as income paid for, and received from, a fund of money. We may think of this fund as a certain amount of capital-value, to distinguish it from the actual capital-goods whose value it expresses.

Herein lies the difference between interest and rent. Rent is thought of as a payment for the use of certain definite capital-goods, but interest is thought of as payment for the use of a certain amount of capital-value. Nevertheless, we must not lose sight of the fact that, back of the sum of money or capital-value on which interest is paid, are the real goods, and that the payment is really made for the use of these goods in both cases. There is, therefore, no fundamental difference between rent and interest; the same income may be called either one or the other, depending on the point of view. If we could put our fingers upon the particular articles of wealth from which the sixty dollars is derived in the above examples, we could call it the rent of those articles; but so long as it is considered simply with reference to a capital-value, it is called interest. We may arrive at the definition, therefore, that *interest is income derived from capital, viewed with reference to the value of the latter.*

Since both the value of the income and the value of the capital which yields it are stated in money terms, one can be expressed as a percentage of the other. It is very common to express interest in this way. If $1,000 worth of capital yields $60 worth of income, the interest is 6 per cent. In this case the value of the capital concerned is called the principal, to distinguish it from the income, or interest. The ratio of the interest to the principal is known as the *rate of interest.* In the above example, this rate is 6 per cent.

As in the case of rent, interest frequently arises out of a loan contract, but there can be interest without such a transaction. The owner of capital receives interest for its use whether he lends it to someone else, or employs it himself. Suppose two business men, A and B, each have $5,000 worth of capital. A invests his in the bonds of a railroad, securing an interest return of 5 per cent, which brings him in an income of $250 per year. Here is a definite loan, and an agreed payment of interest. B, on the other hand, invests his money in a small grocery store. Here no loan is involved, as he runs the store himself. He will nevertheless expect the store to yield him as much return for his money (in addition to all other costs, including wages for his own labor), as if he had loaned it to another. The interest accrues to him just as truly as in A's case. Interest, therefore, does not arise necessarily out of a loan transaction, but is received by the owners of capital wherever it is productively used. Some economists draw a distinction between *explicit interest,* by which they mean that interest which arises where a loan is made and an agreed interest paid upon it; and *implicit interest,* which arises where no loan transaction is involved, but where the capital yields income directly to its owner. However, it is not often necessary to make this distinction. Both forms of income are essentially alike in their nature, and both can be called by the simple term, interest.

We see, then, that the income from capital can be regarded either in its relation to the *piece of wealth* from which it is derived, in which case it is called rent; or in relation to the *value* of the capital from which it is derived, in which case it is called interest. The same income can be looked at from either or both points of view. A man owns a one hundred acre farm, which represents an investment of $20,000. He leases it to a tenant for $12 an acre. This sum is the *rent* of the farm, amounting, in the aggregate, to $1,200 per year. But this $1,200 is also *interest* on his investment, at the rate of 6 per cent. This one item of income, valued at $1,200, is both rent and interest. All income from capital has this dual aspect; it can be called by either the one or the other, depending upon the point of view.

Equipment and Land. — Our immediate problem is to find out what fixes the amount of interest or rent, in order that we may understand how the share of the social income which goes to the owners of capital is determined. In doing this we shall be carrying on that general analysis of the income sharing process with which we have been occupied in the last two chapters. For this purpose, we must bear in mind that some capital is supplied gratis by nature, while other capital results from the investment of savings. The former we call *land,* the latter, *equipment.*

We have here a distinction of great importance for the problem of income sharing, for it indicates a fundamental difference in the conditions of supply for the two kinds of capital. Since the investment of savings is essential to the creation of equipment, the supply of the latter is variable. According to whether men save and invest much or little, the quantity of equipment will be great or small. If its quantity is great, its value will be less than if it were more scarce, and the income which its owners can derive from it will be governed accordingly. Therefore, if we would understand the factors determining the yield of this kind of capital, we must study the conditions which affect the process of saving and investment.

The supply of land, on the other hand, is very nearly fixed. To be sure, its quantity can be increased to some extent by the irrigation of deserts and the drainage of swamps, but, as compared with the total, this is insignificant. For all practical purposes we may say that man cannot materially increase the quantity of land, nor destroy that which is already here. Since it has been here from the beginning, no saving is required to bring it into existence. In this respect the conditions governing the supply of land differ from those governing the supply of equipment; and therefore, the income shares derived from them cannot be explained on the same principles.[1]

We shall find, however, that there are some forms of equipment, so difficult to construct and so durable in character, that it takes a long time to change the amount of them very greatly; for short periods, therefore, they are practically inseparable from the land itself. In these circumstances, the income from equipment cannot be sharply demarcated from that of land. We shall give due consideration to such cases as we proceed, but they will not destroy the validity of the general distinction which we have drawn.

In view of the foregoing, we shall consider the income from equipment as a share distinct from that of land, devoting this chapter to the former. Since equipment arises from the investment of savings, our problem is to analyze the conditions of demand and supply of savings available for investment. When thinking of these in terms of *investible funds,* we shall consider their income as interest. It is this aspect of the problem that we shall take up first. When thinking of the savings as embodied in physical equipment, we shall consider their income as rent. We shall deal with this briefly after the discussion of interest. Let us turn, therefore, to the latter.

B. The Rate of Interest

Consumers' Demand for Investible Funds. — How much will a borrower be willing to pay for the loan of a sum of money which he

---

[1] It is because of this distinction that some economists exclude land from the category of capital, as explained in the third footnote of Chapter IV. The same writers use the words *rent* and *interest* in a sense different from that here adopted. They reserve the word *rent* for the income from land (sometimes employing the term *economic rent* to avoid confusion with business usage), and *interest* for the income from what they call capital (*i.e.,* equipment). They would never speak of the income from land as interest, nor of that from equipment as rent. The whole purpose of this terminology is to bring out clearly the distinction between land and other kinds of wealth. The distinction is a proper one, but the terminology involves a confusion with popular speech, as well as some other difficulties, which were pointed out in the footnote above referred to.

intends to convert into some form of equipment? There are two classes of such borrowers—consumers and producers. Some borrow to obtain the use of consumers' goods. A good example of this is where a man borrows from a building and loan association to finance the building of a home. Other examples are where an automobile, a piano, an electric refrigerator, a phonograph, or a radio, is bought on the installment plan. Each such purchase really involves a loan transaction, in which the price the purchaser pays includes not only the price of the article itself (the principal of the loan), but also interest on the amount he owes from the time he buys the article until it is fully paid for. We may call all borrowings of this sort consumers' loans. When we consider the great number of home building mortgages and installment purchases, it will be realized that the total amount of such loans is of considerable importance.

We may get at the factors determining how much consumers will pay for such loans by considering a simple example. Let us suppose that a man with a fair income, but with little or no savings, is desirous of building a house. He is confronted with the following alternatives: If he waits until he has saved enough from his income to pay the cost of building the house, he must do without it for a very long time. On the other hand, if he borrows enough to build it now, he must pay a premium (interest) for the use of the lender's savings. He must weigh the advantage of immediate possession against the disadvantage of having to pay interest. How much he will pay depends upon (1) the utility to be derived from the use of the goods, (2) his impatience or feeling of urgency for the immediate enjoyment thereof, and (3) his present and probable future paying capacity (income). Each consumer borrower is governed by similar influences. Some, of course, stand ready to pay more than others. It is possible, therefore, to draw up a demand schedule, showing the various quantities of savings that will be taken at each of a series of rates of interest. Like other demand schedules, it will follow the law of demand; i.e., the lower the rate, the greater the quantity that consumers will borrow. A curve representing such a schedule is shown by D_c in Figure 55 (page 521).

Producers' Demand for Investible Funds. — In addition to this demand from consumers, there is the much larger demand from enterprisers, who desire to borrow funds for purposes of production. Here we are dealing with producers' loans. Nearly all enterprisers are borrowers at one time or another. Corporations "float" issues of bonds with which to secure funds for the construction or expansion of their plants, and both corporations and individual business men borrow from banks or acquaintances to obtain warehouses, stores, and fixtures, or stocks of materials and merchandise. The funds so borrowed are savings, invested in equipment (except those used in the purchase of land, which will be considered later). Hence the amount of interest enterprisers will offer depends upon how highly they value the use of such equipment. Since they do not use it for the gratification of their own desires, it has no direct utility for them; they value it only for the salable products which they expect to obtain with its aid. What they are willing to pay depends on its importance to them in the production of those salable commodities. Since the equipment is to be used along with land and labor in production, we are again confronted with the problem of how to determine its importance to the process apart from that of the other agents. Here the principle of marginal productivity enters. Let us consider this principle once more, and see how it applies to the present case.

The Marginal Productivity of Equipment. — In an earlier chapter, we learned that the productive processes of modern industry are not direct, but roundabout. The savage who wants water goes directly to the stream and dishes it out in a crude pail or cup; but the civilized man devotes thousands or millions of hours to preliminary labor, constructing huge dams and reservoirs, powerful pumping machinery, long pipe lines and complicated plumbing. As a result of this roundabout method, he obtains more water, in the long run, for the amount of energy expended. It is the use of equipment, derived from saving and investment, that has made this greater product possible. Tools, which in this case consist of reservoirs, pumps, pipes, and so on, make labor more efficient. The product that results from their use is not only great enough to pay for their cost, but there is a surplus besides. This surplus makes possible the payment of interest by enterprisers, and determines how much they can afford to pay.

The amount of the surplus yielded by equipment will depend upon the quantity of it that is employed, relative to the other agents of production, following the principle of diminishing productivity. As an illustration of this, let us imagine a producer who is about to enter the baking business. He has his choice of using a simple plant with few tools, or a more elaborate one. Suppose he employs comparatively little equipment, using the simplest sort of building in which to conduct his operations, a small inexpensive oven, cheap pans, and a push cart in which to deliver his loaves. Because of the lack of adequate facilities, only a small quantity of bread can be baked at one time, and the process will have to be often repeated. There will be much extra labor required repeatedly to mix and knead the dough, to fire the oven, and to deliver the goods by the slow method of the push cart; while the flimsiness of the plant and tools will require the expenditure of much labor and materials on their repair and replacement. A larger oven would make possible the mixing of a greater quantity of dough and its baking at one operation, with a consequent saving of time. Automatic mixing and kneading machinery will save considerable labor. An auto-truck will make possible the delivery of the product with corresponding economy. More substantial plant and equipment will require proportionately less repair and replacement. Even if we take into consideration the labor and resources required to make all this additional equipment, there will be a saving, for it provides a surplus above its own cost.

However, as the baker elaborates the process still further by the employment of more complex and substantial instruments, there will not be a corresponding increase in the product. Suppose he employs an electric oven in place of one heated by coal. Suppose his pans are made of solid nickel, so that they will not rust, and will last for many years. Suppose belt conveyors are installed to move the materials and bread from place to place within the plant. It is even conceivable that the baker might construct a system of underground pneumatic tubes to the homes of his various customers, through which to shoot the loaves as they come fresh from his ovens. All these are methods of increasing the roundaboutness of the baking process. There is no limit to which it might be carried, but after it had passed a certain point, the increase in the output of bread made by using additional equipment would get progressively smaller.

The reader will recognize that in this situation the marginal productivity of the equipment is declining. When but few tools are employed, each is very important to the output, but when many are used, they must take less productive forms, in which case a little more or less does not make a very great difference in the product. The least productive uses to which any of the equipment of the plant is put are marginal uses. The surplus over its cost yielded by the equipment on this margin will be small, and may disappear entirely. It is the product of the equipment employed at the margin which determines how much the baker is willing to borrow. So long as he can borrow funds which, when invested in equipment, will yield him more than he has to pay for the loan, it will be to his interest to do it; but not otherwise. In short, he will continue to borrow until the value of the marginal product of his equipment has fallen so low as just to equal the price he must pay for its use; and there he will stop.

This baker is not alone in seeking the use of investible funds. There are many competing enterprises whose conduct is determined by similar considerations. They, too, are desirous of obtaining the use of any equipment they can get, so long as its price does not exceed the value of the surplus they expect its employment to yield. So, each will seek to secure more of it until the point is reached where the value of its marginal product is just enough over its cost to pay the interest. Competition tends to bring this margin to nearly the same point in every well-managed enterprise. Just where this point will be depends upon the volume of equipment that can be provided out of the available savings. We may conclude that the demand of producers for investible funds is based on the marginal productivity of equipment. Since the marginal productivity becomes lower as the quantity of equipment becomes greater, we may further conclude that this demand, like that of consumers, follows the law of demand; that is, the greater the quantity of funds offered on the loan market, the lower will be the price that can be obtained for their use.

Summary View of the Demand for Investible Funds. — By bringing together what has been said about consumers' and producers' demands for loans, a picture of the total demand for the use of investible funds may be obtained. This demand is composite, being made up of the two sources just named. The demands of both sets of borrowers are alike in that they follow the law of demand. If only a small supply of funds is available, a few consumer borrowers can be found who will pay a high price for the loan of them, and producer borrowers will also pay a high price because the resulting scarcity of equipment makes its marginal productivity in their industries high. If the supply available is large, however, the funds will have to be loaned to consumer borrowers to whom their utility is less, or whose small incomes permit them to pay only a low price, and to producer borrowers who will pay less, because the greater abundance of equipment makes its marginal productivity in their industries low.

The nature of the resulting demand schedule is pictured graphically in Figure 55 (page 521). Here D_c is supposed to represent the demand of consumer borrowers, D_t the total demand of consumer and producer borrowers combined. By drawing a horizontal line across the two curves from any point on the vertical axis, we can ascertain how much will be borrowed by each group at the corresponding interest rate. For instance, the horizontal line intersecting the curve D_t at G tells us that, if the rate of interest is 5 per cent, the effective demand of consumer borrowers will be 1½ million dollars, and of producer borrowers 4½ million dollars, making a total of 6 millions. The effective demand at any other rate of interest can be found by a similar procedure. Observe that the curve of total demand slopes downward to the right, thereby exhibiting the same characteristic which we have found to be typical of demand curves generally.

The Supply of Investible Funds. — We have already learned that the supply of investible funds comes from saving. This may be either voluntary or involuntary, but it is with the former that we are mainly concerned for the moment, because it is upon voluntary saving that the average amount of investment over long periods of time depends. Therefore, it is the investment of voluntary savings that is the significant supply factor in determining the normal rate of interest. We may postpone the question of involuntary saving until we are ready to consider the fluctuations of market rates of interest about their norms.

In order to understand the influences at work on the supply side of the investment market, we must find the answer to two broad questions: What determines the willingness of people to save, instead of spending all their income in immediate consumption? And, what determines their willingness to invest their savings in productive equipment, instead of hoarding them in stores of near-goods, or in cash? Let us consider each of these questions, in turn.

Willingness to Save. — The capacity of people for saving depends on the size of their incomes. When a man's income is so small that it barely suffices for the subsistence of himself and his family, he cannot save very much; only if he has a surplus above his minimum needs can his savings be substantial. In general, therefore, we may expect the volume of saving to be affected by the size of individual incomes. But saving does not depend on size of income alone, for different persons having the same income will not all save the same amounts. How much each will save depends on his habits of thrift, and his anticipation of future needs. Thrifty people will endeavor to create a fund of savings to meet possible expenses arising from sickness or accident, to provide for old age, and to give support to surviving dependents after death. The institution of insurance has greatly promoted the habit of saving for purposes of this kind. In these cases, the saving is not undertaken primarily for the purpose of creating productive equipment—a store of cash or of near-goods would serve the end desired well enough.

In other cases, saving may be done with the deliberate intention of creating equipment. This is the case with the home-owner who takes out building and loan shares in order that he may accumulate enough to build himself a house; and it is the case with the corporation, whose board of directors decides to reinvest some of the earnings in the business (perhaps for a plant extension), instead of distributing all of the profits in dividends to stockholders.

It is generally held that, given the above factors pertaining to the incomes, habits and propensities of the various members of the population, the amount that will be saved and offered for investment will vary with the inducement that borrowers are disposed to offer. That is, more will be saved and invested when interest is high than when it is low. There is another school, however, which holds that the quantity of savings is determined predominately by sociological and economic factors that are largely independent of the interest rate. The British economist Keynes, for instance, while not denying that the inducement of interest is one of the relevant factors, nevertheless believes that saving depends mainly upon the size of the national income, rising as it rises and falling as it falls. He holds that the inducement of interest is relatively unimportant in determining the amount of savings, but is of great importance in determining what proportion of savings will be put into investments, and what proportion will be held in the form of idle money balances. We must presently consider some of the interesting consequences which follow from this line of thought; but for the moment our task is to develop more fully the customary type of explanation.

The Time Preference Theory. — This explanation is called the time preference theory. According to this theory, the person who saves is giving up present goods in exchange for goods which he expects to receive some time in the future. But most people prefer present goods to future goods. Hence, they will not make the present sacrifice, involved in saving, unless the goods which are expected to result later from the saving exceed in value those which are sacrificed now. This is believed to be one reason why interest has to be paid for invested savings—it is an extra premium (in addition to the principal) to compensate for the sacrifice of waiting.

This trait of human nature (preference for present goods) is known as *time preference,* or *impatience.* It can be expressed mathematically, as a rate, or percentage. For instance, a man who could just be induced to exchange $1,000 in the present for $1,100 a year in the future would be said to have a rate of time preference of 10 per cent, while an individual who would accept $1,050 next year for $1,000 now would have a rate of 5 per cent. The rates of impatience of different communities, and of different individuals in the same community, will differ according to their intelligence, habits, and circumstances. Intelligent, thrifty people save willingly—their rates of time preference are low. Some people would save to meet future needs even if they had to accept less than they give up now—their rates of impatience are negative (*i.e.,* less than zero). Ignorant, shiftless people would not save unless the inducement were very strong—their rates are high. Between these extremes are all possible gradations. Among the factors that affect the rates are: size of income (the rich have lower rates of time preference than the poor); prospective growth or shrinkage of income (the man whose income is declining has a lower rate, because he can foresee a time when his needs will be poorly taken care of, unless he

INTEREST   517

makes provision now); age (a young man, with a growing family, has
more reason to save than an old man with one foot in the grave);
hazards (the person employed in a dangerous occupation has more
need to provide for accidents than have other persons); and so on.

For each individual there is not just one rate of time preference,
but rather a schedule of the rates, at each of which he will save different proportions of his income. To save a small portion of one's
income entails no great sacrifice; the larger the proportion of it set
aside, the greater is the pain of foregoing the consumption of present
goods. Hence, one's rate of impatience is low on small savings, and
rises with each increase in the amount saved. One will offer more
savings for investment when interest is high than when it is low. It is
the joint action of all these forces, some working in one direction,
some in another, that is found in the loan market. The nature of the
combined influences is such that, the greater the amount to be saved,
the higher the inducement that must be offered. In other words,
savings have a supply-price, which is higher for a large quantity of
savings than for a smaller quantity. If plotted as a supply curve, the
latter would slope upward to the right, like a curve of increasing
costs. (See the curve TT in Figure 55, page 521.)

Objections to the Time Preference Theory. — Those who object
to this theory claim that the concept of a rate of time preference, according to which savings will be increased if a higher price is offered for them and decreased if the price falls, does not correspond to
the facts. They stress particularly four important influences affecting
savings, which are believed to be inconsistent with the theory. The latter rests upon the assumption that saving is irksome or distasteful to the
saver; that to do without present goods is a sort of abstinence which
entails a sacrifice that must be paid for. The first objection raised by
the critics is that in many cases this assumption does not hold true.
It is pointed out that the very rich have so large a surplus that they
are quite unable to spend it all for their own use, and that they therefore invest it in equipment as a matter of course. Consequently, the
amount they will save depends on the amount of their surplus, and
bears no definite relation to the price they can obtain for the use
of the savings so accumulated.

In the second place, it is argued that the large volume of savings
accumulated by the reinvestment of corporate earnings does not
involve any question of time preference or abstinence, because the
stockholders do this saving involuntarily. The funds never get into
their possession, for the directors simply decide that it is wise for the
prosperity of the business to use the earnings for extensions to plant,
rather than to distribute them in dividends.

Thirdly, a great deal of saving is accomplished by the state, through taxation. When a city builds an art museum, although it may borrow the funds in the first instance, it eventually redeems the bonds out of taxes levied upon the community. Here the individual is forced to save because public authority deems it wise for the welfare of the citizens; but in this case again, it is held, we cannot speak of a rate of time preference.

Finally, it is pointed out that, if the motive of an individual in saving is to provide himself with a certain income, sufficient to maintain him at his accustomed standard of living, the lower the rate of return on investments, the greater the amount he must save in order to secure such an income. Suppose, for instance, that one is accustomed to living at a scale which involves the expenditure of $5,000 a year. If investments yield a return of 5 per cent, $100,000 of savings will provide such an income; but if the rate falls to 4 per cent, it would take $125,000 to provide it. Hence such persons will save less when the price paid for savings is high than when it is low. This is directly contrary to the time preference theory, which says that, the higher the rate of return, the more people will save. This is an important factor in those savings which go into life insurance funds.

These objections lead to the conclusion that the supply of savings is not controlled by the rate of time preference, but is fixed by the general habits of individuals in regard to savings, by customary standards of living, by business practices and institutions, by governmental policies regarding the erection of public works, and by all the various factors affecting those general sources of savings which were described in a preceding paragraph. This tends to support the view that savings have no definite supply-price, and that their supply is determined largely irrespective of the rate of return on investments.

These criticisms are useful in calling attention to certain forces influencing the supply of savings which are not sufficiently stressed by the time preference theory; but, in the judgment of the present writer, they do not render the analysis invalid. We may recognize that there are some savings the volume of which would remain unchanged whether a higher or lower price were paid to them, and also that there are some savers who would be induced to accumulate more if the price fell and less if it rose, rather than the reverse; but in addition to these there are undoubtedly many more persons to whom saving constitutes a real sacrifice of present goods, and who will therefore be influenced strongly by the prospect of future income to be derived from their capital. Even the rich man finds a point where, if he saves any larger proportion of his present income, he must do without some luxury which he would like to enjoy, and he will not be willing to submit to this abstinence unless some premium in the future is to be obtained by so doing. Hence, it is not incorrect to think that the volume of savings will increase or decrease, according as the inducement offered for their use is higher or lower.

Liquidity Preference. — Be that as it may, it seems fairly certain that funds saved will not be offered for investment unless some reward is to be gained thereby; for nominal savings do not have to be put into equipment—they can be hoarded in the form of money, instead. Modern financial institutions make it possible to hoard money with great safety. All one has to do is to store cash (specie or paper) in a safety deposit box, and the trick is done. Even a bank deposit may, under some circumstances, constitute a fund of idle money which does not enter into investment.

There are a number of reasons why people with surplus funds might prefer to keep them in cash, instead of invest them. For one thing, the funds may be safer in a safety deposit vault. But the chief advantage is that cash is a more "liquid" asset than an investment in equipment. By "liquid" is meant, readily exchangeable for other kinds of goods. When money is saved, the saver presumably expects to use it sometime later, to meet some future need. That need may take a great variety of forms. The money may be wanted to pay medical bills or funeral expenses; it may be wanted to provide a livelihood in old age; or perhaps a favorable business opportunity may arise in which the saver may desire to employ it. If the money has been invested (say in railroad bonds) there may not be a ready market for the bonds at the time when it is needed. Bonds may be low in price, so that the investment cannot be converted into cash without loss. If it has been invested in real estate, it may take a long time to find a buyer for the property; in the meantime, the funds are "frozen." But if the money has been hoarded in the form of cash, it is instantly available for any purpose whatsoever. This is an advantage not to be disregarded lightly. It is not likely that the saver would willingly forego it, unless there was some offsetting gain to be derived from investment. Hence, the prospect of receiving interest is a necessary inducement to investment.

The preference which people have for cash, rather than for an investment in equipment, is called *liquidity preference*. It can be measured as a rate, in the same manner as time preference. That is, by ascertaining the interest premium which would just suffice to induce an individual to invest his surplus holdings of money, instead of hoarding them, we could know what was his rate of liquidity preference. This rate presumably differs from person to person; and any one person would probably be willing to invest a larger proportion of his nominal savings at a high rate than at a low one.

The factors upon which liquidity preference depends were set forth in the chapter on *The Fluctuating Price Level,* where the reasons why people prefer to hold a part of their assets in money, instead of in goods, were explained. According to that explanation, people's holdings of money depend upon: (1) the interval of time that elapses between their successive money receipts—a man must not spend all his money on the day he receives it, he must spread it out over the period that will intervene before the next pay day; (2) the desire to provide for possible contingencies, such as illness, or the need for repairs to one's house; (3) the desire to hold money for speculative purposes. The amount of money that will be held for these three reasons (especially the last) will presumably be affected by the interest rate. If the rate is high, savers may find that they can "pare" somewhat the amounts they need to hold in cash, in order to reap the advantage of a high yield from investment; if the rate is low, they will hold more of their surplus in liquid form. This causal relationship works both ways; a change in the attitudes of people toward the desirability or need of holding cash for the above three reasons will have corresponding repercussions on the interest rate. If they feel it wise to hold a larger part of their assets in cash (*i.e.,* if their liquidity preference rises) proportionately less will be offered for investment, and the rate of interest will go higher; if they reduce their cash holdings (*i.e.,* if liquidity preference falls) more will be offered for investment, and the rate of interest will go down.

Cost and Risk of Lending. — The willingness of savers to invest their surplus is also affected by the costs of making investments, and by the risks of possible loss. A loan transaction often involves a certain amount of administrative detail which must be paid for. This is most conspicuous in the case of banking. The making of loans is a bank's most important function, and the whole cost of maintaining the building, paying the cashiers, clerks, and other employees—in fact, the whole administration of the institution—is one of the expenses involved in the loans it makes. Naturally, the bank must be recompensed for this cost by its customers, and this recompense constitutes a considerable element in the interest which the borrower pays. Similar elements enter to a lesser degree in almost any loan.

Finally, in making a loan or an investment of any kind, there is usually some danger of losing a part or all of one's savings. Businesses may fail; persons to whom funds are entrusted may prove dishonest; natural disasters may occur, or weather conditions may be unfavorable—in fact, any one or all of the property risks discussed in Chapter VII may be present in greater or less degree. Where the risk is insurable, the cost of the insurance must be paid for, and the saver will expect to receive enough income from his loan to meet this expense. Where the risk is not insurable, the lender will nevertheless have it in mind, and unless the borrower pays him a sufficient sum to make it worth his while to assume this risk, he is not likely to make the loan. Therefore, payment for risk is one of the costs a borrower must meet, and is one of the elements included in interest.

Determination of the Rate of Interest. — We have now surveyed the various factors which are at work in the market for investible funds. If we bring these factors together into a single picture we will be able to see how the rate of interest is determined. The mechanism of this determination is represented graphically in Figure 55.

In this diagram, quantities of savings offered for investment are

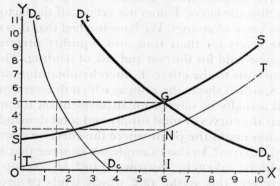

Figure 55. Determination of the Rate of Interest.

measured in millions of dollars, shown on the base line OX. On the vertical line, OY, are measured the various prices that may be paid for the use of savings, expressed in terms of percentages (that is, in interest rates). The composite nature of the schedule of demand for investible savings is shown by the fact that there are two demand curves instead of one. The first of these (D_c) represents the schedule of demand of those who borrow for purposes of consumption, as explained in a previous paragraph. To it is added the demand of producer borrowers, so that the curve D_t represents the schedule of total demand. We have learned that producers' demand rests upon the marginal productivity of the equipment which they can obtain with the funds they borrow. Since both of these schedules follow the law of demand, the curve D_t slopes downward to the right, showing that the effective demand for funds is greater at low rates than at high rates.

The curve S represents the supply prices at which different quantities of savings will be offered for investment. It is made up of two elements. The first of these, represented by the curve T, indicates the combined influence of time and liquidity preference. Since there are some people with low rates of time and liquidity preference, who would be willing to offer funds for investment without the inducement of high rates of interest, a small quantity of savings would be forthcoming even if the rate of interest were fairly low; therefore, this curve begins at a low point on the left side of the diagram. If greater quantities of savings are to be offered, suppliers must be drawn into the market whose rates of time and liquidity preference are higher (including those who would offer small amounts at low rates, but who could be persuaded to offer larger sums if the inducement were greater). Therefore, the curve slopes upward to the right, indicating that the effective supply will be greater, the higher the rate of interest prevailing. But the curve T does not reflect all the factors entering into the supply price of savings. We have learned that it is not enough to compensate savers for their time and liquidity preference alone. They must also be paid for the cost and risk of lending. Therefore, we must add these costs to the curve T, thereby obtaining the complete supply curve S, which shows the rates at which different quantities of savings would actually be offered for investment on the market.

Observe that the curves of total supply and total demand cross at G. This intersection marks the point where the effective demand and effective supply are equal. In this example, we suppose that at 5 per cent $6,000,000 will be taken by borrowers and $6,000,000 offered by lenders. Therefore, this is the rate which tends to prevail in the market. Such a rate is called *the normal rate* of interest. It is the same as the true or equilibrium rate which was discussed in Chapter XI. Market rates of interest will fluctuate about this point, just as market commodity prices fluctuate about their normals.

Gross Interest and Net Interest. — It is desirable to make a distinction between that part of interest which is paid for time and liquidity preference and that part which is paid to compensate for the costs and risks of investment. Accordingly, the line GI in Figure 55, which represents the rate of interest, is divided into two parts, lettered NI and GN, respectively. NI represents the payment for time and liquidity preference. This is what savers receive for sacrificing present goods and for giving up the advantage of holding their assets in liquid form. It is given the name *net interest,* or *pure interest.* It is what investors would receive if they could put their savings into loans which were absolutely free from risk and which involved no administrative costs. However, it seldom (if ever) happens that the price paid for the use of investible funds consists only of net interest. Always there is something extra (GN) to compensate for administrative costs and risks. The total payment, which includes all the elements we have analyzed, is called *gross interest*. It is represented by the line GI in the diagram. The distinction is important in order for us to understand the relation between rates of interest among different investments in the same loan market. This thought will be developed in the next two paragraphs.

The Tendency to Equality of Net Interest Rates. — Some writers speak as if normally there was only one "general" rate of interest, there being a tendency for all loans to be made at the same rate, any difference in the rates yielded by different investments being an accident or an abnormal condition. This is a mistake, if by interest is meant the rates actually paid in the markets—that is, gross interest. There is, however, a long-run tendency towards such rates of interests as will establish the same rate of *net* interest of every investment in a given loan market. Where active competition prevails, there tends to be paid the same premium for time and liquidity preference on all loans, any differences in gross interest being due to differences in the payments for risk or administrative costs.

This is due to the *mobility of savings*. Durable kinds of equipment, once constructed, cannot change their form, of course; and because they are often somewhat specialized, they sometimes cannot even change their uses, except to a limited extent. A textile factory cannot be converted into the equipment of a silver mine, nor can a railroad be made into an ocean liner. Therefore, if silver mining yields higher rates of return than textile manufacturing, or if ocean transportation is more profitable than railroading, nothing can be done about it until the railroad or the factory wears out. The owners of steamships and silver mines will receive high rates of net interest on their investments and the owners of the railroads and textile mills will receive low rates for a time—possibly for a considerable period of years. But with such a situation prevailing, persons with new savings to invest will not be likely to offer them for textile manufacture or railroad building purposes, for they can get a better return if they construct steamships and open up new silver mines—or, what amounts to the same thing, lend to enterprisers who borrow for these purposes. This will cause a gradual shifting of investment from the low-paying to the high-paying industries. As textile mills and railroads wear out, no new equipment taking their place, the scarcity of their products will cause their price to rise, until the income derived from such investments increases sufficiently to attract new savings. They will then be yielding higher rates of interest than before. As new silver mines and steamships are constructed, the increasing supply of their products will cause the price of the latter to fall, until the income from such investments declines. They will then be yielding lower rates of interest than before. Thus, there will have been set in motion forces which, given sufficient time, would bring about an equalization of the rates of net interest yielded in these investments.

But the rates of gross interest would never be equal. Ocean transportation involves risks and costs not found in textile manufacture. It is a more hazardous enterprise. So is silver mining. One never knows how long a rich vein will last nor when a deposit will be worked out, although the science of geology has greatly reduced the element of guesswork in such undertakings. Thus, these industries would have to offer greater inducements to investors than would be necessary in the more stable fields of production. But these differences would just compensate for the extra administrative costs, insurance, and risk in the industries in question; the actual premium offered for time and liquidity preference in the four cases would be equalized by the process of shifting investments.

There is a steady flow of new savings ever seeking the most profitable use they can find. Part of this flow comes from the depreciation funds which business men lay aside to replace their plants when worn out, and part from the surplus earnings of corporations not distributed to stockholders but held for reinvestment. These funds need not be invested in plants identically like the old. They can be put in new businesses altogether, if the old ones do not pay; and frequently they are so shifted. Another part comes from individuals who are continually accumulating new savings. These can be put in the form of any kind of wealth that offers sufficient inducement in income yield. It is these replacement funds, surplus earnings, and new savings which make the equipment of the nation mobile, and which tend slowly to adjust rates of net interest towards equality.

Differences in Rates of Interest. — Such differences as are to be found in the rates of interest yielded by different investments, therefore, must be due to one of the following three groups of causes:

(1) Different rates of both net and gross interest may prevail in *different markets*. While some kinds of equipment can be transported around the world, and although international investments are common, different rates of interest usually prevail in different nations, and even in different parts of the same country. In new countries the rates are usually higher than in old. This is partly due to the scarcity of savings in those countries where large fortunes and surplus wealth have not yet been accumulated, and where enterprisers are very desirous of obtaining equipment with which to exploit the rich natural resources of the region. In old and prosperous countries, the rates of interest are lower, because a larger supply of savings is available and

industries are already so well provided with equipment that its marginal productivity is low. Therefore, investments in such places as South America or Africa yield more than similar investments in England or the United States. Higher rates generally prevail in our own western states than are found in the east. Investors hesitate to send their savings far away because of the real or fancied risk. Hence, the amount of equipment that is exported from the centers of accumulation to the more distant and less developed parts is not sufficient to equalize the rates of interest in the two regions.

(2) Differences in the rates of both net and gross interest, within a given market, may be due to the *lack of a perfect equilibrium* in the demand for and supply of loans. Industries may be in such a state of continual change, the demand for various commodities shifting from one to another, and the conditions of production being subject to influences which raise or lower costs, that the income yielded by given investments is subject to considerable fluctuations. Most equipment is of a more or less elaborate sort which cannot be created in an instant, and which, once constructed, cannot readily be done away with. Hence, the supply of equipment in each industry does not show a perfect response to changes in the demand, and differences in the rates of return on investments result. We shall consider some such cases more fully in a paragraph below. These differences are only temporary, for, as we have just seen, if there is permanently a lower rate of yield in one industry than in another, there will be a shifting of investment from the former to the latter until the difference is wiped out. These temporary fluctuations in the return from investments are much like profits, which are very irregular in their nature. This will be made clear in the chapter on profits (Chapter XXIII). Much of what is said there about profits will apply to temporary variations in interest rates.

(3) Finally, there may be differences in gross interest rates due to *differences in the costs and risks* of making loans. In such cases the pure return, or net interest, is equal; it is only the gross interest that shows differences. The most frequent source of differences of this sort is to be found in the varying degrees of risk attached to divers types of investment. This has already been commented upon. In general, it can be said that, the safer the investment, the lower the interest rate, and the greater the risk, the higher the rate. Old, well-established businesses can usually obtain loans at lower rates than new and unfamiliar ones. Some businesses which are unattractive, and in which people hesitate to invest their savings because of the odium which attaches to them, may yield higher rates of interest than businesses which are in better repute. Investments in pawnbroking, disorderly houses, and

similar undertakings in the big cities, yield high returns for this reason.

Temporary Fluctuations in the Return from Investments. — The proposition that there is a tendency towards equalization of the rates of net interest yielded by invested savings rests on the assumption that the supply of equipment is sufficiently mobile to permit of a ready shifting of investments from channels where the returns are low to those where the returns are high. It was pointed out, however, that certain temporary differences in the rates of yield may result from a lack of perfect mobility, due to the fact that investments once made in permanent form cannot be withdrawn, and that new investments in plant of an elaborate sort cannot be made quickly. The more quickly reproducible and the less durable a given kind of equipment is, the more likely is the rate of return on it to seek the common level. But where the equipment is but slowly reproducible and slowly worn out, it presents a case of temporary fixity of supply, and the income it will yield is for the time being at the mercy of the demand for the particular kind of goods for whose production it is adapted. If the demand for these goods is very great, so that they are yielding a price above their cost of production, part of this excess may be reflected in more than the normal returns to the savings invested in the industry. If the demand for the goods happens to be small, so that they are selling for less than their cost of production, the income may be below that prevailing on other investments. These differences will continue either until more of this kind of equipment can be produced, in the first case, or until that already established is worn out or converted to other uses, in the second case.

For an illustration of the first sort: During the first World War there was a rapid increase in population in certain cities, particularly along the eastern seaboard of the United States, due to the sudden development of shipbuilding, and other activities. There was a temporary shortage of houses to shelter the influx of new workers, with their families, and a shortage of shipyards to build the great number of new ships that were needed. New houses and shipyards capable of meeting the tremendous increase of demand could not be constructed quickly; existing housing facilities, and old shipyards in a position to go ahead immediately with ship construction, had great value, and yielded abnormally high returns.

For an illustration of the opposite sort, where returns are below normal, the shipyards are again a good example. When the war was over, the abnormal demand for ships declined. But here were great quantities of specialized equipment good for but little else than ship construction. Having once been built, their form could not be changed, and they continued as part of the effective supply of shipbuilding facilities, at a time when few such facilities were needed. Ship prices had fallen so low that some of these yards could not be operated profitably. The same thing can happen to consumers' equipment. Dwelling houses in a declining town or district may yield low returns, or none at all, because the demand for them has fallen off. The value of their product has shrunk. The effective supply cannot be curtailed in correspondence with the declining demand, because of their permanent nature. The principles of fixed supply govern, and returns from such investments fall.

In the long run, however, the supply of equipment can be adjusted to the demand for it, so that the returns from it tend to approach the normal rate.

The Rent of Equipment. — The lending or leasing of a particular piece of equipment, such as a factory or a dwelling house, does not differ greatly in principle from the lending of a sum of money, except in one respect. When a man makes a money loan, he gets back his principal intact at the time when the loan matures, and therefore he needs only to charge for the time and liquidity preference, risk, and administrative costs involved in doing without the use of the money and attending to the necessary formalities of the transfer; but when a landlord leases a building to a tenant, he will not receive back his principal intact at the end of the lease. There will be certain wear and tear which results from the use of the building, necessitating certain expensive repairs on the part of the owner from time to time; and, in the course of years, in spite of such repairs, the building will become worthless, either through actual decay, or by becoming too antiquated for further use. The lender (landlord) will expect to be paid for this depreciation by the borrower (tenant). The price paid for the use of the building will include not only interest on its cost, but, in addition, a sum sufficient to keep it in repair and to replace it when it is entirely worn out. If the building will become entirely unfit for use at the end of one hundred years, one one-hundredth part of its cost will be included in its annual rental, in addition to the average amount of yearly repairs required to keep it in good condition during its life. The rent of equipment, therefore, as contrasted with its interest, includes six, instead of four, elements of cost: time preference, liquidity preference, compensation for risk, administrative expenses, maintenance (repairs), and depreciation.

C. The Rôle of Interest in the Economic Process

The Balance Between Consumption, Nominal Saving, and Investment. — We learned in Chapter XI that it is the function of interest to preserve balance in the relations between consumption, nominal saving, and investment. If such a balance is not preserved, the continuity of industry will be interrupted and a general depression may ensue. Now that we have a fuller understanding of interest, it will pay us to consider this problem further.

Let us look for a moment at the vertical structure of industry. As we know, this consists of the series of stages reaching from the consumer back to those successively more remote in the time-chain of production. It is upon this succession of processes that the smooth flow of products from industry to consumers depends. The structure is governed by the volume of investment. An increased amount of investment takes the form of more roundabout processes of production, so that the vertical structure is lengthened. A decreased amount of investment, on the other hand, means a shortening of the vertical structure. Therefore, the rate of interest controls the structure because it controls the amount of investment. This works out as follows: We know that, as the roundabout process is lengthened, the marginal productivity of equipment falls; this means that increasing amounts of savings can be utilized in industry only at progressively lower rates of interest. On the other hand, if the psychological theory of time preference is correct, an increasing volume of savings will be offered for investment only at progressively higher rates of interest. The normal, or equilibrium, rate is fixed at the point where these two influences meet, and this determines how long the roundabout process shall be. Therefore, it fixes the vertical structure of industry. If, for any reason, the rate of interest should fall, the vertical structure would be lengthened; if the rate of interest should rise, the structure would be shortened.

In equating the demand for savings with the supply of them, the rate of interest also tends to establish a harmonious relation between the volume of consumption and the volume of nominal saving. If the theory of time preference is correct, a high rate of interest tends to encourage saving and investment, a low rate of interest, to discourage it. Therefore, a low rate of interest tends to encourage consumption, and a high rate to restrict it. With a given rate of interest prevailing, income recipients tend to spend a certain proportion of their incomes, and to save the rest. If, at that rate of interest, business men can profitably utilize all the nominal savings offered, they will all be invested, and the relations between consumption, saving, and investment will be harmonious. However, if the volume of nominal savings is greater than enterprisers can effectively use in investment, the effective supply will presumably exceed the effective demand, and the rate of interest will fall. This decline in the rate will discourage saving and encourage consumption, at the same time that it makes possible the profitable utilization of more savings in industry. (The roundabout process will be lengthened.) So, the effective demand for savings increases, and the effective supply decreases, until balance is restored. If, at the prevailing rate of interest, the effective demand is greater than the supply, the rate will rise, causing the effective demand to decrease (the roundabout process will be shortened) and consumption to decline (more savings will be offered for investment), until the balance is restored. Thus, there is a rate of interest which will keep consumption, saving, and investment in equilibrium. This is the normal rate.

In Chapter XI we found that these balanced relationships can be upset by monetary factors. Therefore, it is important for us to analyze the relations between money and interest.

Interest and Money. — Although loans of investible funds are usually made in monetary terms, our analysis indicates that money is loaned and invested to be used in the purchase of goods, and that the price which is paid for the funds invested depends, therefore, on what the use of the goods is worth. Hence, the rate of interest does not depend primarily on the demand and supply of money *per se,* but, in the last analysis, on the demand of borrowers for the durable equipment in which savings are invested, and on the willingness of savers to give up the present enjoyment of the goods which the money saved would buy. Because of this, economists have generally held that, in the long run, the quantity of money has nothing to do with the rate of interest.

This is at variance with popular thinking. Because the loans for which interest is paid are usually expressed in money terms, many people are likely to think of interest as primarily a monetary phenomenon. From this it is an easy step to the belief that the quantity of money has an important connection with the rate of interest. When borrowers have to pay high rates of interest, money is said to be scarce, or "tight." At such times there are always some persons who come forward with quack schemes for issuing cheap money (such as paper), thinking thereby to bring lower rates of interest. When interest rates are low, money is said to be plentiful, or "easy," and the idea is current that there is an abundance of it in circulation. It is true that, for the time being, an increase or decrease in the circulation of money will have marked effects upon the interest rate. This will be more fully developed in the following paragraph. But it seems clear that, in the long run, the rate of interest does not depend on this factor. This can be demonstrated by the following line of reasoning: Suppose the circulation of money (MV in the equation of exchange) were doubled. Other things being equal, this would tend to double prices eventually. Then a business man, needing a certain supply of equipment, would have to borrow twice as much money in order to pay for it. Rising prices would have increased the demand for loans of money in the same proportion as the increase in the supply of it. So, after all adjustments were completed, the rate of interest would be the same as before. Similarly, a decreased circulation of money would tend to lower prices, reduce the demand for money loans correspondingly, and leave the rate of interest where it was in the beginning. These are the long-run effects.

In the short run, however, a change in the circulation of money will cause changes in interest, because it does not affect the loan market and the prices of commodities simultaneously, nor does it react upon all prices at once, and to the same degree. For instance, an increased supply of money is likely first to find its way into the bank reserves, making available more loanable funds, which would induce the banks to encourage borrowing. The bank rate of interest would fall, and this might even be reflected in a reduction of the rate on long-time investments. After the money had got into circulation, however, so that it had time to affect prices generally, the demand for loan money would increase sufficiently to bring the rate up to where it had been before, in accordance with the principle just explained. Indeed, for a time it would even rise above its original figure. For we know that the rising prices occasioned by the increase in money would increase the profits of business men, stimulating them to increased borrowings and thereby bringing about that general rise in the rate of interest that usually accompanies the expansion phase of the business cycle. In time, however, as the prices of all things became adjusted to the new level, profits would no longer be increasing, and the demand for loans, relative to the supply of loanable funds, would be no greater nor less than before. It appears, then, that while, temporarily, an increase in the supply of money tends first to lower interest, then to raise it; in the long run it leaves it undisturbed. Similarly, a decrease in the quantity of money might tend at first to raise interest rates, by causing a contraction of bank reserves, then to lower them, by its adverse effects on business profits; but in the long run, it would effect no permanent change.

The thought embodied in the above paragraph can be summed up by putting it in a slightly different way. Given time for an adjustment to be worked out, it does not make any difference in the rate of interest paid for loans whether the amount of money in circulation is abundant or scarce; for all prices will be adjusted to the amount of money then circulating, and both the demand for and supply of savings will be reflected in terms of that level. But *a change in the level,* caused by an increasing or decreasing flow of money, will affect interest rates *during the period of transition,* until the new level is fully established throughout the entire price system. Hence, the circulation of money is an important factor in determining the fluctuations of market rates of interest about their normals.

The Bank Rate of Interest and the Business Cycle. — The deviations of interest rates arising from this cause may seriously disturb the functioning of interest in its work of balancing consumption, saving, and investment. These disturbing effects are aggravated by the fact that short-time rates of interest are determined in large measure by banking policy. While the banks are not immune to the general influences which determine the normal rate of interest, they are particularly sensitive to the volume of money in their reserves. In the chapter on *The Banking System,* it was shown that banks are not dependent for their loans on the volume of nominal savings voluntarily placed in their hands by depositors; they have the capacity to supply funds in the form of deposits which are created by the banking system in its process of lending. Temporarily, this destroys the connection between nominal savings and investment. The volume of loans so created depends chiefly on the demand of enterprisers, in relation to the size of the banks' reserves. The reserves, in turn, are peculiarly sensitive to changes in the volume of money. As a result, monetary changes strongly influence the bank rate of interest. When the reserves are large in relation to enterprisers' demand, the banks depress their rate of interest below the normal, or equilibrium, rate. This means that enterprisers can borrow at a cost which is below the expected marginal productivity of the equipment which they intend to purchase with the funds borrowed. This makes borrowing look profitable. Hence, bank loans expand, and the volume of investment exceeds the volume of voluntary saving. Later, when this process of expanding loans has reached the point where the ratio of reserves to deposits has become dangerously low, the banks reverse their policy. They now raise the rate of interest above the normal. This means that enterprisers must now pay for loans a rate in excess of the marginal productivity of equipment. Borrowing no longer looks profitable. Hence, the demand for loans falls off, and deposits shrink. So, as a result of a bank rate of interest which fluctuates now above, and now below, the normal rate, the volume of investment is thrown out of balance with the volume of voluntary saving, and the balancing functioning of the interest rate is destroyed. In Chapters XI and XII we found this to be an important cause of business cycles.

Here is a type of deviation from normal prices which is due to the peculiarities of our banking institutions. There is probably no parallel to it in the fluctuation of commodity prices about their normals. Notwithstanding it, there is some connection between the bank rate of interest and the normal rate. This is due to the fact that, although bank loans are nominally made for short periods, there is a certain amount of shifting of funds between the short- and long-time markets. In the long-time market, the influences which determine normal rates of interest are more controlling. If the bank rate is too low in relation to the normal rate, some bank funds will find their way into long-time investments. On the other hand, if the bank rate is too high in relation to the normal, money may be withdrawn from the long-time markets in order to take advantage of the short-time rates. This tends to bring the rate down to closer correspondence with the normal. Hence, we may conclude that deviations of the bank rate from the normal tend to correct themselves in time. Meanwhile, however, the deviations may be great enough to cause a marked disturbance of the balance of industry.

Keynes' Theory of Employment Once More. — In Chapter XI we also discussed the interesting theory of the British economist, Keynes, concerning the relation of the interest rate to the total volume of employment in society. We are in a better position to understand this theory, now that we have analyzed the forces which determine the rate of interest. Keynes believes that the volume of nominal saving, instead of adjusting itself to the demand so as to preserve a balance, tends in progressive communities to become so large that the effective supply chronically exceeds the effective demand. This is because, in his view, nominal saving depends mainly on income, and is not sufficiently responsive to the rate of interest. If the level of income in the community is very large, the volume of nominal saving will be correspondingly great; but, because of the declining marginal productivity of equipment which is the result of increasing investment, so large a quantity of savings cannot be invested profitably except at a very low rate of interest. The cost and risk of lending, coupled with obscure psychological influences which tend to keep up the rate of interest, will not permit the rate of gross interest to fall low enough for these savings to be absorbed into investment. Hence, the effective demand for investible funds falls short of the supply.

The drawing of Figure 56 perhaps represents Keynes' views. Here the line SS represents the schedule of supply for investible funds. Its nature is such that none will be offered for investment at less than 3 per cent (Keynes reasons that the minimum supply-price cannot be much below this figure, or perhaps 2½ per cent); but a large amount (here assumed to be 7 mil-lions, for purposes of illustra-tion) will be offered if the rate is 3 per cent, and more if it is higher. The schedule of de-mand, based on the marginal productivity of equipment, is represented by DD. It is such that no more than 5 million dollars of funds can find their way into investment at the rate of 3 per cent. Since inter-est can fall no lower, the unabsorbed nominal savings

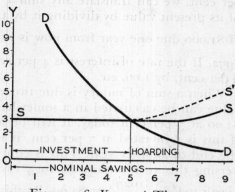

Figure 56. Keynes' Theory.

(amounting to 2 millions) must either be hoarded, in the form of cash, or destroyed in the process of liquidating bank loans. In either case, the level of prices will fall, causing a business depression. This goes on until business activity has been so reduced that the supply curve shifts to the position SS', and the effective supply of savings falls to 5 millions. Then demand and supply will be in equilibrium, and no further shrinkage of business activity need take place. However, the equilibrium so reached is one in which the resources of the community are not fully employed. There is unemployment of both labor and capital. The conclusion to be reached from this analysis is that a high level of prosperity cannot be sustained unless the surplus funds which private industry cannot profitably absorb are taken up by government loans and utilized in a program of public spending.

The controversial nature of this theory, and the reasons for hesi-tancy in accepting it, were set forth in Chapter XI. It rests on the questionable assumptions, (1) that the opportunities for investment are so limited that the marginal productivity of equipment is below the minimum rate of interest, and (2) that the volume of savings is not sufficiently responsive to the rate of interest.

Discounting and Capitalization.[2] — By means of the rate of in-terest, it is possible to ascertain the present value of any future sum of money, or its equivalent in goods. We know that, if the rate of

[2] An excellent discussion of this topic, to which I am indebted, is contained in Chap-ter 6 of Irving Fisher's *Elementary Principles of Economics* (1910).

interest is given, at, say, 5 per cent, a sum of $1,000 invested today will yield $1,050 a year from now. Looking at this relationship the other way round, it appears that a sum of $1,050 a year hence is equivalent to $1,000 now. Therefore, when the rate of interest is 5 per cent, we can translate any sum a year in the future into terms of its present value by dividing it by 1.05. On this reckoning, a sum of $1,000 due one year from now is worth $\frac{\$1,000}{1.05}$, or approximately $952. If the rate of interest is 4 per cent, we divide by 1.04; if it is 6 per cent, by 1.06, etc.

When a sum of money is due two years in the future, its present value can be calculated in a somewhat similar fashion. If we invest $1.00 at 5 per cent today, it will be worth $1.05 in one year; then if this is reinvested at 5 per cent, it will have grown to $1.1025 at the end of another year. This is equivalent to $1.00 × (1.05)². Reversing this relationship, $1.1025 two years in the future will be worth today $\frac{\$1.1025}{(1.05)^2}$, or $1.00. By this calculation, given an interest rate of 5 per cent, the present value of any sum of money two years from now can be found by dividing by (1.05)². If the rate of interest is 4 per cent, we divide by (1.04)²; if 6 per cent, by (1.06)², etc. By a similar line of reasoning, it can be shown that, given an interest rate of 5 per cent, the present value of any sum due three years hence could be found by dividing by (1.05)³; four years hence by dividing by (1.05)⁴; and so on. Calculations based on other interest rates would follow the same general principles.

This process of determining the present value of future sums by means of the rate of interest is known as *discounting*. Discounting makes it possible, given the rate of interest, to ascertain the present worth of any future sum no matter how far distant it may be in time. This has important applications in business. For instance, suppose one owns a $1,000 bond, the principal of which is payable seven years from now, and bearing 5 per cent interest in the meantime. The holder of this bond will receive $50 yearly for seven years, and $1,000 at the end of that time. By discounting this series of future payments at the prevailing rate of interest (which may be different from the interest stipulated in the bond), he can calculate what that bond is worth today. Investment bankers have tables which enable them to make these calculations quickly.

We are now in a position to understand more fully the nature of capitalization, which was briefly described in Chapter II. It follows from the above that the present value of any piece of capital will depend upon the income which it is expected to yield in the future, its probable life, and the rate of interest. Capitalization consists of this derivation of capital values from future income yields, through discounting. The income is said to be capitalized, at the current rate of interest.

Now suppose that we have a piece of very durable capital, such as a plot of land, which lasts indefinitely, and offers the prospect of a continuous stream of income extending far into the future. The discounted present value of these future increments of income will represent an infinite mathematical series, whose aggregate value increases by progressively smaller amounts. The increments of income anticipated in the far distant future are discounted by so much that their present values approach zero as a limit, so that the series, although infinite, has a finite value. It can be demonstrated that this value is expressed by the formula: $V = \frac{100}{r} \times I$, where V is the capital value, r the rate of interest, and I the annual income. To illustrate, if the income yielded by our piece of land is $50 yearly, and the rate of interest is 5 per cent, the present value of the land (V) will be $\frac{100}{5} \times \$50$, or $1,000. This is only common sense, for, if the rate of interest is 5 per cent, a stream of income is $\frac{5}{100}$, or $\frac{1}{20}$, of the value of the capital which yields it; therefore the capital value must be $\frac{100}{5}$, or 20 times, the amount of the income. Similarly, if the rate of interest is 4 per cent, the capitalized value of a stream of income will be $\frac{100}{4}$, or 25 times, the amount of the income. Capital values can be similarly derived from any stream of income extending indefinitely into the future, when the rate of interest is known.

The Income and Capital Value of Old Equipment. — We have seen that the rate of interest is determined, on the demand side, by comparing the yield (marginal product) of equipment with the sums invested therein. Here the initial capital sum with which the yield is compared consists of the cost of constructing the equipment in question. For instance, suppose that a factory, with a long prospective life, is to be constructed at a cost of $100,000, and that it is expected to yield a net income, over the costs of operation, amounting to $5,000. Then the expected yield is 5 per cent of the investment, and the proprietors can afford to bid 5 per cent for the funds needed to finance its construction. It is such calculations as these which determine the schedule of demand for savings, and it is upon this schedule of demand, taken in conjunction with the supply, that the rate of interest will depend in the long run. When the factory has once been built, the yield may be more or less than was anticipated. Suppose, for instance, that the yield is only $4,000. Then, if the prevailing rate of interest is 5 per cent, the value of the factory will fall below its original cost of construction. For, according to the principles of the preceding section, its value will now depend upon its actual yield, capitalized at the current rate of interest. $4,000 capitalized at 5 per cent is only $80,000, and that is all that the factory will be worth. Had the earnings of the factory been greater than was expected—say $6,000—the factory would be worth more than its cost, for $6,000, capitalized at 5 per cent, is $120,000. A change in the prevailing rate of interest will affect these values. For instance, if the factory earns $4,000, and the rate of interest falls to 3 per cent, the capitalized value will be $33\frac{1}{3} \times \$4,000$, or $133,333. If interest rises to 6 per cent, the capitalized value will be only $16\frac{2}{3} \times \$4,000$, which is $66,667. We see then, that a fall in the rate of interest raises capital values and a rise in the rate reduces them.

It follows that the value of equipment, once it has come into existence, is determined, not by what it cost to produce it, but by capitalizing its yield at the current rate of interest. This is applicable not only to equipment, but to all kinds of wealth. In the next chapter we shall find that it is particularly important as applied to land.

Summary

The use of durable capital commands a price which depends upon the value of the income which can be derived from it. If this price is thought of as a lump sum, paid for the use of the physical item of capital, it is called rent; but if it is construed as a percentage of the value embodied in the capital, it is called interest. In analyzing the income from capital, it is necessary to separate equipment from land, because the supply of the former depends upon saving and investment, while the latter is supplied gratis by nature, and its supply is practically fixed.

The rate of interest depends upon the demand for and supply of funds made available for investment by saving. The demand for these funds comes partly from consumers, but chiefly from enterprisers. Consumers' demand depends upon the urgency of their desire for immediate possession of goods whose purchase they cannot finance out of their own resources. Enterprisers' demand depends upon the marginal productivity of the equipment which borrowed funds enable them to create. The supply of investible funds depends upon the following factors: time preference, liquidity preference, costs of lending, and risk of lending. According to the time preference theory, people prefer present to future goods; hence, the amounts they will save depend upon the rate of interest obtainable, so that savings have a supply-price, which rises as the amount of savings called for on the market increases. Some economists dispute this theory, believing that the supply of savings is independent of the rate of interest. Since savers have the option of holding their surplus funds in cash, they will not be offered for investment unless the rate of interest is sufficient to overcome their liquidity preference. The rate must also be high enough to compensate investors for the cost and risk of investing their funds.

By setting the schedule of demand for investible funds against the schedule of supply, based on the above principles, an equilibrium rate is established at the point where the effective demand and the effective supply are equal. This is the normal rate of interest. The gross rate covers all four of the supply factors above mentioned; net, or pure, interest consists of that part of the gross rate which is compensation for time and liquidity preference.

Investment in different branches of industry can be changed by the wearing out of old equipment and by the directing of new funds into the most profitable channels. As a result of this mobility, there is a tendency towards equal rates of net interest throughout the investment market; but gross rates will differ from one industry to another, and from market to market, because of differences in the costs and risks of lending. Since changes in investment from industry to industry take time, there may be considerable deviations from the normal rate over short periods. The rent of equipment includes a charge for maintenance and depreciation, in addition to interest on the invested funds.

The rate of interest regulates the vertical structure of production, and determines the balance between consumption, nominal saving, and investment, by its effects on the supply of, and demand for, savings. This balancing function can be interfered with by the monetary policy of banks; for, although the rate of interest in the long run is independent of the size of the monetary circulation, a change in the latter will affect interest rates temporarily. The bank rate of interest is governed by the ratio of bank reserves to deposits, rather than by the supply of and demand for savings; hence, when bank reserves are large, banks depress their rate of interest below the equilibrium level, and thereby stimulate over-investment. Later, when reserves get low, they raise their rate of interest above the equilibrium level, and thereby retard investment. These influences obstruct the functioning of the interest rate, and contribute to cyclical movements of business activity.

According to Keynes' theory, the supply of savings in prosperous countries is so great that it could not all be invested in industry, except at a very low rate of interest; but, since the rate of interest is prevented from falling to this low level, not all the savings can be absorbed into industry. Hence, some of them are hoarded or liquidated, and the volume of business activity and employment is thereby reduced.

The present value of any future sum of money can be ascertained by discounting it at the current rate of interest. In a similar way, the present value of capital can be ascertained by capitalizing its yield. The value of old capital, once created, is determined in this way, and may deviate from its original cost of production.

REFERENCES AND SUGGESTIONS FOR FURTHER READING

The theory of interest most generally held by contemporary economists is a synthesis of the psychological and productivity approaches. The psychological theory has been most fully elaborated by Irving Fisher in his *The Theory of Interest* (1930). A briefer statement of his views is contained in Chapters 19 to 22, inclusive, of his *Elementary Principles of Economics* (1910). Both the productivity and psychological aspects of the problem are painstakingly developed in Books V, VI, and VII of E. von Böhm-Bawerk's *Positive Theory of Capital* (English translation, 1923), which, while somewhat labored, has greatly influenced thinking on this subject. Two well-balanced, brief summaries of traditional interest theory are to be found in Chapters 3 and 4 of H. G. Brown's *Economic Science and the Common Welfare* (1923), and in Chapter 6 of T. N. Carver's *The Distribution of Wealth* (1904).

A monetary approach, which introduces a new note into interest theory, is offered by J. M. Keynes in Book IV of his *The General Theory of Employment, Interest and Money* (1936). I am indebted to this work for the concept of liquidity preference, but have not followed Keynes' theory in its more general aspects, in which it seems to me to be one-sided and incomplete.

Gustav Cassel, in his *The Nature and Necessity of Interest* (London, 1903) emphasizes the elasticity of demand for savings, and the factors which prevent the rate of interest from falling to zero. H. D. Henderson, in Chapter 8 of his *Supply and Demand* (1922), develops especially the element of involuntary saving.

Chapter XXII

THE INCOME FROM LAND

The Demand for and Supply of Land. — A price is paid for the use of land for the same reason that a price is paid for any other productive agent—it has certain useful productive qualities, and it is scarce. Like other kinds of capital, it is sometimes used for consumption, as when a rich man maintains a game preserve for his hunting or a beautiful lawn to adorn his home. For the most part, however, it is used for production; we may, then, focus our attention upon its productive aspect. The money income that a landowner receives, whether he rents the land to a tenant or uses it himself, depends on the value of the services of the land. Land possesses fertility, by virtue of which crops can be grown upon it; it often contains mineral deposits or other valuable materials; and it affords a solid basis upon which to erect buildings, railroads, and the like. It is upon the importance of these qualities to producers that the demand for the use of land depends. This demand is derived from the demand for the products to which the land contributes. If it is to be used for farming, the farmers' demand for it will depend upon what they can get for their cereals, vegetables, or fruits. If it is to be used for railroads, the demand will depend upon what prices the railroads can charge for their services of transportation. In all such cases, the importance of the land's contribution to the product follows the same general principle of marginal productivity which, as we have seen, determines the demand for productive agents generally. In the case of land which is used at remote stages of production, the marginal product will be discounted for the time that must elapse before its product emerges in consumable form, the same as we found to be the case with wages. So far, we encounter no new principle.

When we come to consider the supply of land, we find certain peculiarities. The outstanding fact is that the quantity of land is practically fixed. In this it differs from the supply of equipment, and it is on that account that we must deal with it separately. If the demand for equipment increases, the higher price then offered for its use will presumably stimulate an increase in saving and investment, so that the effective supply of equipment will increase, thus checking the rise in price. If the demand for equipment decreases, the price offered for its use will fall, saving and investment will presumably be discouraged, and the effective supply will shrink, thereby checking the fall in price. Not so with land. Since it cannot be substantially increased or decreased in amount, the quantity of it offered for use will not respond to changes in the demand. If the demand increases, there will be no tendency for the supply of land to increase; hence there is nothing to check a permanent rise in its price from taking place; if the demand is great enough, the price can soar to very great heights. On the other hand, if the demand for land decreases, the supply of it will not fall off, and there is nothing to check a permanent decline in its price. This may drop to a very low figure —even to the point where the land becomes worthless.[1]

The supply of land differs from that of equipment in a second respect. We learned in the last chapter that the return from equipment tends to a uniform rate of net interest on the costs of its production, because the fund of savings is mobile—it can be turned into this kind of equipment or that, as the demand for the products indicates. So, although the yield of particular equipments may differ for short periods of time, there is a long-run tendency towards uniformity. There is no such tendency in the case of land. Land has no cost of production, and different pieces of land have permanently different characteristics. Some are suited to one crop, some to another; some contain mineral deposits, others do not; some are advantageously situated, others are badly located. Because there is no mobile replacement fund or recurring supply of land which can take any desired form, permanent differences in the yield of different plots of it arise. Each kind of land, and each piece, has its own value, which differs from the others.

However, there is some mobility of land in respect to its different uses, because of the fact that, more often than not, there are several possible employments open to the prospective user of a given piece of land. The case of land that may be used to grow either cotton or peanuts was cited in a previous chapter, and there are hundreds of other examples. In the city there may be a choice between residen-

---

[1] Of course, a particular nation may increase its supply by conquest, but the supply will not respond naturally to economic need for it in the way that that of equipment and most commodities does. A mere rise in the price will not cause more of it to come into being. Also, the supply actually in use may be decreased by the abandonment of some of it; but this does not reduce the amount of land actually available, in the way that the supply of equipment and of most commodities is reduced (by not being produced), when their price falls. The land under such circumstances does not become more scarce.

tial, manufacturing, and mercantile use; near the city, between dairy farming and truck gardening; in the country, between cereal crops and pasture; and so on. An increase in the demand for one product in such cases may cause land to be withdrawn from its other uses and devoted to meeting such an increase. So, the adjustment of the total supply of land among all its possible uses is variable, and the amount employed for any one purpose can and will increase or decrease in response to the demand for it. Therefore, while recognizing the fixity of the supply of land as a whole, our analysis must give due consideration to this variability of the supply of land for any particular use. It will be found that the mobility of land in this respect is not sufficient to prevent important permanent differences in the returns obtainable from different plots.

Factors Determining the Rent of a Piece of Land. — With these general principles as a basis, it is now possible to describe what determines the price paid for the use of any piece of land. For the present, it will be convenient to think of that income as a rent per acre. Later we shall see how this rent may be regarded as interest.

According to the principles already set forth, the rent that will be paid for a piece of land will depend upon the following factors: (1) the particular product (or products) to which the land is suited; (2) its excellence (fertility, location, etc.) for that particular product; (3) the scarcity of that kind of land; (4) the demand for the product, as transmitted to the land according to the principle of marginal productivity. Let us see how these factors coöperate to establish prices for the use of various kinds of land.

Land Rent as Determined by Marginal Productivity. — We may begin with a very simple illustration, in which we suppose that a farmer has several men, equipped with the necessary agricultural implements, working on a single acre of land of a certain kind. Because the land area is so small in proportion to the number of men employed, the working combination is not a very efficient one—the full working capacity of the men cannot be utilized very effectively. Therefore, it would be desirable for the farmer to acquire more land. How much would the use of additional land be worth to him? According to the reasoning developed in previous chapters, its value would depend on what it could add to the product. Successive additions of land will bring into play the principle of diminishing productivity. Here, then, are the elements of the problem.

We can visualize the situation by referring to Figure 57. Here we suppose the product obtained when only one acre of land is used to be 30 bushels, represented by the height of the first column at the left of the drawing. The addition of a second acre (of land of ex-

actly the same kind as the first) is assumed to result in an addition to
product greater than that obtained on the first acre, because the
more efficient combination of agents results in increasing marginal
productivity. Accordingly, the second column is higher than the first,
denoting a marginal product of 35 bushels. If the price of the product
is supposed to be $1 per bushel, this second acre would be worth
$35 to the farmer. After two acres are in use, we suppose the point
of diminishing productivity to have been reached. Therefore, if a
third acre of the same kind of land be now added (using the same

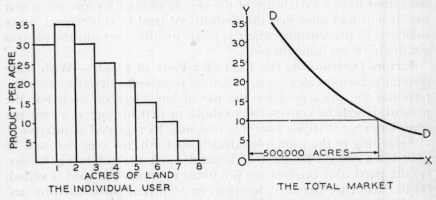

Figure 57. Land Rent Determined by Marginal Productivity.

men and tools as previously), the extra increment of product will be
less than before. Hence, a third acre would not be as valuable to the
farmer. In the drawing, the increment of product from this third
acre, as shown by the third column, is 30 bushels; so that it would
be worth $30. From now on, each additional acre of land adds a
progressively smaller amount to the product; therefore, the additional columns are drawn progressively lower, like a flight of steps.
These steps, representing the successive additions to product which
can be obtained by employing more and more land, measure the
worth of each additional acre to the farmer. It will pay him to rent
more land, just so long as he can get it for a price that will not exceed the extra product which its use will make possible. Continuing
the assumption that each bushel is worth one dollar, he will rent 5
acres if the rent is $20, 6 acres if the rent is $15, 7 acres if the rent
is $10, and 8 acres if the rent is $5. That is his schedule of demand.

If we add together the similar demand schedules of all the users
(actual or potential) of that particular kind of land, we will have the
schedule of demand for the total market. This will give us a demand
curve like that shown in the second half of the drawing. Now, if the

total amount of this kind of land is 500,000 acres, it will rent for $10 per acre. It is a simple case of fixed supply. Since the land costs nothing to produce, it has no supply-price, and must be rented for whatever it will bring. Its value is determined by the marginal demand-price, which, in this case, is based on the value of its marginal product.

While this gives us an insight into the principles on which the rent of land depends, it is not a full explanation, for it does not take account of the differences between various kinds of land, and of the relations between them. Therefore, let us look at the problem in a broader way, in order to get at this aspect of the problem.

Utilization of the Various Classes of Land. — It may be assumed that the available labor and savings of any community will tend to be employed in the most productive manner possible—meaning, by most productive, that manner which yields products of greatest value. The most valuable products can be obtained by applying labor and saving to those lands which are scarcest, in relation to the demands for the goods which can be produced upon them. Those lands which are suitable for building sites in the hearts of our great cities are of this sort. Below them are lands capable of yielding products of only slightly less value, such as city residence and manufacturing sites. Below this follow many other kinds of land, whose products are of continually decreasing value, such as lands used for truck farming, those devoted to the various staple crops, such as wheat, corn, and other cereals, cotton, tobacco, sugar, etc., and finally those suitable only for grazing. These various lands might be classed into almost any number of grades, but we shall think of them as divided altogether into five, which we shall call Classes A, B, C, D, and E. We then have a simplified picture of all the land in the community divided into five groups, ranging from those whose products are of greatest value (Class A) to those whose products are of least value (Class E). There may be yet other lands, too poor to be cultivated at all, which we call waste lands. For the present we exclude mineral lands from the discussion, but we will give due consideration to them later. Not all of the lands within each class are of equal quality; they differ among themselves in their suitability for their particular products, some being of great excellence, others poorer, due to their differing advantages of fertility, location, and other qualities.

The successive gradation of lands is represented by Figure 58. In this drawing, the area included within the lines represents the entire product of industry, expressed in terms of its monetary value, and the part of that value produced on the lands of each class is indicated by the five divisions. The height of the columns expresses the value

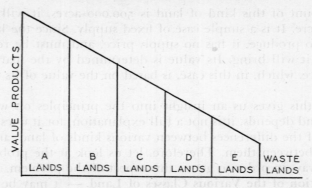

Figure 58. The Utilization of the Various Grades of Land.

of the products produced on the lands in question, showing that on the best A lands the value-product is greatest, falling gradually as we come to the poorer A lands, and so on throughout the entire land area in use. Let us now see how the available labor and equipment of the community can be utilized most productively on these lands.

Since the products of greatest value, in proportion to the labor and saving employed, are to be obtained on the A lands, as much as possible of the labor and equipment will be employed on them. However, the application of more than a certain amount of these productive agents on each acre of the A lands will bring into operation the principle of diminishing productivity. Consequently, any further amount of labor and equipment applied to them will yield smaller increases in physical product, and correspondingly less value-product. In view of this fact, the remaining labor and saving of the community can only be employed in one of two ways: either the best lands must be utilized more intensively, past the point of diminishing productivity, or poorer lands must be used.

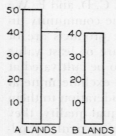

Figure 59. Diminishing Returns in the Utilization of Land.

The situation is represented in Figure 59. We here suppose that labor and saving are applied to each acre of the lands in successive inputs. It is assumed that one input employed on the Class A lands yields a product worth $50, and that from then on diminishing returns begin, so that a second input yields a smaller product, which (at the same price as before) is worth only $40. As an alternative, labor and savings might be transferred to lands of the next lower grade; but, since these lands are poorer, there would be a similar decrease in the value yield, so that the alternative is no better. Observe that, in the drawing, the first input on B lands is represented as yielding the same output ($40) as the second input on the A lands.

From this it appears that, in order to utilize all the labor and savings in a community, it will be necessary to employ some land that is not of the most productive kind, and to carry the use of land beyond the point of diminishing productivity. In bringing successively poorer grades of land into use, it will be found profitable to devote them to different products. Assuming that the A lands are used for business sites, it is probable that the B lands would not be suitably located for this purpose, but that they might be made to yield a product of good value as residence sites. But not all of the labor and savings can be employed in these two ways. In order to dispose of the rest, either both A and B lands must be utilized still more in-

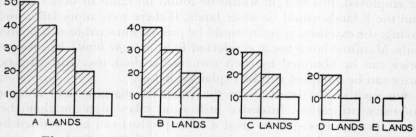

Figure 60. The Value Products of all Grades of Land.

tensively, involving a further tendency to diminishing productivity, or land of still less valuable kinds must be brought into use. Each will be devoted to the product that yields the greatest value, until all the labor and savings are employed as productively as can be. This will not usually require the cultivation of all the land. Generally, all the available labor and savings can be employed without having recourse to the most barren and inaccessible soils; the latter, therefore, will lie idle, constituting the waste land to which reference has been made. Just how far cultivation will be extended to poor soils, and what proportion of the land will be permitted to lie idle, will depend upon the size of the laboring population and the amount of savings to be employed, in relation to the land area at the disposal of the community. In a populous country, all but the very poorest soils will be used, and the best ones will be cultivated very intensively.

We may picture the entire production, when all the labor and savings are employed, by the drawing in Figure 60. On the A lands, which are the most productive, five inputs of labor and savings are represented as being employed, the successive increments of value product resulting therefrom being measured by the five blocks of decreasing size. On the B lands, it does not pay to push the utilization quite so far; therefore, only four inputs of agents are used. On the C, D, and E lands, the inputs are three, two, and one, respectively, and the products are correspondingly less. In each case, the total area of the blocks represents the total value product obtained. On the A lands, this product is 150 (50 + 40 + 30 + 20 + 10 = 150); on the B lands it is 100; on the C lands, 60, and so on. The meaning of the shaded areas will be made clear in a later paragraph.

The Margins of Cultivation. — The poorest land in use is commonly known in economics as *marginal land*. It is also called the *extensive margin of cultivation,* because it marks the outer fringe beyond which land is not utilized. In Figure 60 the extensive margin is found on the Class E lands. If there were less labor and saving to be employed, this margin would be found on lands of better grade, and the E lands would be waste lands; if there were more labor and saving, the extensive margin would be pushed outward to still poorer soils. Marginal lands are also referred to as *no-rent lands,* because no price can be obtained by their owners for their use. Just why no price can be obtained will be explained below.

On each of the lands above the extensive margin there is some intensive utilization. Intensive utilization takes place on them because, in each case, just as great a value-product can be obtained by applying more labor and saving to the higher grade lands as by carrying cultivation extensively to poorer grade lands. Hence, both processes go on side by side, with declining value-productivity resulting. So, when the extensive margin of cultivation is reached, there is also reached on the better lands an *intensive margin,* which may be defined as *that point in the utilization of any piece of land where the least productive unit of labor and saving is applied.* In Figure 60 it is represented by the last block on each grade of land above the poorest E lands. The value-product yielded by the labor and saving applied at the intensive margin in each case tends to equal that of those applied to the extensive margin. If it were not so, labor and savings would be diverted from the less productive to the more productive margins, until their yields at the different points were brought to equality; for the owners of those agents seek the most profitable available use for them. Hence the product at each of the margins in the diagram is shown as having the same value ($10).

Why Marginal Land is No-Rent Land. — The product obtained at the margins of cultivation is the marginal product of the combined labor and saving employed in production. By definition, the marginal product of these agents must be the amount of product depending upon the use in production of a single unit of them. If any enterpriser were to sacrifice a unit of labor and savings, the product he would lose would be only that product which such a unit produces at either the intensive or the extensive margins. For, with his remaining units, he could go on getting the superior product which all units above the margin yield. A glance at Figure 60 will reveal that the amount of product depending on a single unit of labor and savings on any of the lands there shown would be worth $10; that is the product at the margins of cultivation. In arriving at the concept of the margins of cultivation, therefore, we have simply reached, by a different route, the same idea of marginal productivity formerly encountered.

We can now understand why land at the extensive margin yields no rent to its owner. It has already been shown that the price paid for an agent of production will be equal to the value of its marginal product. Therefore, the entire value of the product at the margins of cultivation will be paid to those who furnish the labor and savings employed there. Since, in our illustration, labor and savings at the margin yield products to the value of $10, a unit of these agents combined will be worth $10, and the landowner will get none of this.

While the student is now familiar with the principle that the owner of an agent of production is paid for its use the full value of its marginal product, it may seem strange that the poorest land in cultivation yields no rent. The reason for this may be made clearer by a somewhat different line of reasoning, which leads to the same conclusion. Just beyond the poorest land in use is other land, only slightly less suitable for cultivation. This land, on the frontiers of civilization and elsewhere, is free because no one has any use for it. The prospective user of marginal lands has the option of employing his labor and savings on these free lands, where the product will be only slightly less than on marginal lands, or of employing them at the intensive margin on other lands already cultivated, where, again, the yield will be only slightly less. Rather than pay a rent for marginal lands, he would prefer to adopt one of these alternatives. So, the owner of the marginal lands cannot get any appreciable rent for their use. That there is actually a considerable amount of land in cultivation which yields no return to its owner, a moment's reflection will show. Not only are there scattered farms on the frontiers, in the mountains and elsewhere, which yield no more than ordinary wages to the labor employed on them and the normal return to the savings invested in buildings, fences, tools, fertilizer, and seed; but, even in prosperous farming districts there are usually rented farms whose soil or location is so poor that, after we deduct the ordinary returns for the improvements made upon them in the way of barns, outbuildings, residences, and enclosures, we would find that there would be nothing left which could be regarded as a payment to the owner for the land itself.

The Determination of Land Rent. — We are now in a position to see what it is that determines the amounts of rent that will be paid for these different kinds of land. Labor and savings are not equally productive on all lands; on some lands they produce more than on others. But the prices which these two agents can command must be the same throughout the whole of the market. Wages for labor employed on the best land will not be any higher than the wages for labor of the same kind employed elsewhere; and the same is true of interest. Therefore, labor and savings, no matter where employed, cannot get any more than the value of what they produce at the margins of cultivation. That is their marginal product, and it determines their prices. It follows that, if they produce more on better land, the surplus is attributable to the superior quality of the land itself, and determines what the land is worth. The owner of the land can claim the entire value of this surplus. If a tenant would secure the use of such land, he must pay this value to the owner. From this reasoning we conclude that *the rent of a piece of land is determined by the surplus value product which labor and savings can produce on that land, over what they could produce at the margins of cultivation.* This is known as the *law of land rent*—sometimes called *the Ricardian law,* after the economist David Ricardo. The surplus product here referred to is commonly termed a *differential surplus,* because it measures the difference between what labor and savings can produce on good land, and what they can produce at the margins.

The differential surplus on each kind of land is represented by the shaded areas of the previous drawing (Figure 60). On the A lands, five inputs of labor and savings are employed. The first input yields a product worth $50; but this input, the same as any other, would yield only $10 at the margin. Here, then, is a surplus of $40. The second input yields a product of $40, which is $30 more than could have been produced by the same labor and savings at the margin. The third input yields a product of $30, including a surplus of $20, and the fourth input a product of $20, including a surplus of $10. The fifth input yields only $10, for it is working on the intensive margin; therefore it brings in no surplus at all. From this it appears that the total surplus obtained on the A land is $40 + $30 + $20 + $10, which makes a total of $100. Since this surplus is obtained, the possessor of this land is that much better off than he would be if he had to employ his labor and savings at the margin, therefore that is what the land is worth. It should rent for $100.

The surplus on the B lands is shown in the same way. It is $30 + $20 + $10, or $60 in all; so the land should rent for $60. By the same reckoning, the differential surplus (and rent) of C lands is $30. and of D lands, $10. E land yields no surplus, and commands no rent. The shaded areas of the diagram represent the total differential surplus of all kinds of lands, and the white areas indicate the product of labor and savings at the intensive and extensive margins (*i.e.*, their combined marginal products).

Land Rent as Marginal Product. — The differential surplus of land is also its marginal product. By definition, the marginal product of land is the addition to product that one unit of it will cause, or (what amounts to the same thing) the loss in product that would result if one unit of it were withdrawn. Suppose that a farmer, having 100 acres of C land, could obtain one more of them. He could then transfer to this land some of the labor and savings formerly used in marginal employments on the land he held before. The first input of labor and savings so transferred to the new C land would yield a surplus of $20 over their former employment at the margin, and the second input so transferred would yield a surplus of $10; a third input transferred would yield no surplus at all. It appears, then, that the additional acre would have added $30 to the product. By definition, this is its marginal product; but it is also the differential product, as we previously figured it. Therefore, the marginal product and the differential product are the same thing.

By calculating the loss that would be caused by withdrawal of one acre of land, we get the same result. Suppose that our farmer, with 100 acres of C land, loses one of them by an earthquake. He still has the labor and equipment formerly employed on that acre. The only thing he can now do with these agents is to employ them at the intensive margin on his remaining 99 acres, where they will yield approximately $10 per input, or transfer them to free land on the extensive margin, where they will again yield $10. It appears, then, that what he has lost is the differential surplus of $30 which he formerly obtained from that acre, over what his labor and savings can produce at the margins.

Calculations of the marginal products of the other kinds of land, by the same methods, would lead to an identical conclusion: the marginal product is the same as the differential product. Therefore, the law of rent, which represents it as determined by the differential surplus of land, is in harmony with our general principle, that the shares of income are equal to the value of the marginal products of the productive agents.

The differential analysis of land rent was understood before the marginal productivity theory was evolved; and, because of its early acceptance and long establishment, it is better known. It is simpler, and for some purposes more illuminating than the marginal productivity analysis; but the latter shows more clearly the similarity between the forces determining the value of the income from land and that of the other income shares.

Opportunity Costs and the Margin of Transference. — If the analysis of the last few pages has appeared to regard the supply of land available for any particular purpose as unalterably fixed in amount, that impression must now be corrected. The mobility of land as to its various uses must be allowed for. This mobility, it will be remembered, is a limited one; but it is of sufficient importance to exercise considerable influence upon land rents. An intelligent and well-informed farmer or business man will devote any piece of land to that product which, in proportion to the labor and savings employed, yields the greatest value. Therefore, no piece of land will ordinarily be employed (except temporarily) for one use, if the rent obtained from it in that use is less than might be derived from it if devoted to some other use. This is the now familiar principle of opportunity costs.

In the allocation of lands to their various possible uses, it is found that some plots are so clearly superior for a particular purpose that there will be no question of devoting them to any other. No one would seriously consider using a piece of land in the heart of a great city for any other purpose than as the site for a business building. As to other pieces of land, however, it may be a matter of doubt as to just what product is most advantageous for it. A piece of land lying somewhat outside the center of a city may be only moderately good for business purposes, but excellent for residences. The possible value returns to be derived from either use might be so nearly equal that it is a question which would be more profitable. At such a point there is said to be a *margin of transference*. This term may be defined as *any point where there are alternative uses for land which will yield approximately equal returns*. In this situation each of the possible uses of the land limits the other. Lands inferior for business sites to those on this margin will not be used for that purpose, if they can be made to yield more for residences; and lands superior to this for residences will not be used as such, if they can be made to yield more for business sites. That this mutual limitation, through its effects on the supply of the two kinds of products, affects their costs and values, has already been made clear.[2] If we pass on from the better to poorer residence sites, we may come to a point on the outskirts of the city where there is a margin of transference between residential uses and truck farming. This margin sets the lower limit below which the rents of the residence sites cannot fall, and above which those of truck lands cannot rise (so long as the lands in question are capable of being used for either purpose). There is a margin of transference wherever there is a borderline of advantage among two or more possible uses of land. There may be such a margin between wheat and corn lands, between cotton and tobacco lands, between dairy farming and truck farming lands, between cereal and grazing lands, and so on.

Just where the margin of transference between two uses will be established is a matter of the demands for the two products, and of the quantity of lands suitable for them. If the schedule of demand for one of the products changes, the margin of transference will shift, and the apportionment of land between the two uses will be readjusted, with corresponding changes in their rents, and in the prices of the two products. For instance, if, in the growth of a big city, the demand for residences increases, higher rents can be obtained for residence sites; lands formerly devoted to truck farming will be used for building purposes, and a new margin of transference between residential and truck farming land will be established. As a result, truck lands will be more scarce, and so will truck products. This raises the price of garden vegetables, and their enhanced values will, in turn, be reflected in higher rents for truck lands. The reaction will not stop there, for the higher rents obtainable from truck lands will cause lands, formerly devoted perhaps to cereal crops, to be diverted to truck. So, a new margin of transference between truck and cereal lands is effected, and the effects will be passed on in widening circles to other lands, until a complete readjustment is arrived at. An increase in the demand for any other product tends to produce similar results, and a decrease tends to produce an opposite chain of actions. So, we see that the rent yielded by any kind of land is not fixed entirely by influences peculiar to it, but depends to a very great extent on the rents of other lands used for very different purposes. The discussion also shows very neatly the great intricacy and interdependence of all prices in the modern industrial system.

The Rent of Mineral Lands. Royalties. — The value of the income from lands which contain mineral or other valuable deposits is determined by principles substantially the same as those of lands used for agricultural and building purposes; but differing slightly in two respects.

[2] See the discussion of opportunity costs in Chapter XIV.

In the first place, the price paid for the leasing of mineral land is usually called a *royalty*. This is paid in the form of a price *per unit of product* taken out of the land, not in the form of a certain annual sum *per acre*. On coal lands, there will be a payment by the operator to the owner of so much per ton; on oil lands, it will be so much per barrel; and so on. The amount of the royalty varies according to the quality of the product obtained from the land, and according to the difficulty of getting it out. If land contains exceptionally rich copper ore, well located with reference to transportation facilities, and in such a position that it can readily be extracted, the royalty will be high; if the ore is of poor quality, or difficult to get at, the royalty will be low. The money income derived by the owner of such land will depend on two factors: the amount of the royalty per unit of product, and the amount of product yielded by the deposit. In the case of a rich oil gusher, producing an abundant flow of high grade petroleum, the price per barrel and the number of barrels will both be high, making the owner rich. In other cases, both factors may be small, and the returns will not be so good. It is frequently possible to lease the mineral rights to land without leasing the surface, in which case, farming or other operations can go on upon it at the same time that the deposits are being removed. The land will then yield both a mining royalty and an ordinary agricultural rent.

The second peculiarity about mineral lands is that they contain a limited store of their particular deposit which is irreplaceable. Once the natural supply of mineral is exhausted, the yield ceases forever. This is not the case with other lands. The ability of a site to support a building will never wear out; the fertility of agricultural lands can be depleted, but it is not irreplaceable, and by proper methods of cultivation it can be maintained unimpaired indefinitely. Hence, the owner of the latter types of land receives back his capital practically intact at the end of his lease; but the mine-owner does not. The tenant in the case of building and agricultural land pays only for the *use* of it; the lessee of mineral land pays not only for its use, but also for its depreciation. He may be said to be buying outright a certain annual portion of the store of valuable minerals it contains. It is claimed that, because of this fact, there are no no-rent mineral lands —that even the marginal mine, quarry, or oil well yields a small royalty. Above this marginal royalty, superior mineral lands will yield larger amounts, on the differential principle. An analogy can be drawn between land and equipment in respect to this peculiarity of mineral lands. The owner of a building site or agricultural land is in the position of the lender of a sum of money who expects to receive his principal intact at the expiration of the loan; therefore, he needs only to charge a price for the use of the savings that will reimburse him for doing without them in the meantime. But the owner of mineral lands is in the position of the man who lets a building to a tenant; he must charge the latter, not only for its use, but enough besides to take care of its depreciation while in his possession.

Capitalization of Land Rents. — In the preceding chapter, it was explained that any regular source of income has a selling value determined by capitalizing the income. The rent yielded by a piece of land is such an income. The selling value of any piece of land, therefore, is determined by capitalizing the rent, at the current rate of interest. Suppose that an acre of farm land will yield annually a rent, free from taxes and other deductions, of $5 per acre. Assume also that the rate of interest prevailing on new investments in good long-time securities is about 5 per cent. Then the piece of land in question should be worth $100 per acre; for an investment of $100 in an acre of such land will yield just as much as the investment of an equal amount in other forms of capital. If other possible investments yielded more than $5 for each $100 invested, buyers for the land would not be forthcoming at the price of $100 per acre, and the price of the land would, consequently, fall. If other investments yielded less than $5 for each $100 put in, the land would be more valuable than $100 per acre, and its price would rise. Thus, persons with savings to invest will bid the selling price of land up or down until its value is such that the yield, computed as a percentage of that value, is no greater nor less than that generally prevailing. Therefore, if the rent of a piece of land rises or falls, its selling value will rise or fall correspondingly. Furthermore, if the rate of interest rises, land values will shrink; if the rate of interest falls, land values will rise. Real estate men sometimes speak of the price of land as "twenty years purchase," meaning that its selling value is twenty times its annual value, or rent. This is simply capitalizing its rent at 5 per cent interest. All land values are derived from their rent, by a similar process of capitalization.

There is, in fact, no other basis on which the selling value of land could be computed. Land, not being the product of human industry, has no cost of production, to which its value might conform. The value, therefore, can only be arrived at by figuring it from the income it affords. In this respect land is like equipment, whose value, once it is on the market, is determined by capitalization. But, whereas there is a tendency to keep the yield of equipment to somewhere near a certain percentage of its cost, by the operation of the mobile replacement fund and the volume of new savings, there is no such tendency in the case of land, because of the absence of such a cost.

This tends to confirm what was said in the preceding chapter, about the differences between land and other forms of capital.

Land Rent as Interest. — We can now see how the rent of land can be regarded as interest. Having once ascertained the value of a piece of land, by capitalizing its rent, the land itself can be thought of as a fund of capital-value, and the yield as a percentage of that value. If the services of a piece of land are valued at $1,000 annually, and the rate of interest is 5 per cent, the land will be worth $20,000. The purchaser can think of this investment in terms of that sum of money. The annual rent of $1,000 which he can get from it he can then regard as 5 per cent interest on his money.

It is interesting to note, however, that the income from land can only be regarded as interest by a circular process. For the capital-value of land is not determined independently of the income from it. Before we can obtain its capital-value we must first know what income it yields, and what the rate of interest is. Hence, the rate of interest helps to determine the value of land, but land values have no part in determining it. It is different with new (though not with old) investments in equipment. For here we have the capital-value determined, independently of the income it yields, by its cost of production. By comparing the income yield with this cost, we can derive the rate of interest. Hence the value (cost) of new equipment helps to determine the rate of interest, and is not determined by it.

Market Interferences Affecting the Returns from Land. — As with other economic principles, the forces operating to determine the price paid for the use of land, as explained in the foregoing paragraphs, are to be regarded only as representing strong tendencies. The rent yielded by a piece of land tends just to measure the marginal product or differential surplus of that land; but other influences may interfere with the full realization of that tendency. Just as the market values of commodities may fluctuate above or below their normal values, so the actual rents paid for land may deviate from their normal amounts.

This may be due to the ignorance of tenants, who may be paying more than the land is really worth, because they do not know that their labor and savings could be utilized more productively elsewhere. It may be due to the ignorance or good nature of the owner, who leases his land for less than he might obtain. Especially in the case of urban sites is the rent actually paid likely to be less than the full value of the marginal product of the land. Just what such lands can be made to yield is usually a matter of conjecture. A shrewd business man may see in an advantageous location possibilities not realized by the owner, or by competing bidders. He thereby obtains the land for a moderate price, but makes it yield a great deal more.

Lack of mobility of labor and equipment may also cause the market rents to deviate from the principles laid down. When a farm has once been improved and a family is settled upon it, its yield may be less than was anticipated; yet the improvements cannot be withdrawn, and the family is reluctant to move, as well as being uncertain as to whether they would be likely to do any better elsewhere. Undoubtedly, many farms are being operated for some such reasons as this, where the yield is actually less than a fair return for the labor and savings put upon them. In such a case, the land is not only no-rent land, it is even poorer than that; yet it is cultivated.

Allowance must also be made for the speculative possibility of future changes in the value of the land. If a prospective tenant has reason to believe that the growth of population will enhance the value of a certain city site within ten or twenty years, he may be willing to pay an annual rent greater than the present value of the site, if he can get a lease long enough to ensure his benefiting by the future increase in yield, which he expects to accrue. If there is reason to believe that the yield will decline, a long-time tenant could not be secured at all, except at a rental lower than the present value of the use of the land.

Notwithstanding these obstacles to the operation of the marginal productivity or differential principle, its effects are felt. If the rent of a given piece of land is too low, the owner or prospective tenants will in most cases become aware of that fact, and it will rise; if the rent is too high, similar considerations will usually bring it down in time. So, the price actually paid in the market can be said to tend toward the value of the land's marginal product, or differential surplus, notwithstanding the frequent discrepancies from this principle which can be found.

Similar considerations apply to the selling value of land. In capitalizing the rent, there may be some question as to just what rate of interest is the proper basis of capitalization, and as to what is the proper rent. Ignorance on the part of both buyer and seller, or either one of them, may affect the bargain, and the resulting price will be too high or too low. The speculative element will be apparent here likewise. If there is reason to believe that the yield of land will rise, or that the rate of interest will fall, in anticipation of such changes, the land will sell for a price somewhat higher than the capitalization of its current yield at the current rate. On the other hand, if there is reason to believe that the yield of the land will fall, or that the rate of interest will rise, the present selling price will be somewhat less.

SUMMARY

Because of the peculiarities which differentiate land from other kinds of capital, the rent yielded by a piece of land depends upon the following factors: (1) the products to which it is suited; (2) its excellence for those products; (3) its scarcity; (4) the demand for the product. The labor and savings of a community will be applied to the available land in the way that will yield products of greatest value, which results in the intensive cultivation of the better grades, and a much less intensive cultivation of the poorer grades. The poorest land which it is necessary to use is the extensive margin of cultivation, and the least productive applications of labor and savings on the better lands mark the intensive margin. With land thus utilized, the differential surplus of any particular kind determines the rent it can command. According to this principle, the rent yielded by a piece of land is equal to the difference between the value of the product obtained upon it, and that of an equal amount of labor and savings applied at the margins of cultivation. The differential surplus is the same as the marginal product of the land.

Where there are two or more possible products for which a given kind of land may be used, each of which yields approximately equal returns, there is said to be a margin of transference. Changes in the demand for either of these products will cause a shift in this margin, which will affect the rents yielded by both kinds of land, will also affect the prices of the products concerned, and which may extend its effects to other kinds of lands and other products.

The returns yielded by mineral lands are paid in the form of a royalty per unit of the product removed from it, and not as a lump sum per acre. They differ slightly in principle from the returns from other kinds of land, in that, since the land is not returned to the owner as rich in deposits as it was received, the royalty includes a price paid for depreciation, that is, for the minerals removed.

The selling value of land is obtained by capitalizing its yield (rent) at the current rate of interest. The yield can be regarded as interest, when considered as a percentage return on this capitalized value.

The principles governing the rent of land, and its capitalization, are not to be thought of as operating in every case with mathematical precision, but as being merely tendencies, which may be interfered with by the ignorance of buyers and sellers, by the imperfect equilibriums established in the market, and by the speculative possibilities of future changes in land values.

REFERENCES AND SUGGESTIONS FOR FURTHER READING

A short and illuminating introduction to the principles governing the income from land is that of H. D. Henderson, in his *Supply and Demand* (1922), Chapter 6, to which I am indebted for the idea of the margin of transference, and other material. Another able discussion, which sets forth clearly the concept of the rent of land as its marginal product, is in T. N. Carver's *The Distribution of Wealth* (1904), Chapter 5.

Formerly, the rent of land was not regarded as a cost of production *entering into* the price of commodities, but only as a differential *determined by* the price of the products raised on the land. For this older view see F. W. Taussig, *Principles of Economics* (4th edition, 1939), Chapters 44 to 47, inclusive. In the last-named chapter, also, he shows clearly why many economists prefer not to regard land as a part of capital. For an argument upholding the view that land rents are costs, entering as much into the prices of commodities as any other costs, see H. J. Davenport, *The Economics of Enterprise* (1913), Chapters 12 and 13, and G. Cassel, *The Theory of Social Economy* (English translation, 1923), Chapter 7, and the chapters in Henderson and Carver above referred to.

Chapter XXIII

THE PROFITS OF BUSINESS ENTERPRISE

A. CHARACTERISTICS OF GROSS PROFITS

The Composite Nature of Enterprisers' Gains. — It is the function of the business enterpriser to bring capital and labor together into a working organization. *As an enterpriser* he does not furnish either the capital or the labor himself, but acts merely as an agent for bringing them together, and he determines the broad general policies of the business establishment that results. The capital he borrows, and the labor he hires, often delegating even the labor of supervision to employees. It was explained in Chapter VI, however, that a person who is an enterpriser and nothing but that is seldom found. In practice, enterprisers almost always have some savings of their own invested in their businesses, and (except in corporations) they do some of the labor of management. At the head of many businesses, therefore, we find capitalist, laborer, and enterpriser centered in one person.

The incomes which enterprisers receive from this triple activity are similarly composite. Yet in common parlance these incomes are lumped together under the general term profits. A farmer who owns his own farm and does much of his own labor, in addition to being an enterpriser, does not regard his income as being made up of three parts corresponding to these functions. He simply subtracts from the proceeds of the sale of his crops all his outlays for seed, fertilizer, tools, equipment, interest on borrowed funds, taxes, wages of hired labor, etc., and calls the remainder the profit from his year's operations. Likewise a manufacturer, usually, makes no distinction between that part of his gains which are to be attributed to his own capital, that part which is due to his labor, and that part which comes to him by virtue of his position as enterpriser. He simply knows that he has a certain amount left over from his sales after he has deducted his money outlays, and that amount he regards as his profit. Some business men are beginning to make a distinction between these things; but the practice is not yet general.

The economist, however, with his analytical eye, discerns three elements in such an income. Part of these gains he regards as a payment to the enterprisers for the savings which they have invested in their businesses. In the case of the farmer, it is in the nature of a rent for the use of that part of his farm which he owns free from encumbrances. In the case of the manufacturer, it is a rent for the use of his plant, or interest on the money of his own which he has invested in it. Another part of the gains is equivalent to wages paid to the enterprisers for their labor—whether it be the manual exertion of the farmer, or the mental work of supervision and direction performed by the manufacturer. Finally, a third part is thought of as a payment to the business man for his function as an enterpriser, for assuming the responsibility and determining the general policies of the undertaking. This is in some measure a compensation for the risks he runs as the head of the business; but it cannot be regarded as wholly that, for reasons which will presently appear.

Gross Profits and Pure Profits. — Are all three of these elements to be included in the term profits for purposes of scientific reasoning? They are all enterprisers' gains, surely, and in practice it is often quite impossible to separate them. Yet there are certain differences between them which make it desirable to think of them as distinct in our reasoning. Some economists therefore confine the term profits only to the third of the elements mentioned above, applying the word only to that part of a business man's income which can be regarded as paid to him solely in his capacity as enterpriser. Those parts of his gains which may be thought of as payments for his capital and for his labor are by these writers treated simply as ordinary interest (or rent) and wages, and are not regarded as profits at all. But to this there are objections. The separation cannot always be made in practice, and it is not even satisfactory in theory. For we shall find that the entire income of the enterpriser, from whatever source derived, rises and falls as a unit in response to the influences operating upon profits. It is desirable to acknowledge this unity, while at the same time recognizing the influence of interest, rent, and wage factors. We may solve the difficulty by distinguishing between two kinds of profits—one a broad concept including all the elements which have been mentioned, the other a narrower term. The first we shall call *gross profits,* and the second *pure profits.*

Gross profits include all residual sums left in enterprisers' hands after payment of all business costs due to other parties. These profits may include: (1) income from capital owned by the enterpriser and used in his own business; (2) wages of management, by which is meant payment to the enterpriser for his labor of supervision in his business; and (3) pure profits. We may think of pure profits for the moment as any surplus earned by the enterpriser above ordinary interest or rent on his own capital and ordinary wages of management. In the following section it will be more carefully defined.

Not every business will contain all three of these elements in its gross profits. A few enterprisers, such as brokers and promoters, may be able to carry on with very little investment of their own. Their incomes then consist mostly of wages of management and pure profits, especially the latter. Such cases, however, are in the minority. The profits of corporations, on the other hand, constitute an important class of incomes which ordinarily include only two of the elements above named. The stockholders of a corporation are its enterprisers. They have savings invested in the business, and they assume the ultimate responsibility and risk; but most of them perform practically no labor of supervision. Therefore, their dividends contain elements of interest as well as pure profits, but no wages of management.

Profits and Losses. — There are losses as well as gains in business, and they both arise from the same general sources. A good season will improve the farmer's crops; a bad season will injure them. An increase in the demand for steel rails will increase the earnings of their manufacturers; a decrease in the demand will reduce them. The discovery of a rich mineral deposit in a mine will bring in handsome returns; the petering out of a vein will make it worthless. All the fluctuations and uncertainties of industry which give rise to profits may also give rise to losses. Which way they will work is partly a matter of chance, and partly a matter of the resourcefulness and ingenuity of the enterpriser in meeting and taking advantage of them. Hence, profits and losses are but the positive and negative aspects of the same thing, and must be explained by a common theory.

When is a business truly profitable? If an enterpriser is earning no more from his operations than the current rate of interest on his capital and the prevailing rate of wages for his labor, he is no better off than if he were not in business at all. For he could lend out his capital at interest, hire himself out to an employer for wages, and save himself the responsibility and worry of being an enterpriser. It is for this reason that only the surplus above interest and wages of management is to be regarded as a pure profit. If the earnings are less than such interest and wages of management, it is apparent that the enterpriser is actually in a worse position than if he were not in business for himself. We can truly say, therefore, that in such a case there is actually a deficit. This deficit differs from the surplus presented by the opposite case only in that it is a minus rather than a plus quantity. It springs from the same business operations and the same sort of influences. We can regard it, therefore, as a negative pure profit.

Recognizing, then, that pure profits may sometimes take the negative form of losses, we can give a more accurate definition of them than that of the preceding section. *Pure profits are the difference between the gross profits of a business, and the sum of interest on enterprisers' capital plus wages of management.* We shall think of pure profits ordinarily as a positive quantity, using the term losses to denote their negative aspect; but it must not be forgotten that profits and losses are simply two different sides of the same thing, and that the theory of profits is an explanation of both.

Income from Capital in its Relation to Profits. — An enterpriser is almost perforce a capitalist as well. Without some capital of his own invested in his business he can hardly live up to the responsibilities of his position. Other capitalists will not lend to him, other enterprisers will not have confidence in his ability to fulfill his contracts with them, and his business credit will be very poor, unless he has sufficient investments of his own in his undertakings to assure his creditors of his ability to protect them against loss. In most businesses, therefore, ownership of capital is inseparably associated with the functions of the enterpriser. Nowhere is this more apparent than in corporations, which are the dominant form of business enterprise in modern industry. Here the stockholders are the enterprisers; but they can usually become such only by investing in the capital stock of the company.

The investment of an enterpriser stands on a different footing from that of an ordinary capitalist, however, in that the return derived from it is inseparably mingled with the profits of the business. When a capitalist lends money to a business other than his own, the borrower guarantees to return the principal intact at the end of a certain period, with interest during the meantime at the rate agreed upon. Barring extraordinary risks, the capitalist receives a certain, predetermined income from his savings. The enterpriser-capitalist, on the other hand, gives up a certain for an uncertain return. Instead of receiving a fixed rate of interest, he gets only what he can make his business earn. One year it may be high; another year it may be low. All depends on his ability as an enterpriser; and in part on external conditions beyond his control. So the income from his capital is inextricably entangled with his profits, and virtually becomes a part of them. The corporation again furnishes an excellent illustration of this. The bondholder of a corporation is purely a capitalist; his investment is a loan to the company, on which he is paid yearly a stipulated interest. The stockholder, who is an enterpriser-capitalist, has no such assured income; he shares in the risks of the business, and in successful years his dividends will be high, while in poor years they will be low. So the return on his capital is part and parcel of his profits.

Although in any one year the profits of a given enterpriser are thus indistinguishable from the interest on his capital, the case is different if we take the average profits of a whole industry over a considerable period of years. In such a long-run view it is possible to discern the separate action of interest on the gains of business men, as contrasted with the other elements of their gross profits. The discussion of this can best be taken up after a consideration of wages of management.

Wages of Management. — If an enterpriser is the active head of his business, he is, as has already been stated, a kind of laborer, specializing on the work of superintendence and direction. This links an element of wages with his profits, just as in the preceding case there is involved an element of income from capital. To this element of wages we have already given the name wages of management.

Here again the income which the enterpriser derives from his labor stands on a different footing from that of a hired worker. Many persons are employed by corporations and other business organizations as executives, superintendents, managers, and so on, at definite salaries. In these positions they perform much the same kind of work which an enterpriser performs in directing and supervising his own undertakings. But the enterpriser receives, usually, no such regular, definite wage as they. In going into business for himself he gives up a possible salary for the uncertain, irregular income of business profits. As a result, it is not usually possible to separate his wages of management from the other elements of his gross profits at any given time.

In the case of corporations, however, that is not true. It has already been stated that corporate dividends do not contain the element of wages. In this form of business organization the stockholders delegate the real work of management or supervision to salaried men employed for the purpose. Even the directors occupy themselves only with broad matters of general policy, dealing primarily with the financial and strategic aspects of the business; and for this they, too, frequently draw a salary. So the wages of management appear on the payroll as salaries, and do not constitute a part of the profits of the stockholders.

Where the wage element appears in the gross profits, its separate influence upon them can be observed, like that of interest, only over considerable periods of time. Just how this works out we may now investigate.

Average Profits and Particular Profits, or Profits in the Long and Short Run. — An enterpriser is not compelled to set up in business for himself. If he has savings, he may lend them to someone else at interest. If he has managerial ability, he may accept employment at a salary. Let us imagine a person who has savings amounting to $25,000 and who is a fairly good organizer. We may assume that he might invest his money in good bonds, yielding five per cent interest, and bringing him an income of $1,250 per year. Suppose also that, as an executive for some corporation, he could command a salary of $10,000 per year. Under what conditions would he find it worth while to become an enterpriser? There would be no inducement for him to do so unless he could reasonably expect to make gross profits of at least $11,250 annually. In fact, unless he made a little more than that, there would be nothing to compensate him for the risks and responsibilities of his position, and he would be better off if he did not set up in business. His profits in any one year would not necessarily have to be as great as that; but they should average no less over a period of several years. Suppose now that he goes into business, and after ten years finds that his gains have averaged only $8,000 yearly. The probabilities are that he would consider the venture a failure; and if he could get out of it without sacrificing his capital, he would have a strong motive for doing so.

There is continually going on in industry a series of experiments of this sort. Men leave their employers and set up businesses of their own. Others retire from their own businesses and seek employment with others. Savings are invested by enterprisers in one industry and withdrawn from another. Business men are always alert to an opportunity for profit. Hence, if in the long run the average profits of an industry do not pay the prevailing market rate of interest on the enterprisers' savings, and do not yield wages of management equal to current salaries for similar kinds of labor, enterprisers already established there will tend to withdraw, and new enterprisers will be dissuaded from entering it. There will result a curtailment of products in the industry, until their price rises sufficiently to afford such profits.[1] We may conclude, therefore, that in the long run the average gross profits of an industry cannot fall below the current rate of interest on enterprisers' capital, plus wages of management.

[1] This reasoning reinforces the point emphasized in our analysis of commodity prices, that interest on the enterprisers' savings and wages of management are costs of production just as truly as interest on borrowed savings and the wages of hired employees; for if the price of the commodity does not cover such items, the commodity cannot continue to be produced.

In fact, as will be shown in the next section, it is probable that they would have to be slightly in excess of that amount, to induce business men to assume the risks of their position.

The profits of any particular individual, or of a whole industry in any particular year, however, will not necessarily bear any close relationship to interest and wages of management. It is characteristic of the income of enterprisers that it varies greatly from person to person, and from time to time. It fluctuates upward and downward in a capricious way, as though it were subject to no uniform principles at all. It is the most unstable of all the shares of income. A complete explanation of profits, therefore, must account for the deviations above and below interest and wages of management that are so conspicuous an element in the profits of particular businesses from time to time. By our previous definition, these deviations are pure profits (positive and negative). They are the result of short-run influences, as contrasted with the long-run influence of interest on enterprisers' capital and wages of management. They affect the earnings of this or that individual, as contrasted with the average earnings of a trade. Before endeavoring to show just how these pure profits are determined, it will be well to consider the theory, held by some economists, that profits are to be explained as a reward for risk; for this theory will shed some light upon our problem.

Reward for Risk in its Relation to Profits. — In Chapter VII the nature of the risks incurred by enterprisers was discussed, so that it is not necessary here to go into them in detail. It suffices to recall to the reader that, although enterprisers are not the sole risk-takers of industry, they do assume certain hazards that are peculiar to their position. They produce goods in anticipation of demand, going to certain expense and entering into obligations which they expect to be able to meet out of the selling prices of their products. In this there are two possibilities of loss: the danger that production will be interfered with by some unforeseen occurrence, such as fire, strike, or flood; and the chance that market fluctuations may increase costs or decrease selling prices. Some of these contingencies may be provided for by insurance, but many of them the enterpriser must bear himself. This is particularly true of those arising out of market fluctuations. The uncertain nature of his profits, which, unlike ordinary wages or interest, are not known in advance, leaves him continually in doubt as to how he is going to come out on his year's business. He must pay to the others their shares, and take what is left for himself. At one time this residue may be large; at another it may be very small.

While some persons are fond of taking a chance, it is probably true of human beings in general that they would not be willing to subject themselves to such uncertainty of income without the prospect of some extra reward or premium. Therefore it may be argued that some element of income in addition to interest on the enterpriser's capital and wages of management is necessary if business is to be carried on under a system of free enterprise. It is plausible to include such a reward, therefore, as a part of the pure profits of business men. This reasoning justifies, also, the inclusion of some payment for enterprisers' risks as one of the costs of production entering into the determination of values.

Following this analysis, the writers already referred to explain business profits as primarily a reward for risks. Profits are in this view regarded simply as a necessary inducement to stimulate business, and without which it would not be carried on. It is claimed further, that if all the gains in business were compared with all the losses, the average rate of profits would be shown to be very low. Thus this explanation calls attention to average profits rather than the particular profits of individuals, and points out that this average rate is not excessive. It follows also from the argument that the greater the risks in any particular industry, the higher the average rate of profits in it must be.

As a complete explanation of business profits the theory is unsatisfactory in two respects. In the first place, it accounts only for average profits, ignoring the fluctuations in the earnings of different individuals. The necessity of explaining these particular profits has already been emphasized. In the second place, it is doubtful if the average profits of an industry will show any very close relation to the degree of risk it involves. Human beings will often take great risks against heavy odds, if the stakes are large enough. Suppose that an automobile, worth $1,000, is to be chanced off to the holder of a winning number, and one thousand chances in all are to be sold. On the basis of their mathematical value, each chance should be worth one dollar; yet it would not be difficult to find a thousand persons to buy the tickets at two dollars each. As a group they would give up $2,000 in the hope of gaining half that sum. So in industry, if there is a chance of very high profits, many persons may be induced to have a try at it where there is hope of success for only a few; and while those few may reap tremendous gains, the losses of the remainder may reduce the average to less than zero. According to the risk theory a hazardous industry like gold mining ought to show a high average rate of profits; but if all the losses of the gold-seekers were known, and balanced against the gains, it is not unlikely that the industry would show a net loss.

There are two elements of truth in the theory, however, which shed light upon the problem of business profits. In the first place, as already mentioned, unless a business offers *the possibility* of some recompense above the ordinary returns to labor and capital, enterprisers will not assume the risks; and, in general, the greater the amount of those risks, the greater must be the possibility of extra gains. Gold mining again furnishes a good example of this. The uncertain nature of the industry is well known. One may spend years in fruitless search for the precious metal and die a pauper; or one may strike a bonanza and reap a colossal fortune. It is only the possibility of the fortune that lured so many into the gold rush as to cause enormous losses. But this is not the same as saying that the average returns in the industry are large.

In the second place, the risk theory rightly stresses the connection between profits and the uncertainties of the enterpriser's position. Those uncertainties are a fruitful source of pure profits, and losses. How they give rise to such profits will now be made clear.

B. Sources of Pure Profits

Competition, Uncertainty, and Pure Profits. — Imagine a state of society in which there is perfect competition, and no uncertainty. The competitive forces would be so keen, so immediate in their action, that no seller could get a higher price for his wares than any other; all investments would yield equal rates of return, all producers of a given commodity would have equal costs of production, and prices would correspond exactly to those costs. This would be so, because if any buyer or any seller had an advantage in any of these particulars over his fellows, the latter would quickly learn of it, and would take advantage of the same opportunity until equality was restored. If the student has followed closely the analysis of economic forces in the preceding chapters of this book, he will understand that competition always has a leveling effect wherever its influence is felt; therefore, if it were perfect, complete equality of prices, costs, and earnings would be achieved. If uncertainty were absent, there would be no risks. Each producer would know in advance the demands of consumers, the intentions of his competitors, and the prices he could get for his products when completed. He would be sure, also, of his costs of production, and would not have any catastrophes or interruptions to fear, such as strikes, unfavorable weather, and other accidents that now interfere with the calculations of enterprisers. There would be no losses in business.

In such an ideal society, there would be no pure profits. The only

returns which enterprisers could secure would be interest on whatever savings they had invested in their businesses, and ordinary wages
of management. The reasons for this should already be apparent to
the reader. If an industry or enterprise yielded more than prevailing market rates of interest on the savings invested, competing enterprisers would at once enter that industry with more savings, until
the increased production in the trade lowered the prices of its products, and brought the returns to normal. Likewise, if any industry
or enterprise yielded more than ordinary wages of management, persons previously working for wages as hired employees would be induced to set up businesses of their own in the more lucrative field,
until, as before, the resulting increase in production lowered the
prices of the products of the trade, and reduced the earnings to prevailing wage rates.

Since perfect competition and perfect certainty would eliminate
pure profits, we may conclude that where such profits are to be
found they must be due to the lack of these conditions. The theory
of pure profits here presented, therefore, is that they arise from two
characteristics of the industrial system in which we live: (1) the im-
perfectness of competition, and (2) uncertainty.[2] This explanation
of profits will now be more fully developed.

The Enterpriser's Strategic Position in Relation to Pure Profits. —
Not all the results of imperfect competition and of uncertainty are
reflected in enterprisers' gains. The earnings of both labor and capital are also affected by them. In the discussion of wages and of the income from capital it was shown that the fluctuations of the market
might cause irregularities in wages, interest, or rents, and that occupations or investments involving risks would result in higher earnings
than those which were free from such uncertainties. It may be won-
dered, therefore, why these influences are regarded as being of peculiar
importance in the determination of pure profits.

We can best understand the reasons for this by a moment's consideration of the position occupied by the enterpriser in industry.
He is the center about whom all economic forces play and through
whom they operate. He is the buffer who absorbs most of the shocks
of the industrial system. His relation to the owners of the other
agents of production is one of contract. He employs them at agreed
rates of wages, interest, or rent, and takes his chances on the selling

[2] While this theory assigns an important place to risk as a determinant of pure profits,
it differs from the "reward for risk" theory above discussed in two important respects:
(1) it introduces imperfect competition as an equally important factor, and (2) it does not
establish a direct connection between the degree of risk in an industry and the average
rate of profits prevailing in that industry. On the contrary, it regards profits as being
very irregular and unpredictable, fluctuating with the chances of circumstance. It, therefore, focuses attention on individual profits, rather than average rates of profit.

price of his product. All receipts from the sale of goods pass first into the hands of the enterpriser, and are then paid out by him in wages and interest, or rent, to the laborers and capitalists. Consequently, he is the first one to feel the effects of any decrease in costs or any rise in prices. Changes in demand first affect him. If the price of his commodity is going up, it may be some time before competition makes it necessary for him to pass on a share of this increase in higher wages or higher interest. If interest rates or wages are going down he may not immediately find it necessary to give consumers the benefit of this in lower prices. He feels the effect of every temporary fluctuation in economic forces, but he does not always pass these effects on to the other participants in the productive process. If he is shrewd and quick to take advantage of the irregularities and fluctuations he can enlarge his gains.

In short, the income of the enterpriser is *residual*—it is what is left over after his expenses are paid. Hence it rises and falls with the eccentricities and uncertainties of the market.

External Sources of Pure Profits. — There are some conditions which will cause all or nearly all the producers in a given industry (or group of industries) to profit for a time. These are conditions arising outside of any particular business establishment, and therefore beyond the control of the individual business man. We may call them external sources of pure profits.

A general rise of prices usually increases profits throughout industry. Since the reasons for this have been explained elsewhere, we need only review them briefly here. (1) Business is usually carried on by borrowed funds; hence enterprisers benefit by the gains which all debtors enjoy when prices rise. Since they pay back their debts in dollars of less value than at the time they borrowed them, they profit by the difference. (2) During rising prices, wages and interest rates do not generally keep pace with the prices of commodities. Therefore, enterprisers' selling prices increase more rapidly than their costs, and they pocket the surplus. (3) Finally, since they buy materials and hire labor days, weeks, or months in advance of their sales, they incur their costs at a low level of prices and sell at a higher one, reaping an extra profit. A fall in prices, on the other hand, will produce opposite effects. Enterprisers must then pay their debts in an appreciated dollar, and their costs will not fall as rapidly as their selling prices. Hence, losses will result.

A rise in the price of a particular commodity due to an increase in the demand for it will usually cause profits to those enterprisers who are engaged in producing it. It was shown in the discussion of prices that when the schedule of demand for a good increases, its price rises above its cost for a time, until increased production brings it down again. Meanwhile, the difference represents profits to the producers. Examples of profits arising from this source are not hard to find. During the first World War the American government found itself suddenly in need of great quantities of munitions. The price of these supplies immediately rose, due to their scarcity relative to the enormous demand for them. Huge profits were reaped by those who were fortunate enough to be engaged in war industries at that time. Thus arose a class of business men who were scornfully dubbed "war profiteers." During several recent decades there has been an unforeseen and unprecedented increase in the demand for petroleum and its products. The need for gasoline for automobiles and airplanes, the use of fuel oil in railroad and ocean transportation, the necessity for increasing quantities of lubricating oils, and the development of the many by-products of petroleum which found a ready market, caused a demand which the oil-producing facilities existing at the beginning of this period of growth were entirely inadequate to supply. The price of crude oil and its products soared, and those who were already established in the industry reaped the advantage therefrom. The high gains brought about a rapid expansion of oil production and the opening up of new fields, which are rapidly increasing the supply of oil, so that in time the high profits in this industry may be expected to disappear, if they are not already doing so. On the other hand, if the schedule of demand for a commodity falls off, its price will sink below its cost of production temporarily, and producers will lose.

Uncontrollable variations in the production of commodities will sometimes arise. This is particularly true in agriculture, where climatic conditions cannot be regulated by the producer. Good and bad harvests will occur, causing plentifulness or scarcity of crops, and corresponding fluctuations in their prices. If these changes are favorable to farmers, they will profit; if unfavorable, they will lose.

Internal Sources of Pure Profits. — We may now turn to those sources of profits which affect only certain individual enterprisers, rather than all producers in an industry or group of industries. These arise from some economy or other advantage confined to one establishment or individual, which enables the enterpriser concerned to reap gains not shared by his fellows. We may call these internal sources of pure profits.

One of the most important of these sources is the *individual efficiency of the enterpriser*. A capable and skillful man may be able so to organize his production as to reduce his costs below those generally prevailing in his trade. This may result from more scientific methods of management, greater ability in the handling of men, or other causes. Real organizing and executive ability is a rare human quality. The man who is gifted with it can always keep ahead of his competitors. He sells his goods at the same prices which they obtain for theirs, but he keeps his costs lower. He reaps a differential surplus very similar to that obtained by the owner of superior over marginal land. This is probably the most prolific source of the profits of really successful business men. Their methods are always imitated by their competitors, so that the differential gains of the leader are continually threatened with extinction; but by the time the competing producers have adopted one improved method, the skillful enterpriser has already inaugurated another, thereby maintaining his position in the lead.

Another frequent source of profits is *successful speculation*. All business is carried on in anticipation of demand, and is, therefore, speculative. Costs have to be incurred in advance; future selling prices are somewhat uncertain. The man who can foresee a coming rise or fall in the price of a commodity, and buy or sell accordingly, can turn these fluctuations to his own advantage. Enterprisers who are not so well informed on market conditions, or who lack the venturesome spirit to engage in speculation, partly escape therefrom by contracting out or by hedging, shifting the burden of the risk to the shoulders of those who make speculation their business. This brings profits to the latter, the more conservative business men being then obliged to content themselves with smaller gains. Speculation is not always a source of positive profits, and it is quite possible that on the whole as much is lost as is gained by those who speculate.

The *introduction of novelties* may often bring gains to a producer. For example, the manufacturer of toys at the Christmas season may put on a clever innovation which finds popular approval. Tremendous sales follow, at a price well above the cost of production. The gain is but a temporary one, for in the next season other toy manufacturers will adopt the same idea; but it is a substantial source of revenue when first introduced. In the clothing trades new styles may bring about similar gains; and in many other industries examples of this sort can be found. If the novelty does not take well with the public, however, it may prove a drug on the market, and the expense of introducing it may cause a loss.

Successful bargaining on the part of an enterpriser in the purchase of materials, the hiring of labor, or the securing of capital may be a source of profits. For example, a landlord should always obtain the full value of the use of his real estate as rent. However, this value is not always easy to determine in advance. Particularly in the case of urban building sites, such as advantageous locations for retail stores in the heart of a great shopping district, it is difficult to forecast just what the productive possibilities are. The prospective tenant (an enterpriser) is more likely to know these possibilities than an owner. He offers for such a property a rent somewhat less than he estimates its actual value to be. If he is able to strike a bargain with his landlord on such terms, the difference between the rent he pays and that actually yielded by the site goes into his pockets as profits. Similarly, employers are usually better informed concerning the market for labor than are the employees, and a skillful employer can often secure his labor force at a wage somewhat less than the full value of their marginal product. If other employers are paying that full value, this employer will gain. It is similar with the purchase of raw materials. Any enterpriser who can secure supplies at less than normal rates has an advantage over his competitors which brings in pure profits. A poor bargainer, on the other hand, may pay more than prevailing rates for his means of production, and thereby suffer losses.

Good will is frequently a source of profits. By good will, as was explained in Chapter II, is meant the general esteem in which a business concern is held by the buying public, and which brings it patronage. Good will frequently makes it possible for a business man to obtain slightly better prices for his merchandise than his competitors. His established reputation and the general confidence of consumers in him makes them willing to pay slightly more for his wares rather than buy somewhere else, at lower prices, goods which may be similar, but in which they have less confidence.

Advertising is another source of pure profits. By it good will can be established and so insistent a demand for a certain product can be built up that it can be sold in large volume at high prices in spite of competitors. Huge sums are nowadays spent in advertising campaigns in this country. Often these campaigns have proved to be extremely profitable to their promulgators.

Financial manipulation is a type of business activity that has become very prevalent with the advent of the corporation. Mergers and consolidations, the promotion of new enterprises, and various types of financial wizardry have made many a fortune. A promoter sees an opportunity to consolidate several concerns into a monopoly or near it. For his services in bringing together the parties concerned he receives stock in the new corporation. This he sells for a good round sum after the consolidation is successfully launched. There are all sorts of stock juggling procedures, some of which were described in Chapter VI, which may be made the source of profits.

Some of these are legitimate, others border closely on fraud. They may also be associated closely with monopoly gains, which will be considered presently.

Predatory activities of various kinds are to be found in the business world, which may prove very lucrative to those who take part in them. Some of the sharp financial practices mentioned above are of this sort. The adulteration of food or other goods, misrepresentation, and downright fraud may produce profits. The principle involved here is that something is sold for what it is not, and the purchaser is fooled into paying a price for it as high as he would have had to pay for a genuine article or for one of better quality. The dishonest seller reaps the benefit of the difference.

Transitory and Irregular Nature of These Profits. — Other sources of competitive profits doubtless might be enumerated, but the ones already described are sufficient to illustrate their general nature. The most noteworthy fact about all of them is that they are very irregular and transitory. All pure profits, in fact, rest upon inconstant and unpredictable business influences. This fact has already been mentioned; but it can hardly be overemphasized. Most business men are confronted with some degree of competition. All are eager to take advantage of such chances for gain as have been described. Hence, when (positive) pure profits appear at any point in the industrial system, other producers seek to share in them either by entering the industry, or, if already established there, by imitating the methods of the successful individual. But the influx of new producers into an industry where high gains are widespread brings such an increase in the supply of the commodities concerned that their price falls, causing the surplus gains soon to disappear; while the imitation of one successful producer by his less original competitors quickly makes his differential advantage the common property of all, and in the scramble for the business which ensues the surplus earnings are entirely eliminated. Only by keeping continually one step in the lead of the procession can any producer consistently keep his profits above wages of management and interest on his investment year after year. Notwithstanding this leveling tendency on profits, the irregularities, the innovations, and the changes of all sorts in the industrial system are so numerous that the chances for gain in any industry are never entirely wiped out, and almost always some individuals are enjoying surplus profits while others, less successful, are barely able to meet their expenses, or are even suffering loss. Pure profits are thus ever-present, yet fleeting; universal, yet irregular; enjoyed by a few always, by many for short periods, and to others—less capable, less adaptable, less alert—denied.

Monopoly Profits. — The analysis of profits up to this point has proceeded on the assumption that competition among the producers in each industry prevailed. It is increasingly true in modern times, however, that some restriction of competition approaching monopoly is found in a considerable number of fields of production. Such monopoly is a fruitful source of pure profits. How such monopolies come to exist was set forth in earlier chapters, where we found the causes of monopoly to be: (1) a natural scarcity of some important resource found only in limited regions, such as diamonds; (2) economies of large scale production which bring the costs of the monopoly below those of possible small competitors; (3) control of huge aggregations of capital which give the monopoly irresistible competing power; (4) knowledge of secret processes; (5) legal grants, such as patents and franchises; (6) product differentiation.

The amount of profits which can be made by pure monopolies is governed by the law of monopoly price, which was explained in Chapter XIV. We there learned that a monopoly cannot arbitrarily fix its price at a very high figure and continue to sell its product in undiminished quantity; for consumers will only buy a certain quantity at a given price, and the higher that price the less that quantity will be. If the price is very high, the profit on each unit of goods sold may be great, but the total number of sales will be so small that the aggregate profits will be less than if a lower price were charged. The monopoly must reckon with this, and govern its policy accordingly. If it takes full advantage of its control over the supply, it will fix its price at that figure which will make its marginal costs equal to its marginal receipts. The discussion of this rule in Chapter XIV suffices fully to explain the determination of monopoly profits. According to it, the maximum such profits will be limited by the demand for the commodity, and will be higher or lower as that demand is more or less inelastic.

Few monopolies are complete. There are many producers who are in a position of monopolistic competition of one kind or another. These producers may be able to obtain slightly more than a strictly competitive price and yet less than full monopoly price for their goods. Their profits will be governed accordingly. The country hardware dealer, who has the sole shop of its kind in a rural neighborhood, is in such a position of semi-monopoly. Farmers must either buy of him or go to the expense and inconvenience of journeying to some other place to make their purchases. This enables the dealer in question to charge just a little more than he might be able to do if another dealer was in his community; yet not enough more to drive his customers elsewhere. Some of the factors already mentioned as sources of competitive profits really bring gains to the enterpriser because they put him in a position somewhat near to monopoly. Good will is in this class. The merchant who by successful advertising, efficient service, or long-established reputation is able to build up an insistent demand for his wares can obtain a price somewhat better than his competitors, but less than a 'full monopoly price. From these simple examples up to huge combines which control almost the entire supply of a great staple commodity, all possible gradations can be found, with profits that vary from low to high accordingly. Even in the case of a complete monopoly, however, the price may not be forced up to the point of maximum net returns, and profits will thereby be less than they might be. This may be the result of unwillingness to attract competitors into the field, of fear of retaliation by the public, or of governmental regulation.

SUMMARY

The gains of enterprisers in industry are composed of three elements, which together comprise their gross profits. These elements are: (1) payment for the enterprisers' own capital invested in their businesses, (2) wages of management, and (3) pure profits, which consist of any surplus earned above these two factors. Losses are negative pure profits.

When an enterpriser puts his savings and his labor into a business of his own, he gives up the relatively certain interest which he might have obtained by lending out his funds, and the wages he might have earned as the employee of someone else, and accepts instead the uncertain earnings which he can make his business yield. In the long run, however, the average profits of an industry must return to the enterprisers gross profits at least equal to prevailing rates of interest and wages, or they will withdraw from the industry until the scarcity of its products brings higher prices, yielding profits that will pay these rates. For any one individual, and at any one time, however, interest on enterpriser's capital and wages of management are indistinguishable from profits. The real problem of profits, therefore, is to explain pure profits—that is, to explain the individual deviations above and below interest on enterprisers' capital and wages of management which are to be found in individual businesses from year to year. The theory which explains profits as a reward for risk is unsatisfactory for this purpose because it deals with average rather than individual profits, and because it is not certain that even the average profits of an industry vary directly with the risk involved; but it is true that some expectation of pure profit is necessary to induce enterprisers to assume the risks and responsibilities of their position.

If competition were perfect and there were no uncertainty in society, there would be no pure profits. Pure profits are due, therefore, to imperfect competition and to uncertainty. The enterpriser is in such a position that he acts as a buffer for the industrial system, upon whom all changes, irregularities, and fluctuations first fall. His income is more subject to such influences than the other distributive shares. If such influences are favorable, and he takes good advantage of them, he makes pure profits; if they are unfavorable, or if he is not skillful in adapting himself to them, he makes losses.

Such irregularities and fluctuations which give rise to pure profits and losses may be classed as external (arising from conditions outside a particular enterprise and affecting whole industries or groups of industries), and internal (arising from advantages enjoyed only by particular individuals). Among the external sources of pure profits are: (1) a general rise (or fall) in prices; (2) a rise (or fall) in the price of a particular commodity due to an increase (or decrease) in the demand for it; (3) uncontrollable variations in production. Among the internal sources of pure profits are: (1) individual efficiency (or inefficiency) of the enterpriser; (2) successful (or unsuccessful) speculation; (3) the introduction of novelties; (4) successful (or unsuccessful) bargaining; (5) good will; (6) advertising; (7) financial manipulation; (8) predatory activities. Profits arising from these sources are transitory, tending always to be eliminated by the attraction of new enterprisers into profitable trades, or by the imitation of successful by less original business men.

Where a monopoly controls the production of a commodity it can obtain surplus profits by raising the price. The maximum profits so obtainable are limited by the law of price under pure and monopolistic competition. All gradations of profits from the competitive level up to full monopoly returns are to be found.

REFERENCES AND SUGGESTIONS FOR FURTHER READING

An especially clear and satisfactory account of business profits, which represents them (in competitive industries) as a result of the dynamic fluctuations of industry, is that of H. R. Seager, in *The Principles of Economics* (revised edition, 1923), Chapters 12 and 13. I have used some of Seager's ideas in Part B of this chapter. I am also indebted to Professor F. H. Knight's *Risk, Uncertainty and Profit* (1921), especially Chapters 1, 2, 9, and 10, in which the relation of profits to risk and uncertainty is very ably analyzed. A brief summary of several theories of profits, tending to uphold the view that they are a form of wages paid for rare executive ability, is to be found in F. W. Taussig's *Principles of Economics*

(4th edition, 1939), Chapters 48, 49, and 50. These chapters are excellent in many respects. Alfred Marshall, in his *Principles of Economics* (5th edition, 1907, or later), also treats profits as a sort of wage of business ability in the long run. Raymond T. Bowman's *A Statistical Study of Profits* (1934) treats the subject both statistically and theoretically.

The risk theory of profits is set forth in F. B. Hawley's *Enterprise and the Productive Process* (1907). Maurice Dobb, in *Capitalist Enterprise and Social Progress* (London, 1925), Chapters 5 to 7, gives a critical analysis of profit theories and develops a supply-price theory which makes profits a kind of monopoly gain due to inelasticity of supply. A detailed critical analysis of the various theories of profits, with emphasis upon the importance of differential advantages, is contained in James P. Beddy's *Profits—Theoretical and Practical Aspects* (Dublin, 1940).

Chapter XXIV

CONSUMPTION

A. The Meaning of Consumption

Consumption Defined. — The commodities and services which man produces afford certain utilities or benefits for his enjoyment. In obtaining these benefits the goods are used up and destroyed. Services, such as those of the valet or musician, exist for but an instant, and then are gone. Our clothing is worn out in a few weeks or months, and must then be discarded. Even the houses we live in, durable as they are, gradually weaken and crumble or decay, necessitating occasional repairs and eventual abandonment. All wealth except land is destructible, and even some of the latter's most useful qualities, such as fertility, can be exhausted. In short, in using goods we *consume* them. For this reason, *the use of economic goods in the gratification of desires is known as consumption.*

Consumption may be either *direct* or *indirect*. We directly consume the food which we eat; that is, we obtain satisfaction from it immediately in the very process of using it. In preparing this food, however, certain materials were used which did not immediately gratify anyone's desires. Perhaps it was cooked by gas; the burning up of this gas afforded no direct enjoyment; it was merely a preliminary step. In the manufacture of the gas, coal was used; this use, again, did not yield immediate satisfactions. The consumption of both the gas and the coal was indirect. The utilization of consumers' goods, such as clothing, dwelling houses, newspapers, pleasure automobiles, and so on, is direct consumption. The utilization of producers' goods, such as raw materials, natural resources, tools, factories, office buildings, and so on, is indirect consumption.

Of these two, it is direct consumption that is most significant for the study of the economic process; for producers' goods are only consumed in order that they may yield consumers' goods; and it is upon the demand for the latter that the direction and character of production very largely depend. Consumers decide what things they want and they buy accordingly; producers cater to them. Hence, the choices of ultimate consumers exercise an important influence upon economic life. It is these choices which we now seek to analyze and explain. In using the term consumption, therefore, economists generally refer to direct consumption, unless the contrary is expressly stated; and it is with direct consumption that the present chapter deals.

The Twofold Relation between Consumption and Production. — From one point of view, consumption can be regarded as the end and goal of all economic activity. This was implied in what has just been said about the controlling influence exercised by consumers' choices upon production. Men are placed in the world with various desires, partly inborn, partly acquired. Certain commodities and services are necessary to gratify those desires. Therefore, men produce those commodities and services. Not only do desires drive men to the onerous exertions of production, but they determine what things shall be produced. Each individual governs his consumption according to his desires and to his means. So demands arise. Producers, in their quest for the best opportunities for gain, bring forth supplies of goods in response to those demands. Production in this way is governed and directed by consumption, which is the end of the process.

From another point of view, consumption can be regarded as the beginning. According to this, production is conceived of as the end, to which consumption is only a means. Writers who favor this way of looking at consumption point out that productive activity is a natural outlet for human energy, and they conceive of creative work as part of the purpose of human existence. They believe, also, that in the competition and struggle for existence that characterizes all life, those individuals and those peoples will be strongest and most likely to survive whose production is most efficient. To produce, then, becomes the aim of economic life, and consumption is the means to production. To be an efficient producer one must be well fed, well clothed, and well housed. Not only that, but he must be provided with sufficient recreations and comforts to keep the body sound, the mind alert, and in good spirits; but not with so much luxury and ease as to enervate and demoralize. From this point of view, our standards of consumption could be judged by their productive results. If our consuming habits were such as to maintain vigor and keep us producing to our fullest capacity, they would be economically efficient; if they were such as to make us indolent and unproductive, they would be economically wasteful.

Pure and Applied Economics in Relation to Consumption. — Which of these two points of view is correct? Is production the means to the end of consumption, or is it the end to which consumption is the means? Do we produce in order that we may consume, or consume in order that we may produce? The answer to these questions depends upon the purposes we have in mind in making a study of consumption. We can better appreciate this if we recall the distinction between pure and applied economics which was made in the first chapter of this work—a distinction which has sometimes been ignored by other writers in discussing consumption. Pure economics seeks merely to describe and explain things as they are; applied economics seeks to use the findings of pure economics in promoting human welfare. Pure economics would therefore ask such questions about consumption as: What things do people consume? Why do they consume these things? How does this consumption affect production and other economic processes? Applied economics would ask: What things ought people to consume? How can one direct his expenditures most economically? What standards of consumption will best promote the welfare of society? How can we control consumption so as to realize these standards?

From the standpoint of applied economics, it may be better to regard consumption as a means to the end of production. If we are seeking to control consumption in the interest of the general welfare we must look at it from a philosophical or moral point of view. Perhaps men *ought* to work for the work's sake, and to consume only in ways that will enable them to work most effectively. In an ideal society perhaps this might be realized, and, if we are seeking some criterion to test the economy or waste in our present consuming habits, it is a rule which we may apply.

But from the standpoint of pure economics, we shall get further toward an understanding of economic processes as they are if we look upon consumption as the end to which production is the means. Consider, for instance, the attitude of most workers toward their employment. While the labor of some persons is attractive in itself, that of the great mass of mankind is not so. For the "working classes" labor is a means undertaken not for its own sake, but to provide consumable goods. The desire for consumable goods is for most persons the force which leads them to produce; and, as has already been shown, it is the choices which consumers make that guide production into its established channels. This is the point of view from which the subject will be approached in the present chapter, for we are concerned only with pure economics. We are seeking to learn how the industrial system works—not how it may be improved; hence we want to know what standards of consumption govern the choices of consumers, and what part these choices play in controlling production. It would be interesting to go further and criticize our present standards of consumption, testing how well they promote productivity, and how they might be improved. To do this would carry us beyond the bounds of pure economics, to which this volume is confined. However, in showing how consumption serves as a guide to production, it will be necessary to point out some of its effects upon our wealth and income; and in doing so it will be impossible to avoid some of the applied aspects of the subject. This discussion will be merely incidental, however, and not the primary object of our study.

Consumers and Producers. — We often hear consumers and producers spoken of as if they were two different classes in the community. For instance, there are consumers' leagues, and consumers' coöperative societies, organized to promote the interests of consumers and to protect them against exploitation by producers. Again, low prices are supposed to be favorable to consumers, and high prices to producers. In fact, however, taken collectively, producers and consumers are one and the same set of people. That is, every producer is also a consumer; and most adult consumers are producers. There is not one group of persons who are producers, and another group who are consumers. The interests of producers and consumers as a whole, therefore, are the same. But while an individual usually produces (or helps to produce) only one commodity, he consumes a great many. His individual interest as a producer of that commodity is, therefore, different from his interest as a consumer of other commodities. It would benefit him, for instance, if he could keep the price of his commodity high, while that of other commodities remained low; for by this he would be able to consume relatively much of the produce of others' labor, while they would be able to consume less of his produce. It is obvious, however, that all producers cannot play this game simultaneously, for they are all consumers of each other's goods. Taken as a whole their interests are identical; all will benefit by general abundance of production, and all will lose by its curtailment. Looking at the matter broadly, therefore, it cannot be said that the interests of producers are different from those of consumers.

There are some consumers, however, who are not producers. These are the children, the old, weak, and infirm, the dishonest, the leisure class, and all those persons whose activities were described in Chapter II as unproductive. Only of these would it be correct to speak of as a "class" of consumers as distinct from producers, and to say that their interests were divergent.

B. The Nature of Consumers' Choices

Desires, Scarcity, and Choice. — It is a first principle of consumption that human desires are unlimited. It is almost impossible to conceive of completely satisfying every possible desire. It is doubtful if even the multimillionaire has so much of the world's goods that he could enjoy no more. Even if we admit that one man's wants might be satisfied in full, it will nevertheless remain true that the total desires of all the people in our country are so far from complete fulfillment that, for all practical purposes, we can think of these desires as infinite. There is no danger that we might have so much wealth that we could find no use for it all. We may take it as established, therefore, that the consuming power of a community is indefinitely great.

Over against this enormous multitude of desires for goods we must set the fact that goods are scarce. Nature's resources are limited, and man's productive power likewise. Hence our utmost output of commodities and services must fall far short of giving us all the income we would like to have. We must therefore choose between those things which we will produce, and those which we will go without. If we use our land, labor, and tools for one thing, we cannot use them for something else; we must somehow select those desires which appear to us most urgent, and deny gratification to the rest.

Every consumer is continually making such choices. He has a certain amount of income to spend. He must apportion it in the manner that seems to him best. If he buys a house, he may have to give up the automobile he had hoped to possess. If he spends his money on clothes, he may have to economize on food. So, he expresses his choices in the market, and contributes to the demand for the commodities in question. We have already learned that production follows demand. It remains, therefore, to see what governs the choices of the individual to complete the analysis.

The Consumer's Freedom of Choice. — In most modern communities the consumer is free, nominally at least, to choose what goods he shall buy. That is, no government or autocrat tells him what he shall consume and what he shall not. How he shall spend his income is his affair. We take this for granted; but it is easy to conceive of a society where consumption would be rigorously controlled by the state. Styles might be set by law, menus might be established with just the right proportions of the various food elements to maintain us at maximum health, housing conditions could be supervised in great detail, amusements and reading matter could be severely censored so as to inculcate in the minds of the people only those thoughts which it was deemed best for them to receive, and so on. In fact, totalitarian governments (and even democratic ones in wartime) may control consumption to a very considerable degree. During both the World Wars, raw materials were definitely allocated to this or that industry in this country, production of certain fancy breads and sweetmeats was sharply curtailed, sugar was rationed in doles, and many similar measures were taken. Even in time of peace there is some regulation of this sort. The prohibition amendment, formerly in effect in the United States, practically put a ban on the consumption of alcoholic drinks; housing laws prescribe that people shall not be allowed to live in certain conditions deemed detrimental to the public health; the use of such narcotics as opium and cocaine is banned; the purchase and sale of firearms is restricted; and so on. Nevertheless, the number of such regulations is few, and there is a strong public feeling against sumptuary legislation (as laws controlling consumption are called). There is a general adherence to the principle that the consumer should have full liberty of choice in his expenditures. Any wide departure from this principle, in fact, would undermine the whole system of free enterprise and usher in a régime of communism.

Limits to the Consumer's Freedom of Choice. — While under the present system there are few formal restrictions upon the consumer's freedom of choice, that freedom is nevertheless limited by certain circumstances inherent in economic life.

In the first place, the range of choice open to consumers is limited by the productive power of the community. This depends upon the abundance and richness of their natural resources, the energy and discipline of the people, the amount of productive equipment they have succeeded in accumulating, and the excellence of their productive technique. Among primitive peoples, whose industrial system is not highly developed, the output of goods is not much more than sufficient to provide them with the bare necessities of life. The kind and quantity of food, clothing, and housing they can enjoy is determined largely by the vagaries of climate and natural wealth, the success of the day's hunting and fishing, and the productivity of their crude implements and methods. They can enjoy but few luxuries, and their range of choice must necessarily be very narrow. Among highly civilized peoples, however, living in a region of favorable climate and rich natural resources, with science and invention well developed, and plenty of invested savings, the annual product of industry is enormous, and affords a large surplus over the minimum needs of existence. Such people can enjoy a great variety of luxurious goods, and their range of choice is very wide.

However, even though consumers in general may have a wide range of choice, particular consumers may find their choices limited narrowly by the smallness of their incomes. With the great inequality of incomes which prevails in modern communities, the range of choice open to different consumers is very unequal. In the markets of commerce one person's dollar is as good as another's; he who has the most dollars, therefore, can control the most goods. The poor man, with his meager earnings, must spend them all on the necessaries. He has very little freedom of choice. The rich man, on the other hand, has spread out before him a multitudinous variety of possibilities in the way of diet, clothing, home furnishings, entertainment, literature, art, travel, and a thousand and one other things. He has a liberal range of choice. Since production follows demand rather than need, it is the choices of those consumers, who have the most purchasing power, that exercise the greatest control upon production.

Some writers lay considerable stress, also, upon the power which the producer has to influence the choices of consumers. People are easily led, a well-conducted advertising campaign can stimulate buying, and a clever salesman can cajole his victim into purchasing where the latter had no intention of doing so. It is alleged that these facts make the consumer's freedom of choice more apparent than real. Yet, although admitting that these acts upon the part of producers exercise a considerable effect upon the market, it remains substantially true that the consumer makes his own selection. Alluring as may be the advertisement to smoke one brand of tobacco, there is right beside it an equally strong appeal to choose another; and if the consumer is bombarded with literature aimed at convincing him he should eat more dairy products, this is offset by just as strong a campaign to persuade him to eat more fruit. So, after all, he is forced to choose, and his decision is the controlling influence in the end. Moreover, no matter how well advertised a commodity may be, if it has not some quality which consumers like. it cannot have a permanent market. Advertising and salesmanship, therefore, while they influence consumers and help them in their buying, do not destroy their freedom of choice.

We may conclude, then, that within the limits set by the community's production, and by the income of the individual, each person has substantial liberty to direct his own consumption. But this does not mean that he is an absolute dictator of his own desires, making his decisions independently without being influenced by environing circumstances. There is no absolute freedom of will in that sense. On the contrary, one's choices are the natural reaction of certain tendencies within the individual to the external situation in which he finds himself. They are, therefore, as much subject to scientific laws as any other natural phenomena. We do not yet know as much about these laws as we do about some others, but there are a few things that can be said about them.

The General Mechanism of Consumers' Choices. — The problem raises the whole question of economic motives and their place in human behavior. To discuss this adequately would require a treatise on psychology. Since it is impossible to do justice to the subject in these few paragraphs, we must be content with a few simple observations. According to the findings of psychologists, human behavior is the result of stimuli from the environment acting upon the innate equipment of instincts, appetites, and emotions with which we are endowed at birth. The child sees a flame—that is the stimulus. Curiosity, one of his innate impulses, leads him to touch it. He experiences the feeling of pain. Thenceforth the sight of the flame will recall the sensation of discomfort, and he will avoid touching it. As he goes on through life he meets other stimuli—the sight, feel, odor, or sound of objects and movements about him, the instructions, admonitions, and punishments of parents and teachers, the attentions and associations of relatives and friends, the customs and conventions of the social group in which he is placed, and so on. As a result, his reactions become more complex; much of his behavior loses the spontaneous, instinctive simplicity of his first experience with the flame, and becomes intricate, building up habits which control his conduct quite unconsciously. In a new situation, however, he is called upon perhaps to make a conscious choice between conflicting stimuli. Here his decision may be more or less deliberative, depending on the circumstances. More often, past choices already crystallized into habits guide him without the necessity of his thinking much about the matter; or he accepts by imitation the choices that have been made for him by the conventions of the society in which he lives.

The choices which a consumer makes in deciding what to buy, and what to do without, conform to these general principles. He has his individual instinctive nature, and habits acquired by experience and imitation. He finds himself confronted by a great variety of tempting wares among which he must choose. Shall he buy a new hat, go to Bermuda, purchase a radio set? In deciding he is influenced by a variety of motives. Advertising, by appeals to deep-seated impulses, builds up a strong desire for this or that commodity; a new fashion affected by his social set compels him to fall into line to keep "in the swim"; things to which he has always been accustomed he will continue to use; some new article finds a particularly responsive note in some peculiar trait of his character; and so on. In making his selection, there is often opportunity for him to exercise his individuality, but it is conspicuously true that to a very considerable degree he will be governed by habits, and that much of what he buys will be impressed upon him by the customs of the people with whom he associates. The general direction of his purchases is socially determined. So, his consumption becomes more or less crystallized into a mold, based on acquired habits and social conventions. We express this idea by saying that he has a definite standard of living.

Standards of Living. — *By a standard of living is meant an established, customary mode of consumption.* The term is used mostly to mark off the different ways of life that prevail among the various social classes; it conveys the idea of a general level of prosperity. It is usually measured in terms of the amount of income that each class has to spend. The rich are supposed to have a higher standard than the poor because they have more goods at their disposal, regardless of whether they use their wealth wisely or ill. But our present concern is not so much with the general level of income represented by a standard of living; we are interested in the actual goods that go to make it up. The important thing for the problem of income is that people have adopted certain ways of living which control the commodities that they desire and the choices that they make. If they are used to a certain kind of a house, to certain kinds of food, to certain sorts of dress, and to certain types of recreation, they will direct their consumption according to those standards.

It is characteristic of one's standard of living that it is an established, customary thing, which has been assumed more or less unconsciously. The individual does not sit down and devise the mode of life which he ought to adopt, and then proceed to adopt it. Often he is not even aware that he has a standard of living, or at least has given the matter very little thought. He just grew into it, having acquired it by the home life in which he was brought up, by association with his fellows, and by all the other contacts of his everyday doings. Some writers have tried to formulate a theory as to how the standard is established in the first place; but their ideas on the subject can be little more than conjecture. The important fact is that the standard is here, and that it governs consumption in a general way. If linen collars prevail in our social group, we will buy them. In other groups where this luxury is not regarded as important, it will be dispensed with. In almost every phase of our lives the standard broadly prescribes the goods which we must choose, and we accept, more or less willingly, these ready-made choices. It is, in fact, inconceivable that we should make every choice independently and individually in our consumption. It would be too great a tax on our minds. To accept the conventions in which we are placed is an economy of effort, conserving our intellectual energy for more important decisions. Custom, then, as embodied in the established standards of the various social groups, is a powerful determinant of consumption.

It is characteristic of standards of living that they are clung to with great persistency. We had occasion to note this fact in the discussion of wages. It was there shown (Chapter XX) that if the income of a group of workers falls so low that it makes difficult the maintenance of their standard, they will forego the begetting of children rather than sacrifice the method of living to which they have become accustomed, until scarcity of their numbers causes the wages of their group to rise. In this way there is some tendency for the supply of labor of different grades to adjust itself roughly to the demand for it, so that the resulting wage will permit their accustomed standard of living to be maintained. So an individual will, after supplying himself with the barest necessities of existence, devote his expenditures first to those goods which are regarded as essential to the standard of his group. Only if he has a surplus above this will he extend his consumption to other commodities for which he has an individual liking. In fact, what has come to be a fixed part of the standard is thought of as a necessity, and persons will often deprive themselves of things which an outsider might consider more important, rather than give up some conventional thing. So, we find persons who starve and otherwise injure themselves to "keep up appearances." This indicates that it is largely the desire for the approval of one's fellows that causes standards of living to be clung to with such tenacity. We shall have occasion to discuss this point more fully presently.

In the course of economic development, as the progress of science and invention increases the efficiency of production, assisted by improvements in the quality of the people and habits of thrift leading to a growth in productive equipment, the income of a people rises and makes possible a parallel betterment of the standards of living prevailing among them. This will only be true, however, if the progress in production is more rapid than the growth of population; otherwise the increase in numbers will absorb the enlarged output of industry, leaving per capita income no greater than before. Such an increase in income may be devoted in part to additional savings; but a considerable portion of it is pretty sure to be directly consumed, and the people thereby enjoy more goods than they have previously been accustomed to. In time they will become so accustomed to the new luxuries that these will constitute an established part of their standards of living, and will be clung to with as much persistency as the more elemental necessities. There is continually going on a process of getting used to new luxuries, their gradual adoption into everyday life, and then their passing over into the category of conventional necessaries. So, permanently higher standards of living become fixed, and the persons who are concerned will do all in their power to maintain them. On the other hand, a decadent civilization, or some great catastrophe, may reduce the income of a people and so force their standards of living downward. In time they will become used to the lower level, and commodities which they formerly thought of as necessaries will now be regarded as luxuries.

Upward and downward changes in standards of living, such as these, may not only happen to whole peoples, but there is a similar shifting within the various industrial groups of a nation. As the wages or other incomes of this or that group rise or fall, in response to changes in the demand or supply for their products, they will feel a tendency for their standards of living to be raised or depressed. If the tendency is upward, the group will soon learn to accustom themselves to new ways of spending, and will assume a higher level of consumption. If the tendency is downward, and the group is unable to resist it, they will be forced to curtail their consumption, and will learn to accept the new conditions.

Prestige and Imitation in Consumption. — The desire to be a leader, to receive the admiration and applause of one's fellow men, appears to be one of the most deep-seated characteristics of human nature. It undoubtedly affects strongly the habits of consumption of both the higher and lower economic strata of the population. To appear great in the eyes of others is one of the strongest of the motives which lead men to seek great wealth, among both primitive and more civilized peoples; consequently those who possess unusual riches are likely to use them in ways that will attract attention. This accounts for many of the methods of consumption adopted by the more well-to-do. Among certain primitive tribes there used to be a peculiar custom known as the "pot latch." It consisted in some wealthy chief, who had accumulated a great store of valuable blankets or other goods, inviting his friends to a feast, whereupon he gave them blankets and other wealth in reckless generosity. They were expected, in turn, later to be equally generous, or be disgraced. The purpose of these "pot latches" was apparently to display wealth and to demonstrate the superiority in riches of the giver; for if one could give so much that others who were poorer could not equal the performance, one's prestige among one's people was greatly enhanced, and unsuccessful competitors lost caste.[1] In modern communities we have a similar phenomenon, which Professor Veblen has cleverly called "conspicuous consumption." To possess the most elaborate residence in one's community, to drive the most expensive automobile, to give away huge sums to charity, to wear silk clothing and rare jewels, to go to Florida to spend the winter among "the élite," and to indulge in the countless other more or less subtle ways of displaying wealth commonly practiced by the rich, is to acquire an "invidious distinction" which sets one above one's fellows. It is this desire for social position that prompts many of the modes of consumption adopted by the rich, rather than any direct enjoyment which they get from the use of the goods they buy.

Among the less well-to-do classes, the same motive expresses itself in imitating the consumption of the rich. Even if one's income is not as large as that of the millionaire, if one can do some of the things that he does with his money, one can acquire something of his glory. So, the working girl stints herself to acquire her fur coat and her cheap jewels, the poor have their expensive weddings and funerals, they copy the clothing styles of the social "four hundred," and so on, for the sake of prestige, when, oftentimes, they might better spend their money for some more pressing physical need. But here we are treading on dangerous ground, for who shall say that the craving of human nature for distinction is any less important than that for proper nourishment or other bodily and mental needs? We had better leave that question to the moralist, and content ourselves with the strictly scientific observation that, through the influence of imitation, a considerable part of the standards of living of the poor are impressed upon them from above, by the conspicuous modes of consumption of the rich.

Rational Choice and Marginal Comparisons in Consumption. — So far, our discussion shows that, within the limits set by the production of the community and the size of his income, the individual is free to choose how he shall direct his consumption; but that, in making these choices, he is governed by the general laws of human behavior, and is especially subject to such influences as the physical needs of his being, his accustomed standard of living, the conventions of society, and the prestige which his expenditures give him in the eyes of his neighbors. Given these influences, can we go further and lay down any general rule as to how, in detail, he will

[1] I am indebted for this illustration to an unpublished manuscript by Dr. W. Christie MacLeod.

apportion his income among the range of goods available to him in the market? It is at least possible to describe how he *would* make his expenditures *if he acted rationally*. That is, we can say what mode of expenditure would bring him the maximum amount of gratifications which his income could afford. Let us begin with the assumption that each individual is an "economic man,'" who spends wisely, seeking always the greatest amount of benefit for his money. How would such a man direct his consumption?

In the first place, different goods would have for him different utilities. By utility we mean here (as always in economics) the power which a good has to gratify his desires, taking into consideration all the factors that influence those desires, as above described. One good he might desire for its nutritive elements, another for its ability to confer prestige upon him, another because the conventions of his social group demand it, and another because he has become used to it—he accepts it unquestionably as a part of his standard of living. We can think of him as making a comparison of these desires, and arranging the various goods which he might buy in a scale accordingly, beginning with those which he considers of most importance and ending with those of least.

But here we come upon a second consideration which complicates the calculation; namely, the fact that the utility of a good varies with the quantity of it which we have in our possession. According to the law of diminishing utility, the utility of economic goods diminishes as additional units of them are consumed. That is, if we have but little of some desired commodity, our desire for more of it may be great; but if we already have a considerable quantity, we will be less eager to increase our stock of it. A person may consider one house a necessity, but a second he might regard as of less importance than an automobile. To show the effect that this principle would have on carefully planned expenditures, imagine a housewife who has just 20 dollars a week to spend upon food and clothing for herself and family. A small amount of each will be absolutely necessary. More of each, not only in quantity, but in quality and variety, will increase the enjoyments derived from them. Each additional amount spent for food will make possible tenderer cuts of meat, more expensive vegetables and fruits, and she can set a much better table. Also, each additional expenditure for clothes will make possible better materials, better styles, more changes of garments, adding to the comfort, self-respect, and prestige of the wearers. In both cases, however, the law of diminishing utility will manifest itself. Buying more food or clothing, after a certain point has been reached, will not bring proportionate increases in satisfaction. After a certain minimum of food and clothing has been secured, spending more upon them will add less and less to the enjoyments of the family, until, if more money is available, it becomes a question whether it would not be preferable to use some of it for something else, rather than to improve still further the diet and dress.

We can illustrate the situation by the accompanying diagram. In Figure 61 the numbers along the horizontal axes (OX and O'X') denote increasing expenditures for food and clothing, respectively, and those on the vertical axes (OY and O'Y') the units of utility derived from each additional purchase. For instance, when 11 dollars per

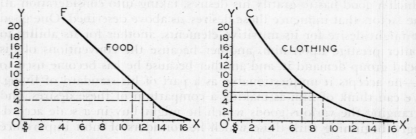

Figure 61. Marginal Comparisons in Consumption.

week is spent for food, 8 units of utility are assumed to be obtained from the eleventh dollar, and 6 more units would be derived if the expenditure was increased to 12 dollars. When 7 dollars per week is spent for clothing, 8 units of utility are derived from the seventh dollar, and 6 units would be added by increasing the expenditure to 8 dollars.

Under these circumstances, how can the housewife best apportion the 20 dollars weekly which she has for food and clothing? If she calculates wisely, she will spend 12 dollars weekly for food, and 8 dollars for clothing; for by so regulating the family consumption more utility will be derived than from any other combination. Suppose, for instance, that she purchased only 11 dollars' worth of food and spent the remaining 9 dollars for clothing. The two curves show that the last dollar so spent for clothing brings in only 5 units of utility, whereas the extra food which could have been bought with that dollar would have yielded 6 units. It would be wiser, therefore, for her to economize a little on clothing and spend the difference on food. Suppose she experimented in the other direction, and spent 13 dollars for food and only 7 dollars for clothing. In that case she would again have done unwisely; for the curves indicate that the last dollar spent on food yields less utility (4 units) than would have been derived from a dollar more spent on clothing (6 units). When she spends just 12 dollars on food and 8 dollars on clothing, therefore, the utility obtainable from her 20 dollars is at its maximum.

What principle does this illustration disclose? It is to be observed that the total utility derived from the expenditure is greatest when the utilities of the last dollar spent for each are equal (in the example, the twelfth dollar spent for food and the eighth spent for clothing each yield 6 units of utility). The utility of the last unit of a series of goods consumed is known as the marginal utility of those goods. More precisely stated, *the marginal utility of a given quantity of goods is the amount of utility dependent upon a single unit of them.* When the housewife consumes 12 dollars' worth of food per week, its marginal utility is that obtained from what can be purchased with a single dollar, and can be determined by the satisfactions of which she (and her family, in this case) would be deprived if she had one dollar's worth less food. In this case, a dollar less spent for food would deprive the family of 6 units of utility; that, then, is the marginal utility of the food to them, when they buy 12 dollars' worth of it. The marginal utility would be greater if they had less food, and less if they had more. Our analysis of the food and clothing leads to the conclusion that when the apportionment of a given amount of money between two different commodities yields equal marginal utilities for a dollar of expenditure, the maximum utility obtainable from that amount of money is reached.

This principle can be extended to all the expenditures of a consumer. If he weighs carefully the goods he purchases with each dollar, he will never spend a dollar for one commodity if he derives less enjoyment from it than he might have obtained if he had used the dollar to purchase something else. If, by buying a little less of this and a little more of that, he deprives himself of less satisfactions from the one than he would obtain from the other, it will be to his advantage to take that course. He will find that as he increases his consumption of any good, its marginal utility will fall, so that he will do better to turn the next portion of his money income to the purchase of something else, and so on, until it is all apportioned in the manner that will bring in a maximum of total utility. This will be achieved when he has so regulated his purchases that the utility of the final dollar's worth of every commodity that he buys is equal.

There is, therefore, a margin in the consumption of every good which marks the point beyond which it is uneconomical to consume more of it. A rational consumer would endeavor to find this margin for each commodity that enters into his consumption and govern his expenditures accordingly. We may say that an economic man will spend according to his *margin of consumption,* which is *that point in the utilization of all the goods he enjoys where a dollar buys goods of equal marginal utility.*

Utility and Disutility in Consumption. — There is another matter which a perfectly economic man would have to consider in regulating his consumption. Not only would he have to measure the marginal utility of one good against that of another, as above explained; but also he would need to balance the gratifications derived from his income as a whole against the pains and discomforts of acquiring that income. The principle of diminishing utility applies not only to the consumption of individual commodities, but also to one's income as a whole. Hence, although our desires are unlimited, it is true that, as the size of our income increases, the enjoyment we get from each addition to it does not increase proportionately. Ten thousand dollars a year brings us more utility than five thousand dollars; but scarcely twice as much. On the other hand, the difficulty of obtaining a very large income is, for any particular individual, greater than it would be for him to obtain a small one. Most persons secure their incomes by working. The longer the hours and the more energetically they work, other things being equal, the more they will earn. To work a little bit, in an easy-going manner, is not very unpleasant. To work long hours at a hard pace is extremely arduous. It involves three elements of disutility. There is, first, the fatigue and monotony of the work itself, trying to the muscles and nerves, and involving all the ennui of continued application to one kind of activity. Secondly, it deprives the individual of the opportunity for consumption. One cannot consume very much or very pleasantly while at work (as most occupations today are carried on); of what use is it, therefore, to pile up extra income beyond a certain amount, if there is no time to enjoy it? Finally, it involves a sacrifice of leisure. One must make a choice between more goods, or more rest and recreation; and there comes a point where the loss of leisure does not compensate for the extra goods. The net result of these conditions is that, as one strives to increase his income, the disutility of obtaining it grows.

Such being the case, a rational individual would seek to balance the utility of consuming his income against the disutility of acquiring it. He would stop working at that point where the utility of an additional installment of income was exceeded by the disutility necessarily suffered in securing it.

Obstacles to Rational Choice. — The above considerations enable the economist to say what constitutes true economy in consumption, from the individual's point of view. True economy is attained when a dollar spent for any good brings in no less utility than it would have brought in if spent for any other good, and when the last installment of income obtained is just balanced by the disutility of acquiring it. Do these principles also explain how human beings actually *do* govern their expenditures in real life? They show how a perfectly "economic man" *would* spend his money; but are we "economic men"? Some writers have answered in the affirmative, and have set forth the foregoing principles as an explanation of how consumption actually is controlled. Others have vigorously denied it, asserting that it is contrary to what we know about the nature of human behavior. The truth probably lies somewhere between these two points of view. Men are neither wholly rational, nor yet wholly irrational; they are not truly "economic," yet not entirely "uneconomic."

As consumers they appear to be less subject to the influence of pecuniary calculations than as producers. A business enterpriser watches with care the prices at which he buys his materials and those at which he sells his product, and endeavors to get the greatest income he can with the least expenditure; but the very same individual may spend that income in a far less rational way. The truth is that consumers are often whimsical, thoughtless, and foolish. They spend frequently without plan or consideration of whether they are getting the greatest possible satisfaction from their money. Hence, while we can properly base an analysis of production and income sharing on the general assumption that business men will follow the opportunities for greatest returns and lowest costs, we cannot assume that the individual consumer apportions his personal income in a similarly systematic manner.

There are many obstacles to interfere with rational choice upon the part of a consumer. The very multiplicity of selections that must be made daily in our expenditures in itself precludes a careful weighing of the utility derived from each one against that which might be obtained by some other purchase. Reflective thinking, of the sort such a comparison would require, takes energy and time; the mind has not sufficient capacity to accomplish it. Nor do we have sufficient information about the goods we buy to apportion our incomes with the greatest possible economy. Advertisements deceive, goods are not standardized so that we can know the exact quality we are getting, we are not informed as well as we might be on such matters as a properly balanced diet, the kinds of dress most conducive to health, the right sorts of amusement, and so on. Then, the influences controlling our behavior are so complex that they cannot be comprehended in the formula of the margin of consumption. First one motive or impulse and then another controls us, and under its spell we buy this or that thing, when, in another mood or under other circumstances, we would have done something quite different. Who has not made a purchase under the influence of some momentary desire which he later regretted and came to recognize as foolish? So, the forces by which our conduct is regulated are so many and intricate that the attainment of true economy in consumption by any individual is almost an impossibility.

The Extent of Rational Choice. — Yet the principle of the margin of consumption is not without *some* effect upon us. There are often times when we weigh with considerable care a contemplated expenditure to decide whether or not it is worth while. This is especially the case where the amount of money involved is large. One may spend a quarter for a magazine to read on the train without hesitating an instant to think whether he might not better keep the quarter for something more desirable, but if it is a question of putting out a hundred dollars for a vacation trip, one is pretty certain to consider with care whether or not it is better to spend the money that way, or to purchase a new rug for one's home, or to save it for future contingencies.

Even in expenditures which are matters of habit, it is not at all certain that considerations of utility were not important in causing the habit to be established; and if there are strong economic reasons for change, it is quite likely that the habit will be broken. Many persons in the northeastern United States, for instance, have for years been in the habit of buying annually a definite number of tons of anthracite coal to heat their homes. This habit was established, probably, by their parents or grandparents before them, who had learned by experience that it was a satisfactory and economical method of heating. In recent years, however, the price of anthracite coal has been rising, while new devices for heating homes by oil or gas have been developed. As a result, many householders are now seriously comparing the cost of heating their homes by anthracite with the cost of installing and operating the oil or gas boilers, with the result that not a few of them are making the change. Meanwhile, a great many others are learning to save on their coal bills by using smaller and cheaper sizes of anthracite, or by substituting soft coal or coke, in place of the fuel they formerly burned. Here we see consumers comparing, dollar for dollar, the advantages (that is, the utility) of one method of heating with that of another, and directing their consumption accordingly. It is a clear case of seeking economy in consumption in the manner outlined in the preceding section.

The number of such comparisons which all of us are constantly making in our daily expenditures is probably greater than we realize. The housewife, in doing the marketing for her family, watches the prices of the various meats and vegetables and arranges her meals accordingly; the business man compares the cost of a ready-made with a made-to-measure suit and decides whether he thinks the superiority of the latter compensates for its higher cost; the little child in the candy store, with five cents to spend, surveys the array of sweetmeats before him, and decides which he wants most only after much weighing of possible delights in his mind. We may be only half conscious of the comparisons we make, and they may appear to lack any semblance of deliberation; yet make them we do. The very fact that our incomes are limited forces us to choose among many alternatives, and in this choosing the marginal utilities of the goods we buy must have influence.

We may conclude, therefore, that consumers' choices are very largely capricious and impulsive, and much less conscious and rational than those of business enterprisers; they follow the principle of economy to only a limited degree. While there is some tendency to weigh the utility of the last dollar's worth of each commodity purchased against the last dollar's worth of every other commodity, and to bring these to equality, this tendency would only be fully realized by a perfectly rational being who never made a choice without careful deliberation. In actual life it is interfered with by the whims and inconsistencies, the ignorance and misinformation, the weakness and thoughtlessness of consumers, as well as by the fact that the motives to human behavior are so complex that the finite mind is incapable of the intellectual effort which so difficult a set of comparisons would require for its complete fulfillment.

C. The Effects of Consumers' Choices

Economy and Waste in Consumption. — In Part B of this chapter we were concerned with the influences which make consumers choose as they do. We were trying to explain merely on what principles they decide how to spend their incomes. We are now concerned with the effects which those expenditures have upon production, and upon the consumers themselves. That these effects must be important will be clear from what has been said already about the relation between consumption and production. Production, in following demand, responds to the choices of consumers, which therefore exercise a dominant influence upon the whole economic process. Not only that, but their choices react decisively upon their own welfare. If consumers choose wisely, the productive resources will be utilized in ways that contribute most effectively to the well-being of society; if they choose badly, the productive resources will be wasted in being utilized for useless or injurious purposes. It is for this reason that the subject of consumption deserves an important place in the study of applied economics. We cannot go into the relation of consumption to welfare in this chapter (except incidentally); but it is appropriate to consider some of the purely economic effects of different standards of consumption.

The Adaptation of Desires to the Environment. — The environment in which a people lives is better suited to the production of some commodities than others. In the United States, for instance, we can raise wheat, corn, and cotton better than we can coffee, tea, or bananas; and we can produce iron and steel manufactures more easily than raw silk or ivory carvings. It follows that, if our desires are limited to the things which we can easily produce, we will be more readily able to gratify them than if we have a taste for things which must be brought from a great distance. If we insist on wearing silk garments and adorning our homes with oriental objects of art, these things must be brought from far-away lands, entailing the expense of transporting them. This is evidenced by the fact that imported articles are usually more expensive than domestic goods.[2] If we are content with the things that can be produced by our own industry, we can come nearer to satisfying our desires.

The principle of adapting consumption to the environment can be applied also to different articles of domestic manufacture. Some things, such as cotton clothing, oak furniture, potatoes, and newspapers, can be produced cheaply, because the environment supplies the raw materials for them in relative abundance, and but little labor and capital are required for their growth or manufacture. Some other things, such as gold and silver objects, jewelry, fancy fruits and vegetables, meat delicacies, elaborately printed and bound books and pictures, and automobiles, are expensive, because the raw materials for them are scarce, or because it requires a great deal of labor and capital for their production. If we have simple tastes, they can readily be gratified by the commodities which the economic conditions render most plentiful; but if our desires are extravagant, they will be much more difficult to gratify.

According as the standards of consumption of a people are closely adapted to the facilities afforded by the economic environment, or are out of harmony with it, they will be the more or less easily attainable. This principle is called by some writers *the law of least social cost*. It may be stated as follows: *Those standards of consump-*

---

[2] However, this is as much due to import duties levied upon the foreign wares as it is to the costs of transportation or production abroad.

tion are most economical which can be satisfied by goods whose cost of production in proportion to their utility is least. Thus, if the tastes of a people are out of harmony with the facilities afforded by their environment and productive technique, their productive energies will be diverted into wasteful channels where they will bring in less utility to the community than if popular tastes were more carefully directed.

This has led some writers to suggest that there is continually going on a testing and sifting of standards of consumption on the basis of their fitness, with the result that those which are detrimental to the economy and welfare of society gradually fall into disfavor, while those which are beneficial become generally accepted. The late Professor Simon Patten said, "Each nation has a strong tendency to love what its environment can furnish with the least expense." [3] Carrying the same idea a little further, Mr. J. A. Hobson believes that some of our economic choices possess an "organic utility," which contributes to the well-being of the group, while others possess disutility, which renders them injurious, and that there is a process of natural selection going on between our desires in which the less advantageous ones are being eliminated.[4] This thought, however, must be regarded rather as the expression of a wish than as the statement of a law. It is an analogy between the struggle for existence and survival of the fittest which goes on in nature among the various forms of life, and a similar rivalry between standards of consumption which is believed to go on in human society. But this is only an unconfirmed theory, and there is little or no evidence to support it.

Necessaries and Luxuries in Consumption. — One of the greatest differences between modern industry and that of a previous period is the great surplus of goods above the minimum needs of existence which it affords. This surplus permits even those in moderate circumstances to enjoy such luxuries as electric lights, daily newspapers, and motion pictures, which the richest nobles of former days never dreamed of. In fact, we have become so used to many of the comforts of the twentieth century that we cease to think of them as luxuries.

This raises the question: What is the difference between a necessary and a luxury? The borderline between them is very difficult to define. There are very few commodities which are an absolute necessity for the maintenance of life. A simple fare of bread and vegetables will provide sufficient nourishment, and some coarse, scanty clothing and a rude hovel will protect the body well enough from the

---

[3] S. N. Patten, *The Consumption of Wealth*, p. 36.
[4] J. A. Hobson, *Work and Wealth*, Chapter X.

ravages of the weather. This is enough of consumable goods to enable human beings to live—as the cave men lived, ages ago. In a sense it might be said that anything above this is luxury. Yet, as the terms are generally used, much more is included in the idea of necessaries, and only the more rare and elegant comforts are regarded as luxuries. When we have once become thoroughly accustomed to the enjoyment of a certain article, which at first we looked upon as a luxury, we gradually come to regard it as a necessary, and would feel a very real hardship if deprived of it. Nearly everyone considers his daily newspaper a necessary, many consider an automobile very essential, and by the millionaire perhaps a winter at Palm Beach would be placed in the same category. Each person has his own concept of what is necessary and what is luxurious, and that which to the poor man is a most extravagant luxury, by the rich man may be considered an important necessary. The truth seems to be that each person regards that as a necessary which is an established part of his standard of living; [5] while those things are luxuries which, because of their expense, are not a part of it, being customarily consumed only by persons in higher income levels. Such a purely relative concept of necessaries and luxuries, however, is too shifting to be very satisfactory for scientific purposes, and economists have long sought a more objective standard.

Two possible alternatives suggest themselves. One is to set up a "minimum standard of living," which will embody the ordinary decencies of life, such as sufficient clothing to provide adequate warmth in winter, and neatness and modesty the year round, enough plain food of sufficient variety to provide a well-balanced, nourishing diet, lodgings of sufficient size and sanitary conveniences to protect health, a common school education, ordinary provision for sickness and old age, a very little reading matter and recreation, and not much else. The contents of such a standard have often been worked out, and the cost of its maintenance for a family of five computed. The elements of this standard we might take as making up the necessaries of life; and all commodities or services in excess of it could then be regarded as luxuries. Another possibility is to define necessaries as those goods which are required to keep up the full industrial efficiency of the individual. This would be different for different individuals. A manual laborer would require good food, plain clothing, decent shelter, and enough rest and recreation to keep up his strength and morale. A musician might require extensive education,

---

[5] It was in this sense that the term "conventional necessaries" was used above (page 587) to refer to those articles which, once looked upon as luxuries by an individual, later come to be regarded as essential.

travel, amusement, and many comforts to develop the intellectual and emotional sides of his nature, as well as mere provision for physical wants. In both cases, all goods in excess of the necessaries for industrial efficiency would be regarded as luxuries. This again gives an unstable, and therefore unsatisfactory, concept of necessaries and luxuries, which varies from person to person. For this reason the "minimum standard" concept of necessaries is to be preferred, and will be accepted for the discussion which is to follow.

The Economic Effects of Luxury. — Without entering upon the moral aspects of luxurious consumption, it is possible to point out certain significant facts about the effects of consuming luxuries upon the direction and efficiency of production, and upon the utility derived by the community from its income. The enjoyment of luxuries may often contribute to industrial efficiency. Directly, it may so increase the happiness and well-being of an individual as to make him a better producer. A healthy, happy worker is more likely to be efficient than an unhealthy, unhappy one. Indirectly, the prospect of rising to a position of luxury may furnish a powerful motive to stimulate the individual to do his best. It is very largely upon this motive, which lies back of the lure of high business profits, that a competitive society relies for efficiency. As was pointed out in the second part of this chapter, it is the desire for social prestige that leads many to consume luxuries. The conspicuous consumption of riches gives preëminence to the spender. It is for the attainment of this preëminence that people strive, and this is a strong incentive for business success that drives the leaders of industry to their achievements. In this way luxury may be said to have had important indirect effects upon productive achievement. Whether or not it would be possible to accomplish equal industrial efficiency without this incentive is one of the moot questions of today, upon the answer to which the possible success or failure of such projected reforms as socialism is likely to hinge.

Carried beyond a certain point, however, luxury may tend to destroy industrial efficiency. It has often been observed that a good man or woman has been spoiled by having too much wealth. It is very easy for the rich to become idle and unproductive. Much luxurious consumption tends in no way to improve the energy or ability of the consumers; it may even injure both their health and their characters. Such consumption, of course, is economically wasteful.

It is probable that the consumption of luxuries beyond a certain point does not yield as much utility as does the consumption of less luxurious articles. According to the law of diminishing utility, the utility derived from additional increments of any particular good diminishes as more of it is consumed. It was stated above that the same principle undoubtedly holds true also of one's income as a whole. That is, as one's income gets larger and larger, the utility derived from each increase is not as great as before. Hence, the expenditure of a hundred dollars by a millionaire upon some luxury does not bring him the same utility that it would to a person in more modest circumstances, who would spend it for something of greater necessity. To the millionaire it might mean merely buying a pedigreed poodle to amuse his wife; to a poor workman it might mean a year's supply of sorely needed clothing. Putting the argument a little differently, to deprive the millionaire of a hundred dollars would cause him little sacrifice, but it might be a terrific hardship for the poor man. The principle is one argument in favor of as great a degree of equality of incomes as is practicable.

These facts attain great significance when we consider again that production is guided by demand, rather than by the needs of consumers. We have said that, in the markets of commerce, everyone's dollar has equal purchasing power. Each rich man has more dollars than a poor man, and thereby diverts some production toward providing luxuries for him which might otherwise have gone to articles of greater utility to the poor. If this luxurious consumption is of the unproductive sort, there is economic waste involved. The surplus incomes of the rich *in the aggregate,* however, are not as large as the combined incomes of the poor and moderately well-to-do; hence the amount of this waste is not as great as might be supposed.

Saving for Future Consumption. — An intelligent consumer, in disposing of his income, thinks not only of the present, but also of the future. He accordingly saves a portion, for his own consumption in later life, for the use of his family, for the establishment of some worthy charity or scientific foundation, or for the mere power and prestige of amassing great wealth. Such saving, as we learned in Chapter IV, usually takes the form of productive investment, and goes to create new equipment for industry. It is by this means that the wealth of society grows, taking the form of railways, factories, warehouses, shops, office buildings, canals, roads, machines, tools, and instruments of production of all kinds. Some of it goes into durable consumers' equipment, such as pianos, dwelling houses, and automobiles. The great majority of it is used in production, and goes to increase the future output of industry. So is the future income of society increased. Saving is refraining or abstaining from present consumption. Its effect is to increase the stream of consumable commodities in the future. The large income enjoyed among civilized peoples today would not be possible were it not for the savings of consumers in the past. The huge industrial plants which turn out goods in such abundance are the result of the thrift of persons in the past who chose not to consume all of their incomes, but to invest a part of them in productive capital.

Economists have given a great deal of discussion to the motives which induce people to save instead of to spend their incomes, because it has an important bearing upon the payment of interest. We have learned something about those motives in our study of the income from savings; therefore it will not be necessary to go into it here. It will suffice to recall that it is a question of how much the consumer prefers present to future goods, which depends on his intelligence and foresight, the habits of thrift which have been bred into him by teaching and up-bringing, his present as compared with his probable future earning power, the likelihood of future risks which might cut off his earning power, the uncertainty of life itself, and so on.

To a very considerable extent, the economic progress of a people depends upon an increasing accumulation of capital in productive equipment. The same applies to the progress of an individual. The nation or the person that consumes all of its income is really a spend-thrift. One writer [6] goes so far as to say that the economic worth of an individual, and the competing power of a nation, can be measured by the difference between their production and their consumption. If there is no surplus, he says, the individual has contributed nothing to society in the first case, and the nation is making no progress in the second. This, however, is a moral preachment based on individual opinion, rather than a scientific fact. It is based on the assumption that production is the end to which consumption is but a means; one who holds the view that consumption is the goal of economic activity may come to a different conclusion. It is possible for an individual to consume annually all that he produces, and yet enjoy an increasing income each year as a result of his increasing skill and ability in his work; can it then be said that he has been a failure? It is equally possible for a nation to consume annually its entire net income, so that there would be no increase in the amount of its capital, and yet there might go on progress in science, invention, and the technique of industry, which would greatly increase its production by enabling it to make more effective use of what equipment it has. Hence it is hardly accurate to make the surplus of production over consumption the sole measure of economic progress; but it cannot be denied that the increasing ac-

6 T. N. Carver, *Principles of National Economy*, Chapters XLI and XLV.

cumulation of capital by saving has been and is a very important factor in the increase of prosperity of modern peoples.

The Effects of Spending as Contrasted with Saving. — Notwithstanding this truth, many persons have failed to understand the productive results that follow from saving. It is a popular fallacy that there is some benefit conferred on the community by spending, which benefit is lost when income is saved. The very rich, when criticized for spending large sums in an extravagant manner, sometimes defend themselves by arguing that their expenditure "circulates money" and "gives employment." For instance, if there is a great ball among the "social four hundred," in which many thousands of dollars are spent for costumes, refreshments, service, and so on, its sponsors may seek to justify the seeming waste, on the ground that thousands of dollars are put in motion, going from one person to another in the community, giving them a profit on some sale and purchasing power with which to buy goods, while at the same time many workers are benefited by being given employment—cooks and waiters are needed to provide the refreshments, tailors and dressmakers to create the costumes, musicians to furnish tuneful melodies for the dancing, taxicab drivers to transport the participants, and so on. At first thought it does indeed seem as if the ball set up a bustle of economic activity which increased the prosperity of the community. But this reasoning is faulty. It rests on the false assumption that a dollar spent is an active one, while a dollar saved is idle. It implies that if money is saved, instead of being spent, it does not circulate, and fewer people are employed. This assumes that saving is nothing but hoarding; it overlooks the fact that savings are usually invested. When money saved is invested, it is really spent, only it is spent for remote-goods instead of near-goods. In advanced industrial communities saving does not take the form of hoarding. We no longer store our surplus funds in a cellar or bury them in the garden. Instead, we invest them in good securities or deposit them in a bank. If we invest them, we turn them over to business men to use in production; and, if we deposit them in a bank, the bank lends our money for a similar purpose. In either case, therefore, the money is loaned to be used in industry. The borrowers spend it—perhaps to build a railroad, to construct a factory, or to lay in a stock of raw materials. So we see that the money circulates just the same, whether we spend it or save it. It also gives employment to labor in either case, for labor must be employed to work upon the railroad, or the factory, or in producing the raw materials.[7]

[7] But see the theory of Keynes (discussed in Chapters XI and XXI) which upholds the view that saving may exceed the opportunities for profitable investment, and so lead to unemployment.

The real difference between spending and saving (if the savings are invested) lies in its ultimate effects upon the wealth of the community. When money is "spent," it is paid out for near-goods, which are then used up and consumed. Goods are thereby destroyed. This is not necessarily a real loss, if sufficient gratification results from the consumption, for the ultimate destiny and purpose of economic goods is to be destroyed in giving benefits to consumers. But if the expenditure was extravagant, goods have been destroyed without giving very much benefit to consumers—they have been "frittered away." When money is saved and invested, it is paid out for the creation of new equipment, usually of a durable sort. The wealth of the community has thereby been increased and more consumable goods will in the future result from it. Goods have been created instead of consumed.

Summary

Consumption is the use of economic goods in the gratification of desires. The use of consumers' goods is direct consumption, while that of producers' goods is indirect. In speaking of consumption, it is usually the direct sort that is meant. Consumption may be regarded as the end for which production is carried on, or as a means to make possible further production. The latter point of view may be useful for applied economics; but for pure economics, the former is more useful. Consumers and producers are not two different classes of society, but they are the same individuals in different capacities.

Since human desires are unlimited and goods are scarce, the consumer must choose which desires he will gratify, and which he will deny. He is nominally free to make this choice as he wills, but is limited by the productive capacity of industry, the size of his individual income, and the advertising and selling methods of producers, which to some extent influence demand. What choices a consumer will make is a matter of psychology, and depends upon the complex reactions between his inborn nature and his environment. He is particularly guided by his standard of living, which is the established mode of consumption to which he has become accustomed. Such standards of living are clung to with great persistency. Consumers' choices are also influenced by imitation and prestige, which lead to conspicuous consumption on the part of the rich, and mimicry thereof by the poor.

A rational consumer would apportion his expenditures in such a way as to establish a margin of consumption, where the marginal utility of the last dollar's worth of each good he purchased would be equal. He also would balance the disutility of the effort expended in acquiring each addition to his income against the extra utility derived from its consumption, and would cease efforts to obtain more income when the two were equal. While such rational calculations may influence consumer expenditures somewhat, many of our expenditures are irrational, whimsical, and habitual.

Production, in following demand, is controlled by consumption; hence, consumption can lead to either economy or waste. The greatest economy is to be attained by choosing only those things which, in the existing environment and technique of industry, can be produced at the lowest cost. Some writers believe that there is a tendency for desires to adjust themselves in obedience to this law, through a process of natural selection; but this is merely conjecture.

The line between necessaries and luxuries cannot be sharply drawn. Necessaries may best be defined as those things which go to make up a minimum standard of living conducive to health and decency. All other goods are luxuries. Some luxury increases the industrial efficiency of the individual, and it is probably a necessary incentive to make people industrious in a competitive society; excessive luxury, however, is injurious to health and character. Also, the consumption of luxuries beyond a certain point does not bring proportionate utility to the consumer; hence there is waste if production is directed to turning out luxuries for the rich when articles of greater utility might be produced for other classes. Saving is abstaining from consumption in the present, and, when accompanied by investment, it results in the accumulation of equipment, which increases the production of consumable goods in the future. Saving and investment therefore promote economic progress. The notion that spending extravagantly benefits society by "circulating money" and "making work" for people is an error; for saving, which in modern society takes the form of investment, also causes the money to circulate and gives employment to workmen.

REFERENCES AND SUGGESTIONS FOR FURTHER READING

The subject of consumption has received an increasing amount of attention in recent years. Two of the most noteworthy works are Hazel Kyrk's *A Theory of Consumption* (1923) and E. E. Hoyt's *The Consumption of Wealth* (1928). The latter is more comprehensive than the former. An older work, which, however, is still worth reading, is S. N. Patten's *The Consumption of Wealth* (1889). For an analysis of the marginal utility theory of consumption see P. H. Wicksteed, *The Common Sense of Political Economy* (London, 1910), Chapters 1 and 2.

In Chapters 9 to 11 of his suggestive book, *Work and Wealth* (1914), Mr. J. A. Hobson has presented an interesting discussion of the relation of consumption to social welfare. The same topic is very differently treated in T. N. Carver's *Principles of National Economy* (1921), Part VI, where the importance of thrift and of standards of consumption that will promote industrial efficiency is very forcefully shown. A brilliantly critical attack on the consuming habits of the well-to-do will be found in Thorstein Veblen's *Theory of the Leisure Class* (1899).

The following texts deal comprehensively with the problems which confront the consumer in the modern industrial system: Margaret G. Reid, *Consumers and the Market* (1938); Leland J. Gordon, *Economics for Consumers* (1939); Charles S. Wyand, *The Economics of Consumption* (1937).

Chapter XXV

THE ECONOMIC PROCESS AS A WHOLE

A. How the Industrial System Functions

A General View of Industry. — This volume was begun with a broad general survey of the industrial system. In its very opening paragraphs we obtained a bird's-eye view of the economic activities of men—we saw raw materials being extracted from the earth in many parts of the world, labor and tools devoted to working them up into finished products, ships and railroads transporting them hither and thither, men buying and selling them in exchange for money, labor and capital getting paid for handling them—a myriad of interdependent and complicated processes, out of which emerged consumable goods (such as the textbook which we used for an illustration) to gratify the desires of men. But at that time we had no clear idea of how it all came about. We saw that it was largely spontaneous—no authoritative hand consciously controlled it—yet somehow there was a system about it which made it accomplish a definite purpose. We set about the task of studying that system, in order to discover upon what principles it functioned. We have now completed that study. We have traced step by step the various processes involved in the operation of the industrial system, so that by this time we should be able to understand how it works. It is an old saying, however, that we sometimes cannot see the forest for the trees, and it may be that, in our study of economics, we have been so busy grasping the details that we have not seen its process as a whole. It is well, therefore, to return to the general picture, and focus our attention once more upon its broadest outlines. In so doing, we will be making a summary, in a very general way, of this whole book. Such is the purpose of the present chapter.

Desires and the Means of Production. — At one end of the economic process stand the desires of men. We are creatures with many wants, hopes, ambitions, and whims. To the fulfillment of these, certain commodities and services are necessary. So varied and numerous are our desires, that there seems to be no limit to the number of such commodities and services we can assume. Hence we make efforts to obtain as many and diverse goods as possible. It is to this end that the economic process is directed. It is driven by the urge of consumers' desires, and is directed toward their fulfillment.

At the other end of the process stand the means of production. These consist of the natural resources embodied in our fertile soil, mineral deposits, forests, wild animal and vegetable life; and also of men themselves, in their capacity as producers. In short, the primary agents of production are nature and man—land and labor. Out of nature, man builds up, through saving, a secondary agent of production, in the form of equipment of many kinds—factories and warehouses, railroads and steamships, machinery and tools. All these agents of production are limited. Land is fixed in area, and offers increasing resistance to our efforts to extract more produce from it —the principle of diminishing returns. The laboring population is likewise more or less fixed, and the capacity of each worker restricted by his intelligence, vigor, and endurance. The quantity of equipment is somewhat elastic, but depends on the thrift and willingness to save of the people. The result of limited agents of production is that goods are scarce, and have to be economized.

This economy is effected through the economic process. With unlimited desires and limited means of production, there is an incentive to develop a productive organization that will make those means yield as much as possible of the kinds of things that are wanted most. It is not to be concluded that the organization which has been developed actually does this in the most efficient manner conceivable. The system is, in fact, full of waste and misdirection. But it has arisen in response to the desires of men, and is guided and controlled mainly by those desires. The economic process is, in short, an unconscious, unplanned adaptation of the means of production to the wants of consumers, through the medium of a complex industrial organization.

The Productive Organization. — One of the outstanding characteristics of that organization is the existence of *specialization*. In each industry, we find a division of labor among the producers. Every individual has his appointed task, and works only upon one product, or part of a product, according to the work which has been allotted him in life, whether by his own choice, his capacities, or the force of circumstances. Not only is there this specialization among individuals, but there is observable also specialization by whole communities, or even nations, upon the particular kinds of industry for which their natural resources are best fitted, or at which tradition and long established custom have rendered them expert. This system of specialization has supplanted an earlier industry (in which each individual or family was a more or less independent economic unit), because it has been found to be more productive.

Along with specialization has come *exchange*. This is an inevitable adjunct to a system of divided labor. When men spend their entire labor upon one product, they must obtain other products through trade. With increasing specialization, therefore, has come commerce of ever-growing complexity, until today we have a great network of trade relations and institutions. In each industry there is a marketing organization to dispose of the product, and between producers and consumers there are wholesale and retail merchants who perform an important function. Commerce is not merely local, but extends its operations across international boundaries until it embraces the whole world. As a necessary means to this wide process of exchange, there is a highly developed system of land and water transportation and communication—the railroads, motor trucks, steamships, airplanes, postal services, telegraphs, and telephones.

A third characteristic of the productive organization is *the time-consuming process* of production. This process is roundabout, in that most of the labor of industry is devoted, not directly to consumable goods, but to producers' goods—to productive equipment at more or less remote stages, which will later yield finished products. Millions of men are employed in mining ore, to be later converted into machines, which will be used to make still other machines, which finally will turn out consumable goods. In agriculture, men are employed to till the soil, in which to plant seed, to grow up and produce more seed, which will again be planted to yield, in time, corn or wheat or cotton goods for human consumption. So it is in every industry. This indirect labor is made possible by the fact that industry produces a surplus of near-goods, out of which those who are working on remote-goods can be maintained. The surplus is in the hands of capitalists, who, by saving instead of consuming their incomes, advance wages to the laborers, for which they will be repaid later (with interest), out of the finished products which will eventually be produced. The time-consuming process causes a great deal of the wealth of a community to be tied up in the form of durable equipment. It is vastly more productive than a direct process, and is largely responsible for the prosperity of modern, as contrasted with primitive, peoples.

The minute specialization of modern industry, with its elaborate plant, requires some scheme of coördination to bring workers and capital together into smoothly running units. In some industries today, as many as ten thousand men or more, with millions of dollars worth of equipment, must be employed in a single enterprise—even under a single roof. To make this possible, several *forms of business organization* have been developed, ranging from the single enterpriser, who has control of a business entirely in his own hands, through the partnership, where a few business men are somewhat loosely associated in a simple form of organization, to the corporation, with its elaborate division of functions. The corporation is a dominant feature of our mining, manufacturing and public utilities industries, and, to a lesser degree, of marketing. In it, large aggregations of capital can be obtained from the savings of many investors, who participate somewhat in the management as stockholders, or simply lend to the business as bondholders; at the same time, it permits unity of action and efficiency of control, by the delegation of powers to boards of directors, and through them, to salaried executives. The elasticity of this form of business organization has aided greatly in the development of large-scale industry and modern industrial methods, although not without allowing also some abuses.

Finally, perhaps the most conspicuous feature of our present productive organization is *the use of money.* Where there is a highly developed system of specialization and its accompanying trade, there must be a medium of exchange. A trade by means of barter would be entirely too clumsy to operate. Our monetary institutions (including banking) meet this need. So universal a characteristic of our economic process have they become, that we measure all wealth and income in money terms (often confuse them, in fact) and carry out all our transactions through the medium of money. We live in a money régime.

Money and the Mechanism of Exchange. — In the beginning, some universally desired commodity was used as money. Gold and silver were especially popular, and early became the accepted medium of exchange. Later the government assumed a monopoly of coining them, thereby establishing uniformity and a guarantee of weight and fineness. Then the difficulties of bimetallism led to the general abandonment of silver, and the establishment of gold as the standard currency of most of the world. But the actual circulation of gold has gradually declined, as nominal currencies were found to provide an even more satisfactory medium. One of these is paper money, issued either by governments or banks.

With the development of exchange, a still more ingenious form of money has been developed by commercial banks. This consists of circulating demand deposits. A bank lends its credit to a client by establishing a deposit for him on its books (for which, of course, the depositor will eventually repay the bank with interest). The client can make payments to others, for goods which he buys, by drawing checks against this deposit, and when the check is returned to the bank, the amount of it will simply be transferred from the credit of the drawer to that of the drawee. Through the clearing (or offsetting) process, deposits can be transferred from bank to bank by similar bookkeeping methods. So, bank deposits circulate from hand to hand, performing the functions of money.

The fundamental fact about this monetary and banking organization is that it substitutes a system of bookkeeping debits and credits for money in the process of exchange. When a manufacturer sells goods and accepts the purchaser's note in payment, discounts the note at his bank and receives a deposit credit, it is as though he had taken his goods to a central accounting office, and been granted credit to the amount of their value. When, later, he draws on the deposit to buy other goods, it is as though he had been debited in the central accounting office with the goods he purchased and his credit canceled. Goods have simply been exchanged for goods, and the transactions offset on the account. Such is the modern banking system.

Paper money and bank credit have so effectually supplanted gold as the medium of exchange that gold is today used almost entirely as a monetary reserve. Our money seems to be gradually becoming a nominal one. While subject to abuses and occasional breakdowns, it performs fairly well the stupendous task of making possible the intricate and multitudinous exchanges of modern industry.

The Productivity of the Economic Organization. — Many factors affect the productivity of this complex system of modern industry, and it would be a bold task to try to enumerate them all. There are certain broad limits which mark the maximum possibility of production at any time, however, which we may discern.

The most obvious of these limiting factors, perhaps, is *the amount and character of the natural resources* of a people. A large land area will support more people than a small one. Other things being equal, a country rich in natural resources will be more prosperous than one poor in this respect. The great expanse of territory embraced in the United States, including, as it does, both temperate and semi-tropical regions, rich agricultural soils, good climate, varied and abundant deposits of iron, coal, copper, silver, oil, and other minerals, vast tracts of forest, and other advantages, has been one of the most important causes of our economic success. All nations recognize the value of abundant natural resources, and their efforts to obtain control over the unexploited regions of the earth have been a great source of war.

Equally important is *the size and character of the population*. Owing to the tendency to diminishing productivity, in any given state of the arts, too large a population may cause such a pressure on the available land of a nation as to reduce its per capita production. This has happened in China and India, and is partly responsible for the low standards of living prevailing among the peoples of those countries. Too small a population may be unable to utilize the land most effectively, which again will mean low per capita production. There is an optimum number of people which, in any given stage of technical progress, will give a maximum output per head. That is the population of most advantageous size for a people to find and maintain.

The relation of population to productivity is not solely one of numbers. There is also the question of quality. Much depends upon the industry, thrift, and intelligence of a people. The economic supremacy of Anglo-Saxon peoples at the present time is probably due, in considerable measure, to their restless energy and inventive genius. Other peoples, of more phlegmatic or easy habits, produce much less, even with equally suitable resources. This may be due partly or largely to the climatic environment of the different peoples, however, and not alone to racial qualities. Thrift is a particularly important economic quality, because upon it depends the accumulation of equipment, upon which the roundabout process depends. A spendthrift people will not accumulate such equipment, and the lack of it will compel them to resort to less roundabout, and therefore less productive, methods.

Finally, the productivity of the economic organization depends also on *the state of science and the arts*. The industrial revolution, which in the century between 1750 and 1850 completely transformed our industrial processes, was a triumph of science and invention. The application of steam and electricity as sources of power, and the development of mechanical contrivances in manufactures, which were the outstanding features of that revolution, increased the income of civilized peoples many fold. Our future progress will depend largely on a continuance of the epoch-making strides in scientific discovery and inventive genius which have characterized the last hundred years. To the economists of the early nineteenth century, the law of population and the law of diminishing returns seemed an insuperable obstacle to continuous progress in economic activity. We have seen, however, that these laws may be offset by continual improvement in the technique of production. A great economist has said, that nature's part in production shows a tendency to diminishing return, but man's part a tendency to increasing return.[1] Recently, man has kept in the lead. So long as he goes on making new discoveries in the laboratory, and applying those discoveries to improving the organization and technique of industry, there is no limit to the possible increase in production.

Prices, and Their Function as Guides to Production. — Up to this point, we have been discussing the machinery for carrying on production, and the conditions affecting the quantity of its total output. But equally important is the direction of that output. Let us now turn our attention to that problem. It must be remembered that our desires are unlimited; but that the means of production which are necessary to the fulfillment of those desires are scarce. It is impossible, therefore, completely to satisfy them, and it becomes necessary to economize in the use of the productive agents. Since there is no human dictator to decree which desires shall be satisfied and which shall not, we must rely upon some natural principle to settle the matter. Prices perform this function by acting as the guides for production. Prices are the expression of consumers' desires, and production responds to these values. They determine what things shall be produced, and what shall not, and the relative quantities of each. Let us briefly review this process.

Each consumer has a certain amount of income to spend. He spends it according to the wants which at the time seem to him most urgent, and so contributes to the demand for this or that commodity. In this way schedules of demand are established. To meet these demands, goods must be produced, requiring more or less of the scarce agents of production. So there arise competing demands for the various kinds of land, for skilled and unskilled labor, for savings, and for business enterprisers. Now, any producer who desires to use some of these means of production must compete with other producers, who also desire to use them. This competition forces each to pay for his agents all that the demand for his product will allow; and these payments constitute his costs of production. The agents of production will naturally go to those who are able to bid most for them, which means that they will go to the production of those commodities for which there is the greatest demand, relative to the quantities of productive agents which their production requires. The production of each good is carried toward the point of equilibrium between the supply and demand where the price equals the optimum costs of production. This simply means that, to produce any more of it, would yield less returns, in proportion to the agents of production employed,

[1] Alfred Marshall, in his *Principles of Economics*.

than could be obtained from some other use of those agents. When we say that a commodity is worth less than its cost, that is just another way of saying that consumers will pay less for that commodity than they would pay for some other produced with the same agents. It is because those agents are worth more in that other use that the cost is above the price in this use.

In this process there is manifest a distinct principle of economy, in that it prevents the diversion of the means of production into channels where there is less demand than in some other channel. If, for instance, too much of the productive agents was being devoted to cotton and not enough to wool growing, the supply of cotton would be large, in relation to the demand for it, and that of wool would be small. This would lead to a price for cotton less than its cost, and for wool above its cost. The high value of wool would stimulate an increase in its production until the price fell to cost; and the low value of cotton would discourage its production until the price rose sufficiently to cover its cost. Equilibrium in the production of the two commodities would then have been reached. So it would be impossible for the productive agents to be turned for very long in one direction, if there was a greater demand for them in some other direction. Values direct them into the channels of greatest demand. This is the mechanism by which the industrial system is controlled. It is the regulator which, spontaneously, without the intervention of any authority, guides the economic process.[2]

Sharing the Product, and the Economy of the Income Sharing Process. — The economy of the pricing process extends beyond merely deciding the commodities that shall be produced, and the quantities of each; it also serves to estimate the economic importance of each agent of production, and to pay the owners of the agents accordingly. In so doing, it helps to economize in the use of those agents of production which are most scarce, by offering the highest prices for them.

In a system of specialization and exchange, each individual does not consume what he himself produces; on the contrary, he sells his own produce, and with the proceeds purchases the produce of others. How much goods he will have to consume in such a system depends on how much he is paid for his own contribution to production. So the question of income sharing arises. All income has its origin in

---

[2] The above reasoning is not to be interpreted to mean that, in following prices, production is guided in the direction of greatest social need or social welfare. Production follows demand, and this depends upon desires backed up by purchasing power, not upon desires alone. Where incomes are unequal, the desires of the rich receive more consideration than those of the poor, regardless of whether this is just, or good, or not. In this connection see the discussion of inequality, below.

production. Each person who contributes either his labor or his capital to production is paid a share of the product. Capitalists contribute capital, and receive rent or interest; laborers contribute their services, and are paid wages; enterprisers put in their capital and their labor of supervision, and obtain profits.

The value of these contributions is determined by the market, on the principle of marginal productivity. It is found that the use of land, labor, and savings in production brings into operation the law of diminishing productivity, so that, the greater the supply of any one of these agents, the less is its marginal contribution to the product. Competition compels enterprisers to pay the full value of this marginal product to the individuals who supply the agents; but no more. Hence, if an agent is scarce relative to others, he who supplies it will get a large share of income, because the value of its marginal product is great; but if the agent is plentiful, he who supplies it will get a less share of income, because the value of its marginal product is small. How abundant or scarce any agent will be depends, in the case of labor, upon the relative numbers of the people in the various non-competing groups, and upon their prudence in the begetting of families, which in turn depends somewhat upon their standards of living. In the case of savings, it depends upon the strength of the motives to saving and investment (as reflected in time and liquidity preference) which prevail among the population. In the case of land, it depends on its area, relative to population and savings, which area cannot be much increased or diminished.

The economy involved in this method of sharing the income of society can be shown by quoting what was said on this point in Chapter XIX: "By setting a high price on the scarce agents and a low price on the plentiful ones, it induces enterprisers to use the scarce agents as sparingly as possible, and to substitute a cheaper for a more expensive one when this can be done. For instance, a wise enterpriser would never permit a skilled workman to do unskilled work, because his time is too valuable to be wasted in that manner when a laborer at much lower wages can be obtained for it. So, the scarce agents are reserved only for their most important uses. The high price of the scarce agents, moreover, stimulates men to increase their supply, thereby adding to the productivity of industry. For instance, if new savings for the construction of industrial plants are scarce, investments in such projects will bring in large incomes. This encourages people to save for the sake of this income, making available a larger supply of such equipment for production. If a certain type of skilled mechanics is scarce, they will obtain high wages. This is a notice to workingmen that more mechanics of that sort are needed.

More persons are thereby persuaded to learn that trade, with the result that the lack of such workers is remedied." These principles, however, must be understood to operate only as tendencies, to which there are many obstacles. Their operation in actual economic life falls far short of perfection.

Income sharing is not a process distinct from that of the determination of prices, but is a part of it. The costs of production which enter into commodity prices are the prices of the agents of production, and these prices determine the income shares. There are a great many consumers' demands competing for products, and the producers of those products competing for the agents of production. Out of the prices of the products, the producers determine what they can afford to pay for the agents, on the basis of the marginal contribution of the agents to the products. Thereby the prices of the products and the shares of income are established simultaneously by competitive bidding in the market.

Prices as the Center of the Economic Process. — The analysis of the past few paragraphs makes it apparent that the price system occupies a central position in the economic process. In it the forces of production and income sharing are both focused. Prices guide production, and they determine the income shares. So fundamentally do they enter into every economic activity, that some writers regard economics simply as the study of prices. Without taking this dubious position, we must recognize the dominant influence of the price system in modern industry.

In doing so, we are merely calling attention once more to the all-pervasiveness of exchange in economic life. Goods are produced almost always to be exchanged (sold) at a price. Out of the proceeds of the sale, enterprisers pay for their costs—the prices of the productive agents. From the prices of the productive agents, those who contribute them derive their money incomes. And at last, they convert these money incomes into real incomes by the purchase of commodities and services—once more involving a price.

Consumption. — In this last act, the converting of money incomes into real incomes, we arrive at consumption. Here the economic process finds its culmination, its goal. After the products find their way into consumers' hands in that last act of purchase, they are used up in gratifying the consumers' desires. This is the ultimate purpose of it all, and is the reward for all the efforts and sacrifices of production. Not all goods are consumed in the *direct* gratification of desires, however; many are used up in production, helping to yield other products which will eventually furnish gratifications.

Consumption, being the goal of the economic process, is at the same time the force which sets the whole in motion. For it is largely the desire to consume which leads people to produce, and which creates the motive for economic activity. It is, moreover, consumers' desires, expressed through demands, which decide what things shall be produced, as we have seen. In the fundamental elements of human behavior which control our choices, therefore, is the ultimate source of economic activity. These choices—built out of instinctive impulses and the influences of the environment, crystallized into habits, social conventions, and standards of living, sometimes rational and reflective, sometimes irrational and whimsical—are the rulers of industry. As they are well or ill adapted to the productive environment, economical or extravagant, the utility derived from industrial activities is great or small. In consumption, therefore, the economic process finds at once its driving power, its goal, and the criterion of its success or failure.

B. SOME DISTINCTIVE CHARACTERISTICS OF THE SYSTEM CALLED "CAPITALISM"

Capitalism. — The system of industry under which we live, and which has been described in this volume, is commonly known as *capitalism*. This term is used by way of contrast with alternative systems of economic organization which have been proposed, such as socialism, communism, and fascism. It derives this name from the fact that, in modern industry, production is carried on with the aid of vast quantities of very valuable and important capital, which is owned, for the most part, by a class of men known as capitalists, who thereby are given a dominant influence and control over the whole process. The term is inapt, however, for the reason that almost any conceivable scheme of industrial organization would be capitalistic, in the sense that production would be time-consuming and round-about—carried on by means of elaborate plant, equipment, tools, and other forms of equipment, at stages more or less remote from consumption. The real difference between the present economic order and others which have been suggested lies, not in the fact that one would be capitalistic and the other not, but in that now the ownership and control of capital is in the hands of particular persons, whereas in other proposed systems it might be in the hands of the state, or of the working classes, through some method of collective management. The present system might better be called one of private property and free enterprise, for these are the outstanding features which differentiate it from other possible systems, and which are had in mind when the term capitalism is popularly applied to it.

In a broad survey of the economic process, we cannot afford to neglect a discussion of these distinctive characteristics, for they are fundamental to an understanding of the present structure of society, and they form the principal bone of contention in much of the agitation for social reform which so heatedly prevails in recent years. In this discussion, we must keep in mind the central purpose of our study. We are not here concerned with the merits and defects of the present system; we are trying to find out only what it is and how it works. We shall not seek to evaluate our present institutions, therefore, but merely to describe them; not to find out whether they are bad or good, but merely what they are. The reader must be on his guard against misinterpreting this attitude. It is not because there are no defects that we do not consider them. An *explanation* of capitalism is not to be construed as a *justification* of it. But in the first chapter of this volume we resolved to confine ourselves to pure (descriptive) economics, because the understanding of our economic system is a necessary prelude to an intelligent appraisal or criticism.

Private Property. — Private property is one of the most basic institutions of our present economic organization. Most of our wealth is owned and controlled by individuals. Nearly all of our land, factories, railroads, mines, warehouses, stores, industrial equipment, houses, furniture, clothing, food, and so on, are privately owned, either by single individuals, or by groups, such as the stockholders of a corporation. They are not common property. One cannot help himself to his neighbor's fruit nor trespass upon his land without his consent. Under our constitution, not even the state can take away one's property without compensation, so that if it is desired to cut a new road through a farmer's land, or to raze his dwelling to make way for some public improvement, he must be paid the fair value of what is taken.

The ownership of property carries with it the right to use that property as one sees fit, to dispose of it by sale or gift, and to prevent the use of it by others. Control extends even after the death of the owner, who may by will decree what shall be done with it; and the law will see to it that his wishes are carried out. These rights are not absolute, and may be restricted if exercised in a manner injurious to other members of society. For instance, if a man maintains a public nuisance on his property, the courts will restrain him, and he may be prevented from using his wealth for dishonest or immoral purposes. But, in general, there is substantial control by the owner; and, within wide limits, he can dispose of his property as he wills.

There can be no doubt that this institution of private property performs an important function. The desire to accumulate wealth appears to be a powerful motive in human life, and leads men to work hard to obtain it. The possibility of acquiring and holding property is a stimulus to economic endeavor and efficiency which plays a considerable part in the industrial process. Its all-pervasiveness, too, entering, as it does, into every business organization and every purchase or sale, differentiating the "capitalist class" from the propertyless "working class," shows it to be fundamental to the present régime. Without it, we would have a very different system, indeed.

There is, of course, some public property. There are some land, some public buildings, and other wealth, owned by the people collectively, through their government. Some of this public wealth, such as public roads, parks, and playgrounds, the people can use freely, it being paid for out of general taxes; other of it, such as municipal water systems or the post office, the users must pay for, just as they would pay a private owner. But this publicly owned wealth is a minor part of the whole; it does not invalidate the general assertion that private ownership of property is inherent in the present industrial system. There is evident a tendency for the government to acquire more and more property, however, and this movement may go very much further. Some people look forward to the eventual abandonment of private property, at least in producers' goods, and its replacement by some scheme of common ownership. It is not inconceivable that such a change may come about; but it is by no means inevitable.

Free Enterprise and Self-Interest. — Along with private property goes freedom of enterprise. By this is meant that each individual is free to employ his person or his wealth in any line of production he cares to. He may choose his own occupation, within the limits set by his capacity and his opportunities. If he wants to set up in business for himself, he may do so, if he can sufficiently convince others of his ability to induce them to lend him the necessary capital. If he has savings to invest, he can put them into whatever industry or enterprise seems to him most advantageous. If he is a wage-earner, he can select his own employer. If he is an employer, he can select his own employees. If he is a farmer, he can decide for himself what crops he will grow. If he is a manufacturer, his is the choice as to what goods he shall produce. Like the right of private property, this freedom of enterprise is not absolute. It is limited by economic conditions, by the knowledge and resourcefulness of the individual, by the existence of monopolies and trade unions, by the conditions of the market, by laws prohibiting certain types of activity which are deemed injurious, and by similar restrictions. Public regulation of private enterprise is certainly growing, and is likely to increase further, rather than to diminish; but it still remains true of our economic system as a whole, that the limits, within which individuals are left free to make their own economic decisions, are fairly wide.

This being the case, the individual is left to follow the dictates of his self-interest. Society relies upon his common sense to act wisely. It is to the individual's economic advantage to do the thing that will yield him the greatest net income, in proportion to the effort and sacrifice put forth; hence, if intelligent and well-informed, he will go into the type of occupation for which he is best fitted, and devote his productive resources to those products which are in greatest demand. That people are often ignorant and unwise, that they are victims of circumstance and opportunity, goes without saying. Hence this principle of self-interest only works out roughly; undoubtedly, in a system of free enterprise many mistakes are made. But such is the process by which the industrial system functions as at present constituted.

We have noted that there is some tendency toward a departure from this principle. There is evident an increasing amount of direction and control of industry by the state. Some businesses, such as the post office and the coining of money, are entirely monopolized by the government. In others, such as the railroads, telegraphs, and telephones, there is a considerable measure of public regulation, through agencies like the Interstate Commerce Commission. There are also child labor laws, compulsory workingmen's insurance schemes, factory legislation, and agricultural crop controls, which interfere to a greater or less degree with perfect freedom of enterprise. Some persons believe that this tendency too, like the gradual encroachments on private property, is destined to go on until the principle of free enterprise is completely overthrown. However this may be, that principle is still effective in most of our economic activities.

Competition. — A natural accompaniment of free enterprise is competition. That competition is almost universal in our economic life, notwithstanding the many sorts of voluntary and involuntary coöperation that are to be found, was shown in Chapter III. There is competition among buyers to secure the available supplies of goods, and among sellers to secure the patronage of the buyers. This applies not only to consumers and producers of the same good, but of widely different goods. There is competition among capitalists for the best investments, and among laborers for the best employments, while capitalists compete with laborers for the lion's share of the industrial product. The principle is, therefore, all-pervasive.

We rely largely upon competition to secure industrial efficiency. That is perhaps its main function in industry. In farming, mining, manufacturing, banking, marketing, and so on, there goes on a continual struggle for existence, in which the less able producers fail and are eliminated. He who is the quickest and surest of judgment, who watches the markets and the costs with the most unerring eye, and who can best foresee coming changes in the demand, the supply, or the conditions of production for a commodity, is most likely to succeed. In each industry, there is a battle to maintain the best markets and the lowest costs. The competition of buyers and sellers tends to keep prices down to the level of costs, and to keep the costs as low as the existing state of productive technique and the ability of the producers make possible. Within each plant, moreover, there is competition among the employees to win promotion to the best positions. So, all along the line, there is a continuous rivalry, which acts as a powerful incentive to efficiency.

Like the other principles we have considered, this one does not work unimpeded. There are monopolies and trade unions, which restrain competition among both employers and workers. Some writers believe there is manifest a tendency toward concentration of industry in the hands of small groups, a tendency which, eventually, will render competition no longer effective. Moreover, there are kinds of competition which cannot be said to work toward efficiency. Competition may take the form of browbeating one's rivals or of deceiving the consumer, in which cases it makes for inefficiency. Also, many persons object to it as unethical; and they hope to see eventually the substitution of some other incentive to efficiency. They believe that men might be made to do their best in a spirit of service to their fellows, or in response to the creative impulses within them, or for the sake of some non-material reward, such as the attainment of a coveted honor or social prestige. However this may be, it is true that, as at present constituted, the economic process does rely largely upon competition to promote efficiency.

Inequality. — Where there is competition, there is bound to be inequality of wealth and income. Such inequality is a conspicuous feature of the present system. As things now are, each person's income is left to the determination of the market. If one owns land, he can get whatever price for the use of his land bidders are willing to pay for it. If he has savings, he derives from them an income determined in a similar bidding process. If his wealth is inherited, rather than earned by himself, it makes no difference. If he is a laborer, he gets whatever wages the market valuation process has fixed as the price of his labor. If he is an enterpriser, he gets, in addition to ordinary wages for his labor and interest on his capital, whatever else his adaptability and ingenuity enable him to obtain in taking advantage of the irregularities and fluctuations of industry. The natural result of such a process of income-getting is that some receive more than others. Some kinds of labor are scarce and highly valued; the fortunate laborers of this sort are well paid. Other kinds of labor are plentiful and poorly paid. Some lands are worth fabulous sums, and, because land is private property, their owners can gain by this worth. Some investments prove profitable, others do not. Some people inherit great wealth from their parents, and others receive little or none in this way. Some enterprisers are successful, others fail.

So, we have extremes of wealth and poverty in society. We have people who are immensely rich, and can lead lives of luxury and leisure. We have others who are miserably poor, and must live in squalor and destitution.

Inequality is inseparably connected with competition in acting as an incentive to efficiency. The fear of poverty on the one hand, and the lure of riches on the other, make men work and strive for economic success. One way to success is to produce commodities of value, and at as low a cost as one's competitors; this makes for efficiency. But it cannot be denied that many people achieve great wealth by sheer luck, or even by dishonesty—people who have not contributed to society products of equal value to what they have received. Hence it is impossible always to establish a direct relation between economic success and economic efficiency.

The existence of inequality has an important bearing upon the economy of the pricing process. If everybody had equal purchasing power, no one would exercise any greater control over the market than his fellows. Each person's desires would have equal opportunity for gratification, and demand would be a true expression of the wishes of consumers. Under such circumstances, in following demand, production would be devoted as nearly as possible to the things which the people wanted. It would correspond with social need, in so far as the people were capable of expressing their needs intelligently. But when inequality prevails, the people with the most money exercise the strongest influence on the market. Demand does not then coincide with the needs of the community. The rich can gratify their whims, and production will be directed to that purpose, while many of the wants of the poor will go uncared for. Inequality, therefore, interferes with perfect economy of production, from a social viewpoint.

Unlike the other characteristics of capitalism which we have so far considered, there seems to be little or no tendency away from the principle of inequality. While the average standards of living today are undoubtedly higher than those of a few generations ago, we still have many people on the verge of starvation, and we have others with private fortunes surpassing anything of the like ever known before. There is, however, a considerable amount of attention being given to the question of inequality, and there are persons who hope to see established a much greater degree of equality than now prevails, just as they hope to see the abandonment or substantial modification of the principles of private property, free enterprise, and competition.

The Distinctive Characteristics of Capitalism are not Necessarily Permanent. — It is a natural trait of human nature to think of that which has been long established, and to which we have always been accustomed, as permanent and unchangeable. From this it is an easy step to the conclusion that whatever has long prevailed is right and desirable. This is evidenced by the opposition from conservatives which always greets any new idea, whether in politics, science, religion, art, or other fields of life, and by the slowness with which innovations find acceptance. So, it is necessary to emphasize once more the fact that, in describing and explaining the basic principles of capitalism, we have not necessarily justified them, nor proved them to be indispensable. We have merely stated what they are, in order that our picture of the economic process might be complete. We must think of them as characteristics of the present system only, which may and do have both merits and defects, and which might be supplanted by other principles, which might or might not work as well or better.

Other schemes of social organization have been conceived of, and seriously proposed, based on very different principles. It is not at all unthinkable that we could have a society where, instead of private property, all property, or at least all the means of production, would be owned and shared by the people in common; where production, instead of being left to the play of free enterprise and self-interest, would be centrally directed in accordance with some carefully worked out plan; where substantial equality of wealth and income would prevail; and where other motives would be relied on to supplant the lure of riches as the incentive to economic efficiency. Nothing is more clearly established than that all aspects of life are being continually subjected to a process of evolution. The basic principles of the present industrial system are, therefore, not to be regarded as eternal and unvarying. They, too, may evolve to different forms. They are not necessarily in their perfect and final shape.

It would be interesting to undertake a critical study of their merits and defects, to seek ways in which they might be improved; but from that fascinating task we must at present refrain. Such a study belongs in the domain of applied economics, to which this description of the general principles of the present industrial system is a necessary preliminary foundation. Having outlined those principles, our task is complete. However, it is to be hoped that the student, having learned something of the operation of the economic world in which he lives, will not be content to rest with such knowledge, but will go on studying that world critically, that he may play a part in finding means by which it may be improved, and in aiding in their realization.

SUMMARY

The economic process which we have been studying is capable of being sketched in a single picture which reveals its general outlines. At one end of the process stand the desires of consumers; at the other, the means of production—land, labor, and saving. To utilize these agents for gratifying those desires, there has developed the elaborate productive organization of modern industry. This organization is characterized by (1) specialization, (2) exchange, (3) the roundabout, time-consuming process of first applying labor to the making of remote-goods, later to be used in turning out near-goods, (4) the coordination of the productive agents in operating units, under single enterprisers, partnerships, or corporations, and (5) the use of money. The productivity of this elaborate organization depends upon the natural resources at the disposal of a people, the size, intelligence, and energy of the population, and the state of science and the arts.

The channels which production shall take are determined by the price system, which guides producers in determining what is the best way to employ the labor and capital at their disposal. Consumers express their choices in demands, and the prices of products respond to these demands. Enterprisers respond to the prices of the products. This effects a certain economy in the use of the productive resources, by preventing them from being devoted to one purpose when they could be made to yield products of greater value (that is, in greater demand) if put to some other purpose. In the same way, there is effected a further economy in the use of the agents of production, through the process of income sharing. The scarcer the agent, the greater is its marginal product. The value of this marginal product determines the price which will be paid for the agent. So, the scarce agents cost the enterprisers most. This stimulates economy in their use, and tends to induce an increase in the supply of the agents which are most wanted. At the same time, this process fixes the shares of income obtained by those whose labor, savings, and land are employed in production.

The process is completed when the products are used up in the act of consumption. Consumption is thus the goal and ultimate controlling influence of industry.

The economic process so described rests on certain distinctive institutions which cause it to be known as "capitalism," by contrast with other proposed systems. These characteristic features are: (1) the institution of private property, (2) free enterprise, (3) competition, and (4) inequality. The system relies upon these institutions to give it efficiency. The right to acquire, use, and dispose of property is a strong inducement to produce goods. Free enterprise allows each to follow his own self-interest, tending to direct him to the kind of work at which he will be most productive, and for which there is greatest demand. Competition, with the inequality which accompanies it, holds up the prospect of great wealth on the one hand, and of poverty on the other, as an incentive to efficient production. Thus it is upon these principles that the economic world in which we live operates and depends for its success. They do not work perfectly, however, and it is not to be concluded that they are permanent and unchangeable, simply because they have been long established. There is, in fact, an observable tendency toward modification of them, and many persons look forward to their eventual replacement by a new system which will be based on different principles.

REFERENCES AND SUGGESTIONS FOR FURTHER READING

The first part of this chapter, dealing in summary fashion, as it does, with the whole field of economics, necessarily draws on a vast wealth of literature, suggestions concerning which have been appended to the preceding chapters of this book. I am unable to cite any single work which undertakes a general survey of the sort here attempted.

There is much critical literature dealing with the basic principles underlying the industrial system, which constituted the subject-matter of the second part of this chapter. A careful critique of the present system, rendering a verdict in its favor, is to be found in F. M. Taylor's *Principles of Economics* (1921), Chapters 42 to 48, inclusive. T. N. Carver comes to similar conclusions, set forth in a stimulating and interesting style, in his *Essays in Social Justice* (1915), especially Chapters 3 to 7, inclusive. Somewhat more critical of present institutions, and ably presented, are the concluding chapters (21 to 25) of H. Clay's *Economics for the General Reader* (American edition, 1918). An able and thought-provoking analysis, expressing frank dissatisfaction with the industrial system, is that of R. H. Tawney, *The Acquisitive Society* (1920). The literature of radical movements, such as socialism, abounds with critical attacks on capitalism. For a good survey of this whole controversy, consult W. N. Loucks and J. W. Hoot, *Comparative Economic Systems* (1938).

INDEX